MW01041011

Learning Disabilities and Related Disabilities

STRATEGIES FOR SUCCESS

Learning Disabilities and Related Disabilities

STRATEGIES FOR SUCCESS

THIRTEENTH EDITION

JANET W. LERNER
Northeastern Illinois University

BEVERLEY H. JOHNS
MacMurray College

CENGAGE
Learning·

Australia • Brazil • Mexico • Singapore • United Kingdom • United States

Learning Disabilities and Related Disabilities: Strategies for Success, Thirteenth Edition
Janet W. Lerner and Beverley H. Johns

Senior Product Manager: Mark Kerr

Content Developer: Kate Scheinman

Outsource Development Coordinator: Joshua Taylor

Product Assistant: Nicole Bator

Associate Media Developer: Renee Schaaf

Marketing Director: Jennifer Levanduski

Senior Marketing Manager: Kara Kindstrom

Art and Cover Direction, Production Management, and Composition: PreMediaGlobal

Manufacturing Planner: Doug Bertke

Rights Acquisitions Specialist: Roberta Broyer

Cover Image: Hero/Fancy/Corbis/Glow Images, Inc.

© 2015, 2012 Cengage Learning

ALL RIGHTS RESERVED. No part of this work covered by the copyright herein may be reproduced, transmitted, stored, or used in any form or by any means graphic, electronic, or mechanical, including but not limited to photocopying, recording, scanning, digitizing, taping, Web distribution, information networks, or information storage and retrieval systems, except as permitted under Section 107 or 108 of the 1976 United States Copyright Act, without the prior written permission of the publisher.

For product information and technology assistance, contact us at **Cengage Learning Customer & Sales Support, 1-800-354-9706**.
For permission to use material from this text or product, submit all requests online at **www.cengage.com/permissions**.
Further permissions questions can be e-mailed to **permissionrequest@cengage.com**.

Library of Congress Control Number: 2013937078

ISBN 13: 978-1-285-43320-2

ISBN 10: 1-285-43320-3

Cengage Learning
200 First Stamford Place, 4th Floor
Stamford, CT 06902
USA

Cengage Learning is a leading provider of customized learning solutions with office locations around the globe, including Singapore, the United Kingdom, Australia, Mexico, Brazil, and Japan. Locate your local office at **www.cengage.com/global**.

Cengage Learning products are represented in Canada by Nelson Education, Ltd.

To learn more about Cengage Learning Solutions, visit **www.cengage.com**.

Purchase any of our products at your local college store or at our preferred online store **www.cengagebrain.com**.

Printed at EPAC Mexico, 07-16

To Eugene—J.L.

To Lonnie—B.J.

BRIEF TABLE OF CONTENTS

ptaxa/iStockphoto.com

3

Specialized Instruction
and Technology   73

Michael Newman/PhotoEdit

4

Educational Settings and the Role of the Family 105

PART III Theoretical Perspectives and Expanding Directions   128

Brian Mitchell/Corbis

5

Theories of Learning   129

Ellen B. Senisi/The Image Works

6

Social, Emotional, and Behavioral Challenges   157

7

Related Disabilities: Autism Spectrum Disorders (ASD) & Attention Deficit Hyperactivity Disorder (ADHD)   189

Inara Prusakova/Shutterstock.com

8

Young Children with Disabilities 215

Steve Debenport/iStockphoto.com

9

Adolescents and Adults With Learning Disabilities and Related Disabilities   247

Spencer Grant/PhotoEdit

10

Understanding The Laws Related To Students With Disabilities 283

Part IV From Theories to Teaching Strategies 306

Bolot/iStockphoto.com

11

Spoken Language Difficulties: Listening and Speaking 307

Maria Uspenskaya/Shutterstock.com

12

Reading Difficulties 341

Tom Odulate/Cultura/Getty Images

13

Written Language Difficulties: Written Expression, Spelling, and Handwriting 383

Courtesy of Elizabeth Crews Photography

14

Mathematics Difficulties 421

14.1 Theories Describing Difficulties
with Mathematics 423

14.2 Students with Mathematics Difficulties
and Students with Mathematics
Learning Disabilities 423
    14.2a Early Number Concepts and
      Number Sense 424

14.3 Characteristics of Students with Mathematics
Disabilities 426
    14.3a Information-Processing Difficulties 427
    14.3b Language and Mathematics Abilities 427

14.3c Math Anxiety 427
    PROFESSIONAL RESOURCE DOWNLOAD:
      TEACHING TIPS 14.1: Guidelines for Dealing
      With Math Anxiety 428

14.4 Students with Mathematics Disabilities
at the Secondary Level 429

14.5 Mathematics Standards 430
    14.5a High Standards and Annual Testing 430
    14.5b Common Core State Standards
      for Mathematics 430

14.6 Learning Theories for Mathematics
Instruction 431
    14.6a Active Involvement 431
      STUDENT STORIES 14.1: Active Involvement
      in Mathematics 432
    14.6b Progression From Concrete Learning
      to Abstract Learning 432
    14.6c Direct Instruction of Mathematics 433
    14.6d Learning Strategies Instruction 433
    14.6e Problem Solving 433
      STUDENT STORIES 14.2: Encouraging a
      Problem-Solving Attitude 434
      PROFESSIONAL RESOURCE DOWNLOAD: TEACH-
      ING TIPS 14.2: Some Problem-Solving
      Examples 435

14.7 Assessing Mathematics
Achievement 435
    14.7a Formal Tests 436
    14.7b Informal Measures 437

14.8 Teaching Strategies to Improve
Mathematics Difficulties 440

14.9 Mathematics Strategies for the General
Education Classroom 440
    PROFESSIONAL RESOURCE DOWNLOAD: Including
      Students in GENERAL EDUCATION 14.1 441

14.10 The Mathematics Curriculum 441
    14.10a The Sequence of Mathematics:
      Grades K–8 441
    14.10b The Secondary Mathematics
      Curriculum 442

Learning Disabilities and Related Disabilities: Strategies for Success, Thirteenth Edition, focuses both on students with learning disabilities and on students with related disabilities. **Learning disabilities** is a category of disability that is identified in special education law. Related **disabilities** are those that are increasingly found in schools that serve children within a cross categorical approach. Students with learning disabilities and students with related disabilities are perplexing in that each individual has a unique combination of talents, characteristics, strengths, and weaknesses. The concepts and strategies presented in this text are broad in scope and are applicable for students with learning disabilities and students with related disabilities. Students with learning disabilities and related disabilities are found in every classroom. Unless these students are recognized and treated, they are destined to have many difficulties throughout life. The primary concerns and goals of this textbook are identifying students with learning disabilities and related disabilities and helping them to succeed in school and in life.

This Thirteenth Edition reflects contemporary views of students with learning disabilities and students with related disabilities, includes the critical advances in research, and recognizes the changes in policies that are occurring in both general education and special education today. The revised text strives to provide a fair and clear explanation of new and controversial issues within the field. In addition to covering new trends, this textbook also presents the basic and classic foundations, concepts, and strategies that have helped teachers, parents, and students over the years.

Audience, Approach, and Purpose

Learning Disabilities and Related Disabilities, Thirteenth Edition, is an introductory textbook written for undergraduate and graduate students who are majoring in general education or special education. It provides a comprehensive view of the field, describes the characteristics of various disabilities, and offers teaching strategies for general education teachers, special education teachers, school psychologists, administrators, language pathologists, counselors, and related professionals. *Learning Disabilities and Related Disabilities* is particularly useful for preservice teachers and in-service classroom teachers who are increasingly responsible for teaching students with special needs within general education or inclusive classrooms. In addition, this textbook provides parents with the necessary background information to better understand their child and their child's problems. Learning disabilities and related disabilities are conditions that impede learning for many children, adolescents, and adults, affecting their schooling and adult lives. Their problems can lead to serious difficulties in school learning, and those difficulties often continue into adulthood. Our multidimensional approach to learning disabilities and related disabilities enables readers to gain a comprehensive overview of this complex subject. Teachers must understand the diverse theoretical approaches within the field of disabilities. They must know procedures for evaluating students; possess skills in the art of clinical teaching; and be familiar with teaching methods, strategies, and materials. Teachers must also be familiar with the implications of the special education laws.

New and Updated for the Thirteenth Edition

The text coverage and special features are designed to help new teachers be successful in their future classrooms and with their future students. Below is a brief list that outlines some of the key revisions that we have made within the new edition:

New Colorful Design

This edition is a full-color text with an appealing interior design and larger page size to help enhance student learning.

New Learning Objectives

New Learning Objectives correlated to the main sections in each chapter show students what they need to know to process and understand the information in the chapter. After completing the chapter, students should be able to demonstrate how they can use and apply their new knowledge and skills.

New Standards Included with Each Chapter

At the start of every chapter, a list of standards addressed within the chapter appears. In chapters 1–10, the standards come from the Council of Exceptional Children Initial Level Special Education Standards as Approved by the National Council for the Accreditation of Special Education. In Chapters 11–14, the Common Core Standards are discussed.

New Professional Resource Downloads

New Professional Resource Download Downloads include tips, boxes, figures, and tables in the textbook plus a complete Sample IEP for students to download, often customize, and use to review key concepts and in the classroom! Look for the Digital Download label that identifies these items.

New Did You Get It? quizzes

New Did You Get It? quizzes allows students to measure their performance against the learning objectives in each chapter. One question for each learning objective is featured in the textbook to encourage students to go to *MindTap* take the full quiz, and check their understanding.

TeachSource Video Cases

TeachSource Video Cases feature footage from the classroom to help students relate key chapter content to real-life scenarios. Critical-thinking questions, artifacts, and bonus video help the student reflect on the content in the video.

New Chapter on Special Education Law and Regulations

This edition provides a new chapter, Chapter 10, that focuses on the laws, regulations, and court cases that impact students with disabilities.

New Coverage of English Language Learners (ELLs)

Special consideration is given across the text to English Language Learners (ELLs)—students whose native language is not English and who are not yet proficient in English. Marginal icons throughout the chapters highlight where this material is covered. Preservice teachers must learn about the unique needs of ELL students who have mild disabilities. These issues are discussed in Chapter 11, and across the book as well.

New Marginal Key Terms and Definitions

As an additional study aid, this edition features key terms and their definitions in the text margins, next to where the boldface key terms are defined in the text. At the end of each chapter, a list of the key terms appears, and at the end of the book, there is a comprehensive glossary of key terms.

Cross-Categorical Emphasis

Many states are changing their teacher certification policies and certifying special education teachers *cross-categorically,* using a designation such as "mild disabilities" or in some cases, "mild/moderate disabilities." The designation of "mild disabilities" often includes students that qualify for special education services within several different categories—such as learning disabilities, intellectual disabilities, emotional/behavior disorders, and other disabilities—depending on the individual state's certification rules. To meet the new certification requirements of their states, college-level teacher preparation programs now include broader, cross-categorical courses of study for teaching students with varying disabilities. This text can be used in these broader courses (often entitled "Teaching Students With Mild Disabilities"), as well as the more traditional courses about "Students With Learning Disabilities." The concepts presented in this text are broad in scope and are applicable to both types of courses. For example, the topics and coverage on the law, assessment, response-to-intervention (RTI) procedures, and instructional strategies readily apply to students with both learning disabilities and related disabilities.

More Coverage on Instruction in General Education Classes

The educational setting for the majority of students with learning disabilities and related disabilities is the general education classroom, and teaching these students becomes the responsibility of the general education teacher. Each chapter of the textbook addresses strategies for the general education teacher to instruct students with learning disabilities and related disabilities—both within special text boxes and within each chapter's narrative.

Today, many students with learning disabilities and related disabilities receive instruction in general education classes or inclusive classrooms. There are many benefits of inclusion. General education classrooms can provide students with disabilities greater access to their general education peers, raise expectations for student performance, help general education students be more accepting of diverse students, and improve coordination between regular and special educators.

Response-to-Intervention (RTI)

RTI is a process for instructing all students and also affects the determination of eligibility of students with learning disabilities and related mild disabilities. RTI is comprehensively addressed in Chapter 2, and discussed wherever relevant throughout the text.

Web-Based Resources

Students today want to investigate certain topics further through the Internet. Throughout this textbook, we have provided the URLs of websites relevant to the topics being discussed. These website references enable students to identify high-quality, accurate website content more easily. In addition, greater coverage of certain topics and a variety of learning resources are provided on the website that accompanies this textbook.

Chapter Coverage and Key Revisions within the Thirteenth Edition

- The field of special education is changing and Chapter 1 provides the latest information about the field, including changes and new directions. It provides an overview of the field of learning disabilities and other related disabilities. It also discusses the neuroscience and the study of the brain.
- Chapter 2 explains the importance of assessment to plan appropriate instruction. A significant part of the chapter is devoted to response to intervention, including benefits and concerns about the use of RTI as a sole assessment tool for students with learning disabilities. Curriculum-based measurement is reviewed and the details of a comprehensive evaluation are provided. The IEP process is detailed and included in the chapter for the first time, as

are present levels of academic achievement and functional performance. A sample IEP is provided as a Digital Download.

- Chapter 3's new content is devoted to specialized instruction, clinical teaching, and differentiating instruction. Discussion focuses on the difference between specialized instruction and accommodation and modifications. Part of the chapter is focused on effective instructional strategies for general education and also on the importance of task analysis.

- Chapter 4 describes the continuum of alternative educational settings for students with disabilities and how the decision about the appropriate placement is made. Included in this chapter is also a description of the art of collaboration with educators and families.

- Chapter 5 provides a comprehensive description of the theories of learning including development psychology, behavioral psychology, and cognitive psychology. Also included in this chapter is a description of learning strategies.

- Chapter 6 is devoted to the social, emotional, and behavioral challenges that students with learning disabilities and related disabilities often exhibit. An explanation of the importance of functional behavioral assessment and a positive behavior intervention plan based on that assessment is stressed. Also included is a description of Positive Behavioral Interventions and Supports. An explanation about why school suspension is an ineffective intervention is provided.

- A thoroughly revised Chapter 7 includes information about new research and medications for ADHD. Chapter 7 also addresses related Autism Spectrum Disorders, such as autism and Asperger's syndrome and includes the latest information from the Diagnostic and Statistical Manual 5. A description of nonverbal learning disorders is also provided.

- Chapter 8 is devoted to young children with disabilities and describes the developmental indicators of problems in young children and stresses the importance of assessment. The chapter provides an overview of laws impacting young children and provides multiple strategies for working with young children, including those children who are in general education classes.

- What is happening to our students with learning disabilities and related disabilities after they exit the school system is covered in Chapter 9. This chapter explores the characteristics and needs of adolescents and adults with learning disabilities and related disabilities. Effective inclusionary strategies for the general education classroom are provided and the learning strategies model is described. Characteristics of postsecondary programs are discussed.

- Chapter 10, the newest addition to this edition, provides an explanation of the federal laws and regulations that impact students with disabilities. It also covers the Supreme Court cases that have had major implications for services for students with disabilities.

- Chapter 11 includes an explanation of the types of language problems exhibited by students with learning disabilities and related disabilities, difficulties encountered by students who are English-Language Learners, and types of language assessment. It also includes a discussion of the use of technology.

- Chapter 12 focuses on phonemic awareness, word recognition, comprehension, and fluency with a multitude of practical reading strategies for struggling readers.

- Chapter 13 stresses the importance of teaching writing so that students can achieve the Common Core Standards. Instructional strategies that focus on the Common Core are provided.
- Chapter 14 focuses on mathematical difficulties with particular attention given to the Common Core Standards for Math and the instructional strategies to meet those standards.
- Updated citations. Current citations and many updated citations appear throughout the textbook.

Additional Student Learning Aids and Special Features

To make this textbook easy to read and appealing to use, we have added many valuable features to the Thirteenth Edition (as noted above in the "New and Updated" section) and retained those learning tools from previous editions that were the most successful.

QUOTATIONS at the beginning of each chapter help to focus the reader and to provide stimulating insights.

TEACHING TIPS BOXES provide examples of practical instruction models, methods, and strategies for teaching students with learning disabilities and related mild disabilities. Many of these are now also Digital Downloads.

STUDENT STORIES are interspersed throughout each chapter. These short illustrative vignettes are real-life situational snapshots of students that illustrate the topic under discussion. Reflective questions are posed to readers at the end of each Student Story.

INCLUDING STUDENTS IN GENERAL EDUCATION BOXES offer ideas and strategies for teaching students with learning disabilities and/or related mild disabilities included in general education classes. Many of these are now also Digital Downloads.

I HAVE A KID WHO.... These brief, accessible case studies allow students to apply the content that they have read in each chapter, and are accompanied by reflective questions.

CHAPTER SUMMARIES at the end of each chapter highlight, in a clear point-by-point format, the major ideas presented in the chapter.

QUESTIONS FOR DISCUSSION AND REFLECTION follow the summary section at the end of each chapter and offer an opportunity to pull together and elaborate on the major ideas of the chapter.

MindTap™: The Personal Learning Experience

MindTap for Lerner/Johns, *Learning Disabilities and Related Mild Disabilities*, 13e represents a new approach to teaching and learning. A highly personalized, fully customizable learning platform with an integrated eportfolio, MindTap helps students to elevate thinking by guiding them to:

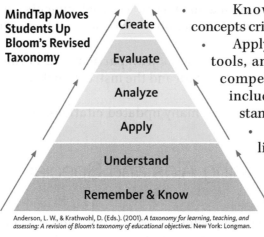

MindTap Moves Students Up Bloom's Revised Taxonomy

Create
Evaluate
Analyze
Apply
Understand
Remember & Know

Anderson, L. W., & Krathwohl, D. (Eds.). (2001). *A taxonomy for learning, teaching, and assessing: A revision of Bloom's taxonomy of educational objectives.* New York: Longman.

- Know, remember, and understand concepts critical to becoming a great teacher;
- Apply concepts, create curriculum and tools, and demonstrate performance and competency in key areas in the course, including national and state education standards;
- Prepare artifacts for the portfolio and eventual state licensure, to launch a successful teaching career; and
- Develop the habits to become a reflective practitioner.

As students move through each chapter's Learning Path, they engage in a scaffolded learning experience, designed to move them up Bloom's Taxonomy, from lower- to higher-order thinking skills. The Learning Path enables preservice students to develop these skills and gain confidence by:

- Engaging them with chapter topics and activating their prior knowledge by watching and answering questions about authentic videos of teachers teaching and children learning in real classrooms;
- Checking their comprehension and understanding through Did You Get It? assessments, with varied question types that are autograded for instant feedback;
- Applying concepts through mini-case scenarios—students analyze typical teaching and learning situations, and then create a reasoned response to the issue(s) presented in the scenario; and
- Reflecting about and justifying the choices they made within the teaching scenario problem.

MindTap helps instructors facilitate better outcomes by evaluating how future teachers plan and teach lessons in ways that make content clear and help diverse students learn, assessing the effectiveness of their teaching practice, and adjusting teaching as needed. MindTap enables instructors to facilitate better outcomes by:

- Making grades visible in real time through the Student Progress App so students and instructors always have access to current standings in the class.
- Using the Outcome Library to embed national education standards and align them to student learning activities, and also allowing instructors to add their state's standards or any other desired outcome.
- Allowing instructors to generate reports on students' performance with the click of a mouse against any standards or outcomes that are in their MindTap course.
- Giving instructors the ability to assess students on state standards or other local outcomes by editing existing or creating their own MindTap activities, and then by aligning those activities to any state or other outcomes that the instructor has added to the MindTap Outcome Library.

MindTap for Lerner/Johns, *Learning Disabilities and Related Mild Disabilities*, 13e helps instructors easily set their course since it integrates into the existing Learning Management System and saves instructors time by allowing them to fully customize any aspect of the learning path. Instructors can change the order of the student learning activities, hide activities they don't want for the course, and—most importantly—create custom assessments and add any standards, outcomes, or content they do want (e.g., YouTube videos, Google docs). Learn more at www.cengage.com/mindtap.

Instructor Ancillaries

Online Instructor's Manual and Test Bank An online Instructor's Manual accompanies this book. It contains information to assist the instructor in designing the course, including sample syllabi, discussion questions, teaching and learning activities, field experiences, learning objectives, and additional online resources. For assessment support, the updated test bank includes true/false, multiple-choice, matching, short-answer, and essay questions for each chapter.

Online PowerPoint Slides These vibrant, Microsoft PowerPoint lecture slides for each chapter assist you with your lecture by providing concept coverage using images, figures, and tables directly from the textbook!

Cengage Learning Testing Powered by Cognero

- Author, edit, and manage test bank content from multiple Cengage Learning solutions.
- Create multiple test versions in an instant.
- Deliver tests from your LMS, your classroom or wherever you want.

Acknowledgments

Learning Disabilities and Related Disabilities grew out of our experiences from working in public schools with students who had learning disabilities, serious learning difficulties, social problems, and emotional/behavioral challenges. We also learned by teaching courses on learning disabilities, emotional/behavioral disorders, and special education in colleges and universities. This textbook was influenced greatly by the feedback from students in our courses. Students, colleagues, and organizations also alerted us to new concepts, programs, assessment instruments, and intervention strategies. We are indebted to many scholars, researchers, authors of books and articles, speakers at conferences, and educators in school districts and universities with whom we have worked.

We extend our thanks to the following reviewers who read the manuscript at various stages and provided helpful suggestions and criticisms:

Dawn Atlee, *Southern Illinois University, Carbondale*
Patricia Clark, *University of Maine Augusta*

Rebecca Cohen, *Pima Community College*
Barbara Cordasco, *Georgian Court University*
Tara Cosco, *Glenville State College*
Karen Coughenour, *Francis Marion University*
Ken Dobush, *Bridgewater State College*
Robin Ennis, *Georgia State University*
Patricia Frawley, *Fairleigh Dickinson University*
Leah Hoover, *Kentucky Wesleyan College*
MeShelda Jackson, *Benedictine University*
Jane Leatherman, *Indiana University–Purdue University Ft. Wayne*
Linda McCuen, *Anderson University*
Amy Nissley, *East Texas Baptist University*
Danielle Parisi, *Montclair State University*
Melissa Phillips, *Brandman University*
Peggy Rawn, *Loyola Marymount University*
Valerie Roderick, *ASU/Mary Lou Fulton Teachers College*
Lynn Stafford, *Rockford College*
Roben Taylor, *Jacksonville State University*
Doris Tyler, *North Carolina Central University*
Alandra Weller-Clarke, *Benedictine University*
Glenda Windfield, *Jackson State University*
Roberta Wohle, *Fairleigh Dickinson University*
Jie Zhang, *SUNY College at Brockport*

We also wish to acknowledge Kate Scheinman, freelance development editor at Cengage Learning, who skillfully guided us through the process of writing this book.

Janet Lerner acknowledges her first college instructor in special education, a stimulating and provocative scholar and writer, the late Dr. Samuel A. Kirk, who played a significant role in the inception of this book. She also thanks her family—Susan, Laura, Dean, James, Aaron, Lee, Sue, Anne, and Sarah. Finally, she recognizes her husband, Eugene, who continues to provide the encouragement and support every author needs.

Beverley Johns wants to thank the professor who most influenced her career, Dr. Beth Sulzer-Azaroff, for her guidance and inspiration. She values the long dedication of Janet Lerner to the field of learning disabilities and greatly appreciates being her co-author. Her family (James, Martha, Jim, Craig, Babs, Luverne, Judi, and Jan, and Don) has provided the training, discipline, and encouragement that every author must have. Her husband, Lonnie, is a source of constant support and personal security.

Janet W. Lerner
Beverley H. Johns

JANET W. LERNER is professor emeritus at Northeastern Illinois University, where she served as professor and chairperson of the Department of Special Education. She received the J. E. Wallace Wallin Special Education Lifetime Achievement Award from the Council of Exceptional Children. She was awarded the Romaine P. Mackie Award from the Pioneers Division of CEC. Dr. Lerner served as a general education teacher, a special education teacher, and a reading specialist at the elementary, middle school, and high school levels. She has taught at several colleges and universities in the fields of learning disabilities, reading instruction, and special education. She served as coeditor of the journal *Learning Disabilities: An Interdisciplinary Journal,* a publication of the Learning Disabilities Association of America. Dr. Lerner has authored and coauthored numerous journal articles and books, including *Young Children With Special Needs* (2006) and *Reading Problems: Diagnosis and Teaching Strategies* (2010). Dr. Lerner is currently an adjunct professor in the PACE program at National Louis University.

BEVERLEY HOLDEN JOHNS has 35 years' experience working with students with learning disabilities and emotional/behavioral disorders within the public schools of Illinois. She is now a learning and behavior consultant and an adjunct instructor for MacMurray College. She is the 2000 recipient of the CEC Outstanding Leadership Award from the International Council for Exceptional Children, past international president of the Council for Children with Behavioral Disorders, and she is the 2007 recipient of the Romaine P. Mackie Leadership Service Award. She served as president of the International Association of Special Education from 2006 to 2010. She presented the first Marden lecture at the University of Hong Kong. Johns is the lead author of 10 books (and coauthor of 4 others). She is listed in *Who's Who in America, Who's Who of American Women, Who's Who in American Education,* and *Who's Who Among America's Teachers.* She has chaired ISELA, the Illinois Special Education Coalition (whose membership includes 13 statewide organizations), for 30 years. She is a past president of the Learning Disabilities Association of Illinois, and was the national state president's representative serving on the Board of LDA of America. She has presented workshops across the United States and Canada; in San Juan, Puerto Rico; Sydney, Australia (keynote), Warsaw, Poland; Hong Kong, China; Lima, Peru; and Riga, Latvia.

energyy/iStockphoto.c

Learning Disabilities and Related Disabilities: Characteristics and Current Directions

A teacher affects eternity; he can never tell where his influence stops.

—Henry Adams

LEARNING OBJECTIVES

After reading this chapter, you should be able to:

1.1 Describe key changes in special education

1.2 Describe the categories of learning disabilities and other related disabilities

1.3 Describe the neurosciences and the brain

1.4 Identify new issues and directions in special education

Part 1 of this book consists of Chapter 1, "Learning Disabilities and Related Disabilities: Characteristics and Current Directions." In this chapter, we consider (1) some significant changes in special education, (2) the category of learning disabilities and the history of learning disabilities, (3) related other disabilities, (4) neurosciences and study of the brain, and (5) major current issues in the field of special education.

STANDARDS Addressed in This Chapter:

Council for Exceptional Children Initial Level Special Educator Preparation Standards as approved by the National Council for the Accreditation of Teacher Education

CEC Initial Preparation Standard 1: Learner Development and Individual Learning Differences

- 1.0—Beginning special education professionals understand how exceptionalities may interact with development and learning and use this knowledge to provide meaningful and challenging learning experiences for individuals with exceptionalities.
- 1.1—Beginning special education professionals understand how language, culture, and family background influence the learning of individuals with exceptionalities.

- 1.2—Beginning special education professionals use understanding of development and individual differences to respond to the needs of individuals with exceptionalities.

CEC Initial Preparation Standard 6: Professional Learning and Ethical Practice

- 6.0—Beginning special education professionals use foundational knowledge of the field and their professional Ethical Principles and Practice Standards to inform special education practice, to engage in

lifelong learning, and to advance the profession.

- 6.2—Beginning special education professionals understand how foundational knowledge and current issues influence professional practice.
- 6.3—Beginning special education professionals understand that diversity is a part of families, cultures, and schools, and that complex human issues can interact with the delivery of special education services.

learning disabilities
A disorder in one or more of the basic processes involved in understanding spoken or written language. It may show up as a problem in listening, thinking, speaking, reading, writing, or spelling, or in a person's ability to do math, despite at least average intelligence. The term does not include children who have learning problems that are primarily the result of visual, hearing, or physical handicaps, mental retardation, or emotional disturbance, or of environmental, cultural, or economic disadvantage. Individuals with learning disabilities encounter difficulty in one or more of seven areas: (1) receptive language, (2) expressive language, (3) basic reading skill, (4) reading comprehension, (5) written expression, (6) mathematics calculations, or (7) mathematics reasoning.

mild disabilities
A grouping of students with different disabilities for instruction, such as learning disabilities, mild intellectual disabilities, emotional disturbances, and other disabilities.

mild/moderate disabilities
A term that includes both students with mild disabilities and students with moderate disabilities.

Intellectual disabilities
The term *intellectual disabilities* has replaced the term *mental retardation* and is characterized by significant limitations both in intellectual functioning and in adaptive behavior as expressed in conceptual, social, and practical adaptive skills. The disability originates before age 18.

This book focuses both on students with learning disabilities (a category in special education) and on students with **disabilities.** Learning disabilities and related other disabilities are conditions that impede learning for many children, adolescents, and adults, affecting their schooling and their adult lives. Some states have categorical certification and programs for specific categories of special education, such as for learning disabilities or emotional/behavioral disorders. Some states have noncategorical (or cross-categorical) certification and programs for students with mild/moderate disabilities.

1.1 Recent Changes in Special Education

A number of recent significant changes have occurred in the field of special education (U.S. Department of Education, 2012). Based on data from the 2012 report:

- **The term** *Intellectual Disabilities* **replaces the term Mental Retardation.** The term "mental retardation" has been in the federal law for special education for over 50 years, but over time it has taken on a pejorative connotation. In October 2010, the law changed the term to "intellectual disabilities."
- **Although Learning Disabilities remains the largest category of disability, the percentage of children identified with learning disabilities has decreased considerably.** Over 4.4% of the population ages 6 through 21 were identified with learning disabilities in 2000, but in 2012 this percentage decreased to 4.0% (U.S. Department of Education, 2012).
- **The category of "Other Health Impaired" (OHI) has increased significantly.** The category of OHI includes children with "attention deficit/hyperactivity disorder" (ADHD). Because an increasing number of students are identified with ADHD, the category of OHI has increased significantly. Almost 1% of the general population is identified with OHI (U.S. Department of Education, 2012).

- **The number of children identified with "Autism" has increased significantly.** This is in part due to the expanded designation of autism to include "autism spectrum disorder." In 2000, 1% of the population was identified with autism, but this percentage increased to 3% (U.S. Department of Education, 2012). The Centers for Disease Control and Prevention (CDC) reported that a new estimate of American children having autism spectrum disorder is 1 in 50 (CDC, 2013).
- **Common Core Standards**

Over the next several years, most schools will be working to implement the common core standards since the majority of the states have adopted them. These will have major implications for students with disabilities as educators work to provide universally designed procedures to ensure that students with disabilities have access to the standards. All educators will also be working to task analyze the common core skills to determine the specific strategies that will be utilized to ensure progress in the standards. An increasing emphasis on differentiated instruction will be necessary to include all students in the common core. Specific attention to vocabulary development and critical thinking will be essential.

These standards are designed to result in uniform expectations and are sequential. New assessments based on these standards will be utilized. There is a strong emphasis within the common core on critical thinking skills, literacy, collaborative work, text complexity and on 21st century skills for career preparation.

According to the National Governors' Association for Best Practices, teachers, parents, and community leaders have weighed in to help create the Common Core State Standards. The standards communicate what is expected of students at each grade level. Provided teachers are given adequate training and support, these standards will allow teachers to be better equipped to know exactly to how to help students learn and establish individualized benchmarks for them. The Common Core Standards focus on the core conceptual understandings and procedures and give students the opportunity to master them. (National Governors Association Center for Best Practices, 2010).

The concepts and strategies presented in this text are broad in scope and are applicable for students with disabilities. Table 1.1 describes some of the characteristics of students with disabilities.

In the following section, we briefly review the major categories of special education. Specifically, we review the categories of Intellectual Disabilities, Social/Emotional Disturbance, Learning Disabilities, and Other Disabilities.

1.1a Intellectual Disabilities

The term *Intellectual Disabilities* is used in the 30th Annual Report to Congress (U.S. Department of Education, 2012) instead of *mental retardation*, which was previously used in the special education law (IDEA-2004). Many special educators and parents have long felt that the term *mental retardation* is stigmatizing and demeaning. In response to this concern, the American Association for Mental Retardation (AAMR), the foremost organization supporting the needs of people with mental retardation, in February 2007 changed its name to the

TABLE 1.1

Common Learning and Behavioral Characteristics of Students With Related Other Disabilities

Characteristic	Description
Disorders of attention	Does not focus when a lesson is presented; short attention span, easily distracted, poor concentration; may display hyperactivity
Poor motor abilities	Difficulty with gross motor abilities and fine motor coordination (exhibits general awkwardness and clumsiness)
Psychological processing differences	Problems in processing auditory or visual information (difficulty in interpreting visual or auditory stimuli)
Poor cognitive strategies for learning	Does not know how to go about the task of learning and studying; lacks organizational skills; passive learning style (do not direct their own learning)
Oral language difficulties	Underlying language disorders (problems in language development, listening, speaking, and vocabulary)
Reading difficulties	Problems in learning to decode words, basic word-recognition skills, or reading comprehension
Writing difficulties	Performs poorly in tasks requiring written expression, spelling, and handwriting
Mathematics difficulties	Difficulty with quantitative thinking, arithmetic, time, space, and calculation facts
Poor social skills	Does not know how to act and talk in social situations; difficulty with establishing satisfying social relationships and friendships

© Cengage Learning

American Association on Intellectual Disabilities (*http://www.aaidd.org*). The law and many agencies and organizations now refer to *intellectual disabilities* rather than to *mental retardation.* On September 24, 2010, Congress passed S. 2781 known as "Rosa's Law," which changed the term *mental retardation* to *intellectual disabilities* in all laws that refer to individuals with disabilities. In "Rosa's Law" an intellectual disability shall mean a condition previously referred to as mental retardation or a variation of this term, and shall have the same meaning with respect to programs or qualifications for programs for individuals with such conditions. (S. 2781, September 24, 2010).

In 2002, the AAMR's definition of mental retardation was revised as follows:

> Mental retardation is characterized by significant limitations both in intellectual functioning and in adaptive behavior as expressed in conceptual, social, and practical adaptive skills. The disability originates before age 18.

adaptive behavior
Skills that people need to function in their everyday lives, such as independent skills and social responsibility. Part of the definition of mental retardation.

The revised definition recognizes that mental retardation is a set of conditions that blends together intelligence and adaptive behavior. Adaptive behavior refers to practical skills, such as self-care skills, independent skills, or social skills. The levels of mental retardation are structured by the level of supports that the student needs. Thus, mental retardation is a particular state of functioning that begins in childhood and is characterized by limitations in both intelligence and adaptive skills (Kirk et al., 2009; Hunt & Marshall, 2013).

Students with mild intellectual disabilities can learn academic skills, but their learning rate is slow and they will need sufficient supports along the way.

TABLE 1.2

Levels of Support Needed by Students With Intellectual Disabilities

1. Intermittent support	Support provided as needed, and not at all times. This level is similar to mild intellectual disabilities.
2. Limited support	Support provided on a regular basis for a short period of time. This level is similar to moderate intellectual disabilities.
3. Extensive support	Support provided on an ongoing and regular basis. This level is similar to severe intellectual disabilities.
4. Pervasive support	Support consists of constant high-intensity help across environments and involves more staff members. This level is similar to profound intellectual disabilities.

© Cengage Learning

Levels of Intellectual Disabilities When levels of intellectual disabilities were based on IQ scores, they were defined with the terms *mild, moderate, severe,* or *profound.* Currently four levels of intellectual disabilities are based on the level of support that students need (Table 1.2).

Prevalence of Intellectual Disabilities Most students with intellectual disabilities considered mild (87%) are likely to be in programs for mild disabilities. About 16% of all students with intellectual disabilities are in general education classes for 80% or more of the day, and 29% are in regular classes for 40% to 79% of the day (U.S. Department of Education, 2012). About 8% of all students with disabilities are in the category of intellectual disabilities. Useful websites for intellectual disabilities include *http://thearc.org* (the ARC) and *http://www.aaidd.org* (American Association on Intellectual and Developmental Disabilities). Children with intellectual disabilities are found in every economic, racial, cultural, and language group.

1.1b Emotional/Behavioral Disorders

The term used in the federal law is *emotional disturbance* (Individuals with Disabilities Education Improvement Act (IDEA-2004). *Emotional Disturbance* is defined in the federal IDEA-2004 regulations, shown in Table 1.3.

TABLE 1.3

Emotional Disturbance as Defined in Federal Law
(IDEA-2004 Regulations)

A condition exhibiting one or more of the following characteristics over a long period of time and to a marked degree that adversely affects educational performance—

A. An inability to learn that cannot be explained by intellectual, sensory, or health factors;

B. An inability to build or maintain satisfactory interpersonal relationships with peers and teachers;

C. Inappropriate types of behaviors or feelings under normal circumstances;

D. A general pervasive mood of unhappiness or depression; or

E. A tendency to develop physical symptoms or fears associated with personal or school problems

© Cengage Learning

TeachSource Video Case Activity

Watch the TeachSource Video Case entitled "Foundations: Aligning Instruction with Federal Legislation." In this video a teacher, a specialist, an intern, and the principal discuss the federal laws of the Individuals with Disabilities Education Act (IDEA) and No Child Left Behind Act (NCLB), and the implementation of these laws.

QUESTIONS

1. What problems did these educators discuss in the process of implementing these laws?

2. What are the differences between IDEA and NCLB?

©Cengage Learning 2015.

No Child Left Behind Act (NCLB)
The 2001 revision of the Elementary and Secondary Education Act of 2001. Public Law 107–110.

emotional/behavioral disorders (EBD)
Students who have emotional disorders or behavioral disturbances. Many states use the designation EBD to refer to both conditions.

emotional disorders
Involves feelings about oneself, such as depression or low self-esteem, that can interfere with a person's outlook on life and the ability to learn.

behavioral disorders
Disabilities that result in an adverse effect on educational performance and are characterized by one or more of these problems: An inability to build or maintain satisfactory interpersonal relationships with peers and teachers; inappropriate types of behaviors or feelings under normal circumstances; general pervasive mood of unhappiness or depression; or a tendency to develop physical symptoms or fears associated with personal or school problems.

Many experts note that there are problems with the federal definition; and instead, they suggest using the term *emotional/behavioral disorders* (EBD) (Kauffman & Landrum, 2009; Forness & Knitzer, 1992; Stichter, Conroy, & Kauffman, 2008). Forness & Knitzer (1992) indicate that the term *emotional/behavioral disorders* has several advantages over the federal term of *emotional disturbance.* It (a) reflects terminology that reflects current professional preference, (b) includes both disorders of emotion and behavior, (c) focuses on behaviors that occur within the school, and (d) excludes minor or temporary problems.

Many states and school programs use the term emotional/behavioral disorders (EBD). Emotional/behavioral disorders interfere with learning, and students with this type of disability present a significant challenge to teachers and others. Often students with emotional/behavioral disorders are included in programs for mild disabilities.

Characteristics of Emotional/Behavioral Disorders The characteristics of emotional disorders and behavioral disorders differ. Emotional disorders involve feelings about oneself. For example, the student may feel so chronically sad or depressed or have such a low self-concept that these feelings interfere with the individual's outlook on life and ability to learn.

Behavioral disorders involve more overt problems, such as aggressive or antisocial behavior. Often behavioral and emotional challenges are interdependent or overlap with each other and are interrelated. A student who feels poorly about himself or herself may engage in specific behaviors that lead to being socially isolated. A student who is depressed may engage in withdrawal behavior, which leads to poor peer relationships. Moreover, emotional and behavioral challenges occur in diverse populations, and they are found in every economic, racial, cultural, and language group.

Students with emotional/behavioral disorders are discussed in detail in Chapter 6, "Social, Emotional, and Behavioral Challenges." Chapter 6 also describes teaching strategies and the needed supports for students with emotional and behavioral challenges.

Prevalence of Emotional Disturbance About 7% of all students with disabilities are identified under the category of emotional disturbance (see Table 1.4). About 35% of these students are in general education classes (80% or more of the day) and 21% are in general education classes for 40% to 80% of the day (U.S. Department of Education, 2012).

TABLE 1.4

Categories of Children With Disabilities, Ages 6–17

Type of Disability	Percent of Population	Percent of All Disabilities
High-Incidence Categories		
Learning disabilities	5.36	46.2
Language impairment	2.29	19.7
Intellectual disabilities	0.98	8.4
Emotional disturbance	0.92	7.9
Other health impairment	0.99	8.5
Low-Incidence Categories		
Autism	0.32	2.8
Hearing impairment	0.14	1.2
Orthopedic impairment	0.12	1.0
Visual impairment	0.05	0.1
Traumatic brain injury	0.04	0.3
Developmental delay	0.15	1.3
Multiple disabilities	0.23	2.0
Deaf-blindness	0	0
All disabilities	11.60	100.0

Source: From U. S. Department of Education. (2012). Thirtieth annual report to Congress on the implementation of the Individuals with Disabilities Education Act. Washington, DC: Westat.

1.1c The Series of Special Education Laws

There have been a series of special education laws, as shown in Table 1.5. Under this series of laws, all children and youth ages 3 through 21 with disabilities have a right to a free and appropriate public education. Further, each state must have a special education plan that is in compliance with the federal law.

TABLE 1.5

Series of Special Education Laws

Year	Number	Name of Law
1975	P.L. 94-142	The Education of All Handicapped Children Act
1986	P.L. 99-457	The Education for All Handicapped Children Act Amendments
1990	P.L. 101-476	The Individuals with Disabilities Education Act of 1990
1997	P.L. 105-117	The Individuals with Disabilities Education Act of 1997
2004	P.L. 108-456	The Individuals with Disabilities Education Improvement Act of 2004

© Cengage Learning

Public Law 94-142

The Education for All Handicapped Children Act, Public Law 94-142 was passed by Congress in 1975. The law guarantees a free and appropriate public education to children with disabilities. This law was reauthorized in 1990 and 1997 as the Individuals with Disabilities Education Act (IDEA). The most recent version is the 2004 Individuals with Disabilities Education Improvement Act (IDEA-2004).

Special education laws are considered civil rights legislation that guarantees education to individuals with disabilities. The first law providing for students with disabilities was called the Education for All Handicapped Children Act (Public Law 94-142), passed by Congress in 1975. The most recent law in the series is the *Individuals with Disabilities Education Improvement Act of 2004* (IDEA-2004).

1.1d Learning Disabilities

Students with learning disabilities are typically included within the designation of "high incidence disabilities." A more detailed discussion of learning disabilities is given in the next section. A concise description of learning disabilities is that it is a neurological condition that interferes with a person's ability to store, process, or produce information. It can affect the person's ability to read, write, speak, spell, compute math, reason, and can also affect one's attention, memory, coordination, social skills, and emotional maturity (Learning Disabilities Association of America, 2009). There are several other widely used definitions of learning disabilities, which are presented in the next section, on the category of learning disabilities.

About 40% of all students with disabilities are identified under the category of learning disabilities. About 55% of these students are in general education classes for 80% or more of the school day, and about 31% are in regular classes for 40% to 79% if the school day (U.S. Department of Education, 2012). Students with learning disabilities are often included in groups of mild disabilities. Children with learning disabilities are found in every economic, racial, cultural, and language group.

1.1e Other Disabilities

Children with other disabilities are often included in the designation *high incidence disabilities*, depending in large measure on the individual state's certification requirements for special education teachers, as well as specific programs that are in the schools. For example, in Illinois, the initial certification for special education teachers certifies teachers to teach seven different categories of disabilities: learning disabilities, intellectual disabilities, emotional/behavioral disturbance, orthopedic impairments, traumatic brain injury, autism, and other health impairments. Thus, types of other disabilities that may be included in mild disabilities depend on individual state certification regulations and school programs. Children with other disabilities are found in every economic, racial, cultural, and language group.

> ### Did You Get It?
> The U.S. Department of Education has pointed to several trends in its 2012 Annual Report to Congress. One such change pertains specifically to the category of "Learning Disabilities," a category whose number of identified students has _____ in recent years.
> **a.** virtually remained the same
> **b.** decreased slightly
> **c.** decreased markedly
> **d.** increased dramatically

1.2 The Category of Learning Disabilities: A Field in Transition

A learning disability is a neurological condition that interferes with a person's ability to store, process, or produce information, affecting the person's ability to read, write, speak, spell, or compute mathematics. It can also interfere with attention, memory, coordination, and social skills. If provided with the right support and interventions, students with learning disabilities can succeed in school and have a successful, and often distinguished, career later in life. Parents and teachers can help the student achieve success by both fostering the student's strengths and knowing the student's weaknesses.

The enigma of the youngster who encounters extraordinary difficulty in learning, of course, is not new. Throughout the years, children from all walks of life, in all cultures, nations, and language groups have experienced serious difficulties in learning. The condition of learning disabilities has been recognized for over 50 years, and its recognition offered a welcome explanation for misunderstood children who were encountering serious problems in school and in learning.

1.2a Prevalence of Learning Disabilities

Beginning in 2000, the number of students identified with learning disabilities in the public schools has decreased. In 1997, 4.4% of the population were identified with learning disabilities. By the year 2006, the number had dropped to 4.0%. This decrease in learning disabilities occurred, even though the numbers of students eligible for special education continued to grow—increasing 16% over the past 7 years (see Figure 1.1). Probably, some students are being identified in other areas of disabilities, such as ADHD or Autism Spectrum Disorder.

Several possible reasons for this decrease in the prevalence of students identified with learning disabilities are suggested by Cortiella (2009) in the *State of Learning Disabilities*. They include:

- Shifts of students to other disability categories, such as ADHD, which is included in the category, Other Health Impairments, or Autism.

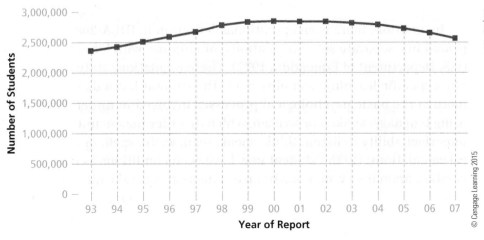

FIGURE **1.1**
Students With Learning Disabilities

© Cengage Learning 2015

- Expansion and attention to early childhood education.
- Improvements in reading instruction provided in general education.
- Shifts in identification approaches, including the use of Response-to-Intervention (RTI).

1.2b Definitions of Learning Disabilities

The Federal Definition The most widely used definition of learning disabilities first appeared in 1975 in Public Law 94-142, the Education for All Handicapped Children Act. It also has been incorporated in the series of revisions of this law, including the federal Individuals with Disabilities Education Improvement Act of 2004 (IDEA-2004): The definition of learning disabilities in the federal law forms the basis of many state definitions, and it is used by many schools. The definition of learning disabilities in the federal law IDEA-2004 is:

> The term "specific learning disability" means a disorder in one or more of the basic psychological processes involved in understanding or in using language, spoken or written, which disorder may manifest itself in imperfect ability to listen, think, speak, read, write, spell, or to do mathematical calculations. Such term includes such conditions as perceptual disabilities, brain injury, minimal brain dysfunction, dyslexia, and developmental aphasia. Such term does not include a learning problem that is primarily the result of visual, hearing, or motor disabilities; of mental retardation; of emotional disturbance; or of environmental, cultural, or economic disadvantage.
>
> —*Source:* U.S. Department of Education. 2012. The Individuals with Disabilities Education Improvement Act of 2004 (IDEA-2004). Washington, DC.

To summarize, the federal definition of learning disabilities includes the following major concepts (some of which have become controversial):

1. The individual has a *disorder in one or more of the basic psychological processes.* (These processes refer to mental abilities, such as memory, auditory perception, visual perception, oral language, and thinking.)
2. The individual has *difficulty in learning*, specifically, in speaking, listening, writing, reading (word-recognition skills and comprehension), and mathematics (calculation and reasoning).
3. The problem is *not primarily due to other causes*, such as visual or hearing impairments, motor disabilities, intellectual disabilities, emotional disturbance, or economic, environmental, or cultural disadvantage.

In addition, there is an operational definition in IDEA-2004 that first appeared in a separate set of regulations for children with learning disabilities (U.S. Department of Education, 1977). These regulations state that a student has a specific learning disability if: (1) the student has a disorder in one or more of the basic psychological processes involved in understanding or in using language, spoken or written, which disorder may manifest itself in the imperfect ability to listen, think, speak, read, write, spell, or do mathematical calculations; (2) the student may have such conditions as perceptual disabilities, brain injury, minimal brain dysfunction, dyslexia, and developmental aphasia; (3) the student does not achieve at the proper age and ability levels in one or more specific areas when provided with appropriate learning experiences; and (4) the student has a severe discrepancy between achievement and intellectual ability in one or more of these seven areas: (a) oral expression, (b) listening comprehension, (c) written expression, (d) basic reading skills, (e) reading comprehension, (f) mathematics calculation, and (g) mathematics reasoning.

To determine eligibility for services for a student with learning disabilities, the school may consider whether a severe discrepancy exists between the student's apparent ability for learning and his or her low level of achievement. As noted later in this chapter and in Chapter 2, "Assessment and the IEP Process," the school may also consider the student's *response-to-intervention* to determine eligibility.

Other Significant Definitions of Learning Disabilities Two other significant definitions of learning disabilities are offered by the National Joint Committee on Learning Disabilities and the Interagency Committee on Learning Disabilities. Additional definitions of learning disabilities have been developed by other organizations and in other countries.

National Joint Committee on Learning Disabilities (NJCLD) The **National Joint Committee on Learning Disabilities (NJCLD)** is an organization of representatives from 14 professional organizations and disciplines involved with learning disabilities. The NJCLD definition includes the following highlights (National Joint Committee of Learning Disabilities (NJCLD), 1990; National Center for Learning Disabilities, 2009):

- Heterogeneous (or diverse) group of disorders
- Significant difficulties in the acquisition and use of listening, speaking, reading, writing, reasoning, or mathematical skills
- Disorders are intrinsic (or inherent) to the individual, presumed to be due to central nervous system dysfunction
- Occurs across the life span
- Often problems in self-regulatory behaviors, social perception, and social interaction
- May occur concomitantly with other disabilities, (e.g., sensory impairment, mental retardation, serious emotional disturbance) or with extrinsic influences (such as cultural differences, or insufficient or inappropriate instruction). They are not the result of those conditions or influences.

Interagency Committee on Learning Disabilities (ICLD) The **Interagency Committee on Learning Disabilities (ICLD)** is a government committee that was commissioned by the U.S. Congress to develop a definition of learning disabilities. ICLD includes representatives of 12 agencies within the Department of Health and Human Services and the Department of Education. The ICLD definition includes social skills deficits as a characteristic of learning disabilities (Interagency Committee on Learning Disabilities, 1988).

Diagnostic and Statistical Manual of Mental Disorders (*DSM* 5) The Diagnostic and Statistical Manual of Mental Disorders (DSM 5), published in May 2013, represents 36,000 individuals in the field of mental health. This includes many physicians and psychologists. The definition for this organization in its 5th edition is not *learning disabilities.* Instead, they use the terms *reading disorders, written expression disorders,* and *mathematics disorders* (American Psychiatric Association, 2013).

National Joint Committee on Learning Disabilities (NJCLD)
An organization of representatives from several professional organizations and disciplines involved with learning disabilities.

Interagency Committee on Learning Disabilities (ICLD)
A committee commissioned by the U.S. Congress and made up of representatives from 12 agencies of the Department of Health and Human Services and the Department of Education to develop a federal definition of learning disabilities.

1.2c Common Elements in the Definitions of Learning Disabilities

The various definitions of learning disabilities have several elements in common: (1) neurological factors, (2) cognitive processing factors, (3) difficulty in academic and learning tasks, (4) discrepancy between potential and achievement, and (5) exclusion of other causes. The nature of each of these elements and the problematic issues that surround them are briefly described in the following section.

 Neurological Factors Although not always stated directly, implied in many of the definitions is the view that learning disabilities are related to neurological factors. All learning originates within the brain and, consequently, a disorder in learning can be caused by a dysfunction in the central nervous system, which is an organic system comprising the brain and the spinal cord. In many cases, the neurological condition is difficult to detect by medical examination or external medical tests. Central nervous system dysfunction is therefore usually determined through observation of behavior. Neuroscience and medical research report growing evidence of the neurological basis for learning disabilities through functional Magnetic Resonance Imaging (fMRI) studies (Shaywitz, 2003; Sousa, 2001).

Cognitive Processing Factors Cognitive processing factors refer to an uneven development of the various components of mental functioning. Mental ability is not a single capacity; rather, it is composed of many underlying mental abilities. For the individual with learning disabilities, these component abilities do not develop in an even fashion. That is, whereas some of the components are maturing in an anticipated sequence or rate, others are lagging in their development, thereby appearing as symptoms of the learning problem. Students with learning disabilities manifest strengths and weaknesses in different mental processes. A key phrase in the federal definition that refers to this component of the definition is *a disorder in one or more of these basic psychological processes.*

Difficulty in Academic and Learning Tasks Individuals with learning disabilities encounter different types of problems in learning. One child's challenge may be in the acquisition of speech and oral language; another's may be in reading, arithmetic, handwriting, motor skills, or writing. As noted earlier, the operational portion of the federal definition identifies seven specific academic areas of learning in which learning disabilities can be detected.

Discrepancy Between a Student's Potential for Learning and Academic Achievement The most controversial component in the definitions of learning disabilities is the identification of a gap between what the student is potentially capable of learning and what the student has in fact learned or achieved. The operational portion of the federal definition states that the child with learning disabilities has a severe discrepancy between achievement and intellectual ability in one or more of seven areas.

To determine if a discrepancy exists between potential and achievement, one must (1) determine the student's potential for learning, (2) the student's current achievement level, and (3) the degree of discrepancy between the

---

severe discrepancy
A significant difference between a child's current achievement and intellectual potential.

current achievement level
A student's present stage of performance in an academic area.

student's potential for learning and the actual achievement level. This evaluation process entails a number of issues, such as the use of IQ tests to determine a student's potential for learning and the degree of severe discrepancy needed to ascertain a learning disability. Some states quantify the learning disability discrepancy using one of several forms of "discrepancy formulas" to determine if a child is eligible for learning disabilities services. (Visit the Student website for more information on these eligibility formulas.)

Exclusion of Other Causes This component of the definition reflects the notion that learning disabilities are not primarily the result of other conditions, such as intellectual disabilities; emotional disturbance; visual or hearing impairments; or cultural, social, or economic environments.

In practice, however, the exclusion component of the definition of learning disabilities becomes difficult to implement because children often exhibit co-occurring (or comorbid) problems. Teachers who work with children with other disabilities often observe that many students appear to have two problems—their primary disability plus their learning disabilities. There is growing acceptance that other conditions often co-occur with learning disabilities (Silver, 2006).

1.2d Gifted and Talented Children With Learning Disabilities

Some children with learning disabilities also may be gifted and talented (Vukovic & Siegel, 2006; Lovett & Lewandowski, 2005). Characteristics of giftedness include spontaneity, inquisitiveness, imagination, boundless enthusiasm, and emotionality; and these same traits are often observed in children with learning disabilities. Often, children with learning disabilities, like gifted children, seem to require a great deal of activity. They may find the general education classroom environment uninviting, or they may have trouble attending to the classroom instruction. If their learning needs are not being met, they may respond by becoming fidgety, inattentive, and even disruptive. It is especially important that difficulty with school for these children does not lead to the withholding of learning opportunities, which can develop into frustration, failure, or depression.

Gifted and talented individuals with learning disabilities can become high-achieving adults. Successful adults with learning disabilities may find the world of work to be quite different from the world of school. Studies show that many highly successful people have learning disabilities. In fact, one

Some children with learning disabilities can also be gifted or talented.

study shows that 30% to 40% of 300 individuals who had achieved a high level of financial success had learning difficulties in school (Kantrowitz & Underwood, 1999; West, 2003). A major business magazine, *Fortune,* did a cover story on chief executive officers (CEOs) of major corporations who have learning disabilities (Morris, 2002). There appears to be a strong, positive side to learning disabilities that requires further research (West, 2003).

1.2e Characteristics of Learning Disabilities

Many different characteristics are associated with learning disabilities. However, each individual is unique and will display only some of these characteristics. No one individual displays all of the characteristics and traits. Some students have disabilities in mathematics, whereas others excel in mathematics. Attention problems are symptomatic for many students with learning disabilities, but not for all. Further, certain characteristics are more likely to be exhibited at certain age levels. For example, young children are more likely to be hyperactive than adolescents. In addition, deficits are manifested in different ways at different age levels. For example, an underlying language disorder may appear as a delayed speech problem in the preschooler, as a reading disorder in the elementary pupil, and as a writing disorder in the secondary student. Moreover, these characteristics are also found among students with mild disabilities. The implications of each of these learning and behavioral characteristics are complex, and they are discussed in detail throughout this book.

Gender Differences Clinics and schools identify four times more boys than girls who have learning disabilities. However, gender research shows that there actually may be as many girls with learning disabilities as boys, but they are not being identified. Boys and girls with learning disabilities have different characteristics. Boys tend to exhibit more physical aggression and loss of control; however, they also exhibit visual-motor abilities, spelling ability, and written language mechanical aptitude. Girls with learning disabilities tend to have more cognitive, language, and social problems and to have severe academic achievement deficits in reading and math. Girls tend to be more verbal and display less physical aggression. Girls with learning disabilities who are not identified are an underserved group that is at significant risk for long-term academic, social, and emotional difficulties (Cortiella, 2009; Shaywitz, 2003).

Explanations of why more boys than girls are identified with learning disabilities include *biological causes* (males may be more vulnerable to learning disabilities), *cultural factors* (more males may be identified because boys tend to exhibit more disruptive behaviors that are troublesome to adults), and *expectation pressures* (the expectations for success in school may be greater for boys than for girls).

1.2f Characteristics at Different Stages of Life

When the initial small group of concerned parents and professionals first sought to obtain help for their children and to promote the field of learning disabilities in the 1960s, their efforts focused on the pressing needs of the elementary-level child. Today, we recognize that learning disabilities become evident at many stages of life and that the problem appears in a different form at each stage.

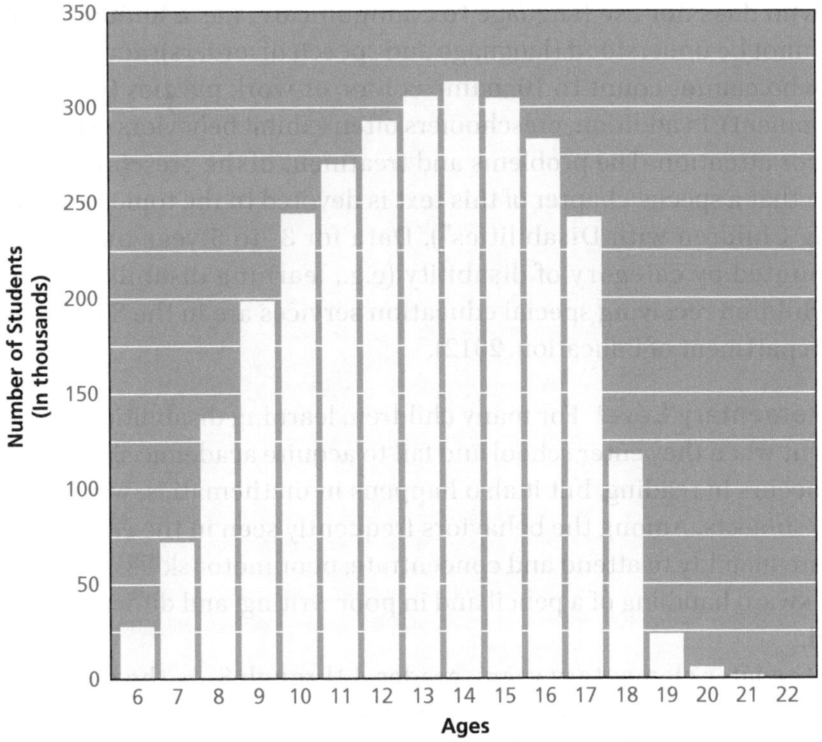

FIGURE **1.2**
Age Distribution of Students With
Learning Disabilities

[Bar chart: Y-axis labeled "Number of Students (In thousands)" ranging from 0 to 350 in increments of 50. X-axis labeled "Ages" from 6 to 22. Bars show approximately: age 6 ≈ 25, age 7 ≈ 75, age 8 ≈ 140, age 9 ≈ 200, age 10 ≈ 245, age 11 ≈ 270, age 12 ≈ 295, age 13 ≈ 310, age 14 ≈ 315, age 15 ≈ 305, age 16 ≈ 280, age 17 ≈ 245, age 18 ≈ 120, age 19 ≈ 25, age 20 ≈ 5, ages 21–22 ≈ 0]

Source: To assure the free appropriate public education of all children with disablities. Twenty-eight annual report to congress in the Implementation of the individual with Disabilities Education Act, by the U.S. Department of Education, 2008. Washington, DC: Westat.

Figure 1.2 illustrates the number of children identified with specific learning disabilities at each age, from ages 6 to 21 (U.S. Department of Education, 2012). The number of students gradually increases from age 6 to 9, a majority of students are in the 9 to 14 age range, and the number decreases sharply from age 16 to 21. This pattern suggests that substantial numbers of children with learning disabilities are identified in the age range of 9 through 14. Most children are not identified until age 9, and the decrease during the late teen years may relate to the large school dropout rate of adolescents with learning disabilities.

Each age group (preschoolers, elementary children, adolescents, and adults) needs different kinds of skills. Therefore, certain characteristics of learning disabilities assume greater prominence at certain age levels.

The Preschool Level Because growth rates are so unpredictable at young ages, educators are generally reluctant to identify preschoolers under a categorical label such as *learning disabilities*. Very young children (under age 6) who appear to have learning disabilities are often identified with a noncategorical label such as *developmental delay*. Legislation for preschool children with disabilities includes two different laws. (1) Ages birth to age 3 for infants and toddlers, and (2) ages 3 to age 6 for preschoolers. Preschool children are further discussed in Chapter 8, "Young Children With Disabilities." Experience and research show that intervention programs for infants and toddlers (ages birth to 3) and preschool children (ages 3 to 6) are very effective and that intervention efforts have a high payoff (Lerner, Lowenthal, & Egan, 2003).

Among the characteristics displayed by preschool children with developmental delays are poor motor development, language delays, speech disorders, and slow cognitive and concept development. Common examples of problems at the preschool level are the 3-year-old child who cannot catch a ball, hop, jump, or play with manipulative toys (poor motor development); the 4-year-old child who does not use language to communicate, has a limited vocabulary, and cannot be understood (language and speech disorders); and the 5-year-old child who cannot count to 10, name colors, or work puzzles (poor cognitive development). In addition, preschoolers often exhibit behaviors of hyperactivity and poor attention. The problems and treatment of the preschool child are so unique that a special chapter of this text is devoted to the topic (see Chapter 8, "Young Children with Disabilities"). Data for 3- to 5-year-old children are not counted by category of disability (e.g., learning disabilities), but 5.8% of all children receiving special education services are in the 3 to 5 age group (U.S. Department of Education, 2012).

The Elementary Level For many children, learning disabilities first become apparent when they enter school and fail to acquire academic skills. The failure often occurs in reading, but it also happens in mathematics, writing, or other school subjects. Among the behaviors frequently seen in the early elementary years are inability to attend and concentrate; poor motor skills, as evidenced in the awkward handling of a pencil and in poor writing; and difficulty in learning to read.

In the later elementary years, grades 4 through 8, as the curriculum becomes more difficult, problems may emerge in other areas, such as social studies or science because more higher-level thinking skills are required. Emotional problems also become more of an impediment after several years of repeated failure, and students become more conscious of their poor achievement. For some students, social problems and the inability to make and keep friends increase in importance at this age level. About 40% of all children with learning disabilities are in the 6 to 11 age group (U.S. Department of Education, 2012).

The Secondary Level A radical change in schooling occurs at the secondary level, and adolescents find that learning disabilities begin to take a greater toll. The tougher demands of the middle school and high school curricula and teachers, the turmoil of adolescence, and the continued academic failure combine to intensify the learning disability. Adolescents are also concerned about life after completing school. They may need counseling and guidance for college, career, and vocational decisions. To worsen the situation, a few adolescents find themselves drawn into acts of juvenile delinquency or are tempted to drop out of school.

Because adolescents tend to be overly sensitive, some emotional, social, and self-concept problems often accompany a learning disability at this age. Most secondary schools have programs for adolescents with learning disabilities. Although this age group is considered throughout this text, some of its unique features and some special programs for adolescents are discussed in Chapter 9, "Adolescents and Adults With Learning Disabilities and Related Mild Disabilities." About 60% of all students with learning disabilities are in the 12 to 17 age group (U.S. Department of Education, 2012).

The Adult Years By the time they finish schooling, some adults overcome their learning disabilities, are able to reduce them, or have learned how to compensate or circumvent their problems. For many adults, however, the learning problems continue, and vestiges of their disorder continue to hamper them in adulthood. Both reading difficulties and nonverbal social disabilities may limit their career development and may also hinder their ability to make and keep friends. Many adults voluntarily seek help in later life to cope with their learning disabilities.

1.2g Some Eminent People With Learning Disabilities

The life stories of some individuals who eventually became eminent, successful contributors to society reflect their travails with serious learning disabilities. Student Stories 1.1, "Childhood Memories," describes the childhood stories of such people with learning disabilities. These persons of eminence, fortunately, were somehow able to find appropriate ways of learning, and they successfully overcame their initial failures.

STUDENT **STORIES 1.1**

Childhood Memories

Charles Schwab, the founder of the successful and innovative stock brokerage firm, struggled with severe reading problems throughout his life. Schwab explains that he coped by developing his other abilities, such as the capacity to envision, to anticipate where things are going, and to conceive a solution to a business problem (Kantrowitz & Underwood, 1999). Schwab believes his reading problem forced him to develop these skills at a higher level than is attained by people for whom reading comes easily: "I've always felt that I have more of an ability to envision, to be able to anticipate where things are going, to conceive a solution to a business problem than people who are more sequential thinkers" (West, 1997, p. 349). A website for Charles Schwab is at *http://www.schwablearning.org*.

Nelson Rockefeller, who served as vice president of the United States and governor of the state of New York, suffered from severe dyslexia, a type of learning disability that involves extreme difficulty in learning to read. His poor reading ability kept him from achieving good grades in school, and his learning disability forced him to memorize his speeches during his political career. In describing his feelings about growing up with a learning disability, Rockefeller (1976) recalled,

I was dyslexic...and I still have a hard time reading today. I remember vividly the pain and mortification I felt as a boy of eight when I was assigned to read a short passage of scripture at a community vesper service and did a thoroughly miserable job of it. I know what a dyslexic child goes through... the frustration of not being able to do what other children do easily, the humiliation of being thought not too bright when such is not the case at all. But, after coping with this problem for more than 60 years, I have a message of hope and encouragement for children with learning disabilities and their parents (pp. 12–14)

As a child, Thomas Edison, the ingenious American inventor, was called abnormal, addled, and mentally defective. Writing in his diary that he was never able to get along at school, he recalled that he was always at the foot of his class. His father thought of him as stupid, and Edison described himself as a dunce.

Auguste Rodin, the great French sculptor, was called the worst pupil in his school. His teachers diagnosed Rodin as uneducable and advised his parents to put him out to work, although they doubted that he could ever make a living.

Woodrow Wilson, the scholarly 28th president of the United States, did not learn his letters until he was 9 years old and did not learn to read until age 11. Relatives expressed sorrow for his parents because Woodrow was so dull and backward (Thompson, 1971).

Albert Einstein, the theoretical physicist, did not speak until age 3. His search for words was described as laborious and, until he was 7, he formulated each sentence, no matter how commonplace, silently with his lips before speaking the words aloud. Schoolwork did not go well for young Albert. One teacher predicted that "nothing good" would come of him. Einstein's language disabilities persisted throughout his adult life. When he read, he heard words. Writing was difficult for him, and he communicated badly through writing. In describing his thinking process, he explained that he rarely thought in words; it was only after a thought came that he tried to express it in words at a later time (Isaacson, 2007; Patten, 1973).

REFLECTIVE QUESTION

1. How did these early years of academic struggle affect the lives of these individuals?

1.2h The Cross-Cultural Nature of Learning Disabilities

The condition of learning disabilities is a universal problem that occurs in all cultures and nations in the world. The problem is not confined to the United States or to English-speaking countries. Accumulating research shows that in all cultures and societies there are children who seem to have normal intelligence but who also have severe difficulty in learning language, acquiring reading or writing skills, or doing mathematics. The International Academy for Research in Learning Disabilities (IARLD), an organization dedicated to fostering international research on learning disabilities, publishes a journal called *Thalamus* and has a website at *http://www.iarld.com.*

Clinical reports of the personal travails of children from all corners of the world are remarkably similar. In the following excerpt, for example, a Chinese adult remembers his first baffling failure in a Chinese school; the story parallels the bewildering episodes that children with learning disabilities face in U.S. schools (Lerner & Chen, 1992).

> My first recollection of learning problems occurred at age 7, when I entered the first grade in school in Taiwan. My teacher wrote characters on the blackboard and the pupils were to copy this board work into their notebooks. I clearly remember that I was simply unable to perform this task. Observing how easily my classmates accomplished the assignment, I was perplexed and troubled by my inability to copy the characters and words from the board.

Research reports about learning disabilities come from many parts of the world: South Korea, (Kim, Rhee, Burns, & Lerner, 2009), the Netherlands (Van der Lief & Morfidi, 2006; Stevens & Werkhoven, 2001), Great Britain (Wedell, 2001), Scandinavia (Lundberg & Hoien, 2001), New Zealand (Chapman, 1992), Germany (Opp, 2001), Italy (Fabbro & Masutto, 1994), Mexico (Fletcher & DeLopez, 1995), Portugal (da Fonseca, 1996), Canada (Wong & Hutchinson, 2001), Australia (Elkins, 2001), Russia (Korkunov et al., 1998), South America (Bravo-Valdivieso & Miiller, 2001), and Israel (Shalev et al., 1998). The problem appears in children learning an alphabet-based system of written language, such as English, and with children learning a logographic (pictorial) system of written language, such as Chinese (Hsu, 1988) or Japanese (Tsuge, 2001).

1.2i History of the Field of Learning Disabilities

This section offers a brief history of the field of learning disabilities. A more detailed history appears on the student section of the Education CourseMate, under Additional Information for Chapter 1.

The term *learning disabilities* was first introduced in 1963, when a small group of concerned parents and educators met in Chicago to consider linking the isolated parent groups active in a few communities into a single organization. Each of these parent groups identified the children of concern under a different name, including children with *perceptual handicaps*, brain-injured children, and *neurologically impaired children*. To unite these groups, they needed to agree on a single term to identify the children of concern. When the term *learning disabilities* was suggested at this meeting by Sam Kirk (Kirk, 1963), it met with immediate approval. The organization today known as the Learning Disabilities Association of America (LDAA), *http://www.ldaamerica.org*, was born at this historic meeting.

brain injured child
A child who before, during, or after birth has received an injury to or suffered an infection of the brain. As a result of such organic impairment, there are disturbances that prevent or impede the normal learning process.

During the 50 years since learning disabilities were first recognized, the field has wrestled with many controversial issues, and our notion of learning disabilities is different from what it once was (Hallahan, 2007). Although the term *learning disabilities* had immediate appeal and acceptance, the task of developing a definition of learning disabilities that is acceptable to all has proved to be a formidable challenge. Indeed, defining this population is considered so overwhelming that some have likened learning disabilities to Justice Potter Stewart's comment on pornography: impossible to define, "but I know it when I see it." The most influential definition of learning disabilities is in the federal law IDEA-2004.

Learning disabilities was first identified as a category of special education in federal law in 1975 (PL 94-142). These were heady days for parents, who finally had a sensible explanation of their child's problems and for educators who were passionately committed to instructing students with learning disabilities and providing the kind of intensive, relentless, iterative individualized instruction they needed (Hallahan, 2007).

Prior to the establishment of the field of learning disabilities (1800–1930), there was a period of broad scientific research on the functions and disorders of the brain. Many of the early brain researchers were physicians who were involved in investigating the brain damage of adult patients who had suffered a stroke, an accident, or a disease. These scientists gathered information by studying the behavior of patients who had lost some brain function, such as the ability to speak or to read. Through autopsies of many of these patients, the scientists were able to link the loss of functions to specific damaged areas of the brain.

This brain research became the foundation of the field of learning disabilities (1930–1960), when the scientific studies of the brain were applied to the clinical study of children and were then translated into ways of teaching. Psychologists and educators developed instruments for assessment and for methods of teaching students with learning disabilities. During the transition phase, terminology changed many times, with various terms being used to describe the problem—*brain-injured children, minimal brain dysfunction*, and, finally, *learning disabilities*.

The term *brain-injured child* was first used by Alfred Strauss and Laura Lehtinen (1947), pioneers who identified brain-injured children as a new category of exceptional children. Strauss and Lehtinen hypothesized that a brain injury could occur during one of three periods in the child's life: *before* birth (prenatal stage), *during* the birth process, or at some point *after* birth (postnatal stage). These scholars believed that as a result of such organic impairment, the normal learning process was impeded. Many of these children previously had been classified as mentally retarded, emotionally disturbed, autistic, aphasic, or behaviorally maladjusted. A large number of children exhibited such severe behavioral characteristics that they were excluded from the public schools.

One characteristic of the brain-injured child is a perceptual disorder, which is a disturbance in the ability to perceive objects, relations, or qualities—a difficulty in the interpretation of sensory stimulation. For example, one teacher noted that when she wore a particular dress with polka dots, the children with perceptual disorders seemed compelled to touch it to verify what they thought they perceived. Figure 1.3 illustrates the ambiguity in perception that the normal observer senses, and which can help a normal observer understand the

perceptual disorder
A disorder in which the student is unable to recognize and interpret information received through the senses.

FIGURE **1.3**
Do You See a Young Woman or
an Old Woman in This Picture?

Source: Illustration by W. E. Hill in Puck, 1915.

minimal brain dysfunction (MBD)
A term that refers to mild or
minimal neurological abnormality
that causes learning difficulties.

unstable world of the child with a perceptual disorder. In this figure, we are asked to determine whether the picture is the face of an old woman or a young woman. Do you see a young woman or an old woman in this picture?

In Figure 1.4 one is asked to look at the drawing and then to sketch it from memory. (Even copying this figure while viewing it may prove to be difficult.) These illustrations produce a perceptual confusion, much like that experienced by a child with perceptual disorders.

Strauss's work with brain-injured children laid the foundation for the field of learning disabilities by perceiving similar characteristics in a diverse group of children who had been misdiagnosed by specialists, misunderstood by parents, and often discarded by society.

The term minimal brain dysfunction (MBD) is defined as a mild or minimal neurological abnormality that causes learning disabilities, and the term *MBD* was recommended as a way to identify these children by the U.S. Department of Health, Education, and Welfare (Clements, 1966). MBD was used to describe children with near-average intelligence and with certain learning and behavioral disorders associated with deviations or dysfunctions of the central nervous system. Many medical professionals employed the term *MBD* when diagnosing children.

Learning disabilities successfully serves as a recognized way to refer to individuals with problems that are the concern of this text.

Learning disabilities became an established discipline in schools throughout the United States. The field grew rapidly as programs for learning disabilities were developed, teachers were trained, and children began to receive services.

One of the first public school programs for learning disabilities was established in Syracuse, New York (Cruickshank et al., 1961). By the 1960s and 1970s, public school programs for learning disabilities were rapidly established throughout the nation. Several strong forces promoted this development, including parental pressures, an increase of professional information, the availability of teacher training programs, and state laws requiring services for students with learning disabilities. All of this took place before the passage of the first comprehensive special education law in 1975, the Education for All Handicapped Children Act (PL 94-142).

Most of the early programs were for students at the elementary level. In these early programs, children with learning disabilities were placed in separate classes, a setting that followed the traditional instructional programs in special education at that time. Later in this period, resource room programs were introduced, and the secondary schools also began to serve adolescents with learning disabilities. Many new tests and teaching materials were developed during this period to serve the growing number of students identified under the category of learning disabilities.

FIGURE **1.4**
Examine This Drawing;
Try to Copy or Sketch
It From Memory

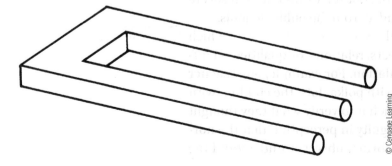

© Cengage Learning

1.2j The Common Core Standards

Learning Disabilities is the largest category, accounting for 40% of all disabilities, Intellectual Disabilities accounts for 0.9%, and Emotional Disturbance accounts for 0.7.% of all disabilities. The category "Other Health Impaired" (OHI), which includes ADHD, accounts for 8.5% of all disabilities.

The designation "Other Disabilities" refers to Low-incidence categories and accounts for approximately 1% of children receiving special education services. Other Disabilities consists of several categories of exceptionality, and often these students are included in the group of Mild Disabilities. For a student to be eligible for special education services, the student must have an identified category of disability that adversely impacts educational performance.

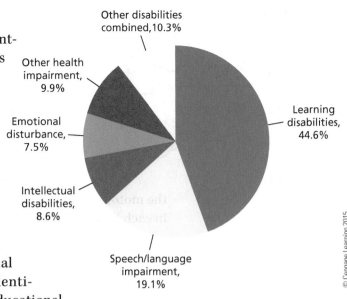

© Cengage Learning 2015

FIGURE **1.5**
Composition of Students With All Learning Disabilities

Did You Get It?

In terms of a "federal" definition of learning disabilities, which of the following is not one of the component criteria?
- **a.** The disability has no possible cause other than learning-related.
- **b.** The individual experiences at least one form of emotional and/or behavioral difficulty in addition to his or her learning disability.
- **c.** A difficult in learning exists.
- **d.** The disorder affects at least one psychological process.

1.3 Neurosciences and Study of the Brain

Informed educators need up-to-date information about the brain and learning. Scientific investigations that attempt to unravel the mysteries of the human brain and learning are fascinating in themselves. Knowledge about the brain is increasing rapidly and promises to further our understanding of the enigma of learning disabilities. Recent neuroscience advances have new technologies to study the brain and its role in learning (Dehaene, 2009; Sousa, 2001).

The neurosciences are the cluster of disciplines that investigate the structure and functions of the brain and the central nervous system. In this section, we briefly examine two facets of the neurosciences: (1) the structure and functions of the brain and (2) recent brain research.

neurosciences
Disciplines that are involved with the study of the brain and its functions.

1.3a The Brain: Its Structure and Functions

All human behavior, including learning, is mediated by the brain. The process of learning is one of the most important activities of the brain. From a neurological perspective, difficulty in academic learning and reading represents a subtle malfunction in this most complex organ of the human body (Dehaene, 2009; Sousa, 2001). Figure 1.6 shows the four major lobes of the brain.

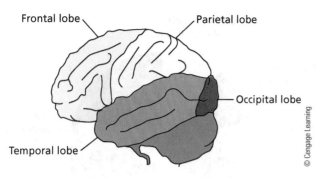

Frontal lobe
Parietal lobe
Occipital lobe
Temporal lobe

© Cengage Learning

FIGURE **1.6**
The Brain

cerebral hemisphere
One of the two halves (the right hemisphere and the left hemisphere) that constitute the human brain.

The Cerebral Hemispheres The human brain is composed of two halves, the right hemisphere and the left hemisphere, which appear on casual inspection to be almost identical in construction and metabolism. Each cerebral hemisphere contains (1) a frontal lobe, (2) a temporal lobe, (3) an occipital lobe, and (4) a parietal lobe, as shown in Figure 1.6. The motor area of each hemisphere controls the muscular activities of the opposite side of the body. Thus, the movements of the right hand and foot originate in the motor area of the left hemisphere. Both eyes and both ears are represented in each hemisphere (Kibby & Hynd, 2001).

Right Brain, Left Brain: Differences in Function Although the two halves of the brain appear almost identical in structure, they differ in function, and these differences appear very early in life.

The left hemisphere reacts to and controls language-related activities. For more than 90% of adults, language function originates in the left hemisphere, regardless of whether the individual is left-handed, right-handed, or a combination of the two. Language is located in the left hemisphere in 98% of right-handed people and in about 71% of left-handed people (Hiscock & Kinsbourne, 1987).

The right hemisphere deals with nonverbal stimuli. Spatial perception, mathematics, music, directional orientation, time sequences, and body awareness are located in the right hemisphere.

Thus, even though visual and auditory nerve impulses are carried to both cerebral hemispheres simultaneously, it is the left hemisphere that reacts to linguistic stimuli, such as words, symbols, and verbal thought. Consequently, adult stroke patients with brain injury in the left hemisphere often suffer language loss, in addition to an impairment in the motor function of the right half of the body.

This duality of the brain has led to speculation that some people tend to approach the environment in a "left-brained fashion," whereas others use a "right-brained approach." Left-brained individuals are strong in language and verbal skills, while right-brained individuals have strengths in spatial, artistic, and mechanical skills. These differences in brain function warrant further discussion because the concept may provide some insight into differences in the need for differentiated learning.

Cerebral Dominance Samuel Orton, a physician and early investigator of reading and language difficulties, theorized that the reversal of letters and words (which he called *strephosymbolia*, or twisted symbols) was symptomatic of a failure to establish *cerebral dominance* in the left hemisphere, which is the location of the language area (Orton, 1937). Current findings support Orton's early theories, showing that the left hemisphere does specialize in the language function and the right hemisphere controls nonverbal functions. However, the two hemispheres of the brain do not operate independently; there are many interrelating elements and functions. The learning process depends on both hemispheres and their interrelating functions. Inefficient functioning of either hemisphere reduces the total effectiveness of individuals and affects their acquisition and use of language (Dehaene, 2009; Shaywitz, 2003; Shaywitz et al., 2002; Kibby & Hynd, 2001).

Lateral Preference The issue of lateral preference is the subject of a related controversial theory, which proposes a relationship between learning disorders and a tendency to use either the right or left side of the body or a preference for the right or left hand, foot, eye, or ear. The term *consistent laterality* refers to the tendency to perform all functions with one side of the body. *Mixed laterality* is a tendency to mix the right and left preference in the use of hands, feet, eyes, and ears. A student's laterality may be tested through observation of simple behaviors—such as throwing a ball, kicking a stick, seeing with a tube, and listening to a watch—or through more sophisticated means used in neuropsychology. There are mixed research findings about the relationship between reading ability and lateral preferences (Biegler, 1987; Obrzut & Boliek, 1991).

lateral preference
A tendency to use either the right or left side of the body or to favor using the hand, foot, eye, or ear of one side of the body.

1.3b Recent Brain Research

Research on the brain and its relationship to behavior and learning has accumulated slowly, in part because some technologies for studying the structure and function of the brain have only recently become available. Today, neuroscientists can vastly extend their studies of the structure and functions of the brain because of technological advancements that have created opportunities for a better understanding of the brain and its relationship to learning and learning problems.

Many of the brain research investigations involve studies of individuals with the condition of dyslexia, which is a puzzling type of learning disability that interferes with learning to read. (See Chapter 12, "Reading Difficulties," for more information about dyslexia.) Individuals with dyslexia encounter severe difficulty with reading. It is not a matter of intelligence; instead, dyslexia appears to be related to brain structure and function. Additional information about dyslexia can be found at the website for the International Dyslexia Association at *http://www.interdys.org.*

dyslexia
A severe reading disorder in which the individual cannot learn to read or does not acquire fluent and efficient reading skills. Research suggests that there is a connection between dyslexia and neurological dysfunction.

The act of reading is an extremely complex human task that requires an intact and well-functioning brain and central nervous system. Modern brain imaging methods reveal the brain areas that activate when a reader deciphers printed words. Moreover, recent brain imaging studies show that people with dyslexia exhibit significant differences in brain functioning (Dehaene, 2009). Student Stories 1.2, "Recollections of Individuals With Dyslexia," illustrates the serious challenges for people with dyslexia.

For almost a century, scientists suspected that there was a neurological basis for dyslexia and that the difficulty in acquiring reading skills stemmed from neurological differences in brain function. With the growing knowledge about the brain and its relationship to reading, there is finally convincing evidence that people with dyslexia do indeed differ in their brain structure and function from persons who do not have reading problems (Dehaene, 2009; Lyon et al., 2001; Shaywitz, 2003; Zeffrino & Eden, 2000).

A series of research studies to investigate the mystery of dyslexia occurred in a relatively short period of time. This research involved (1) postmortem anatomical studies, (2) genetics studies, (3) computed tomography (CT), (4) positron-emission tomography (PET), and (5) functional magnetic resonance imaging (fMRI). Each of these research studies revealed a piece of the puzzle of the brain and reading.

postmortem anatomical studies
Autopsy studies of the brain of persons with a history of dyslexia.

The following stories told by individuals with dyslexia, a severe reading problem, reveal the frustration they faced in school and the strengths they developed as they met the challenges of life.

- Tom Cruise, the successful movie actor, recalls, "When I was about 7 years old, I had been labeled dyslexic. I'd try to concentrate on what I was reading, then I'd get to the end of the page and have very little memory of anything I'd read....I would go blank, feel anxious, nervous, bored, frustrated, dumb. I would get angry. My legs would actually hurt when I was studying. My head ached. All through school, and well into my career, I felt like I had a secret."

Source: From "My struggle to read," by Tom Cruise, *People,* July 21, 2003, 60–64.

The Label of Dyslexia. Two students reflect on the effect of having the label of dyslexia.

- Mary said she was "thrilled" when told that she had dyslexia. She said that the diagnosis and label brought her relief. She could now better assess her abilities and recognize why and where she was having difficulty learning. Also, the label positively affected her parents, prompting them to realize the struggle she underwent in order to do well in school.

- Jackie said the label of dyslexia gave her a "feeling of peace and assurance that [she] wasn't an oddity." She noted, "The label of LD is a label, and as [with any] label[,] stereotypes will always surface. But that label is also part of me. It's as much a part of me as my middle name, as my smile, as my love of lilacs."

Source: From H. McGrady, J. Lerner, & M. Boscardin, "The Educational Lives of Students With Learning Disabilities," in P. Rodis, A. Garrand, & M. Boscardin, *Learning disabilities and life stories* pp. 177–193. Copyright 2001 by Pearson Education. Adapted with the permission of the publisher.

REFLECTIVE QUESTIONS

1. What kinds of memories of school do people with dyslexia have?

2. What reaction do Mary and Jackie have to the label of "dyslexia"?

Postmortem Anatomical Studies Postmortem anatomical studies—autopsy studies—of individuals with dyslexia show strong evidence that the brain structure of dyslexic individuals is different from that of individuals without dyslexia. The brain tissue of eight people—six men and two women—was studied. Some of these individuals were young men who died suddenly, often in motorcycle accidents. At the time of death, their brains were donated for study to an ongoing dyslexia research center at Harvard Medical School's Department of Neurology at Beth Israel Hospital in Boston. The postmortem anatomical brain studies found a remarkable and consistent abnormality in the structure of the brain in these individuals. This abnormality was found in an area of the brain known as the *planum temporale*, which lies on the superior surface of the temporal lobe. In the left hemisphere, this area is the center of language control. In the postmortem studies of dyslexic cases, this area (i.e., the language area) of the left hemisphere was smaller and had fewer brain cells than that of nondyslexic individuals. However, this same area in the right hemisphere was larger and contained more cells than are found in nondyslexic individuals (Galaburda et al., 2006; Galaburda, 1990; Powers, 2000).

genetics of dyslexia
The inheritability of dyslexia.

Genetics Studies Knowledge of the genetics of dyslexia and its role in the inheritability of dyslexia increased significantly in the last decade (Fisher & DeFries, 2002; Snowling, Gallagher, & Frith, 2003; Pennington, 1995). Two types of genetic studies are (1) family studies and (2) twin studies.

Family studies The family studies began with a study conducted in Scandinavia, which showed that dyslexia aggregates in families (Hallgren,

1950). Since then, more extensive family studies continue to show strong evidence that the tendency for severe reading disabilities is inherited and appears to have a genetic basis (Snowling et al., 2003; Pennington, 1995).

Twin studies The twin studies research provides further evidence that genetics plays a significant role in dyslexia. Research showed that twins have similar characteristics in terms of reading disabilities, even when they are raised separately (DeFries et al., 1997).

Computed Tomography **Computed tomography (CT)** is a computerized series of X-rays that build a three-dimensional image of the brain. Using this technology, researchers were able to see the structure of the brain for the first time (Shaywitz, 2003).

Positron-Emission Tomography Positron-emission tomography (PET) was the first technology developed to measure the brain at work. PET measures blood flow to the brain regions through the use of a radioactive compound that is injected into the bloodstream (Hauser et al., 1993). Much has been learned about the brain through PET technology. However, this technology is difficult to use because it is an invasive procedure, and it also requires elaborate equipment.

positron emission tomography (PET)
A procedure that permits one to measure metabolism within the brain.

1.3c Advances With Functional Magnetic Resonance Imaging (fMRI)

An immense breakthrough in the study of the brain during the reading process came about in the 1990s with the development of the technology of functional magnetic resonance imaging (fMRI). This device has several advantages: (1) it allows neuroscientists to view regions of the human brain as the person is reading, (2) it is a noninvasive procedure, and (3) it is a relatively easy procedure for use with children. The fMRI shows which parts of the brain are receiving the most blood or are the most active at any point in time. The studies conducted at Yale University with the fMRI provide much information about the human brain during reading tasks (Dehaene, 2009; Gorman, 2003; Shaywitz, 2003; Shaywitz et al., 2004). Figure 1.7 shows three areas of the left hemisphere of the brain that are used during the act of reading (Gorman, 2003; Kotulak, 2004; Shaywitz, 2003; Shaywitz & Shaywitz, 1999). Further information about fMRI can be found at *http://www.fmri.ucsd.edu.*

functional magnetic resonance imaging (fMRI)
The fMRI is used to study the live human brain at work.

1. In the frontal lobe (*left interior front gyrus*) is the phoneme producer. This region of the brain, called *Broca's area*, is used to link letters to sounds and is associated with the ability to say words aloud.
2. In the parietal lobe (*left parietotemporal area*) is the word analyzer. This region of the brain, called *Wernicke's area*, is involved with analyzing words.
3. In the occipital lobe (*left occipitotemporal area*) is the automatic detector. This region of the brain is involved with integrating learned words and storing and retrieving words.

All of these areas work simultaneously during reading, much like "sections of an orchestra playing a symphony" (Shaywitz, 2003).

The fMRI studies show that beginning readers and children with reading disabilities or dyslexia rely heavily on the front of the brain, which is the

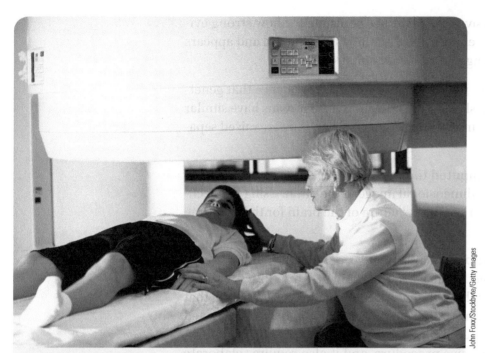

Neuroscientists are using functional magnetic resonance imaging (fMRI) to study the working brain of children as they read.

phoneme producer region, as they concentrate on, and try to say, the sounds of phonemes. They also rely heavily on the *word analyzer* region of the brain, as they try to decode words. As readers became more skilled, they activate the *automatic detector* region of the brain, as they automatically recognize familiar words on sight. The fMRI research also shows that even after gaining reading skills, individuals with dyslexia continue to have difficulty accessing the reading areas at the back of the brain (i.e., the automatic detector region of the brain), and they rely more heavily on the phoneme producer region and the front of the brain. Hence, there is a neurological explanation for why these individuals read more slowly and require extended time (Shaywitz, 2003).

Some fMRI research suggests that physical changes occur as a result of academic intervention with children who are dyslexic (Aylward et al., 2003; Shaywitz, 2003). One of the fMRI studies conducted at Yale University found that the areas of the brain changed after children were given intensive reading instruction, using phonologically based reading instruction. This study showed that the brains of poor readers started off with only the first two areas of the brain activated; however, after a year of reading instruction, their reading ability leaped ahead, as did the word storage area of the brain, which began to activate, just like that of the good readers (Shaywitz et al., 2004). Another study by Simos and colleagues (2007) also found changes in brain activity after intensive reading instruction.

A research study using fMRI was conducted in China on children as they read using the Chinese writing system. Similar to fMRI Western studies, the Chinese study also showed differences between the brain scans of normal and dyslexic readers. However, the Chinese symbolic writing system puts demands on different parts of the brain than Western alphabetic writing systems. The Western alphabetic writing system requires abilities in phonological awareness of spoken words. The Chinese writing system requires abilities

FIGURE **1.7**
An fMRI image shows activation patterns in the brain while a person is engaged in an activity. This illustration shows the activation locations of some reading activities

Phoneme Producer

Word Analyzer

Automatic Detector (Integrating learned words, storing and retrieving words)

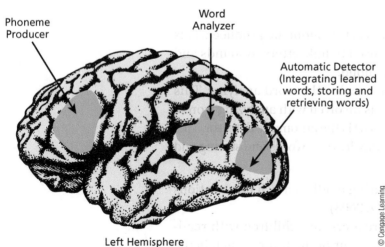

Left Hemisphere

with pictorial and visual symbols. The fMRI study with Chinese dyslexic children showed that they had difficulty in the left middle frontal gyrus, located in front of the brain on the left, the area of the brain that maps written symbols to meaning. The researchers suggest that dyslexic children using the Chinese writing system need instruction in linking visual shapes, sound, and meaning of visual characters (McGough, 2004).

The fMRI studies also demonstrate that particular parts of the brain specialize in particular activities (Carr, 2006). While the individual is being studied with the fMRI, the scientists are able to stimulate the visual area, the auditory area, memory systems, and other areas of the brain. This research using fMRI gives credence to the psychological processing and cognitive processing theories of learning and learning disabilities (Dehaene, 2009; Carr, 2006; Sousa, 2001).

Did You Get It?

Ricardo is able to memorize the dates of inauguration for each of the Presidents of the United States. However, when he is asked which of two presidents comes first in chronological order (Polk and Reagan for example), he is consistently unable to answer accurately. Time-sequencing is controlled by

a. The left hemisphere.
b. The right hemisphere.
c. Both the left and right hemispheres.
d. The medulla oblongata.

1.4 New Issues and Directions

A number of current issues and directions are occurring in special education and general education that affect students with learning disabilities and related mild disabilities. In the following section, we briefly review a few of these issues and directions.

1.4a More Inclusive Placements

Today, many students with learning disabilities and related mild disabilities receive instruction in general education classes or inclusive classrooms. There are many benefits of inclusion. General education classrooms can provide students with disabilities greater access to their general education peers, raise expectations for student performance, help general education students be more accepting of diverse students, and improve coordination between regular and special educators (Cawley et al., 2002; Elbaum, 2002). The philosophy and practice of inclusion are discussed in detail in Chapter 4, "Educational Settings and the Role of the Family."

Most students with learning disabilities and related disabilities are served in general education classes. In addition, students may have a disability but they have a 504 Plan and receive instruction in the general education classroom. Success in an inclusive classroom requires the collaborative effort of the classroom teacher and the special education teacher (Schwarz, 2006). The strategies in the

Including Students in GENERAL EDUCATION 1.1

- **Begin each lesson with a review of what has been learned.** Students often forget what has been accomplished thus far, especially with an intervening weekend or vacation. A review is helpful to assist students in remembering what has been learned.

- **Tell students the goal of the lesson.** It is important for students to understand the purpose for a particular lesson.

- **Place students with special needs near the teacher.** Reorganizing the seating helps students concentrate on the lesson and not become distracted. It also helps teachers observe the students' responses during the lesson.

- **Teach all students study skills.** All students in the class will benefit from learning study skills. Explain the procedure for study skills and model the activities for studying.

- **Allow sufficient practice of the concepts or skills.** Students with disabilities and related mild disabilities may process slowly, and they need many examples and opportunities to practice the concepts and skills they are learning.

- **Use differentiated instruction.** Take into account the learning styles and learning needs of all students in the class. Students with learning disabilities and related mild disabilities often have different styles of learning. It is important to teach the lesson in several different ways to respond to different interests, styles of learning, and personal talents.

- **Summarize what has been learned at the end of each lesson.** After the lesson is completed, help all students pull the different parts of the lesson together and summarize what they have learned.

Professional Resource Download

feature *Including Students in General Education 1.1*, "Some Overall Strategies," are targeted for students with learning disabilities and related mild disabilities. However, these basic strategies will benefit all students in the general education classroom. Inclusion must be done responsibly to ensure that the students receive the services designed to meet his or her needs in whatever setting the student is placed.

1.4b Response-to-Intervention (RTI)

response-to-intervention (RTI)
The Individuals with Disabilities Education Improvement Act of 2004 advocates the procedure of teaching all students with evidence-based instructional materials through general education in order to judge the students response to this intervention. RTI is also identified as a procedure that may be used for assessing children with learning disabilities.

Response-to-Intervention (RTI) RTI is a procedure for teaching *all* students in general education classes. Under the law (IDEA-2004) and the Regulations for IDEA-2004 (2007) schools are permitted to use RTI to identify students with learning disabilities or a comprehensive evaluation. RTI is briefly mentioned is this section, but it is discussed in greater detail in Chapter 2, "Assessment and the IEP Process."

Briefly, RTI is a prevention model to limit or prevent academic failure by providing "evidenced-based teaching procedures" for all students in general education. The RTI procedure provides for increasing intensity levels of support for those students who do not respond adequately to the instruction (Renaissance Learning, 2009; O'Conner, 2007; Division for Learning Disabilities, 2007; Vaughn, 2006; Learning Disabilities Association, 2006, *http://www.ldaamerica.org/news/responsiveness.asp*).

The Regulations for IDEA-2006 state that when determining whether a child has a specific learning disability, schools can use the RTI procedures.

The law also notes that the schools may also determine a child's eligibility for learning disabilities services by using a comprehensive evaluation procedure that may include a measurement of a severe discrepancy between achievement and intellectual ability (Fuchs, Fuchs, & Hollenbeck, 2007).

1.4c Standards for Teachers

Standards refers to the setting of achievement standards by individual states for the field of education. The Council for Exceptional Children (CEC), with the approval of the National Council for Accreditation of Teacher Education (NCATE), developed seven for the initial preparation of special education teachers. For more information, visit the CEC website at *http://www.cec.sped.org*. These initial preparation standards refer to all areas of special education. Table 1.6 shows the seven initial level special educator preparation standards for special education and where each standard is addressed in this text. Statewide assessment standards are discussed in greater detail in Chapter 2, "Assessment and the IEP Process."

standards
The identification of the specialized knowledge and skills and the assurance that practicing professionals are able to practice their profession effectively.

1.4d Assistive and Instructional Technology

Today's children live in a technological society with an ever-changing influx of new computer-based technologies. They have more comprehensive and faster world-wide links to commerce, communication, and culture. Schools must prepare students to deal with these dramatic changes so that they can fully participate and compete in the increasingly complex technological workplace.

Society readily recognizes the benefits of computer-based technologies for typically functioning children. However, there are even greater benefits for students with learning disabilities and related mild disabilities. Computer applications can help level the playing field by allowing them to succeed in the general education environment. For many students with learning disabilities and related mild disabilities, their ease in operating computers is an area of strength that helps them overcome areas of severe difficulty, such as their abilities to read and write. Research shows that often students who have academic problems have a special facility with computers (Belson, 2003; Hasselbring & Glaser, 2000; Raskind & Higgins, 1998a, 1998b). Specific applications of computer technology appear within pertinent chapters throughout this book.

The **Assistive Technology Act,** passed in 2004, recognizes the need for persons with disabilities to access and use assistive technology devices and provided funding to support assistive technology (PL 108-364). The reauthorization of the Assistive Technology law was passed in 2010 and was renamed the Twenty-First Century Communications and Video Accessibility Act of 2010 (PL 111-260) Assistive technology for students with disabilities is defined as "any item, piece of equipment, or product system, whether acquired commercially off the shelf, modified, or customized, that is used to increase, maintain, or improve functional capabilities of individuals with disabilities" (Individuals with Disabilities Education Act, 2004 Regulations, 34 C.F.R. 300). Table 1.7 lists some ways the students with learning disabilities and related mild disabilities can use computers.

assistive technology
Any technology that enables an individual with a disability to compensate for specific deficits. It includes low-tech or high-tech equipment.

TABLE 1.6

Council for Exceptional Children Initial Level Special Educatior Preparation Standards as Approved by the National Council for the Accreditation of Teacher Education

A Correlation Chart with Learning Disabilities and Related Disabilities: Strategies for Success, 13th Edition.

CEC Initial Preparation Standards	Description	Chapters
Standard 1— Learner Development and Individual Learning Differences	Beginning special education professionals understand how exceptionalities may interact with development and learning and use this knowledge to provide meaningful and challenging learning experiences for individuals with exceptionalities.	1, 2, 3, 4, 5, 6, 7, 8, 9, 11, 12, 13, 14
Standard 2— Learning Environments	Beginning special education professionals create safe, inclusive, culturally responsive learning environments so that individuals with exceptionalities become active and effective learners and develop emotional well-being, positive social interactions, and self-determination.	3, 4, 6, 7, 8, 9
Standard 3— Curricular Content Knowledge	Beginning special education professionals use knowledge of general and specialized curricula To individualize learning for Individuals with exceptionalities.	3, 5, 7, 11, 12, 13
Standard 4— Assessment	Beginning special education professionals use multiple methods of assessment and data-sources in making educational decisions.	2, 3, 6, 7, 8, 9, 11, 12, 13, 14
Standard 5— Instructional Planning and Strategies	Beginning special education professionals select, adapt, and use a repertoire of evidence-based Instructional strategies to advance learning of individuals with exceptionalities.	2, 3, 4, 5, 6, 7, 8, 9, 11, 12, 13, 14
Standard 6— Professional Learning and Ethical Practice	Beginning special education professionals use foundational Knowledge of the field and their Professional Ethical Principles and Practice Standards to inform Special education practice, to engage in lifelong learning, and to advance the profession.	1, 4, 6, 8, 9, 10
Standard 7— Collaboration	Beginning special education professionals collaborate with families, other educators, related service providers, individuals with exceptionalities, and personnel from community agencies in culturally responsive ways to address the needs of individuals with exceptionalities across a range of learning experiences.	4, 8, 9

Source: Council for Exceptional Children, Professional Standards (2012). Arlington, VA: Council for Exceptional Children.

TABLE 1.7

Ways Computers Can Be Used by Students With Learning Disabilities
and Related Mild Disabilities

- **E-mail.** E-mail is widely used by students with learning disabilities and related mild disabilities. With e-mail, students can send and receive electronic messages, make friends, communicate with other students, and teachers can communicate with the entire class through a listserv. Students can obtain a free Yahoo! e-mail address through *http://www.yahoo.com*. Teachers can also communicate with parents through e-mail.

- **The Internet.** Students enjoy using the Internet. They can conduct research or get background material for writing assignments. Students should receive instruction in Internet safety.

- **Social Networking.** Examples of popular social networking sites include *MySpace, Facebook,* and *Twitter.* Many students with mild disabilities and learning disabilities are using such social networking sites to build online communities and to communicate with friends

- **Electronic Storybooks.** Electronic storybooks on CD-ROM offer high-interest stories, and words can be highlighted or read aloud by the computer.

- **Word Processing.** Word processing is a boon for students with learning disabilities who have difficulty in handwriting, spelling, and written composition.

- **Voice Recognition Devices.** A voice recognition device allows the user to dictate through a microphone. The device then translates the user's speech into a form that the computer can say. One specifically used speech recognition tool is Dragon Naturally Speaking. More information can be found on the website, *http://www.scansoft .com/naturallyspeaking.*

- **Text Readers.** Text reader devices are known as text-to-speech applications. Such devices convert printed text into synthetic or digital speech. An excellent text reader program is the Kurzweil Reading Program. More information can be found on the website, *http://www.kurzweiledu.com.*

- **Texting.** Students are getting more experience with abbreviated written communication when they text their friends or their families.

© Cengage Learning 2015

JGI/Blend Images/Jupiter Images

Often students who have academic problems have a special facility with computers.

I didn't learn how to write until I learned how to use a computer. This sounds ironic, but in my past, writing was spelling, and because I could not spell, I could not write. When I discovered a word-processing system with a spell check, I finally understood that writing involved putting thoughts and ideas into some kind of written form. Knowing that the computer would catch my spelling errors, I began to ignore my spelling. Then I began to look at writing as content.

Source: C. Lee & R. Jackson (1992), *Faking It: A Look Into the Mind of a Creative Learner.* Portsmouth, NJ: Heinemann

REFLECTIVE QUESTION

1. How did the ability to use a computer change this individual's view of writing?

In Student Stories 1.3, "Using a Computer," we learn how important computers were to one student with learning disabilities.

1.4e Universal Design for Learning

Universal Design for Learning (UDL)
A policy of designing solutions for people with disabilities that are useful for others in the general population.

A model of technology use was developed by the organization Universal Design for Learning (UDL). UDL emphasizes the idea that every curriculum should include alternatives to make learning accessible and appropriate for individuals with different backgrounds, learning styles, abilities, and disabilities in widely varied learning contexts. The website for UDL is *http://www.cast.org*.

I Have a Kid Who...
TIGER, *a Student With a Reading Problem*

Tiger G. is 9 years old and in the third grade at the Lincoln Elementary School. He moved into the school district this fall and is in Ms. Jackson's general education classroom. Tiger seems to try hard, but reading is very difficult for him. He is not able to copy words from the chalkboard onto paper. He does not seem to understand the phonics instructions, nor does he complete his phonics assignments. He has a very limited sight vocabulary. Overall, Tiger's reading is at about the first-grade level. His math skills are good; he enjoys math and can easily keep up with the math work in the class. Tiger participates with the class in oral activities, but he is very quiet and cannot keep up with the reading in the class.

Tiger has become very unhappy in school. Ms. Jackson had a conference with Tiger's mother, who said he does not want to come to school and that getting Tiger to school each day is a hassle. Tiger's mother also told Ms. Jackson that he was very slow in his language development. Tiger is good in sports, likes to play baseball, and has made some friends. The major problem that Tiger has is in the area of reading.

Tiger's mother said that she is eager to have the school conduct an evaluation of Tiger, and requested an evaluation. The IEP team reported the following scores in their assessment: WISC-IV (Wechsler Intelligence Scale for Children, 4th ed.): A full-scale IQ was 125. Achievement Tests: Reading Word Recognition, Grade 1.2; Reading Comprehension, Grade 1.6; Spelling, Grade 1.5; Arithmetic, Grade 3.6.

The IEP team concluded that Tiger has a learning disability. He has the potential to achieve much higher in reading but needs intensive reading intervention in a small group situation.

Note: Adapted from the popular annual session that has been held at the Learning Disabilities of America Conference for 29 years, moderated by Dr. Jerry Minskoff. In the session, a member of the audience offers a problem and a group of experts tries to answer the problem, often with assistance from the audience.

QUESTIONS

1. Why do you think the IEP team decided that Tiger has a learning disability?

2. What are Tiger's strengths? What are Tiger's areas of need?

Many strategies can be utilized effectively to facilitate the inclusion of students with learning disabilities and to pave the road in a manner that fosters success and positive outcomes. Which of the following is not one of the recommended strategies?
   a. Teaching students how to study.
   b. Utilizing the practice of undifferentiated instruction.
   c. Reviewing comprehensively what has been learned in past lessons.
   d. Ending each lesson with a summarization of what has been learned.

Chapter Summary

- There are many key changes in special education.
- Specific learning disabilities is the largest category of disabilities.
- Other disabilities are related to learning disabilities.

- The neurosciences and the brain are an important topic.
- There are a number of new issues and directions in special education

Questions for Discussion and Reflection

1. Describe the category of learning disabilities. How do mild disabilities differ from categorical disabilities?
2. How have the roles of teachers of special education and learning disabilities changed? Discuss the new responsibilities.
3. All students are tested with tests based on standards. What are some implications of this testing for students with learning disabilities?
4. Describe some ways that computers can be used by students with disabilities.
5. Describe four distinct historical phases in the development of the field of learning disabilities.

Key Terms

adaptive behavior (p. 6)
assistive technology (p. 31)
behavioral disorders (p. 8)
brain-injured children (p. 20)
cerebral hemisphere (p. 24)
current achievement level (p. 14)
dyslexia (p. 25)
emotional disorders (p. 8)
emotional/behavioral disorders (EBD) (p. 8)
genetics of dyslexia (p. 26)
Interagency Committee on Learning Disabilities (ICLD) (p. 13)
functional magnetic resonance imaging (fMRI) (p. 27)
lateral preference (p. 25)
learning disabilities (p. 4)
intellectual disabilities (p. 4)

mild disabilities (p. 4)
mild/moderate disabilities (p. 4)
minimal brain dysfunction (MBD) (p. 22)
National Joint Committee on Learning Disabilities (NJCLD) (p. 13)
neurosciences (p. 23)
No Child Left Behind Act (NCLB) (p. 8)
perceptual disorder (p. 21)
positron emission tomography (PET) (p. 27)
postmortem anatomical studies (p. 25)
Public Law 94-142, Education for All Handicapped Children Act (1975) (p. 10)
Response-to-intervention (RTI) (p. 30)
severe discrepancy (p. 31)
standards (p. 31)
Universal Design for Learning (UDL) (p. 34)

monkeybusinessimages/iStockphoto.

2

Assessment and the IEP Process

LEARNING OBJECTIVES

After reading this chapter, you should be able to:

2.1 Describe uses of assessment information

2.2 Explain eligibility to special education services

2.3 Describe response-to-intervention (RTI)

2.4 Explain the comprehensive evaluation

2.5 Describe the individualized education program (IEP)

2.6 Describe how to obtain assessment information

2.7 Explain testing and accountability

2.8 List examples of tests

2.9 Describe test-taking strategies in the general education classroom

Well, that's the news from Lake Wobegon, where all the women are strong, all the men are good looking, and all the children are above average.

—Garrison Keillor

Part II, "The Assessment-Teaching Process," includes the three chapters that highlight the interrelated elements of the assessment-teaching process: assessment (Chapter 2), clinical teaching (Chapter 3), and educational settings (Chapter 4).

When assessment is linked with teaching, it helps teachers understand and teach a struggling student. If attention is paid to only one of these components, it splinters the effort and shortchanges the student. For example, routinely teaching skills or using methods or materials without considering a student's unique problems may be ineffective because such teaching does not address the student's unique needs. Similarly, if assessment only results in selecting a diagnostic label, the procedure does not provide guidelines for aiding the student's learning.

STANDARDS Addressed in This Chapter:

Council for Exceptional Children Initial Level Special Educator Preparation Standards as Approved by the National Council for the Accreditation of Teacher Education

CEC Initial Preparation Standard 1: Learner Development and Individual Learning Differences

- 1.0—Beginning special education professionals understand how exceptionalities may interact with development and learning and use this knowledge to provide meaningful and challenging learning experiences for individuals with exceptionalities.
- 1.1—Beginning special education professionals understand how language, culture, and family background influence the learning of individuals with exceptionalities.
- 1.2—Beginning special education professionals use understanding of development and individual differences to respond to the needs of individuals with exceptionalities.

CEC Initial Preparation Standard 4: Assessment

- 4.0—Beginning special education professionals use multiple methods of assessment and data sources in making educational decisions.
- 4.1—Beginning special education professionals select and use technically sound formal and informal assessments that minimize bias.
- 4.2—Beginning special education professionals use knowledge of measurement principles and practices to interpret assessment results and guide educational decisions for individuals with exceptionalities.
- 4.3—Beginning special education professionals in collaboration with colleagues and families use multiple types of assessment information in making decisions about individuals with exceptionalities.
- 4.4—Beginning special education professionals engage individuals with exceptionalities to work toward quality learning and performance and provide feedback to guide them.

CEC Initial Preparation Standard 5: Instructional Planning and Strategies

- 5.1—Beginning special education professionals consider an individual's abilities, interests, learning environments, and cultural and linguistic factors in the selection, development, and adaptation of learning experiences for individuals with exceptionalities.

I n Chapter 2, "Assessment and the IEP Process," we examine the uses of assessment, look at the RTI approach to eligibility, and review the Comprehensive Evaluation approach to eligibility. We also investigate the influence of the law on the IEP process, review ways to obtain assessment information, and provide examples of assessment measures.

2.1 Uses of Assessment Information

Assessment is the process of collecting information about a student that will be used to form judgments and make decisions concerning that student. Assessment procedures are used to identify the nature of the student's challenges and to plan instruction. To be eligible for special education services, a student must be identified—or *classified*—within a special education category within the law. The more important reason for assessment is to obtain information that can be used to plan ways to help the student learn. Assessment serves several purposes:

1. **Screening.** The screening process is a cursory evaluation that is used to detect pupils who may need a more comprehensive evaluation.
2. **Referral.** The referral process seeks additional assistance from other school personnel. On the basis of observation and classroom performance, the teacher (or others) requests an evaluation of a student.
3. **Classification.** The classification process is used to determine a student's eligibility for services. Students are assessed to judge the need for services and to identify the category of disability and whether the disability has an adverse impact on educational performance.
4. **Instructional planning.** The instructional-planning process develops an educational program for an individual student. The assessment information is used to formulate instructional goals and to develop specific plans for teaching.

5. **Monitoring pupil progress.** It is important to review a student's progress. Several approaches to monitoring can be used, including standardized formal tests, informal measures, and a continuous monitoring procedure.

Did You Get It?

The process of student assessment can be broken up into five parts. Which part refers to determining a prospective student's eligibility to receive disability-related services?

   a. classification
   b. screening
   c. referral
   d. planning

2.2 Determining Eligibility for Special Education Services

IDEA-2004 brought about significant changes in the way students are identified for special education services (IDEA, 2004, with regulations of 2006). For identifying students with learning disabilities, the final regulations for the law indicate that states: (1) must not require a severe discrepancy between intellectual ability and achievement, (2) must permit the use of a process based on the child's response-to-interventions, and (3) may permit the use of other alternative research-based procedures to determine whether the child has learning disabilities (Regulations for the Individuals with Disabilities Education Improvement Act of IDEA-2004, 2006; Division for Learning Disabilities, 2007).

Two ways that schools can determine eligibility for special education services are (1) the response-to-intervention (RTI) approach, or (2) a comprehensive evaluation of the student with suspected disabilities. In this chapter, we discuss both approaches.

Did You Get It?

The Individuals with Disabilities Education Improvement Act of 2004 (IDEA 2004) mandates that an individual student _____ demonstrate a severe discrepancy between intellectual ability and achievement.

   a. must always
   b. must usually
   c. need not
   d. must conditionally

2.3 Response-to-Intervention (RTI)

Response-to-intervention (RTI) is a procedure that is intended to identify students who are having academic difficulties when the problems first become apparent by using response-to-intervention (RTI) (IDEA-2004; Regulations for IDEA-2004, 2006). RTI is a practice to be used with *all* students, including students in general education classes, students who are considered at-risk for school

response-to-intervention (RTI)
The Individuals with Disabilities Education Improvement Act of 2004 advocates the procedure of teaching all students with evidence-based instructional materials through general education in order to judge the students response to this intervention. RTI is also identified as a procedure that may be used to assess children with learning disabilities.

failure, and students with suspected disabilities (including students with suspected mild disabilities and learning disabilities). The goal of RTI is to prevent academic failure for all of these students (Fuchs & Vaughn, 2012; Division for Learning Disabilities, 2007; Renaissance Learning 2009; Fuchs & Deshler, 2007).

Since 2003 when RTI was still an emerging idea, RTI has become a major force in education reform. It is collated into federal law as a method for evaluation of students with learning disabilities (IDEA, 2004, 2006). It is integrated in the laws of all 50 states in various forms (Fuchs & Vaughn, 2012).

2.3a Tiers of Instruction in RTI

Although there are several different versions of RTI, many descriptions of RTI use three tiers (or levels) of intervention (see Figure 2.1). Each tier represents a level of intervention or instruction. Students with differing needs receive more intensive instruction. RTI is most successful as a screening tool for reading and mathematics (Fuchs & Vaughn, 2012).

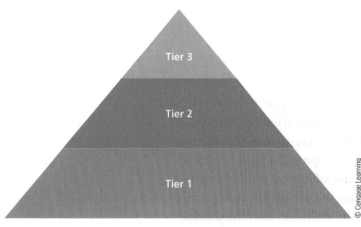

FIGURE **2.1**
A Three-tiered Model of RTI

The RTI model proposes that if a student responds well to the evidence-based interventions, at Tier 1 (first level), the student does not have a disability. However, students who do not respond positively to the RTI instruction at Tier 1 are given more intensive instruction in the next level (Tier 2). If the student still does not respond or learn after intensive intervention at Tier 2, the student receives still more intensive intervention in a smaller group at Tier 3. Finally, students who do not respond positively to interventions at Tier 3 may then be considered for an evaluation for special education (Fuchs & Vaughn, 2012, Renaissance Learning, 2009; Division of Learning Disabilities, 2007).

To summarize, RTI targets *all* students. Students in general education classes, students considered to be at-risk for learning failure, including students with suspected learning disabilities, and students with suspected mild disabilities. Students who respond well to the instruction in the RTI procedure at Tiers 1, 2, or 3 are *not* considered eligible for special education services. Students who are *not* learning with the RTI interventions are considered to be "nonresponders" and may be referred for a special education evaluation (Fuchs & Vaughn, 2012; Renaissance Learning, 2009; Division for Learning Disabilities, 2007). The three tiers of intervention that are commonly used:

- **Tier 1. High-quality instruction in general education and monitoring of student progress.** It is anticipated that about 80% of students will be served in Tier 1. Students who do not respond adequately to Tier 1 go on to Tier 2.
- **Tier 2. More intensive evidenced-based instruction while progress monitoring continues.** Often support teachers, such as reading specialists, instruct students at Tier 2. It is anticipated that 10–15% of students are in Tier 2. Students who do not respond adequately to Tier 2 go on to Tier 3.
- **Tier 3. Highly intense, evidenced-based interventions taught in small groups or individually, while progress monitoring continues.** Tier 3 is meant to include 5–10% of students. Students who do not respond adequately to Tier 3 may be considered for a comprehensive evaluation

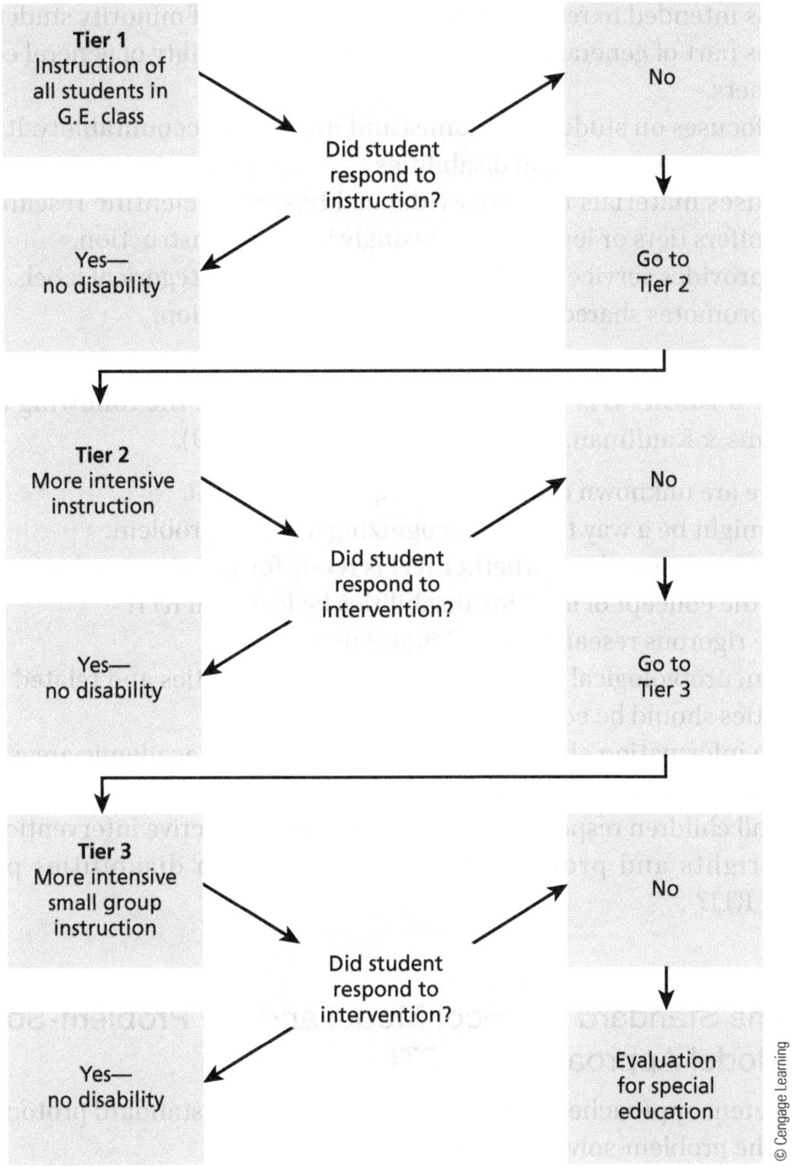

FIGURE **2.2**
A Decision Flow Chart for the
Three Tiers of RTI

Tier 1
Instruction of
all students in
G.E. class

Did student
respond to
instruction?

No

Yes—
no disability

Go to
Tier 2

Tier 2
More intensive
instruction

Did student
respond to
intervention?

No

Yes—
no disability

Go to
Tier 3

Tier 3
More intensive
small group
instruction

Did student
respond to
intervention?

No

Yes—
no disability

Evaluation
for special
education

© Cengage Learning

(Renaissance Learning 2009; Division for Learning Disabilities, 2007; Denton, 2006; Bradley, Danielson, & Doolittle, 2005). A decision flow chart of the three tiers of RTI is shown in Figure 2.2.

- **It must be noted that at any time in this process when a student has a disability or is suspected of having a disability, the school district cannot use RTI to delay or deny an evaluation for eligibility under the Individuals with Disabilities Education Act.** (Memo to State Directors of Special Education from Melody Musgrove, Director of Office of Special Education Programs, United States Department of Education, January 21, 2011.)

2.3b Benefits and Concerns About RTI

Benefits of RTI The benefits of RTI include the following (Fuchs & Vaughn, 2012; Renaissance Learning, 2009; Division of Learning Disabilities, 2007).

- RTI focuses on earlier identification and prevention of disabilities, thereby reducing the number of students referred to special education.

- RTI is intended to reduce the over-identification of minority students.
- RTI is part of general education and the responsibility of general education teachers.
- RTI focuses on student outcomes and increased accountability. It includes all suspected categorical disabilities.
- RTI uses materials that are evidenced based or scientific research based and offers tiers or levels of increasingly intensive instruction.
- RTI provides services to students without using categorical labels.
- RTI promotes shared responsibility and collaboration.

Concerns About RTI Concerns about RTI include the following (Denton, 2012; Johns & Kauffman, 2009; Wanzek & Vaughn, 2009).

- There are unknown costs of fully implementing RTI.
- RTI might be a way to delay recognizing a child's problem.
- Questions arise about whether RTI is ready for wide-scale adoption.
- Will the concept of learning disabilities be lost with RTI?
- More rigorous research on RTI is still needed.
- The neurobiological correlates of learning disabilities and related mild disabilities should be considered.
- More information about older students and other academic areas of learning besides reading are needed.
- Not all children respond well to even the most effective interventions.
- Are rights and protections for students with disabilities provided with RTI?

2.3c The Standard Protocol Model and the Problem-Solving Model Approaches to RTI

Two different approaches for RTI are proposed: (1) the standard protocol model and (2) the problem-solving model.

- In the standard protocol model to RTI, specific approaches and instructional programs are developed and implemented using prescribed procedures for academic or behavioral problems at each stage of instruction. At each level of intervention, instruction is standardized, meaning that consistent instructional methods are implemented for a specific length of time. The procedures for teaching and assessing the performance and growth of the students who responded poorly to general class instruction are the same for all students in the small group (Division for Learning Disabilities, 2007).

problem-solving model to RTI
Focuses on individualized intervention for one student.

- In the problem-solving model to RTI, each student's failure to respond to intervention is given an individually tailored plan for the next level of instruction or support. It is essentially a case-by-case approach to addressing individual students' unique needs. The problem-solving model relies on teacher assistance teams or instructional support teams already established in most schools. (Division for Learning Disabilities, 2007)

An example of the RTI procedure is shown in Student Stories 2.1, "Lucy and the RTI Process."

STUDENT STORIES 2.1
Lucy and the RTI Process

Lucy is 6 years old and in the first grade at The Pine School. The Pine School is using the response-to-intervention procedure with students. Lucy received Tier 1 RTI instruction in her general education class but did not respond well to this intervention. Her general education first grade teacher said that Lucy had difficulty recognizing sounds and did poorly with beginning reading lessons. Progress monitoring also showed that Lucy was not learning through the Tier 1 intervention. Lucy is now in Tier 2, which provides more intensive instruction and is taught by the reading specialist at The Pine School. Lucy is responding positively to Tier 2 instruction and she is not being considered for a special education evaluation.

REFLECTIVE QUESTION

1. How did the RTI procedure indicate that Lucy does not have a disability?

2.3d Progress Monitoring

Progress monitoring is used to determine whether students are making appropriate gains in learning in the instructional program. It is an assessment procedure to measure a student's academic performance and to evaluate the effectiveness of instruction. Progress monitoring is typically done on a regular and frequent schedule. The teacher measures the student's academic performance on a regular basis (weekly or monthly) and charts the academic performance (Division of Learning Disabilities, 2007; Fuchs & Fuchs, 2006; Council for Exceptional Children, 2004). For more information, visit the website for the National Center on Student Progress Monitoring at *http://www.studentprogress.org*.

Many progress-monitoring programs are prepackaged, and many enable teachers to use computers to produce the graphs and charts that they need to see how individual students are progressing. Figure 2.3 shows a

progress monitoring
Assessment procedures to measure the student's academic performance and evaluate the effectiveness of instruction.

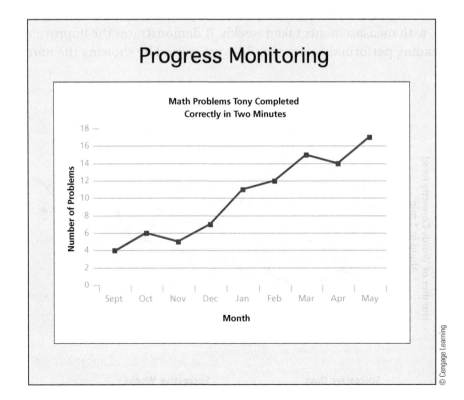

FIGURE **2.3**
Progress Monitoring

progress-monitoring chart for mathematics for Tony, grade 2. It shows how many math problems Tony completed correctly during 2-minute mathematics measurements over a 10-month period.

A useful software program for conducting curriculum-based measurement and progress monitoring in several different academic areas is AIMS-web, which measures reading, early literacy, early numeracy, mathematics, spelling, and written expression. It also provides for monitoring in the behavioral areas. The website for AIMSweb is *http://www.aimsweb.com.*

2.3e Curriculum-Based Measurement

curriculum-based measurement (CBM)

Assessment designed to measure student performance on the student's curriculum activities and materials. The student's performance on an academic task is repeatedly measured and charted to assess changes in learning performance.

One progress-monitoring procedure is curriculum-based measurement (CBM). Curriculum-based measurement is a procedure designed to test what a student actually does in the student's school or classroom curriculum. The assessment requires that the student actively perform some task through frequent and repeated measures.

Curriculum-based measurement (CBM) is described as a procedure for assessing the growth of basic skills (Deno, 2003). First, the teacher determines the area of the curriculum or the goal for the student in the student's IEP. Then, the student's progress is measured through frequent, systematic, and repeated measures of that learning task. Performance results are graphed or charted so that the student's progress is clearly observable to both the teacher and the student. CBM performance samples are 1 to 3 minutes long, and they are charted to display the student's performance changes over successive time periods, such as days or weeks.

In Figure 2.4, CBM is used to monitor growth in reading through frequent measurements of the number of words the student reads aloud during 1-minute reading samples, which are the base-line period over three successive days, as shown in the left side of the figure. The right side of Figure 2.4 shows the progress achieved after a targeting instructional program is used for 14 successive weeks, with measurements taken weekly. It demonstrates the improvement in oral reading performance over the 14-week period by showing the number of

FIGURE **2.4**
A Curriculum-based Measurement Chart Monitoring an Individual Student's Progress

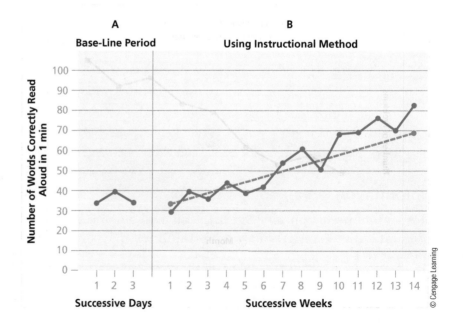

words read correctly in successive 1-minute reading samples. The dashed line shows the IEP goal, which is reading 65 words per minute within 14 weeks (Deno, 2003). CBM can be used to measure many academic areas: spelling, writing, mathematics, and reading (Spinelli, 2006; Bender, 2004).

Did You Get It?

Responsiveness-to-intervention (RTI) is an assessment strategy used to identify _____ students who are experiencing learning-related difficulties as early as possible.
- **a.** disabled
- **b.** special-needs
- **c.** "lagging"
- **d.** any-and-all

2.4 The Comprehensive Evaluation

The comprehensive evaluation is another way to determine a student's eligibility for special education services. A comprehensive evaluation entails collecting information about an individual student that can be used to form judgments and make critical decisions about the student and to plan appropriate instruction. Comprehensive evaluations are used by the schools in the process of preparing for an individualized education program (IEP) for a student (Hallahan & Cohen, 2008; Salvia, Ysseldyke, & Bolt, 2007). The RTI process cannot be used to delay-deny an evaluation for eligibility under the Individuals with Disabilities Education Act (U.S. Department of Education Office of Special Education and Rehabilitative Services, January 21, 2011).

> **comprehensive evaluation**
> Entails collecting information about an individual student that can be used to form judgments and make critical decisions about the student and to plan appropriate instruction.

The comprehensive evaluation of students with suspected disabilities has been used since the passage of the first special education law in 1975. Many other professionals use comprehensive evaluations, as well: psychologists, physicians, and other health professionals.

The U.S. Supreme Court has upheld the right of students with suspected disabilities to have a comprehensive evaluation. In the case *Forest Grove School District v. T.A. (08-305)*, decided on June 22, 2009, the Supreme Court ruled that under IDEA-2004, a student has the right to a timely and appropriate evaluation to make certain that decisions about eligibility to special education are correct. In this case, the Supreme Court determined that the parent should receive reimbursement for the tuition at a private school because, in part, the school district did not provide a comprehensive evaluation for the student (Cohen, 2009; Wright & Wright, 2009).

2.4a Information Obtained in a Comprehensive Evaluation

Several kinds of information would be included in a comprehensive evaluation for a student with suspected learning disabilities (Division for Learning Disabilities, 2007):

- Observational data that describes the student's behavior
- Educationally relevant medical findings

- Data to exclude visual, hearing, or motor disability; mental retardation, emotional disturbance, cultural factors, environmental, or economic disadvantage; or limited English proficiency
- Data from standardized measures and qualitative analysis of the student's ability to listen think, speak, read, write, spell, and do mathematics
- Summary of the student's strengths and weaknesses and the basis for determination of a Specific Learning Disability if found
- Recommendations based on the data that inform individualized instruction, state necessary accommodations or modifications, and identify behavioral and learning supports needed
- Review of RTI information, if used
- A comparison of a student's intellectual ability (potential for learning) and the student's actual achievement

For students with suspected mild or moderate disabilities, a comprehensive evaluation provides evaluation data that would indicate reduced ability levels, significant attention problems, sensory impairments, or behavior disorders (Division for Learning Disabilities, 2007).

2.4b The Discrepancy Between Intellectual Ability and Academic Achievement

One of the most controversial issues in the comprehensive evaluation of students with suspected learning disabilities is the evidence of a severe discrepancy between intellectual ability and the student's actual achievement. As noted earlier, the final Regulations for the Individuals With Disabilities Education Improvement Act of 2004 (2006) permits (but does not require) schools to use evidence of a severe discrepancy between intellectual ability and achievement as one criterion for determining if the child has learning disabilities. Actually, the discrepancy factor is but one component that is considered in the comprehensive evaluation of a child.

Discrepancy between achievement and intellectual ability has been a component in the comprehensive evaluation. Briefly it is based on the concept that the student has the intellectual potential for learning but is not meeting this potential in his or her academic performance (Hallahan, 2007; Hallahan & Cohen, 2008).

The discrepancy means that the student's achievement (what the student has actually learned) is compared to the student's intellectual ability (what the student is potentially capable of learning). A student's intellectual ability is often measured with an IQ score, and IQ tests have been under severe criticism.

It is important to keep in mind that cognitive tests or tests of intellectual ability provide much more than a single score of intelligence. It is also necessary for teachers to know the student's strengths and affinities, as well as areas that are difficult for the student, and to recognize that each student has a "different kind of mind" (Scherer, 2006).

discrepancy score
A mathematical calculation for quantifying the discrepancy between the student's current achievement and his or her potential.

A discrepancy score is a mathematical calculation for quantifying the discrepancy between achievement and intellectual ability (or potential for learning). There are several different formulas for calculating a discrepancy score, and these formulas are explained on the Student Website. Discrepancy should be seen as a critical marker with specific learning disabilities seen as a category that is based on underachievement; not based solely on low achievement. Discrepancy is a reliable criterion (Batsche, Kavale, & Kovaleski, 2009).

Concerns About the Discrepancy Factor The concerns about the aptitude–achievement discrepancy factor include:

- **Quantitative and qualitative information should be combined.** Many parents and teachers are concerned about the use of quantitative discrepancy scores for making decisions about their child and contend that there is no substitute for clinical judgment and actual experience (Chalfant, 1989; Mastropieri, 1987).
- **Using an IQ score for measuring an individual's potential may not be useful.** IQ tests do not necessarily measure intelligence. Moreover, an IQ score can be adversely affected by the student's culture or native language. In addition, the student could have a lower IQ score because of the nature of the disability itself (Stuebing et al., 2009; Fletcher et al., 2004).
- **Children who are poor achievers often have similar learning characteristics, whether they have high IQ scores or low IQ scores.** Research shows there are many similarities between two poor readers regardless of their IQ scores (Stuebing et al., 2009; Fletcher et al., 2004).
- **Discrepancy formulas vary from state to state.** States and school districts differ in their discrepancy formulas for identifying learning disabilities. Thus, a child could be identified as having a learning disability in one state but may be denied services after moving to another state.

An example of the use of the discrepancy model is shown in Student Stories 2.2, "Ozzie: Using the Discrepancy Construct."

STUDENT STORIES 2.2
Ozzie: Using the Discrepancy Construct

Ozzie is 8 years old and in the third grade at The Lincoln School. The Lincoln School evaluates students suspected of having learning disabilities with standardized norm-referenced testing, which includes the discrepancy model. Ozzie is having much difficulty in reading and mathematics, and the general education classroom teacher called upon the prereferral intervention team to suggest methods of instruction for Ozzie. The teacher tried using these methods, but they were not successful with Ozzie. Ozzie's parents and his teacher are concerned about Ozzie's lack of progress, and a referral for a special education evaluation is made. A multidisciplinary evaluation team gives several kinds of tests, including a test of cognitive abilities and a test of reading achievement. As a part of the IEP (individualized education program), the team finds that Ozzie has a discrepancy between his intellectual ability and achievement. The IEP team determines that Ozzie has a learning disability.

REFLECTIVE QUESTION

1. How was the discrepancy procedure used in the evaluation of Ozzie?

Did You Get It?

The justices in the Supreme Court case *Forest Grove School District v. T.A.* (2009) ruled that under the principles of IDEA-2004, a student has the right to a comprehensive evaluation to determine eligibility, an evaluation that is both appropriate and "_____."
- **a.** fair
- **b.** timely
- **c.** objective
- **d.** sensitive

2.5 The Individualized Education Program (IEP) and Stages of the IEP

IDEA-2004 offers all students with disabilities a *free, appropriate public education (FAPE),* This means that special education and related services are provided at public expense and meet the standards of the state education agency. The education includes appropriate preschool, elementary school, or secondary school instruction and provides conformity with the individualized education program (IEP).

A major provision of the special education law is the requirement that each public school child who receives special education and related services must have an individualized education program (IEP) (IDEA-2004). The IEP is a written statement for each child with a disability. Each IEP is designed for one student and should be a truly *individualized* document. The IEP creates an opportunity for teachers, parents, school administrators, related services personnel, and students (when appropriate) to work together to improve educational results for children with disabilities. The IEP is the cornerstone of a quality education for each child with a disability.

Procedural safeguards are provided in federal law, and they are designed to protect the rights of children and parents. The term parents' rights is used in IDEA-2004 as a procedural safeguard to protect the rights of parents and families. Parents' rights have been considerably expanded through the series of special education laws, and these rights are summarized in Table 2.1.

The IEP follows a sequence of stages. As shown in Figure 2.5, there are three broad stages: *referral, assessment,* and *instruction.* Each of these stages is subdivided, making six stages in all. These six stages meet the legislative mandates of the IEP.

individualized education program (IEP)
The written plan for the education of an individual student with a disability that impacts educational performance. The plan must meet requirements specified in the rules and regulations of IDEA.

procedural safeguards
Regulations in federal law that are designed to protect the rights of students with learning disabilities and their parents.

parents' rights
Used in IDEA-2004 for procedural safeguards to protect the rights of parents.

mediation
A process of resolving disputes between the parent and the school in a nonadversarial fashion.

TABLE 2.1

Rights and Procedural Safeguards for Parents and Families

1. Parents must *consent in writing* to several phases of the IEP process: (1) to having their child evaluated; (2) to the IEP, including plans and placement as set forth in the written IEP; and (3) to the 3-year reevaluation plan.

2. The assessment must be conducted in the student's language and form most likely to yield accurate information on what the child knows or can achieve academically, developmentally, and functionally. The findings must be reported in the parents' native language.

3. The school or local education agency (LEA) must ensure that tests are not *racially or culturally discriminatory.*

4. Parents have the *right to see all information* that is collected and used in making decisions. Parents can request an explanation of all evaluation procedures, tests, records, and reports.

5. Parents have the *right to mediation* at no cost. Mediation is voluntary; it is defined as a process of resolving disputes between the school district and the parents of a child with a disability in a nonadversarial fashion.

6. An additional dispute resolution process called a "resolution session" can be convened.

7. Parents and students have the *right to an impartial, due process hearing* if they disagree with the IEP decision or if the voluntary mediation is unsatisfactory. There are certain provisions to have the school pay attorneys' fees if the parents prevail in a lawsuit.

8. The *confidentiality* of the student's reports and records is protected under the law.

© Cengage Learning

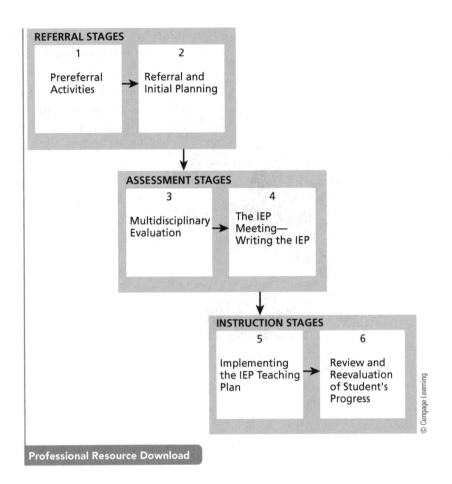

FIGURE **2.5**
Stages of the IEP Process

REFERRAL STAGES

1	2
Prereferral Activities	Referral and Initial Planning

ASSESSMENT STAGES

3	4
Multidisciplinary Evaluation	The IEP Meeting— Writing the IEP

INSTRUCTION STAGES

5	6
Implementing the IEP Teaching Plan	Review and Reevaluation of Student's Progress

© Cengage Learning

Professional Resource Download

2.5a **Referral Stages**

The referral stages begin the IEP process and involve two components: the pre-referral activities and the referral activities.

Stage 1: Prereferral Activities An instructional support team (or a teacher-assistance team) develops prereferral activities for a student who is encountering difficulties in the general education classroom to be used by the general education classroom teachers. Before referring a student for a special education evaluation, teachers use these interventions with the child. If the interventions are successful, the student does not need to be referred for an evaluation. Most school districts now require evidence that a prereferral process has occurred before a referral is initiated. (Some have identified RTI as a prereferral process.)

The instructional support team is a peer group of colleagues to help the classroom teacher analyze the student's academic and/or behavioral problems and recommends interventions and accommodations for the classroom. The classroom teacher then initiates the suggested methods to help the student. The prereferral stage is important because the decision to refer a student for a multidisciplinary evaluation has serious consequences. Once a student is referred, the probability is high that the student will be declared eligible for services (Salvia, Ysseldyke, & Bolt, 2007). The instructional support team responds to the teacher's prereferral request, using the general steps listed in Teaching Tips 2.1, "Tasks of the Prereferral Instructional Support Team" (Chalfant & Pysh, 1993; Clark, 2000; Spinelli, 2006).

referral stages
The initial stages of the IEP process. They include the prereferral activities and the referral activities.

instructional support team
A teacher-assistance team that develops prereferral activities for a student before a referral is made.

prereferral activities
Preventive procedures taken prior to referral for special education evaluation and intended to help regular teachers work more successfully with the child in the regular classroom.

referral
The initial request to consider a student for a special education evaluation.

Stage 2: Referral and Initial Planning The initial referral of a student for special education evaluation can come through several sources: the parent, the teacher, other professionals who have contact with the student, or a self-referral by the student. After a referral is made, school personnel must follow it up. Parents must be notified of the school's concern and must give written permission for an evaluation. In addition, decisions must be made about the general kinds of evaluation data needed and the people who will be responsible for gathering this information.

A collaboration team considers a student's strengths and weaknesses and explores possible interventions for that student.

2.5b Assessment Stages

assessment stages
This is the stage during which tests are given (multidisciplinary evaluation) and decisions are made (the case conference or IEP meeting).

The assessment stages are the core of the process and involve the tasks of evaluation and developing and writing the IEP.

Stage 3: Multidisciplinary Evaluation At this stage, specialists representing various disciplines obtain pertinent information by assessing academic performance and behavior in areas related to the suspected disability. For example, specialists for the multidisciplinary evaluation might include a school psychologist, school social worker, school nurse, speech and language pathologist, learning disabilities specialist, or reading specialist.

multidisciplinary evaluation
The assessment process in which specialists from several disciplines evaluate a child and coordinate their findings.

The law (IDEA-2004) outlines the procedures for gathering information for the evaluation. Several features of the law regulate the evaluation. The tests must be appropriate, validated for the purpose used, and as free as possible from cultural or racial bias. Evaluation materials must be administered in the student's native language. The evaluation team must represent several disciplines and must include at least one teacher or specialist in the area of the suspected disability. The specialists on the multidisciplinary evaluation team administer tests and obtain other evaluation data.

Stage 4: The IEP Meeting—Writing the IEP After the multidisciplinary evaluation has been conducted, the information is gathered, and the parents are contacted for the IEP meeting. It is at this meeting that the eligibility for special education is determined and the IEP is written.

IEP meeting
A meeting attended by parents, school staff, and sometimes the student to make decisions about the individualized education plan (IEP).

The Participants at the IEP Meeting According to IDEA-2004, the participants on the IEP team must include the following:

1. The parents of the child with a disability
2. Not less than one regular education teacher of such child (if the child is, or may be, participating in the regular education/special education environment)

3. Not less than one special education teacher, or where appropriate, not less than one special education provider of such child
4. A representative of the school or school district who
   a. Is qualified to provide, or supervise the provision of, specially designed instruction to meet the unique needs of children with disabilities
   b. Is knowledgeable about the general education curriculum
   c. Is knowledgeable about the availability of resources of the school or school district
5. An individual who can interpret the instructional implications of evaluation results, who may be one of the other members of the team
6. At the discretion of the parent or the agency, other individuals who have knowledge or special expertise regarding the child, including related services personnel as appropriate
7. Whenever appropriate, the child with a disability

Contents of the Child's IEP The contents of the IEP must include these components (IDEA-2004):

1. A statement of the child's present levels of academic achievement and functional performance
   a. How the disability affects the child's involvement and progress in the general education curriculum
   b. For preschool children, how the disability affects the child's participation in appropriate activities
   c. For children with disabilities who take alternate assessments aligned to alternate achievement standards, a description of benchmarks or short-term objectives
2. A statement of measurable annual goals, including academic and functional goals designed to
   a. Meet the child's needs that result from the child's disability, in order to enable the child to be involved in and make progress on the general education curriculum
   b. Meet each of the child's other education needs that result from the child's disability
3. A description of how the child's progress toward meeting the annual goals will be measured and when the periodic reports on the progress the child is making toward meeting the annual goals (such as through the use of quarterly or other periodic reports, concurrent with the issuance of report cards) will be provided
4. A statement of the special education and related services and supplementary aids, based on peer-reviewed research to the extent practicable, to be provided to the child, and a statement of the program modifications or supports for school personnel that will be provided for the child. The special

TEACHING **TIPS 2.1**

Tasks of the Prereferral Instructional Support Team

The following steps describe one model of the prereferral process:

1. A general education classroom teacher who notes a child with a problem in learning requests help from a school collaboration team for a student of concern.
2. The prereferral instructional support team follows up this request by exploring with the classroom teacher some possible interventions for the child.
3. The classroom teacher then tries the suggested interventions in the general education classroom.
4. If further decisions are needed, a member of the collaboration team observes the student in the classroom and then consults further with the classroom teacher.
5. If the student's problem persists, the teacher makes a formal referral for a special education evaluation.
6. A response-to-intervention procedure can be used to provide scientific research-based interventions.

Professional Resource Download

education outlined must include the delivery of specialized instruction based on the individualized needs of the child and be determined by the evaluation information.

5. An explanation of the extent to which the student will not participate with nondisabled children in the regular class and in regular class activities

6. A statement of individual appropriate accommodations that are necessary to measure the academic achievement and functional performance of the child on state and district-wide assessments

7. The projected date for the beginning of the services and modifications, and the anticipated frequency, location, and duration of those services and modifications

8. Appropriate transition assessments and services, beginning no later than the first IEP to be in effect when the child is 16, and updated annually (transition is described in more detail in Chapter 9, "Adolescents and Adults With Learning Disabilities and Related Mild Disabilities").

Related Services In addition to determining the necessary special education services, the IEP team also determines the need for related services that may be required to enable a child with a disability to benefit from special education. Related services may include transportation and developmental, corrective, and other supportive services. Such assistance may include speech-language specialists and auditory services, psychological services, physical and occupational therapy (including therapeutic recreation), social work services, counseling services (including rehabilitation counseling), orientation and mobility services, and medical services for diagnostic and evaluation purposes.

2.5c Instruction Stages

instruction stages
This stage is part of the IEP process and includes implementing a teaching plan, and reviewing and reevaluating the student's progress.

The instruction stages occur after the written document (the IEP) has been completed, and they involve the teaching and monitoring of the student's progress.

Stage 5: Implementing the IEP Teaching Plan This is the teaching portion of the assessment-teaching process. It occurs after the IEP document has been written. During this stage, the student is taught in the agreed upon setting and receives specialized instruction designed to help the student reach the goals set forth in the IEP. This stage involves implementing the IEP plan through teaching (see Chapter 3, "Clinical Teaching," and Chapter 4, "Educational Settings and the Role of the Family").

Stage 6: Review and Reevaluation of the Student's Progress This stage calls for the review and reevaluation of the IEP plan in terms of the student's progress. The IEP must include explanations that show how this evaluation will be accomplished, who will conduct the evaluation, and what assessment instruments and criteria will be used. IDEA-2004 requires that the child's parents be informed of their child's progress toward reaching annual goals as frequently as parents of nondisabled children are informed. One way to do this is to send the parents a progress report that accompanies the student's report card.

2.5d Evaluating Students With Learning Disabilities and Related Disabilities

Federal law describes a number of dimensions to be considered in the process of evaluating students with learning disabilities and related disabilities (IDEA, 2004).

Observing the Student in the Classroom A classroom observation of the student is required to provide information about the student's behavior in school and the ways in which that behavior affects academic performance.

Recognizing the Student's Strengths and Clusters of Characteristics Students with learning disabilities and related disabilities have many strengths, and it is important to recognize and encourage these strengths. For example, some children will do well in math or computer applications, yet they may have difficulty with reading skills. Some children have strong social skills and acquire many friends, others do well in artistic and creative endeavors, and some children excel at physical activities and sports. It is important to recognize the child's strengths and to use those recognized strengths when determining the child's teaching plan.

It is also helpful to look for clusters of characteristics in evaluating a student. For example, a student with a severe handwriting problem may also have difficulty with other fine-motor skills. Likewise, a student with a reading problem may also have an underlying oral language disorder. A student who does poorly in oral expression may have a history of delayed speech, speech-motor difficulties that affect articulation, and difficulty with remembering words.

Considering the Concerns of Parents and Families IDEA-2004 emphasizes strengthening the role of parents and ensuring that families have meaningful opportunities to participate in the education of their child at home and at school. The law recognizes the key role that parents have in their child's education.

Setting Annual Goals The IEP must include a statement of measurable annual goals in academic and functional areas, if necessary, the annual goals are general estimates of what the student will achieve in one year. These goals should represent the student's most essential needs and priorities for each subject area and should address the specific deficit areas of the student. For example, an annual goal in mathematics could be that the student learns to multiply and divide at a specific level. Goals should be based on (1) how the disability impacts learning and (2) deficit areas in the present levels of academic achievement and functional performance (PLAAFP).

To remember how to write goals and present levels of academic achievement and functional performance, remember the mnemonic **MOO**:

M—Measurable
O—Observable
O—objective

When Writing a Goal, It Is Critical that It Be Written in Measurable, Observable, and Objective Terms so that You Are Able to See Whether the Student Has Gained Meaningful Benefit Here are a few examples of

annual goals
General estimates of what the student will achieve in one year. These goals should represent the most essential needs of the student. Annual goals are part of the written individualized education program.

goals that utilize MOO and are based on present levels of academic achievement and functional performance that also utilize MOO:

- **PLAAFP**—Erica currently can execute a one-step direction with no more than 5 words given by an adult 3 out of 5 times.
- **Goal**—Given a one-step direction with no more than 7 words, Erica will be able to execute the direction 4 out of 5 times.
- **PLAAFP**—Jamar can currently read with comprehension at the second grade level.
- **Goal**—Jamar will be able to read 3 one-paragraph passages and answer 3 who, what, or when questions about what was read at the third grade level with 70% accuracy.
- **PLAAFP**—Rafael currently knows his 2s multiplication facts and can do 5 one-digit problems involving his 2s multiplication facts with 95% accuracy.
- **Goal**—Given the 3s multiplication facts, Rafael will be able to complete 5 one-digit problems involving his 3s multiplication facts with 95% accuracy.

Once the Goals are Completed, Then the Specialized Instruction Required to Meet Those Goals Can Be Planned As an example, Erika may need to be taught to repeat the direction immediately after she hears it. She may need to be taught to make herself a note. She may need to be taught how to zero in on key words in the direction. Erika has an auditory memory problem so she will need to be taught to follow the directions taking into account that she has trouble remembering what she hears.

- **In Education CourseMate, you will find an activity designed to assist you in determining whether PLAAFP and goals are written in MOO terms.** Also on the website you will find a sample IEP completed.

When Developing Statements of PLAAFP and Goals Remember That It Is Critical That a Stranger Be Able To Understand the Specific Needs of the Student Many of the students with whom we work may be mobile and may also change teachers. Another teacher should be able to pick up the IEP of the student and be able to know exactly where the student is functioning.

Determining Educational Settings and Services What specific special education and related services are needed, including the specialized instruction that is required to individually meet the student's needs? How will the special education teacher provide the specialized instruction? To what extent will the student attend general education classes? What accommodations will be made within the general education classroom? These decisions are related to the educational setting in which the student receives instruction (see Chapter 4, "Educational Settings and the Role of the Family"). In addition, decisions must be made about the extent to which the student will be placed in the least restrictive environment (i.e., with students who do not have disabilities). In IDEA-2004, the general curriculum is presented to be the appropriate beginning point for planning an IEP for a student, and the general education curriculum is the preferred course of study for all students.

Monitoring Progress How will the student's progress be monitored and measured? It is necessary to determine whether annual goals are being met. What measurement instruments will be used? Who will be responsible for administering them? Also, any accommodations that will be needed for the statewide

TABLE 2.2

Sample Format for IEP Annual Goal in Mathematics

Instructional Area: Mathematics
Annual Goal: Student will learn multiplication and division computation skills
Meeting the Annual Goal

Progress Reports to Parents	Tests, Materials, and Evaluation Procedures to Be Used	Criteria of Successful Performance	Evaluation Schedule	Educational Accommodations
1. Student will add numbers involving 2 renamings	Student will compute 20 addition problems requiring 2 renamings	85% accuracy	End of first grading period	Student will participate in statewide assessment in mathematics
2. Student will subtract numbers involving 2 renamings	Student will compute 20 subtraction problems requiring 2 renamings	85% accuracy	End of second grading period	• Allow double time for math assessment • Permit student to use a calculator during the math test
3. Student will multiply and divide through products of 81	Student will compute a fact sheet containing 20 multiplication and division facts and products through 81 within a specified time	65% accuracy	End of third grading period	
4. Student will multiply 2-digit numbers by 1-digit numbers	Appropriate mastery test will be included in mathematics text	75% accuracy	End of fourth grading period	
5. Student will divide numbers by 2-digit divisors	Appropriate mastery test will be included in mathematics text	75% accuracy	End of fifth grading period	

© Cengage Learning

tests must be included in the IEP. A sample format for evaluating annual goals appears in Table 2.2.

The website of the National Center on Student Progress Monitoring offers information on progress monitoring: *http://www.studentprogress.org*.

2.5e Special Factors to Consider in the IEP

A number of special factors must be considered in the evaluation of students with learning disabilities and related mild disabilities. Federal law requires a functional behavioral assessment (FBA) and positive behavioral intervention and support for children with behavioral challenges. When behavior interferes with learning, a functional behavioral assessment must be conducted in order to develop a behavior intervention plan. This subject is addressed in detail in Chapter 6, "Social, Emotional, and Behavioral Challenges." We address two other special factors here: **English-language learners** and **assistive and instructional technology.**

English-Language Learners Society is becoming more responsive to the growing needs of an increasingly diverse population. English-language learners (ELL) (students with limited English proficiency) comprise the

functional behavioral assessment (FBA)
Evaluating a child's behavior problems by analyzing the behavioral unit and the specific purpose of the behavior.

English-language learners (ELL)
Students who speak a language other than English and have a limited proficiency with English.

▶❚❚ TeachSource Video Case Activity

©Cengage Learning 2015.

Watch the TeachSource Video Case entitled "Assessment in the Middle Grades: Measurement of Student Learning." In this video, the math teacher, Mr. Somers, demonstrates how teaching and assessment are linked.

QUESTIONS

1. How does Mr. Somers use individualized teaching and group teaching to prepare students for the standardized math test?

2. How does Mr. Somers use tests to gauge his own teaching as well as student learning?

---

assistive technology
Any technology that enables an individual with a disability to compensate for specific deficits. It includes low-tech or high-tech equipment.

---

instructional technology
Use of technology, such as computers, for teaching.

---

fastest growing population in our nation. In the largest school districts in the United States, English-language learners make up almost one-half of the children entering school at the kindergarten level. IDEA requires that if the child has limited proficiency in English, the IEP team must consider the child's language needs as they relate to the child's IEP.

Assistive and Instructional Technology IDEA-2004 requires that the IEP team must consider whether the child needs assistive technology devices or services. Assistive technology is defined as any technology that enables an individual with a disability to compensate for specific deficits. It includes low- and high-tech equipment. Instructional technology refers to software and programs used in teaching.

- The term *assistive technology* refers to equipment or products designed to help the functional capabilities of a child with a disability. For example, a speech-recognition system that allows a person to operate a computer by dictating or speaking into it is such a device.
- The term *assistive technology services* refers to any service that directly assists a child with a disability in the selection, acquisition, or use of an assistive technology device. For example, teaching a child who has a disability in writing the needed keyboarding skills for word processing would be an assistive technology service.

The IEP should describe the nature of the child's disability and the required assistive technology devices and services.

"I'm not an underachiever. You're an overexpecter."

Randy Hall

Did You Get It?

The individualized education program (IEP) guaranteed by IDEA-2004 is an individualized plan with what goal for a student who has demonstrated a disability?

- **a.** Guarantee a successful outcome.
- **b.** Provide the student with the resources needed for success.
- **c.** Provide a multidisciplinary and comprehensive team of staff and support personnel with the framework to work together to achieve success.
- **d.** Create an opportunity for the student to be reintroduced into a setting that does not specifically cater to students with disabilities.

2.6 Obtaining Assessment Information

Assessment information can be gathered from several sources: (1) the case history or interview; (2) observation; (3) standardized norm-referenced tests; (4) curriculum-based measurement and progress monitoring; (5) alternate assessment; and (6) informal measures. Often, several kinds of information are compiled at one time or one assessment procedure may lead to another. For example, observation of a student may suggest that a specific test should also be used. Or the detection of speech misarticulation accompanied by the student's frequent misunderstandings of the examiner's conversation could suggest an auditory difficulty and lead to a decision to administer a test of auditory acuity or auditory discrimination.

2.6a Case History

Information obtained through a case history contributes clues and insights about the student's background and development. During an interview, parents share information about the child's prenatal history, birth conditions, neonatal development, the age of developmental milestones (sitting, walking, toilet training, and talking), the child's health history (including illnesses and accidents), and learning problems of other members of the family. The student's school history can be obtained from parents, school records, and school personnel (e.g., teachers, nurses, and guidance counselors).

Interviewers must try to establish a feeling of mutual trust, taking care not to ask questions that might alarm parents or make them defensive by indicating disapproval of their actions. Further, interviewers should convey a spirit of cooperation, acceptance, and empathy while maintaining a degree of professional objectivity to guard against excessive emotional involvement and consequent ineffectiveness.

Skillful interviewers are able to obtain much useful information during the case history interview, gathering information in a smooth, conversational manner. Case history information and impressions are integrated with knowledge obtained through clinical observation, traditional tests, and alternative assessment measures. Table 2.3 illustrates the kind of information obtained through the case history interview.

Many case-history interview forms are available. Some forms are quite lengthy and extensive, procuring information in many domains. Adaptive behavior scales that question the extent to which individuals adapt themselves

case history
A compilation of the student's background, development, and other information. Case-history information is usually obtained from parents and from the student's school and medical histories. Often this information is obtained by interview.

adaptive behavior scales
A rating scale of information provided by an informant who knows the child (such as the parent). It is usually obtained during an interview with the parent and provides information about the student's self-help skills, communication skills, daily living skills, socialization, and motor skills.

TABLE 2.3

Case History Information

Identifying Information

Student: Name, address, telephone, date of birth, school, grade

Parents: Father's name and occupation, mother's name and occupation

Family: Siblings' names and ages, others in the home

Clinic: Date of interview, referral agency, name of examiner

Birth History

Pregnancy: Length, condition of mother, unusual factors

Birth conditions: Mature or premature, duration of labor, weight, unusual circumstances

Conditions following birth: Normal, needing special care

Physical and Developmental Data

Health history: Accidents, high fevers, other illnesses

Present health: Habits of eating and sleeping, energy and activity level

Developmental history: Age of sitting, walking, first words, first sentences, language difficulties, motor difficulties

Social and Personal Factors

Friends

Sibling relationships

Hobbies, interests, recreational activities

Home and parental attitudes

Acceptance of responsibilities

Attitude toward learning problem

Educational Factors

School experiences: Skipped or repeated grades, moving, change of teachers

Preschool education: Kindergarten, nursery school

Special help previously received

Teachers' reports

Student's attitude toward school

© Cengage Learning

observation
Careful watching of a student's behavior, usually in the classroom setting.

to the expectations of nature and society are often used. An informant (usually the mother) provides the information during an interview. We list here some commonly used adaptive behavior scales.

- **Vineland Adaptive Behavior Scales.** These scales assess the domains of communication, daily living skills, socialization, and motor functions for ages birth to 19 (American Guidance Services, *http://ags.personalassessments.com*).
- **Hawthorne Adaptive Behavior Scales.** This inventory is used to interview an informant, and it yields information about self-help skills, communication skills, social skills, academic skills, and occupational skills for ages 6 to 9 (Hawthorne Educational Services, *http://www.hes-inc.com*).

2.6b Observation

According to Yogi Berra, "Sometimes you can observe a lot just by watching." Observation of the student is a required part of the assessment of a student, and the information that it produces can make a valuable contribution. Many attributes of the student may be inadequately identified through testing or case study interviews, but the skillful observer can often detect important characteristics and behaviors of the child in the classroom setting.

Observation of student behavior can corroborate findings of other assessment measures. For example, a skillful observer can note whether the student is attending to the lesson or is engaged in other activities. Observation is also useful for shedding light on a student's general personal adjustment. How does the student react to situations and people? What is the student's attitude toward the learning problem? Motor coordination can be appraised by observing the student's movements and gait. Can the student hop, skip, or throw and catch a ball? How does the student attack a writing task? Is there a contortion of the body while writing? How does the student hold a pencil?

Must the student expend an inordinate effort in trying to make the handwriting presentable?

Language is readily assessed through observation. Is there evidence of articulation problems or infantile speech patterns? Does the student have difficulty finding words? Does the student possess an adequate vocabulary? Does the student speak easily, haltingly, or perhaps excessively? Does the student use complete sentences or single words and short, partial phrases? Are there misarticulations (e.g., *aminal* or *psghetti)?* What is the student's primary or native language and facility with English?

Games and toys offer activities for making observations of the student and also serve as a way to build rapport. Can the student zip a zipper, tie a shoelace, button clothing, or lock a padlock?

Observations of everyday classroom behavior can provide much information. For example, while reading, how does the student react to an unknown word? Does the student stop and look to the teacher for help, look at the initial consonant and then take a wild guess, attempt to break the word into syllables, or try to infer the word from the context?

2.6c Standardized Norm-Referenced Tests

Standardized norm-referenced tests are frequently used in our schools. In developing a norm-referenced test, test publishers give the test questions to a large number of children of the same age. This group is called the *norm-referenced group* because the test norms are based on their performance. When a student's achievement on a standardized test is analyzed, the scores of an individual student are compared with the scores of students of comparable age or grade in the norm-referenced group.

norm-referenced tests
Standardized tests that compare a child's performance to that of other children of the same age.

Formal standardized tests are statistically designed so that one-half of the student scores will be below the mean (average), and one-half will be above the average. Of course, communities want all of their children to score above average. Standardized tests require strict procedures in administration, scoring, and interpretation. Standardized tests

formal standardized tests
Commercially prepared tests that have been used with and standardized on large groups of students. Manuals that accompany the tests provide derived scores on student performance, such as grade scores, age scores, percentiles, and standard scores.

- are usually available in more than one form so that a student can be tested more than once without being able to obtain a higher score due to practice.
- are accompanied by manuals that (a) give directions for administration, scoring, and interpretation; (b) provide information about grade norms, age norms, percentile ranks, or some other form of scaled scores; and (c) provide information on validity (the degree to which the test measures what it is supposed to measure). Manuals also show reliability (consistency or similarity of performance). A reliability coefficient of 0.90 indicates that if the test were given to the student again, it is 90% likely that the student would obtain a score in the same range.

Teachers should know the techniques of using and interpreting tests. Frequently, the value of a test may not be so much in the final test score as in the measurement of a particular subtest performance, the profile of all the subtest scores, or the clinical observations of the student during the test. The evaluator who has had extensive experience with a test may find that some parts used alone yield the necessary information.

The integrity of formal tests is judged on (1) *standardization*—on what group was the test standardized? (2) *reliability*—are the test results consistent? and (3) *validity*—does the test measure what it claims to measure? Norm-referenced tests can be useful in the assessment process. It is important to know the limitations of a test and to use its information in proper perspective. A single score provides only a small part of the information, so teachers should not overgeneralize the implications of a specific test. If multiple sources of data are used in the assessment, test scores can provide a rich harvest of leads for assessment and teaching.

Some commonly used standardized tests are described in this chapter and in Chapter 11, "Spoken Language Difficulties: Listening and Speaking;" Chapter 12, "Reading Difficulties;" Chapter 13, "Written Language: Written Expression, Spelling, and Handwriting;" and Chapter 14, "Mathematics Difficulties."

Standardized testing is criticized for a number of reasons: (1) It does not provide enough information about the students; (2) the tests may not assess what students are learning in class; (3) the tests may be biased against culturally diverse populations; and (4) the pressure for students to attain high test scores may sway teachers to use class time to prepare students for taking the tests.

2.6d Informal Assessment Measures

Disenchantment with standardized testing led educators to turn to informal assessment procedures. Interest in informal assessment is growing because it evaluates the student in the natural setting, uses the school curriculum, and capitalizes on what the student actually does in the classroom. Informal assessment approaches encourage students to produce, construct, demonstrate, or perform a response.

informal assessment measures
Ways of evaluating performance that are not formal standardized tests. These can include teacher-made tests, diagnostic teaching, commercial nonstandardized tests, curriculum-based assessment, and so on.

Informal assessment measures are useful and practical assessment procedures that measure student achievement on the ordinary materials and activities they are currently working with in the classroom. A major advantage of using classroom materials for informal tests is that the assessment is as close as possible to the expected behaviors. Informal tests also give teachers freedom in administration and interpretation. For example, a teacher can encourage the student during the assessment or give the student more time to complete the test. Such adjustments put students at ease and help ensure that they will put forth their best effort. Informal assessment measures can also be given more frequently than formal tests, and they can be administered over a period of time rather than in a single session. In addition, informal assessment measures can use a variety of materials and procedures, they can be given during regular instruction periods, and they are less expensive than formal tests.

In this section, we present several informal measures for teachers to use: (1) portfolio assessment, (2) informal graded word-recognition tests, (3) informal arithmetic tests, and (4) criterion-referenced tests. Some informal tests are also provided in other pertinent chapters, such as the informal reading inventory (see Chapter 12, "Reading Difficulties"), informal motor tests (where is new location of motor tests), and tests of phonological awareness (see Chapter 11, "Spoken Language Difficulties: Listening and Speaking").

Portfolio Assessment

In portfolio assessment, multiple samples of a student's actual classroom work are collected over an extended period of time. This portfolio is used to evaluate the student's current achievement level and progress over time. Portfolio assessment is often used to measure reading and writing progress. Samples of student work can be used to determine achievement and progress in all academic areas.

portfolio assessment
A method of evaluating student progress by analyzing samples of the student's classroom work.

A portfolio might contain the following kinds of materials: selected samples of daily work done in the classroom, academic classroom tests (e.g., in spelling or mathematics), checklists of behavior, sample stories, writing drafts at various stages of development, science projects, art samples, a teacher's observational notes, or the results of group projects.

In deciding what samples to collect, the teacher must first consider the goals of the instructional program, and the samples should then reflect these goals. For example, the portfolio might include samples of the objectives in the IEP. Students can be responsible for organizing their own portfolios. Because portfolios serve as mirrors of the process of learning in the classroom, they should be available for student-teacher conferences or for parent conferences (Salend, 1998).

Informal Graded Word-Recognition Test

This type of test can be used as a quick method to determine the student's approximate reading level. It is also useful in detecting the student's errors in word analysis. An informal graded word-recognition test can be constructed by selecting words at random from graded basal reader glossaries. Table 2.4 illustrates such a list; the words were selected from several basal reader series and from graded reading vocabulary lists. The informal graded word-recognition test can be given as follows: (1) type the list of words selected for each grade on separate cards; (2) duplicate the entire test on a single sheet; (3) have the pupil read the words from the cards while the examiner marks the errors on the sheet, noting the pupil's method of analyzing and pronouncing difficult words; and (4) have the pupil read from increasingly difficult lists until three words are missed. The level at which the student misses only two words suggests the instructional level at which the pupil is able to read with help. The level at which one word is missed suggests the pupil's independent reading level (i.e., the level at which the pupil can read alone).

The level at which three words are missed suggests a frustration level, and the material is probably too difficult.

Alternate and informal assessment measures are useful and practical alternative assessment procedures that test students on the ordinary materials that they are currently working with in the classroom.

Informal Arithmetic Test

An informal arithmetic test can be easily devised to point out weaknesses in a student's basic computational skills. The informal survey test illustrated in Figure 2.6 can be used for

TABLE **2.4**

Informal Graded Word–Recognition Test

Preprimer	Primer	Grade 1	Grade 2
See	day	about	hungry
Run	from	sang	loud
Me	all	guess	stones
dog	under	catch	trick
At	little	across	chair
come	house	ive	hopped
down	ready	boats	himself
You	came	hard	color
said	your	longer	straight
Boy	blue	hold	leading

Grade 3	Grade 4	Grade 5	Grade 6
arrow	brilliant	career	buoyant
wrist	credit	cultivate	determination
bottom	examine	essential	gauntlet
castle	grammar	grieve	incubator
earned	jingle	jostle	ludicrous
washed	ruby	obscure	offensive
safety	terrify	procession	prophesy
yesterday	wrench	sociable	sanctuary
delight	mayor	triangular	tapestry
happiness	agent	volcano	vague

© Cengage Learning

FIGURE **2.6**
Informal Arithmetic Survey
Test: Sixth-Grade Level

ADDITION					
	300	35		234	123
	60	24		573	324
	406	6	271		
	+ 3	+ 18	+ 389	+ 261	+ 452

SUBTRACTION					
	765	751	7,054	8,004	90,327
	− 342	− 608	− 3,595	− 5,637	−42,827

MULTIPLICATION					
	37	45	721	483	802
	× 10	× 83	× 346	× 208	× 357

DIVISION					
	2⟌36	12⟌36	6⟌966	16⟌1,061	13⟌8,726

© Cengage Learning

sixth-grade students. The difficulty level of the test could be increased or decreased, depending on the grade level being tested. The informal arithmetic test should include several items of each kind so that a simple error will not be mistaken for a more fundamental difficulty.

Criterion-Referenced Tests Criterion-referenced tests *describe* rather than *compare* performance, measuring mastery levels rather than grade levels. In contrast, *norm-referenced tests* (traditional standardized tests) compare the pupil's performance to that of other children of the same age. This difference can be illustrated in a nonacademic area of learning, such as swimming. In criterion-referenced terms, a child would be judged as being able to perform certain tasks, such as putting his or her face in the water, floating, or doing the crawl stroke. In contrast, in norm-referenced terms, the child would be tested and judged to swim as well as an average 9-year-old child.

criterion-referenced tests
Tests that measure the student's abilities in specific skills (rather than tests that compare a student to others in a norm group).

Criterion-referenced tests are useful because they provide a way to show growth. It is often difficult to show that a student has improved in terms of percentiles, stanines, or even grade-level scores, but the teacher can show that the student has learned certain specific skills, in terms of mastery, of criterion-referenced measures.

Did You Get It?

Obtaining information to assess an individual student is a multifaceted and complex endeavor. Which activity is used to most formally and objectively obtain comprehensive background information about the student you are assessing?

a. Process monitoring.

b. An informal question-and-answer session.

c. Grades from all previous institutions.

d. A case history.

2.7 Testing and Accountability

Under the No Child Left Behind Act (2001), each state must develop and implement a statewide assessment system that is aligned to the state standards in reading/language arts, math, and science. Under IDEA-2004, each state must have achievement goals that are measured by statewide tests for all public schools.

Common core standards have been adopted in most states, and the states must administer statewide assessments to measure the progress of students in meeting these standards. Many states have now adopted the common core standards, and statewide testing is being updated so that it is based on those standards.

2.7a Including Students With Disabilities in Testing

IDEA-2004 specifically requires that, as a condition of a state's eligibility for educational funding, children with disabilities must be included in general statewide and districtwide assessment programs. IDEA-2004 also addresses timelines and reporting requirements and mandates that states

- Provide for the participation of children with disabilities in general statewide and district-wide assessments, with appropriate accommodations in administration, if necessary

- Provide for the conducting of alternate assessment of children who cannot participate in the general assessment programs
- Make available and report to the public on results of the assessment of disabled children with the same frequency and in the same detail as they report the assessment results of nondisabled children

This regulation means that children with disabilities must participate in the statewide tests and that any accommodations that are needed for this testing must be included in each student's IEP. Further, reports to parents about the child with disabilities must be made in the same detail and with the same frequency as reports about other children. Thus, if report cards are issued on a quarterly basis for all children, then progress reports must be issued for students with disabilities.

2.7b Accommodations for Testing

accommodations for assessment
Tools such as extended timelines, large print, interpreters, etc., that enable students to access the same assessment but don't change the content that are made in testing students with disabilities.

IDEA-2004 permits *accommodations* in statewide testing for students with disabilities. However, these accommodations for assessment must be written into the student's IEP. Teachers need much support and guidance in planning for and implementing these accommodations. Accommodations cannot jeopardize the integrity of the test. Figure 2.7 provides examples of common assessment accommodations for students with disabilities.

IDEA-2004 requires that states develop guidelines for accommodations that allow students with disabilities the opportunity to participate in state-level assessments. Most states have developed guidelines for accommodations (Yell, Shriner, & Katsiyannis, 2006). Accommodations for students with disabilities serve to level the playing field for these students. A concern about accommodations is whether they invalidate the psychometric qualities of the test. For example, does giving extended time on a test nullify the validity of the test (Johnson, Kimball, & Brown, 2001)? There are several studies on the effects of extended time on the test scores of postsecondary students with learning disabilities. Students with learning disabilities had significantly

FIGURE **2.7**
Examples of Common Assessment Accommodations for Students With Disabilities

TIMING	SETTING
• Extend time to complete the test	• Provide a distraction-free environment
• Allow frequent breaks during testing	• Give to small groups
• Alter time of day that test is administered	• Give in hospital setting
• Administer test in several sessions over the course of the day	• Use a study carrel
• Administer test in several sessions over several days	• Give the test in a separate room
	• Administer test over several sessions

PRESENTATION	RESPONSE
• Modify the test format, use enlarged print, use fewer items on a page	• Use computer for writing tests
• Use audiocassettes	• Dictate to scribe
• Read test aloud to student	• Tape record answers
• Repeat the direction	• Put answers in booklet instead of answer sheet
• Use magnification devices	• Allow students to use a word processor instead of handwriting
• Use computers to read test	

© Cengage Learning

better scores after being allowed extended time, whereas students without learning disabilities did not improve their scores by using extended time (Weaver, 2000).

2.7c Alternate Assessments for Students With Significant Cognitive Disabilities

States must develop guidelines for *alternate assessments* based on alternate achievement standards to be used with students with significant cognitive disabilities who are unable to participate in the general state assessment. Alternate assessments refer to another way to measure performance. The alternate assessments should be included in the student's IEP. This type of assessment can be used with 1% of the students with the most significant intellectual disabilities.

alternate assessments
A different test based on alternate achievement standards as determined by the state for no more than 1% of the total population of students. The students must be those with the most significant intellectual disabilities.

Regulations for Alternate Assessments Based on Modified Academic Achievement Standards In April 2007, the U.S. Department of Education issued final regulations concerning the ability of states to create alternate assessments based on modified achievement standards for up to 2% of students with disabilities. The responsibility for the determination of whether the student should take such an assessment is made by the IEP team and that decision is made when the IEP team is reasonably certain that the student will not achieve grade-level proficiency because of the nature of their disability (Regulations, 34 C.F.R. Parts 200 and 300, 2007). The next section describes the regulations for accommodations and alternate assessments.

Alternate Assessments With Modified Academic Achievement Standards This type of assessment is developed by each state and has a less rigorous expectation of mastery of grade-level academic content standards.

STUDENT STORIES 2.3

Accommodations for Statewide Testing

The Oregon Statewide Assessment System (OSAS) measured performance in the area of written-language assessment. These tests did not allow the use of word processors and spell checkers, even for students with learning disabilities who were using these accommodations in their classrooms. Many students with learning disabilities did so poorly on the statewide written-language test that they did not achieve the certificate of mastery. Furthermore, Oregon had not developed alternate assessments for students with learning disabilities, nor was there a fully developed appeals process.

The Oregon legal case involved students with learning disabilities who were denied the certificate of mastery because they had failed the written-language test. The parents of these children filed a class-action lawsuit against the Oregon Department of Education. The settlement of this lawsuit required that appropriate accommodations for students with learning disabilities be developed. Students with disabilities in the area of written language were given the opportunity to use a word processor and a spell checker for the written-language test.

REFLECTIVE QUESTIONS

1. Why do you think that the Oregon Department of Education did not want to allow word processors or spell checkers on the written-language test?

2. Do you believe that the use of word processors or spell checkers for students with disabilities would have given students an unfair advantage over other students without disabilities? Justify your answer.

Modified academic achievement standards must be based on a state's grade-level academic content standards for the grade in which the student with disabilities is enrolled. The state's academic content standards are not modified. Such an assessment can be used with another 2% of the students with disabilities (Regulations, 34 C.F.R. Parts 200 and 300, 2007).

In summary, all students will be assessed in the required subject areas in one of these ways:

1. Regular assessment without accommodations
2. Regular assessment with accommodations
3. Alternate assessments based on the grade-level academic achievement standards
4. Alternate assessments based on modified academic achievement standards
5. Alternate assessments based on the alternate academic achievement standards

Did You Get It?

Which piece of legislation mandated that individual states propose, develop, and implement statewide assessment measures to ensure adherence to state standards in a broad range of academic subjects, ranging from reading to science?

a. Americans with Disabilities Act (ADA)
b. No Child Left Behind Act (2001)
c. Section 504 of the Rehabilitation Act of 1973
d. Educational Assessment Act of 2010

2.8 Examples of Tests

In this section, we provide examples of some of the assessment tests.

2.8a Tests of Intelligence and Cognitive Abilities

Intelligence tests and tests of cognitive abilities provide information about the student's aptitude for learning and specific cognitive attributions. Certain intelligence tests are administered by psychologists; others may be given by teachers with appropriate training. Commonly used individual cognitive or intelligence tests that are typically administered by psychologists are:

- **The Wechsler Intelligence Scale for Children, 4th edition (WISC-IV)** provides four index scores—Verbal Comprehension, Perceptual Reasoning, Working Memory, Processing Speed—with 16 subtests of mental ability. Harcourt Brace & Co.
- **The Stanford-Binet** has 15 subtests grouped into four areas—Fluid Reasoning, Knowledge, Quantitative Reasoning, Visual-Spatial Processing, Working Memory. Riverside Publishing
- **Kaufman Assessment Battery for Children II (K-ABC)** offers a nonverbal composite and a mental processing/fluid-crystallized index, plus individual scale scores. Western Psychological Services

Table 2.5 lists some tests of cognitive ability that can be given by teachers with appropriate training.

TABLE 2.5

Tests of Cognitive Ability That Can Be Given by Teachers With Training

- Tests of Cognitive Ability of the Woodcock-Johnson III. Tests of Cognitive Abilities Riverside Publications

- The Slosson Intelligence Test—Revised is a relatively short screening test. Slosson Educational Publications

- The Detroit Tests of Learning Aptitude—4 (DTLA-4) are intended for use with children ages 6 to 17. Pro-Ed

- The Detroit Tests of Learning Aptitude—Primary—2 are intended for younger children, ages 3 to 12. Pro-Ed

- The McCarthy Scales of Children's Abilities are designed to assess young children, ages 2.5 to 8.5. Harcourt Assessment

- The Illinois Test of Psycholinguistic Abilities—Third Edition (ITPA-3) was one of the first tests of mental processes designed expressly to analyze subskills of mental function. Pro-Ed

- The Goodenough-Harris Drawing Test estimates intellectual maturity through an analysis of a child's drawing of a person. Harcourt Assessment

© Cengage Learning

Woodcock-Johnson Psychoeducational Battery III The Woodcock-Johnson Psychoeducational Battery III, Complete Battery (WJ-III) Normative update provides a conormed set of tests for measuring general intellectual ability, specific cognitive abilities, scholastic aptitude, oral language, and academic achievement. It can be used on subjects from age 2 to 90+ and for grade K through graduate school. The WJ-III consists of two assessment instruments: (1) tests of cognitive abilities and (2) tests of achievement. The WJ-III can be administered by teachers with appropriate training. The WJ-III Cognitive Performance Clusters are shown in Table 2.6.

The Woodcock-Johnson Psychoeducational Battery III—Tests of Achievement is a battery consisting of 22 achievement tests that can be combined to form score clusters. The clusters include (1) oral expression, (2) listening comprehension, (3) basic reading skills, (4) reading comprehension, (5) phoneme/grapheme knowledge, (6) math calculation, (7) math reasoning, and (8) written expression.

The Wechsler Intelligence Scale for Children, 4th edition (WISC-IV) The WISC-IV is probably the most common intelligence test used to measure intelligence. The WISC-IV has four factors of intelligence: (1) verbal comprehension, (2) perceptual reasoning, (3) working memory, and (4) processing speed.

1. **Verbal comprehension.** Ability to use and understand language
2. **Perceptual reasoning.** Ability with nonverbal and perceptual skills
3. **Working memory.** Ability to hold information in short-term memory
4. **Processing speed.** Ability to work quickly

2.8b Commonly Used Achievement Tests

General test batteries measure performance in academic skills in reading, arithmetic, spelling, and grammar. Table 2.7 lists the commonly used standardized achievement tests.

TABLE 2.6

The WJ-III Cognitive Performance Clusters

The WJ-III Cognitive Performance Clusters
The WJ-III cognitive tests include certain clusters representing broad categories of cognitive abilities that are casually related to cognitive performance. The clusters are the result of a combination of tests. They include the following:

- Verbal ability—Standard scale
- Verbal ability—Extended scale
- Comprehension/knowledge
- Long-term retrieval
- Visual-spatial thinking

Other Clinically Useful Clusters
- Phonemic awareness
- Working memory

© Cengage Learning

TABLE 2.7

Commonly Used Achievement Tests

Test	Areas Tested	Type	Publisher
Woodcock-Johnson III Tests of Achievement	Oral language, reading, writing, math	Individual, norm-referenced	Riverside Publishing
Peabody Individual Achievement Test-Revised	General Information, reading recognition, reading comprehension, written expression, mathematics, spelling	Individual, norm-referenced	American Guidance Services
Kaufman Test of Individual Achievement II	Reading, math, written language, oral language	Individual, norm-referenced	American Guidance Service
Brigance Diagnostic Comprehensive Inventory of Basic Skills	Listening, reading, writing, math	Individual, criterion-referenced	Curriculum Associates
Woodcock Reading Mastery Tests-Revised	Reading	Individual, standardized	American Guidance Services
Key Math Diagnostic Arithmetic Test, Revised	Math	Individual, standardized	American Guidance Services

© Cengage Learning

The Wechsler Intelligence Scale for Children, 4th edition (WISC-IV), is recognized as the most commonly used test for assessing and measuring intelligence. Which category of memory is not one of the four categories of intelligence the test measures?

a. working memory
b. mathematical manipulation
c. verbal comprehension
d. processing speed

2.9 Test-Taking Strategies in the General Education Classroom

The general education teacher, with the collaboration of the special education teacher, is responsible for administering the state's standard performance tests to all students in the inclusion class. Including Students in General Education 2.1, "Test-Taking Strategies in the General Education Classroom," offers some strategies to help students to prepare for and take these tests (Spinelli, 2002). Websites with useful information on test-taking strategies are *http://www.charliefrench.com/test_tips.htm* and *http://www.testtakingtips.com*.

Including Students in GENERAL EDUCATION 2.1

Test-Taking Strategies in the General Education Classroom

- Prepare students for test taking by suggesting that they get enough rest and nourishment before taking the test.

- Provide students with opportunities to practice working under standardized conditions in simulated situations.

- Give students practice in filling in the appropriate circle with quick, dark strokes inside the circle or bubble. Most standardized tests require students to record their responses by filling in circles on separate answer sheets.

- Separate answer sheets from the test. Instruct students to mark answers on the test booklet and then have the students practice transferring their marked responses to the answer sheet.

- Instruct students to eliminate any answers that they know are incorrect. Provide students practice in eliminating wrong answers and discuss why they are wrong.

- Explain to students that guessing at an answer is usually better than leaving the question blank.

- Teach students to use their time efficiently by not wasting time on items they do not know. Students should have practice in monitoring their time as they take the test.

- Encourage students to request accommodations, as appropriate for their disabilities, such as extended time, assistive technology, and testing in smaller groups.

- Look for accommodations for testing that are written in the student's IEP.

Professional Resource Download

I Have a Kid Who...

Courtney is 6 years 3 months old and is in first grade at the Washington Elementary School. She is having much difficulty with phonological awareness of language sounds, and she does not recognize rhyming words. Washington School uses the response-to-intervention (RTI) model for teaching students who are considered to be at risk. Courtney's scores were very low on a September screening test on phonemic awareness and she was identified as a student who was at risk for school failure. She received instruction in her first-grade general education class in a Tier 1 intervention program using scientifically based materials. Courtney's performance was monitored for eight weeks under Tier 1 instruction, with a curriculum-based measurement (CBM) assessment given each week. At the end of eight weeks of intervention in Tier 1, the curriculum-based assessment measures showed that Courtney's scores were below the criterion for a positive response. Courtney was then placed into a Tier 2 intervention program. In Tier 2, she received more intensive instruction

delivered by a reading teacher, using scientifically based materials. She received intervention in the Tier 2 group for 30 minutes daily. The reading teacher and the first grade classroom teacher also worked collaboratively on techniques that were effective for Courtney. At the end of the Tier 2 instruction, progress monitoring showed that Courtney's scores had increased substantially and that she was making good progress in her reading skills. Progress-monitoring scores showed that Courtney was responsive to the Tier 2 instruction. Because Courtney responded positively to the Tier 2 intervention, she was not identified as a child with a disability. Courtney's progress will be monitored closely by the first-grade classroom teacher and the reading teacher for the remainder of first grade.

QUESTIONS

1. How did Courtney respond to the Tier 1 instruction?
2. How did Courtney response to the Tier 2 instruction?

Did You Get It?

There are many strategies that can help a child to perform as well as possible and motivate the child's efforts toward a successful outcome. Which strategy is not a recognized intervention strategy?
   a. providing practice sessions and simulations on test-taking processes
   b. educating the student on the importance of proper rest before the testing
   c. teaching time-management and efficiency-boosting skills
   d. counseling the child on the implications and ramifications of subpar performance

Chapter Summary

- Describe uses of assessment information
- Explain eligibility for special education services
- Describe response-to-intervention (RTI)
- Compare the comprehensive evaluation
- Describe the Individualized Education Program (IEP)

- Explain stages of the IEP
- Describe how to obtain assessment information
- Explain testing and accountability
- Describe test-taking strategies

Questions for Discussion and Reflection

1. Describe the 6 stages of the individualized education program (IEP) process. What is the purpose of each stage?
2. The Individuals With Disabilities Education Improvement Act (IDEA-2004) requires that important procedural safeguards be used with students with learning disabilities and students with related mild disabilities. Discuss 4 parents' rights or procedural safeguards.
3. IDEA-2004 specifies the participants for the IEP meeting. Name and describe the role of each of the participants.
4. Write 4 goals utilizing MOO.
5. What are the 5 ways to obtain data for an evaluation of a student with learning disabilities? Give examples of information that might be obtained by using each method.
6. Compare and contrast standardized norm-referenced tests with informal or alternate assessment measures.
7. Describe several accommodations that can be made for testing students with disabilities.
8. What is response-to-intervention (RTI)?

Key Terms

accommodations for assessment (p. 64)
adaptive behavior scales (p. 57)
alternate assessments (p. 65)
annual goals (p. 53)
assessment (p. 000)
assessment stages (p. 50)
assistive technology (p. 56)
case history (p. 57)
criterion-referenced tests (p. 62)
comprehensive evaluation (p. 45)
curriculum-based measurement (CBM) (p. 44)
discrepancy score (p. 46)
English-language learners (ELL) (p. 55)
formal standardized tests (p. 59)
functional behavioral assessment (p. 55)
IEP meeting (p. 50)
individualized education program (IEP) (p. 48)

informal assessment measures (p. 60)
instruction stages (p. 52)
instructional support team (p. 49)
instructional technology (p. 56)
mediation (p. 48)
multidisciplinary evaluation (p. 50)
norm-referenced tests (p. 59)
observation (p. 58)
parents' rights (p. 48)
portfolio assessment (p. 61)
prereferral activities (p. 49)
problem-solving model to RTI (p. 42)
procedural safeguards (p. 48)
progress monitoring (p. 43)
referral (p. 50)
referral stages (p. 49)
response-to-intervention (RTI) (p. 39)

ptaxa/iStockphoto.cc

CHAPTER 3

Specialized Instruction and Technology

Tell me and I forget. Show me and I remember. Involve me and I understand.

—Chinese Proverb

LEARNING OBJECTIVES

After reading this chapter, you should be able to:

3.1 Explain specialized instruction

3.2 Differentiate specialized instruction from accommodations and modifications

3.3 Explain clinical teaching

3.4 Define differentiated instruction

3.5 Give examples of controlling instructional variables

3.6 Describe how to build self-esteem and motivation

3.7 Give examples of how to work with students in general education

3.8 List accommodations for students with learning disabilities and related disabilities

3.9 Describe effective instructional strategies for general education

3.10 Explain task analysis

3.11 Give an example of how to provide Technology in the classroom.

STANDARDS Addressed in This Chapter:

Council for Exceptional Children Initial Level Special Educator Preparation Standards as approved by the National Council for the Accreditation of Teacher Education

CEC Initial Preparation Standard 1: Learner Development and Individual Learning Differences

- 1.0—Beginning special education professionals understand how exceptionalities may interact with development and learning and use this knowledge to provide meaningful and challenging learning experiences for individuals with exceptionalities.

- 1.1—Beginning special education professionals understand how language, culture, and family background influence the learning of individuals with exceptionalities.

- 1.2—Beginning special education professionals use understanding of development and individuals differences to respond to the needs of individuals with exceptionalities.

CEC Initial Preparation Standard 2: Learning Environments

- 2.0—Beginning special education professionals create safe, inclusive, culturally responsive learning environments so that individuals with exceptionalities become active and effective learners and develop emotional well-being, positive social interactions, and self-determination.

- 2.2—Beginning special education professionals use motivational and instructional interventions to teach individuals with exceptionalities how to adapt to different environments.

CEC Initial Preparation Standard 3: Curricular Content Knowledge

- 3.0—Beginning special education professionals use knowledge of general and specialized curricula to individualize learning for individuals with exceptionalities.

- 3.1—Beginning special education professionals understand the central concepts, structures of the discipline, and tools of inquiry of the content areas they teach, and can organize this knowledge, integrate cross-disciplinary skills, and develop meaningful learning progressions for individuals with exceptionalities.

- 3.3—Beginning special education professionals modify general and specialized curricula to make them accessible to individuals with exceptionalities.

CEC Initial Preparation Standard 4: Assessment

- 4.4—Beginning special education professionals engage individuals with exceptionalities to work toward quality learning and performance and provide feedback to guide them.

CEC Initial Preparation Standard 5: Instructional Planning and Strategies

- 5.0—Beginning special education professionals select, adapt, and use a repertoire of evidence-based instructional strategies to advance learning of individuals with exceptionalities.

- 5.1—Beginning special education professionals consider an individual's abilities, interests, learning environments, and cultural and linguistic factors in the selection, development, and adaptation of learning experiences for individuals with exceptionalities.

- 5.2—Beginning special education professionals use technologies to support instructional assessment, planning, and delivery for individuals with exceptionalities.

- 5.4—Beginning special education professionals use strategies to enhance language development and communication skills of individuals with exceptionalities.

- 5.5—Beginning special education professionals develop and implement a variety of education and transition plans for individuals with exceptionalities across a wide range of settings and different learning experiences in collaboration with individuals, families, and teams.

- 5.6—Beginning special education professionals teach to mastery and promote generalization of learning.

I n Chapter 3, we review the teaching portions of the assessment-teaching process and discuss the meaning of specialized instruction. We also look at the important role of Technology in designing specialized instruction.

3.1 Specialized Instruction

specialized instruction
Tailor made instruction designed for an individual student that is based on the specific needs of that student and that provides remediation and compensation.

Instruction based on the individualized needs of the students constitutes specialized instruction. It is what is special about special education. It is the instruction that is unique to a particular child. Provided with a thorough assessment of the student, the special education teacher plans instruction based on the individualized needs of the student. One size does not fit all. Rather we provide the instruction that is needed by the child. One student may need a specific multisensory approach to teach him reading because he has poor auditory and visual memory skills; another may need to be taught a specific learning strategy because she does not know how to take tests well and has a high degree of anxiety. One student may need a fading approach to learn his math facts Another student may be preparing for a job in a laundromat and needs to be taught how to fold clothes utilizing a particular folding board. Figure 3.1 reflects the critical components in designing an appropriate approach to instruction for the student with special needs.

FIGURE **3.1**
Providing Appropriate
Instruction

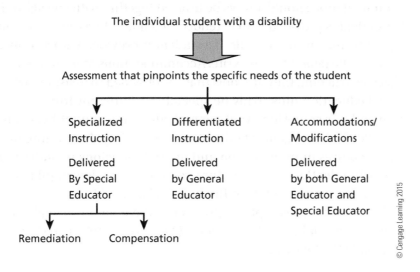

© Cengage Learning 2015

FIGURE **3.1**

Did You Get It?

In the words of the authors of your text, "this is what is special about special education." Educational principles that always put the needs of the student above any other consideration are the hallmark of _____.

a. person-first language
b. specialized instruction
c. special needs education
d. individualized educational plans

3.2 Differentiate Specialized Instruction from Accommodations and Modifications

Oftentimes we hear individuals discussing the accommodations and modifications a student needs. If the child cannot read, we may provide them with someone who can read the material to them. This is not enough and this is not specialized instruction. The student must also be taught to read in the specialized way in which he or she can learn. Services for students with disabilities must include specialized instruction provided by a credentialed special educator. That special education must include remediation of the specific disability. In the case of students who cannot read, students must be taught to read in a way that is appropriate for them. The student must also be taught compensatory strategies for his or her reading disability. The student will need to be taught how to use context clues, how to attack a word he or she does not know, and what techniques help as they struggle with reading.

This differentiated instruction takes place within the general education classroom and involves the classroom teacher using techniques that are designed to meet the range of diversity within the classroom. Accommodations and modifications are provided to students to assist them. Accommodations will be discussed later in this chapter; they are tools provided to students, such as extended timelines or large print materials. Accommodations do not change content. Modifications, on the other hand, change the content of material being learned.

Accommodation should always be utilized together with specialized instruction. If a student is provided with extended timelines, then the student must also be taught time management skills. If a student is provided with a scribe, the student must also be taught how to write. Accommodations or modifications are not specialized instruction; they are tools that are provided to assist in instruction.

Special education must truly be special. It is different from the typical instruction and it is something that general education cannot be. (Kauffman & Hallahan, 2005). Good general education is certainly demanding but special education requires more precision and more dimensions including pacing or rate, intensity, relentlessness, structure, reinforcement, low pupil teacher ratio, monitoring, and assessment. (Kauffman & Hallahan, 2005).

Kirk's diagnostic-prescriptive approach is the pillar of special education. It is what makes special education special. (Minskoff, 1998). The steps in the approach include the following:

1. Assessment of a child's special physical, intellectual, social, emotional, and educational needs.
2. Determination of the focus of the instruction through the development of the annual goals and short-term objectives of the IEP.
3. Decisions about how instruction should be delivered through task analysis and specialized instructional techniques.
4. Measurement of the child's progress. (Kirk & Chalfant, 1984).

Did You Get It?

Which of the four following steps of Kirk's "diagnostic-prescriptive approach" is neither complete nor accurate in the form in which it is stated?
  a. Step #1: Assessment of a child's physical and educational needs
  b. Step #2: Determination of instructional focus, goals and objectives via the IEP
  c. Step #3: Determination of viable and effective instructional methods is crystallized
  d. Step #4: Ongoing assessment of the child's progress

3.3 Clinical Teaching

Assessment is only a starting point. The process continues with teaching—a special kind of teaching that is required to help students who encounter difficulty in learning, which we call clinical teaching. Clinical teaching embodies methods and strategies to reach students with learning disabilities and related disabilities.

clinical teaching
Teaching that designs learning experiences to the unique needs of an individual learner.

3.3a What Is Clinical Teaching?

Clinical teaching implies a concept and attitude about teaching. Clinical teachers enjoy teaching, they believe that they can make a difference in the life and learning of a student, and they are jubilant when a student shows that he or she "gets it" with the "aha" moment. Several terms describe this special kind of teacher, such as *effective teachers, specialized instruction, remedial teachers, educational therapists,* or simply *good teachers.* All of these concepts describe a teacher who is enthusiastic, sensitive, optimistic, and serious about student learning. Clinical teaching does not require any one particular instructional system or educational setting. Clinical teaching can reflect the teaching of special education teachers, of general education classroom teachers, of secondary subject matter teachers, or of collaboration teams.

The goal of clinical teaching is to tailor learning experiences for the unique needs of an individual student. By using information gathered through the evaluation of the student, along with an analysis of the student's specific learning characteristics, the clinical teacher designs a plan of instruction for that student. Assessment does not stop when teaching begins. In fact, the essence of clinical teaching is that assessment and instruction are continuous and interwoven. The clinical teacher modifies the teaching as new needs become apparent.

Many different intervention strategies can be used in clinical teaching. A clinical teacher is a "child watcher," carefully observing what the student is doing. For example, by observing the kinds of errors a student makes, the clinical teacher can obtain information about the student, such as the student's current level of development, way of thinking, or underlying language system. A student's oral reading errors can provide insight into the student's way of thinking.

Clinical teaching can be viewed as a cycle. The student is evaluated, and then a unit of work based on the evaluation is taught. After teaching, the student is again evaluated to determine what has been learned. If the student performs well, the clinical teacher knows that the teaching has been successful and plans for the next step of learning. If the student performs poorly, the teacher must reassess the teaching plan, analyze the errors to try to determine the cause of the failure to learn, and develop a new course of action for teaching. This clinical teaching cycle is shown in Figure 3.2.

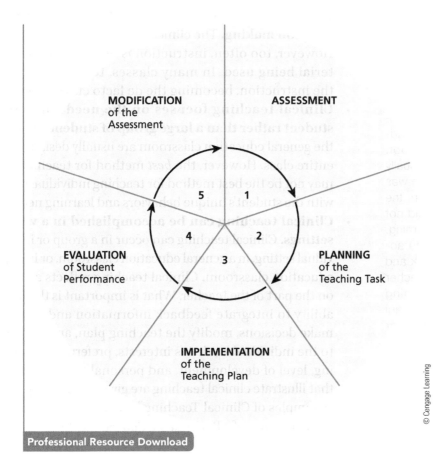

FIGURE **3.2**
Stages of the Clinical Teaching Cycle

© Cengage Learning

Professional Resource Download

- Sammy had difficulty going from the overhead transparency the teacher was showing to the class to the work he was doing at his desk. His teacher realized that this difficulty reflected Sammy's problem with visual perception. The teacher gave Sammy a printed copy of the material on the transparency so that he did not have to make the transfer from the transparency to the work at his desk.

- Debby failed the arithmetic word problem on the test. Her teacher observed that Debby could read the words and perform the arithmetic calculations, but she could not picture the items to be calculated in the word problem. The clinical teacher recognized that Debby's arithmetic failures were related to her difficulty in visualization and spatial orientation. The teacher noted that Debby could not remember how to get to school, to the store, or to her friend's house, and she constantly lost her way. Her teacher directed the teaching toward strengthening Debby's visualization skills and her ability to visualize the situation in the word problem.

- Saul, a high school student, was failing in most of his subjects. He appeared to be uninterested and uninvolved in his school courses. Although his word-recognition skills were good, his reading comprehension was very poor. When questioned in class, Saul usually blurted out his first answer, which was typically wrong. His reactions were the same in his written work. Saul did not have a dependable system for learning. He did not know how to become actively involved in the learning task and responded impulsively. Saul's teacher recognized that he lacked learning strategies to go about learning. Saul was taught specific strategies for learning.

Professional Resource Download

The five stages of the clinical teaching cycle are:

1. **Assessment.** This is the process of gathering evidence about a student's skills or knowledge. It can be administered through a test or as an integral part of instruction.
2. **Planning of the teaching task.** The assessment information is used to plan the instruction.
3. **Implementation of the teaching plan.** This stage involves the actual teaching.
4. **Evaluation of student performance.** The teacher now evaluates how well the student has responded to the teaching.
5. **Modification of the assessment.** Now, it may be necessary to modify the assessment.

Note that the response-to-intervention (RTI) model for teaching (discussed in Chapter 2, "Assessment and the IEP Process") shifts the sequence of these stages. With RTI, the first stage is to teach the student, and then to determine the student's response to the instruction.

3.3b Qualities of Clinical Teaching

Many critical decisions must be made about what and how to teach. In many respects, teaching remains an art. One can never tell where a teacher's influence stops. Clinical teaching is unique in the following ways:

- **Clinical teaching requires flexibility and continual decision making.** The clinical teacher is a decision-maker. However, too often, instruction is determined by the material being used. In many classes, textbooks dominate the instruction, becoming the de facto curriculum.
- **Clinical teaching focuses on the needs of a unique student rather than a large group of students.** Lessons in the general education classroom are usually designed for the entire class. However, the *best* method for teaching a class may not be the best method for teaching individual students, with the student's unique behaviors and learning needs.
- **Clinical teaching can be accomplished in a variety of settings.** Clinical teaching can occur in a group or in an individual setting, in a general education classroom, or in a special education classroom. Clinical teaching reflects an attitude on the part of the teacher. What is important is the teacher's ability to integrate feedback information and be ready to make decisions, modify the teaching plan, and be sensitive to the individual student's interests, preferred way of learning, level of development, and personal feelings. Examples that illustrate clinical teaching are given in Teaching Tips 3.1, "Examples of Clinical Teaching," and Student Stories 3.1, "A Remembrance of a Remarkable Clinical Teacher."

A grateful student wrote the following remembrance of Grace Fernald, a remarkable clinical teacher.

I was the oldest of eight children. Even when very young, my parents talked with me about the world and the politics of the day—we were in the middle of World War II. I liked learning about things. With my second-grade teacher, my otherwise happy world seemed to come to an end. While I was well behaved in school, everything I did or said, from the teacher's perspective, was wrong. While only a second grader, I knew I wanted to be a doctor and a medical researcher and, in my heart, I believed I would be able to do those things well. She asked to see my parents. Because of all the young children at home, my father came alone. It was after school, and I was at one end of the room sitting quietly. I can remember hearing her tell my father I was retarded and, of course, would never be a doctor. I can also remember him patiently, but very firmly, telling her he disagreed about my intelligence and that I would be whatever I wanted.

My parents revered education. They called UCLA and were given the name of Grace Fernald, who agreed to see me in her private practice. I remember Dr. Fernald's house from the first visit. I thought it was grand. It was, to me, a very big Spanish home in a very nice area of Westwood (what is now called Little Holmby Hills). It had a tall, vaulted ceiling of wood and big timbers with a huge stone fireplace. I was amazed by the furniture, which I thought must be antique, and enjoyed looking at the oriental carpets. There were many shelves with books. Everything was very neat and very quiet.

Dr. Fernald was friendly, gray-haired, with a wonderful smile. After talking to my parents, she took me into her office. It was a small office with a big desk and many, many books. It seemed quite cozy and comfortable. We talked. She then told me I would be given an IQ test. It was fun. At a couple of points we both laughed at some of the questions: "If you fire two bullets at somebody and the first bullet kills the person, what does the second bullet do?" She also did some other testing. I did not feel at all nervous. At the end, she told me that I had done just fine and would be learning to read and spell very quickly. She and I were going to impress Miss Potter. And, we did!

Dr. Fernald's kinesthetic approach involved writing in the air as well as tracing words in large written or scripted format. In those visits, Dr. Fernald was always cheerful and always smiling. As a child, I felt I had a new friend, one who I knew was helping me in very important ways. I wanted to do well.

By the summer, Dr. Fernald decided I should enroll in the class being taught at UCLA for children with my type of problem. My parents taught me to take the big blue bus from Pico and Robertson in West Los Angeles directly to the UCLA bus stop and to navigate to the other side of campus across its various little ravines to the wood school building near Sunset Boulevard that housed Dr. Fernald's program. The building was a simple, barracks-style green structure that smelled very much of wood, cheap drawing paper, and the type of paint that children used many years ago. In the course of getting back and forth to her building I, of course, explored many buildings and many ravines!

The class had fewer than 16 pupils. We sat two pupils to a table. For every two pupils, there was a student teacher who was a UCLA trainee. Dr. Fernald was in the background circulating among the pupils and the student teachers.

She did not run the class, but was clearly in charge. The student teachers rotated being in charge of the class. The method of instruction was quite interesting. Every day, each pupil had to dictate a story to his or her student teacher. It could be as long as you wanted—mine were quite long! The teacher wrote it all down. The next day she (all the student teachers were, as I remember, young women) would bring the story back, typed up on a special typewriter that made letters that I recall as being about a half inch in height. We then read our stories to the student teachers from the neatly typed manuscript. We then would practice some of the words of the story, which were written on big cards (in my mind's eye, the cards were about 2- or 3-inches high and about 10-inches long). We would trace the words and learn to spell them. While one of the student teacher's pupils was reciting his story (most of the pupils were boys), the other pupil was doing the word practice, including softly repeating his story and tracing words. There was some work involving the group as a whole with larger cards.

Dr. Fernald always seemed to be in a good mood and seemed to have an individual relationship and concern for each of the pupils and student teachers. Some students had trouble behaving themselves. She was stern about the class being a place to learn. Students who could not behave in the class had to leave and go outside. I remember one or two of those students had to leave the class permanently.

The sessions lasted a half day. They included recess breaks as well as some time for painting. Much of that was finger painting, dipping our hands into chalky paints, which had a rather nice smell.

Once I got the notion of reading, I became quite avid. I tried to explain to Miss Potter what I was learning from Dr. Fernald. But Miss Potter made it quite clear that she was not interested.

(continued)

STUDENT STORIES 3.1 *(continued)*

Forty-five years after the experiences in this story, I was again at UCLA. Having spent 25 years on the Stanford faculty and holding an endowed chair there, I was invited to become Dean for Neuroscience and Research at the UCLA Medical School. I spent 4 years there before coming to New York. The ravines at UCLA had been filled in. There are far more buildings, and Grace Fernald's simple wood classrooms were torn down for a new business school. But UCLA still has a Grace Fernald School, and it is considered one of the crown jewels of the institution.

I had episodically thought of Grace Fernald—particularly as I made various professional transitions. In my current positions as Chair of Psychiatry at the New York Hospital Cornell Medical Center with responsibility for its Payne Whitney Clinic and editor of one of the major scientific journals of psychiatry, I have sometimes wondered what Grace Fernald would have thought. How did life change for some of the other boys as a result of her help and ministrations? I still use aspects

of the Fernald method to this day. I did not know her as a leader in her field—though I came to recognize that. Rather, I knew Dr. Fernald as a teacher who clearly loved helping children who had problems and who—with my two remarkable parents—made possible for me the future I dreamed of.

Source: This remembrance appeared at *http://historyliteracy.org/98_ spring /Fernald_stu.html*. Reprinted with the permission of Dr. Jack D Barchas. Dr. Barchas wrote this tribute when he was Chair of Psychiatry at the New York Hospital Cornell Medical Center and editor of *Archives of General Psychiatry*

About Grace Fernald: In her book, which was first published in 1943, Grace Fernald described the multisensory methods she used (Fernald, 1943/1988). Fernald created one of the first reading clinics for students with reading problems at UCLA, and she also had a private practice.

REFLECTIVE QUESTION

1. What impact did this clinical teacher have on Jack?

Did You Get It?

The term "clinical teaching" describes a particular method of teaching that applies to the educational professional. In this regard, inherent and critical in being an educational "clinician" is a specific and special
  a. curriculum
  b. lesson-plan
  c. training course and framework
  d. mindset

3.4 Differentiated Instruction

differentiated instruction
Teaching that seeks to find that special method that will be successful for each student within a group.

The term differentiated instruction reflects the philosophy of teaching that enables teachers to reach the unique needs of each student, capitalizing on the student's strengths and weaknesses. Differentiated instruction embodies the qualities of clinical teaching by giving students multiple options for taking in information and making sense of ideas (Hall, Strangman, & Meryer. 2011; Tomlinson, Brimijoin, & Narvaez, 2008; Tomlison, 2001). One of the biggest mistakes we make in teaching is to treat everyone equally when it comes to learning. By recognizing that not all students are alike, differentiated instruction applies an approach to teaching and learning that gives students multiple options for taking in information and making sense of ideas.

Children do not respond well to a one-size-fits-all curriculum. Children process information differently from one another; some form images, others form words, and others form sentences. Differentiated instruction takes their individual needs into account with teaching by responding to each student's personal talents, interests, varying background knowledge, and distinct experiences. In differentiated instruction, the teacher seeks to find that special method that will be successful for an individual student to help that student learn (Bender, 2006). A website for differentiated instruction through universal design is *http://www.cast.org*.

3.4a Multiple Intelligences

The concept of "multiple intelligences" presents another view of differentiated learning. Many parents and teachers correctly observe that their children may encounter learning problems in school, but they have incredible talents that are generally undervalued or not well represented in school curricula. Multiple intelligences is a view of learning that reflects the idea that people possess different kinds of intelligences that are not represented in the school curriculum. Howard Gardner (1983, 1993, 1999) suggests that there are at least eight different types of intelligence. Each type of intelligence calls for a distinctive approach for teaching (Table 3.1).

multiple intelligences
Many different talents or intelligences, such as verbal or linguistic intelligence and visual or spatial intelligence.

TABLE 3.1

Gardner's Multiple Intelligences

Type of Intelligence	Description	Symbol
Verbal/linguistic	Related to words and language (qualities of *writers* and *poets*)	
Logical/ mathematical	Abilities with quantitative thinking, numbers, and logical patterns (qualities of *mathematicians* and *scientists*)	
Visual/spatial	Abilities to visualize objects and to create internal mental images and pictures (qualities of *artists, architects,* and *engineers*)	
Musical/rhythmic	Sensitivities to tonal patterns, rhythms, and musical expressiveness (qualities of *musicians*)	
Bodily/kinesthetic	Related to abilities to control one's physical movement (qualities of *athletes* and *dancers*)	
Interpersonal	Skills in dealing with other people (qualities of *salespeople* and *politicians*)	
Intrapersonal	Inner states of being, self-reflection, and knowledge of one's self (qualities of *persons with accurate self-knowledge*)	
Naturalistic	Attuned to nature, animals, and plant life (qualities of *farmers, forest rangers,* and *gardeners*)	

Source: Adapted from *Frames of mind: The theory of multiple intelligences*, by Howard Gardner, 1983, New York: Basic Books.

3.4b Differentiated Instruction and Teaching Approaches

In this section, we describe some of the teaching approaches to meet the unique learning needs of students who learn differently. Teachers should know and have at their disposal many strategies to meet the needs of an individual student, and teachers should not be overly dependent on a single teaching approach. Such a flaw is exemplified in Student Stories 3.2, "A Fable for Teachers." The point of the fable is that each student (or animal) is different, and that one method cannot be relied on as the *best* way for teaching in every case. There is no magic formula for teaching a child. Teachers need to have a wide range of instructional approaches at their disposal, and they need to be imaginative and flexible enough to adapt them to the particular needs of each child.

In the following sections, we look at two distinctive approaches to teaching students who learn differently: (1) cognitive processing, and (2) direct instruction and mastery learning.

cognitive processing
The mental processes involved in thinking and learning, such as perception, memory, language, attention, concept formation, and problem solving.

Cognitive Processing The notion of cognitive processing refers to the different ways that children process information within the brain as they learn (Sousa, 2001). Federal law permits states to use of research-based procedures for determining if a child has a learning disability (IDEA, 2004; Regulations for IDEA, 2006). Many states allow the use of a procedure that determines if a student exhibits a pattern of strengths and weaknesses in areas of cognitive processes that interfere with learning (Schultz, 2009).

Identifying a student's cognitive processing approach to learning has given meaning to the most salient components of the federal definition of learning disabilities, which is *a disorder in one or more of the basic psychological processes*

STUDENT STORIES 3.2

The Animal School: A Fable by George Reavis

Once upon a time the animals decided they must do something heroic to meet the problems of a "new world" so they organized a school. They had adopted an activity curriculum consisting of running, climbing, swimming and flying. To make it easier to administer the curriculum, all the animals took all the subjects.

The duck was excellent in swimming. In fact, better than his instructor. But he made only passing grades in flying and was very poor in running. Since he was slow in running, he had to stay after school and also drop swimming in order to practice running. This was kept up until his webbed feet were badly worn and he was only average in swimming. But average was acceptable in school so nobody worried about that, except, the duck.

The rabbit started at the top of the class in running but had a nervous breakdown because of so much makeup work in swimming.

The squirrel was excellent in climbing until he developed frustration in the flying class where his teacher made him start from the ground up instead of the treetop down. He also developed a "charlie horse"

from overexertion and then got a C in climbing and D in running.

The eagle was a problem child and was disciplined severely. In the climbing class, he beat all the others to the top of the tree but insisted on using his own way to get there.

At the end of the year, an abnormal eel that could swim exceeding well and also run, climb and fly a little had the highest average and was valedictorian.

The prairie dogs stayed out of school and fought the tax levy because the administration would not add digging and burrowing to the curriculum. They apprenticed their children to a badger and later joined the groundhogs and gophers to start a successful private school.

Does this fable have a moral?

Source: This story was written when George Reavis was the Assistant Superintendent of the Cincinnati Public Schools back in the 1940s. This content is in the public domain and free to copy, duplicate, and distribute.

REFLECTIVE QUESTION

1. How does this fable illustrate the statement that "one size does not fit all"?

(IDEA, 2004). Information about a student's cognitive processing can be linked to the student's ability to perform academically (Flannagan, Ortiz, Alfonso, & Mascolo, 2006; Kavale, Holdnack, & Mostert, 2005).

Cognitive processes are thinking procedures that learners use in learning and performing academic tasks. Several different distinctive cognitive processes are identified by Schultz, 2009; Mather and Jaffe, 2002; and Flangan, et al., 2006:

- **Fluid intelligence**—mental operations when a person is presented with a novel task
- **Crystallized intelligence**—a person's general fund of knowledge
- **Short-term memory**—ability to apprehend and hold information for a very short time
- **Visual processing**—ability to think with visual patterns and stimuli
- **Auditory processing**—ability to notice and discriminate separate sounds
- **Long-term storage and retrieval**—ability to store new or previously acquired information and fluently retrieve that information
- **Processing speed**—ability to fluently and automatically perform cognitive tasks

Cognitive process occurs within the brain. Figure 3.3 illustrates how information can be perceived in different ways. What do you see in this figure? The written word *Liar*, or a profile of a face? (Turn the figure sideways.) How do different perceptions affect the interpretation of this figure? Perception occurs in the brain.

Here are two examples of cognitive processing and applications for teaching:

- Jeff's teacher is aware of his difficulty with auditory processing so his teacher understands why Jeff has so much difficulty in learning phonics. Jeff's teacher therefore makes accommodations in how she teaches phonics that consider Jeff's difficulty in auditory processing.
- Susan has difficulty with visual perception and cannot remember printed words. Her teacher uses strategies to help her recognize printed words.

© Cengage Learning

FIGURE **3.3**
Visual Perception—Liar, Liar, Optical Illusion

---

direct instruction
A method associated with behavioral theories of instruction. The focus is directly on the curriculum or task to be taught and the steps needed to learn that task.

Direct Instruction and Mastery Learning Direct instruction is a method of teaching the academic skills of the curriculum in a structured and controlled manner. With direct instruction, the curriculum and the tasks that the student is to learn are first analyzed. Then the desired academic curriculum skill is carefully sequenced so that the teacher teaches each step in sequence. The student practices and repeats each step of the sequence until the skill is mastered. Research shows that direct instruction is very effective, and that students do learn the academic skills with this procedure (Carnine, Silbert, & Kame'enui, 1990; Mainzer et al., 2003).

Cognitive strategies are thinking processes that learners use to perform academic tasks

Rhoda Sidney/The Image Works

Characteristics of direct instruction include:

- Teaches academic skills directly
- Is teacher directed and controlled
- Uses carefully sequenced and structured materials
- Provides student mastery of basic skills
- Sets goals that are clear to students
- Allocates sufficient time for instruction
- Uses continuous monitoring of student performance
- Provides immediate feedback to students
- Teaches a skill until mastery of that skill is achieved

mastery learning
The steps of a subject are put in sequential order. Mastery learning determines if the child has learned (or mastered) each step.

Mastery learning is an outcome of direct instruction. The student must learn each of a sequence of skills in order to learn a task. Learning each skill of a task is likened to climbing the rungs on a ladder. Each rung must be touched in climbing to the top; the student who misses some rungs may fall off. The skill of reading, for example, is analyzed as consisting of many subskills; by mastering the component subskills, the student should master the skill of reading.

Did You Get It?

The concept of "differentiated teaching" takes into account that once information is presented, unique students will intake and "_____" that information in and by a myriad of unique styles, manners, and processes.

a. internalize
b. make sense of
c. value
d. store

3.5 Controlling Instructional Variables

The teacher and the school can do relatively little about many factors linked with learning disabilities and related mild disabilities. The home environment or the genetic or biological makeup of the student may be key elements contributing to the learning problem, but such variables cannot be modified by the teacher. Other factors, however, can be changed by teachers, and these factors should receive careful consideration. Variables in learning that can be readjusted by teachers include the difficulty level, space, time, and language.

3.5a Difficulty Level

readiness
The state of maturational development that is necessary before a skill can be learned.

zone of proximal development (ZPD)
A term, used by Vygotsky, envisioning a range of levels of difficulty for a student. The lower end is very easy, the upper end beyond the student's capacity. The ZPD is the midpoint and is an appropriate level for learning.

The *difficulty level* of material is an extremely important consideration. Difficulty level can be modified to meet a student's present performance and tolerance levels. The concept of readiness, which is defined as the state of maturational development that is necessary before a skill can be learned, applies here, as does Lev Vygotsky's notion of the zone of proximal development (ZPD). The zone of proximal development is a concept that envisions a range of difficulty levels for a student, with the ZPD at the midpoint of a student's capacity and an appropriate level for the student's learning (Vygotsky, 1962). (See Chapter 5, "Theories of Learning.") Many students fail tasks simply because the tasks are too difficult and the required level of performance is beyond their present skill level. Expecting a student to perform a task far beyond her or his skill level can result in a complete breakdown in learning. A synthesis of intervention research shows that "control of task difficulty" is a critical feature of effective intervention (Vaughn, Gersten, & Chard, 2000).

Many skills or responses must be overlearned so that they can become automatic. Many skills must be internalized or become automatic before they can be used quickly in new situations or transferred to new situations. The internalization permits a shift from the conscious, cognitive level to the automatic response, or habitual level. For example, in reading, the student initially may use phonic skills in a conscious, deliberate way to decode words; but later, the process must become automatic for effective reading.

3.5b Space

Space refers to the physical setting, which should be conducive to learning. Among the ways to modify space are using partitions, cubicles, screens, special rooms, quiet corners, and removing distracting stimuli. Space also involves the student's work area, such as the size of the paper and the desk surface. The school environment should not be a distraction from learning, but rather should enhance learning.

The goal of space control is to slowly increase the amount of space with which the student must contend. Gradually, students must internalize their own controls so that they can get along in an unmodified space environment.

3.5c Time

There are a number of ways to control *time* in the teaching setting. Lessons for students with a very short attention span can be limited so that they can be completed in less time. For example, one row of mathematics problems can be assigned instead of an entire page. The work page can be cut into squares or strips to shorten the time required to complete one section. Fewer spelling words can be given in a spelling assignment. In timed exercises, the allotted time can be increased. Time can be broken into shorter units by varying the types of activity so that quiet activities are followed by livelier ones. Planned activity changes, such as having the student come to the teacher's desk or walk to a shelf to get supplies, can be useful breaks during long lessons. Homework assignments can be shortened. The goal is to gradually increase the time that the student works on a task.

3.5d Language

Language can also be modified to enhance student learning. To ensure that language clarifies rather than confuses, teachers should examine the wording of their directions. The language should match the student's level of understanding. For students whose first language is not English, it is especially critical that the teacher's language be clear, precise, and unambiguous. Using a visual support, such as a chart, can be helpful in understanding the language.

For some students, the language quantity must be reduced to the simplest statements. Techniques to simplify language include: (1) reducing directions to "telegraphic speech," or using only essential words; (2) maintaining visual contact with the learner; (3) avoiding ambiguous words and emphasizing meaning with gesture; (4) speaking in a slow tempo; (5) touching the student before talking; and (6) avoiding complex sentence structure, particularly negative constructions.

Did You Get It?

Zone of proximal development (ZPD) refers to the _____ of a student's abilities being the optimal/most appropriate level to facilitate learning when he or she is presented with a range of difficulty levels and variables.

   a. apex

   b. low-end

   c. midpoint

   d. 80% mark

3.6 Building Self-Esteem and Motivation

Robert Louis Stevenson observed that life is not so much a matter of holding good cards but of playing a poor hand well. This observation expresses the plight of students with learning disabilities and related mild disabilities and the call for teachers to help students learn how to play their hand well. Clinical teaching requires an affirming and positive teacher-student relationship. Although effective teaching requires objectivity and a thorough knowledge of the curriculum, skills, and methods, it also requires a subjective understanding of the student as an individual with feelings, emotions, hopes, and dreams (Brooks & Goldstein, 2002; Brooks, 2000). Students often feel lost and frightened because they have suffered years of despair, discouragement, and frustration. Sometimes they experience feelings of rejection, failure, and hopelessness about the future that affect every subject they study in school and every aspect of their lives. The emotional plight of students who are failing is further explored in Student Stories 3.3, "The Emotional Plight of Students With Learning Disabilities and Related Disabilities."

3.6a Self-Esteem

A problem in learning can impinge upon every aspect of the student's world. It is important to recognize the emotional impact of failure on the student. Not only are parents and teachers displeased with the child, but the parent's anxiety also often becomes uncontrollable. The parents wonder whether their child is unable to learn or is just plain lazy. Even the most loving parents can become so alarmed at their child's inability to learn that they will tend to punish, scold, and threaten, or even reward with the hope of producing desired results. Teachers also feel frustrated by their inability to reach the child. A student's problems in learning do not begin and end at the classroom door; they pervade every aspect of the child's life. They interfere with everything important to the child—from riding a bicycle to making friends, from knowing how to behave at recess to being an effective student (Silver, 2003, 2006).

3.6b Fostering Motivation

An important responsibility for the clinical teacher is to motivate students who have been failing and to attract them to learning. In discussing motivation, Rick Lavoie (2007) uses the phrase, "Batteries Not Included: Motivating the Struggling

This box describes the emotional feelings of failure.

For 12 long years of school and after, the student with learning disabilities contends with a situation for which he or she can find no satisfactory solution. When schoolwork becomes insurmountable, the student has few alternative resources. Adults who are dissatisfied with their job may seek a position elsewhere or find solace outside of work or may even choose to endure these difficulties because of a high salary or other compensations. For the student, however, there is no escape; he or she is subjected to anything from degradation to long-suffering tolerance. Proof of inadequacies appears daily in the classroom. In the end, the student is held in low esteem, not only by classmates, but also often by his or her family.

Source: Roswell, R. and Natchez, G. (1977) *Reading Disability*. New York: Basic Books.

REFLECTIVE QUESTION

1. For a student with learning disabilities, what factors can lead to low self-esteem?

Learner." Lavoie observed that teachers lack training and exposure to the basic tenets of motivation. Each student responds to a different form of motivation. If a motivational strategy works, do more of it; if it doesn't, do something else. Lavoie identifies eight different forces of motivation: (1) the need to have friends, (2) the need for independence, (3) the need to be important, (4) the need to know, (5) the need to assert, (6) the need for control, (7) the need to be recognized, and (8) the need to have affiliations and belong to a group. Because each student responds to a unique set of motivators, teachers cannot count on motivating all students by using one solitary motivational approach (Lavoie, 2007).

When a student experiences success in learning, it has a beneficial effect on personality, enhances feelings of self-worth, and rekindles an interest in learning. Such teaching can be considered therapeutic (Brooks, 2000). (See Chapter 6, "Social, Emotional, and Behavioral Challenges," for a further discussion of ways to build self-esteem.)

3.6c Building Rapport

A good relationship between the teacher and student is an essential first step in clinical teaching. Much of the success in clinical teaching depends on the establishment of healthy rapport. The teacher must accept the student as a human being worthy of respect in spite of a failure to learn. A healthy relationship implies compassion without over-involvement, understanding without indulgence, and a genuine concern for the student's development. The clinical teacher's relationship with a student should provide a new atmosphere of confidence and acceptance. Because it may be extremely difficult for a parent or a family member to retain an accepting, yet objective,

Success in learning has a beneficial effect on personality, enhances feelings and self-worth, and rekindles an interest in learning.

attitude, the student becomes very sensitive to the parent's disappointment. Parents are often unaware of their child's reaction to their efforts. For example, one well-intentioned father in a public library helping his son pick out a book and listening to him read, was overheard saying, "I'll tell you that word one more time, and then I don't want you to forget it for the rest of your life." This is not an attitude that is conducive to learning. Children need to see a word dozens of times before they readily recognize the word.

3.6d Sharing Responsibility

Involvement of both the student and the teacher is another factor in clinical teaching. Students should participate in both the analysis of their problems and the evaluation of their performance. In the same collaborative spirit, the student should also take an active role in designing lessons and choosing materials.

3.6e Providing Structure

Providing structure and establishing routines are important factors for introducing order into the chaotic lives of students with learning problems. Many students need and welcome such order. Structure and routine can be provided in many aspects of teaching—in the physical environment, in knowing the specific schedule for the day, in the sequence of activities, and in the manner in which lessons are taught.

3.6f Conveying Sincerity

Students are skillful in detecting insincerity, and they will soon detect dishonesty if a teacher tells them they are doing well when they know otherwise. Instead, the teacher might try to minimize anxiety about errors by saying that many students have similar difficulties and by conveying confidence that together they will find ways to overcome the difficulties.

3.6g Showing Success

Success is similar to a vitamin. If you don't get enough of it growing up, you suffer a very severe deficiency that could result in long-term problems (Levine, 2002). Self-esteem cannot be injected or taught; it is a result of many success experiences (Richardson, 2003). Students should become aware of and appreciate their successes. Students should know what they can do well, and teachers and families should help them pursue their areas of strengths. Many students and adults with learning disabilities and related mild disabilities achieve success by understanding the nature of their learning problems and learning to use their strengths.

Lessons must be designed and materials selected to permit students to experience success. For example, the teacher can obtain books at the reading levels that meet the students' areas of interest. In addition to selecting the appropriate level of difficulty of teaching materials, the teacher can make students conscious of their success and progress by:

- Praising good work
- Using extrinsic rewards as reinforcement
- Developing visual records of progress through charts and graphs

3.6h Capitalizing on Student's Interests

The chance of successful achievement increases when a teacher provides materials based on the student's special interests. Teachers can find student interests through conversations with the student or by administering interest inventories. By finding materials in the student's area of interest, teachers can give the student a strong motivation to learn.

Students have a range of reading interests that include sports, adventure and action, history, science, biography and memoir, mysteries, and humor. Valuable reading lessons can be developed from materials that students have an interest in—*TV Guide,* newspapers, baseball and football programs, music, popular magazines, and even computer manuals. The first real interest in reading shown by some high school students is stimulated by the need to pass a written test in order to get a driver's license. Engaging this interest, some teachers have successfully used the driver's manual as material to teach reading. A favorite author or series books have been the impetus for other youngsters to become readers. The right book can be a powerful tool to build interest, provide motivation, and improve academic learning. The following are some examples of students who made great strides once an interest had been tapped.

© Cengage Learning 2015.

▶❚❚ **TeachSource** Video Case Activity

Watch the TeachSource Video Case entitled "Academic Diversity: Differentiated Instruction." In this video, a third-grade teacher instructs her students in written expression. She differentiates her lesson for academically diverse students by providing different instruction for three groups: children who learn the lesson easily, children who need significant support, and individualized instruction for children who have difficulty in creating the written document.

QUESTIONS

1. Based on watching the video case and reading the chapter, what are your ideas for differentiating instruction for diverse learners when teaching written expression?

2. How can differentiated instruction be used in teaching reading?

- Antonio, an eighth-grade boy with learning disabilities, found the first book he ever read from cover to cover, *The Incredible Journey,* so fascinating that he was completely oblivious to class changes, ringing bells, and classroom incidents from the time he started the book until he completed it.
- Maria developed an interest in successful women who had, in her words, "made it." Her teacher helped her find many books and articles that related stories of successful women in many fields. Her reading improved dramatically after she read these materials.
- Dave had a keen interest in the Chicago Cubs baseball team. His teacher helped him find newspaper stories about the games and biographies of the players. His interest led him to read more, and his reading improved.
- Sometimes a television show or a movie based on a book can spark an interest. After seeing a television show about *Robinson Crusoe,* Juan, who had severe reading problems, was introduced to a simplified version of this book. His teacher reported that he became so immersed in the story that he would grab the book as soon as he entered the room.

Once in a while, dramatic changes occur in a student's attitude and outlook because of clinical teaching. When such a change occurs because of a book the child has read, it is sometimes called bibliotherapy. Learning about

bibliotherapy
A technique of using characters in books to help children work through personal problems.

the experiences of others can foster release and insight as well as hope and encouragement. Students with personal problems (e.g., children who are short, overweight, unpopular, or who have physical or academic disabilities) identify with book characters who suffer similar problems and are helped by the characters' resolution of their problems (Sridhar & Vaughn, 2002). For example, Peter, a seventh-grade student with learning disabilities, was fascinated by Houdini, the great escape artist. Peter read all the books he could find on Houdini in the school library and in the public library. During this period of extensive reading about Houdini, Peter's teachers observed personality and attitude changes, as well as tremendous improvement in his reading.

Did You Get It?

In recognizing and targeting what makes a student tick, it might be helpful to remember Lavoie's eight forces of motivation. Which of the following four forces is not one of those recognized by the author?

a. A need for recognition
b. A need to control
c. A need to manipulate
d. A need to feel important

3.7 Including Students with Learning Disabilities and Related Disabilities in General Education

Most students with learning disabilities receive their instruction in general education classrooms. About 87% of students with learning disabilities spend at least a portion of their school day in general education classrooms. This includes about 55% (who are in the regular classroom for 80% or more of the day) and 32% (who are in the regular class for 40% to 70% of the school day). Only 12% of students with learning disabilities are in the regular classroom for less than 40% of the day. (U.S. Department of Education, 2012).

3.7a Section 504 Students

As noted in Chapter 1, some students with disabilities receive instruction in the general education classrooms under the law known as Section 504 of the Rehabilitation Act of 1973. The law of Section 504 falls under the purview of a federal agency called *Office of Civil Rights.* It is *not* a law of Department of Education and IDEA (Individuals With Disabilities Education Improvement Act-2004). Section 504 is a civil rights law that prohibits discrimination against individuals with disabilities. The provisions in the Americans with Disabilities Act Amendments (ADAA) (2008) applies to students in Section 504.

Under Section 504, a student may have a disability but the student may not be eligible for special education services under a state's diagnostic criteria for that disability. These students may be entitled to Section 504 services in the general education classroom. The Section 504 plan is an accommodation plan that outlines the specific accommodations that are needed for the student. Section 504 students will not have an IEP but they may have a Section 504 plan. The 504 plan may include the following: specialized instruction, modifications to the curriculum, and accommodations (Zirkel, 2009; *http://www.wrightslaw.com/info/sec504.index.htm*; *http://www.concordspedpac.org/section504.html*).

Students identified as Section 504 students are served in the general education classrooms, and they are entitled to "reasonable accommodations in general education classrooms." States must have accommodation guidelines for Section 504 students.

reasonable accommodations The phrase used in Section 504 of the Rehabilitation Act to describe what can fairly easily be done in a setting to make adjustments for an individual with a disability.

3.7b Student Diversity in General Education

In today's pluralistic society, most general education classrooms have students from many different ethnic, language, and cultural populations. Some culturally and linguistically diverse students were born in the United States or Canada; others are recent immigrants from all parts of the world. Some students are English-language learners (ELL) and have limited English proficiency. ELL students are discussed in more detail in Chapter 11, "Spoken Language Difficulties: Listening and Speaking."

Understanding the cultures and language backgrounds of students is essential for effective teaching, and teachers should appreciate the unique contributions of each culture. By the time children enter school, they have already absorbed many of the values and behaviors of the culture in which they were raised, which has major ramifications for school success. The child's language is one obvious consideration. If the school expects all students to be fluent in English, students from families that speak another language will be at a disadvantage. Another consideration is that many schools expect students to work independently and to compete for grades and recognition. This expectation may be in conflict with the attitudes of cultures in which cooperation and peer orientation are valued more than the qualities of independence and competitiveness (Hernandez, 2001; Montgomery, 2001). For students with learning disabilities and related disabilities, their learning problems are compounded by dimensions of the student's culture and language (Hernandez, 2002).

With the increase in cultural and linguistic diversity in our schools, teachers must recognize the impact of culture and language on a student's behavior and performance in school. Knowledge and respect for differences among cultural and language groups will help teachers provide more successful experiences for all students.

Teachers should create an atmosphere that builds on the cultural and linguistic diversity of students (Montgomery, 2001). Teaching Tips 3.2, "Culturally Responsive Teachers," offers ways to do this.

TEACHING TIPS 3.2
Culturally Responsive Teachers

- Accept and welcome culturally diverse students into their classrooms and recognize the need for these students to find relevant connections among their peers and with the subject matter of the tasks teachers ask them to perform.

- Establish a classroom atmosphere that respects individuals and their cultures by providing current and relevant bulletin boards that display positive and purposeful activities and events involving various cultures. Have a book corner with a variety of culturally diverse literature and have language arts and social studies programs that offer opportunities to showcase written and oral reports pertaining to student heritage and cultural traditions.

- Use a range of culturally sensitive instruction materials and methods, including interdisciplinary arts and journal writing.

- Foster an interactive classroom environment so that students can engage in shared inquiry and discovery. One way to *do* this is to provide cooperative learning *groups* that bring students with diverse backgrounds together. Guided and informal group discussions offer *opportunities for* students to learn from one another.

- Collaborate and communicate with culturally diverse families and professionals.

Professional Resource Download

Did You Get It?

By law, students are entitled to accommodations within the realm of the general education classroom. Which of the following terms precedes the word "accommodations" to fully describe that which a student has a right to in this context?

a. Comprehensive
b. Reasonable
c. Average
d. Sensible

3.8 Accommodations for Students with Learning Disabilities and Related Disabilities

The following accommodations will help students with learning disabilities and related disabilities in the general education classroom: (1) increasing attention, (2) improving the ability to listen, (3) adapting the curriculum, and (4) helping students manage time.

accommodations
Refers to adjustments within a general education program to meet the needs of students with disabilities. Required under Section 504 of the Rehabilitation Act and IDEA.

Some accommodations for students with disabilities in the general education classroom are described in Including Students in General Education 3.1, "Accommodations for the General Education Classroom."

3.8a Increasing Attention

A short attention span is a characteristic of many students with learning disabilities and related mild disabilities. Students may initially be attentive, but their attention soon wanders. The following activities will help students attend and prolong their concentration.

- Shorten the task by breaking a long task into smaller parts; assign fewer problems—for example, fewer spelling words or mathematics problems
- Shorten homework assignments by giving fewer problems
- Use distributed practice; instead of a few long and concentrated practice sessions, set up more short, spaced, and frequent practice sessions

Including Students in GENERAL EDUCATION 3.1

Accommodations for the General Education Classroom

- Change the setting. Give instructions or tests in a separate room, in a carrel, or in a small group.
- Change the scheduling. Extend the time and the breaks for testing and instruction.
- Change the type of presentation. Use large print; give verbal directions instead of written directions, or tape-record the directions.

- Change the expectations for responses. Have students answer questions orally or point to the answer; students can mark in a booklet instead of on an answer sheet.

Source: Council for Exceptional Children, 2001; U.S. Department of Education, 2000b.

Professional Resource Download

- Make tasks more interesting to keep students' interest; encourage students to work with partners, in small groups, or in interest centers
- Alternate highly interesting tasks and less interesting tasks
- Increase the novelty of the task; tasks that are new or unique are more appealing and will increase attention

3.8b Improving the Ability to Listen

We erroneously assume that students know how to listen. Students with learning disabilities and related mild disabilities frequently miss important instructions and information because they are not actively listening. They may even be unaware that a message is being given. Teachers expect students not just to hear or recognize the words that are spoken, but also to comprehend the message. The following strategies can help students acquire better listening skills.

- Make instructions simple by using short, direct sentences; give one instruction at a time, and repeat it as often as necessary; make sure that students know all the vocabulary being used.
- Prompt students to repeat instructions after listening to them; later, have the students repeat to themselves information they have just heard to build listening and memory skills.
- Alert students by using key phrases—for example, "This is important," "Listen carefully," or "This will be on the exam"; some teachers use prearranged signals, such as hand signals or switching the lights on or off before giving directions.
- Use visual aids (such as charts, pictures, graphics, and key points on a chalkboard or overhead transparencies) to illustrate and support verbal information.

3.8c Adapting the Curriculum

Often the teacher can change, modify, or adapt the curriculum without sacrificing its basic integrity. Even a small change can be beneficial for the student.

- Select high-interest materials to reinforce the basic curriculum; use manipulatives, or hands-on materials, whenever possible; create activities that require active participation, such as talking through problems and acting out steps—many students learn better when they actually do something in addition to just listening and observing.
- Use visual aids to supplement oral and written information; use learning aids, such as computers, calculators, and tape recordings to increase motivation.
- Accommodate test-taking, allowing students to take tests orally instead of writing the answers; teach students how to cross out incorrect answers on multiple-choice tests.

3.8d Help Students Manage Time

Managing time is a common problem area for many students with learning disabilities and related mild disabilities. They are pulled away from the task at hand and become involved with new challenges. They become procrastinators, a trait they retain into their adult lives. The following activities are designed to help students with time management.

- Students can develop a sense of time and what must be accomplished in a given time span by making a spreadsheet, bar chart, or pie chart with a computer to illustrate time use.
- Set up a specific routine and adhere to it; when disruptions occur, explain the situation to students, as well as appropriate ways to respond.
- During the school day, alternate activities that are done sitting and those that involve standing and moving about.
- Make lists that will help students organize their tasks; have students check off tasks as they complete them.
- Use behavior contracts that specify the amount of time allotted for specific activities.

Did You Get It?

Beau is diagnosed with a learning disability and has a secondary diagnosis of acute anxiety disorder. He simply "decompensates" when he is in a crowded room where a test is being given. Which of the following would represent an effective and reasonable accommodation for him?

a. A slightly easier test
b. A personalized change of venue for taking the test
c. Verbal directions instead of written
d. Dispensing altogether with formalized testing

3.9 Effective Instructional Strategies for General Education

Effective instructional strategies for students in the general education classroom include (1) peer tutoring, (2) explicit teaching, (3) promoting active learning, (4) scaffolded instruction, (5) executive functions, and (6) learning strategies instruction.

3.9a Peer Tutoring

peer tutoring
A method of instruction in which the student is taught by a peer or classmate.

Peer tutoring is a strategy for the general education classroom in which two children work on learning tasks together. One child is the *tutor* and serves as a teacher; the other child is the *tutee* and serves as the learner. The children work in pairs, so peer tutoring supports one-to-one teaching in the general education classroom. The peer tutor helps the tutee learn, practice, or review an academic skill that the classroom teacher has planned. Examples of peer tutoring tasks are saying aloud or writing spelling words, reading sentences, or solving a mathematics problem. Types of peer tutoring include *same-age peer tutoring* (in which one student in the classroom tutors a classmate) and *cross-age peer tutoring* (in which the tutor is several years older than the tutee (Greenwood, Maheedy, & Delquardi, 2002).

Both the tutor and the tutee benefit from the peer-tutoring experience. For the tutee, there are gains in academic achievement. The child is able to learn more effectively from a classmate whose thinking processes are closer to that of the child than that of an adult. For the tutor, there are also academic benefits because the best way to fully learn something is to teach it to someone else. The experience also offers the tutor a sense of accomplishment. Other advantages of peer tutoring are that the tutor serves as a model of appropriate academic and nonacademic behavior and the relationship between the two children provides opportunities for establishing additional social relationships within the classroom.

Research consistently shows that peer tutoring is a successful and valid strategy (Fischer, Schumaker, & Deshler, 1995; Fuchs & Fuchs, 1998; Greenwood et al., 2002). It is also relatively easy for teachers to implement. Peer tutoring is a practical way to provide support for children with learning disabilities and related mild disabilities in the general education classroom, and *more* importantly, children like peer tutoring.

Active learning capitalizes on students' interests and encourages active involvement in learning.

Classwide peer tutoring is a more organized version of peer tutoring that involves the entire class. For this activity, tutor-tutee pairs work together on a classwide basis. At the beginning of each week, all students are paired for tutoring, and these pairs are then assigned to one of two competing teams. Tutees earn points for their team by responding to the tasks presented to them by their tutors. The winning team is determined daily and weekly on the basis of the team with the highest point total (Greenwood, 1996; Utley, Mortweet, & Greenwood, 1997).

3.9b Explicit Teaching

Many students with learning disabilities need explicit teaching. Like *direct instruction,* explicit teaching means that the teacher clearly states what is to be taught and explains what needs to be done. Students are not left to make inferences from experiences that are unmediated by such help. In explicit instruction, students are provided with models of appropriate methods for solving problems or explaining relationships. They are amply supported during the stages of the learning process, and they are provided with adequate practice (Gersten, 1998; U.S. Department of Education, 1997). Teaching Tips 3.3 provides some principles of explicit teaching.

explicit teaching
The process in which the teacher clearly states what is to be taught and thoroughly explains the concepts, provides multiple models, provides needed support, and provides ample opportunities for practice.

TEACHING TIPS 3.3

Principles of Explicit Teaching

- Provide students with an adequate range of examples to exemplify a concept or problem-solving strategy.

- Provide models of proficient performance, including step-by-step strategies (at times) or broad generic questions and guidelines that focus attention and prompt deep processing.

- Provide experiences where students explain how and why they make decisions.

- Provide frequent feedback on quality of performance and support so that students persist in performing activities.

- Provide adequate practice and activities that are interesting and engaging.

Source: From "Recent Advances in Instructional Research for Students With Learning Disabilities: An Overview," by R. Gerstein, 1998, *Learning Disabilities Research & Practice,* 75(13), pp.162–170. Reprinted with the permission of Laurence Erlbaum Associates, Inc.

3.9c Promoting Active Learning

active learning
Dynamic involvement in the
learning process.

Learning is not a spectator sport. The importance of instruction that promotes active learning is advanced by research in contemporary cognitive psychology. Active learners (1) attend to instruction, (2) attribute results to their own efforts, (3) relate tasks and materials to their knowledge and experience, and (4) actively construct meaning during learning. Instruction for active learning capitalizes on the child's interests, stresses the importance of building background knowledge prior to teaching, and encourages the active involvement of students. Active learning emphasizes the concept that learning and behavior emerge from the interaction of three components: (1) the learning environment, (2) the learner, and (3) the teaching material. Ways to promote active learning are offered in Teaching Tips 3.4, "Guidelines for Promoting Active Learning."

3.9d Scaffolded Instruction

Scaffolding refers to abundant teacher supports at the initial stage of a student learning a task. An analogy is made to the scaffold used by builders. A building scaffold is a temporary structure used to support a building in the early stages of construction that is removed when it is no longer needed. Similarly, in teaching the metaphor of a scaffold describes supports that the teacher provides for the student in the early stages of learning a task. These supports are removed when they are no longer necessary (Pea, 2004; Gibbons, 2002).

TEACHING TIPS 3.4

Guidelines for Promoting Active Learning

Encourage interactive learning	Learning emerges from the interaction of three components: the environment, the learner, and the teaching material. Teachers should interrelate these three components.
Recognize the importance of prior experience	Integrate the children's background knowledge and experience into the learning activities. Learning is dependent on what children already know.
Prepare children for the lesson	Preparation for learning leads to improved understanding, motivation, and storage of information. Expose children to key concepts before they are presented in the lesson.
Encourage active involvement	When children are actively involved in their learning, they are more successful learners than when they take a passive role in the learning process.
Structure lessons for success	There is a positive correlation between learning, self-concept, and positive attitudes. Teachers should structure lessons to provide opportunities for children to experience success.
Teach "learning to learn" strategies	Teachers can help children become aware of their learning processes. For example, asking children how they found a solution to a problem will assist them in understanding the strategies they use to learn.

Professional Resource Download

The concept of scaffolded instruction is often linked to Vygotsky's (1962) notion of the zone of proximal development (ZPD). The term *ZPD* refers to the difficulty level for effective learning; it is neither too easy nor too difficult for the child (the "Goldilocks" approach to instruction; see the section titled "Developmental Psychology" in Chapter 5). Also, Vygotsky notes that learning depends upon the social interaction of an experienced adult (teacher) and the learner (student). The teacher provides the support or scaffolding that the student needs during the initial stage of learning the task (Pea, 2004; Gibbons, 2002; Rosenshine, 1997).

For scaffolding to be successful, a child must enter an exchange with some prior understanding of what is to be accomplished (Pea, 2004). Examples of scaffolds include (1) simplified problems, (2) modeling of the procedures by the teacher, (3) thinking aloud by the teacher, and (4) teacher mediation to guide the student to think through the problem.

scaffolded instruction
Teacher supports for the student, particularly at the initial stage of learning a task.

3.9e Executive Functions

The *executive functions* have been called the brain's CEO (Sousa, 2001). Executive functions are the ability to control and direct one's own learning. They orchestrate resources like memory, language, and attention to achieve a goal. As a type of traffic manager that activates, monitors, and controls a person's actions and learning, executive functions regulate thinking processes (Keeley, 2006; Swanson & Sa'ez, 2003; Barkley, 2001). Examples of executive functions are planning what one will do tomorrow, deciding things in the environment to pay attention to, and deciding how to respond to a challenging task. Executive functions disorders are characterized by the situations described in Teaching Tips 3.5.

Difficulty in organizing their lives is an executive functioning problem for many students with disabilities and related mild disabilities. Their lack of organizational skills results in incomplete assignments, unfinished homework, and procrastination. Students need to learn how to plan ahead, how to gather appropriate materials for school tasks, how to prioritize the steps to complete an assignment, and how to keep track of their work.

A news report of a well-organized bank robber was reported in Kansas. The police obtained a search warrant and searched the bank robber's home. The police found a "to-do list" that included the reminder "ROB A BANK." The police were able to apprehend the robber through the evidence in the robber's to-do list.

Teaching Tips 3.6, "Organization Steps," offers ways to help students organize.

3.9f Learning Strategies Instruction

Instruction in learning strategies is increasingly being used as a teaching method for students with learning disabilities and related mild disabilities. These students tend to be inefficient learners because they lack systematic ways of learning, remembering, or directing their

TEACHING **TIPS 3.5**
Examples of Executive Functions

- Planning and organizing
- Identifying what needs to be done
- Determining the sequence of a task
- Carrying out steps in an orderly way
- Beginning tasks
- Evaluating how one is doing
- Taking feedback or suggestions

Source: Keely, 2006.

TEACHING TIPS 3.6

Organization Steps

- Provide clear routines for *placing* objects—especially regularly used objects such as books, assignments, and outdoor clothes—in designated places so that they can be found easily

- Provide students with a list of materials needed for a task; limit the list to only those materials necessary to complete the task

- Provide a schedule so that students know exactly what to *do for each* class period. Use *picture cues* to illustrate the schedule

- Make sure students have all homework assignments before leaving school; write each assignment on the board and have students copy it, or write the assignment for a student in a pocket notebook

- Provide students with pocket folders to organize materials—for example, place new work on one side and completed work in chronological order on the other. Use a different color folder for each subject

- Make a to-do list. Making a to-do list is one of the key strategies for improving executive functioning. Once students learn to depend on to-do lists, they incorporate them into many of life's activities. Write down activities that the student should *do, and* then have the student check each item off as it is accomplished. For example, a student could make a written list of things to *do* to prepare for an *upcoming* test and then check each one off as it is finished: The list might include (1) re-read the chapter to prepare for the test, (2) go over your class notes on the chapter, (3) write down the key vocabulary words often given at the end of the chapter, (4) make an outline of the chapter using the topic headings used in the book, (5) make flash cards of the key words, and (6) test yourself on the key words.

Professional Resource Download

---

learning strategies instruction
A series of methods to help students direct their own learning, focusing on how students learn rather than on what they learn.

learning. Learning strategies instruction helps students learn the secrets of being a successful student, how to study, how to integrate new materials with what they already know, how to monitor their learning and problem solving, and how to remember or to predict what is going to happen. Research supports learning strategies as an effective way to teach students with learning disabilities and related mild disabilities (Mainzer et al., 2003; Swanson, 1999b).

Instruction in learning strategies helps students take charge of their own learning; thus, they become active learners and acquire a repertoire of learning strategies (Deshler, Ellis, & Lenz, 1996). The model for teaching learning strategies was developed at the University of Kansas Institute for Research on Learning. There are eight steps: (1) pretesting, (2) describing the strategy, (3) teaching modeling, (4) verbal practice, (5) controlled practice, (6) advanced practice, (7) post-testing, and (8) generalization.

Applications of learning strategies are presented in several sections of this textbook—Chapter 5, "Theories of Learning," Chapter 9, "Adolescents and Adults With Learning Disabilities and Related Disabilities," and Chapter 12, "Reading Difficulties."

The procedures for learning strategies instruction include the following:

1. Provide elaborate explanations
2. Model learning processes
3. Provide prompts to use strategies
4. Engage in teacher-student dialogue
5. Ask process-type questions

Did You Get It?

In both process and principle of peer-tutoring, it is generally agreed upon that there is one primary benefactor.
  a. Yes — the tutee
  b. No — the tutor and tutee benefit mutually
  c. Yes — the tutor
  d. It depends whether the tutor is part of the school's regular staff or not

3.10 Task Analysis

The purpose of task analysis is to plan the sequential steps for learning a specified skill. Task analysis breaks down the complexity of an activity into easier steps; these steps are organized as a sequence, and the student is taught each step of the sequence. The goal is to move the student to the desired level of skill achievement. The skill of buttoning, for example, entails a sequence of component subskills: grasping the button, aligning the button with the buttonhole, and so forth. The teacher must consider the following: (1) What are the important, specific educational tasks that the student must learn? (2) What are the sequential steps in learning this task?, and (3) What specific behaviors does the student need to perform this task? The procedures of task analysis are given in Teaching Tips 3.7, "Steps of Task Analysis."

The following list provides examples of the task analysis of instruction sequences to reach a curriculum goal:

- **Task analysis of long division** includes the steps (or subskills) of estimating, dividing, multiplying, subtracting, checking, bringing down the next digit, and then repeating the process. Each step must be planned for, taught, and assessed.
- **Task analysis of writing a report** by using the school library includes the skills of knowing alphabetical order, using the card catalog (or a computer station), finding books on a subject, using a book index to find information on a topic, getting a main idea from reading, and knowing language usage skills (Slavin, 2000).
- **Task analysis of recognizing a word** might include the skills of recognizing initial consonants, recognizing short vowels, and blending.

task analysis
A teaching approach that analyzes an activity by breaking it down into a sequence of steps.

TEACHING TIPS 3.7
Steps of Task Analysis

Step 1. Clearly state the learning task (the behavioral objective).

Step 2. Break the learning task into the steps necessary to learn the target skill, and place these steps into a logical teaching sequence.

Step 3. Test informally to determine the steps that the student can already perform.

Step 4. Begin teaching, in sequential order, each step of the task analysis sequence.

Professional Resource Download

Did You Get It?

Task analysis is a highly effective means and method for teaching; this is of primary importance when teaching those students who have disabilities. The main goal of this analysis has to do what in relation to the task-at-hand?
  a. Making it more enjoyable
  b. Lessening frustration levels of the student who is tackling it
  c. Reducing the complex to the achievable
  d. Teaching easy ways of doing things

3.11 Technology in the Classroom

Technology should be viewed as a tool for learning and can supplement the specialized instruction that is being provided by the special educator. Students enjoy using technology in the classroom. It offers them an opportunity for active learning. Students who are technologically savvy are eager to share their knowledge with others. Using technology in the classroom increases student motivation and self esteem. Students want to learn how to use the Internet. Here are some suggested websites.

3.11a Websites

The following websites are designed for children:

http://kids.yahoo.com
http://www.coolmath4kids.com
http://www.kidsknowit.com

- A popular video for teaching mathematics is that of Salman Khan. You can find this website by going to http://on.ted.com/SalKhan

3.11b Useful Technology for Writing and Creating Documents

The following provide some samples of websites that assist students in writing

Co:Writer *http://www.donjohnston.com*
Kidspiration *http://www.kidspiration.com*
PowerPoint *http://office.microsoft.com/en-us/publisher/default.aspx*
Read Please! *http://www.readplease.com*
Smilebox for creating slideshows: *http://www.smilebox.com*
Voki for creating a talking avatar: *http://www.voki.com*
Free website creation for educators: *http://education.weebly.com*

There are multiple ways that technology can be utilized within the classroom. It can be used to support and enhance the delivery of instruction, it can be used by students as a tool to complete assignments, and it can be used as an effective means of communication.

Technology to Support and Enhance Instruction
Teachers use technology to provide instruction to students. They may utilize PowerPoint slides or prezi to provide visuals. They may download information about a given country. They may utilize the Smartboard for interactive instruction. They may use survey tools to get their students' opinion about a given topic.

More teachers are utilizing Skype as a way to feature speakers from other parts of the country. Some classrooms have a relationship with a classroom from another country that they are studying and

▶❚❚ TeachSource Video Case Activity

© Cengage Learning 2015.

Watch the TeachSource Video Case entitled "Teaching Technology Skills: An Elementary School Lesson on PowerPoint." In this video, young children learn to use the technology of PowerPoint.

QUESTIONS

1. How can teachers instruct children to use computer technology?
2. What is PowerPoint?

they use Skype to have a discussion with a classroom in Japan. Some teachers create podcasts that are short lectures about a critical topic and the student can listen to the podcast using her iPod or iPhone.

Voki is an online tool that allows the teacher to create a talking avatar. The teacher creates a character, tells it what to say, and then publishes the character with the message. This is an excellent way to gain student attention (Elliott, 2012).

Many teachers now have webpages as part of their school's website and they can utilize the webpage to provide a preview of the lecture or provide clues to a key vocabulary word that will be in the lecture. Teachers can also create their own free website utilizing weebly for education.

Some teachers have utilized Facebook as a way to enhance instruction. However be advised that some schools will not allow its use so the teacher must always check the school district's policy. Teachers who are allowed to use it create a separate account and only allow their students to utilize it for specific educational purposes. They may pose questions about a topic that they are discussing and the students can respond.

Online discussion boards are an excellent tool for teachers to use to post a question about what is being studied and all students are expected to provide one or two responses to the question.

Technology as a Tool for the Student to Complete Assignments In place of having students complete traditional assignments such as papers or book reports, students can be encouraged to do a podcast about a topic or they can put together a PowerPoint presentation about a given topic. YouTube is now available for education and students can prepare a YouTube about a given topic.

Students can also monitor their own progress in mastering spelling words or math facts by charting their work using a spreadsheet.

Students can be allowed to research a given topic utilizing technology.

For writing, students can blog utilizing such programs as WordPress (*http://www.wordpress.com*).

When expecting students to complete assignments utilizing technology, it is critical that the teacher be cognizant of whether the student has access to technology at home. The family may not have consistent electricity in the home or may not have consistent internet access; if that is the case, the student will need to be provided time to utilize school provided computers.

Technology as a Communication Tool Technology can be utilized to post homework assignments, to post helpful hints to students about how to complete an assignment, and to provide reminders to students about assignments that are due. For parents, helpful hints can be provided about the topic that is being discussed in class. Reminders can also be posted to parents about important school events.

Some teachers utilize dialogue journals with their students. Students create an e-mail specifically for school use and their journal can be sent to the teacher on e-mail. The teacher can then respond personally to the student.

Some teachers are texting parents or students to provide reminders about specific activities or assignments.

The rapid changes in technology make it very important for teachers to stay current with what is available, know what the technology policies of the school district are, keep any use of technology appropriate for school use, and supervise students' use of technology.

I Have a Kid Who...

THE CASE OF BECKY C. *Describes the Influence of a Clinical Teacher*

Becky C. is in the first semester of third grade. In first grade, she was completely baffled by the letters and words. Becky continued to struggle with reading in second grade. Her reading problems are continuing in third grade. She complains that the third grade teacher yells at her a lot. Becky is in a general education third-grade classroom. Becky does not want to go to school and has lost self-esteem. Becky likes art and seems to have a special talent for drawing, cartooning, and painting.

You are the special education teacher collaborating with Becky's general education teacher. You believe that

Becky can learn and you take on the job of being a clinical teacher for Becky. You want to tailor learning experiences for Becky's unique needs.

QUESTIONS

1. What steps can you take to build Becky's self-esteem and give her confidence that she can learn?
2. How can you use Becky's talent in art to build her reading skills?
3. How can you help Becky see the progress she is making?

Did You Get It?

Technology is now an integrated and inextricable component of the educational process. Technology can and should be regarded as all but which of the following?
   a. An adjunct
   b. A surrogate
   c. Supplementary
   d. A partner

Chapter Summary

- Specialized instruction is at the heart of special education and is delivered by a special educator based on the individual needs of the student.
- Clinical teaching requires tailoring learning experiences to the unique needs of a particular student.
- Differentiated instruction is required to meet the individual needs of students with learning disabilities and related disabilities.
- One of the critical options available to teachers is to change certain variables in the school setting: difficulty level, space, time, and language. By modifying these elements, the teacher controls certain variables that affect learning.

- It is important to build the student's self-confidence.
- Most students with learning disabilities and related disabilities are in general education classrooms.
- It is essential to know instructional strategies for general education.
- Task analysis involves analyzing the small sequential steps of a specific skill.
- Technology can be utilized to supplement instruction, allow students to complete assignments, and as a communication tool.

Questions for Discussion and Reflection

1. What is meant by the term "specialized instruction"?
2. What is meant by clinical teaching?
3. Teachers can do little about many of the factors related to learning disabilities. Some variables, however, can be controlled or adjusted by the teacher. Describe and give an example of three instructional variables that teachers can change.
4. Why is it important to consider ways to accommodate students with learning disabilities and related disabilities in the general education classroom? Name three ways that general education classroom teachers can make accommodations for students.
5. Other students in the classroom may complain that it is not fair to make modifications and accommodations for students with disabilities because the students are not all being treated in the same way. How would you respond to these comments?
6. Describe task analysis. Give an example of an instructional sequence (or the steps to learning a specific skill).

Key Terms

accommodations (p. 92)
active learning (p. 96)
bibliotherapy (p. 89)
clinical teaching (p. 76)
cognitive processing (p. 82)
differentiated instruction (p. 80)
direct instruction (p. 83)
explicit teaching (p. 95)
learning strategies instruction (p. 98)

mastery learning (p. 84)
multiple intelligences (p. 81)
peer tutoring (p. 94)
readiness (p. 84)
reasonable accommodations (p. 91)
scaffolded instruction (p. 97)
specialized instruction (p. 74)
task analysis (p. 99)
zone of proximal development (ZPD) (p. 84)

Michael Newman/PhotoEdit

Educational Settings and the Role of the Family

Don't walk behind me; I may not lead. Don't walk in front of me; I may not follow. Just walk beside me and be my friend.

—Albert Camus

LEARNING
OBJECTIVES

After reading this chapter, you should be able to:

4.1 Describe important concepts about educational settings

4.2 Explain the least restrictive environment

4.3 Describe the continuum of alternative placements

4.4 Describe different types of educational settings

4.5 Explain collaboration partnerships between general education and special education teachers

4.6 Describe how a student's learning disabilities affect families and parents.

STANDARDS Addressed in This Chapter:

These standards have been approved by the National Council for the Accreditation of Teacher Education

CEC Initial Preparation Standard 1: Learner Development and Individual Learning Differences

- 1.2—Beginning special education professionals use understanding of development and individual differences to respond to the needs of individuals with exceptionalities.

CEC Initial Preparation Standard 2—Learning Environments

- 2.0—Beginning special education professionals create safe, inclusive, culturally responsive learning environments so that individuals with exceptionalities become active and effective learners and develop emotional well-being, positive social interactions, and self-determination.

- 2.1—Beginning special education professionals through collaboration with general educators and other colleagues create safe, inclusive, culturally responsive learning environments to engage individuals with exceptionalities in meaningful learning activities and social interactions.

CEC Initial Preparation Standard 5—Instructional Planning and Strategies

- 5.5—Beginning special education professionals develop and implement a variety of education and transition plans for individuals with exceptionalities across a wide range of settings and different learning experiences in collaboration with individuals, families, and teams.

CEC Initial Preparation Standard 6—Professional Learning and Ethical Practice

- 6.3—Beginning special education professionals understand that diversity is a part of families, cultures, and schools, and that complex human issues can interact with the delivery of special education services.

CEC Initial Preparation Standard 7—Collaboration

- 7.0—Beginning special education professionals collaborate with families, other educators, related service providers, individuals with exceptionalities, and personnel from community agencies in culturally responsive ways to address the needs of individuals with exceptionalities across a range of learning experiences.

- 7.1—Beginning special education professionals use the theory and elements of effective collaboration.

- 7.2—Beginning special education professionals serve as a collaborative resource to colleagues.

- 7.3—Beginning special education professionals use collaboration to promote the well-being of individuals with exceptionalities across a wide range of settings and collaborators.

The educational setting is a critical element of the assessment-teaching process. In this chapter, we examine educational settings for teaching students with learning disabilities and related mild disabilities. We focus on the following topics: (1) important concepts about educational settings, (2) types of educational settings, (3) collaboration and promoting partnerships between general education teachers and special education teachers, and (4) parents and families of students with disabilities.

4.1 Important Concepts About Educational Settings

A key decision that is made by the IEP (Individualized Education Program) team is to determine the setting or educational environment in which students with learning disabilities and related mild disabilities will receive instruction. We discuss two key concepts in the law that guide decisions about a student's educational environment: (1) the least restrictive environment (LRE) and (2) the continuum of alternative placements.

Did You Get It?

Who determines the appropriate setting where a student with learning disabilities will undergo instruction?

- **a.** teachers and parents together
- **b.** the school board
- **c.** the entire IEP team
- **d.** teachers, parents, and the student

4.2 Least Restrictive Environment

An important provision in special education law pertaining to educational settings is the *least restrictive environment* (LRE). The Individuals with Disabilities Education Improvement Act of 2004 (IDEA-2004) calls for instructing students with disabilities in the least restrictive environment—that is, with peers who do not have disabilities—to the greatest extent appropriate. LRE serves as the cornerstone of the inclusion movement.

4.2a Inclusion

With increasing frequency, the recommended educational setting for students with disabilities is the general education classroom, which is often referred to *as inclusion*. IDEA-2004 requires that students with disabilities receive instruction in the least restrictive environment and that they have access to the general education curriculum.

For effective instruction for students in general education, it is essential to provide suitable supports for students with disabilities.

The inclusion of students with disabilities in general education settings continues to expand. Figure 4.1 shows that about 54% of students with disabilities receive instruction inside the regular class over 80% of the school day, 24% receive instruction in the regular class for 40% to 70% of the school day, 17% receive instruction in the regular class for less than 40% of the school day, and 5% receive instruction in other environments.

4.2b The Philosophy of Inclusion

Inclusion is based on the conviction that all children with disabilities have a right to participate in environments as close to normal as possible and to benefit socially and academically from being in the central school and society. The underlying philosophy supporting inclusion is that maximum integration with typically developing children is highly desirable and should be a major goal (Scanlon, Gargiulo & Metcalf, 2010; Boyle & Scanlon, 2010).

The philosophical contention of inclusion includes the normalization of children through integrated regular classes and the elimination of labels for children with disabilities. An additional hope for inclusion is the underlying belief that a large part of a child's problem would disappear by doing away with labels (Gargiulo & Metcalf, 2010; Boyle & Scanlon, 2010).

An argument for inclusion is that successful adults with disabilities have learned to function comfortably

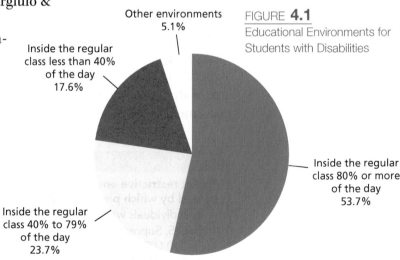

Other environments
5.1%

Inside the regular class less than 40% of the day
17.6%

Inside the regular class 40% to 79% of the day
23.7%

Inside the regular class 80% or more of the day
53.7%

FIGURE **4.1**
Educational Environments for Students with Disabilities

Source: 30th Annual Report to Congress on the Implementation of the Individuals with Disabilities Act. (2012): Washington, DC: U.S. Department of Education. (based in 2008 data)

in society and in the community—in an unrestricted environment composed of all people. To promote normalization and experiences in the greater society, inclusion aims to ensure that, to the extent appropriate, students with disabilities have experiences in school with students who do not have disabilities.

4.2c Mainstreaming

Mainstreaming was an early procedure in which students with disabilities were placed selectively in a general education classroom for instruction, when teachers believed the students would benefit from an integrated placement. Students with learning disabilities and other mild disabilities were carefully integrated into general classrooms, perhaps for a single subject. The goal of mainstreaming was to increase slowly the amount of time that the students would spend in the general education classroom. The mainstreaming plan was carefully worked out and monitored for each student by special and general education teachers.

With mainstreaming, the starting point for the student was the special education classroom. The student was then integrated into a regular or general education classroom. In contrast, with inclusion, the starting point for a student with special education needs is the general education classroom with the student receiving special education services either within or outside that classroom.

4.2d Guidelines for Effective Inclusion

To make inclusion settings more effective, it is essential to provide sufficient support through multidisciplinary teams of professionals who mutually adjust their collective skills and knowledge to create unique, personal programs for each student. Ideally, all staff members should be involved in making decisions, teaching, and evaluating the student's needs and progress.

Effective inclusion requires that teachers (1) consider the student and the family, (2) be committed to the goals of inclusion, (3) have adequate resources and supports, and (4) engage in ongoing professional development (Salend, 2008; Friend & Bursuck, 2006; Smith et al., 2002). Including Students in General Education 4.1 describes some practical strategies for Inclusion.

4.2e Changes in Educational Placements

As noted earlier, the inclusion movement is rapidly escalating within our schools. The steady increase of the placement of students with all disabilities in general education classes is striking. In the 21 years between 1987 and 2008, the percentage of students with learning disabilities who had only general education class placement increased from 17% to 54% (U.S. Department of Education, 2012).

Did You Get It?

"Least restrictive environment" is a principle put forth, championed, and passed by which piece of legislation or governmental body?
  a. Individuals with Disabilities Education Improvement Act of 2004 (IDEA-2004)
  b. U.S. Supreme Court in *Florence Co. School District Four v. Shannon Carter,* 510 U.S. 7, (1993)
  c. No Child Left Behind Act
  d. The Education for the Handicapped Children Act

Including Students in GENERAL EDUCATION 4.1

Practical Strategies

- **Use a team approach.** The general education classroom teacher should use a team approach to share responsibility with special education teachers and related professionals. General education classroom teachers are sometimes hesitant and even fearful about providing for the needs of special students in their classrooms and a team approach alleviates these fears.

- **Provide supportive services.** Students with learning disabilities and related mild disabilities who are served in the general education classroom often need supportive services. The special education teacher can be helpful in obtaining and providing supportive services.

- **Plan for social acceptance.** Many students with learning disabilities and related mild disabilities experience difficulty in being accepted socially by their peers in the general education classroom. By itself, placement in a general education classroom may not lead to greater social interaction or increased social acceptance. Social planning is needed.

- **Teach students appropriate classroom behavior.** Students may have to be taught acceptable classroom behaviors. As predictors of success in the classroom, acceptable classroom behaviors are even more important than academic competencies. Essential behaviors for classroom success include (1) interacting positively with other students, (2) obeying class rules, and (3) displaying proper work habits.

- **Use coteaching strategies.** The general education teacher and the special education teacher should use collaborative planning and teaching in the classroom.

Professional Resource Download

4.3 Continuum of Alternative Placements

Another important concept is the continuum of alternative placements. This provision in the law specifies that schools should make available an array of educational settings to meet the varied needs of students with disabilities. The placement options include (1) general education classes, (2) resource rooms, (3) separate classes, (4) separate schools, and other types of placements as needed, such as a (5) residential facility, or (6) a home-bound or hospital setting.

Table 4.1 contains a brief list, with explanations, of educational services for students with all categories of disabilities. The options are ordered from the least restrictive to the most restrictive environment. As noted earlier, the term *least restrictive environment* refers to the concept that as much as possible students with disabilities are educated in an environment with students who do not have disabilities.

The placement of students with disabilities with nondisabled students in general education classes is considered the least restrictive option. Placement in a separate class or a separate school in which only students with disabilities are served is a more restrictive environment. It is important that teachers not lose sight of the continuum of placement options and the fact that some students with learning disabilities need more than an inclusive setting can offer (Johns, 2003; Crockett & Kauffman, 2001; Zigmond, 2003b, 2007).

continuum of alternative placements
An array of different settings that should be available in a school system to meet the varied needs of students with disabilities.

TABLE 4.1

Continuum of Alternative Placement Options

Least Restrictive ↑	General education class	Includes students who receive most of their education program in a general education classroom and receive special education and related services outside this classroom for less than 21% of the school day. It includes children placed in a general education class and receiving special education within this class, as well as children placed in a general education class and receiving special education outside this class
	Resource room	Includes students who receive special education and related services outside the general education classroom for at least 21%, but not more than 60% of the school day. This may include students placed in resource rooms with part-time instruction in a general education class
	Separate class	Includes students who receive special education and related services outside the general education classroom for more than 60% of the school day. Students may be placed in a separate class with part-time instruction in another placement or placed in separate classes full-time on a regular school campus
	Separate school	Includes students who receive special education and related services in separate day schools for more than 50% of the school day
	Residential facility	Includes students who receive education in a public or private residential facility for more than 50% of the school day.
Most Restrictive ↓	Homebound or hospital setting	Includes students placed in and receiving special education in homebound or hospital programs

© Cengage Learning

4.3a The Case for the Continuum of Alternative Placements

Many scholars believe that the research evidence for one special education delivery model over another is still inconclusive (Zigmond, 2003b, 2007). The case for the continuum of alternative services includes the following:

Students with disabilities need intensive teaching in small instructional groups. Many students with learning disabilities and related mild disabilities need intensive, systematic, and explicit instruction from teachers who are trained and highly skilled in delivering such services. Moreover, instruction for these students is most effective in a small instructional groups, which is difficult to provide in a general education class (Vaughn, Elbaum, & Boardsman, 2001; Zigmond, 2003a, 2007).

General and special educators should work together to provide individualized instruction. The issue of *where* students receive instruction is very complex and there are no simple answers. It is important to recognize that the placement or the setting is not a treatment. The setting itself is less important than what goes on in the setting. General education teachers and special education teachers can work together to provide individualized instruction within a general education classroom setting (Holloway, 2001; McLeskey et al., 2004; Murawski & Dieker, 2004; Zigmond, 2003, 2007; Murawski & Swanson, 2002).

Many parents and professionals worry that many of the needs of students with learning disabilities and related mild disabilities cannot be met in an inclusion classroom. The reality is that labels are indispensable in special education and that even if general education is excellent, special education is still needed (Kauffman, 2007). Does the stigma come from the label or from the child's failure to learn? For example, reading disabilities would not exist in a society that does not value literacy. The reality is, however, that we live in a society that does value literacy, and a person who does not know how to read suffers in this society (Kauffman & Hallahan, 1997).

Many students with learning disabilities and related disabilities need individualized instruction and intensive teaching, which is difficult to provide in a general education classroom setting. As a result, research shows that students with learning disabilities are often neglected (Zigmond, 2003a). The concern is that one size does not fit all, and lumping all students with learning disabilities into the general education classroom ignores the notion of individualized instruction (Crockett & Kauffman, 2001; Foorman & Torgesen, 2001; Johns, 2003).

Empirical research does not identify *one* educational setting as the "most effective." Moreover, no one educational setting is effective for all students. What is much more important than the setting is the question, "What kinds of instructional and learning opportunities are (or can be) made available to students within different educational settings?" More important than the educational setting is the kind of instruction students receive. Students with learning disabilities need instruction that takes into account their individual differences, and they need explicit instruction to learn (Zigmond, 2003).

Did You Get It?

The law applying to the continuum of alternative placements stresses the least restrictive environment, mandating that _____ be made available to accommodate the needs of students with diagnosed disabilities.
   a. a single resource
   b. several resources
   c. an array of resources
   d. unlimited resources

4.4 Types of Educational Settings

In selecting an educational setting for a particular student, the IEP team should consider (1) the severity of the disability, (2) the student's need for related services, (3) the student's ability to fit into the routine of the selected setting, (4) the student's social and academic skills, and (5) the student's level of schooling (primary, intermediate, or secondary). Teams often recommend a placement that combines elements of several types of educational settings.

Parents must agree to the educational setting in writing. If parents and school personnel disagree, parents can ask for mediation at no cost to them, the school can request a "resolution session," or the parent may request a due process hearing (Individuals with Disabilities Education Improvement Act, 2004).

educational setting
The student's placement for instruction.

In what types of settings are students with learning disabilities and related mild disabilities currently receiving instruction? The U.S. Department of Education (2008) reported information on the educational environments of students with disabilities in terms of the percentage of time students were outside the general education class. The classifications for educational environments are: outside the general education class (1) less than 21% of the time out of the regular class, (or the general education classroom) (2) 21–60% of the time out of the regular class (or the Resource Room), and (3) over 60% of the time out of the regular class (or the special class).

4.4a Environmental Options

As indicated earlier, most students with learning disabilities and related mild disabilities are instructed in general education classrooms. Data from the U.S. Department of Education (2012) show that 87% of students with learning disabilities are in general education classes. This number includes both students whose educational placement is in the general education classroom only (52%) and those students who are both in a resource room for part of the day and in a general education classroom for the rest of the day (35%). About 12% of students with learning disabilities receive instruction in separate classes. A small percentage (1%) are in other settings, such as separate schools, residential facilities, or homebound/hospital settings (U.S. Department of Education, 2012). The various educational settings are described in this section. Most students with learning disabilities and related mild disabilities receive services through general education classrooms, resource rooms, or special classrooms.

Sometimes a combination placement is a viable alternative for a particular student. For example, a student could be in a special class for a portion of the day or the week and in a general education classroom for the remainder of the time.

general education classroom
The regular class, in which most students in school receive instruction.

General Education Classroom As shown in Table 4.1, students in a general education environment are outside of this class for less than 21% of the day for special education and related services (U.S. Department of Education, 2012). The general education classroom is considered the least restrictive environment in terms of being with students who do not have disabilities. Effective integration of students with disabilities into the general education classroom requires careful planning, teacher preparation, team effort, and a complete support system. Mere physical placement in a general education classroom is not enough to ensure academic achievement or social acceptance. Students

Teacher helping students.

with learning disabilities and related mild disabilities have specific needs that require targeted and specialized instruction and attention.

Ideally, general and special educators share responsibility for teaching. The special educator may collaborate with the general education classroom teacher, provide materials for the student, or actually teach the student within the general education classroom. The general education classroom teacher must also have the skills, knowledge, and willingness to work with students with learning disabilities and related mild disabilities.

The composition of students in today's general education classroom is changing dramatically. The general education classroom is likely to include the following: most students in the general education classroom do not have disabilities, some students in general education classrooms have disabilities that have been identified through an IEP, some students who do not have an IEP but are eligible to receive accommodation may have a Section 504 Plan (see the example of a Section 504 plan in Figure 4.2), some students in the general education classroom have suspected but undiagnosed disabilities, and some students in the general education classroom may be English-language learners (ELL) and have limited English proficiency. Thus, the general education classroom today has many different types of students with special needs. The percentage of students with disabilities in general education classrooms is increasing, while the percentage in other settings is decreasing.

ELL

Student: _____ School: _____ Grade: _____

Date of
Implementation: _____ Termination: _____ Review: _____

Statement of Student's Achievement as it Relates to this "Plan": _____
_____

INTERVENTION/ STRATEGY	IMPLEMENTOR(S)	MONITORING DATE	COMMENTS

© Cengage Learning

Specific Accommodations Needed

FIGURE **4.2**
Section 504 Plan for Students in General Education

Resource Room Students in a resource room are outside of the general education environment for 21% to 60% of the day for special education and related services (U.S. Department of Education, 2012). A resource room is an educational setting that provides educational services to students with disabilities on a regularly scheduled basis for part of the day. Students spend the remainder of the school day in a general education classroom. The resource room offers flexibility in terms of the curriculum offered, the time students spend in the program, the number of students served, and the teacher's time. As noted in Figure 4.1, the percentage of students receiving resource room instruction is decreasing.

resource room
A special instructional setting, usually a room within a school. In this room, small groups of children meet with a special education teacher for special instruction for a portion of the day. Children spend the remainder of the day in the general education classrooms.

Care must be taken in scheduling students for a resource room session. For example, if the pupil enjoys physical education, the teacher should avoid pre-empting this period for the resource room session. In addition, the classroom teacher must be consulted about the optimum time for the student to leave the classroom. Resource rooms should be pleasant and have an abundant supply of materials. Because students with learning disabilities and related mild disabilities often have short attention spans, it is wise to provide a change of pace by planning several activities during a teaching session.

Separate Class Students in a separate class are outside the general education environment for more than 60% of the day for special education and related services (U.S. Department of Education, 2012). The separate class within the school was one of the first placements used in the public schools to provide education to students with disabilities. Separate classes are typically small, containing about 6 to 15 students at a time. The separate class offers the opportunity for highly individualized and closely supervised intensive instruction. Even with the growing inclusion movement, the percentage of students with learning disabilities placed in special classes is about 12%.

Some separate classes are *categorical* (consisting only of students with one category of disability (such as learning disabilities); others are *cross-categorical* (consisting of students with various mild or moderate disabilities). Often schools cluster the categories of learning disabilities, emotional disturbance, or mental retardation in special classes.

Separate classes are beneficial for certain students who appear to have a better self-concept than similar students in general education classrooms, possibly because regular class competition sets achievement criteria that these students cannot meet. With its lower teacher–pupil ratio, separate classes can offer more intensive individualized instruction in which students spend more time learning. The separate classroom may provide the most appropriate setting for the kind of intensive and comprehensive intervention needed by students with the most serious and severe learning difficulties.

Separate School Often private (but sometimes publicly supported) separate schools are special educational facilities established specifically for students with disabilities. Some students attend the separate school full time. Other students attend the separate school only half a day and may spend the balance of the school day in the public school.

The disadvantages of separate schools include the high expense to parents, the traveling distance, and the lack of opportunity to be with students in the general education population. The advantages of separate schools are that they often serve students with learning disabilities and related mild disabilities well, and they sometimes provide the only feasible option for certain students. Successful pilot programs are often developed at separate schools, which are then used in other settings.

Residential Facility Full-time placement for students away from their homes can be provided by residential facilities . The students receive education in a public or private residential facility. Relatively few students have disabilities that are severe enough to warrant such placement. However, in some cases—if the community lacks adequate alternative facilities, if the behavioral manifestations are extremely severe, or if the emotional reaction among other members

separate class
A special class for children with disabilities taught by a teacher with special training. Children in a separate class usually spend most of the day in this setting.

separate schools
Schools for students with learning disabilities that students attend during the day. They return home after school.

residential facilities
Educational institutions in which students live away from home and receive their education. A residential facility may be sponsored by a government agency or may be privately managed.

of the family is debilitating—residential placement on a 24-hour basis may be the best solution for both the student and the family.

The disadvantages of residential facilities are that they remove the student from home and neighborhood and provide fewer opportunities for social experiences in the larger community. However, for certain youngsters, residential placements become the most appropriate choice, and they have successfully helped many students learn, adjust to the world, and achieve very rewarding careers and lives.

Homebound or Hospital Setting Students in homebound or hospital settings often have a medical condition requiring these placements. Often the school sends teachers to the home or hospital settings to provide instruction.

One-to-One Instruction The type of instruction known as one-to-one instruction occurs when one adult works with one student. It is not an educational environment identified in IDEA-2004. The research shows that it can lead to substantial improvement in student achievement. One-to-one instruction works because the teaching is highly individualized, and the student receives intensive instruction over a period of time by a skilled teacher who can tailor the instruction to the specific student needs. Sometimes students need one-to-one instruction, and they tend to do well with this individualized instruction (Slavin, 2000; Vaughn, Gersten, & Chard, 2000).

> **one-to-one instruction**
> Teaching with one teacher and one student.

In the real world, of course, the cost for schools to provide a teacher for each student is impractical, so parents must often turn to private specialists or clinics to receive this highly individualized form of instruction. Therefore, it is important for schools to seek ways to get as close as possible to one-to-one instruction (Slavin, 2009). Methods for providing individualized instruction include using computer instruction and aides and volunteers as tutors in the classroom. Aides or volunteers must be supervised by an appropriately certified teacher.

Computers offer a way to individualize teaching. A good computer software program is like a tutor because it presents the information, gives students abundant practice, assesses their level of understanding, and provides additional information if it is needed. Computer programs can be quite effective in presenting ideas and in using pictures or graphics to reinforce concepts. Because most students are motivated by the computer, they will work longer and harder than they will with paper-and-pencil tasks. Students utilizing computer programs must be monitored closely to ensure that they are actually working on the designated program and are benefiting from it.

Using *aides and volunteers* offers another procedure to approximate one-to-one instruction. The volunteer movement is alive and growing. Some 60 reading and literacy groups, such as *Literacy Volunteers of America* and the *Laubach Program,* support one-to-one programs, using volunteer adult tutors. Moreover, research demonstrates that tutoring works by increasing a student's reading achievement, confidence, and motivation, in addition to providing a sense of control of the student's reading ability. Even when a student receives the very best in-class instruction, some students still require extra time and assistance to meet the high levels of reading skills needed in school, in the workplace, and throughout life. Tutors can provide the explicit instruction that produces positive results (Center for the Improvement of Early Reading Achievement, 1998; Snow, Burns, & Griffin, 1998a). Tutoring is especially critical during long school breaks, such as summer vacation. Research shows that during these vacation periods, students lose many skills they have learned (Wasik, 1998). Tutoring should be conducted by a well-trained individual who coordinates efforts with the classroom teacher and who gears instruction based on the individualized needs of the student as delineated by the IEP. When teacher aides or volunteers are used, it is important to remember that the teacher is the one who is responsible for planning the instruction for the student. The aide or volunteer must work under the supervision of a teacher who is knowledgeable about how to deliver the specialized instruction needed by the student.

Did You Get It?

When a parent or guardian does not agree with the planned-for educational setting—for any reason whatsoever—he or she can take steps to resolve an impasse. Which step or right is inaccurate in relation to this process?

a. A parent or guardian *must* agree in writing to the proposed placement

b. A parent or guardian can request a resolution session

c. A parent or guardian can request a no-cost mediation session

d. The parent or guardian may request a due-process hearing

4.5 Collaboration: Partnerships Between General Education Teachers and Special Education Teachers

As a greater number of students with learning disabilities and related mild disabilities receive their instruction in general education classrooms, procedures that promote partnerships between general education and special education teachers become especially important. For successful inclusion of students, it is important to find ways to facilitate a team effort.

4.5a Collaboration

collaboration
Teachers working together to plan and teach a child, usually a general education teacher and a special education teacher.

Collaboration is a style of interaction that provides a way for individuals or groups to work together. Through collaboration, two or more individuals interact in a supportive manner that benefits each member, as well as the people they are supporting. The process of collaboration involves people with diverse areas of expertise (such as classroom teachers, special education teachers, and related professions) who work together to find creative solutions to mutually defined problems. Collaboration is essential for effective inclusion (Friend & Cook, 2010; Walther-Thomas, Korinek, & McLaughlin, 2000). Successful collaboration requires the following ingredients (Friend & Cook, 2010):

- Mutual goals
- Voluntary participation
- Equality among participants
- Shared responsibility for participation and decision making
- Shared responsibility for outcomes
- Shared resources

Some principles and strategies for effective collaboration are given in Teaching Tips 4.1, "Effective Collaboration."

4.5b What the General Education Teacher Needs

The responsibilities of the general education classroom teacher are increasing as the inclusion movement continues to expand. Classroom teachers today are accountable for a wider range of students, including more children with disabilities and other special needs. What kinds of supports should be provided for general education teachers who are responsible for inclusion?

- **Participation in the IEP.** The Individuals with Disabilities Education Improvement Act of 2004 requires that general education classroom teachers be part of the individualized education program (IEP) team. Being on the IEP team helps classroom teachers understand the problems, strengths, and needs of students with disabilities.
- **Reduced class size.** Having many students with special needs in a general education classroom makes the teaching task more difficult. A smaller class size could help teachers cope with this added responsibility.
- **Time for planning.** Time should be allocated during the school day for general education classroom teachers to plan with the special education teacher and other professionals for meeting the needs of students with disabilities.
- **Paraprofessionals.** Paraprofessional personnel and aides in the classroom can help general education classroom teachers meet the needs of each student.
- **Volunteers.** Many schools are successful in attracting volunteers to help in the classroom. Senior citizens and volunteers from business organizations sometimes can be recruited to assist.
- **Collaboration with special educators.** Special educators should be available to help general education classroom teachers solve problems, discuss issues, and manage the many situations that they confront in the classroom.
- **Continuum of alternative placements.** Some students with special needs will require more than the inclusive, general education classroom can offer. For these students, other placement options, such as the resource room or special classes, are needed.
- **Availability of related professionals.** The IEP may indicate that the services of related professionals, such as speech-language experts or occupational therapists, are needed for a student. It is important that such services be provided.
- **Opportunities for learning.** General education classroom teachers need to be supported when seeking additional training by attending conferences, seminars, workshops, or learning activities.

▶❚❚ TeachSource Video Case Activity

©Cengage Learning 2015.

Watch the TeachSource Video Case entitled "Inclusion: Classroom Implications for the General and Special Educator." In this video, a general education teacher in a classroom receives support from special education specialists. This video shows the work of occupational and speech therapists with students in the general education classroom.

QUESTIONS

1. Based upon what you read in the chapter, do you find the classroom profiled within this video case to be an effective inclusion classroom? Give some specific examples of its effectiveness.

2. How can an educational therapist help students with learning disabilities and related mild disabilities?

TEACHING TIPS 4.1

Effective Collaboration

Principles for Collaboration	Activities That Work
Establish *common* goals *Successful* partners share *mutual goals* and a *common* philosophy.	✓ Develop a relationship ✓ Engage in small-scale efforts initially ✓ Develop common perceptions
***Participation* should be voluntary** *Collaboration cannot* be *forced* by directives from superiors. Individuals must take mutual responsibility for a problem and freely seek solutions.	✓ Involve key stakeholders ✓ Invite participation
Recognize equality among participants Each person's contribution is equally valued. Each person has equal power in decision making.	✓ Use names, not titles, when interacting ✓ Rotate and share team roles ✓ Structure ways to facilitate participation
Share responsibility for participation and decision making Each person should share the responsibility for participation and decision making.	✓ Share perspectives about the problem ✓ Balance between coordination of tasks and division of labor ✓ Brainstorm before decision making ✓ Establish clear delineation of agreed upon actions as follow-up procedures
Share accountability for outcomes Everyone shares, whether the outcome is successful or not. If the outcome is successful, they share the credit. When it is unsuccessful, they share responsibility for the failure.	✓ Acknowledge risks and potential failure ✓ Celebrate success together ✓ Learn from the failure together
Share resources Each person has resources to contribute.	✓ Identify respective resources ✓ Use joint decision making about resource allocation

Professional Resource Download

4.5c What the Special Education Teacher Needs

The responsibilities of special educators and learning disabilities teachers are difficult to define because they are changing so rapidly. Special education teachers are expected to wear many hats because they are responsible for (1) setting up programs to identify, assess, and instruct students; (2) participating in the screening, assessment, and evaluation of students; (3) collaborating with general education classroom teachers to design and implement instruction; (4) knowing both formal assessment measures and alternate assessment methods; (5) participating on IEP teams; (6) implementing the IEP through direct intervention, coteaching, and collaboration; (7) interviewing and holding conferences with parents; and, perhaps most important, (8) helping students to develop self-understanding and to gain the hope and the confidence that is necessary to cope with and to overcome their learning disabilities.

To accomplish these goals, effective special education teachers need to have two different kinds of competencies: (1) competencies in professional knowledge and skills (having the information and proficiencies for testing and teaching) and (2) competencies in human relationships (the art of working with people).

4.5d Coteaching

Coteaching occurs when two or more teachers deliver instruction to a diverse group of students in a general education classroom. Coteaching between general educators and special educators has become a common method for delivering instruction to all students in a general education classroom. The teaching is shared by all teachers involved. Coteaching can be mutually satisfying, but the teachers must be willing to share and accept responsibility. In fact, coteaching has been likened to a marriage. To be successful, the teachers have to make a 100% effort (Friend & Cook, 2010; Friend & Bursuck, 2002; Gately & Gately, 2001). There are several types of coteaching, and they are described in Table 4.2.

coteaching
The process of two professionals working together within an instructional setting to seek a joint solution. Often refers to the joint efforts of the special education teacher and the general education classroom teacher to work together in the general education classroom

TABLE 4.2

Types of Coteaching

Type	Description
One teaches, one supports One group: One lead teacher, one supportive teacher	One teacher has primary instructional responsibility. The other teacher serves in a supportive role (e.g., observes, tutors, manages behavior)
Station supportive teaching Two groups: Each teacher teaches one group	Divide the content into two parts; then divide the groups into two groups (A and B). Teacher 1 teaches half of the content to Group A, while Teacher 2 teaches the rest of the content to Group B. Then the groups switch. Teacher 2 teaches the rest of the content to Group A, and Teacher 2 teaches the rest of the content to Group B
Parallel teaching Two groups, two teachers: Each teacher teaches one-half of the class	Each teacher instructs half of the class. Both teachers use the same instructional materials. Teachers may differ in their instructional styles. Essentially, the class is smaller, so students have more opportunities to participate
Alternative teaching Two groups: One small, one large	The class is divided into two groups—a large group and a small group. One teacher teaches the large group; one teacher teaches the small group. More intensive and direct instruction is usually used in the small group
Team teaching Both teachers share leadership in teaching the group	Both teachers are equally engaged in the instructional activities. For example, Teacher 1 may begin the lesson by introducing vocabulary while Teacher 2 provides examples to place the words in context

© Cengage Learning

4.5e Strategies to Make Coteaching Work

The following activities can help promote the spirit of coteaching.

- **Make time for coteaching activities.** Productive work requires space, time, and the assurance of uninterrupted sessions. If planning, communicating, and evaluating are not specifically scheduled, there will be insufficient time in the busy school day for these purposes.
- **Recognize that the skills in coteaching and collaboration are learned through developmental processes.** Coteachers must go through developmental stages as they learn to understand each other and to work together.
- **Use coaching strategies.** Coaching is a way to help students with learning disabilities and related mild disabilities. The special education teacher might take on the role of a coach, giving instructions or demonstrating a specific skill, while the general education classroom teacher learns the skill. The coteachers then decide on the skills that they wish to teach.
- **Encourage open communication.** Communication is key to coteaching. If problems are allowed to persist without an opportunity for face-to-face communication, dissatisfaction increases and misunderstandings develop. To avert such situations, oral and written communication must be clear. Effective coteachers are active listeners; they are sensitive to the contributions and ideas of others and recognize nonverbal messages. In addition, effective coteachers give and ask for continuous feedback; they are willing to say "I don't know," and they also give credit to others, when applicable.

One example of how two teachers share classroom responsibilities cooperatively is given in the Teaching Tips 4.2, "Strategies for Two Teachers Working Together."

Did You Get It?

Linda, a general educator, and Eduardo, a special educator, are teachers in the same diverse general education class and share equal time as main instructor to address the needs of students with and without special needs. Linda and Eduardo are

a. paraprofessionals
b. team teachers
c. parallel teachers
d. dual educators

4.6 Families and Parents

Children with learning disabilities and related mild disabilities claim a tremendous emotional toll on parents. Families and parents face many of the same problems as teachers do, but in greatly magnified intensity. The child is in school for a few hours a day in a limited and controlled situation; but, for families and parents, their responsibility encompasses 24 hours a day, 7 days a week, with no vacations, in all types of situations, and with all types of demands.

TEACHING TIPS 4.2

Strategies for Two Teachers Working Together

Activities of Teacher 1	Activities of Teacher 2
✓ Lecturing to the class	✓ Writing notes of key ideas on the board during the lecture
✓ Giving instructions orally	✓ Writing instructions on the board
✓ Giving instructions orally	✓ Checking for understanding with a small group or individual students
✓ Checking for understanding with the large group	✓ Working with the other half of the class in preparing for a debate
✓ Working with one half of the class in preparing for a debate	✓ Providing suggestions for modifications, accommodations, and diverse learners
✓ Creating basic lesson plans for standards, objectives, and content curriculum	✓ Reviewing homework with small groups
✓ Providing large group instruction	✓ Providing modifications
✓ Providing enrichment activities	

Source: Adapted from "Tips and strategies for coteaching at the secondary level," by W. Murawski & L Dieker, 2004, *Teaching Exceptional Children*, 36, p. 56. Reprinted with permission of the Council for Exceptional Children.

It is important for school personnel to consider the strengths of the family. Involvement of parents and families through family–school collaboration is encouraged by informal communication, such as written notes between school and home, parental involvement in the classroom and in extracurricular activities, face-to-face conferences, telephone contact, and e-mail messages (Turnbull, Turnbull, Shank, & Smith, 2004).

Parents can play a crucial role in helping their child. They must (1) be informed consumers, continually working to learn more about the problem of learning disabilities; (2) be assertive advocates, seeking the right programs for their child at home, in school, and in the community; (3) work to ensure that their child's legal rights are being recognized; and (4) be firm in managing their child's behavior while remaining empathetic to their child's feelings, failures, fears, and tribulations. Parents must also give time and attention to other members of the family and try to make a life for themselves.

Parenting a child with disabilities is challenging, but it can also be rewarding. Parents need support from the school, the extended family, and other professionals. With this support, encouragement, and the sharing of expertise, the child can emerge from the school years academically, emotionally, and socially intact, as well as prepared for the challenges ahead.

There are no easy answers or simple solutions for parents of children with disabilities. The feature Student Stories 4.1, "Parents' Thoughts," offers several accounts of the parent's role in helping their child.

- All during the evaluation process, I continued to search for a school for Allegra. I applied to many schools in the city, and one by one they rejected her. It was the same each time, a voice on the phone telling me, "She doesn't belong here." With each rejection came a deeper sense of despair. As the list grew shorter, my despair began to be overcome by something close to panic.

- I was frightened. I didn't know what to do. What in the world can anyone do if a child is denied a basic education? Her future was falling apart before my eyes. I knew the only chance she stood of making it in this world was to find a school, *any* school, that would accept her; yet, with each one I continued to hear, "She doesn't belong here."

Source: From *Laughing Allegra* (p. 40), by A. Ford, 2003, New York: New Market Press

- My son has a learning disability.... I remember his coming home from first grade and crying over his reader. He could not decode! The only way he managed to get through first grade was to memorize the readers he brought home. He accomplished this by going over and over them with me. I don't think his teacher was ever aware that he memorized.

- Teacher comments were predictable: "He is just immature." "He could do it if he would just try." "He's just sloppy because he rushes through his work." "He's just lazy." If only they had been with him as he cried over his homework.

Source: From "A mother's thoughts on inclusion," by M. Carr, 1993, *Journal of Learning Disabilities*, 26(9), 590.

- No one would accuse Kerri ... of lacking smarts or motivation. The ... fifth grader has an IQ of 118 and enthusiasm to spare. Unfortunately, she's never had an aptitude for linking letters to sounds. She recognizes many words by their appearance on the page, but at 11, she still can't spell or write. Common sense says she's dyslexic. But, (by the standards set in her state) Kerri is not entitled to special help. It's sad. She may waste her time in school until she fails badly enough to qualify as learning disabled.

Source: From *Overcoming dyslexia* (p. 29), by S. Shaywitz, 2003, New York: Alfred A. Knopf.

REFLECTIVE QUESTION

1. What are some common themes in the above stories?

4.6a Sensitivity to the Cultural and Linguistic Diversity of Families

In the process of interacting with families, teachers should strive to be responsive to cultural views and attitudes about disabilities. Teachers should realize that there are cultural differences in attitudes about communication, personal space, eye contact, wait time, tone of voice, and touching. Teachers should be sensitive to these issues in interacting with families (Lerner, Lowenthal, & Egan, 2003).

4.6b Suggestions for Parents

Some useful things parents *can* do are presented in Teaching Tips 4.3, "Suggestions for Parents and Families."

Teachers may also wish to recommend reading materials to parents to help them become better acquainted with learning disabilities and with ways of helping their children. Table 4.3 lists a selection of appropriate books and websites for parents.

4.6c Parents' Rights

IDEA-2004 strengthens the rights of parents and families in the educational process of their children. A fundamental provision of the law is the right of

TABLE 4.3

Books and Websites for Parents and Families

Books

Barkley, R. (1995). *Taking charge of ADHD: The complete authoritative guide for parents.* New York: Guilford Press.

Ford, A. (2003). *Laughing Allegra.* New York: New Market Press.

Goldstein, S., & Mather, N. (1998). *Overcoming underachievement: An action guide to helping your child succeed in school.* New York: John Wiley.

Hall, S., & Moats, L. (1999). *Straight talk about reading: How parents can make a difference during the early years.* Chicago: Contemporary Press.

Lavoie, R. (2005). *It's so much work to be your friend: helping the child with learning disabilities find social success.* New York: Simon and Schuster, A Touchstone Book.

Lerner, J., Lowenthal, B., & Lerner, S. (1995). *Attention deficit disorders: Assessment and teaching.* Pacific Grove, CA: Brooks/Cole.

Osman, B. (1997). *Learning disability and ADHD: A family guide to learning and learning together.* New York: John Wiley.

Silver, L. (2006). *The misunderstood child: A guide for parents of children with learning disabilities.* New York: Three Rivers Press. Crown Publishing.

Smith, S. (1991). *Succeeding against the odds: Strategies and insights from the learning-disabled.* Los Angeles: Jeremy P. Tarcher.

Websites

Children and Adults with Attention Deficit Hyperactivity Disorder: *http://www.chadd.org*

Learning Disabilities Association of America: *http://www.ldaamerica.org*

Schwab Learning: *http://www.schwablearning.org*

© Cengage Learning

parents to participate in the educational decision-making process. Parents have the right to:

- A free, appropriate public education for their child
- Request an evaluation of their child
- Notification whenever the school wants to evaluate their child or change the child's educational placement
- Informed consent (parents understand and agree in writing to teaching plans and may withdraw their consent at any time)
- Obtain an independent evaluation of their child
- Request a reevaluation of their child
- Have their child tested in the language that the child knows best
- Review all of their child's school records
- Participate in their child's individualized education program (IEP) or individualized family service plan (IFSP) for young children
- Be informed of their child's progress at least as often as parents of children who do not have disabilities

1. **Be alert to what your child is good at or likes to do.** By discovering an area of interest or a talent, you can give your child a new chance for success. Even small tasks, such as folding napkins or helping with specific kitchen chores, can give your child a sense of achievement.

2. **Do not push your child into activities for which the child is not ready.** The child may react by trying half-heartedly to please you; rebelling, either actively or passively; or just quitting or withdrawing into a world of daydreams. When a child is forced to meet arbitrary and inappropriate standards imposed by the adult world, learning becomes painful rather than pleasurable.

3. **Simplify family routine.** For some children, mealtime can be an extremely complex and stimulating situation. Your child may be unable to cope with the many sounds, sights, smells, and so on. It may be necessary at first to have the child eat earlier and then gradually join the family meal—perhaps starting with dessert. Search for other such examples in your routines.

4. **Try to match tasks to the child's level of functioning.** Think about the child's problem and find some way to help. For example, easy-to-wipe surfaces and break-proof containers can reduce mess and breakage when the child uses these materials. Drawing an outline of the child's shoes on the closet floor can indicate left and right.

5. **Be direct and positive in talking to your child.** Try to avoid criticizing; instead, be supportive and provide guidance. For example, if your child has trouble following directions, ask him or her to look at you while you speak and then to repeat what you have said.

6. **Keep the child's room simple and in a quiet part of the house.** As much as possible, make the room a place to relax and retreat.

7. **Help your child learn how to live in a world with others.** When a child does not play well with other children, parents may have to go out of their way to plan and guide social experiences. This may mean inviting a single child to play for a short period of time, arranging with parents of other children for joint social activities, or volunteering to be a girl scout leader or boy scout leader.

8. **Children need to learn that they are significant.** They must be treated with respect and allowed to *do* their own work. They should learn that being a responsible and contributing member of the family is important—probably more important than learning the academic skills demanded by the school.

9. **Keep your outside interests.** Try to relinquish your child's care to a competent babysitter periodically. Parents need time off for independence and morale boosting.

Professional Resource Download

4.6d The Family System

A family of five is like five people lying on a waterbed. Whenever one person moves, everyone feels the ripple (Lavoie, 1995).

It is useful to view the family as a system. The fundamental idea of the family systems theory is that whatever happens to one part of a family or system affects all the other parts. In the family system, all members of the extended family are interdependent, and each member has an interactive effect on all other members. The family system involves the child, parents, siblings, grandparents, other people living in the home, or those who are part of the child's family.

The entire family system is affected by a child with learning disabilities or with related mild disabilities. Day-to-day living can be stressful from the start. As infants, these children may be irritable, demanding, and difficult to soothe, which can make parents feel incompetent, confused, and helpless. As the child enters school and begins to face learning failure, the parents may have feelings of guilt, shame, or embarrassment. As they become frustrated, they may blame each other for their child's problems. One parent may accuse the other of being too strict or too lenient in raising their child, putting extra strain on the marital relationship. Siblings and other family members are also affected when a brother or sister has learning disabilities. The siblings may be embarrassed or feel angry or jealous if their parents pay more attention to the sibling with learning disabilities. For these reasons, it is necessary in some cases to include the entire family in the treatment process, with counseling for the family system as an important part.

4.6e Stages of Acceptance

When parents are faced with the quandary of a child with a disability, they are likely to pass through a series of predictable stages of acceptance (Kübler-Ross, 1969; Lavoie, 1995). These stages are universal and apply to anyone who experiences a loss. In this case, the parents have lost their hope for a normal child.

Some parents go through a mourning process when first told that their child has learning disabilities. The stages in the process are shock, disbelief, denial, anger, bargaining, and acceptance. For each parent, the number of stages or the length of time spent in each stage is different. Often, too, the parent returns to an earlier stage.

Parents can play a critical role in helping their child.

- *Shock* is the numb, distancing feeling that engulfs the parents when the bad news is being delivered.
- *Disbelief* is the stage in which parents do not believe the diagnosis.
- *Denial* is a stage in which parents refuse to even consider that the child has a disability and seeks an alternative diagnosis. Some examples of statements of denial include "There's nothing wrong," "That's the way I was as a child—not to worry," and "He'll grow out of it."
- *Anger* occurs as the denial breaks down and the child's condition becomes more real and apparent. Angry feelings are exhibited when parents say things like "Why did this happen to me?" or "It isn't fair," "The teachers don't know anything," or "I hate the neighborhood, this school, and this teacher."
- *Bargaining* is evident when the parent decides that dedication will somehow alleviate their child's condition. For example, they may say, "Maybe the problem will improve if we move."
- *Acceptance* is the stage at which the parents can look past the disability and accept the child as he or she is. A stage beyond acceptance is to *cherish* the child for those differences and for how that child has made the parents' lives better.

stages of acceptance
The different emotions parents go through when they learn they have a child with disabilities.

This roller coaster of emotions has a profound impact upon the parent and upon interactions with the child. Because the two parents will probably not go through these stages at the same time, each parent must learn to respect the other's right to travel through the stages at a different rate.

The goal is to reach acceptance so that the parent is able to make decisions that are unclouded by undue emotion. When parents accept their child along with their child's disabilities, they are then able to provide for the child's special needs while continuing to live a normal life and tending to family, home, civic, and social obligations.

4.6f Parent Support Groups and Family Counseling

Establishing healthy parental attitudes and ensuring parent–teacher cooperation are, of course, desirable goals. Parent support groups and family counseling can help in meeting these goals.

parent support groups
Small groups of parents who meet to obtain information about their children with disabilities and to discuss common problems.

Parent support groups offer parents a way to meet regularly in small groups to discuss common problems. They can be organized by the school, family service organizations, professional counselors, or parent organizations, such as the Learning Disabilities Association (LDA). The opportunity to meet with other parents whose children are encountering similar problems tends to reduce the parents' sense of isolation. Furthermore, such parent support groups have been useful in alerting the community, school personnel, other professionals, and legislative bodies to the plight of their children. To find local parent groups, see the LDA website at *http://www.ldaamerica.org.*

Parent support groups and family counseling offer the following benefits:

- Help parents to understand and to accept their child's problem
- Reduce anxieties stemming from apprehension about the psychological and educational development of their child; parents can discover that they are not alone and that other parents have similar problems and have found solutions
- Help parents realize that they are an integral part of their child's learning, development, and behavior; they can learn to perceive their children differently and to deal with their problems more effectively
- Help parents learn about discipline, communication skills, behavioral management, parent advocacy, special education legislation, social skills development, helping one's child make friends, home management, and college and vocational opportunities

4.6g Parent–Teacher Conferences

Parent–teacher conferences are a bridge between the home and school. Both parents and teachers tend to shy away from these private conferences, parents fearing what they will hear and teachers fearing that parents will react negatively. Yet, these conferences, at which the student's progress and problems are discussed, should be viewed as an opportunity to help the student. Parents and teachers can work together to enhance progress.

In setting up a conference, teachers should reassure parents that they are going to communicate with someone who cares about their child. Teachers must impart a sense of confidence without being arrogant and should convey a sincere interest in the student and respect for the parents. Parents also want to know what they can do at home.

Did You Get It?

Although most parents ostensibly have unconditional love for their children, you would be irresponsible to minimize the "_____" toll that children with disabilities can place on their parents.
- **a.** financial
- **b.** emotional
- **c.** devastating
- **d.** abusive

I Have a Kid Who...

BERNICE *and a Coteaching Team*

Bernice, age 9, is in fourth grade in the general education class. Bernice's IEP indicates that she has learning disabilities, and her IEP has goals for improving her reading fluency. Ms. George is her general education teacher, and Mr. Peters is the special education teacher who works in Bernice's class. Ms. George and Mr. Peters have formed a collaborative arrangement to work with students who have special needs. Whereas Ms. George works with most of the class in a large group, Mr. Peters works with students who require special attention in a small group in the class. Several other students in the fourth grade need help in developing reading fluency. Mr. Peters has a group of 4 students in the general education class who need help in building skills in reading fluency.

Mr. Peters plans to use these strategies for building reading fluency with this small group in the general education class: repeated reading, using predictable books, choral reading, and the neurological impress method.

QUESTIONS

1. How can Mr. Peters use *repeated reading* with his small group of students?
2. How can Bernice benefit from the neurological impress method?
3. What read-along technology could Mr. Peters use?

Chapter Summary

- Important concepts about educational settings
- The least restrictive environment
- Continuum of alternative placements
- Types of educational settings
- Collaboration: Partnerships between general and regular educators

Questions for Discussion and Reflection

1. Discuss two key concepts about educational settings that are features of the special education law. Do you think these two features are compatible or in conflict? Explain your position.
2. Discuss some of the recent trends in educational settings. How do you think these trends will affect students with learning disabilities and related mild disabilities?
3. Describe the advantages and shortcomings of the inclusion placement model.
4. Compare and contrast the three most common educational settings for students with learning disabilities and related mild disabilities.
5. Discuss activities for coteaching between the special education teacher and the general education teacher.
6. Discuss the various needs of the general education teacher and the special education teacher.

Key Terms

collaboration (p. 116)
continuum of alternative placements (p. 109)
coteaching (p. 119)
educational setting (p. 111)
general education classroom (p. 112)
one-to-one instruction (p. 115)

parent support groups (p. 126)
residential facilities (p. 114)
resource room (p. 113)
separate class (p. 114)
separate schools (p. 114)
stages of acceptance (p. 125)

Brian Mitchell/Corbis

Theories of Learning

Theories are working concepts to be modified in the light of new knowledge. Those who teach without theories may follow the road that leads nowhere.

—John Dewey

Part III examines underlying theories and new directions in the fields of learning disabilities and related disabilities. The topics in Part III include key theories of learning (Chapter 5); social, emotional, and behavioral challenges (Chapter 6); autism spectrum disorder and attention deficit hyperactivity disorder (ADHD) (Chapter 7); young children with disabilities (Chapter 8); adolescents and adults with learning disabilities and related disabilities (Chapter 9); and special education law (Chapter 10).

STANDARDS Addressed in This Chapter:

CEC Initial Level Special Educator Preparation Standards as approved by the National Council for the Accreditation of Teacher Education

CEC Initial Preparation Standard 1: Learner Development and Individual Learning Differences

- 1.0—Beginning special education professionals understand how exceptionalities may interact with development and learning and use this knowledge to provide meaningful and challenging learning experiences for individuals with exceptionalities.

- 1.1—Beginning special education professionals understand how language, culture, and family background influence the learning of individuals with exceptionalities.

- 1.2—Beginning special education professionals use understanding of development and individuals differences to respond to the needs of individuals with exceptionalities.

CEC Initial Preparation Standard 3: Curricular Content Knowledge

- 3.1—Beginning special education professionals understand the central concepts, structures of the discipline, and tools of inquiry of the content areas they teach and can organize this knowledge, integrate cross-disciplinary skills, and develop meaningful learning progressions for individuals with exceptionalities.

CEC Initial Preparation Standard 5: Instructional Planning and Strategies

- 5.1—Beginning special education professionals consider an individual's abilities, interests, learning environments, and cultural and linguistic factors in the selection, development, and adaptation of learning experiences for individuals with exceptionalities.

- 5.4—Beginning special education professionals use strategies to enhance language development and communication skills of individuals with exceptionalities.

- 5.5—Beginning special education professionals develop and implement a variety of education and transition plans for individuals with exceptionalities across a wide range of settings and different learning experiences in collaboration with individuals, families, and teams.

- 5.6—Beginning special education professionals teach to mastery and promote generalization of learning.

Chapter 5 discusses the underlying theories and new directions in learning disabilities and related areas of special education.

5.1 The Role of Theory and Theories of Learning

theories
The purpose of theory is to bring form and coherence, and meaning to what is observed in the real world, underlying concepts explaining what is observed.

"If you don't know where you are going, any road will take you there." This advice is as applicable to teaching as it is to other facets of life. Theories help us understand the complexities of learning. By shedding light on the nature of the learning problems students encounter, theories guide and act as a basis for instruction. Those who teach without a theory may follow the road that leads nowhere.

Theories are meant to be working statements; they are not meant to be ideas "frozen into absolute standards masquerading as eternal truths" or "programs rigidly adhered to" (Dewey, 1946, p. 202. 1998). A theory is a working concept to be modified in the light of new knowledge. John Dewey considered theory the most practical of all things because it provides a guide for action, clarifies and structures thought, and creates a catalyst for further research.

Theory is constantly evolving and serves as a guide to systematize knowledge. The purpose of theory is to bring form, coherence, and meaning to what we observe in the real world (Dewey, 1998). Theory building is a process. It builds on the shoulders of the giants who have come before. Every discipline is built on the concepts and ideas contributed by earlier scholars. The current theory is challenged, modified, and strengthened as researchers and practitioners test the theory's relevance and usefulness. The modified theory in turn leads to new forms of assessment and instructional practices. The theories generated in studying learning disabilities and related mild disabilities have produced significant applications to many areas of both special education and general education.

In this chapter, we examine the contributions of three major theories in psychology and their implications for learning disabilities and related disabilities: (1) developmental psychology, (2) behavioral psychology, and (3) cognitive psychology

Did You Get It?

Which of the following does not represent an adequate conceptualization of what an effective and contributory theory is or must be in actuality?

a. A working statement

b. A regarded theory that leaves room for future modification

c. A rigid standard demanding strict adherence

d. A guide for action

5.2 Developmental Psychology

Developmental psychology offers an important perspective for understanding difficulties in learning. A key notion in developmental psychology is that the maturation of cognitive skills (or thinking) follows a sequential progression. A child's ability to learn depends on the child's current maturational status. Further, this maturational view implies that attempts to speed up or bypass the developmental process may actually create problems. Jean Piaget, the celebrated Swiss developmental psychologist, remarked, "Every time I describe a maturational sequence in the United States, an American asks 'How can you speed it up?'" In this section, we discuss: (1) developmental variations, (2) Piaget's maturational stages of development, (3) stages of learning, and (4) the implications of developmental psychology for learning disabilities and related disabilities.

5.2a Developmental Variations

The term developmental variations refers to differences in the rates of specific components of development. Further, each individual has a preset rate of growth for various human functions, including cognitive abilities. Discrepancies among the various abilities indicate that various abilities are maturing at different rates, with some abilities lagging in their development. Bender (1957) called these variations "maturational lags." This maturational perspective implies that many children with learning problems are not so different from other children; rather, their developmental differences are more a matter of *timing*.

The developmental perspective suggests that society may actually create many learning problems. For example, if the school curriculum sets expectations for student performance in terms of age, learning problems can occur when children are pushed into performing academic tasks before they are able to do so. In this way, the demands of schooling can cause failure by requiring students to perform beyond their readiness, or ability, at a given stage of maturation.

developmental variations
Differences in rate of development in different areas of learning within an individual.

Vygotsky (1978), the influential Russian developmental psychologist, recognized the importance of teaching at the appropriate difficulty level for the student. He reasoned that children can learn when instruction is directed toward what Vygotsky called their *zone of proximal development (ZPD)*, Vygotsky envisioned a range of difficulty levels of tasks for a student: (1) a level that is very easy for a student to do independently, (2) a middle level that a student can accomplish with assistance, and (3) a level that is much too difficult for successful student learning, or a frustration level. Vygotsky recommends that instruction should be geared to the middle level, which he called the ZPD (zone of proximate development). Some liken this to the "Goldilocks" level because it is neither too easy nor too hard; rather, it is just right. If a child's abilities do not mesh with the instructional level, learning cannot occur.

Many studies demonstrate that, often, young children manifest variations in development that lead to academic problems (Koppitz, 1973; Silver & Hagin, 1966, 1990; De Hirsch, Jansky, & Langford, 1966; Vellutino, Scanlon, & Lyon, 2000). Molfese and Molfese (2002) found developmental variations in learning in the areas of social executive functions, language, and reading skills. More information can be found at the website: *http://www.nichd.nih.gov*.

5.2b Piaget's Maturational Stages of Development

Jean Piaget, a Swiss psychologist, is recognized as a pioneer in developmental psychology and spent his life studying the intellectual development of children. Piaget's observations of the maturational stages of thinking in children showed that cognitive growth occurs in a series of invariant and interdependent stages. At each stage, the child is capable of learning only certain cognitive tasks. As the child goes through a series of maturational or developmental stages, the child's ability to think and learn changes with age. The quantity, quality, depth, and breadth of learning that occurs depend upon the stage during which the learning takes place (Piaget, 1970; Brainerd, 2003; Meece, 2002). Additional information about Piaget can be found at the website: *http://www.piaget.org*.

Piaget provided a schematic description of the typical child's stages of development:

Sensorimotor Stage: Birth to Age 2 The first two years of life are called the sensorimotor stage. During this stage, children learn through their senses and movements and by interacting with the physical environment. By moving, touching, hitting, biting, and so on, as well as by physically manipulating objects, children learn about the properties of space, time, location, permanence, and causality. Some children with learning disabilities need more opportunities for motor exploration. (Motor learning is discussed in Chapter 8, "Young Children With Disabilities.")

Preoperational Stage: Ages 2–7 Piaget called the next five years of life, ages 2 to 7, the preoperational stage. During this stage, children make intuitive judgments about relationships, and they also begin to think with symbols. Language now becomes increasingly important, and children learn to use symbols to represent the concrete world. They begin to learn about the

sensorimotor stage
One of Piaget's developmental stages of learning. During this stage, children learn through senses and movements and by interacting with the physical environment.

preoperational stage
One of Piaget's developmental stages of learning. During this stage, children make intuitive judgments about relationships and also begin to think with symbols.

properties and attributes of the world about them. Their thinking is dominated largely by the world of perception. (Perception is discussed in Chapter 8, "Young Children with Disabilities;" language is discussed in Chapter 11, "Spoken Language Difficulties: Listening and Speaking.")

One characteristic of the preoperational stage is that young children can attach only one attribute or function to an object. For example, 3-year-old Josephine was confused when her mother was the emergency substitute teacher in her nursery school class. Josephine was visibly baffled and upset as she exploded, "You can't be a teacher; you're a mother!"

Concrete Operations Stage: Ages 7–11 The period between ages 7 and 11 is called the concrete operations stage. Children are now able to think through relationships, to perceive consequences of acts, and to group entities in a logical fashion. They are better able to systematize and organize their thoughts. However, their thoughts are shaped in large measure by previous experiences, and they are linked to the concrete objects that they have manipulated or understood through the senses. For example, at this stage, a child can recognize a set of 4 objects without physically touching and counting them.

concrete operations stage
In Piaget's theory, the stage at which children can systematize and organize thoughts on the basis of past sensual experience.

Formal Operations Stage: Age 11 The fourth stage, the formal operations stage, commences at about age 11 and reflects a major transition in the thinking process. At this stage, instead of observations directing thought, thought now directs observations. Children now have the capacity to work with abstractions, theories, and logical relationships without having to refer to the concrete. The formal operations period provides a generalized orientation toward problem-solving activity.

formal operations stage
In Piaget's theory, the stage at which children can work with abstractions.

The transition from one level to the next depends on maturation, and the stages are sequential and hierarchical. An implication for teaching is that students need many opportunities and experiences to stabilize behavior and thought at each stage of development. Yet, the school curriculum frequently requires students to develop abstract and logical conceptualizations in a given area without providing sufficient opportunity for students to go through the preliminary levels of understanding. Attempts to teach abstract, logical concepts divorced from any real experiential understanding on the part of the students may lead to inadequate and insecure learning. The teacher may think students are learning the concepts, but they may be giving only surface verbal responses. Some examples of surface learning without understanding are given in Student Stories 5.1, "Developmental Theory and Maturation."

Mark Boulton/Alamy

The social environment significantly influences learning.

Illustrations of young children who have surface verbal skills without an in-depth understanding of concepts are frequently amusing.

- One kindergarten child explained with seemingly verbal proficiency the scientific technicalities of a spaceship being shot into orbit. His apparently precocious explanation ended with "and now for the blastoff . . . 10-3-8-5-6-11"

- The maturation of the cognitive ability to categorize objects was apparent when each of three children, ages 7, 9, and 11, was asked to pack clothes for a trip in two suitcases. Sue, the 11-year-old, was adult like in her thinking, packing day clothes in one suitcase and night clothes in another. Dean, the 7-year-old, had no organizational arrangement and randomly proceeded to stuff one suitcase with as much as it would hold and then to stuff the second with the remainder. Laura, the 9-year-old, made an organizational plan that called for clothes above the waist to go in one suitcase and clothes below the waist to go in the second. The top parts of pajamas and a two-piece bathing suit were placed in one suitcase and the bottoms in the other. Each child had categorized in a manner appropriate to the individual child's maturational stage.

- Children must understand early learning concepts before moving to more difficult abstract concepts and logical thinking in the primary grades. For example, one-to-one correspondence is an essential concept for learning mathematics—understanding that one object in a set is the same number as one object in a different set. In working with 6-year-old Jennine, the teacher placed 5 small buttons in a glass, one at a time, and then placed 5 large buttons in another glass, one at a time. Jennine said the glass with the large buttons contained more buttons. She had not grasped the concept of one-to-one-correspondence.

- Piaget used the following experiments to illustrate that children's concepts about *conservation* develop according to their maturational stage of thinking. In one of Piaget's conservation experiments, 2 balls of clay of equal size were placed on a scale to demonstrate to the child that they were equal. When one ball of clay was then flattened, 8-year-olds were likely to predict that they were still the same weight. Four-year-olds, however, said that the flattened ball weighed more. In another experiment, an equal amount of liquid was poured in each of 2 identical glasses. When the liquid from one glass was then emptied into a tall, thin container, 5-year-olds were convinced that the tall, thin glass contained more liquid, but 7-year-olds knew there was no difference in volume. From experiments such as these, Piaget concluded that the child's ability to understand the principles of conservation develops naturally through the maturational process.

REFLECTIVE QUESTION

1. How do these cases illustrate the importance of maturation in learning?

5.2c Stages of Learning

stages of learning
The stages a person goes through in mastering material, such as acquisition, proficiency, maintenance, and generalization.

Students need a period of time to fully *know* a concept that is being taught. In general, learners do not fully comprehend, or know, a concept the first time that they are exposed to the concept. Rather, they go through developmental stages of learning before they fully understand the concept. As indicated in Figure 5.1, the developmental stages of learning include (1) exposure, (2) grasping the knowledge, (3) independence, and (4) application. Teachers need to provide appropriate instruction to help students who encounter difficulty in learning to move from one learning stage to the next. These students need abundant support at each stage, and they may move from one stage to the next at a slower rate than other students. The types of practice that are most effective also vary with the stage of learning. In the early stages of acquisition, students need frequent feedback that elaborates and explains the intricacies of the new skill or information. In the later stages of learning, where students are building

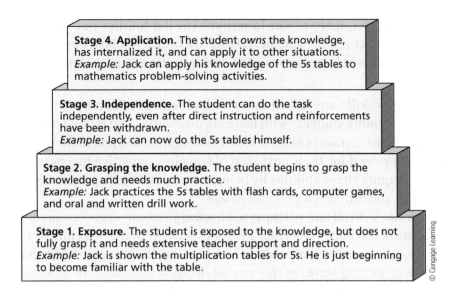

FIGURE **5.1**
Stages of Learning

Stage 4. Application. The student *owns* the knowledge, has internalized it, and can apply it to other situations. *Example:* Jack can apply his knowledge of the 5s tables to mathematics problem-solving activities.

Stage 3. Independence. The student can do the task independently, even after direct instruction and reinforcements have been withdrawn. *Example:* Jack can now do the 5s tables himself.

Stage 2. Grasping the knowledge. The student begins to grasp the knowledge and needs much practice. *Example:* Jack practices the 5s tables with flash cards, computer games, and oral and written drill work.

Stage 1. Exposure. The student is exposed to the knowledge, but does not fully grasp it and needs extensive teacher support and direction. *Example:* Jack is shown the multiplication tables for 5s. He is just beginning to become familiar with the table.

© Cengage Learning

facility with the new skill or consolidating the new knowledge, massed practice is the most effective. Students often need support to generalize or apply a new skill. Simple acquisition does not assure that a person can use the skills flexibly in a variety of contexts.

5.2d Implications of Developmental Psychology for Learning Disabilities and Related Disabilities

What are the implications of developmental psychology for students with learning disabilities and related disabilities? A major cause of these students' school difficulties is immaturity. All individuals have a natural development time for the maturation of various skills. What is sometimes thought to be a learning problem may be merely a lag in a student's maturation of a certain process.

1. Research shows that younger children in the early grades tend to have more learning problems than older children placed in those grades, which is a phenomenon called the *birth-date effect.* When each student's month of birth was compared with the percentage of children referred for learning disabilities services, the younger children (those born near the cutoff date for school entrance) were much more likely to be referred for learning disabilities services (Nichell, Pederson, & Rossow, 2003; Diamond, 1983; Di-Pasquale, Moule, & Flewelling, 1980).

2. The educational environment may actually hinder rather than assist the child's learning by making intellectual demands that require cognitive abilities that the child may not have yet developed. Cognitive abilities are qualitatively different in children from those of adults. Cognitive abilities develop sequentially; as children mature, their ways of thinking continually change. Schools must design learning experiences to enhance children's natural developmental growth.

3. The concept of *readiness* refers to the state of maturational development and prior experiences that are needed before a target skill can be learned. For example, readiness for walking requires a certain level of development of the neurological system, adequate muscle strength, and the development of

certain prerequisite motor functions. Until a toddler has these abilities, attempts to teach the skill of walking are futile. To illustrate readiness in a different area of learning, learning multiplication requires knowledge about addition.

Readiness skills are picked up in an incidental fashion by some learners. However, for young students with learning disabilities and related mild disabilities, explicit instruction is needed to help strengthen the precursor or readiness abilities they need for their next step of learning. Sensitive teachers can help students acquire these abilities by being aware of the young students' stage of maturation and any developmental delays.

Ironically, with all our attempts to be *scientific* about decisions made in education, one of the most important decisions—when to teach a child to read—is based on *astrology*. The star under which the child is born, or the birth date, is the key determining factor of this crucial decision because it determines when the child enters school and begins formal school learning.

We now turn to another major theory in psychology, behavioral psychology, and its implication for learning disabilities and related mild disabilities.

Did You Get It?

The Piagetan stage in which a child sheds his or her entirely concrete view of the world and begins to think in symbolic terms is referred to as the _____ stage of development.

   a. preoperational
   b. concrete operations
   c. sensorimotor
   d. formal operations

5.3 Behavioral Psychology

Behavioral psychology helps us understand how behavior is learned, and this branch of psychology significantly influences the way we teach. For over 60 years, since the seminal work of B. F. Skinner, who is considered to be the father of behavioral psychology, the concepts of behavioral psychology have flourished, creating major and productive applications for promoting learning. In special education, the individual education program (IEP) is an application of the behavioral approach. The IEP requires the use of observable and measurable behavior. In the IEP, the student's current levels of performance are measured and documented goals are determined, and plans for measuring the achievement of these goals and objectives are formulated. Behavioral theories thus provide a systematic foundation for research, assessment, and instruction (Tuckman & Monetti, 2013; Slavin, 2009). Behavioral theories of learning and instruction are based on the following concepts:

1. Human behavior is shaped by behavioral principles, such as positive reinforcement, and is a function of consequences.
2. Modifying behavior requires direct focus on the behavior of concern (for example, talking, reading, paying attention, subtraction).

3. The objective of the teaching should be clearly specified.
4. The target behavior is observable and measurable.
5. The effectiveness of the intervention requires frequent measurement.

In the following section, we discuss (1) the behavioral unit, (2) functional behavioral assessment and positive behavioral support, (3) direct instruction, (4) behavioral analysis, and (5) implications of behavioral psychology for learning disabilities and related mild disabilities.

5.3a The Behavioral Unit

Behavioral psychology is based on the behavioral unit, which has three key events called A, B, and C. The ABC model is illustrated in Figure 5.2. A is the antecedent event (or stimulus), B is the target behavior (or behavior response), and C is the consequent event (or reinforcement).

To illustrate the relationship among the three behavioral events, the teacher's goal, in this example, is to have Bonnie lengthen the time she engages in silent reading. The *antecedent event* (or stimulus) is the teacher's action, which is assigning a silent reading period. The *target behavior* (or behavior response) occurs when Bonnie reads for 2 min. The *consequent event* (or reinforcement) occurs when the teacher reinforces Bonnie's reading behavior by praising her or giving her a reward.

There are critics of reinforcement theory. In his popular book, *Punished by Rewards: The Trouble With Gold Stars, Incentive Plans, A's, Praise, and Other Bribes,* Alfie Kohn (1995) derides rewards as bribes that do not lead to long-term changes in behavior.

5.3b Functional Behavioral Assessment and Positive Behavioral Support

A feature of the Individuals with Disabilities Education Improvement Act of 2004 (IDEA-2004) is the requirement that the IEP for a student with a disability who has challenging behaviors must include a functional behavioral assessment and positive behavioral supports. Briefly, *functional behavioral assessment* is the evaluation of the child's behavior; *positive behavioral support* is the intervention to change that behavior (Lewis & Sugai, 1999; Polloway, Patton, & Serna, 2001; U.S. Department of Education, 2000a; Yell, Rozalski, & Drasgrow, 2001).

Functional Behavioral Assessment When a student displays a challenging behavior, it is serving a purpose or function for the student. In the three events of the behavioral unit (refer to Figure 5.2), this is the antecedent event that triggers the student's observable behavior. Through the functional behavioral assessment, the child's antecedent behavior is described and analyzed to discover what needs this challenging behavior is fulfilling for the student. For example,

behavioral unit
In behavioral psychology, the core unit that constitutes an action and its environment. It consists of the antecedent event, the target behavior, and the consequent event.

antecedent event
In behavioral psychology, the situation that precedes the target behavior.

target behavior
In the behavioral unit, A-B-C, the target behavior is "B," the actual behavior of the student.

consequent event
In behavioral psychology, the reinforcement that follows the behavior.

| A
Antecedent
Event
Stimulus | → | B
Target
Behavior
Response | → | C
Consequent
Event
Reinforcement |

© Cengage Learning

FIGURE **5.2**
Components of the Behavioral Unit

Joshua makes jokes and loud noises whenever he is asked to read aloud. His functional behavioral assessment reveals that Joshua acts this way to avoid reading aloud because his poor reading ability embarrasses him.

Positive Behavioral Support Once the teacher understands the reason for the student's antecedent behavior, the teacher looks for a substitute activity for reading aloud—a positive behavioral support. For example, the teacher could privately inform Joshua ahead of time about the passage that he will be asked to read, and then have him practice reading the passage with a peer. A functional behavioral support would prepare Joshua for being called upon to read aloud. This support would eliminate the need for Joshua's interruptive behavior.

Detailed information about functional behavioral assessment and positive behavioral supports is presented in Chapter 6, "Social, Emotional, and Behavioral Challenges."

5.3c Direct Instruction

direct instruction
A method associated with behavioral theories of instruction. The focus is directly on the curriculum or task to be taught and the steps needed to learn that task.

Direct instruction is an instructional practice stemming from behavioral theory. The approach called *Direct Instruction* was a teaching program initially developed for disadvantaged students and has been used in the Reading Mastery Series (Englemann & Bruner, 1974). The Direct Instruction program has been shown to be effective with children who are considered at risk because of poverty (Carnine et al., 2004). Critical features of the Direct Instruction include lessons based on carefully sequenced skills, much repetition and practice, and fully scripted lessons. The web address for the Direct Instruction programs is *http://www.sra-4kids.com.*

The concepts of direct instruction have come to be used as a more general term to refer to the structured teaching of academic skills. (Note that the general term of direct instruction is not capitalized.) Direct instruction systematically centers on the task to be learned. By focusing on the academic skills that the student needs to learn, direct instruction structures the environment to ensure that the student learns these skills (Algozzine, 1991). Direct instruction has these qualities (Carnine et al., 2004; Algozzine, 1991; Rosenshine, 1986; Rosenshine & Stevens, 1997):

- Teaches academic skills directly
- Is teacher directed and controlled
- Uses carefully sequenced and structured materials
- Provides student mastery of basic skills
- Sets goals that are clear to students
- Allocates sufficient time for instruction
- Uses continuous monitoring of student performance
- Provides immediate feedback to students
- Teaches a skill until mastery of that skill is achieved

explicit teaching
The process by which the teacher specifies the skill to be taught and explicitly teaches the necessary skills.

Explicit teaching is similar to direct instruction and is also based on a behavioral orientation. In explicit teaching, teachers are clear about the specific skills to be taught and they precisely teach each step or skill rather than leave it up to the student to make inferences from the student's own experiences in order to learn (Gersten, 1998).

5.3d Behavioral Analysis

Behavioral analysis is another application of behavioral psychology to teaching. Behavioral analysis requires that teachers analyze a specific task that students are to learn to determine the subskills needed to accomplish that task. These subskills are then placed in an ordered and logical sequence. Teaching involves helping the students accomplish the specific task by learning each skill they have not yet mastered. Students are taught each of the subskills that they do not know. By learning all of the subskills, the students accomplish the desired complex behavior.

For example, the steps involved in teaching a child to swim illustrate the behavioral analysis approach. First, analyze the steps involved in swimming (e.g., floating, treading water, holding one's breath under water, and kicking). Next, teach the child each skill in its sequence, help the child combine the skills, and finally, observe the child swimming across the pool. Although this example does not demonstrate an academic task, the same behavioral procedures would apply to teaching reading, mathematics, or writing. Teaching Tips 5.1 describes the steps that are involved in behavioral analysis. For more information on managing student behavior, visit the website "Dr. Mac's Behavior management Site" at *http://www.behavioradvisor.com*.

behavioral analysis
The process of determining the subskills or steps needed to accomplish a task.

5.3e Implications of Behavioral Psychology for Learning Disabilities and Related Disabilities

Behavioral theories have far-reaching implications for teaching students with learning disabilities and related mild disabilities:

1. Direct instruction and explicit teaching are effective methodologies. It is important for students to receive direct instruction in academic tasks. Teachers should understand how to analyze the components of a curriculum and how to structure sequential behaviors.
2. Direct instruction can be combined with many other approaches to teaching. When the teacher is sensitive to a student's unique style of learning and particular learning difficulties, direct instruction can be even more effective. For example, for the student who lacks phonological awareness the sensitive teacher can anticipate difficulties in learning phonics during a direct instruction lesson. To learn the skill, this student will need more time, practice, review, and alternative presentations of the concepts. The sensitive clinical teacher will use knowledge of the curriculum and of the individual student in planning instruction.
3. Functional behavioral assessment and positive behavioral support can help a student with behavioral challenges. These methods provide a valuable means to understand undesirable behavior and a way to meet a student's needs.

Including Students in General Education 5.1, "Behavioral Strategies," offers strategies based on behavioral psychology for the general education classroom.

TEACHING TIPS 5.1
Steps In Behavioral Analysis

1. State the objective to be achieved or the task to be learned in terms of student performance
2. Analyze the subskills needed to perform that task
3. List the subskills to be learned in their sequential order
4. Determine which of these subskills the student does not know
5. Teach one subskill at a time; when one subskill has been learned, teach the next subskill
6. Evaluate the effectiveness of the instruction in terms of whether the student has achieved the objective or learned the task

Professional Resource Download

Including Students in GENERAL EDUCATION 5.1

Behavioral Strategies

Methods for using behavioral strategies in the general education classroom:

Set goals and objectives

- Structure learning tasks as clear academic goals
- Use task analysis to break goals into manageable steps

Provide rapidly paced lessons and carefully sequenced materials

- Sequence and structure materials and lessons to help students master one step at a time
- Use a fast pace so that learning becomes automatic through overlearning

Offer a detailed explanation and many examples

- Make sure the student understands the task
- Provide detailed and redundant instructions and explanations

- Use many examples
- Ask many questions

Provide many opportunities to practice the new skill

- Offer many practice activities
- Help students develop automaticity so that they can do the activity with ease

Give students feedback and correction

- Help students learn new material through teacher feedback
- Give immediate, academically focused feedback and correction

Monitor student progress

- Actively monitor student progress to check on learning
- Make adjustments in teaching as necessary

Professional Resource Download

Did You Get It?

A fundamental principle of behavioral theory is that any target behavior—that which we focus on and attempt to modify under certain conditions—must be both observable and

a. changeable.
b. objective.
c. measurable.
d. detrimental.

5.4 Cognitive Psychology

We now discuss the third major theory of psychology, cognitive psychology, and review its implications for learning. The field of cognitive psychology studies the human processes of learning, thinking, and knowing. Cognitive abilities are clusters of mental skills that are essential to human functions. They enable one to know, be aware, think, conceptualize, use abstractions, reason, criticize, and be creative. Theories about the nature of cognitive and mental processes lead to a better understanding of how human beings learn and how the cognitive characteristics affect learning. Cognitive theory also offers a guide for teaching students with learning disabilities and related mild disabilities.

Concepts in cognitive psychology have been broadly elaborated over the years, and changes in the field of learning disabilities reflect these elaborations. We explore a progression of ideas from cognitive psychology that have influenced the teaching of students with learning disabilities and related mild disabilities: (1) cognitive processing refers to the mental activities that an

cognitive abilities
Clusters of human abilities that enable one to know, be aware, think, conceptualize, reason, criticize, and use abstractions.

cognitive processing
The mental processes involved in thinking and learning, such as perception, memory, language, attention, concept formation, and problem solving.

140   CHAPTER 5 Theories of Learning

individual uses in learning; (2) the *information-processing model* is a model of learning that emphasizes the flow of information within a person's mind and the memory systems; (3) *cognitive learning theories* offer a contemporary view of how people learn, think, and acquire knowledge; and (4) automaticity, in cognitive learning theory, the condition in which learning has become almost subconscious and therefore requires little processing effort.

automaticity
In cognitive learning theory, the condition in which learning has become almost subconscious and therefore requires little processing effort.

5.4a Cognitive Processing

As noted earlier, a critical element of the federal definition of learning disabilities in the Individuals with Disabilities Education Improvement Act of 2004 (IDEA-2004) is that students with learning disabilities have disorders in one or more of the *basic psychological processes* that are needed for school learning. The term *psychological processing disorders* refers to the difficulties that students with learning disabilities encounter in cognitive processing. Many students with learning disabilities and related mild disabilities have difficulties in underlying cognitive processes including such areas as visual perception, auditory perception, and tactile-kinesthetic perception, in language skills, and in memory functions. These students need special teaching or differentiated instruction to meet the challenges of differences in cognitive processing.

psychological processing disorders
A phrase in the federal definition of learning disabilities that refers to disabilities in visual or auditory perception, memory, or language.

The term *psychological processing disorders* has been used to describe students with learning disabilities since the first special education law in 1975 (P.L. 94-142). For educators, psychologists, parents, and other professionals, the fresh notion of psychological processing disorders offered a refreshing and hopeful new way to view students who were failing to learn, as well as suggesting new ways to teach these students. For parents, it offered an encouraging and logical means for understanding a child's difficulty in learning, without blaming the child for not trying, the teachers for not teaching, or parents for poor parenting (Smith, 2001; Vail, 1992; Vaughn, Gersten, & Chard, 2000).

Teachers can determine a student's cognitive processing strengths and weaknesses through observations, samples of their work, or tests. Knowledge about the student's cognitive processing strengths and weaknesses can help teachers plan appropriate instruction for that student. For example, students who have difficulty in auditory processing often have difficulty with instructional approaches that are primarily auditory, such as phonics. Student with difficulty in visual processing might experience obstacles in learning by methods that are primarily visual. An example of a school curriculum that considers a student's cognitive processes is given in Student Stories 5.2, "A School That Considers Cognitive Processes."

TeachSource Video Case Activity

© Cengage Learning 2015

Watch the TeachSource Video Case entitled "Using Information Processing Strategies: A Middle School Science Lesson." In this video, a middle school science teacher uses information-processing strategies in teaching a chemistry lesson. She uses various ways to present the information: visual, writing, auditory, reading. She says she tries to cover the various "habits of mind" that students have.

QUESTIONS

1. How can a teacher use information-processing strategies to teach a lesson?

2. Based upon what you read in the chapter, do you find the science lesson profiled within this video case to be an effective way to teach science? Why or why not?

3. Give some specific examples of its effectiveness, or questions you might have about the information-processing lesson.

An example of a school curriculum that makes good use of information about the student's cognitive processes is the Lab School of Washington, DC, which is a school for students with learning disabilities (Smith, 2005). Sally Smith, the founder and director of the Lab School, recognized that many of the children attending the school displayed much difficulty with auditory and linguistic learning, yet they excelled in the visual arts. Therefore, she used the arts and experiential, hands-on learning to teach these students. Instead of learning through typically structured, text-based lessons in social studies and history, these children are taught through academic clubs for grades one through six.

These clubs include the Cave Club, the God's Club, the Knights and Ladies Club, the Renaissance Club, the Museum Club, and the Industrialists Club. The children participate in a single club for an entire year during one-half of the school day. The clubs teach content, vocabulary, history, and geography through the visual arts. For example, in the Renaissance Club, the children build scaffolding and actually paint a replica of the ceiling of the Sistine Chapel.

REFLECTIVE QUESTION

1. What is the role of the visual arts in this curriculum?

5.4b The Information-Processing Model of Learning

information-processing model
A systems approach to cognitive processing. The information processing model emphasizes the flow of information, the memory system, and the interrelationships among the elements of cognitive processes.

The information-processing model of learning traces the flow of information during the learning process, from the initial reception of information, through a processing function, and then to an action. There are *inputs,* such as auditory stimuli; *processing functions,* which are cognitive processes such as associations, thinking, memory, and decision making; and *outputs,* which are actions and behaviors. Using the analogy of a computer, the human brain takes in the information (input), stores and locates the information (memory systems), organizes the information and facilitates operations and decisions (central processing system—executive functions), and generates responses to the information (output). Research in the neurosciences on the brain and learning are supportive of the information-processing model (Pugh et al., 2005; Sousa, 2001; Shaywitz et al., 2004).

Figure 5.3 is a pictorial diagram of the information-processing system. The information-processing model provides a useful way to conceptualize the processes of learning by depicting the components of input, output, memory, and an executive control function (Greeno, Collins, & Resnick, 1996; Lyon & Krasnegor, 1996; Swanson, 1996). To illustrate this flow of information, a student is shown a word (input stimulus). The student searches his or her memory to recognize the word and to determine its sound and its meaning (processing and executive function), and, finally, the student says the word (output performance). If the memory of the word has decayed or is lost, the student will be unable to recognize or say the word.

multistore memory system
The central idea in the information-processing model of learning. Information is seen as flowing among three types of memory: the sensory register, short-term memory, and long-term memory.

Central to the information-processing model is the multistore memory system. The multistore memory system conceptualizes a flow of information among three types of memory: (1) sensory register, (2) short-term memory (and working memory), and (3) long-term memory (Swanson & O'Conner, 2009; Atkinson & Shiffrin, 1968; Broadbent, 1958). For more information about information processing, visit *http://www.intime.uni.edu/model/information/proc.html.* The three memory types are shown in Figure 5.3 within the dotted frame.

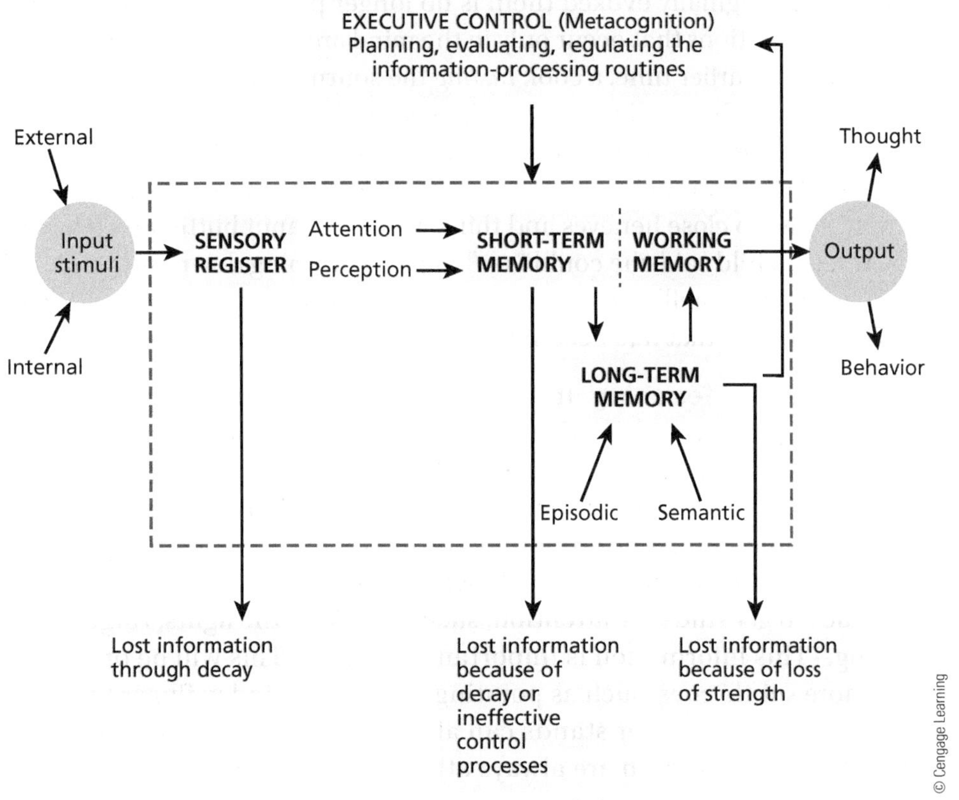

FIGURE **5.3**
An Informational Processing
Model of Learning

FIGURE **5.3** An Informational Processing Model of Learning

The components and the flows of information of the information-processing model of learning are discussed next.

Sensory Register Information is first received through the senses—vision, hearing, touch, smell, and taste. Stimuli can be from internal sources or from external sources. Most of the stimuli that bombard one's input receptors are unimportant, are not attended to, and do not reach the sensory register. However, once the mind attends to selected input stimuli, that information flows into the first memory system, the sensory register. The sensory register system serves as an input buffer, which helps to interpret and maintain the information from the input receptor long enough for it to be perceived and analyzed. Perception is important at this stage because it gives meaning to the stimuli. Perception depends upon the individual's past experiences and ability to organize and attach meaning to the stimulus event. To illustrate how past experiences shape perception, a 3-year-old child was asked to identify a square shape printed on a page. His personal and unique perception of the shape was clear when he responded, "That's a TV."

Along with perception, attention is critical at this stage. Subconscious decisions about what stimuli should receive attention are constantly being made. Attention and associated disorders are covered in more depth in Chapter 8, "Young Children With Disabilities," and in Chapter 7, "Autism Spectrum Disorders and Attention Deficit Hyperactivity Disorder (ADHD)."

Sensation, attention, and perception take place when the stimulus is present; they are ongoing activities. Memory pertains to sensations and data *already* received and perceived. Memory (imagery or "the mind's eye") is our ability to store and retrieve previously experienced sensations and perceptions when the

sensory register
The first memory system in the information-processing model that interprets and maintains memory information long enough for it to be perceived and analyzed.

perception
The process of recognizing and interpreting information received through the senses.

stimulus that originally evoked them is no longer present. Examples of sensations and perceptions that occur only in the mind are a musician *listening* to music played at an earlier time, a cook *tasting* the sourness of a lemon to be used, a carpenter *feeling* the roughness of sandpaper used yesterday in a job, and a gardener *smelling* the sweetness of lilacs while looking only at the buds on the tree. A 3-year-old child was helped to understand the nature of memory. Her mother asked the child to close her eyes and think about a peanut butter and jelly sandwich. Yes, the child said she could "see" the jelly dripping down the sides of the bread, she could "smell" the peanut butter, and she could even "taste" the first bite. The sandwich that had become so vivid existed in her memory.

Implications for Teaching Information-processing theory suggests that a copy of an experience is stored very briefly, perhaps for a few seconds, in the sensory register. Unless there is an effort to pay attention to it, the information is immediately lost from the sensory register. The significance for teaching is that the student must be attending; the lesson must be planned to initially spark the attention of the student. Teachers use a number of verbal and nonverbal cues to get students' attention, such as flicking the lights, ringing a bell, or saying, "This information is important," or even, "This will be on the test." Other more subtle cues, such as pointing, placing the index finger to the lips, or even where the teacher stands can also be used to direct or redirect students' attention. Children are always attending to something. The teacher's challenge is to focus the attention on the material being taught.

short-term memory

A second memory storage within the information-processing model. It is a temporary storage facility used for working memory as a problem receives one's conscious attention.

Short-Term Memory (STM) Short-term memory is also a temporary storage facility. With the first system, the sensory register, the individual is not consciously aware of information. In short-term memory, however, the individual becomes very consciously aware of information, but short-term memory is considered a relatively passive temporary system. When a person thinks of a new problem, the new information replaces the old information in short-term memory. The old information either decays and is lost or is placed into long-term storage (Swanson & O'Connor, 2009; Swanson, Zheng, & Jerman, 2009; Swanson, 1996). Short-term memory is similar to the material you work with on the computer screen. To return to the computer analogy, the information is temporary, and it will be lost when the power is turned off unless the information has been saved.

working memory

An active system of remembering what has been learned to apply that memory to a complex cognitive task. While information is in working memory it demands attention to complete the current task at hand.

Working Memory (WM) Working memory is also a temporary memory system, but it is differentiated from short-term memory in that working memory is an active system and is used in complex cognitive tasks. The individual actively uses information and transforms it into a cognitive or thinking activity. It is in working memory that the individual not only receives the current pertinent information through the person's conscious attention, but the person can act on it, solve a problem, or develop a cognitive plan. It is in working memory that a person can build, take apart, or rework ideas for eventual storage in long-term memory. When something is in working memory, it generally captures our focus and demands our attention (Swanson & O'Conner, 2009; Hambrick & Engle, 2003; Hutton & Towse, 2001; Sousa, 2001).

Implications for Teaching In terms of teaching, we should recognize that information remains in short-term memory for a short period of time. Unless it is acted on in some way, information in short-term memory will be lost. Working memory is also a temporary memory system, but it is more active than short-term memory. A common characteristic of students with disabilities is they have difficulty remembering verbal information (Mastropieri & Scruggs, 2010). Students can extend the time that information stays in short-term memory by actively thinking about it in working memory, which can help to move it to long-term memory. Teaching Tips 5.2, "Strategies for Improving Memory," offers some strategies for improving memory.

Long-Term Memory and Retrieval Long-term memory is the permanent memory storage. To learn and retain information for long periods of time, information must be transferred from short-term and working memory to long-term memory. It is thought that information placed into long-term memory remains there permanently. It is evident from neurological research and clinical experiences that memories remain in long-term storage for a very long time (Semb & Ellis, 1994). The problem people face in long-term memory is not storage, but retrieval; that is, how to recall (or remember) information stored in long-term memory. As was shown in Figure 5.3, information from short-term memory is lost unless it is saved in long-term memory. Before one can think about a problem, the stored information must be retrieved from long-term memory and placed into short-term or working memory (or consciousness). Using the computer analogy again, when one wishes to work on a saved file, the saved file must be loaded into the desktop (short-term or working memory).

Two types of long-term memory are *episodic* and *semantic*. Episodic memories are images—visual and other sensory images of events in one's life. The episodic memory of one's first carnival, for example, might be triggered by the sound of a merry-go-round. Semantic memories consist of the storage of general knowledge, language, concepts, and generalizations. The retrieval of odd bits of long-term memory is sometimes triggered by strange events. One such event occurred at a recent national education conference when a participant noted a vaguely familiar woman in the lobby. After observing her for several minutes, he walked up to her and blurted out "Hilltop 5-4260." Indeed, that had been her telephone number some 25 years earlier. Although the conference participant recalled the telephone number, he could not remember her name.

Implications for Teaching The way information is stored in long-term memory helps with the process of retrieval. Through instruction in learning strategies, teachers can help students with the retrieval process (Mastropieri & Scruggs, 2010). Chapter 9, "Adolescents and Adults with Learning Disabilities and Related Mild Disabilities," discusses learning strategies and Chapter 12, "Reading Difficulties," discusses some of the strategies used in reading to improve vocabulary or semantic

long-term memory
Permanent memory storage that retains information for an extended period of time.

retrieval
Recalling information from long-term memory.

TEACHING TIPS 5.2
Strategies for Improving Memory

- **Rehearsal or repeating the information.** Rehearsal slows the forgetting process and helps in transferring the information to long-term memory. For example, when you look up a telephone number, repeating the number may help you to remember it long enough to dial it.

- **"Chunking" or grouping the information.** It is easier to remember *grouped* information than isolated bits of information. For example, a social security number can be grouped into three chunks: a chunk of three numbers, a chunk of two numbers, and a group of four numbers, as in 123-44-1830.

- **Organizing the information.** The organization of information makes the information less complicated and relates the parts to one another. For example, food can be organized in four basic food groups—dairy, grains, fruits and vegetables, and meats.

- **Key words.** This is a mnemonic technique in which a word is linked to another word that is familiar (Mastropieri & Scruggs, 1998). The linkage is that part of the word (e.g., the initial sound or rhyming element) that is similar to the key word. The key-word method is useful when pairs of items, such as foreign language words, technical words, or names, have to be learned. For example, when you are introduced to someone, you will more easily recall the person's name if you link the name with a characteristic, such as "tall Tony" or "blue-eyed Bonnie."

Professional Resource Download

memory. The following strategies help with the storage and retrieval of information in long-term memory:

1. Organizing schemes. Many of the recommended study techniques are methods of organizing information to make it easier to recall from long-term memory. For example, in studying a country in social studies, use a word web to link key information about the country, such as the weather, crops, rivers, and so on.

2. Using prior knowledge. New information that is linked to something the student already knows is much easier to retrieve. To know something is not only to have received information, but also to have interpreted the information and related it to other knowledge. Teachers must recognize that learning depends on what the student already knows, and that the student must build links between old and new knowledge. For example, Abe already knows quite a lot about dinosaurs. A new type of dinosaur has just been discovered, so Abe links this new dinosaur information with the old information that he already knows.

3. Making the information meaningful. Students can strengthen their long-term memory if they make the information meaningful by linking it to something they already know. Learning depends on what one already knows (or prior knowledge). Teachers can help students by providing background knowledge and linkages to what is already in the long-term memory. For example, Betty has come across the concept of the Electoral College in the news. That term becomes more meaningful when she links it with information she already knows about elections. Betty has developed a spreadsheet of Electoral College votes for each state and the total number of electoral votes for each presidential candidate. She can illustrate this spreadsheet with a bar graph.

executive control
A component in the information-processing model that refers to the ability to control and direct one's own learning. It is also referred to as *metacognition*.

Executive Control Executive control is the component of the information-processing model that refers to the ability to control and direct one's own learning, thinking, and mental activity. The term *metacognition* is often used in conjunction with executive control. Metacognition is discussed in more detail later in this chapter. Executive control (1) directs the flow of thinking, (2) manages the cognitive processes during learning, and (3) keeps track of what information is being processed. It involves the planning, evaluating, and regulating of the information-processing routines. Executive control determines which mental activities occur and which processing components receive system attention resources, or one's concentration. One's motivation and goals are important factors in directing the priorities and the problems that will receive attention (Lavoie, 2007; Lyon & Krasnegor, 1996; Swanson, 1996).

Executive control is similar to the operating system of a computer. The operating system intervenes and controls the allocation and interface between the program and the resources of the system. It keeps track of what each program is doing and when the program needs to use some system resources, such as a disk drive or print instructions.

Implications for Teaching It is not enough to memorize information; students must also have the executive control to decide to use the information. Research shows that students must learn to activate and select the strategies to use the information they have (Deshler, Schumaker, Lenz, & Bulgren, 2001; Deshler et al., 1996; Lenz, Ellis, & Scanlon, 1996). Learning strategies instruction for controlling one's thinking are discussed in greater detail in Chapter 9, "Adolescents and Adults With Learning Disabilities and Related Disabilities."

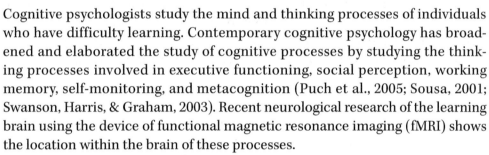

Did You Get It?

In an instructional situation, and against the backdrop of information-processing theory, a teacher must be cognizant of the fact that unless _____ is provided to a particular stimulus, experience, principle, or fact, it is at risk of being lost from availability and can become irretrievable.

a. memorization
b. consciousness
c. attention
d. reward

5.5 Cognitive Learning Theories

Cognitive psychologists study the mind and thinking processes of individuals who have difficulty learning. Contemporary cognitive psychology has broadened and elaborated the study of cognitive processes by studying the thinking processes involved in executive functioning, social perception, working memory, self-monitoring, and metacognition (Puch et al., 2005; Sousa, 2001; Swanson, Harris, & Graham, 2003). Recent neurological research of the learning brain using the device of functional magnetic resonance imaging (fMRI) shows the location within the brain of these processes.

To succeed in the general education classroom, students must learn complex concepts, have good problem-solving skills, and know how to organize information on their own. They often have limited background knowledge for many academic activities and need sufficient feedback and practice to retain abstract information (Swanson, Harris, & Graham, 2003; Gersten, 1998; Vaughn et al., 2000).

A number of instructional strategies stem from cognitive theories of learning, which help students with learning disabilities grasp the concepts and subject matter of the general education curriculum. Some of the effective and validated instructional approaches are discussed in Chapter 3, such as scaffolded instruction, learning strategies instruction, and peer tutoring. In this section, we will discuss several additional effective cognitive learning strategies: (1) apprenticeships, (2) graphic organizers, (3) concept maps, and (4) mind mapping.

5.5a Cognitive Learning Strategies

Apprenticeships Apprenticeships refer to the kind of teaching that occurs in a setting in which a knowledgeable adult and a learner work jointly on a real-life problem. Learning in such a setting is geared to solving a genuine problem rather than just reading about the problem. Apprenticeships are motivating for learners, and apprentices increase generalization because student apprentices learn through experience how the knowledge they have acquired applies to the real world (Gersten, 1998). In some European countries, apprenticeships become an alternative to postsecondary education. For example, a young adult might work with a carpenter as an apprentice to learn the skills of carpentering.

Graphic Organizers Graphic organizers are visual representations of concepts, knowledge, or information that incorporate both text and pictures. They make it easier for a person to understand the information by allowing the mind to see complex relationships. Research shows that graphic organizers have proven to be very useful for students with learning disabilities (Baxendell, 2003; Sabbatino, 2004). Graphic organizers commonly used include

graphic organizers
Visual representations of concepts, knowledge, or information that incorporates both text and pictures to make the material easier to understand.

- Venn diagrams
- Hierarchical (top-down) organizers
- Word webs
- Concept maps
- Mind mapping

In the following sections, we discuss concept maps and mind mapping, which also are effective cognitive learning strategies.

Concept Map With a concept map, a student or a teacher can cluster ideas and words that go together. The activity serves to activate the student's construction of a concept. Figure 5.4 shows part of a concept map that a 13-year-old student created on the topic of team sports to prepare for a writing project. For more information on concept maps, see *http://www.thinkingmaps.com.*

mind mapping
A technique that employs a pictorial method to transfer ideas from a student's mind onto a piece of paper.

Mind Mapping Mind mapping is a technique that employs a pictorial method to transfer ideas from a student or from a group of students onto a large piece of paper, a transparency, or a large class chart. Ideas are produced randomly, and certain words or ideas will trigger other ideas, which will lead to other suggestions or pictures. It is much easier to mind map than to create an outline because the ideas do not have to be organized or sequenced. Figure 5.5 shows a mind map that a group of students constructed on the topic of homework.

FIGURE **5.4**
Concept Map of Team Sports

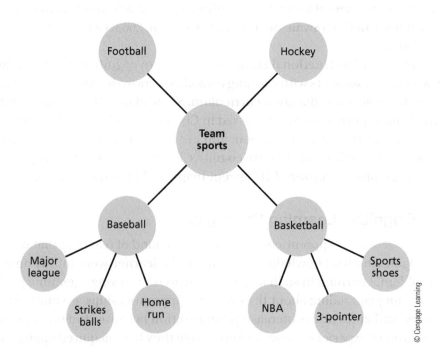

© Cengage Learning

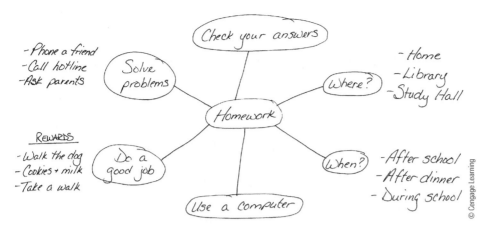

FIGURE **5.5**
Mind Mapping on Homework

5.5b **Metacognition**

Metacognition refers to the awareness of one's systematic thinking about learning. It is the ability to facilitate learning by taking control and directing one's own thinking processes. People exhibit metacognitive awareness when they do something to help themselves learn and remember, such as compiling shopping lists to remember what to buy, outlining difficult technical chapters to help themselves understand and recall the material, or rehearsing and repeating what they have just learned to help stabilize and strengthen their learning. These behaviors indicate an awareness of one's own limitations and the ability to plan for one's own learning and problem solving (Swanson, 1996). Student Stories 5.3, "Metacognitive Shopping Behavior," offers other examples of metacognition.

Efficient learners use metacognitive strategies, but students with learning disabilities and related disabilities tend to lack the skills to direct their own learning. However, once they learn the metacognitive strategies that efficient learners use, students can apply them in many situations. The metacognitive strategies needed for school learning include (1) classification, (2) checking, (3) evaluation, and (4) prediction (Creel, Fore, Boon, & Bender, 2006; Gersten, 1998; Kluwe, 1987).

Classification Classification is a technique for determining the type, status, or mode of a learning activity. Individuals ask themselves "What am I doing here?" or "Is this activity important to me?" For example, Jose, while comparing words in Spanish with words in English, says to himself, "Knowing this will help me learn English."

Checking Checking involves taking steps during the process of problem solving to determine one's progress, success, and results. For example, a person may say, "I remember most of the lesson," "My planning is pretty detailed and careful," "I still have a long way to go before I get there," or "There is something I do not understand here."

Evaluation Evaluation goes beyond checking and provides information about quality. For example, an individual may think, "My plan is not good enough to rule out any risks" or "I have done a good job."

Prediction Prediction provides information about the possible alternative options for problem solving and possible outcomes. The person may think,

metacognition
The ability to facilitate learning by taking control and directing one's own thinking process.

A common example of metacognitive behavior that is familiar to most people is the activity of planning for grocery shopping. Most people must engage in this activity, and they have developed plans that work for them. The following grocery-shopping plans are metacognitive behaviors that are based on prior knowledge and experience. They include ways to enhance memory (e.g., through writing, visualization, or review) and to organize and prepare for future activities (e.g., making meals, eating, and entertaining). When groups of people were asked how they plan for their grocery shopping, their answers differed widely, revealing a correspondingly wide range of metacognitive styles. Some of their answers follow.

- I keep a pad of paper in a convenient spot; as I discover needs during the week, I jot them down on the notepad. I take this list with me to the store, and it becomes my guide for shopping.

- I think about what I need, and I write a list just before going shopping. I take this list with me and then check each item on the list as I take it off the grocery shelf.

- I open my kitchen cabinets just before going shopping, and the visualization of missing items gives me enough information to complete my grocery shopping.

- I walk up and down the aisles, and items that I need just pop up.

- I buy only items that are on sale, and I stock up on these items.

- I carefully plan my shopping to use the coupons I have acquired.

- I go to the store and just buy food that looks as though it would be good to eat. When I get home, I usually find that I forgot to buy the necessary items, so I have to go back to the store again. I guess I do not plan well for shopping.

- To avoid impulsive buying, I always eat something before I go shopping.

- I plan on how much money I will spend, use a calculator, and stop when that amount is reached.

REFLECTIVE QUESTION

1. What are your metacognitive shopping behaviors?

"If I decide to work on this problem, the technical details will be hard to accomplish. I will have to get someone to help me with them" or "I should be able to finish the paper in four days."

5.5c Implications of Cognitive Psychology for Teaching

Cognitive psychology analyzes how people learn and, therefore, it offers strategies for teaching. Teaching strategies based on cognitive psychology can help students learn to attend, to remember, to understand, to think, and to enjoy learning.

Did You Get It?

Ms. Arturo-Fernandez, science teacher and knowledgeable botanist, works side by side with one of her students, Matt, on a long-term project: devising an irrigation system to water plants in the school garden. This relationship represents a(n)
  a. apprenticeship.
  b. concept-map.
  c. tutelage.
  d. formal educational collaboration.

5.6 Learning Strategies Instruction

In this section, we discuss some instructional applications of cognitive theories: (1) learning strategies, (2) the social interactions of learning, and (3) interactive dialogues. We also review the implications of learning strategies instruction for students with learning disabilities and related mild disabilities.

5.6a Learning Strategies

The learning strategies approach to instruction is a series of methods that focuses on *how* students learn rather than on *what* they learn. Efficient learners can count on a number of learning strategies to help them learn and remember. Students with learning disabilities and related mild disabilities lack such a repertoire of learning strategies. When teachers help students acquire learning strategies, students *learn how to learn.* What strategies are employed by people who learn in an efficient and well-functioning manner? Successful learners control and direct their thinking processes to facilitate learning. They are active learners. They ask themselves questions, and they organize their thoughts. They connect and integrate the new materials that they are trying to learn with prior experience and with knowledge that they already possess. They also try to predict what will come next, and they try to monitor the relevance of the new information. In other words, good learners have discovered how to go about the business of learning, and they have at their disposal a repertoire of cognitive strategies that work for them (Deshler et al., 2001; Swanson & Deshler, 2003; Lenz & Deshler, 2001; Deshler et al., 1996; Lenz et al., 1996).

Students who do not possess these functional learning strategies become passive learners. They do not know how to control and direct their thinking in order to learn, how to gain more knowledge, or how to remember what they have learned. They may lack interest in learning because past learning experiences were dismal exercises in failure and frustration. Not believing that they can learn, these students do not know how to go about the task of learning. As a consequence, they become passive and dependent learners, exhibiting a style that is called learned helplessness.

Students must first become aware of and acquire learning strategies to facilitate their learning and remembering. Fortunately, research shows that once they have received learning strategies instruction, they become privy to the best-kept secrets about how to achieve academic success, and they consequently use these strategies in many contexts (Deshler, 2003; Lenz & Deshler, 2001; Gersten, 1998; Mainzer et al., 2003).

The strategies intervention model (SIM) is an instructional method for teaching learning strategies to adolescents (Deshler, 2003; Lenz & Deshler, 2001; Deshler et al., 1996). The SIM learning strategies were developed over many years at the University of Kansas Center for Research on Learning (Deshler et al.,2001; Lenz & Deshler, 2001; Swanson & Deshler, 2003; Deshler et al., 1996; Lenz et al., 1996). (See Chapter 9, "Adolescents and Adults With Learning Disabilities and Related Disabilities," for a more complete discussion of the strategies intervention model.)

Learning strategies can be used in every area of the curriculum—in the teaching of reading, writing, mathematics, social studies, and science. In addition, learning strategies for specific academic areas are woven throughout various parts of this textbook.

learning strategies approach
A series of methods to help students direct their own learning, focusing on how students learn rather than on what they learn.

active learners
Students who are involved with their learning and contribute to the learning process.

passive learners
Adolescents with learning disabilities who tend to wait for teacher direction instead of being actively involved in the learning situation.

learned helplessness
A trait of students with learning disabilities in which they exhibit passiveness and do not take on the responsibility for their own learning.

strategies intervention model (SIM)
An instructional method for teaching learning strategies to adolescents with learning disabilities.

5.6b The Social Interactions of Learning

The social environment significantly influences learning. The learning process is more than an individualistic, student-centered activity. The social interactions between the teacher and the student, as well as social interactions among students, are critical ingredients in the learning process. Theories that emphasize the social context of learning include Vygotsky's (1978) social influences of learning and interactive dialogues. These theories are reviewed in this section. (See also Chapter 6, "Social, Emotional, and Behavioral Challenges," for more information on social interactions.)

Vygotsky: The Social Influences of Learning The social nature of cognitive development and the role that interpersonal relationships plays in this development were observed more than 70 years ago by Lev Vygotsky, a Russian psychologist. Vygotsky (1978) observed that social influences are crucial in the learning processes. Learning is an interpersonal, dynamic social event that depends on at least two people, with one person better informed or more skilled than the other. Human learning occurs as a transfer of responsibility, be it learning to play the violin, doing arithmetic, learning Spanish, reading, writing, or repairing an automobile. All of these learning abilities pass along the interpersonal plane. While much learning and development occurs naturally, students who are not learning well require a more careful analysis of the task relative to the student's current ability. Learning and cognitive development are enhanced when the student works collaboratively with a slightly more skilled learner.

5.6c Interactive Dialogues

interactive dialogues
Discussions between the teacher and children in the class.

Interactive dialogues are conversations between students and a teacher. Research shows that the use of interactive dialogues is an effective intervention strategy, particularly in teaching reading comprehension and writing. The research shows that interactive dialogues are most effective when used with small, interactive groups of six or fewer students. The role of the teacher and the students is to explore ideas and to think critically about the topics under discussion (Vaughn et al., 2000; Wong, 1999). Interactive dialogues are often used as a strategy to improve reading comprehension. The students discuss a story they have read. The teacher listens to what the students say and guides the discussion.

reciprocal teaching
A method of teaching through a social interactive dialogue between teacher and student that emphasizes the development of thinking processes.

An application of the interactive dialogue, called reciprocal teaching, has been used to teach reading comprehension strategies (Palinscar, Brown, & Campione, 1991). Palinscar and colleagues successfully taught the following reading comprehension strategies through reciprocal teaching:

1. The teacher and the students read the material silently.
2. The teacher explains and models summarizing, questioning, clarifying, and predicting by saying aloud the thoughts that are used.
3. The students read another passage and take the responsibility of modeling and saying their thoughts aloud.
4. Each student demonstrates abilities in summarizing, questioning, clarifying, and predicting.

Social interactions between the students and their teacher are central ingredients in the learning process.

5.6d Implications of Learning Strategies Instruction

The approaches of learning strategies instruction have practical teaching implications. Once students are taught effective learning strategies, they can use them in many learning situations. They can become active, involved learners who accept responsibility for their own learning. Effective learning occurs in a social context where the interrelationship between a student and a teacher is critical.

I Have a Kid Who...

SPECIAL STUDENTS *Learn Strategies for Social Studies*

Ben, Cory, Jennifer, Sally, John, Bob, Mary, and Luisa were all seventh-grade students in Ms. Weiss's resource room. They were also in Mr. Keene's general education social studies class. Mr. Keene was a new teacher at the school, and these students liked Mr. Keene very much. When Mr. Keene announced that there would be a test in two weeks on the social studies chapter in their textbook, this group of students wanted to do well on the test. They asked Ms. Weiss if she would help them prepare for the social studies test. Ms. Weiss agreed to spend the next two weeks in the resource room preparing for the social studies test. The social studies text had key vocabulary words at the end of the chapter. So Ms. Weiss had the students analyze each word—the root words, prefixes, and suffixes—and discuss the meaning of each word. They took the topic headings in the chapter and made an outline of the chapter. They explained each chart, picture,

and graphic feature to Ms. Weiss. They acted out parts of the text. They developed questions to ask each other. When the test results came out, this group of students in the resource room scored much better than the rest of the class. Some of the general education students complained to the principal that it wasn't fair because the students in the resource room had help studying the chapter.

QUESTIONS

1. If you were the principal, how would you answer the charge that is was not fair?

2. What role do you think motivation played in doing well in the test?

3. What strategies from this chapter did Ms. Weiss use in her teaching?

Did You Get It?

A scenario in which a learner becomes passive, dependent on others, loses faith in him or herself, and "learns" to become unable to extricate him or herself from given situations, is referred to as learned

    a. inability.
    b. hopelessness.
    c. helplessness.
    d. vulnerability.

Chapter Summary

- Theory has an important role in serving as a guide to learning.
- Developmental psychology stresses the natural progression of the child's growth and the sequential development of cognitive abilities. A state of readiness is needed for the child to acquire certain abilities. Forcing a child into trying to learn before that state of readiness has been reached can lead to academic failure.
- Behavioral psychology provides an approach to learning disabilities that emphasizes (1) explicit teaching and (2) direct instruction. The behavioral unit consists of (1) the antecedent event, (2) the target behavior, and (3) the consequent event. Explicit teaching means that teachers are clear about what needs to be accomplished. Direct instruction focuses on the teaching of needed academic skills.
- Cognitive psychology deals with the human processes of (1) learning, (2) thinking, and (3) knowing. A group of theories about learning disabilities stem from cognitive psychology: (1) differences in cognitive processing, (2) the information-processing model of learning, and (3) cognitive learning theories
- The learning strategies approach focuses on *how* students learn rather than on *what* they learn. Students learn to use strategies that enable them to control their own learning.

Questions for Discussion and Reflection

1. Why is theory important in the study of learning disabilities and disabilities?
2. Discuss developmental psychology as it applies to learning. How can developmental delays lead to learning disabilities?
3. How do the principles of behavioral psychology apply to teaching students with learning disabilities and related mild disabilities?
4. What are the basic concepts of cognitive psychology?
5. What are the three memory systems of the information-processing model? How are these systems related? How can the information-processing model of learning be applied to teaching students?
6. What is meant by the term *metacognition?* Discuss the learning problems of students with regard to metacognitive strategies.
7. What are interactive dialogues? How can they be used to teach students?

Key Terms

active learners (p. 151)

antecedent event (p. 137)

automaticity (p. 140)

behavioral analysis (p. 139)

behavioral unit (p. 137)

cognitive abilities (p. 140)

cognitive processing (p. 141)

concrete operations stage (p. 133)

consequent event (p. 137)

developmental variations (p. 131)

direct instruction (p. 138)

executive control (p. 146)

explicit teaching (p. 138)

formal operations stage (p. 133)

graphic organizers (p. 148)

information-processing model (p. 142)

interactive dialogues (p. 152)

learned helplessness (p. 151)

learning strategies approach (p. 151)

long-term memory (p. 145)

metacognition (p. 149)

mind mapping (p. 148)

multistore memory system (p. 142)

passive learners (p. 151)

perception (p. 143)

preoperational stage (p. 132)

psychological processing disorders (p. 141)

reciprocal teaching (p. 152)

retrieval (p. 145)

sensorimotor stage (p. 132)

sensory register (p. 143)

short-term memory (p. 144)

stages of learning (p. 134)

strategies intervention model (p. 151)

target behavior (p. 137)

theories (p. 130)

working memory (p. 144)

Ellen B. Senisi/The Image Works

6

Social, Emotional, and Behavioral Challenges

The teacher's primary task is to structure or order the environment for the pupil in such a way that work is accomplished, play is learned, love is felt, and fun is enjoyed—by the student and the teacher.

—James Kauffman and Timothy Landrum (2009)

LEARNING OBJECTIVES

After reading this chapter, you should be able to:

6.1 Articulate social, emotional, and behavioral challenges and discuss how they are observed and are related.

6.2 Articulate social challenges faced by students and provide examples of why social skills are important in today's society.

6.3 Explain how emotional challenges interfere with academic learning.

6.4 Explain the behavioral challenges that result in school suspension and the need for positive behavioral supports to keep students in school.

6.5 List and explain at least five strategies to improve social competencies.

6.6 Explain at least three strategies for students with emotional challenges, including strategies for self esteem.

6.7 Explain five strategies for students with behavioral challenges, including the importance of the behavior intervention plan.

6.8 List and explain five behavior management strategies, including contracting, reinforcement, cognitive behavior modification, and time out.

STANDARDS Addressed in This Chapter:

As approved by the National Council for the Accreditation of Teacher Education

CEC Initial Preparation Standard 1: Learner Development and Individual Learning Differences

- 1.0—Beginning special education professionals understand how exceptionalities may interact with development and learning and use this knowledge to provide meaningful and challenging learning experiences for individuals with exceptionalities.

- 1.2—Beginning special education professionals use understanding of development and individual differences to respond to the needs of individuals with exceptionalities.

CEC Initial Preparation Standard 2: Learning Environments

- 2.0—Beginning special education professionals create safe, inclusive, culturally responsive learning environments so that individuals with exceptionalities become active and effective learners and develop emotional well-being, positive social interactions, and self-determination.

- 2.1—Beginning special education professionals through collaboration with general educators and other colleagues create safe, inclusive, culturally responsive learning environments to engage individuals with exceptionalities in meaningful learning activities and social interactions.

- 2.2—Beginning special education professionals use motivational and instructional interventions to teach individuals with exceptionalities how to adapt to different environments.

- 2.3—Beginning special education professionals know how to intervene safely and appropriately with individuals with exceptionalities in crisis.

CEC Initial Preparation Standard 4: Assessment

- 4.3—Beginning special education professionals in collaboration with colleagues and families use multiple types of assessment information making decisions about individuals with exceptionalities.

CEC Initial Preparation Standard 5: Instructional Planning and Strategies

- 5.0—Beginning special education professionals select, adapt, and use a repertoire of evidence-based instructional strategies to advance learning of individuals with exceptionalities.

- 5.1—Beginning special education professionals consider an individual's abilities, interests, learning environments, and cultural and linguistic factors in the selection, development, and adaptation of learning experiences for individuals with exceptionalities.

CEC Initial Preparation Standard 6: Professional Learning and Ethical Practice

- 6.0—Beginning special education professionals use foundational knowledge of the field and their professional ethical principles and practice standards to inform special education practice, to engage in lifelong learning, and to advance the profession.

- 6.1—Beginning special education professionals use professional ethical principles and professional practice standards to guide their practice.

- 6.2—Beginning special education professionals understand how foundational knowledge and current issues influence professional practice.

- 6.3—Beginning special education professionals understand that diversity is a part of families, cultures, and schools, and that complex human issues can interact with the delivery of special education services.

I n this chapter, we discuss social, emotional, and behavior challenges. These challenges can interfere with a student's learning and the quality of his or her entire life. We also describe strategies and interventions to help students with social, emotional, and behavioral challenges.

6.1 Overview of Social, Emotional, and Behavioral Challenges

Many students with mild disabilities and students with learning disabilities have social, emotional, or behavioral challenges that are apart from their academic difficulties. These challenges may involve:

- **Social challenges,** which are difficulties in interrelating with others, in making and keeping friends, and in meeting the social demands of everyday life
- **Emotional challenges,** which involve feelings about oneself. For example, the student may feel so chronically sad or depressed or have such a low self-concept that these feelings interfere with the individual's outlook on life and the ability to learn.
- **Behavioral challenges,** which are problems manifested by aggressive, antisocial, and similar behavior

Social, emotional, and behavioral challenges occur in children in all populations, and they are found in students from diverse economic, racial, cultural, and language groups. Often the social, emotional, and behavioral challenges are interdependent; they overlap with each other, or they are interrelated problems. For example, students who feel poorly about themselves may engage in specific behaviors that can lead to social isolation. A student who is very depressed may engage in withdrawal behavior, which leads to poor peer relationships and social isolation. Some examples of students with social, emotional, or behavioral challenges are described below:

- Marty struggled in school in acquiring academic skills. In fact, Marty and his family spent so much of their time and energy in improving his academic skills that Marty had no time available for making friends or building a social life. Marty's concentration on academics was successful in that he graduated from high school and went on to technical school to become a successful computer programmer. However, with no time given for Marty to make friends and learn how to interact with peers, Marty now finds that he still has no friends as an adult.
- Katie had emotional challenges throughout her elementary school years. Katie is now in college, but she still struggles with depression, a poor self-concept, and a high degree of test anxiety.
- Jerod takes a very long time to complete an assignment. A comprehensive evaluation indicates that Jerod has an obsessive-compulsive disorder. He wants to make sure that his work is "perfect" before he turns it in. Jerod's need for perfection is part of his obsessive-compulsive disorder.

Imagine going to work every day and being faced with tasks that are too difficult for you. Even the most resilient person would eventually give up and start looking for another job. Yet students do not have this option. They are supposed to stay in school and face tasks every day that are too difficult for them to accomplish. No wonder many students become extremely frustrated and give up. They know they have many strengths and things they can do well. Yet they are struggling with hard academic tasks, and they do not understand why they are struggling so much. Investigations of the relationship between academic underachievement and externalizing behavior show that students may act out to avoid aversive academic tasks (Farley et al., 2012, Lane and Beebe-Frankenberger, 2004). Students with behavioral problems present a major challenge to school personnel because they often present both academic and behavioral deficits (Farley et al., 2012; Nelson, Benner, & Moody, 2008). Teachers should explore the "cause" of negative behaviors in school and then plan interventions that consider those causes. Teachers must be sensitive to the stresses that many students with learning problems face—they are expected to try to do academic tasks that are extremely difficult for them. They may respond by giving up, acting out, or putting their head down on their desk and trying to rest. They are tired—doing work that is difficult is tiring and what may appear as work refusal may be exhaustion from demanding tasks.

It is also important to find strengths that students have while assisting them in the areas in which they struggle. Two examples of such students are described in Student Stories 6.1, "Students with Challenges."

- **Mark.** Mark has a learning disability that affects his reading. His classroom teacher expects pupils to read aloud in a round-robin type of reading exercise. During reading class, Mark clowns around and engages in numerous attention-seeking behaviors until the teacher gets tired of his behavior and sends Mark to the office. The consequence of the teacher's action is that Mark does not have to read.

- **Wendy.** Wendy displays behavioral challenges. During her seventh-grade math lessons, she tears up her math papers and throws them in the trash. Her classroom teacher is sure Wendy can do the work but she just will not do it. In reviewing her records, Wendy's teacher notes that her latest individual achievement test scores show that her math skills are at a third-grade level.

REFLECTIVE QUESTIONS

1. What could Mark's teacher do in place of expecting him to read aloud in a round-robin type of reading?

2. What should Wendy's math teacher do now that she has the information about Wendy's achievement test scores?

Did You Get It?

When Solomon, a child with a learning disability and a secondary behavioral disorder, refuses to work, cooperate, and interact at the end of the day, what is the last thought his teacher should consider?

   a. He is probably exhausted from the challenges he has faced.

   b. It's not easy for him.

   c. He's got a lot to carry on his young shoulders.

   d. He's acting out and pushing buttons.

6.2 Social Challenges

social skills
Skills necessary for meeting the basic social demands of everyday life.

Social skills consist of skills that are necessary to meet the basic social demands of everyday life. Deficits in social skills are among the most crippling types of problem that a student can have. In terms of total life functioning, a social disorder may be far more intimidating than an academic dysfunction. A social disorder affects almost every aspect of life—at school, at home, and at play (Silver, 2006). Social challenges involve the student's ability to interact with others. When students are not aware of the nuances of social situations, they are unsure of how to act or how to make friends. It is estimated that one third of students with learning disabilities also have problems with social skills (Elksnin & Elksnin, 2004; Bryan, 1997; Voeller, 1994). Some individuals with learning disabilities are less socially skilled than their same-aged peers (Gresham et al., 2006). If they are asked to use cognitive social behaviors, they are less able to do so than their peers. If they are asked to solve a social problem, they may jump to a solution quickly rather than use problem-solving strategies to arrive at the best answer to the problem. If pressured, they tend to engage in antisocial behaviors (Schumaker & Deshler, 1995). Students with learning disabilities accounted for 52% of all students with disabilities who experienced disciplinary actions during the 2007–2008 school year. Learning disabilities is the second most common disability found among incarcerated juveniles (Cortiella, 2011).

Some students who have social difficulties do quite well in academic domains, while other students have both social and academic difficulties. Also, it is important to recognize that not all students with learning disabilities and related mild disabilities encounter difficulties with social skills (Gresham et al., 2006). In fact, for many, the social sphere is an area of strength. These students are socially competent at making and maintaining friends, and they work at pleasing teachers and parents (Haager & Vaughn, 1997).

Difficulties in the social arena are also characteristic of students with autism, and nonverbal disabilities (see Chapter 7, "Autism Spectrum Disorders and Attention Deficit Hyperactivity Disorder").

Students who have problems with social relationships may lack sensitivity to others, have a poor perception of social situations, and suffer social rejection. They may exhibit a wide range of poor social traits, such as impulsiveness, low tolerance for frustration, and problems in handling day-to-day social interactions and situations (Sridhar & Vaughn, 2001; Wong & Donahue, 2002; Bryan, 1997).

Having a social challenge puts a child at a great disadvantage. In school and in other environments, students need well-developed social and interactive skills in dealing with peers and adults. Although these students want to be accepted socially, they often do not know how to engage in appropriate social behaviors. Our job as educators is to help students learn how to improve their ability to respond appropriately in social situations. A story of a student with social difficulties is described in the feature Student Stories 6.2, "Bill: A Student With Social Challenges."

Myrleen Pearson/Alamy

Children need well-developed social and interactive skills in dealing positively with peers and adults.

Bill feels isolated—he doesn't feel like he belongs to any social group at school. One day, a group of students is huddled together planning something. They ask Bill if he wants to join them. Bill is pleased that he has been asked to join a group. It seems that the group is plotting a bomb threat at the school. They ask Bill if he would call in the bomb threat the next day. They assure Bill that he won't get caught and they will allow him into their group permanently if he will do just this one thing for them. The next morning Bill calls in the bomb threat. A police investigation occurs and Bill is arrested, has to appear in court, and is suspended. When Bill tries to tell the police officers what happened, the police question the other students who obviously don't admit that they had anything to do with the event.

REFLECTIVE QUESTION

1. What interventions other than suspension could have been provided for Bill?

Did You Get It?

Of the 23 students in your class, 15 have a learning disability. According to statistics, if your class is demographically representative, you have approximately how many children in your class with both a learning disability and some deficit in social skills?

a. 1
b. 3
c. 5
d. 7–8

6.3 Emotional Challenges

Emotional challenges often interfere with academic learning. When students are troubled by emotional challenges, it is arduous for them to focus on academic tasks. Students may be preoccupied with other problems that prevent them from successfully completing the academic tasks.

6.3a Relationship Between Learning Difficulties and Emotional Challenges

The emotional development of typically developing students can be very different from the emotional development of students with learning problems. Successful achievers have a multitude of gratifying experiences to develop important basic feelings of self-worth, and they have hundreds of opportunities for self-satisfaction, as well as the enjoyment of pleasing others. When students are achieving, the parent-child relationship is mutually satisfying because normal accomplishments stimulate parental responses of approval and encouragement. As a result of students' own feelings of accomplishment and their awareness of the approval of those around them, achieving students develop a sense of self-worth and a prideful identity. Successful achievers establish healthy identifications with their mothers, fathers, and other key figures in their lives, building feelings of self-worth, a tolerance for frustration, and a consideration for others (Lavoie, 2007; Silver, 2006).

In contrast, the emotional development of students who encounter learning problems follows a very different pattern. If the central nervous system is not intact and is not maturing in a normal manner, disturbances in motor and perceptual development lead to dissatisfaction with one's self. Failed attempts at mastering tasks induce feelings of frustration, rather than feelings of accomplishment. Instead of building self-esteem, the thwarted attempts produce an attitude of self-derision and, at the same time, these thwarted attempts fail to stimulate the parents' normal responses of pride. Parents, therefore, may become anxious and disheartened, reactions that can result in either rejection or overprotection.

With such a developmental scenario, it is not surprising that many students with mild disabilities and students with learning disabilities develop emotional challenges. These students may react by either internalizing or by externalizing their emotional problems. An internalizing reaction may take the form of a conscious refusal to learn, a resistance to pressure, clinging to dependency, quick discouragement, a fear of success, sadness, and withdrawal into a private world. An externalizing reaction can take the form of overt hostility, acting-out behaviors, excessive anger, fighting with other children, and defiance toward teachers.

The environment should be a place in which the student can be successful. It is important to restructure tasks to assure success. These students do have many strengths and interests, and teachers and families must find those areas of strengths and capitalize on them. By recognizing students for their accomplishments, teachers reduce feelings of inadequacy, decrease anxiety, and increase student beliefs in themselves.

It is not unusual for students with serious emotional or behavioral problems to also have a coexisting learning disability (Kauffman & Landrum, 2009). If the problems are so severe that they interfere with further learning and life activities, the student may be referred for psychological or psychiatric counseling (Silver, 2006).

internalizing
Disorders that are inward, such as refusal to learn, resistance to pressure, withdrawal, clinging to dependency, or sadness.

externalizing
Conduct disorders that encompass a broad range of antisocial behaviors such as aggressive acts, theft, vandalism, arson, lying, truancy, and running away.

6.3b Characteristics of Emotional Challenges

In this section, we describe several characteristics of emotional challenges.

Depression Many students with emotional challenges suffer from depression and a general pervasive mood of unhappiness. Depression may be a reaction to the stress and frustration of school demands, to the lack of friendships and social interactions, or may stem from a biochemical predisposition. Signs of depression include (1) loss of energy, (2) loss of interest in friends, (3) difficulty in concentration, and (4) feelings of helplessness, which occasionally are expressed through suicidal talk (Silver, 2006; Rutter, 2003; Gorman, 1999).

Lack of Resiliency Although a person's feelings of self-worth may be threatened by continual failure, it is interesting to note that not all individuals who face difficulties in life develop low self-esteem. Some have remarkable resiliency and are able to preserve self-confidence and self-worth (Goldstein & Brooks, 2005; Brooks & Goldstein, 2002; Freiberg, 1993; Keogh, 2000). Their resilience seems to come from a mix of internal and external factors (Sorensen et al., 2003). Resilience has been described as "a buffering process"—it doesn't eliminate risks or the adverse conditions that one might face but it helps individuals deal with those conditions effectively (Brooks & Goldstein, 2004). What are the factors that enable individuals to keep on trying, and how can the school help build resilience? Self-worth is gained through mastery of a skill or task, through perceived respect from peers, and through feelings of competence. Students who believe that they have competencies in areas other than academic work are less likely to be devastated by school failure. To maintain their sense of self-worth, students need a support system from teachers, from parents and families, and from peers who acknowledge that these students possess specific competencies. The support system preserves student self-worth by keeping failure to a minimum; increasing the visibility of nonacademic talents, skills, and competencies; and emphasizing *learning* goals over *performance* goals. For example, the student can be given credit for performing a task in the correct manner (a learning goal) even though the final answer may not be accurate (the performance goal).

It is fascinating to observe individuals who have achieved greatness and maintained a sense of belief in their self-worth and in what they were doing despite having faced years of rejection and ridicule. Examples include Gertrude Stein, the famous poet, who submitted poems to editors for about 20 years before one was finally accepted for publication; Vincent van Gogh, who sold only one painting during his lifetime; and Frank Lloyd Wright, who was rejected as an architect during much of his life. So, too, many individuals with learning disabilities have overcome failure and rejection because they strongly believed in themselves. The stories of adults with learning disabilities who have succeeded against the odds are inspiring, and their resilience is evident in their success (Hart, 2009; Gerber & Brown, 1997; Gerber & Reiff, 1991; Smith, 1991).

Anxiety Students with learning disabilities and related mild disabilities display more symptoms of anxiety than their peers. The demands and pressures of school and high-stakes testing provoke increased anxiety and even panic. These students feel that events beyond their control are happening to them. When they encounter these situations, they feel hopeless and become frozen and panicked during these periods of intense pressure. Anxiety may cause students to miss class, to tune out, and to become disorganized. Feelings of anxiety are real and must be understood by teachers and families (Gorman, 1999). One student had such high anxiety when she took a high-stakes assessment test that she spelled her last name incorrectly. Some test-taking tips are provided in Chapter 9, "Adolescents and Adults With Learning Disabilities and Related Mild Disabilities."

It is important to accent students' strengths to build their belief in their self-worth.

Steve Skjold/Alamy

Did You Get It?

Loss of interest in what was previously valued; in friends and acquaintances; and possible suicidal thoughts, talk, and ideation can and should all be considered signs of

a. depression.
b. learning disabilities.
c. behavioral disorders.
d. panic disorder.

6.4 Behavioral Challenges

Students with learning disabilities and related mild disabilities sometimes exhibit co-occurring behavioral challenges. These behavioral challenges must be considered in planning instruction (Farley et al., 2012; Burns et al., 2009; Haydon et al., 2009; Buck et al., 2000; Scott, 2003). When students struggle with learning, they may become so frustrated that they act out or refuse to work. Because they cannot get attention for strong academic skills, they may seek to get attention for inappropriate behaviors.

6.4a Suspensions of Students

Some students engage in behaviors in an attempt to be accepted by peers, or they impulsively engage in a behavior, not realizing the consequences of their behavior. Thus, they get into trouble. Students with disabilities have higher rates of suspension than youth without disabilities. An analysis of data from the U.S. Department of Education based on the 2009–2010 school year showed that 13% of students with disabilities in kindergarten through grade 12 were suspended compared to 7% of students without disabilities in urban middle schools (Losen & Skiba, 2012). Studies of students with learning disabilities and students with attention deficit disorders show that these students have a higher risk of being suspended. When academic tasks become very difficult, these students may respond with disruptive behaviors that result in suspensions (Johns & Carr, 2012; Krezmien, Leone, & Achilles, 2006).

If the student is suspended or expelled, the IEP (Individualized Education Team) team must make a manifestation determination. This means that the IEP team must decide whether the presenting problem behavior is a result of the student's disability and whether the current IEP is being implemented. If the behavior is a result of the disability or if the services on the IEP were not being met, services must continue for students with disabilities who have been suspended or expelled because of their behavior.

manifestation determination
The process that the IEP undertakes in order to determine whether a student's behavior is the result of a disability.

Of concern is the number of students reported to either be suspended from school for more than 10 school days or to be removed to an interim alternative educational setting for drugs or weapons. According to the Civil Rights Data Collection's 2009–2010 statistics based on data from 72,000 schools in 7,000 districts that serve approximately 85% of American students, it was reported that 1 in 5 black males and 1 in 10 black females received an out-of-school suspension (Lewin, 2012). In 10 states in urban middle schools more than 25% of black students with disabilities were suspended in 2009–2010 (Losen & Skiba, 2012). In a Texas study reported in 2011, almost 60% of the students in grades 7 through 12

Alex, a seventh grade student with autism, was going to be expelled because he was spending too much time in the bathroom. The IEP team convened and determined that spending too much time in the bathroom was not related to Alex's disability of autism. As a result of a complaint by the parent, a more thorough investigation of the situation occurred. Alex loved to watch water spinning and going down the drain. When Alex would go into the restroom, he would repeatedly flush the toilet so he could watch the water spin. This behavior was specifically noted in elementary school reports and evaluations. Further exploration also found that Alex was to receive social work services for 60 minutes weekly. Alex was receiving no social work services because the previous social worker had left and was not replaced this year. In this case, Alex could not be expelled and had to be provided appropriate services.

REFLECTIVE QUESTIONS

1. What should the IEP team have done prior to convening the manifestation determination?

2. Develop a plan to reduce the amount of time that Alex spends in the bathroom.

had received an in-school suspension, an out-of-school suspension, or had been expelled. Out of all of the students who were suspended, students who qualified for special education constituted 75%. About 76% of the students identified as having a learning disability had at least one disciplinary action (Fabelo et al., 2011; Johns & Carr, 2012).

One-third of youth with learning disabilities are suspended or expelled from school at some point (Cortiela, 2011). In certain school districts, students who have disabilities are 2 to 3 times more likely to be subjected to discipline than those students without disabilities (Cortiela, 2011).

Unfortunately, a result of suspension is that students fall further behind academically. Suspension disengages them from the school system and increases the likelihood that they will drop out of school. Suspension also allows the student to escape the situation and does nothing to teach the student appropriate behavioral skills. It is our responsibility as educators to work to keep our students in school.

6.4b Functional Behavioral Assessment and Positive Behavioral Supports

The Individuals With Disabilities Education Improvement Act of 2004 (IDEA-2004) requires that if the child's *behavior* interferes with his or her learning or the learning of others, the IEP team will consider strategies and supports to address the child's behavior. Moreover, if a child with disabilities displays behavior that impedes his or her learning or that of others, the IEP team must be able to evaluate the child's behavior through a *functional behavioral assessment* and to design *positive behavioral supports* to change the student's troublesome behavior (Institute of Education Sciences of the U.S. Department of Education, 2008, Center for Effective Collaboration and Practice, 1998; Smith, 2000; Sugai & Homer, 1999; U.S. Department of Education, 2000a). (See the Center for Effective Collaboration and Practice website at *http://cecp.air.org*, the Positive Behavioral Intervention and Supports website at *http://www.pbis.org*, the Families and Advocates Partnership for Education website at *http://www.fape.org*, and Dr. Mac's Amazing Behavior Management Advice Site at *http://www.behavioradvisor.com*.)

Functional Behavioral Assessment (FBA) A functional behavioral assessment (FBA) involves determining the cause, or antecedent event, that triggers the child's behavior. The concept of functional behavior assessment is not new. It is based on the applied behavior analysis procedure called *ABC*: antecedent, behavior, consequence (see Figure 6.1).

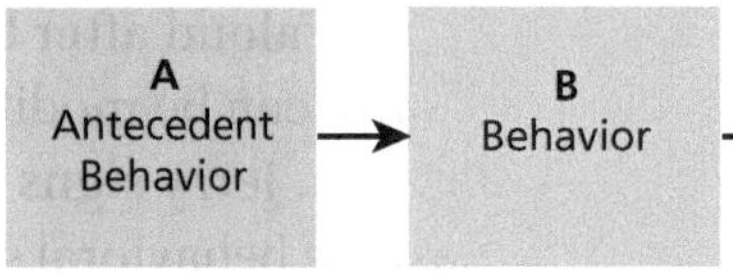

Figure 6.2 illustrates these three behavioral events.

Functional behavioral assessment requires a thorough look at factors that may be contributing to behavioral concerns. Some examples of behavioral concerns are

- When the teacher asks Charlie to read (antecedent event), he begins to disturb others in the classroom by hitting them.
- Jerry swears and uses inappropriate language when asked to do an independent math task.
- Sylvia refuses to copy from the chalkboard in the classroom. Upon further investigation, it is learned that Sylvia has a vision problem and cannot see the board. Rather than admitting that she cannot see, Sylvia refused to copy from the board.
- Cultural factors also must be considered as part of a thorough functional assessment. For example, the teacher, Mr. Jones, demands that the student look at him and give him eye contact when he speaks to the student. Yet in that student's culture, eye contact is a sign of disrespect.

Five important outcomes gained from the functional assessment process are (O'Neill et al., 1997; Fox & Gable, 2004):

1. A clear description of the problem behavior
2. Identification of the events, times, and situations that predict when a problem behavior will and will not occur
3. Identification of the consequences that result in the maintenance of the behavior
4. Development of summary statements or hypotheses that describe the problem behavior, in what situations it occurs, and what maintains the behavior
5. Collection of direct observation data that support the summary statements

Positive Behavioral Supports (PBS) Positive behavioral supports are strategies to change a student's troublesome behavior and to increase positive behavior or to replace an undesirable behavior. For example, Charlie is only asked

---

A Antecedent Behavior → **B** Behavior → **C** Consequences

© Cengage Learning 2015

FIGURE **6.1**

Functional Assessment: ABC Behaviors

functional behavioral assessment (FBA)
Evaluating a child's behavior problems by analyzing the behavioral unit.

positive behavioral supports
Positive methods that assist students in learning new ways of behaving.

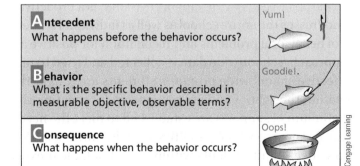

FIGURE **6.2**

Example of ABC: Antecedent Event, Behavior, and Consequent Event

to read aloud after he has practiced and prepared to do this task. Charlie's response can be modified by rewarding him when he responds in a more suitable fashion. Jerry signs a contract to respond using appropriate language. These positive behavioral supports are based on strategies of behavior management.

Questions that should be asked to develop positive behavioral supports include (1) What happened? (2) What happened before? (3) What happened after? (4) How can the student's response be changed? What can the adult do to assure that the adult is encouraging the student to engage in appropriate behavior? The steps for developing positive behavioral supports include (1) collecting and reviewing the student's background information and data, (2) functional behavioral assessment, and (3) writing a plan to change the student's behavior (Buck et al., 2000). A website for positive behavioral supports can be found at *http://www.pbis.org/main.htm*.

IDEA-2004 stipulates that if a child's behavior impedes the child's learning or the learning of others, the IEP shall consider strategies, including positive behavioral interventions and supports, to address the behavior. Positive behavioral support as a general term refers to the culturally appropriate applications of positive behavioral interventions and systems to achieve socially important behavior change (Center for Effective Collaboration and Practice, 1998; U.S. Department of Education, 2002).

Strategies to implement positive behavioral interventions include

- A desirable replacement behavior should be taught to the student. For example, if the student throws a math book, an alternative math assignment could be given so that the student is successful in completing a math assignment.
- Modify the environment to increase the effectiveness of the replacement behavior. For example, the student would receive a consequence for throwing the book such as being removed from the math class but the student would still be expected to complete the math assignment in a different setting.
- Throughout the process, the student must be taught the appropriate behaviors and must be recognized positively for engaging in those behaviors.

Positive Behavioral Interventions and Supports (PBIS) is a nationwide project funded by the U.S. Department of Education, Office of Special Education Center to establish school-wide systems that are based on positive recognition of appropriate behavior. Current updates on that project can be found on the website at *http://www.pbis.org/main.htm*.

School-Wide Positive Behavior Support (SWPBS) Throughout the country, schools are being encouraged to promote positive learning climates for their students. School-wide positive behavior support (SWPBS) is a proactive school-wide approach that addresses the entire school as well as individual students. It focuses on prevention of behavioral problems and recognition for positive actions of students. In this approach, school-wide data is collected and used to make decisions and plan an effective school wide program, students are taught the behavioral expectations within the school and are recognized for meeting those expectations, and a continuum of supports are established to meet the needs of students (Flannery, Sugai, & Anderson, 2009). In PBIS schools, universally designed interventions are designed for all students within the school. Clear expectations are set and students are recognized for performing those expectations. Students are

school-wide positive behavior support
A process used within the entire school that is based on identification of problem behaviors through data collection, clear expectations for appropriate behavior, and recognition of positive behaviors.

taught the expectations. They may get special tickets that are good for a drawing or can be cashed in for special prizes. For those students who need more than the universally designed interventions, secondary interventions are put into place. The student may need more individual attention, may need additional interventions, or may need a closer look at the reasons for the behavior. There will be those students who fail to respond to either universal or secondary interventions and those students will need tertiary interventions. They may need to be referred for a comprehensive case study evaluation that includes a thorough functional assessment. They may need additional support services such as those offered by a school social worker or a school psychologist.

6.4c Specific Functions of Behavior

Behavior is communication, and our job as educators is to ascertain what the student is telling us. By recognizing the function of the student's behavior, the educator can change either the antecedents or the consequences in order to meet the need of that student. Function-based interventions can make meaningful and lasting change (Gage, Lewis, & Stichter, 2012; Lane et al., 2006; Liaupsin et al., 2006). In order to assess the function of the behavior, it is important for the general educator and the special educator to work collaboratively. Oftentimes it is difficult for a teacher to see the function of the behavior because he or she may be too close to the situation and can't always see what is driving the behavior. However, another individual may be able to see the function of the behavior more clearly.

The general educator may not have the time to collect the necessary data on how many times a student engages in a specific behavior and at what times of day and during what specific academic activities a behavior is occurring. If the special educator can take the time to observe in the classroom and collect the data, it assists the team in determining appropriate behavioral interventions.

The major purposes of behavior are described below.

Purpose of Behavior 1: Access Some examples of engaging in a specific behavior to gain attention, power, and control are:

Example 1: Jerry likes to get attention from the teacher and has learned that he can get attention by getting out of his seat without permission. Each time Jerry gets out of his seat, the teacher tells him to sit down (thus giving Jerry attention for inappropriate behavior). A teacher can meet this need for attention by changing the consequence. If the teacher gives Jerry attention when he is sitting in his seat, the teacher is meeting his need for attention.

Example 2: Sammy wants access to power and control, and he gets that power and control by bullying other students. With the increase in bullying in the schools, it is critical that educators look at the function of bullying behavior and recognize that students may be engaging in such behaviors in order to gain power and control. In this example, the teacher can change antecedents that result in Sammy getting power and control for appropriate behavior rather than the inappropriate behavior of bullying. The teacher can build in choices in assignments. Sammy can do his assignment with a blue pen or a red pen, or Sammy can choose any 10 math problems, or Sammy can be provided opportunities to do assistive work with another student.

Purpose of Behavior 2: Escape/Avoidance Engaging in a specific behavior to avoid doing a task because the student fears embarrassment or failure. Students may engage in specific behaviors because they think that the task is too difficult for them or there is too much of the task. Questions that teachers should ask when they suspect that the student is trying to escape a task are

Is the task at the appropriate level for the student? Is the student embarrassed in front of his or her peers? Most students do not want their peers to know that they cannot complete a task so rather than embarrass themselves, they may engage in inappropriate behaviors that allow them to escape the task.

Can the student read the assignment? Does the student understand the vocabulary used in the assignment? The teacher should look at a task in advance to review the vocabulary and see if the student understands those vocabulary words.

Is there too much to do at one time? Often students are overwhelmed at the sight of a task, such as when there are too many words on a page or too many math problems on the page.

Does the student have emotional feelings about the task? The student may have had a negative experience in a history class previously and therefore wants to avoid doing any task related to history.

Is the physical appearance of the worksheet overwhelming to the student? Is the worksheet crowded with too many different directions or difficult-to-read type?

Does the student understand the directions for the task? Does an assignment take into account the way the student learns best? If the student has an excellent visual memory but is weak in processing auditory information and remembering what he or she hears, the student probably will be frustrated if the student is in a classroom where the teacher uses straight lecture.

In the case of escape/avoidance, the teacher can change the antecedent, specifically the type of assignment, so that the student is able to complete the task. For example, Maria has difficulty with written expression and refuses to write in her journal because written work is difficult for her. The teacher could allow Maria to record her thoughts for the journal into a tape recorder and they could later transcribe the information.

Purpose of Behavior 3: Sensory Stimulation Some students engage in behaviors as a result of sensory overstimulation or not enough sensory stimulation.

Examples: There is too much noise, or the child needs movement, or the child has an oral need to suck on something, or the child is overly sensitive to the feel or texture of certain clothes. Difficulties with touch processing might contribute to clumsiness and awkwardness (Myles et al., 2004). The student might be overstimulated by bright lights or too many details on a sheet of paper (Myles, Adreon, & Gitlitz, 2006). For a description of how FBA drives the behavior intervention plan, see the sample behavioral intervention plan for Jerod in Student Stories 6.4.

Did You Get It?

Suspension or expulsion from school of a child with a disability results in a process known as "manifestation determination." This action is and must be initiated by

    a. parents or guardians.

    b. school administrators.

    c. the IEP team.

    d. Child Protective Services (CPS).

6.5 Strategies to Improve Social Competencies

Students who are socially competent learn social skills effortlessly through daily living and observation. Students with social challenges need conscious effort and specific teaching to learn about the social world, its nuances, and its silent language. Just as we teach students to perform academic work (to read, write, spell, do arithmetic, and pass tests), we should teach students with social challenges how to live with and relate to other people.

6.5a Improving the Student's Self-Perception

Scrapbooks can help the students put together information about themselves. The students should include pictures of themselves at different stages of growth, pictures of their families and pets, a list of their likes and dislikes, anecdotes about their past, accounts of trips, awards they have won, and so on. One group of secondary students with social challenges enjoyed making a PowerPoint presentation entitled "About Me."

6.5b Improving Nonverbal Communication

Spoken language is only *one* means of communication. People also communicate by means of a "silent language" that relies on gestures, stance, or facial expressions. Students with social challenges need help interpreting communication messages conveyed by this silent language. We list here some ways of providing this help.

1. **Pictures of faces.** Collect pictures of faces and have the students ascertain whether the faces convey the emotion of happiness or sadness. Other emotions to be shown include anger, surprise, pain, and love.
2. **Gestures.** Discuss the meanings of various gestures with the students, such as waving good-bye, shaking a finger, shrugging a shoulder, turning away, tapping a finger or foot, and stretching out arms.
3. **DVDs, CDs, and story situations.** Find pictures, short DVDs, or story situations in which the social implications of gesture, space, and time are presented, and help the students to identify the emotional content of communication.
4. **What the voice tells.** Help students learn to recognize implications in the human voice, beyond the words themselves, by having the students listen to a voice on a tape to determine the mood of the speaker. Is the speaker happy, sad, or angry? Role playing with different emotions is also effective.

6.5c Cognitive Learning Strategies for Social Skills

Often students with social challenges respond impulsively in social situations. They act without considering what is required, without thinking through the possible solutions, or without thinking about the consequences of various courses of action. Through instruction in the strategies of self-verbalization and self-monitoring, students can be taught self-control to keep from giving immediate, nonreflective responses. Students can learn to ask themselves questions such as "What am I supposed to be doing?" In other words, they are taught to stop and think before responding. Teachers can model social learning strategies by talking out loud with such thoughts as "Does this problem have similarities to other problems I have encountered?" or "What are three possible solutions?" The students then practice these skills of self-verbalization, or thinking aloud.

Cognitive learning strategies instruction is effective for helping students acquire social skills (Deshler, Ellis, & Lenz, 1996; Lenz & Deshler, 2003). Social strategies instruction can change patterns of responses in social situations. When students learn to develop new cognitive responses to social problems, they begin to think about the consequences of social actions. Cognitive learning strategies can teach students: (1) to stop and think before responding, (2) to verbalize and rehearse social responses, (3) to visualize and imagine the effect of their behavior, and (4) to preplan social actions. Including Students in General Education 6.1, "Social Skills," presents several social skills strategies.

Including Students in GENERAL EDUCATION 6.1

Social Skills

- **Judging behavior in stories.** Read or tell an incomplete story that involves social judgment. Have the students anticipate the ending or complete the story. A short video of a social situation provides an opportunity to discuss critically the activities of the people in the video. For example, discuss the consequences of a student's rudeness when an acquaintance tries to begin a conversation, or the consequences of a student making a face when asked by her mother's friend if she likes her new dress, or the consequences of a student hitting someone at a party.

- **Grasping social situations through pictures.** A series of pictures can be arranged to tell a story that involves a social situation. Have the students arrange the pictures and explain the story. Comics, readiness books, beginning readers, and magazine advertisements are all good source materials for such activities. The series can also include pictures that are on transparencies.

- **Learning to generalize newly acquired social behaviors.** After students learn socially appropriate behaviors, they must learn to generalize these

behaviors to many settings, such as an inclusive classroom, the home environment, playgrounds, and other social situations. Students need many opportunities to practice and maintain newly acquired skills. Collaboration between special education teachers and general education teachers is needed to make plans for generalizing in inclusive classrooms.

- **Learning conversation skills.** Students must learn how to converse with others. They must learn how to extend greetings, introduce themselves, find a topic to talk about, listen actively, ask and answer questions, and say good-bye.

- **Friendship skills.** Students must learn how to make friends, give a compliment, join group activities, and accept thanks.

- **Game-playing skills.** Social skills can be taught to students through the activity of playing games with others. The instruction involves social modeling, behavioral rehearsal, and behavior transfer while playing games.

Professional Resource Download

Did You Get It?

After Annabelle is taught appropriate, positive, and constructive behaviors and she begins to acquire them, the next, critical step is
  a. learning situational specificity of these new behaviors.
  b. challenging the validity of these new behaviors.
  c. generalization of the behaviors across situations and settings.
  d. discussing these behaviors in-depth and formally contracting to display them regularly

6.6 Strategies for Students With Emotional Challenges

Student accomplishments can increase the ability to learn and strengthen emotional outlook. Successful experiences build feelings of self-worth, self-confidence, and self-respect. Teachers should help students accomplish an educational task so that their feelings of self-worth and self-esteem are enhanced. The beginning of a mutual reinforcement cycle is also the beginning of effective treatment (Silver, 2006). Teaching Tips 6.1, "Strategies for Improving Self-Esteem," offers ways to build self-esteem.

TEACHING TIPS 6.1

Strategies for Improving Self-Esteem

- Build a *rapport* with the student. Teachers can provide a type of therapy through skilled and sensitive clinical teaching. Try to gain the student's confidence and show sincere interest in the student.
- Provide students with tasks at which the students will be successful.
- Provide positive feedback and rewards for student successes.
- Find the student's areas of interest or hobbies and try to build lessons on these interests.
- Show enthusiasm with the student's successes.
- Make learning fun and enjoyable.
- Find ways to visually show that the student is learning by using charts or graphs.
- Use an approach such as *bibliotherapy,* a technique to help students understand themselves and their problems through books with characters that are learning to cope with problems similar to those faced by the students. By identifying with a character and working out the problem with the character, students are helped with their own problems. Books designed to explain the learning problem to the students are also useful.
- Engage the students in *circle time* activity in which *participants* are seated in a circle and are encouraged to share their feelings, learn to listen, and observe others. The program seeks to promote active listening, focus on feelings, give recognition to each individual, and promote greater understanding. Sample magic circle topics include "It made me feel good when I . . . ," "Something I *do very* well is . . . ," and "What can I *do for* you . . . ?"
- Use art, dance, music, and other *creative media* as therapy techniques for promoting emotional involvement.

Professional Resource Download

Did You Get It?

"_____" utilizes characters and situations from literature, characters who are dealing with the same issues as your student, and situations commonly encountered by your student to increase self-esteem and self-awareness.

a. Characterization awareness
b. Literatherapy
c. Literary infusion
d. Bibliotherapy

6.7 Strategies for Students With Behavioral Challenges

Many students with learning disabilities and related mild disabilities display disruptive or antisocial coping behaviors when they are faced with challenging and frustrating work. In this section, we discuss a variety of instructional strategies for students with behavioral challenges. Including Students in General Education 6.2, "Behavioral Challenges," offers some strategies for helping students with behavioral challenges in general education classes.

Including Students in GENERAL EDUCATION 6.2

Behavioral Challenges

- Seating placement. Seat the student in a place with minimal extraneous distraction and where you can readily ascertain if the student is attentive. Place the student away from windows and doors.

- Plan varied activities. Modify the classroom routine to enable the student to get up and move around the classroom periodically. Have the student pass out papers or put books away.

- Provide structure and routine. Establish a routine and follow it each day. If something unusual occurs, prepare the students by explaining what event will happen and when the event will occur.

- Require a daily assignment notebook. The assignment notebook helps the students to organize time, know what is to be done, and designate when it has been accomplished.

- Make sure you have the student's attention before you begin. Use an attention signal, such as a hand sign or eye contact to gain the student's attention.

- Make directions clear and concise. Directions should be consistent with daily instructions. Simplify complex directions and avoid multiple commands. State directions in a positive way. "I need you to start your math" is an example of a positive, short direction.

- Break assignments into workable chunks. If workbook or assignment sheets are cluttered and confusing, adapt them by breaking them into smaller parts. Less material will be on the page, and the material will be better organized. Give extra time as needed. Some students may work at a slower pace and may require extra time to complete the task. Teach students how to manage the time that is provided.

- Provide feedback on completed work as soon as possible.

- Encourage parents and families to set up appropriate study space at home.

- Make use of learning aids. Many students enjoy using computers, calculators, and other learning aids.

- Find something that the child does well and encourage that interest.

6.7a Developing an Effective Behavioral Intervention Plan

Earlier in this chapter, we discussed conducting a functional behavioral assessment to determine a behavioral intervention plan. Sometimes school personnel do a thorough job of functional assessment, but then create a "one size fits all" behavioral intervention plan. The behavioral intervention plan should be based on the individual needs of the student. Student Stories 6.4, "A Behavioral Intervention Plan for Jerod," gives an example of how a behavioral assessment can be used to develop a behavioral intervention plan.

6.7b Creating a Positive Classroom Environment

Children may feel threatened, or even defeated, by the demands placed on them in school. Students crave a sense of competence and achievement, which can be theirs when educators provide the right structure for success (Johns, 2004). A positive classroom environment is important in the process of conducting a positive behavioral intervention plan. Teaching Tips 6.2, "Strategies for Creating a Positive Environment," offers methods for achieving this goal.

Errorless Learning Techniques   Errorless learning techniques offer students the chance to succeed by accentuating what the students do well. Two strategies that result in errorless learning are fading and backward chaining. These instructional strategies require conducting a task analysis on the activities that are expected.

fading
A gradual removal of supports

backward chaining
The teacher gradually constructs a backward chain, or a chain in reverse order from that in which the chain is performed.

In the strategy called *fading,* the teacher gives the student maximum cues to begin with and then fades those cues away until the student is able to do the task on his or her own (Johns, 2004). For example, if the student is learning cursive writing, the teacher can provide a model of the letter to be written and the student merely traces over the letter. The teacher then reinforces the student for writing the letter. When the student is able to do this, the teacher can then prepare a model with dotted lines and the student traces over the dotted lines. The teacher then reinforces the student with praise. The last step is for the student to write the letter on his or her own. Let's look at an example of fading used to increase middle school and high school students' compliance with classroom rules. When students switch from class to class, it is sometimes difficult for them to comply with different teachers' rules. Perhaps one teacher expects students to raise their hand before speaking; another teacher is not concerned with that behavior. Middle school and high school teachers should have their rules posted in an obvious spot in the classroom. This is an excellent visual prompt for students. During the first two weeks of school, each teacher reviews the rules of his or her classroom. When students comply with the rules, the teacher remembers to thank them for doing so. After the first two weeks, the teacher fades his or her verbal prompt and simply points to the rules and reminds the students of the importance of following the posted rules. The teacher again thanks students for following the rules and may write a short personal note to students who have followed the rules. After the first month of school, the teacher leaves the rules posted but no longer provides a verbal reminder. However, the teacher continues to positively reinforce students who follow the rules but does not do so as often as he or she did the first month of school.

On page 177, you will find an explanation of the importance of a behavior intervention plan and reference to the plan that has been created for Jerod.

Strategies for Meeting the Social and Emotional Needs of Students

1. **Model positive and peaceful behavior.** The teacher is a positive role model for the students—do as I say and as I do. At least 70% of comments that the teacher makes to students must be positive comments (Johns & Carr, 2009). Work to ensure that the student is treated respectfully because reprimanding a student in front of his or her peers is not respectful. Praise should be specific to the behavior desired. For example: "Thank you for raising your hand"; "I like the way you waited in line quietly"; "Thanks for walking in the halls." If the student gets something wrong, the teacher should utilize the opportunity to reteach the skill rather than reprimand the student.

2. **Provide routine, structure, and organization within the classroom.** Students need routine and structure so that they know what will happen and when it will happen. The teacher should provide a written or picture schedule that is posted in a highly visible place so students know what will happen and when. If the schedule is going to be changed during the day, the teachers should prepare students for that change and reward them for making the adjustment. For students with problems with organizational skills, teachers should help them become better organized. A good motto is "A place for everything and everything in its place." The more we can provide labels for where items go, the better it is for the student. At the same time, we are teaching the student a useful life long skill.

3. **Establish clear expectations in the classroom.** Teach expectations for classroom behavior, and be firm, fair, and consistent in fulfilling the expectations. Rules or expectations should be kept short and simple, and they should be based on observable behaviors. For example: "Raise your hand before speaking"; "Keep your hands to yourself"; "Walk quietly in the hall." Post rules as a reminder for students. Picture cues are effective for students who have difficulty reading; post

written hallway rules with simple pictures alongside them as a visual reminder. Spend time teaching the students the meaning of the rules and providing examples. Provide reinforcement to those students who *do* follow the rules. Expectations are meaningless if they are not backed up with reinforcement for compliance and consequences for noncompliance (Johns & Carr, 2009; Barbetta, Norona, & Bicard, 2005).

4. **Create an environment of caring and success.** Set the students up for success by utilizing errorless learning techniques (discussed in the next section). Our job as educators is to show students that we genuinely care about them and that we are their cheerleaders for success. Establish high expectations and show them that they have many strengths on which they can capitalize. It is critical that we provide supports to our students, learn about their lives, and reflect frequently on our role in developing a caring relationship with our students. The way that the teacher interacts with students during the initial stages of relationship building is a determining factor in promoting either a positive or a negative relationship (Mihalas et al.,2009).

5. **Understand and respect the diverse cultures and backgrounds of students in the class.** Help students foster pride in their cultural backgrounds. Create lessons in diversity based upon the students' backgrounds, neighborhoods, and life experiences (Johns, Crowley, & Guetzloe, 2002).

6. **Make the classroom as physically appealing and beautiful as possible.** The classroom should be an inviting place where the students want to be. Little things such as real or silk plants can give the classroom a beautiful look. Rocking chairs offer the students an opportunity to move while they read. A reading corner with comfortable chairs may be more inviting for a student to go to read. Lamps will give the room a softer light.

Professional Resource Download

In *backward chaining*, the teacher gradually constructs a backward chain, which is a chain in a reverse order from that in which the chain is performed. The last step is established first; then the next to the last step is taught and linked to the last step (Martin & Pear, 2003; Johns, 2004). An example of backward chaining occurs in teaching a student to tie shoes. The teacher does all of the steps except pull the bow. The student does that and is praised for doing so. The student then does the last two steps, and so forth.

Jerod is a fifth-grade student with learning disabilities who is very resistant to completing math assignments. When the teacher presents him with a worksheet to complete in math (antecedent), he rips the paper up and throws it on the floor each time (behavior); the teacher then sends Jerod to the office (consequence). The function of the behavior is escape—Jerod actually has done a good job of communicating that he doesn't like to do math worksheets, and he has learned that if he rips the paper up he will be sent to the office. The functional assessment showed that Jerod does have the skills to do fifth-grade level math work but worksheets are difficult for him because of visual-motor perception difficulties. He is easily overwhelmed by a paper with many math problems. However, Jerod has strong computer skills and loves to read books about Superman.

The Behavior Intervention Plan for Jerod

A behavioral intervention plan is created. The replacement behavior desired is the completion of written math assignments at the fifth-grade level. The goal is for him to complete 20 math computation problems with 95% accuracy. The goal is then broken down into benchmarks.

1. Jerod will complete 5 math computation problems with 95% accuracy.
2. Jerod will complete 10 math problems with 95% accuracy.
3. Jerod will complete 15 math problems with 95% accuracy.
4. Jerod will complete 20 math problems with 95% accuracy.

As part of the plan, the teacher agrees to give Jerod only 5 math problems at one time. Each of the math problems will be enlarged so they are easy to read. Jerod is told that when he completes the 5 math problems he will be able to spend 5 minutes reading his book on Superman. A self-management system is also developed in which Jerod is allowed to graph on the computer using the Excel program to show how many math problems he completes each day. When Jerod does 5 math problems successfully, the teacher will add a new problem, gradually working up to Jerod doing 10 math problems.

In this behavioral intervention plan, the Premack principle (first you do this and then you can do that—the process of doing a non-preferred activity followed by a preferred activity) for reinforcement is used, and Jerod's work is rewarded when he successfully completes the math problems. Self-management is built into the system by using Jerod's strength in computers as Jerod graphs his own progress.

In the event that Jerod refuses to do the assignment and throws the assignment on the floor, Jerod will lose the privilege of reading his Superman book, but he will not be sent to the office.

REFLECTIVE QUESTIONS

1. Why is it important that a self-management system be built into any behavioral intervention plan?
2. If this plan was not making a positive difference for Jerod after three weeks, what might you do?

Let's look at another example. The teacher is concerned that two young children are not able to play cooperatively together. The teacher wants them to be able to throw a ball back and forth. The teacher decides that she will engage in the game with the two students. She throws the ball back and forth to the students, never expecting the students to throw to each other. She then praises them for playing ball together. She has done all but the last part of the chain. After the students have become accustomed to doing that, she then throws the ball to each student and they throw it back to her. She then throws the ball to one of the students and expects one of the students to throw the ball to the other student and the other student is to catch it. She then praises both students. In the next step, she throws the ball to one of the students—he catches it and throws it to the next student and then throws the ball to the teacher. In the next step, the teacher begins the game by throwing the ball to one student who throws it to the other student and they throw it back and forth—teacher is praising the students for playing together. In the last, the teacher removes herself completely from the game and the students throw it back and forth.

6.7c Restructuring Academic Work to Make It User Friendly

The following ideas are designed to restructure academic tasks to make them less intimidating and more fun for the student.

Build choice into assignments to give students power and control. For example, allow students to choose *where* they work on the assignment or *what color* pen is used. Structure two or more different assignments and allow students to choose which assignment they want to do. Allow students to choose the order in which they perform the assignment. Research shows that building in choices about curricula results in higher rates of on-task behavior and work completion (Strout, 2005; Jolivette et al., 2002). Further, when a preferred task is assigned rather than a non-preferred task, students have a higher level of engagement (Cole et al., 1997). In a study of students' academic choices and their impact on academic performance, it was found that students who had significant cognitive or behavioral problems benefited more under conditions of student choice than experiments with general education students. For general education students, factors that may moderate the impact of student choice include the nature of the task, the background of the students, and feedback during the performance of the task (Von Mizener & Williams, 2009).

Use response cards. Response cards serve to increase student opportunity to respond and provide a high degree of academic engagement. For example, teachers often ask questions when instructing a group. Students who know the answers raise their hands, whereas students who don't know the answers look down and hope the teacher does not call on them. Instead, the teacher can utilize a variety of response-card strategies. For example, the teacher can give each student a small white board, an index card, or a small blackboard. When the teacher asks the question, all of the students write down what they believe is the answer. After sufficient wait time, the teacher asks the students to hold up their answer. When instructing with new material, elicit four to six responses a minute from students who should then be able to respond with 80% accuracy. Increasing opportunities to respond has a positive effect on academic outcomes and classroom behavior (George, 2010; Blood, 2010; Haydon et al., 2009; Lambert et al., 2006; Council for Exceptional Children, 1987; Sutherland, Alder, & Gunter, 2003).

Use traveling assignments for worksheets. Instead of giving a student a worksheet with 100 math problems, cut the worksheet into strips and tape the strips up around the room. Students take a clipboard around the room and answer the questions. This activity has the advantage of breaking the task down into small steps and allowing students to move as they complete the assignment.

6.7d Self-Management Strategies

self-management
Using behavior strategies to take charge of one's own activities

Teach students to manage their own behaviors at any early age. Self-monitoring during independent seatwork can improve student accuracy in computation of basic math skills (Hodge et al.,2006). Learning self-management fosters independence for students and discourages the sense of helplessness. The following steps can help students with self-management (Little, 2000).

- Identify the behavior(s) that the student will monitor or evaluate. Make sure that the behavior description is written in Measurable, Observable, and Objective terms (MOO).
- Clearly state the expectations by which students will judge their own performance.
- Use a contract for self-monitoring, in which students define positive behavior, how it will be monitored, and how it will be rewarded.
- Make random checks to gauge the accuracy of student-completed forms.
- Provide specific praise and corrective feedback.

Another effective self-management strategy is goal setting. Following are steps for teaching this strategy.

1. First, teachers model the strategy by writing a goal for themselves for a short period. Depending on the level of the student, the teacher may want to set a goal for a half day.
2. Then the teacher assists the student in writing a goal for a half day. At the end of the designated time period, the teacher and the student evaluate if each has met the established goal. As the student gets accustomed to the process of goal setting, the teacher can then have the student write a goal for the entire day.
3. Eventually students should write a goal for the week and monitor their progress each day.

goal setting
The teacher models setting a goal. Teacher helps student in setting a goal. Students set the goal and monitor progress toward the goal.

6.7e Positive Strategies for Passive-Aggressive Behaviors

Some students may exhibit passive-aggressive behavior. For example, aggression is exhibited through their refusal to do something. They can make adults angry because they just do not do what is expected of them. What is passive-aggressive behavior?

passive-aggressive behavior
A student shows aggression by refusing to do something.

- Simultaneous, combined passive and aggressive behavior that is both conforming and irritating to others
- Behavior that is more destructive to interpersonal relationships than aggression
- Acts of passive aggression that are covert, insidious, and could last a lifetime
- Anger that is expressed indirectly (Long & Long, 2002)

When a student thinks the specific academic tasks are too difficult, or the student just decides that he or she is not going to do the task, the teacher may react by becoming very angry. Even though the student has not acted out overtly, the student's behavior has brought out overt aggression on the part of the adult. The following strategies can help teachers proactively deal with passive-aggressive behavior:

Recognize that the student is engaging in passive-aggressive behavior. For example, Randy pretends that he does not understand what is to be done or that he did not hear the directions. Teachers should be very clear in giving directions so that the student understands what to do. It helps to provide visual cues along with directions.

Avoid engaging in "begging" behavior. For example, the student sits and will not do the task. The teacher knows that the student is able to do the task. The teacher asks the student to get the task done multiple times. The student further avoids doing the task, seeing that the teacher is getting upset. Provide clear directions no more than two times. When the student does what the teacher wants the student to do, the teacher should praise the student for the effort.

Acknowledge normal feelings of anger. Long & Long (2002) suggest these steps: (1) Recognize that you are feeling angry toward the student but do not express your anger through aggressive and passive-aggressive behavior to the student; (2) Talk to yourself reminding yourself that you will not allow the student to get to you and that you should stop and count to 15 to yourself to calm yourself down. It is important to remember that if the student is not going to do a task, you cannot make him or her do it; and (3) establish some specific routines that increase the likelihood that the student will perform the task. The following interventions help deal with feelings of anger.

- **Use an "I" message.** For example, the teacher might say "I am having difficulty dealing with your behavior right now. I need to wait a few minutes. We need to discuss this situation but not right now."
- **Request that the student start a task.** If a student engages in passive-aggressive behavior when the teacher tells the student to get the entire task done, the student may become overwhelmed and, in all probability, will not complete the task. Instead, just ask the student to start the task.
- **Provide power and control by giving assignments that incorporate choices.** Give two assignments and ask the students to choose one. Or the students can choose when or where they do a certain task.
- **Utilize behavioral momentum.** Prior to giving a difficult task, the teacher can give the student an easy task to do (one that the teacher knows the student will be able to do successfully). When the student completes the task, the teacher reinforces the student for completing the task. The teacher then gives another task to the student that is easy for the student to do. When the student completes the task, the teacher provides a reinforcement. The teacher then gives a more difficult task. Students will be more confident that they can do the task because they have gained momentum by successfully doing the simpler tasks. This technique is called behavioral momentum.

behavioral momentum
Before giving a student a difficult task, give the student at least two easy tasks. The student gains confidence by completing the easy tasks and gains momentum to accomplish a more difficult task.

Did You Get It?

A teaching technique in which a teacher initially provides frequent cues, only to diminish those cues incrementally as the student becomes more task aware and adept is
   a. attenuation.
   b. fading.
   c. prompting regression.
   d. hint mitigation.

6.8 Behavior Management Strategies

Students with behavioral challenges can benefit from behavior management strategies. Many teachers intuitively use many behavior management procedures, but precise application of behavior management requires that the procedures are systematic and that the behaviors to be changed are observable and measurable. In the following sections, we describe several behavioral management activities.

6.8a Contingency Contracting

The *contingency contract* is a written agreement between the student and the teacher. An example of a contingency contract is shown in Figure 6.3. The idea that something desirable can be used to reinforce something the student does not wish to do is the essence of contingency contracting. This method is also called "Grandma's Rule" because grandmothers are alleged to promise, "If you finish your vegetables, you can have your dessert." For example, Dave, who likes to play ball, is allowed to play after he finishes his spelling work. Another name for this procedure is the Premack principle, which is based on the premise that a nonpreferred activity is reinforced with a preferred activity. As an example, the student does not like doing math problems but loves to color in a coloring book. If the student completes 5 math problems, he can color for 1–2 minutes. For an older student who likes to draw or listen to his iPod, the student can do a set number of math problems and then can have 5 minutes to draw or listen to music.

6.8b Time-Out

Time-out is a procedure in which a disruptive student is removed from the instructional activities and placed in a designated isolated area for a short period of time. Isolation does not have to be complete to be effective, but it does need to remove the student from the group. Time-out can be a powerful technique to manage disruptive behaviors in children, but it should be used cautiously. If implemented properly, time-out offers an effective means of managing behavior. Several conditions will increase the likelihood of success with this method (Johns & Carr, 2009; Alberto & Troutman, 2003):

- Time-out should be brief, from 1 to 5 minutes, with young children requiring the least amount of time. A common rule of thumb is no more than 1 minute for every year of the child's age.
- During a time-out, the teacher and the other children should ignore the student.
- Actively assist the student's return from time-out by directly engaging the child in ongoing activities (Groteluschen, Borkowski, & Hale, 1990; McGrady, Lerner, & Boscardin, 2001).
- Time-out is only effective if the teacher also reinforces the child when the child is engaging in the appropriate behavior. As an example, the teacher

contingency contracting
A behavioral management strategy that entails a written agreement between the student and the teacher stating that the student will be able to do something he or she wants if he or she first completes a specified task

premack principle
The principle where a student must complete a non-preferred activity and then is allowed to do a preferred activity for a specified period of time

time-out
A behavior management method in which a child is removed from a group for a short period of time

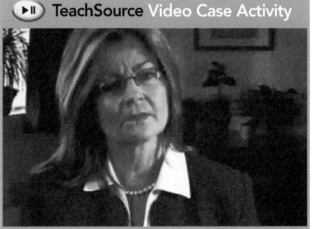

TeachSource Video Case Activity

Watch the TeachSource Video Case entitled "Classroom Management: Handling Students With Behavior Problems." In this video case, a team of school professionals is trying to better understand Peter's behavior.

QUESTIONS

1. What do you think were the antecedents of Peter's behaviors in both of the classrooms?
2. Because behavior is communication, what do you think Peter was trying to communicate with his behavior?
3. What were some of the positive interventions that were utilized with Peter?

© Cengage Learning 2015

FIGURE **6.3**
Contingency Contract

Bryce is a sixth grade student who refuses to take his assignment notebook home with him at night and to return it to school. He takes his books home but not his assignment notebook and as a result he doesn't know what to do and his parents don't know what to do to assist him. Bryce is in general education classes and the remainder of his day is in a special education classroom. His special education teacher has exposed him to a variety of types of assignment notebook and Bryce likes the one he has but doesn't take it home. He leaves the special education classroom at the end of the day with the notebook and his books but the notebook does not get home. It is found that he hides it in his locker on his way to the bus. Bryce loves to draw but has been losing his drawing time because he has to complete makeup assignments. The special education teacher, the general education teachers, the principal, Bryce, and his mother meet to create a contract for Bryce as follows:

CONTRACT BETWEEN BRYCE AND HIS TEACHERS

This contract is an agreement that each evening Bryce agrees that he:

1. will take his assignment notebook home with homework assignments recorded and the books he needs
2. complete all of his homework assignments, and return the assignments the next day completed.
3. Books and the assignment notebook will be returned.

Each day that Bryce returns the above completed items to his special education teacher first thing in the morning, his special education teacher agrees to give him the following:

1. 20 minutes of free drawing time.

Each week that Bryce has returned all of the items each day, Bryce will receive a coupon to excuse him of his choice of one homework assignment from his classroom teachers.

Signed:

Student _____

Parent _____

Special Education teacher _____

Classroom teachers _____

_____

_____

_____

Building Principal _____

Date:

This contract will remain in effect for the remainder of the school year.

© Cengage Learning

may have decided to use time-out because the student is engaging in an inappropriate behavior with a peer—the student has taken an item away from a peer or the student has made a negative comment to a peer. Time-out will not work unless the teacher also reinforces the student when the student shares an item with a peer or engages in appropriate and respectful conversation with a peer (Johns & Carr, 2009).

- Seclusionary time-out—time out where the student is removed to a separate room—should be used very cautiously and only as a last resort when other means of time out have been exhausted. An increasing number of states have laws and regulations that govern its use and those must be followed. Be sure to research those laws and regulations as well as your school board's policy before implementing any type of seclusionary time out.

6.8c Cognitive Behavior Modification

Cognitive behavior modification is a self-instructional approach to learning. It requires that individuals learn to motivate themselves through (1) talking to themselves aloud, (2) giving themselves instruction on what they should be doing, and (3) rewarding themselves verbally for accomplishments (Meichenbaum, 1977). Cognitive behavior modification stresses techniques that give students the tools to control their own behavior (Robinson, 2007; Fitzpatrick & Knowlton, 2009).

The self-instructional cognitive behavior modification program involves the following steps:

1. First, the teacher models or performs a task while talking to himself or herself aloud as the students observe.
2. The students then perform the same task while talking to themselves, under the teacher's guidance.
3. The students quietly whisper the instructions to themselves while going through the task.
4. The students use inner (or private) speech while performing the task.
5. Finally, the students self-monitor their performance by telling themselves how they did. For example, "I did well" or "Next time I should slow down."

Cognitive behavior modification has often been used with adults in such settings as weight-loss programs. Students with learning problems can use the procedure for all kinds of learning, schoolwork, and homework. The goal of cognitive behavior modification is not only to change the person's behavior, but also to increase the person's awareness of his or her behavior and the thinking associated with the behavior.

6.8d Using Reinforcements

Reinforcement theory offers a major tool for behavior management. The use of reinforcements provides an important strategy for teaching students appropriate behavior and for managing behavior. Reinforcements are used to increase or to change behavior. By identifying reinforcements that a student wants, teachers can construct a reward system that will promote the desired behavior. Positive and immediate reinforcements are the most effective in fostering the desired behavior. Stars, stickers, raisins, tokens, points, praise, flashing lights, or simply the satisfaction of knowing that the answer is correct are common reinforcers. Examples of reinforcements:

- After Annette reads five pages, she receives *two tokens that are exchangeable for a small toy.*
- In teaching reading to Serena, the desired behavior is having her say the sound equivalent of the letter *a* every time a stimulus card with the letter *a* is shown. For each correct response, Serena immediately receives a positive reinforcement, such as *a piece of low-sugar cereal, stars, points, praise,* or *attention.*

To use reinforcements successfully, the teacher must

1. Identify potential reinforcers that will motivate the student and accelerate performance on a specific task.
2. Identify the student's responses or behaviors that should trigger the reinforcer. Responses and behaviors must be observable and clearly defined.
3. Arrange the environment so that the student receives reinforcement for the desired behavior. A reward system should be devised so that

cognitive behavior modification
A self-instructional approach to learning. It requires individuals to talk to themselves out loud, give themselves instruction on what they should be doing, and reward themselves verbally for accomplishments.

reinforcement theory
A behavioral concept of learning based on using rewards or reinforcement

behavior management
Using behavioral strategies to direct an individual's activity in an appropriate manner

reinforcement
An event following a response that increases the likelihood that the person will make a similar response in similar situations in the future

reinforcements are offered on a predetermined schedule for the desired behaviors.

4. Eventually, have the student make independent instructional decisions, such as making corrections and establishing reinforcement values. Including the student in the modification of the reward system is helpful as the student is moved to a system of naturally occurring reinforcers.

Teaching Tips 6.3, "Finding Reinforcers," offers ideas on finding appropriate reinforcers.

6.8e Home-School Coordination

home-school coordination
A behavior management strategy for helping a child learn. Progress at school is reinforced at home.

Programs of home-school coordination are intended to improve the behavior of students by combining school and home efforts. Behavioral goals are established for the student, and each day the teacher indicates the goals the student has met. These behavior-management sheets are sent home, signed by the parent to acknowledge the teacher's comments, and then returned to the school. The student is reinforced at home for the positive behaviors displayed at school. As educators work to establish a positive relationship with the parents, it is important that they recognize the efforts of the parents—when the

---

TEACHING TIPS 6.3

Finding Reinforcers

The success of behavior management depends upon finding the appropriate reinforcer to increase the target behavior. What is viewed as desirable by one student may hold little interest for another. To find a successful reinforcer, observe the students to see what they choose to *do* in their free time or request such information from the students and their parents. Reinforcers can be *extrinsic,* which is something external, such as food or toys, for older students it might be time to listen to music on the iPod, time to look at an appropriate teen magazine, or time to talk with a friend; or reinforcers can be *intrinsic,* which is something internal, such as the satisfaction of mastering a task. The reinforcement can be social, such as praise or approval from a teacher or parent. A personal note from the teacher can be very reinforcing to an older student and can assist in establishing a positive relationship. It can be a token to be exchanged for a later reinforcement or it can take the form of a privilege. A good reinforcement for any individual is simply the one that works for that individual. Several suggested reinforcements are

- *Foods:* edible seeds, low-sugar cereal, popcorn, raisins, and fruit or fruit roll-ups. If food is used as a reinforcer, the amount should be kept to a minimum. Before considering the use of food, it is imperative that we work with the family to determine whether the child may have specific food allergies to different products. The use of food should always be paired with positive verbal

reinforcement—praise—so that the use of food can be faded as soon as possible. Low-calorie and healthy foods are always preferred if they are reinforcing to the student.

- *Play materials:* Baseball cards, toy animals, toy cars, marbles, jump ropes, gliders, crayons, coloring books, clay, dolls, kits, balls, puzzles, comic books, balloons, games, and yo-yos may be appropriate for younger students. Older students may like stress balls, fidgets that twist, pencils or pens that have a particular smell, or baseball or basketball cards.

- *Tokens:* Marks on the blackboard or on the student's paper, gold or silver stars, marbles in a jar, plastic chips on a ring, poker chips, tickets, and washers on a string. Older students like to earn raffle tickets for a drawing at a specific time.

- *Activities or privileges:* Having computer time, presenting at show and tell, going first, running errands, having free time, helping with cleanup, taking the class pet home for the weekend, leading the songs, seeing a video, listening to music, and doing artwork. Older students like getting to leave for lunch a few minutes early or getting to leave for home a few minutes early. Arrangements must be made ahead of time for such privileges. If the school allows cell phones, they may want to earn the privilege of getting to text message for five minutes.

Professional Resource Download

parent helps with homework, when the parent gets the student to school on time each day, when the parent answers notes from the teacher. Parents need to be reinforced for their efforts and appreciate a "Thank you, I really appreciate your support." Below find a true example of an experience one of the authors had:

Michael, a freshman in high school, had come to an alternative school for students with significant behavioral disorders. His mother, a single parent, was working two jobs to support the family of four. Through recognition of Michael's appropriate behavior and many opportunities for his success, Michael became a model student—he had perfect attendance, he thrived academically and emotionally. The author, the principal of the school, would often call his mother to brag about how Michael was doing. The author stressed how much she appreciated all of the cooperation she received from the mother. When Michael's mother would come in for conferences, the author would talk about how she admired the mother for managing to do all that she did. The author established a positive relationship with the mother.

Michael did so well that he was systematically integrated back to his home high school. The time came for the IEP where Michael was returned to his school full-time with consultation services by a resource special education teacher. Michael did well for a few weeks and then started acting up and exhibiting increasing behavior problems; the home school called for a new IEP because they wanted to return him to the alternative school. Further investigation showed that the school was giving positive recognition to Michael but no one had established a positive relationship with Michael's mother. No one was calling her when Michael was doing well. Because her need for positive support was not being met, she began to sabotage his new placement, wanting him to go back to the alternative school. It was critical for the school's guidance counselor and the resource special education teacher to frequently contact the mother to support her. That was all that was needed to resolve the issue.

A sample home-school behavior-management sheet is shown in Figure 6.4.

FIGURE **6.4**

Home-School Behavior Management Sheet

Student: _____   Teacher: _____

Week beginning: _____

Use (S) for satisfactory performance.
Use (U) for unsatisfactory performance.
Use (N) for items that do not apply.

	Mon	Tues	Wed	Thurs	Fri
1. Homework turned in					
2. Began work within 3 min. of assignment					
3. Followed directions					
4. Followed class and school rules					
5. Paid attention to teacher					
6. Raised hand to speak					
7. Other					

If 80% of applicable boxes are checked, the student will receive 20 min of computer time.

Teacher's initials: _____

COMMENTS AND SIGNATURE

	Teacher	Parent
Monday	_____	_____
Tuesday	_____	_____
Wednesday	_____	_____
Thursday	_____	_____
Friday	_____	_____

- Parent signs chart daily
- Child takes chart home daily
- Child returns chart to school daily
- Child receives daily reward

© Cengage Learning

I Have a Kid Who...

MARIO, *a Student With Behavioral Challenges*

Mario recently moved to Jefferson School and he is in the fifth-grade classroom of Mrs. Holden. There is no record that he has received any special education services before. During the first week of class, Mario urinated on another student in the classroom. He also had an incident where he soiled his pants while outside after lunch. He complained to the teacher that the lights were too bright in the classroom. Mrs. Holden went to the principal to see if the principal could get any background information from Mario's previous school. When the call is made, the principal learns that a case study evaluation was in progress but had not been completed because Mario moved. His previous school reported that Mario would become very upset when anyone would get close to him or when he would get dirty. The previous school had received a psychiatric report that Mario has Asperger's syndrome and ADHD.

The school personnel at his new school decide to initiate a case study evaluation. During the parent interview, Mario's mother reports that he is one of two children in the home and his father is unknown to him. Mario's mother is very concerned about how Mario is doing both at home and at school. Mario will not comply with his mother's requests, and he is obsessed with the notion that if he gets dirty, his arms will fall off. He has a special interest in Superman and likes to watch those videos most of the time, if allowed to do so.

While waiting for the case study evaluation, Mrs. Holden continued to work with Mario. On at least five occasions, when a fellow student touched him accidentally, he screamed for three minutes. Mario completes little work in the classroom—only about 20% of all assignments across all subject areas except for math. Mario does like to read but does not like math and refuses to do any math work. His achievement test scores from his previous school show that he is able to do fifth-grade work in reading recognition and comprehension. His math skills are at a third-grade level.

Within the next three weeks, Mario soils his pants 5 more times. Each time he becomes upset, goes into the bathroom, and won't come out until the principal calls his mother to come and get him. Mrs. Holden is frustrated and puzzled. She awaits the IEP eligibility meeting, hoping she will get some help with Mario.

QUESTIONS

1. If you were Mrs. Holden, what would you do to help Mario until the case study evaluation is done?

2. What might Mario's behavior be communicating to Mrs. Holden?

3. How could Mrs. Holden accentuate Mario's strengths within the classroom?

Did You Get It?

"Tommy, if you are able to go each week without becoming verbally abusive to your peers, I will allow you to have extra time to use the binoculars on Friday, something I know you like to do. If you agree, let's draw up a contract." The technique used by the teacher talking to Tommy is _____ contracting.

    a. opportunistic
    b. exigency
    c. contingency
    d. circumstantial

Chapter Summary

- An increasing number of students come into today's classrooms with social, emotional, and behavioral challenges. These challenges may be related to each other and behaviors exhibited by students may either be internalizing problems or externalizing problems.
- It is critical that we teach students appropriate social skills in order for them to function in today's society.
- There is a relationship between learning difficulties and emotional challenges.
- Behavioral challenges often result in suspensions that disengage students from schools and to prevent such disengagement, schools must utilize functional behavioral assessments and positive behavior supports.
- There are a number of effective strategies to improve social competencies.
- Strategies for students with emotional challenges include strategies for building positive self-esteem.
- Strategies for students with behavioral challenges include the development of behavior intervention plans.
- Effective behavior management strategies include reinforcement, contracting, cognitive behavior modification, and appropriate use of time out.

Questions for Discussion and Reflection

1. Why do you think challenges in social skills are called "the most crippling type of problem that a student can have"? What are common indicators of social challenges?
2. Describe functional behavioral assessment and positive behavioral supports.
3. What is reinforcement? How can effective reinforcers be identified? What types of reinforcers might be appropriate for adolescents?
4. What academic strategies can be utilized to reduce behavioral problems?
5. Discuss "resiliency." Why is the quality of resiliency important to individuals who have difficulty in learning?

Key Terms

backward chaining (p. 175)
behavior management (p. 183)
behavior momentum (p. 180)
cognitive behavior modification (p. 183)
contingency contracting (p. 181)
externalizing (p. 163)
fading (p. 175)
functional behavioral assessment (FBA) (p. 167)
goal setting (p. 179)
home-school coordination (p. 184)
internalizing (p. 163)

manifestation determination (p. 165)
passive-aggressive behavior (p. 179)
positive behavioral supports (p. 167)
premack principle (p. 181)
reinforcement (p. 183)
reinforcement theory (p. 183)
school-wide positive behavior support (p. 168)
self-management (p. 178)
social skills (p. 160)
time-out (p. 181)

BestPhotoPlus/Shutterstock.com

Related Disabilities: Autism Spectrum Disorders (ASD) and Attention Deficit Hyperactivity Disorder (ADHD)

They are able who think they are able.

—Virgil

LEARNING OBJECTIVES

After reading this chapter, you should be able to:

7.1 Discuss Autism Spectrum Disorder (ASD)

7.2 Discuss Attention Deficit Hyperactivity Disorder (ADHD)

7.3 List the characteristics of ADHD

7.4 List treatments for ADHD

7.5 Demonstrate methods of teaching for students with ADHD

STANDARDS Addressed in This Chapter:

CEC Initial Level Special Educator Preparation Standards as approved by the National Council for the Accreditation of Teacher Education

CEC Initial Preparation Standard 1: Learner Development and Individual Learning Differences

- 1.0—Beginning special education professionals understand how exceptionalities may interact with development and learning and use this knowledge to provide meaningful and challenging learning experiences for individuals with exceptionalities.

- 1.2—Beginning special education professionals use understanding of development and individual differences to respond to the needs of individuals with exceptionalities.

CEC Initial Preparation Standard 2: Learning Environments

- 2.2—Beginning special education professionals use motivational and instructional interventions to teach individuals with exceptionalities how to adapt to different environments.

CEC Initial Preparation Standard 3: Curricular Content Knowledge

- 3.3—Beginning special education professionals modify general and specialized curricula to make them accessible to individuals with exceptionalities.

CEC Initial Preparation Standard 4: Assessment

- 4.0—Beginning special education professionals use multiple methods of assessment and data-sources in making educational decisions.

- 4.3—Beginning special education professionals in collaboration with colleagues and families use multiple types of assessment information in making decisions about individuals with exceptionalities.

- 4.4—Beginning special education professionals engage individuals with exceptionalities to work toward quality learning and performance and provide feedback to guide them.

CEC Initial Preparation Standard 5: Instructional Planning and Strategies

- 5.0—Beginning special education professionals select, adapt, and use a repertoire of evidence-based instructional strategies to advance learning of individuals with exceptionalities.

- 5.1—Beginning special education professionals consider an individual's abilities, interests, learning environments, and cultural and linguistic factors in the selection, development, and adaptation of learning experiences for individuals with exceptionalities.

- 5.4—Beginning special education professionals use strategies to enhance language development and communication skills of individuals with exceptionalities.

- 5.5—Beginning special education professionals develop and implement a variety of education and transition plans for individuals with exceptionalities across a wide range of settings and different learning experiences in collaboration with individuals, families, and teams.

We devote this chapter to two related disabilities: Autism Spectrum Disorders (ASD) and Attention Deficit Hyperactivity Disorder (ADHD).

7.1 Autism Spectrum Disorder

autism spectrum disorder (ASD)
A range of disorders that are included within the category of autism, including autism and Asperger's syndrome.

Autism spectrum disorders (ASDs) consist of a group of developmental disabilities that are caused by problems with the brain. Scientists do not know yet exactly what causes this disability (Hunt & Marshall, 2012). The term autism spectrum disorder (ASD) includes several types of conditions with a wide range of symptoms, differences in when symptoms start, and different levels of severity, from very mild to severe. However, they share some similar symptoms, such as problems in social interaction. In its milder forms, only a few of the characteristics of autism are present or they are in a very mild form. In 2007, the Centers for Disease Control and Prevention (CDC) estimated a prevalence rate of 1 in 150. In 2009, the CDC found a significantly higher prevalence of autism spectrum disorders—1 in 110 children. In 2012, the CDC reported that 1 in 88 children in the United States is being diagnosed with autism—nearly a doubling of the prevalence since the CDC began tracking these numbers. Autism can now officially be declared an epidemic in the United States (Centers for Disease Control and Prevention, 2012). In 2013, The CDC reported that 1 in 50 children is being diagnosed with autism (Centers for Disease Control and Prevention, 2013).

Autism was first identified as a separate category of disability in the federal legislation, IDEA, in 1990. Before 1990, autism was included in the category of other health impaired (OHI) and prior to that in the category of emotional disturbance.

The American Psychiatric Association publishes a reference manual entitled the *Diagnostic and Statistical Manual of Mental Disorders, Fifth Edition (DSM-5),* which provides criteria for the diagnosis of all mental disorders (2013). The *DSM-5* is widely used by medical specialists, psychologists, and others. Autism was identified in the *DSM-IV-TR,* but the category was changed in DSM-5 (2013) to autism spectrum disorder. That is, the original multicategorical diagnosis has been changed to a single diagnostic category (Stetka & Volkmar, 2012). (DSM-5 published in May 2013 by the American Psychiatric Association).

Diagnosing ASD can be difficult because there is no physical medical test, such as a blood test. ASD is typically diagnosed through the child's behavior and development. In addition, there is no medication that can cure autism spectrum disorders. Four times as many boys as girls are identified with ASD. It is recommended that treatment begin as early as possible, by age 3 (Eunice Kennedy Shriver National Institute of Child Health and Human Development, 2008; Centers for Disease Control and Prevention, 2009).

7.1a Types of Autism Spectrum Disorders

Autism Spectrum Disorders has been defined in the *DSM-5* (American Psychiatric Association, 2013) as the following:

A. Persistent deficits in social communication and social interaction across multiple contexts, as manifested b the following, currently or by history:

  1. Deficits in social-emotional reciprocity, ranging, for example from abnormal social approach and failure of normal back-and-fort conversation; to reduced sharing of interests, emotional, or affect; to failure to initiate or respond to social interaction.

  2. Deficits in nonverbal communicative behaviors used for social interaction, ranging, for example, from poorly integrated verbal and nonverbal communication; to abnormalities in eye contact and body language or deficits in understand and use of gestures; to a total lack of facial expressions and non-verbal communication.

  3. Deficits in developing, maintaining, and understanding relationships, ranging, for example, from difficulties adjusting behavior to suit various social contexts; to difficulties in sharing imaginative play or in making friends; to absence of interest in peers.

B. Restricted, repetitive patterns of behavior, interests, or activities as manifested by at least two of the following, currently or by history (these examples are illustrative, not exhaustive).

  1. Stereotyped or repetitive motor movements, use of objects, or speech.

  2. Insistence on sameness, inflexible adherence to routines, or ritualized patterns of verbal or nonverbal behavior.

  3. Highly restricted, fixated interests that are abnormal in intensity or focus.

  4. Hyper- or hypoactivity to sensory input or unusual interest in sensory aspects of the environment.

C. Symptoms must be present in the early developmental period but they may not become fully manifested until social demands exceed limited capacities, or may be masked by learned strategies in later life.

D. Symptoms cause clinically significant impairment in social, occupational, or other important areas of current functioning.

E. The disturbances are not better explained by intellectual disability or global developmental delay. An intellectual disability and autism spectrum disorder frequently co-occur.

Previously the DSM-IV provided for different diagnosis of autistic disorder, Asperger's disorder, or pervasive developmental disorder not otherwise specified. Now children who were previously diagnosed with those disorders are to be given the diagnosis of Autism Spectrum Disorder.

This is a significant change in the diagnosis.

Asperger's Syndrome Virtually unknown as a specific condition until the 1990s, Asperger's syndrome is now recognized as a relatively common disability. Asperger's syndrome was first brought to the attention of the psychiatric community in 1944 by Hans Asperger (1944), a Viennese physician, who published an article describing the unusual social isolation of a group of children with whom he was working. However, Asperger's syndrome did not gain wide recognition until the disorder was included in the American Psychiatric Association's *DSM-IV* (American Psychiatric Association, 1994).

It is important to note that three previous autism diagnoses—autism, Asperger's, and Pervasive Developmental Disorders—have been replaced with the single diagnosis of autism spectrum disorders as per the DSM-5 released in May, 2013 (Moran, 2012 and American Psychiatric Association, 2013).

Individuals with Asperger's syndrome often have severe difficulty in social interactions. Asperger's syndrome is characterized by a reluctance to accept change; an inflexibility of thought; and an all-absorbing, narrow area of interest. Children with Asperger's syndrome are usually extremely good at rote memory skills (e.g., repeating facts, figures, dates, times) and many excel in mathematics and science. There is a range of severity of symptoms within the syndrome; the very mildly affected child often goes undiagnosed, and many others may just appear odd or eccentric (Baker & Welkowitz, 2005). Children with Asperger's syndrome lack an understanding of the rules of social behavior, such as eye contact, proximity to others, gesture, and posture. They often display emotional vulnerability and stress, and, as a result, problems of poor self-esteem, poor self-concept, and depression are common. In individuals with Asperger's syndrome, characteristics of difficulty with social competence can include (Baker & Welkowitz, 2005):

- Frequent misunderstanding of the social communication of others
- Lack of empathy or seeing the perspective of others
- Poor play skills
- Frequent conflicts with others
- The target of teasing or bullying

Usually, children with Asperger's syndrome receive instruction in the general education classroom, but they often have academic difficulties because of their poor organizational skills, poor problem-solving skills, and poor motor skills that interfere with their academic achievement. To succeed in the general education classroom, children with Asperger's syndrome need the support of special educators and related services personnel familiar with this diagnosis. They need help in developing social skills, in academic planning and programming and in support for their sensory issues. Direct instruction of social skills

---

Asperger's syndrome
Qualitative impairment in social interactions, impulse control, and self-motivation. Included in the disability category of autism.

Temple Grandin, Ph.D., is one of the most accomplished and well-known adults with autism, possibly with Asperger's syndrome. She has written widely about living with autism and the many challenges and hardships she has faced. She also describes how she learned to live with her problems and succeed in the "neurotypical" world. Temple Grandin became an associate professor at Colorado State College in animal husbandry and in livestock handling. Her book *Animals in Translation* (2005) is a best seller. She speaks around the world on both autism and cattle handling.

Temple Grandin describes in detail the difficulty she has with sound sensitivity and with overstimulating sound sensations. She relies on visual thinking and images. She explains that her reaction to being touched was like a wild horse, flinching and pulling away. She believes that the reaction of an autistic child and a wild horse are similar. According to Grandin, the process of taming a wild animal has many similarities to an autistic child's reaction to touch (Grandin, 2008). For more information about Temple Grandin, go to the website at *http://www.autism .org/temple/visual.html*.

REFLECTIVE QUESTION

1. Why does Temple Grandin think that children with autism spectrum disorder and wild horses are similar?

is critical. With suitable support and instruction, most children with AS can be successful in school. Many students with AS are able to attend college and enjoy a variety of successful careers (Goldstein, Naglieri, & Ozonoff, 2008; Baker & Welkowitz, 2005; Myles, Cook, Miller, Rinner, & Robins, 2000).

Student Stories 7.1 relates the story of Temple Grandin, a very successful person with Autism Spectrum Disorders.

Often students with ASD have an intense interest in a specific topic and they acquire a broad knowledge about that subject. For example, one student with ASD had acquired a broad knowledge of Chicago restaurants. If given a location in the city or suburbs, he could tell you the name of a restaurant, its location, type of cuisine, and the price range for that restaurant. He used his knowledge to make a Microsoft Access directory of Chicago restaurants. Another student's expertise was in geography. Classmates could count on him knowing the capital of any country or the major rivers in the states.

Every student with ASD is different and no one intervention will be effective with every student (Goldstein, et al., 2008; Safran, 2002; Baker & Welkowitz, 2005). Teaching Tips 7.1, "Supporting Students with Autism Spectrum Disorders," offers some ways to work with students with ASD in the school environment. Figure 7.1 gives an example of the Social Story.

A helpful website for Asperger's syndrome is OASIS, Online Asperger Syndrome Information and Support, at *http://www.AspergersSyndrome.org*.

Helpful websites for Asperger's syndrome include

- Online Asperger's Syndrome Information and Support (OASIS), http:// aspergersyndrome.org. This website has general information about Asperger's syndrome.
- Asperger's Syndrome Coalition of the United States, *http://www.asperger.org*.
- The Online Resource and Community for Those With Asperger's Syndrome, *http://www.wrongplanet.net*. This website is for young adults with Asperger's syndrome, who often refer to themselves as "Aspies."

- **Use Social Stories.** A strategy for increasing social knowledge is the use of social stories. (See the website of The Gray Center for Social Learning and Understanding at *http://www.thegraycenter.org*.) These stories are often about problematic social situations, and they offer a way for students to discuss the "how and what" of social situations. A companion strategy is "comic strip situations." Students discuss a comic strip that implies a social situation. See Figure 7.1 for an example of a social story comic strip, entitled Jitters, used with a young child with Asperger's.

- **Provide Direct Instruction in the "What" and "How" of Social Relationships.** Direct instruction can be used to teach specific reactions to social situations. For example, Barbara can be taught three polite refusals when she does not want help, such as "No thank you," *or* "I am fine right now, thanks."

- **Circle of Friends.** In the "Circle of Friends" strategy, an adult facilitates interactions between the child with Asperger's syndrome and classmates. The teacher might talk about the characteristics of Asperger's syndrome (with parental permission). The peers then participate in ways to include the child in a social group of children.

- **Sensory Integration.** Sensory integration refers to the processes that the nervous system uses to integrate sensory information. In schools, the occupational therapist is the related professional who can work with classroom teachers to help students with sensory integration dysfunction. (For additional information about sensory integration, see Chapter 8, "Young Children With Disabilities.")

Professional Resource Download

FIGURE **7.1**

"Jitters" A Social Story Comic Strip

© Cengage Learning

7.1b Nonverbal Learning Disorders: A Related Condition

The condition of nonverbal learning disorders (NVLD) is capturing the attention of many psychologists, physicians, and researchers. Children with NVLD may function well in academic areas but have problems in the social sphere. The condition of NVLD is not identified within the special education law (IDEA-2004); however, NVLD is recognized as a disorder in the field of neuropsychology. NLVD is believed to have a neurodevelopmental basis that involves a dysfunction in the brain's right hemisphere.

Children with NVLD have difficulty understanding the subtle cues that are inherent in nonverbal communication and that play such an important role in social interaction. For example, these children cannot read facial expressions to discern if a person is sad, happy, or angry. They may not know how to initiate friendships or recognize the idea of personal space. These social cues are normally grasped intuitively through observation and living, but children with NVLD need to be taught these social skills through direct and explicit instruction (Rourke, 1995; Thompson, 1997; Boyle and Scanlon, 2010).

One mother described her daughter's NVLD as a serious difficulty in visual-spatial imagery, noting that her daughter could not find her way to a friend's house nor was she able to visualize where her classroom was at school. She had to remember words and verbal labels to keep from getting lost (Martin, 2004).

Students with NVLD often have a high verbal intelligence, they tend to be early talkers, and they are highly verbal. Because they do well in reading and decoding in the primary years, their nonverbal learning problems are frequently missed. Children with NVLD often have poor visual-spatial abilities, poor nonverbal problem-solving abilities, and low arithmetic skills. Problems with NVLD become more evident in the later elementary school years, during adolescence, and in the adult years (Dimitrovsky et al., 1998; Rourke, 1995; Thompson, 1997).

People with NVLD often have difficulty adapting to new situations. Despite their high verbal intelligence and high scores on receptive and expressive language measures, they inaccurately read nonverbal signals and cues, and they lack the social ability to comprehend nonverbal communication cues. If they do not perceive subtle cues in the environment, they do not know when something has gone far enough, and they cannot interpret the facial expressions of others. Normally, these social cues are intuitively grasped through observation; however, individuals with NVLD need to be taught these social skills through direct and explicit

nonverbal learning
disorders (NVLD)
Poor skills in nonacademic areas of
learning, such as poor social skills

TeachSource Video Case Activity

© Cengage Learning 2015

Watch the TeachSource Video Case entitled "Including Students With High-Incidence Disabilities: Strategies for Success." The teacher, Martha Cleveland, discusses the needs of students with high-incidence disabilities, such as attention deficit hyperactivity disorder, nonverbal learning disorders, and Asperger's syndrome. She points out that special strategies are required to accommodate the learning needs of these students in the elementary classroom. Discuss these questions after you view the video.

QUESTIONS

1. How can graphic organizers help students to organize their thoughts?
2. How can computer technology be used to help children develop graphic organizers?
3. The video mentions that these children have problems with executive functions. What are executive functions?

instruction (Dimitrovsky et al., 1998; Thompson, 1997; Tsatsanis, Furst, & Rourke, 1997).

Adults with NVLD often have serious difficulty in the workplace. Their problems include poor self-concept, mental health problems, difficulty in social relationships, and terse or curt response styles. Transitions are difficult because these individuals like routine and find it difficult to take on new responsibilities and assignments. Unable to reflect on the nature and seriousness of their own problems, they tend to attribute their failures, as well as their successes, to others, instead of to themselves. Their coping mechanisms are often misinterpreted as *emotional* or *motivational* problems (Price, 1997; Rourke, 1995; Thompson, 1997; Tsatsanis et al., 1997). A useful website for NVLD is LD Online, *http://www.nldline.com.*

Did You Get It?

Autism spectrum disorder diagnosis rates have been increasing sharply in the U.S. in recent years to the most current prevalence rate of 1 case per every 50 children. The Centers for Disease Control and Prevention (CDC) now considers these disorders

    a. epidemic.
    b. pandemic.
    c. widespread.
    d. catastrophic.

7.2 Attention Deficit Hyperactivity Disorder (ADHD)

attention deficit hyperactivity disorder (ADHD)
Difficulty in concentrating and staying on a task. Accompanied by hyperactivity. The condition of ADHD is identified and defined by the American Psychiatric Association's *Diagnostic and Statistical Manual of Mental Disorders*, Fifth Edition.

attention deficit disorder (ADD)
Difficulty in concentrating and staying on a task. It may or may not be accompanied by hyperactivity. Used by the U.S. Department of Education.

Attention deficit hyperactivity disorder (ADHD) is a common cooccurring condition for children with learning disabilities. (The terms *cooccurring, coexisting,* and *comorbidity* are used to indicate that a condition occurs along with another condition.) Research indicates that between 25% and 40% of the children with learning disabilities have cooccurring ADHD and that between 30% and 65% of the children with ADHD have cooccurring learning disabilities (Goldstein, 2007; Centers for Disease Control and Prevention, 2005; Silver, 2006; Fletcher et al., 2000). (See the website of Children and Adults With Attention Deficit Hyperactivity Disorder at *http://www.chadd.org.*)

Attention deficit hyperactivity disorder (ADHD) is a condition of the brain that makes it difficult for children to control their behavior in school and social settings. It is one of the most common chronic conditions of childhood and affects between 4% and 12% of all school-age children. About three times more boys than girls are diagnosed with ADHD (American Academy of Pediatrics, 2001).

Two different terms are used to refer to this condition: (1) attention deficit hyperactivity disorder (ADHD) is the terminology in the *DSM-5*, which is used by physicians and psychologists (American Psychiatric Association, 2013) and (2) attention deficit disorder (ADD), which is used by the U.S. Department of Education and many schools. Both terms refer to the same disorder.

We will use the term *ADHD* because it is being used more frequently in the literature. With increasing frequency, physicians and psychologists are identifying children with ADHD.

There are several active support groups that can provide additional information to parents of children with ADHD and to the professionals who work with them:

- CHADD, Children and Adults With Attention Deficit Disorder: *http://www.chadd.org*
- National Resource Center on ADHD, A Program of CHADD: *http://www.help4adhd.org*
- ADDA, Attention Deficit Disorder Association: *http://www.add.org*
- AD-IN, Attention Deficit Information Network, Inc.: *http://www.addinfonetwork.com*

Did You Get It?

Attention deficit hyperactivity disorder (ADHD) is rooted in _____, which makes it difficult or impossible for children to concentrate in various settings and situations.
- **a.** the brain
- **b.** the entire central nervous system
- **c.** unknown cause
- **d.** the circulatory system

7.3 Characteristics of ADHD

ADHD is a chronic neurological condition characterized by (1) inattention, (2) impulsiveness, and (3) hyperactivity. Inattention refers to the child's inability to concentrate on a task. Impulsiveness is the tendency to respond quickly without thinking through the consequences of an action. Hyperactivity refers to behavior that is described as a constant, driving motor activity in which a child races from one endeavor or interest to another. Many individuals with ADHD show problems in each of these areas, but some will have only one or two of these behaviors (Silver, 2006; Elison, 2006).

Children with ADHD have difficulty staying on task, focusing attention, and completing their work. Roughly one-half of all children with ADHD have a cooccurring learning disability. They are easily distracted, rushing from one idea or interest to another, and they may produce work that is sloppy and carelessly executed. They give the impression that they are not listening or have not heard what they have been told. Children with ADHD have attention problems, impulsive behavior, and problems with hyperactivity. They often display symptoms of age-inappropriate behavior (Barkley, 2005; Accardo et al., 2000; Haber, 2000; Lerner, Lowenthal, & Lerner, 1995; Rappley, 2004; Silver, 2004, 2006). Children with ADHD are known to turn off some peers during their first contact because of their difficulty in joining other children in a social interaction (Hund and Landau, 2012). In addition, students with ADHD often have deficits in academic achievement (Scheffler, et al., 2009). An example of a young child with ADHD is presented in Student Stories 7.2.

inattention
Not concentrating on a task

impulsiveness
A characteristic of attention deficit disorder, in which the child reacts quickly without careful thought

hyperactivity
A condition characterized by uncontrollable, haphazard, and poorly organized motor behavior. In young children, excessive gross-motor activity makes them appear to be on the go, and they have difficulty sitting still. Older children may be extremely restless or fidgety, may talk too much in class, or may constantly fight with friends, siblings, and classmates.

Ryan's parents have come to dread the phone calls from his teacher. He is only 6 years old, but he is already viewed as a discipline problem. When Ryan was 3, his nursery school teacher informed his parents that Ryan's pushy behavior interfered with the play of his classmates. The nursery school teacher described him as an undisciplined child. At age 4, his preschool teacher said that the other children complained about Ryan's aggressive behavior. At age 5, his kindergarten teacher described him as a wild boy who ran about the room knocking toys off the shelf and interrupting other children. His classmates did not want to play with him because he was so aggressive.

Now Ryan's first-grade teacher compares him to a tornado. When Ryan enters a room, he changes the tone from a peaceful and quiet class to total pandemonium. Ryan's distraught parents are reluctant to take him anywhere because of his sudden tantrums. He has never been invited to a birthday party and has no playmates. Ryan's parents finally sought help from a pediatric neurologist, who diagnosed Ryan as having ADHD.

REFLECTIVE QUESTION

1. What were some of the characteristics of Ryan's behavior?

7.3a Symptoms of ADHD

For a diagnosis of ADHD, symptoms must meet the following three criteria (American Psychiatric Association, 2013):

1. **Severity.** The symptoms must be more frequent and severe than are typical of other children at similar developmental levels.
2. **Early onset.** At least some of the symptoms must have appeared before the child reaches age 12.
3. **Duration.** The child's symptoms must have persisted for at least 6 months prior to the diagnosis.

7.3b Symptoms of ADHD at Different Ages

Symptoms of ADHD change at different stages of life. Young children, elementary-age children, adolescents, and adults tend to exhibit different sets of behaviors.

- **Young children** with ADHD exhibit excessive gross-motor activity, such as running or climbing. They are described as being "on the go," "running like a motor," and "having difficulty sitting still." They may be unable to sit still for more than a few minutes at a time before beginning to wriggle excessively. It is the *quality* of the motor behavior that distinguishes this disorder from ordinary over-activity because hyperactivity tends to be haphazard and poorly organized. For example, 4-year-old Jerry, who has ADHD, grabs a toy from another child, and he hits the child if the toy is not given to him.
- **Elementary-age children** with ADHD may be extremely restless and fidgety. They are likely to talk too much in class and may constantly fight with friends, siblings, and classmates. For example, 8-year-old Sarah always blurts out the answer without raising her hand or waiting to be recognized.
- For **adolescents** with ADHD, hyperactivity may diminish, but other symptoms may appear, such as behavioral problems, low self-esteem, in-attentiveness, or even depression. For example, 13-year-old Lorraine has such low self-esteem that she believes even her imaginary friend is too busy to talk to her.

- **Adults** with ADHD often have organizational problems, social relationship difficulties, and job problems. For example, 27-year-old Joshua cannot keep a job because he does not follow through in completing job assignments.

ADHD affects children in all environments and in all ethnic and language groups, disrupting the child's home life, education, behavior, and social life. At home, children with ADHD have difficulty accommodating home routines and parental expectations. They may resist going to bed, refuse to eat, or break toys during play. At school, they have trouble completing their class work, often missing valuable information because of their attention problems. They speak aloud out of turn and find themselves in trouble for their behavior. Their social interactions may be undermined by their impulsivity, hyperactivity, and inattention, which hamper their ability to make and keep friends (Lavoie, 2006). In terms of gender, more boys than girls are diagnosed with ADHD. However, research suggests that the prevalence rate is equal for boys and girls, but boys are more likely to be identified. This gender difference may due to the fact that boys are more likely to engage in aggressive behavior (Shaywitz, Fletcher, & Shaywitz, 1995).

7.3c Assessment

An assessment is a necessary step before decisions can be made about eligibility for services and treatment. The diagnosis of ADHD is usually based on the observation of behaviors. The criteria for these behaviors are described in the *DSM-5* (American Psychiatric Association, 2013). Mayes and colleagues (2012) found that core ADHD symptoms are part of autism spectrum disorder and a thorough evaluation is critical to determine the nature of the student's disability. Those authors recommend that children who are being evaluated for ADHD should be screened for autism spectrum disorders (Mayes et al., 2012).

7.3d Types of ADHD

The American Psychiatric Association's DSM-5 uses the term Attention-Deficit/ Hyperactivity Disorder and defines it as follows:

A. Persistent pattern of inattention and/or hyperactivity-impulsivity that interferes with functioning or development, as characterized by (1) Inattention and/or (2) Hyperactivity and impulsivity.

For inattention, six (or more) of the following symptoms have persisted for at least 6 months to a degree that is not consistent with developmental level and negatively impacts directly on social and academic/occupational activities. For individuals 17 and older at least five symptoms are required:

a. Often fails to give close attention to details or makes careless mistakes in schoolwork, at work, or during other activities.
b. Often as difficulty sustaining attention in tasks or play activities.
c. Often does not seem to listen when spoken to directly.
d. Often does not follow through on instructions and fails to finish schoolwork, chores, or duties in the workplace.
e. Often has difficulty organizing tasks and activities.

f. Often avoids, dislikes, or is reluctant to engage in tasks that require sustained mental effort.

g. Often loses things necessary for tasks or activities.

h. Is often easily distracted by extraneous stimuli.

i. Is often forgetful in daily activities.

For Hyperactivity and impulsivity, there are six or more of the following symptoms that have persisted for at least 6 months and are inconsistent with developmental level and negatively impact social and academic/occupational activities. For those 17 and older at least five symptoms are required:

a. Often fidgets with or taps hands or feet or squirms in seat.

b. Often leaves seat in situations when remaining seated is expected.

c. Often runs about or climbs in situations where it is inappropriate. In adolescents or adults, may be limited to feeling restless.

d. Often unable to play or engage in leisure activities quietly.

e. Is often "on the go" acting as if "driven by a motor."

f. Often talks excessively.

g. Often blurts out an answer before a question that has been completed.

h. Often has difficulty waiting his or her turn.

i. Often interrupts or intrudes on others.

Additional criteria specify that several inattentive or hyperactive-impulsive symptoms were present prior to age 12 years, are present in two or more settings, and there is clear evidence that the symptoms interfere with, or duce the quality of, social, academic or occupational functioning. The symptoms also do not occur exclusively during the course of schizophrenia or another psychotic disorder and are not explained by another mental disorder.

Also included in the diagnosis of Attention-Deficit/Hyperactivity Disorder is

A. Other Specified Attention-Deficit/Hyperactivity Disorder which applies to the presentation in which symptoms characteristic of attention-deficit/hyperactivity disorder that cause clinically significant distress or impairment in social, occupational or other important areas of functioning predominate but do not meet the full criteria for attention-deficit/hyperactivity disorder or any of the disorders in the neurodevelopmental disorders diagnostic class.

B. Unspecified Attention Deficit/Hyperactivity Disorder which applies to presentations in which symptoms characteristic of attention-deficit/hyperactivity disorder that cause clinically significant distress or impairment in social/occupational, or other important areas of functioning predominate but do not meet the full criteria for attention-deficit/hyperactivity disorder or any of the disorders in the neurodevelopmental disorders diagnostic class. This category is used in situations in which the clinician chooses not to specify the reason that the criteria are not met. Table 7.1 explains the criteria for ADHD in DSM-5.

7.3e Rating Scales

rating scales
A ranking of student behavior as judged by a parent, teacher, or other informant.

Rating scales are frequently used assessment measures for students with ADHD and are based on reports of behavior observed by teachers and parents (Barkley, 2005). Table 7.2 shows the most frequently used rating scales.

TABLE 7.1

Criteria for Subtypes of Attention Deficit/Hyperactivity Disorder as per the DSM-5 (American Psychiatric Association, 2013).

Inattention

a. Often fails to give close attention to details or makes careless mistakes in schoolwork, at work, or during other activities.

b. Often as difficulty sustaining attention in tasks or play activities.

c. Often does not seem to listen when spoken to directly.

d. Often does not follow through on instructions and fails to finish schoolwork, chores, or duties in the workplace.

e. Often has difficulty organizing tasks and activities.

f. Often avoids, dislikes, or is reluctant to engage in tasks that require sustained mental effort.

g. Often loses things necessary for tasks or activities.

h. Is often easily distracted by extraneous stimuli.

i. Is often forgetful in daily activities.

Hyperactivity and Impulsivity

a. Often fidgets with or taps hands or feet or squirms in seat.

b. Often leaves seat in situations when remaining seated is expected.

c. Often runs about or climbs in situations where it is inappropriate. In adolescents or adults, may be limited to feeling restless.

d. Often unable to play or engage in leisure activities quietly.

e. Is often "on the go" acting as if "driven by a motor."

f. Often talks excessively.

h. Often has difficulty waiting his or her turn.

e. Is often "on the go" acting as if "driven by a motor."

i. Often interrupts or intrudes on others.

Also included in the diagnosis of Attention-Deficit/Hyperactivity Disorder is

a. Other Specified Attention-Deficit/Hyperactivity Disorder.

b. Unspecified Attention Deficit/Hyperactivity Disorder.

Source: American Psychiatric Association, 2013. *Diagnostic and Statistical Manual-5*. Washington, D.C. American Psychiatric Publishing.

TABLE 7.2

Rating Scales for Assessing ADHD

Rating Scale	Publisher
Attention Deficit Disorder Evaluation Scale	Hawthorne Educational Services
Behavior Assessment System for Children (BASC)	American Guidance Services
Child Behavior Checklist for Ages 2–3	University of Vermont, Department of Psychiatry
Child Behavior Checklist for Ages 4–16 Conners Rating Scales	University of Vermont, Department of Psychiatry Multi-Health Services

© Cengage Learning

FIGURE **7.2**
Rating Scale of Student
Behavior

	POOR				GOOD	
	1	2	3	4	5	
AUDITORY COMPREHENSION						
1. Ability to follow oral directions						1
2. Comprehension of class discussion						2
3. Ability to retain auditory information						3
4. Comprehension of word meaning						4
SPOKEN LANGUAGE						
5. Complete and accurate expression						5
6. Vocabulary ability						6
7. Ability to recall words						7
8. Ability to relate experience						8
9. Ability to formulate ideas						9
ORIENTATION						
10. Promptness						10
11. Spatial orientation						11
12. Judgment of relationships						12
13. Learning directions						13
BEHAVIOR						
14. Cooperation						14
15. Attention						15
16. Ability to organize						16
17. Ability to cope with new situations						17
18. Social acceptance						18
19. Acceptance of responsibility						19
20. Completion of assignments						20
21. Tactfulness						21
MOTOR						
22. General coordination						22
23. Balance						23
24. Ability to manipulate						24

© Cengage Learning

We provide one rating scale that can be used by teachers in Figure 7.2. It is a 24-point rating scale designed to help teachers identify pupils with learning disabilities in their classes. Teachers rate the 24 behaviors, from auditory comprehension to motor skills, on a 5-point scale (with 1 indicating poor behavior; 5, good behavior; and 3, average behavior). The highest possible score is 120 (5 × 24). In one study, the mean score of the children classified as normal was 81, and the score of the children identified as having learning disabilities was 61 (Myklebust & Boshes, 1969).

7.3f Eligibility of Children With ADHD for Special Services

The condition of ADHD is not identified as a separate category of disability in the Individuals With Disabilities Education Improvement Act of 2004 (IDEA-2004). However, Table 7.3 lists several significant laws that were passed by the U.S. Department of Education allowing children with ADHD to be eligible for special education services under the existing categories of disabilities.

7.3g Implications of the Law for Children With ADHD

The following laws provide legal protections for students with ADHD:

Special Education Services Children with ADHD may be eligible for special education services under the category of "other health impaired" in IDEA-2004. The law describes "other health impaired," when applied to children with ADHD, as heightened alertness to environmental stimuli that results in limited

1991	Clarification of Policy to Address the Needs of Children With Attention Deficit Disorders Within General and/or Special Education
1999	The Regulations for Individuals With Disabilities Education Act of 1997 (IDEA-1997)
2004	The Individuals With Disabilities Education Improvement Act of 2004

alertness with respect to the educational environment (U.S. Department of Education, 1999).

A child with ADHD may also be eligible for special education services under other existing categories of special education, in addition to other health impaired, such as the categories of learning disabilities or emotional disturbance.

Section 504 Services A child with ADHD may be eligible for services under the legislation of Section 504 of the Rehabilitation Act of 1973, even if that child is not eligible for special education services. Section 504 mandates that any agency receiving federal funds provide reasonable accommodations for people with disabilities.

According to Section 504, if the child is found to have "a physical or mental impairment that substantially limits a major life activity," such as learning, the school must make an individualized determination of the child's educational needs, and reasonable accommodations must be provided within the general education classroom (Section 504 of the Rehabilitation Act).

7.3h Increase in the Number of Children Identified With ADHD

ADHD is estimated to affect 9.5% of the school-age population (Centers for Disease Control and Prevention, 2010). In IDEA (2004), the condition of ADHD is included in the category of *other health impaired* (OHI). The number of children identified under the category of other health impaired has increased substantially since ADHD was included in this category. Since the issuance of the 1991 Clarification of Policy to address the needs of children with ADHD and the clarification within the Regulations for Individuals With Disabilities Education Act of 1997, more children with ADHD are being identified. The number of students identified in the category of other health impaired increased from 53,165 in 1991 to 489,806 in the year 2008, as shown in Figure 7.3. The increase in children in the other health impaired category is mostly due to the inclusion of children with ADHD.

7.3i Educational Settings for Students With ADHD

Most students with ADHD are in general education classes as indicated in Table 7.4 About 83% of students in the category of other health impairments (OHI) are in general education classes at least part of the time. Students in the category OHI are served in the following educational settings (U.S. Department of Education, 2012) as indicated in Table 7.4.

FIGURE **7.3**
Increase in "Other Health
Impaired" Category

Source: From the United States
Department of Education. 1991–2008.
To assure the free, appropriate public
education of all Children with Disabilities.
Annual Reports to Congress on the
Implementation of the Individuals with
Disabilities Act. Washington, DC: U.S.
Government Printing Office.

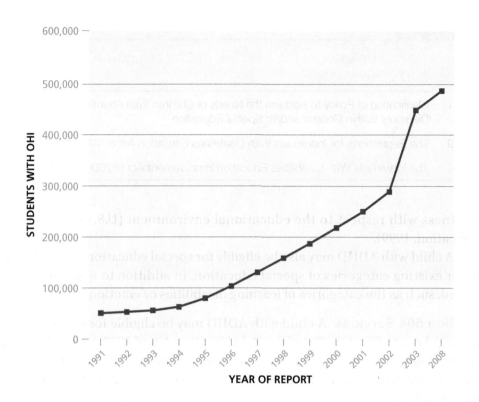

TABLE 7.4

Educational Environments for Students With Other Health Impairments,
Ages 6–21

General Education Class (outside regular class less than 21%)	54%
Resource Room (outside regular class 21–60%)	29%
Separate Class (outside regular class more than 60%)	14%
Other Environments	3%

Source: U.S. Department of Education. (2012). To assure the free appropriate public education of all children with
disabilities. Thirtieth Annual Report to Congress on the Implementation of the Individuals with Disabilities Education Act.
Washington, DC: U.S. Government Printing Office.

7.3j Response-to-Intervention and Eligibility of Students With ADHD

In Chapter 2, "Assessment and the IEP Process," we describe the new procedure called response-to-intervention (RTI). Under IDEA-2004 and the Regulations for IDEA-2004 (2006) schools may use the procedure of RTI to determine the eligibility of students with ADHD for special education. RTI is a procedure for providing interventions to all students who are at-risk for school failure (Hallahan et al., 2007; Zirkel, 2007; Learning Disabilities Association of America, 2006).

Schools may use the RTI procedure with students whose behavior suggests ADHD in the process of determining eligibility for special education. In the RTI procedure, a child with suspected ADHD would receive intervention within general education in various tiers of intervention. Students who do not respond positively would be eligible for an evaluation. (See Chapter 2, "Assessment and the IEP Process," for additional information about RTI.)

Did You Get It?

You can use the acronym SED to remember the diagnostic criteria for ADHD/ADD. "S" refers to severity, "E" to early onset, and "D" to

a. duration.
b. disruptiveness.
c. deficit.
d. direction.

7.4 Treatments for ADHD

7.4a American Academy of Pediatrics Guidelines for Treatment

The American Academy of Pediatrics (2001) established the following guidelines for pediatricians for the treatment of children with ADHD.

- Primary care clinicians should establish a treatment program that recognizes ADHD as a chronic condition.
- The treating clinician, parents, and child, in collaboration with school personnel, should specify appropriate target outcomes to guide management.
- The clinician should recommend stimulant medication and/or behavior therapy as appropriate to improve target outcomes for children with ADHD.
- When the selected management for a child with ADHD has not met target outcomes, clinicians should evaluate the original diagnosis, use all appropriate treatments, and adhere to the treatment plan and presence of coexisting conditions.
- The clinician should provide a systematic follow-up for the child with ADHD. Monitoring should be directed to target outcomes and adverse effects, with information gathered from parents, teachers, and the child.

Several different kinds of treatments are prescribed for children with ADHD.

7.4b Multimodal Treatment

A multimodal treatment plan combines several approaches for treating children with ADHD. Multimodal instruction includes (1) effective educational instruction, (2) behavior management strategies, (3) family and child counseling, (4) home management, and (5) medication. A student's improvement is greatest when all components of the treatment are present and are working in conjunction with each other (Silver, 2006; Accardo et al., 2002).

multimodal treatment plan
Combines several approaches to treating children with ADD/ADHD, which refers both to attention deficit disorders and attention deficit hyperactivity disorder

7.4c Medication

Medication is prescribed for many children with ADHD to improve their attention and to control their hyperactive behavior. In fact, medication is prescribed in 56% of all cases of ADHD (Scheffler et al., 2009). The ideal medication should control hyperactivity, increase attention span, and reduce impulsive and aggressive behavior without inducing side effects, such as insomnia, loss of appetite,

TABLE 7.5

Psychostimulant Medications Used for Treatment of ADHD

Brand Name	Generic Name	Duration of Action
Ritalin	Methylphenidate	short (3–5 hours)
Dexedrine	Dextroamphetamine	short (3–5 hours)
Adderall	Combination of dextroamphetamine and amphetamine	long (8 hours)
Concerta	Contains a type of Ritalin	long (8 hours)
Focalin	Generic	short (4 hours)
Vyvanse	Lisdexamfetamine	long (8 hours)

© Cengage Learning

drowsiness, or other serious toxic effects. Finding the ideal medication for a child is not an easy task, and it requires close cooperation among physicians, school personnel, and family members (Silver, 2006; Accardo & Blondis, 2000; Powers, 2000).

psychostimulant medications
Medications, including Ritalin, that are initially prescribed for a child with attention deficit disorder

Psychostimulant Medications Psychostimulant medications are the most widely used type of medication prescribed for ADHD and are very effective for most children. About 75% to 85% of individuals with ADHD improve with the use of psychostimulants. Psychostimulant medications include Ritalin, Dexedrine, Adderall, Concerta, and Vyvanse (Silver, 2006; Accardo & Blondis, 2000; Rappley, 2004). Table 7.5 provides more details about these psychostimulant medications.

The usefulness of psychostimulants in reducing hyperactivity was first reported more than 50 years ago when children taking the psychostimulant Benzedrine showed longer attention spans and an improved ability to concentrate, with a corresponding decrease in hyperactivity and oppositional behavior (Bradley, 1937).

Research on ADHD suggests that psychostimulant medications affect the brain of children with ADHD by increasing the arousal or alertness of the central nervous system (Hervey et al., 2006; Accardo & Blondis, 2000; Barkley, 2005). It

neurotransmitters
The chemicals that transmit messages from one cell to another across the synapse (a microscopic space between nerve cells)

is thought that these individuals do not produce sufficient neurotransmitters—chemicals within the brain that transmit messages from one cell to another across a gap, or synapse—and that the psychostimulants work by stimulating the production of the chemical neurotransmitters needed to send information from the brain stem to the parts of the brain that deal with attention. The psychostimulant medications appear to lengthen the children's attention spans, control impulsivity, decrease distractibility and motor activity, and improve visual-motor integration (Barkley, 2005; Powers, 2000; Rappley, 2004). The psychostimulant medications most frequently prescribed for ADHD are Ritalin, Dexedrine, Concerta, Adderall, and Vyvanse. The duration of effect for Ritalin, Dexedrine, and Focalin is short, 3 to 5 hours. Consequently, unless a second dose is taken during the school day, the effects of a morning dose of either of these medications will wear off during the course of the day. The psychostimulants Adderall, Concerta, and Vyvanse are taken in one daily dosage, and the effects are long lasting, 8 or more hours.

The side effects of stimulant medications include insomnia and loss of appetite, but these effects are usually transient and diminish as tolerance develops (Barkley, 2005). For a few children, a more serious side effect of Ritalin is that it can trigger tics or Tourette's syndrome. If one of these side effects occurs, the medication must be changed.

A *rebound effect* sometimes occurs with children on psychostimulants. The child's behavior can significantly deteriorate in the late afternoon or evening after a daytime dose of the stimulant. This wearing off of the medication can cause the child to temporarily exhibit more impulsivity, distractibility, and hyperactivity than was previously observed (Barkley, 2005). If this occurs, additional low doses may be needed in the late afternoon.

Strattera A medication that is not a psychostimulant for the treatment of ADHD is Strattera. Because Strattera is not a psychostimulant medication, it is not subject to the same restrictions as other medications used for most other treatment of ADHD. Strattera only needs to be given once daily (Silver, 2006; Kratochvil et al., 2002; Rosenthal, 2003).

Other Medications As noted, about 75% to 85% of children with ADHD show general improvement with psychostimulant medications. For those who do not improve, other medications are used. These include Wellbutrin, Catapres, Tenex, and Strattera (Silver, 2006).

The use of psychostimulants for ADHD is associated with rapid improvement in attentiveness, hyperactivity, impulsivity, scholastic performance, handwriting skills, family life, and socialization based on objective tests and subjective evaluations by parents, teachers, and clinicians. In addition, psychostimulant medication appears to help children with ADHD improve their self-esteem and self-image, and it enables children with ADHD to express feelings of greater control over themselves and their lives (Silver, 2006; Powers, 2000).

7.4d Neurochemistry of Psychostimulant Medications

In this section, we look at the neurochemistry of psychostimulant medications, which are often prescribed for children with ADHD. Individuals with ADHD do not release enough of the needed chemicals to send information from the brain stem to other parts of the brain. A deficiency in the production of the neurotransmitters *dopamine* and *norepinephrine* results in decreased stimulation and a consequent dysfunction of the neural circuits underlying attention.

The brain is a complex information network made up of millions of nerve cells called neurons. Information moves through the brain as nerve impulses that are transmitted from cell to cell by neurotransmitters. An impulse travels along the cell body from a sending neuron to a receiving neuron. A small space, called a *synapse,* is between the sending neuron and the receiving neuron. The impulse causes the sending cell to release chemicals—or neurotransmitters— from tiny sacs located at the synapse between the sending cell and the receiving cell. A diagram of the neurotransmitter system is shown in Figure 7.4.

Individuals with ADHD have an insufficiency in the neurotransmitter activity within the brain stem. The psychostimulant medications increase the production of the chemicals, leading to a decrease in the behaviors associated with

neurons
Nerves within the brain

FIGURE **7.4**
The Neurotransmitter System

Source: Adapted from *The Dana
sourcebook of brain science:
Resources for secondary and
postsecondary teachers and students,*
2003. New York: Dana Press, p. 138.

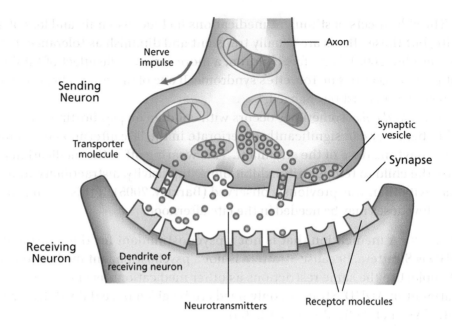

ADHD, such as inattention, impulsivity, and hyperactivity. Thus, medication, through its action on the neurotransmitters, improves the child's attention, motivation, motor responses, activity level, restlessness, and responsibility (Silver, 2006; Lerner et al., 1995; Powers, 2000; Rappley, 2004).

Did You Get It?

Which treatment is not usually included in multimodal plans for the effective treatment of ADHD?
a. medication
b. individual and family counseling
c. psychotherapy
d. behavior management skills and techniques

7.5 Methods for Teaching Students With ADHD

To accommodate students with ADHD, it is necessary to consider the three primary traits of ADHD: (1) inattention, (2) impulsivity, and (3) hyperactivity. Because most students with ADHD are in a general education classroom setting, it is important for both the special education teacher and the general education classroom teacher to be familiar with these methods (Silver, 2006; Barkley, 2005; Lerner, Lowenthal, & Lerner, 1995).

7.5a Increasing Attention

Inattention is a major symptom of individuals with ADHD. The student may be attending, but attending to the wrong stimuli. For example, the student may be attending to what is going on outside, to noises in the classroom, or even to his or her own thoughts. There are several distinct but interrelated phases of attention.

1. **Coming to attention.** The first phase, coming to attention, requires students to be alert, steady, and motivated for the lesson.

2. **Focusing attention.** The next phase, focusing attention, requires vigilance and the energy to examine problems carefully and to develop an interest in the problems to be solved. Students with ADHD must learn to focus their attention, to slow down, to become more deliberate and reflective, and to monitor their responses before answering.

3. **Sustaining attention.** The third phase, sustaining attention, requires that students concentrate for an extended period of time. The ability to focus and attend to a task for a prolonged period is essential for the students to receive the necessary information and to complete certain academic activities. To learn many academic skills, such as reading, students must work hard and keep attending over many days, weeks, or even months. Teaching Tips 7.2, "Increasing Attention," describes some methods for helping students increase attention.

TEACHING TIPS 7.2
Increasing Attention

- Place the student near the front of the room.
- Place the student away from noisy or distracting locations, such as windows and hallways.
- Place the student away from students with behavior problems. Place the student with well-behaved students.
- Keep the routines simple and direct.
- Alert the student by using key words and phrases, such as "this is important."
- Use visual aids; write out key points.
- Increase the novelty of the task.

Professional Resource Download

7.5b Managing Impulsivity

Impulsive students act out physically and/or verbally. Often, they will shout out answers without raising their hands or waiting for recognition. Particularly challenging for impulsive students are transition times, when class activities shift from unstructured activities to structured activities. After a stimulating activity, such as recess or a physical education period, impulsive students have difficulty settling down. Teaching Tips 7.3, "Managing Impulsivity," offers suggestions for managing impulsivity.

7.5c Reducing Hyperactivity

Students who are hyperactive present challenges for classroom teachers. These students cannot sit in their seats for prolonged periods; they may get up to sharpen their pencils 12 times during each class. They need to move frequently within the classroom and be active. They will probably respond to an increase in hands-on activities and opportunities for movement while engaging in a nonactive activity such as a lecture. As an example, they may increase their attention by being able to doodle on a piece of paper or being able to squeeze a fidget toy. Such students may simply pace back and forth because

Young boy reading Chess Book.

Florian Franke / Alamy

they cannot sit quietly. One student with ADHD reported that she retained information that she needed to memorize much better when she was able to write her notes on small index cards, and that she would go home and pace back and forth as she read and reread the information on the index cards. Teaching Tips 7.3, "Managing Hyperactivity," provides methods for managing hyperactivity in the classroom.

TEACHING TIPS 7.3

Managing Impulsivity

- **Adapt the curriculum.** Small changes in the curriculum can be helpful. Students with ADHD need a stimulating, active curriculum that will hold their attention and motivate them to complete the activity at hand.
- **Help students learn to wait.** Give the student some substitute verbal or motor responses to use while waiting. Instruct the student about how to continue on

easier parts of tasks, or how to do a substitute task, while awaiting the teacher's help.

- **Help students manage time.** Give short assignments and tasks and reduce the amount of work involved. Alternate activities that are done while sitting with those that involve standing and moving about.

Professional Resource Download

Including Students in GENERAL EDUCATION 7.1

Students With ADHD

Limit Distractions

- Seat student near the teacher
- Seat student away from noisy places
- Seat student with well-behaved students and away from students with problem behaviors
- Keep routines simple and direct

Increase Attention

- Shorten the task—break it into smaller parts
- Shorten homework assignments
- Use distributed practice (i.e., many shorter sessions)
- Make tasks more interesting (e.g., work with partners, interest centers, groups)
- Increase the novelty of the task

Improve Organization

- Provide clear classroom rules and teacher expectations
- Establish routines for placing objects in the room
- Provide a list of materials for each task
- Check that student has homework before leaving school; use assignment books
- Use a different colored folder for each subject

Improve Listening Skills

- Keep instructions simple and short
- Have students repeat instructions aloud, then to themselves
- Alert students by using key phrases, such as "this is important" or "listen carefully"
- Use visual aids, charts, pictures, graphics, transparencies; write key points on chalkboard

Help Students Manage Time

- Set up a specific routine and adhere to it
- Make lists to help students organize tasks
- Use behavior contracts that specify the time allotted for activities

Provide Opportunities for Moving

- Permit students to move in class (e.g., sharpen pencils, get papers, get materials)
- Alternate activities (e.g., standing, sitting, moving)
- Allow students to work while standing or while leaning on their desks
- Have work centers in the classroom
- Use computers (e.g., allow children to go to computers during work time)

Professional Resource Download

I Have a Kid Who...

TONY, a Student With ADHD

Tony is a student with attention deficit hyperactivity disorder (ADHD) with impulsivity and hyperactivity. He currently attends a fifth-grade general education class. Tony is trying to work on a computer program that does not seem to be working. Tony tells his teacher that the computer program was installed incorrectly, but his teacher tells him that it is working and he should get back to work. Tony feels himself getting extremely frustrated and agitated, and his foot is tapping louder and faster. He feels that he must get out of the classroom before he explodes. He asks his teacher, "Can I go to the bathroom?" His teacher says, "No, Tony. Get back to work." Tony gets out of his seat and starts pacing around the classroom, muttering to himself. The voice of the teacher and the laughter of the other students in the class is deafening. He feels he must block it out. Tony starts banging his head against the wall. The teacher asks someone to go get the principal, quickly.

QUESTIONS

1. Should the teacher anticipate this kind of problem in a student with ADHD with hyperactivity and impulsivity?

2. Should the teacher have allowed Tony to leave the classroom?

3. Do you think this was the best educational setting for Tony?

7.5d Accommodations for the General Education Classroom

Teachers must make accommodations in the general education classroom to adjust for the behaviors of students with ADHD. Including Students in General Education 7.1, "Students With ADHD," lists some of the target behaviors, along with accommodations that can be made to achieve those behaviors for students with ADHD.

Many of the characteristics of Asperger's syndrome appear to be similar to NVLD. However, Roman (1998) claims they are different disorders. AS is part of the autism spectrum, but NVLD is not recognized in IDEA-2004 or in the *DSM-IV-TR*. NVLD is recognized in the field of neuropsychology. Some parents report that their child has had both diagnostic labels, and diagnosis appears to some extent to reflect the orientation of the examiner.

Did You Get It?

Verbal prompts in the form of _____ are effectively used to inform the child with ADHD/ADD that a particular fact, concept, or subject is of primary importance.
   a. key words and phrases
   b. raising ones voice several decibels
   c. mnemonics
   d. animation of verbal pitch and tone

Chapter Summary

- Autism spectrum disorders include a group of conditions, including classic autism disorder, pervasive developmental disorder-not otherwise specified, and Asperger's syndrome. The prevalence of autism spectrum disorders is increasing.
- Children with NVLD often have poor visual-spatial abilities, poor nonverbal problem-solving abilities, and low arithmetic skills.
- Attention deficit hyperactivity disorder and learning disabilities are common cooccurring conditions.
- The term *attention deficit hyperactivity disorder (ADHD)* is defined by the American Psychiatric Association and used by physicians and psychologists.
- The characteristics of ADHD change with age. Young children, elementary-age children, adolescents, and adults all display different characteristics of ADHD.
- For a diagnosis of ADHD, symptoms must meet the criteria of (1) severity, (2) early onset, and (3) duration.
- The *Diagnostic and Statistical Manual of Mental Disorders, Fifth Edition, Revised (DSM-5)* describes three types of ADHD: (1) Attention-Deficit/Hyperactivity Disorder, (2) Other Specified Attention-Deficit/Hyperactivity Disorder, and (3) Unspecified Attention-Deficit/Hyperactivity Disorder.
- Laws that make children with ADHD eligible for special education services are (1) the 1991 Clarification of Policy to Address the Needs of Children With Attention Deficit Disorders Within General and/or Special Education, (2) 1999 Regulations for IDEA-1997, and (3) the Individuals With Disabilities Education Improvement Act of 2004.
- The number of children identified with ADHD is increasing.
- Medication is an important part of the treatment of children with ADHD. Psychostimulant medications are widely used and are effective medications for ADHD. There are also other medications and alternative therapies used for children with ADHD.
- Teaching methods for students with ADHD are used by special education teachers and general education teachers. These teaching methods include strategies of (1) increasing attention, (2) managing impulsivity, and (3) reducing hyperactivity.

Questions for Discussion and Reflection

1. Many children today are diagnosed with ADHD. Describe the characteristics of children with ADHD at different developmental stages.
2. What are some of the settings for serving children with ADHD in the schools? What is the educational setting for most students with ADHD?
3. Many children with ADHD receive medication as part of their treatment. Discuss the kinds of medication that children with ADHD receive.
4. Describe two related neurodevelopmental conditions.

Key Terms

Asperger's syndrome (AS) (p. 192)
attention deficit disorder (ADD) (p. 196)
attention deficit hyperactivity disorder
　(ADHD) (p. 196)
autism spectrum disorder (ASD) (p. 190)
hyperactivity (p. 197)
impulsiveness (p. 197)

inattention (p. 197)
multimodal treatment plan (p. 205)
neurons (p. 207)
neurotransmitters (p. 206)
nonverbal learning disorders (NVLD) (p. 195)
psychostimulant medications (p. 206)
rating scales (p. 200)

Inara Prusakova/Shutterstock.com

CHAPTER 8

Young Children With Disabilities

All children can learn, if we can learn how to teach them.

—Sister Joanne Marie Kliebhan

LEARNING OBJECTIVES

After reading this chapter, you should be able to:

8.1 Discuss the importance of the early years

8.2 List strategies for working with young children in general education

8.3 Outline the importance of the law and young children with disabilities

8.4 Explain the laws and programs related to Head Start

8.5 List the developmental indicators of problems in young children

8.6 Discuss the impact of motor on development and learning

8.7 Explain perceptual development in young children

8.8 Outline the steps in assessing young children

8.9 Discuss early childhood programs and practices

8.10 List early intervention strategies

STANDARDS Addressed in This Chapter:

CEC Initial Level Special Educator Preparation Standards as approved by the National Council for the Accreditation of Teacher Education

CEC Initial Preparation Standard 1: Learner Development and Individual Learning Differences

- 1.0—Beginning special education professionals understand how exceptionalities may interact with development and learning and use this knowledge to provide meaningful and challenging learning experiences for individuals with exceptionalities.
- 1.1—Beginning special education professionals understand how language, culture, and family background influence the learning of individuals with exceptionalities.
- 1.2—Beginning special education professionals use understanding of development and individual differences to respond to the needs of individuals with exceptionalities.

CEC Initial Preparation Standard 2: Learning Environments

- 2.2—Beginning special education professionals use motivational and instructional interventions to teach individuals with exceptionalities how to adapt to different environments.

CEC Initial Preparation Standard 4: Assessment

- 4.0—Beginning special education professionals use multiple methods of assessment and data-sources in making educational decisions.
- 4.1—Beginning special education professionals select and use technically sound formal and informal assessments that minimize bias.
- 4.3—Beginning special education professionals in collaboration with colleagues and families use multiple types of assessment information in making decisions about individuals with exceptionalities.

CEC Initial Preparation Standard 5: Instructional Planning and Strategies

- 5.0—Beginning special education professionals select, adapt, and use a repertoire of evidence-based instructional strategies to advance learning of individuals with exceptionalities.
- 5.1—Beginning special education professionals consider an individual's abilities, interests, learning environments, and cultural and linguistic factors in the selection, development, and adaptation of learning experiences for individuals with exceptionalities.
- 5.4—Beginning special education professionals use strategies to enhance language development and communication skills of individuals with exceptionalities.
- 5.5—Beginning special education professionals develop and implement a variety of education and transition plans for individuals with exceptionalities across a wide range of settings and different learning experiences in collaboration with individuals, families, and teams.

CEC Initial Preparation Standard 6: Professional Learning and Ethical Practice

- 6.2—Beginning special education professionals understand how foundational knowledge and current issues influence professional practice.

CEC Initial Preparation Standard 7: Collaboration

- 7.0—Beginning special education professionals collaborate with families, other educators, related service providers, individuals with exceptionalities, and personnel from community agencies in culturally responsive ways to address the needs of individuals with exceptionalities across a range of learning experiences.
- 7.1—Beginning special education professionals use the theory and elements of effective collaboration.
- 7.2—Beginning special education professionals serve as a collaborative resource to colleagues.
- 7.3—Beginning special education professionals use collaboration to promote the well-being of individuals with exceptionalities across a wide range of settings and collaboration.

In this chapter, we review programs and intervention for young children with special needs. Services for young children are available today because of national and state policies that support early intervention services for young children with disabilities. Schools and agencies are expanding their early intervention programs for young children. It is important for elementary and secondary teachers to know about the nature of a child's early development and school experiences, and to be aware of the links between early intervention and later learning (Gargiulo & Kilgo, 2005).

8.1 The Importance of the Early Years

The early childhood years are crucial for all children, but for the child with special needs these years are especially critical. Research from several disciplines confirms what early childhood educators have long observed—that the early years of life are crucial for establishing a lifelong foundation for learning. If the opportunities are missed for children to develop intellectually and emotionally during these critical years, precious learning time is lost forever.

Children do not *begin* to learn when they enter formal schooling at age 6. During the first 6 years of their lives, young children learn at a rapid pace. In fact, from the moment of birth, they are engaged in continuous and intense learning. By the time they reach school age, they should have mastered many skills. Parents and families need to actively promote learning during the preschool years. Otherwise, their child's intellectual abilities will not grow optimally during these vital years. When children start school already behind their peers, they may never be able to catch up, to keep up, or to take advantage of all the efforts schools make to help them. With early identification of young children who show signs of learning difficulties, children can receive valuable early intervention services (Gargiulo and Kilgo, 2005; Allen, Cowdery, 2009; Bowe, 2007; Lerner, Lowenthal, & Egan, 2003).

8.1a Benefits of Early Intervention

Perhaps the most promising success stories in education today are the reports of special programs for young children who have disabilities or who are at risk for disabilities because of environmental and other conditions that make them likely to develop disabilities. The formative stages in child development and family life occur during the early years. These early years make a significant difference in a child's growth and development. When problems are recognized early, the likelihood that child will experience failure in school can, to a large extent, be prevented or reduced (Wolery & Bailey, 2004).

at risk
Children who are at-risk have factors that led to poor general development and learning failure.

Early childhood special education programs are designed to (1) identify young children, birth through age 5, who have special needs and are likely to encounter difficulty in school and (2) provide early intervention for these children. Research demonstrates that early intervention is beneficial for children with disabilities, for their families, and for society (Guralnick, 2005; Wolery & Bailey, 2004).

Early Intervention Helps Children With Disabilities   Early intervention accelerates cognitive and social development and reduces behavioral problems. Many conditions can be alleviated, other difficulties can be overcome to a large extent, and some problems can be managed so that the child can live a better life. Early intervention can avert the occurrence of secondary problems that compound the original difficulty.

Early Intervention Benefits the Families of Young Children With Special Needs   In the family-centered intervention approach, the child is viewed as part of a family system. When parents and family members are empowered to be an integral part of the intervention process, the family becomes an essential element in the process of teaching the child and improving child–adult interactions.

Early Intervention Benefits Society   Early intervention programs offer a substantial financial savings for the community by reducing the number of children who need special education services. It also empowers families to work positively with their young children and can strengthen family capacity.

In summary, early intervention accomplishes the following (Wolery & Bailey, 2004; Guralnick, 2005; Lerner et al., 2003; Schweinhart, Barnes, & Weikart, 1993):

- Promotes substantial gains in all developmental areas (intellectual, physical, cognitive, language, psychosocial, and self-help)
- Inhibits or prevents secondary disabilities
- Reduces family stress
- Reduces dependency and institutionalization
- Reduces the need for special education services at school age
- Saves the nation and society substantial health care costs and education costs

8.1b Considerations of Cultural Diversity for Young Children

Many children and families who participate in programs for young children with special needs have diverse linguistic and cultural backgrounds. Cultural differences may occur in parent–child interactions, values of the family, the family's perceptions of disabilities, and attitudes toward seeking help. Families in the majority culture usually value qualities such as independence, self-help, and individual achievement. For example, the majority culture encourages early self-feeding skills, but in some cultures, children are fed by caregivers until they are 3 years old. Some cultures, such as that of Native Americans, value the qualities of contributing to the group and community more than competitive individual achievement. In certain cultures, the family may be ashamed that they have a child with a disability and may neglect their child with special needs. In some cultures, children are expected to be quiet and not initiate language and communication. Children whose first language is not English may have difficulty recognizing words or the sounds (phonemes) of the English language.

Sensitivity to cultural diversity is extremely important for teachers who work with young children and their families. Teachers should communicate with family members in a way that is respectful and clear. Teachers should understand that some families may be reluctant to accept suggestions from the school. Children from diverse cultures and languages should be encouraged to demonstrate their knowledge through drawing, collaboration, or performance in small group discussions (Lerner et al., 2003).

The U.S. Department of Education (2012) provides data on the race/ethnicity of young children with disabilities. Table 8.1 shows the percentage of young children with disabilities receiving special services. The percentages of young children with disabilities in all racial/ethnic groups are similar to the percentages in the general population.

Children at risk dramatically improve when early intervention and work with families are provided.

creo77/Shutterstock.com

8.1c Young Children At Risk

Young children who are considered at risk have factors that lead to poor general development and learning failure. Although children who are at risk may not be eligible under the law for special services, they are at high risk for becoming children with disabilities unless early intervention services are provided. States have the option to serve children who are at risk; however, they are *not* required to provide services for this group under the law.

Among the factors that affect young children at risk are poverty, disrupted families, or abusive parents. Other risk factors are prenatal substance exposure; exposure to alcohol, tobacco, and nicotine; and illegal drug use (Gargiulo & Kilgo, 2005; Keogh, 2000). Research shows that when early intervention and work with families are made available, children who are at risk dramatically improve. For example, low-birth-weight infants show significant gains in cognitive and behavioral function when they receive comprehensive early intervention consisting of home visits, parent training, parent group meetings, attendance at a child development center, pediatric surveillance, and community referral services (Lambie, 2006; Gopnick, Meltzoff, & Kuhl, 1999; Keogh, 2000). See *http://www.childrenatrisk.org*.

The critical effect of the infant's environment on the early development of the brain is demonstrated through scientific evidence (Dehanene, 2009; Gopnick et al., 1999; Huttenlocher, 1991). During the early months and first years of life, the *synapses,* or interconnecting links between the neurons in the brain, grow at a phenomenal rate. The brain rapidly increases in size and becomes more efficient. The environmental influences and the child's experiences during the earliest years of life play a major role in brain development and affect intelligence and the ability to learn. Research on early brain development shows that

- Environment affects the number of brain cells, the connections among the brain cells, and the way the brain cells are wired. Brain development is much more vulnerable to environmental influences than was previously suspected.
- Brain development before age 1 is more rapid and extensive than previously realized.
- The influence of the early environment on brain development is long lasting.
- Early stress has a negative impact on brain function.

TABLE 8.1

Percent of Preschool Children With Disabilities Receiving Services by Race/Ethnicity

American Indian/Alaskan Native	3.0%
Asian/Pacific Islander	5.1%
Black (not Hispanic)	5.1%
Hispanic	4.5%
White (Not Hispanic)	4.9%

Source: U.S. Department of Education (2012) Thirtieth Annual report to Congress on the Implementation of the Individuals with Disabilities Education Act, 2008. Office of Special Education Services. U.S. Department of Education.

Did You Get It?

Missed learning opportunities for intellectual and emotional development during the vital, early years of childhood are a serious concern. Such a period of missed development can take

    a. months to make up for.
    b. a few years to make up for.
    c. a decade or more to make up for.
    d. can never be made up for.

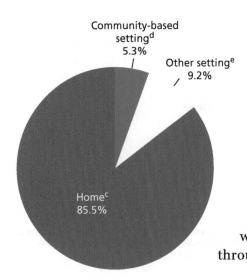

8.2 Strategies for Young Children in General Education

The most frequent educational placement for young children with special needs is in a general education preschool classroom (U.S. Department of Education, 2012). This means that general early childhood teachers must plan for teaching both typically developing young children and young children with disabilities and special needs. Including Students in General Education 8.1, "Young Children With Special Needs," offers some suggestions for meeting the needs of both populations, while Figure 8.1 shows the percentage of infants and toddlers, birth through age 2, in each of the primary intervention settings.

FIGURE **8.1**

Percentage[a] of infants and toddlers birth through age 2 served under IDEA, Part C, by primary early intervention setting[b]: Fall 2006

Source: U.S. Department of Education, Office of Special Education Programs, Data Analysis System (DANS), OMB #1820-0557: "Report of Program Settings Where Early Intervention Services Are Provided to Children with Disabilities and Their Families in Accordance with Part C," 2006. Data were updated as of July 15, 2007. For actual data used, go to https://www.ideadata.org/Archive/ARCArchive.asp. These data are for the 50 states, the District of Columbia, Puerto Rico, and the four outlying areas.

> ### Did You Get It?
>
> In a general educational setting, young children without disabilities and their peers with disabilities should _____ share curriculum.
> **a.** minimally
> **b.** partially
> **c.** mostly
> **d.** completely

8.3 The Law and Young Children With Disabilities

The special education law, Individuals With Disabilities Education Improvement Act (IDEA-2004), requires that services be provided for two different age groups of young children with disabilities: (1) *preschoolers,* ages 3 through 5, and (2) *infants* and *toddlers,* birth to age 3. The provisions in the law are different for each of these two age groups in terms of eligibility and the state agency that is responsible for the services. For infants and toddlers, a predominant focus is on serving families. For preschoolers, the focus is on intervention practices for the child Table 8.2 shows the percentage of children identified for ages birth to age 2 and for age 3 through age 5 that are receiving services through special education.

8.3a Preschool Children: Ages 3 Through 5

Preschool children with disabilities, ages 3 through 5, are eligible to receive the same full rights under the law that older children have. These provisions are specified in Part B of IDEA-2004. Table 8.3 shows the disabilities classification for children ages 3–5.

The following list summarizes the provisions in the law for preschoolers with disabilities:

- Each state must provide a free, appropriate public education, along with related services, to all eligible children with disabilities, ages 3 through 5.

Including Students in GENERAL EDUCATION 8.1

Young Children With Special Needs

- Early childhood general education teachers and special education teachers should collaborate in planning the curriculum for all children in the preschool class.

- Young children with special needs and young children without special needs should share a common curriculum.

- Adaptations are needed for young children with diverse learning styles and abilities.

- Both child-initiated activities and teacher-initiated activities should be used.

- Play experiences should foster active engagement and interaction of all children.

- Activities should be appropriate for each child's stage of development.

- Activities should nourish social relationships for all children.

- Activities should promote communication among children.

- Cultural and linguistic diversity of all children should be considered.

Professional Resource Download

- States may select to identify preschool children either noncategorically, such as by *developmental delay,* or by the category of disability, such as *learning disability.* Any state that adopts the term *developmental delay* has the option to apply it to children ranging from age 3 to age 9.

- For children ages 3 through 5, the child study team may use either the IEP or the individualized family service plan (IFSP). The IFSP is a plan for young children that includes the family as well as the child. The plan used must ensure due process, confidentiality, and the child's placement in the least restrictive environment.

- The lead agency for preschool children ages 3 through 5 is the state education agency. The law gives each state's education agency the responsibility of implementing Part B of IDEA-2004 for preschool children by working with local education agencies or other contracted service agencies.

TABLE 8.2

Percentage of Children Receiving Services Through Early Intervention or Special Education

Percentage of Birth to Age 2 and Age 3 Through Age 5	
Birth to age 2	3.9%
Age 3 through Age 5	5.8%

© Cengage Learning 2015

individualized family service plan (IFSP)
A plan for young children that includes the family as well as the child

8.3b Infants and Toddlers: Birth Through Age 2

The policies for infants and toddlers, birth to age 3 with disabilities are contained in Part C of IDEA-2004. Services for infants and toddlers with disabilities are not mandated, but Part C authorizes financial assistance to the states through state grants. The family system is recognized as critical in the child's development. The teams must use an IFSP (individual family service plan), which includes services for the family as well as for the child.

TABLE 8.3

Disability Classifications for Children Ages 3 Through 5 Served Under IDEA

Disability classification[b]	Percent
Autism	89.4
Developmental delay	64.1
Emotional disturbance	60.4
Intellectual disabilities	71.4
Specific learning disabilities	69.7
Orthopedic impairments	66.7
Other health impairments	57.2
Speech or language impairments	88.3
Low-incidence disabilities[c]	61.6
Total	77.4

Source: U.S. Department of Education, Institute of Education Sciences, National Center for Special Education Research (NCSER), 2008.

The number of infants and toddlers with disabilities is increasing, with 3.9% of the general population of infants and toddlers (birth to age 3) and their families receiving services (U.S. Department of Education, 2012). With recent advances in medical technology, neonates with very low birth weights and substantial health problems survive and may be children at risk. Newborns may also have other kinds of problems. For example, there are 375,000 drug-exposed babies and 2,000 HIV-infected babies born each year. These fragile infants usually need highly specialized medical attention, and they and their families also require services that medical professionals cannot provide. Infant specialists and infant/toddler service coordinators (or case managers) are key members of the interdisciplinary team in neonatal intensive care units and in child-care centers (Lerner, Lowenthal, & Egan, 2003; U.S. Department of Education, 2012).

8.3c Number of Preschool Children Receiving Special Education Services

The number of preschool children receiving special education services has been increasing. About 5.8% of all preschool children (ages 3 through 5) with disabilities receive special education services through the schools (U.S. Department of Education, 2012).

8.3d Educational Environments

educational environments
The student's placement for instruction

The term educational environments refers to the educational setting for young children with disabilities. As shown in Figure 8.2, the U.S. Department of Education (2012) reports that preschool children with disabilities are served through many different educational environments.

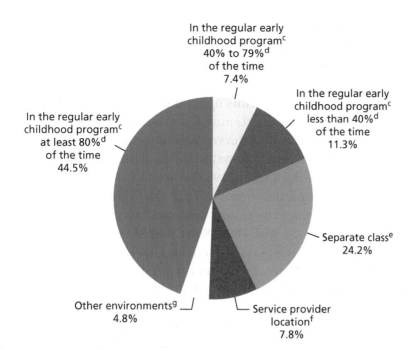

In the regular early childhood program[c] 40% to 79%[d] of the time
7.4%

In the regular early childhood program[c] less than 40%[d] of the time
11.3%

In the regular early childhood program[c] at least 80%[d] of the time
44.5%

Separate class[e]
24.2%

Other environments[g]
4.8%

Service provider location[f]
7.8%

FIGURE **8.2**
Percentage[a] of children ages 3 through 5 served under IDEA, Part B, by educational environment[b]: Fall 2006

Source: U.S. Department of Education, Office of Special Education Programs, Data Analysis System (DANS), OMB #1820-0517: "Part B, *Individuals with Disabilities Education Act*, Implementation of FAPE Requirements," 2006. Data were updated as of July 15, 2007. For actual data used, go to https://www.ideadata.org/Archive/ARCArchive.asp. These data are for the 50 states, the District of Columbia, Bureau of Indian Education schools, Puerto Rico, and the four outlying areas.

Did You Get It?

For young children (from 3- to 5 years-old) who are eligible for disability-related services, the multidisciplinary team is presented with a choice of using the individualized educational plan (IEP) or the individualized _____ plan.
  a. childhood education (ICEP)
  b. infant and toddler (IITP)
  c. family services (IFSP)
  d. youth in education (IYEP)

8.4 Head Start: Laws and Programs

Head Start was first launched in 1964 under the administration of President Lyndon Johnson, within the Office of Economic Opportunity, and it is now administered by the Administration for Children and Families. Head Start was intended to provide preschool education to the nation's low-income children ages 4 and 5 and to offer early educational experiences to low-income children who might otherwise come to school unprepared and unmotivated to learn. Head Start has become one of the most influential and massive federal social experiments in the history of early childhood education. In 1972, Head Start legislation was amended to include children with disabilities, reserving 10% of its total enrollment for children with disabilities who also met the economic requirements for being served by Head Start. The 10% of disabilities in Head Start include the following (Allen & Cowdery, 2009):

- Intellectual disabilities
- Deafness or serious hearing impairments
- Serious special impairments
- Crippling orthopedic impairments
- Chronic health disabilities
- Learning disabilities

Head Start
A preschool program intended to provide compensatory educational experiences for children from low-income families who might otherwise come to school unprepared and unmotivated to learn. Head Start is sponsored by the Office of Child Development.

In 2007, the Improving Head Start for School Readiness Act of 2007 was passed. The goal of this legislation is to help more children arrive a kindergarten ready to succeed. This law aligns Head Start performance standard with State early learning standards.

Head Start created a fortuitous opportunity to investigate the impact of early intervention. Several heartening longitudinal studies showed impressive long-term effects of early intervention for environmentally at-risk children. Individuals who had participated in Head Start were evaluated some 15 years later (Lazar & Darlington, 1982). The study followed up on 820 Head Start participants, comparing them with a group of children who did not have the Head Start experience. The results demonstrated that the Head Start program was extremely successful. Head Start participants were less likely to be placed in special education classes, were less likely to be retained and to repeat a grade, consistently scored higher on intelligence tests, and were more likely to finish high school by the age of 18. The research showed that early intervention prevents school failure and reduces the need for remedial programs (Head Start Bureau, 1993). In addition to education, Head Start offers services for health, parental involvement, and social services (Administration for Children and Families, 2001).

8.4a Head Start Studies

Along with other early intervention research, Head Start studies demonstrate the benefits of early intervention. In terms of cost-benefit analysis, society has received its money back with interest. On the completion of schooling, students who receive early intervention are more likely to be gainfully employed—to be taxpayers rather than tax receivers—and to be citizens who contribute to society. "Every dollar invested in quality early childhood education can save society $4 to $17 in remedial and correction costs. That's a pretty good return on investment" (Bolton, P., 2007, p. 2).

8.4b Early Head Start

The purpose of Early Head Start is to serve low-income women and their very young children. The first programs opened in 1995. The program provides services for pregnant women, infants, and toddlers that focus on prevention and promotion of healthy habits and positive parent–child interactions. Early Head Start programs work closely with the schools to provide a smooth transition for children and families (Allen & Cowdery, 2009).

▶❚❚ **TeachSource** Video Case Activity

© Cengage Learning 2015

Watch the TeachSource Video Case entitled "Home-School Communications: The Parent-Teacher Conference." In this video, a kindergarten teacher is holding a conference with a mother. The teacher uses actual samples of the child's work to illustrate how the child is progressing over the year. The teacher explains to the mother that all children in the class are different and have different strengths.

QUESTIONS

1. How does the kindergarten teacher use the child's work in the parent-teacher conference?

2. How does the teacher respond to the mother's concerns?

3. How does the teacher put a positive note in the parent-teacher conference?

Did You Get It?

A major change was implemented to the Head Start Program in 1972. The program would now allocate _____ of the placement space within its services to children with disabilities whose families otherwise met enrollment criteria.

  a. 5%
  b. 10%
  c. 25%
  d. 50%

8.5 Developmental Indicators of Problems in Young Children

Developmental indicators are early signs of problems in young children. Signs of problems can be observed in the child's motor development, auditory processing, visual processing, speech and language development, or attention abilities. Often, the child will excel in some areas of development, while displaying significant lags or difficulty in others. Learning does not suddenly begin when a child reaches age 5 or 6 and enters school. During the preschool years, children are earnestly and actively engaged in learning. During these early years, children master many preacademic skills and acquire a vast amount of knowledge, information, and abilities that are needed later for learning of academic subjects (Kirk, 1987). In the preschool years, children acquire skills in visual and auditory perception, extend their facility to attend, expand memory and thinking skills, and learn to understand and use language. The levels to which children acquire these skills can act as developmental indicators, which are predictive of later difficulty in academic achievement. However, early intervention can help preschool children reduce or overcome these potential problems (Lerner et al., 2003). Some early warning signs in preschool children are:

developmental indicators
Early precursors or signs of learning disabilities

- Late talking, compared with other children
- Delayed gross and/or fine motor problems
- Pronunciation problems
- Slow vocabulary growth, often unable to find the right word
- Difficulty rhyming words
- Trouble learning numbers, the alphabet, days of the week
- Extremely restless and easily distracted
- Trouble interacting with peers
- Poor ability to follow directions

Some useful early childhood websites are:

- First Signs: *http://www.firstsigns.org*
- Division for Early Childhood: *http://www.dec-sped.org*
- National Dissemination Center for Children With Disabilities: *http://www.nichcy.org*
- Family Village of the University of Wisconsin: *http://www.familyvillage.wisc.edu*
- LD Online: *http://www.ldonline.org*

8.5a Common Developmental Indicators

Developmental indicators of disabilities may appear as difficulties with gross-motor skills, fine-motor skills, auditory processing, visual processing, communication and language skills, or attention.

Gross-Motor Skills A common precursor for some children with learning disabilities is an awkwardness in gross-motor skills, which require children to use large muscles when moving their arms, legs, torso, hands, and feet. Young children with gross-motor problems appear clumsy in walking, jumping, hopping, running, skipping, throwing, and catching skills.

Fine-Motor Skills Fine-motor activities involve the small muscles used to move fingers and wrists, as well as eye-hand coordination and coordination of the two hands. Children with problems in fine-motor skills tend to be slow in learning to dress themselves, in learning eating skills, in using buttons and zippers, and in using pencils and crayons. Problems in fine-motor development are evident when children have difficulty doing puzzles, playing building games, accomplishing art projects, and using scissors in cutting activities. In the later elementary years, fine-motor difficulties are evident in slow and laborious handwriting.

Auditory Processing An important precursor of learning disabilities involves auditory processing. The ability to interpret what is heard provides an important pathway for learning. Children who have difficulty learning to read show early signs of difficulties with auditory processing abilities. These children can hear, but their difficulty lies in processing what they hear.

Visual Processing Visual processing abilities play a significant role in school learning, particularly in reading. Children with visual processing difficulties can see, but they encounter problems in visual discrimination of letters and words, visual memory, or visual closure.

Communication and Language Skills Difficulty in acquiring speech and understanding and using language are among the most common symptoms of difficulty. The ability to use language to communicate one's thoughts is central to learning. Children with communication or language disorders have difficulty understanding the language of others (listening), responding to instructions, initiating communications, explaining, engaging in conversations, and communicating with others. Delays in speech and language acquisition are discussed in Chapter 11, "Spoken Language Difficulties: Listening and Speaking."

Problems with Attention Some young children have behaviors related to attentional problems and display behaviors of hyperactivity, inattention, and impulsivity. These preschoolers cannot regulate or manage their activity levels to meet the demands of schooling. They act as if they were driven by a motor, running and climbing about excessively, being in constant motion, fidgeting and squirming when sitting, and making loud noises. Young children with inattention problems have difficulty concentrating on a task, are easily distracted, shift from one activity to another, and do not finish what they start. Parents and teachers complain that these children do not listen. They may be impulsive, unable to inhibit their responses to immediate events, and do not consider the consequences of their behavior before acting. They tend to blurt out answers before their teachers have finished the question. These youngsters also find it difficult to share and take turns with their classmates (Warner-Rogers et al., 2000). (See Chapter 7, "Autism Spectrum Disorders and Attention Deficit Hyperactivity Disorders.)

Did You Get It?

Developmental indicators, in the context of early special education, refer to what criteria?
  a. progress made
  b. signs of problems
  c. established developmental goals and objectives
  d. age-appropriate levels of development

8.6 Motor Development and Learning

Parents, teachers, physicians, and other professionals often describe the young child as awkward or as lacking manual dexterity. Parents frequently report that their child was slow in acquiring motor skills, such as using eating utensils, putting on clothes, buttoning a coat, catching a ball, or riding a bicycle.

Throughout history, philosophers and educators have written about the close relationship between motor development and learning. Plato placed gymnastics at the first level of education in the training of the philosopher-king. Aristotle wrote that a person's soul is characterized by both body and mind. Spinoza advised, "Teach the body to do many things; this will help you to perfect the mind and to come to the intellectual level of thought." Piaget (1952) emphasized that early sensorimotor learning establishes the foundation for later, more complex perceptual and cognitive development. Indeed, a recurring theme throughout the history of special education is the concern for motor development (Francks et al., 2003; Itard, 1962; Montessori, 1912; Sequin, 1970).

The *Diagnostic and Statistical Manual of Mental Disorders (DSM-5)* American Psychiatric Association 2013. The criteria is the DSM-5 is:

A. The acquisition and execution of coordinated motor skills is substantially below that expected given the individuals's chronological age and opportunity for skill learning and use. Difficulties are manifested as clumsiness, as well as slowness and inaccuracy of performance of motor skills.

B. The motor skills deficit in Criterion A significantly and persistently interferes with activities of daily living appropriate to chronological age and impacts academic/school productivity, prevocational and vocational activities, leisure, and play.

C. Onset of symptoms is in the early developmental period.

D. The motor skills deficits are not better explained by intellectual disability or visual impairment and are not attributable to a neurological condition affecting movement. (American Psychiatric Association, 2013). The special education law (IDEA-2004) recognizes the need for physical education for all exceptional children. The child's IEP can designate the use of related services, such as adapted physical education or occupational therapy (OT).

Occupational therapists (OTs) are health professionals who provide therapy for a variety of motor disorders. Motor activities are typically part of the curriculum in early childhood special education programs. Student Stories 8.1, "Motor Coordination Problems," describes a student with motor coordination difficulties.

occupational therapist (OT)
A therapist who is trained in brain physiology and function and who prescribes exercises to improve motor and sensory integration

Tony, age 6, is failing in math, and he also shows signs of immature motor development and poor awareness of his own body.

Tony was evaluated because he was doing poorly in school, particularly in reading and arithmetic. An individual intelligence test indicated that his cognitive skills were above average and a screening test for vision and hearing show no abnormalities. His oral language skills were good for his age. At first, Tony's posture gave the impression of being unusually straight, almost military in bearing. During the motor testing, however, it was evident that this seemingly straight posture was actually rigidity. When a required movement was made, he was unable to make a correction within his body position, and lost his balance. He was unable to walk a straight line and lost his balance and fell. He was unable to catch a large ball, and lost his balance trying. Although he had been given swimming lessons several times, he was still unable to swim. He could not ride a bicycle, and Tony could not participate in any ball games. Evidence of poor motor skills appeared in many academic activities. For example, his handwriting was almost illegible. Tony's father, who had excelled in athletics and had won several sports championships in high school and college, had little patience for playing with a son who did not learn motor skills easily. In fact, because of Tony's abysmal failure in sports, his father told the evaluator that his son was not "a real boy."

REFLECTIVE QUESTION

1. What do you think was Tony's major problem?

8.6a The Importance of Motor Development

Early childhood general educators view motor growth as a cornerstone of child development. Motor activities are typically included in the general education curriculum for preschool children. For preschoolers with disabilities who have deficits in motor coordination, balance, rhythm, or body image, the intervention strategies include methods for building motor skills, spatial awareness, and motor planning (Cook, Klein, & Tessier, 2008; Lerner et al., 2003).

Providing motor activities can bring about many unanticipated and probably immeasurable improvements for the young child. It can help a child become happier, more confident, and more available for learning; it can also foster social interactions. When the motor curriculum requires the child to go *through, under, over, between,* and *around* obstacles, the child is also learning important cognitive and language skills.

8.6b Key Concepts of Motor Development

Movement and motor experiences are crucial for human development. Difficulty in motor coordination is a serious problem for many children with disabilities. Some children exhibit motor behaviors that are typical of a much younger child. Examples of such motor behaviors are overflow movements (when the child performs a movement with the right arm, the left arm involuntarily performs a shadow movement), poor coordination in gross-motor activities, difficulty in fine-motor coordination, poor body image, and lack of directionality. These children perform so poorly in the physical education activities for their age that they are easily spotted in gym class. They frequently disturb others in the classroom by bumping into objects, falling off chairs, dropping pencils and books, and appearing generally clumsy.

Gross-motor skills involve the large muscles of the neck, trunk, arms, and legs. Gross-motor development involves postural control, walking, running, catching, and jumping. To provide stimulation for gross-motor development, children need safe environments that are free from obstacles, and they need much encouragement from parents and teachers.

Fine-motor skills involve the small muscles. Fine-motor coordination includes coordination of the hands and fingers and dexterity with the tongue and speech muscles. Children develop fine-motor skills as they learn to pick up small objects, such as beads or chunks of food, cut with a scissors, grasp and use crayons and pencils, and use a fork and spoon. They need ample opportunities for building with blocks, manipulating small toys, stringing beads, buttoning, and rolling and pounding (Cook et al., 2008).

Through the normal activities of play, children have many opportunities for motor learning.

The normal activities of play offer children many opportunities for motor activity. On the playground, children's muscles move as they reach, grasp, run, stoop, or stretch. In the typical play environment, the child develops motor skills by playing with toys, using clay, or painting. Playing games can also help build self-concept, social relationships, and acceptance by peers. Motor activities—such as riding bicycles, playing games, and dancing—signal the emergence of various developmental levels. The inability to accomplish these activities with reasonable proficiency may precipitate a chain of failure (Squire & Bricker, 2007).

Sometimes children receive instruction in motor skills through an adapted physical education program, which is a special physical education program that has been modified to meet the needs of children with disabilities. Helping children with disabilities take advantage of the same physical, emotional, and social benefits of exercise, recreation, and leisure activities that other children enjoy is important in inclusive environments. Movement games can help young children adjust to general classroom environments. For example, the child's attention span can be lengthened through games and physical activities that require increasing the ability to pay attention. Learning letters can become a physical activity if large letters made of rope are placed on a playground and games are devised in which the student runs or walks over the shapes of letters. Activities that involve the total body may also serve to focus the attention of the hyperactive child (Cratty, 1988, 2004).

8.6c Perceptual Motor Development

The relationship between perceptual motor learning and learning disabilities was formulated by one of the pioneers in the field of learning disabilities, Newell Kephart (1963, 1967, 1971). Through perceptual motor learning, the child

perceptual motor learning
The integration of motor learning and visual perceptual learning

integrates motor behaviors and perception (visual, auditory, tactile, and kinesthetic perception). Children who have normal perceptual motor development establish a solid and reliable concept of the world, a stable perceptual motor world, by the time they encounter academic tasks at age 6.

In contrast, children with difficulty with perceptual motor development must contend with a perceptual motor world that is unstable and unreliable. In order to deal with symbolic materials, these children must make some rather precise observations about objects and events. Children with perceptual motor problems are confused when confronted with symbolic materials because they have not established a stable perceptual motor world. For example, one child could not understand or perceive a square because he lacked sufficient motor experiences with squares. Another child could not rely on her visual observations, so she had to touch things to assure herself that what she was seeing was real.

8.6d Sensory Integration

sensory integration (SI)
A theory stemming from the field of occupational therapy that physical exercises can modify the brain

Sensory integration (SI) provides another approach to motor development. The theory of sensory integration comes from the field of occupational therapy and is based on the relationship between the neurological processes and motor behavior (Ayres, 1994; Kranowitz, 2006; Goldey, 1998; Williamson & Anzalone, 1997).

Occupational therapists are trained in the relationship between brain physiology and function. Specific physical therapies and exercises are designed to modify the motor and sensory integration functions of patients. Occupational therapists use sensory integration therapy with children who have disorders in several sensory integration functions, which interfere with the awareness of their body and body movements. Sensory integration methods are often used in early childhood special education programs.

Three systems are involved in sensory integration: (1) the tactile system, (2) the vestibular system, and (3) the proprioceptive system (Kranowitz, 2006; Silver, 2006; Clark, Mailloux, & Parham, 1989).

Tactile System The *tactile system* involves the sense of touch and the stimulation of skin surfaces. Some children have problems in *tactile defensiveness;* they experience discomfort when touched by another person. Infants with tactile defensiveness do not like to be held or touched. Older children may complain about being bothered by a tag on the back of a shirt, by a seam on a sock, or by clothes that are uncomfortable. These children may lash out and fight when they are brushed against while they are lining up. These children need to learn to tolerate more tactile contact.

Methods of sensory integration used by occupational therapists for tactile defensiveness include touching and rubbing skin surfaces, using lotions, and brushing skin surfaces.

Vestibular System The *vestibular system* involves the inner ear and enables individuals to detect motion. The vestibular system allows children to know where their head is in space and how to handle gravity. Children with vestibular disorders fall easily and do not know how to adjust their bodies for the position of their heads or for other body movements.

Therapy for vestibular disorders used by occupational therapists consists of exercises in body planning and balance. It includes activities such as spinning in chairs, swinging, and rolling on a large ball to stimulate the vestibular system.

Proprioceptive System The *proprioceptive system* involves stimulation from the muscles or within the body itself. Disorders in this system may involve *apraxia,* which is a difficulty in intentional performance of certain body movements. Children with an apraxia problem cannot plan how to move their bodies without bumping into walls, and they cannot direct movements, such as buttoning, tying, skipping, or writing. Therapies for proprioceptive stimulation used by occupational therapists include having the child use scooter boards and engage in other planned motor behaviors.

Did You Get It?

A young child is given intervention to increase her integration of visual, auditory, and tactile skills into her physical movement skills. This intervention aims to develop/improve _____ learning.

a. compensatory-motor
b. fine-motor
c. kinesthetic-motor
d. perceptual-motor

8.7 Perceptual Development

Perception is the process of recognizing and interpreting sensory information. It is the intellect's ability to give meaning to sensory stimulation. For example, a square must be perceived as a whole configuration, not as four separate lines. Because perception is a learned skill, the teaching process can have a direct impact on the child's perceptual facility.

> **perception**
> The process of recognizing and interpreting information received through the senses

Several dimensions of perception have implications for understanding learning disabilities: (1) the perceptual processing concept, (2) overloading the perceptual systems, (3) auditory perception, (4) visual perception, and (5) tactile and kinesthetic perception.

8.7a Perceptual Processing Concept

The perceptual processing concept is based on the premise that children learn in different ways. Some learn best by listening (auditory), some by looking (visual), some by touching (tactile), and some by performing an action (kinesthetic). Adults, too, have individual learning styles. Some learn best by listening to an explanation; others know that to learn something they must read about it or watch it being done. Still others learn best by writing something down or by going through the action themselves. Some students with learning disabilities appear to have a much greater facility in using one perceptual or learning style over another. Student Stories 8.2, "Auditory and Visual Perception Difficulties," describes contrasting perceptual difficulties of two children.

> **perceptual processing concept**
> A theory that learning problems are related to difficulty in mental processes

Research on brain function, using brain-imaging technologies (such as fMRI), shows that different perceptual systems do exist in different areas within the brain. Sensitive teachers use information about a child's style of learning and perceptual strengths and weaknesses in teaching academic skills. For example, the child who has great difficulty with the auditory perception of the sounds in words (or a deficit in awareness of phonemes) is likely to have difficulty learning phonics. Of course, the child will have to learn to decode words to acquire reading fluency. However, recognizing the child's auditory difficulties alerts the teacher to the child's area of difficulty and helps in teaching the child. The child may need additional practice in recognizing sounds in words.

8.7b Overloading the Perceptual Systems

For a few children, the reception of information from one input system interferes with information coming from another. These children have a lower tolerance for receiving and integrating information from several input systems at the same time. An analogy might be made to an overloaded circuit that blows out when it cannot handle any more electrical energy. Unable to accept and process an excess of data, the perceptual system becomes overloaded. Symptoms include confusion, poor recall, refusal to do the task, temper tantrums, or catastrophic responses.

If a child presents such symptoms, teachers should be cautious about using multisensory techniques and should change the method of instruction. One teacher reported that a second-grade girl with learning disabilities was not

STUDENT STORIES 8.2
Auditory and Visual Perception Difficulties

Sandra: Auditory Perception Difficulties

Eight-year-old Sandra failed many tasks that involved auditory learning. She could not learn nursery rhymes, was unable to take messages over the telephone, forgot spoken instructions, and could not discriminate between pairs of spoken words with minimal contrast or a single phoneme difference *(cat-cap)*. She could not tap out the number of sounds in words and found phonics instruction baffling. Sandra was failing in reading, yet she had passed the reading readiness test with ease because it tested performance skills that required visual learning. At first, Sandra could not remember the arithmetic facts, but there was a sudden spurt in her arithmetic achievement during the second half of first grade. She explained that she solved her arithmetic problems by putting the classroom clock in her head. By *looking* at the minute marks on the clock to perform arithmetic tasks, Sandra did well with visual tasks, but poorly in auditory processing, particularly in recognizing sounds in words.

John: Visual Perception Difficulties

In contrast, John, at age 8, performed several years above his age level on tasks that required auditory processing. He had easily learned to say the alphabet in sequence. He also learned poems and nursery rhymes; remembered series of digits, phone numbers, and verbal instructions; and quickly learned to detect phonemes or sounds in words. Visual tasks, however, were difficult. John had much trouble putting puzzles together, seeing and remembering forms in designs, doing block arrangements, remembering the sequence and order of things he saw, and recalling what words looked like in print.

REFLECTIVE QUESTION

1. How would you compare the strengths and weaknesses of Sandra and John?

making progress when taught through simultaneous auditory and visual instruction. The teacher reduced the auditory input by not talking and instead taught reading and arithmetic through visual pictures and examples. The girl now could understand and made great strides in both reading and arithmetic.

Sometimes children learn by themselves to adapt their own behavior to avoid overloading. One boy avoided looking at an individual's face when he engaged in conversation. When asked about this behavior, the boy explained that he found he could not understand what was being said if he watched the speaker's face while listening. The visual stimuli, in effect, interfered with the boy's ability to comprehend auditory information.

8.7c Auditory Perception

Auditory perception, which is the ability to recognize or interpret what is heard, provides an important pathway for learning. Accumulating research shows that many poor readers have auditory, linguistic, and phonological difficulties (Lyon, 1998; Stahl & Murray, 1994). These children do not have a problem in hearing or in auditory acuity. Rather, they have difficulty with auditory perception. Because abilities in auditory perception normally develop during the early years, many academic teachers mistakenly presume that all students have acquired these skills. Auditory subskills include (1) phonological awareness, (2) auditory discrimination, (3) auditory memory, (4) auditory sequencing, and (5) auditory blending. (See LD Online, Visual and Auditory Processing Disorders, *http://www .ldonline.org/ article/6390.*)

Phonological Awareness A necessary ability for learning to read is the ability to recognize that the words we hear are composed of individual sounds within the word. This ability is called phonological awareness. For example, when an individual hears the word *cat,* the ear hears it as one pulse of sound. But the individual who has acquired phonological awareness knows that the word *cat* is made up of three sounds (or *phonemes):* /c/a/t/. The child who lacks phonological awareness does not recognize that *cat* has three separate sounds.

phonological awareness
A child's recognition of the sounds of language. The child must understand that speech can be segmented into syllables and phonemic units

Children who have trouble learning to read are often completely unaware of how language is put together. They are unable to recognize or isolate the sounds of words or the number of sounds in a word. For example, when hearing the word *kite,* they cannot tap out three sounds. These children also cannot recognize similarities in words. They have difficulty recognizing words that rhyme (e.g., *right, fight,* and *night*) and alliteration in words (e.g., *cat* and *cap*). As a result, these children cannot understand or use the alphabetic principle needed for learning phonics and decoding words.

Skills in phonological awareness abilities are formed during the preschool years. It is very important to assess these abilities before children are taught to read and to provide training for children who have not acquired phonological abilities. Fortunately, research shows that young children can develop phonological awareness through specific instruction and that such teaching has a positive effect on reading achievement (Jennings, Caldwell, & Lerner, 2010; Ball & Blachman, 1991; Lerner, 1990; Liberman & Liberman, 1990; Stahl & Murray, 1994). Phonological awareness as it relates to reading is also discussed in the chapters on oral language and reading. An informal test of phonological awareness is shown in Chapter 11, "Spoken Language

TABLE 8.4

Tests for Assessing Motor and Perceptual Development

Tests for Assessing Motor Development

Bruininks-Oseretsky Test of Motor Proficiency 2: http://ags.pearsonassessments.com

Peabody Developmental Motor Scales-2: http://www.wpspublish.com

Tests for Assessing Perceptual Development

Detroit Tests of Learning Aptitude-Primary-2: http://www.proedinc.com

Detroit Tests of Learning Aptitude-4 (reversed letters, word sequences): http://www.proedinc.com

Illinois Test of Psycholinguistic Abilities (ITPA–3); auditory sequential memory, sound blending, and auditory closure: http://www.proedinc.com

Bender-Gestalt Visual Motor Test: http://www.wpspublish.com

Developmental Test of Visual–Motor Integration: http://www.wpspublish.com

Developmental Test of Visual Perception: http://www.wpspublish.com

© Cengage Learning

Difficulties: Listening and Speaking." Table 8.4 lists some formal tests of auditory perception.

8.7d Visual Perception

visual perception
The identification, organization, and interpretation of sensory data received by the individual through the eye

Visual perception is the identification, organization, and interpretation of sensory data received by the individual through the eye, and it plays a significant role in school learning, especially in reading. Students have difficulty in tasks requiring the visual discrimination of letters and words, as well as of numbers, geometric designs, and pictures. Figure 8.3 shows several examples of visual perception tasks.

Visual Perception and Reversals There is an important difference between the perceptual world of *objects* and the perceptual world of *letters* and *words*. During the prereading stage of development, children make a perceptual generalization that an object retains the same name or meaning regardless of the position it happens to be in, the direction it faces, or the modification of slight additions or subtractions. A chair, for example, is a chair regardless of whether it faces left or right, back or front, upside down or right side up. Whether it is upholstered, has additional cushions, or even has a leg missing, it is still called a *chair.* The child makes similar generalizations about dogs; no matter what its position, size, color, or quantity of hair, a dog is still called a *dog.*

When beginning to deal with letters and words, however, the child finds that this perceptual generalization no longer holds true. The placement of a circle on a stick from left to right or top to bottom changes the name of the letter from b to d or to p or q. The addition of a small line changes c to e. The direction the word is facing changes it from was to saw, from no to on, and from top to pot.

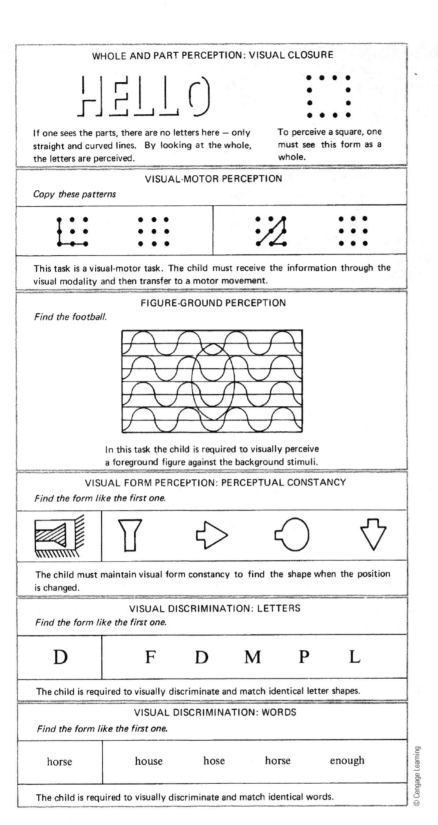

FIGURE **8.3**
Examples of Visual Perception
Tasks

Some students fail to make the necessary amendments to earlier perceptual generalizations they have formulated. One incident of such confusion happened during a teachers' strike. A boy with this type of difficulty looked at the picket signs and asked why the teachers were picketing if the strike had been called off. The sign was lettered *ON STRIKE,* but the boy read it as *NO STRIKE.* In another such example, a student reversed the letters when making a Christmas card. He printed *IEON* instead of *NOEI.*

Learning activities and materials should be concrete, real, and relevant to the lives of young children.

Frances Roberts/Alamy

8.7e Tactile and Kinesthetic Perception

The tactile and kinesthetic systems are two perceptual systems for receiving information. The term *haptic* is sometimes used to refer to both systems.

Tactile Perception Tactile perception is obtained through the sense of touch via the fingers and skin surfaces. The ability to recognize an object by touching it, to identify a numeral that is drawn on one's back or arm, to discriminate between smooth and rough surfaces, and to identify which finger is being touched are all examples of tactile perception.

tactile perception
Perception obtained through the sense of touch via the fingers and skin surfaces

kinesthetic perception
Perception obtained through body movements and muscle feeling, such as the awareness of positions taken by different parts of the body and bodily feelings of muscular contraction, tension, and relaxation

Kinesthetic Perception Kinesthetic perception is obtained through body movements and muscle feeling. The awareness of positions taken by different parts of the body and bodily feelings of muscular contraction, tension, and relaxation are examples of kinesthetic perception.

The tactile and kinesthetic systems are important sources of information about object qualities, body movement, and their interrelationships. Most school tasks, as well as most acts in everyday life, require both touch and body movement. Tactile and kinesthetic perceptions play important roles in learning.

Did You Get It?

Randall learns most effectively by hearing, Malcolm learns most effectively by seeing, and Juan is a "hands-on" learner. Understanding how children take in and utilize information, and thus learn from it, is inherent to a model referred to as the perceptual _____ concept.

    a. integration
    b. processing
    c. implementation
    d. operation

8.8 Assessing Young Children

A major trend in assessment practices today is to use informal, functional assessment measures instead of relying solely on formal standardized tests and testing procedures. There is more authentic assessment and observation of the child in a natural environment (Lerner et al., 2003).

8.8a Phases of Early Identification and Assessment

Four separate but related phases of identification and assessment of preschoolers with disabilities are (1) child-find, (2) screening, (3) diagnosing, and (4) evaluating, as shown in Figure 8.4. Many different tests and assessment procedures can be used.

Figure 8.4 explains the process of determining whether a young child may have a disability from child find through individualized evaluation.

Child-Find This first phase, child-find, refers to ways of finding young children with disabilities in the community. Emphasis is on making initial contact and increasing the public's awareness of services. Preschool children are not usually in the public school system, and communities must therefore make a concerted effort to seek them out. Communities develop methods, such as radio announcements, posters, signs in day-care centers and libraries, and local newspaper articles to alert families of young children.

Screening This second phase, screening, attempts to identify children who need further study. Screening involves surveying many children to identify those who *may* need special services. School districts often encourage families to bring *all* 3- through 5-year-old children in for free evaluation services, even if the family does not suspect a disability. The screening is a short, low-cost assessment of children's vision and hearing, speech and language, motor skills, self-help skills, social-emotional maturity, and cognitive development.

Many school systems use screening interviews or questionnaires with the parents of all incoming kindergarten children. Questions are designed to detect those children who are likely to have learning difficulty. Table 2.5 in Chapter 2, "Assessment and the IEP Process," provides some questions that might be used in such a screening interview.

Diagnosing The third phase, diagnosing, consists of determining the extent of developmental delay and devising an intervention program. In this phase, the child receives a comprehensive evaluation through formal and authentic measures to determine if the child needs special education services. A multidisciplinary team determines the nature of the problem, its severity, and the intervention and educational setting that the child needs.

Evaluating The fourth phase, evaluating, concentrates on measuring progress, judging whether a child should remain in a special education program, and planning for transition. This stage of the assessment helps determine whether the child still needs special education services, what skills the child has learned and still lacks, and what new placement will be needed.

8.8b Areas of Assessment

To evaluate a child's developmental delay, the assessment typically includes an evaluation of cognitive, motor, communication, perceptual, social, and adaptive development (Gargiulo & Kilgo, 2005; Lerner et al., 2003).

Cognitive Development This evaluation includes the assessment of the child's abilities in thinking, planning, and concept development. Examples of cognitive tasks are identifying colors; naming parts of the body; rote counting (up to 10 or so); showing an understanding of one-to-one correspondence ("Show me 3 blocks"); demonstrating place concepts (on, under, corner, between, middle); identifying given concepts (round, bigger); naming letters; or sorting chips by color, size, and shape.

4. EVALUATING: Measure progress, plan for transition

3. DIAGNOSING: Determine extent of delay, plan intervention

2. Identify children who need further study

1. CHILD-FIND: Locate children, increase public awareness

© Cengage Learning

FIGURE **8.4**

Stages of the Assessment Process for Young Children With Disabilities

child-find
Ways of locating young children with disabilities in the community

screening
A type of assessment using ways to survey many children quickly to identify those who may need special services

developmental delay
A term designating that a child is slow in a specific aspect of development, such as in cognitive, physical, communication, social/emotional, or adaptive development. It is considered a noncategorical label for identifying a young child for services

Motor Development The assessment of motor development includes the child's overall physical development, gross-motor skills, and fine-motor development. Examples of tasks the child is asked to perform include catching a ball or bean bag, jumping, hopping, skipping, building a 4-block design, touching fingers (copying the tester's demonstration by consecutively touching each finger on one hand to the thumb of the same hand and then repeating the task on the other hand), cutting various patterns with scissors, matching and copying shapes and letter formations, and writing one's own name. The child's visual and auditory acuity are also often assessed. Table 8.4 lists tests for assessing motor and perceptual development.

Communication Development This evaluation includes speech and language skills and the abilities to understand and use language. Evaluators might assess articulation by having children say certain words. They can be asked to repeat numbers and sentences spoken by the evaluator; to describe pictures; to answer problem-solving questions; or to state their first and last names, gender, age, address, and phone number. An auditory test—for example, that has children copy a series of clapping patterns—may also be included.

Social and Emotional Development The child's social and affective interactions are recorded through observational notes made by the evaluators. Typical observations include how well the child relates to adults and to other children.

Adaptive Development This category refers to the child's self-help skills. It includes such areas as independent toileting skills, dressing skills, eating skills, and the ability to separate from parents.

Did You Get It?

Child-find, the earliest stage of planned intervention in a four-pronged system of childhood assessment for students with disabilities, involves which activity?

a. formalized testing for eligibility
b. development of the IEP or IFSP
c. finding children in need of services
d. an initial interview with the IEP team

8.9 Early Childhood Programs and Practices

8.9a Recommended Practices: The Division of Early Childhood

A leading professional organization for early childhood special education is The Division for Early Childhood (DEC), which is a component of the Council of Exceptional Children. The website is *http://www.dec-sped.org*. DEC has proposed the following recommended practices for early childhood special education:

- **The right of all children to be included in natural settings.** This means that teaching should occur within the context of daily routines in natural environments.
- **The importance of individualization.** The teaching should meet the individual needs of each child.

- **The assessment procedures should be informal and in natural environments.** The use of standardized assessment tests should be de-emphasized.
- **The assessment and curriculum should be integrated.** Testing and teaching should not be isolated; they should be combined.
- **Encourage child-initiated activities.** A child-centered approach to teaching young children with special needs is encouraged.
- **Use active engagement to learn independent functioning.** In activity-based instruction, the teacher follows the child's lead to discover the child's interests, motivation, and choice of activities.

8.9b Using Computer Technology

For young children with learning disabilities and related mild disabilities, computers offer many opportunities to explore, play, and learn. Their computer experiences become an integral part of their overall development. Computers bestow a unique magic on children who have special needs by empowering them with a sense of independence and control. The value of the computer may be greater for exceptional youngsters than for others in the population. It is widely acknowledged that computers enable ordinary people to do extraordinary things, but for the child who has special needs, the computer does even more. It enables extraordinary people to do ordinary things.

Computers can help young children develop independence, self-help skills, motor control, visual and auditory concepts, language skills, and cognitive skills. Young children with disabilities who use computers are able to control their environment and to make decisions. Even social skills can be encouraged through cooperative computer activities. Computer activities can help families and teachers meet IEP and IFSP goals (Bowe, 2007; Lewis, Church, & Tsantis, 2006). Computers can creatively present colors; distinguish differences, such as larger and smaller; illustrate concepts, such as above and below; and help with shape and letter recognition, counting, matching, and sequencing.

Adaptive peripherals are particularly useful with young children. Speech synthesizers allow the computer to talk to the child. Switches can be plugged into the computer, allowing the child to use the computer without the keyboard. Interactive White Boards are very useful (Whitby, Leininger, & Grillo, 2012). With the TouchWindow, the child can directly touch the screen to control the computer. Most important, young children with disabilities like using the computer. It is an enjoyable, motivating way of learning.

Did You Get It?

The Division for Early Childhood (DEC) stresses which approach in its charter document of recommended practices for early special educational?
   a. curriculum centered
   b. community centered
   c. child centered
   d. teacher centered

8.10 Early Intervention Strategies

In this section, we describe representative activities for teaching young children with disabilities. The activities include (1) motor development activities, (2) auditory processing, (3) visual processing, and (4) tactile and kinesthetic processing.

8.10a Motor Development Activities

Motor development activities are a particularly useful part of the early childhood curriculum. The teaching strategies for motor development targets three areas: (1) gross-motor activities, (2) fine-motor activities, and (3) body awareness activities.

Gross-Motor Activities Gross-motor activities involve the ability to move various parts of the body. The purpose of these activities is to develop smoother, more effective body movements and to increase the child's sense of spatial orientation and body consciousness. Gross-motor activities are grouped as (1) walking activities, (2) throwing and catching activities, and (3) other gross-motor activities. Teaching Tips 8.1, "Activities for Gross-Motor Development," lists suggested activities for building gross-motor skills.

Courtesy of Elizabeth Crews Photography

Motor activities help young children develop motor skills. The balance beam is commonly used in the early childhood program.

Fine-Motor Activities Fine motor activities involve the small muscles, for example, the coordination of the hands and fingers. Teaching Tips 8.2, "Activities for Fine-Motor Development," lists suggested activities for building fine-motor skills.

8.10b Auditory Processing

Many young children with learning disabilities and related mild disabilities need specific practice to acquire auditory processing skills. In Teaching Tips 8.3, "Auditory Processing Activities," we suggest strategies for phonological awareness, listening to sounds, auditory discrimination, and auditory memory.

8.10c Visual Processing

Abilities in visual perception are necessary for academic learning. Children who can read letters and numbers, copy geometric patterns, and match printed words tend to do well in first-grade reading. In Teaching Tips 8.4, "Visual Processing Activities," we suggest some visual processing activities.

8.10d Tactile and Kinesthetic Processing

Teaching Tips 8.5, "Tactile and Kinesthetic Processing Activities," provides activities that enhance tactile and kinesthetic processing abilities.

TEACHING TIPS 8.1
Activities for Gross-Motor Development

Walking Activities

1. **Forward, backward, and sideways walk.** Children walk to a target goal on a straight or curved path marked on the floor. The path may be wide or narrow, but the narrower the path, the more difficult the task. A single line requiring tandem walking (heel-to-toe) is more difficult than a widely spaced walk. A slow pace is more difficult than a running pace. Walking without shoes and socks is more difficult than walking with shoes. Students walk through the same course backward and sideways. In variations, children walk with arms in different positions, carrying objects, dropping objects such as balls into containers along the way, or focusing eyes on various parts of the room.

2. **Stepping-stones.** Put objects on the floor for stepping-stones, identifying placements for right foot and left foot by colors or by the letters *K* and *L*. The student is to follow the course by *placing* the correct foot on each stepping-stone.

3. **Line walks.** Draw lines in colors on the floor. Lines can be curved, angular, or spiral. Place a rope on the floor and have the students walk along the side of the rope. A variation is to place a ladder flat on the ground. Students walk between the rungs, forward and backward, and then hop through the rungs.

Throwing and Catching Activities

1. **Throwing.** Balloons, wet sponges, beanbags, yarn balls, and rubber balls of various sizes can be used to throw objects at targets, to the teacher, or to one another.

2. **Catching.** Catching is a more difficult skill than throwing. Students can practice catching the previously mentioned objects thrown by the teacher or by other students.

3. **Ball games.** Various types of ball games help develop motor coordination. Examples include balloon volleyball or rolling-ball games, bouncing balls on the ground, and throwing balls against the wall. If children find that throwing and catching a rubber ball is too difficult, a rag ball can be used. Rag balls are made by covering rags or discarded nylon hosiery with cloth.

Professional Resource Download

TEACHING TIPS 8.2
Activities for Fine-Motor Development

Fine-Motor *Activities*

1. **Tracing.** Students trace lines, pictures, designs, letters, or numbers on tracing paper, plastic, *or* stencils. Use directional arrows, color cues, and numbers to help children trace the figures.

2. **Water control.** Children carry and pour water into measured buckets from pitchers to specified levels. Smaller amounts and finer measurements make the task more difficult. Coloring the water makes the activity more interesting.

3. **Cutting with scissors.** Choose cutting activities that are appropriate for the child's developmental level. The easiest activity is cutting straight lines marked near the edge of the paper. A more difficult activity is cutting a straight line across the center of the paper. A piece of cardboard attached to the paper helps guide the scissors.

4. **Stencils or templates.** Children draw outlines of geometric shapes. Templates can be made from cardboard, wood, plastic, or foam containers. Two styles of templates are (1) a solid shape and (2) frames with the shape cut out.

5. **Lacing.** A piece of cardboard punched with holes or a pegboard can be used for this activity. A design or picture is made on the board, and then the student follows the pattern by weaving or sewing through the holes with a heavy shoelace, yarn, or cord.

6. **Paper-and-pencil activities.** Coloring books, readiness books, dot-to-dot books, and kindergarten books frequently provide good paper-and-pencil activities to practice fine-motor and eye-hand development.

7. **Clipping clothespins.** Clothespins can be clipped to a line or to a box. The child can be timed in this activity by counting the number of clothespins clipped in a specified time.

8. **Copying designs.** The child looks at a geometric design and copies it on paper.

(continued)

Body Awareness Activities

The *purpose* of these activities is to help children develop accurate images of the location and function of the parts of the body.

1. **Pointing to body parts.** Children point to the various parts of the body: nose, right elbow, left ankle, and so forth. This activity is more difficult with the eyes closed. The child can also lie on the floor and be asked to touch various parts of the body. This activity is more difficult if performed to a rhythmic pattern—using a metronome, for example. As a variation, make a robot from cardboard that is held together at the joints with fasteners and can be moved into various positions. The child can move the limbs of the robot on command and match the positions with his or her own body movements,

2. **"Simon says."** This game can be played with the eyes open or closed,

Professional Resource Download

3. **Life-size drawing.** Children lie on a large sheet of paper, and the teacher traces an outline around them. Next, the children fill in and color the clothes and the details of the face and body,

4. **Games.** Games such as "Looby Loo," "Hokey-Pokey," and "Did You Ever See a Lassie?" help develop concepts of left, right, and body image,

5. **Following instructions.** Instruct the child to put the left hand on the right ear and the right hand on the left shoulder. Other instructions might be to put the right hand in front of the left hand or to turn right, walk two steps, and turn left,

6. **Twister.** Make rows of colored circles on the floor, an oilcloth, or a plastic sheet, or use the commercial game. Make cards instructing the student to put the left foot on the green circle, the right foot on the red circle, and so on.

TEACHING TIPS 8.3

Auditory Processing Activities Listening *to Sounds*

1. **Listening for sounds.** Children close their eyes and listen to environmental sounds—for example, sounds of cars, airplanes, animals, and other outside sounds; and sounds in the next room. Recorded sounds of planes, trains, animals, and bells can be played back to the students, who are then asked to identify them,

2. **Sounds made by the teacher.** Children close their eyes and identify sounds that the teacher makes. Examples of such sounds include dropping a pencil, tearing a piece of paper, using a stapler, bouncing a ball, sharpening a pencil, tapping on a glass, opening a window, snapping the lights, leafing through a book, cutting with scissors, opening a drawer, jingling money, or writing on a blackboard,

3. **Shaking sounds.** Place small, hard items, such as stones, beans, chalk, salt, sand, or rice, into containers with covers. Have the children identify the contents by shaking the containers and listening,

4. **Listening for sound patterns.** Have children close their eyes or sit facing away from the teacher. Clap hands, play a drum, or bounce a ball, Rhythmic patterns can be made—for example, slow, fast, fast. Ask students how many counts there were, or ask them

to repeat the patterns. As a variation on the previous suggestion, use a cup and a book, for example, to tap out sound patterns.

Auditory Discrimination

1. **Near or far.** With eyes closed, the students judge from what part of the room a sound is coming and whether it is near or far,

2. **Loud or soft.** The students learn to judge and to discriminate between loud and soft sounds that the teacher produces,

3. **Find the sound.** One student hides a music box or a ticking clock, and the other students try to find it by locating the sound.

Auditory Memory

1. **Do this.** Place five or six objects in front of the student and give the student a series of directions to follow. For example, "Put the green block in Jean's lap, place the yellow flower under John's chair, and put the orange ball into Joe's desk." The list can be increased as the student improves in auditory memory.

(continued)

2. **Following directions.** Give the student several simple tasks to perform. For example, "Draw a big red square on your paper, put a small green circle underneath the square, and draw a black line from the middle of the circle to the upper right-hand corner of the square." Such activities can be tape recorded for use with earphones at a listening center.

3. **Nursery rhymes.** Have children learn nursery rhymes and poems and play finger games.

4. **Going to the moon.** Update the game of "Grandmother's Trunk" or "Going to New York." Say, "I took a trip to the moon and took my spacesuit." The student repeats the statement, but adds one item, such as "helmet." Pictures may be used to help with auditory memory.

Professional Resource Download

TEACHING TIPS 8.4
Visual Processing Activities Visual Perception

1. **Pegboard designs.** Using colored pegs, students reproduce colored visual geometric patterns on a pegboard from a visual model made by the teacher or shown on a printed page.

2. **Blocks.** Children reproduce models using parquetry blocks. Have children use wood or plastic blocks that are all one color or have faces of different colors to match geometric shapes and have them build copies of models.

3. **Puzzles.** Students assemble puzzles. Subjects such as people, animals, forms, numbers, or letters can be cut into large pieces for the child to assemble.

4. **Classification.** Students group or classify objects by shapes, sizes, and colors. The objects can be placed in a box or bowl. They can be chips, coins, buttons, beans, and so on.

5. **Matching geometric shapes.** Place shapes on cards and have the students play games requiring the matching of these shapes. Collect jars of different sizes with lids, mix the lids, and have students match the lids with the jars. Make a domino-type game by making sets of cards decorated with sandpaper, felt, self-adhesive covering, or painted dots; have students match the cards with one another.

6. **Playing cards.** A deck of playing cards provides excellent teaching material to match suits, pictures, numbers, and sets.

7. **Letters and numbers.** Visual perception and discrimination of letters are important reading readiness skills. Games that provide opportunities to match, sort, or name shapes can be adapted to letters and numbers. Bingo cards can be made with letters. As letters are called, the student recognizes and covers up the letters.

Visual Memory

1. **Identifying missing objects.** Expose a collection of objects. Cover and remove one of the objects. Show the collection again, asking the student to identify the missing object.

2. **Ordering from memory.** Expose a short series of shapes, designs, or objects. Have the student place another set of these designs in the identical order from memory. Playing cards, colored blocks, blocks with designs, or mahjongg tiles are among the materials that might be used for such an activity. Show a toy, number, letter, or word for a brief time and then have the child recall it.

3. **Stories from pictures.** On a flannel board, place pictures of activities that tell a story. Remove the pictures and have the pupil tell the story by depending on visual memory of the pictures.

Professional Resource Download

TEACHING TIPS 8.5

Tactile and Kinesthetic Processing Activities

1. **Feeling various textures.** Children feel various textures, such as smooth wood, metal, sandpaper, felt, flocking, sponge, wet surfaces, and foods. Attach different materials to small pieces of wood. The student touches the boards without looking and learns to discriminate and match the various surfaces.

2. **Feeling shapes.** Place various textures that are cut into geometric patterns or letters on boards. Children can touch them and discriminate, match, and identify the shapes. The shapes can also be made of plastic, wood, cardboard, clay, or the like.

3. **Feeling weights.** Fill small cardboard spice containers to different levels with beans, rice, and so on. Have the child match weights through shaking and sensing the weights.

Professional Resource Download

I Have a Kid Who...

LORINDA: *A Preschooler With Developmental Delay*

Lorinda was identified during the local school district's preschool screening program as a high-risk child who needed further assessment and intervention. She performed poorly on tests requiring expressive language skills and on social measures. At the time of the preschool screening, Lorinda's age was 3 years 9 months.

During the interview with Lorinda's mother, the school obtained additional information. Linda was born 6 weeks prematurely, and she weighed a little more than 4 pounds at birth and had trouble breathing. She frequently suffered from colds during her first 2 years, and between the ages of 2 and 3, she had at least eight serious ear infections. Motor development seemed to be normal; she sat up, walked, and crawled at the same ages that her siblings had performed these activities. Her language development, however, was slower than the other children in her family. Although she seemed to understand language when spoken to, she could not use it to make her wants known. She did not use any words until she was 2 years old and even now uses only very short sentences, such as "Me want pizza" or "Him break cup." She often uses the wrong word or simply points to what she wants. She still has temper tantrums, which seem to be triggered by her inability to communicate her needs.

Her mother described her as an "overactive" child compared with the other children. She would "tear the house apart," break the crib, and take all her toys apart. She never sat down, except to watch television, and that activity usually lasted for only a few minutes. When Lorinda turned 3, her mother tried to enroll her in a small play at school, but after a few days the director said she could not stay because of her extreme hyperactivity. Without provocation, she grabbed toys from other children and hit or scratched her classmates.

Lorinda's mother had suspected that Lorinda was different, but everyone had told her not to worry—that Lorinda would outgrow her disruptive behavior. The mother expressed relief at having her daughter in the special preschool program. At last, someone else recognized Lorinda's problem and would be working to help her. The hours Lorinda would be in school would offer her mother the first break since Lorinda was born, and her mother was looking forward to receiving help from the school on home behavior management.

QUESTIONS

1. How was Lorinda's problem identified?
2. What are Lorinda's strengths?
3. What are Lorinda's weaknesses?
4. In what educational setting do you think Lorinda should receive services?

Did You Get It?

Many games that might seem childish can be used effectively to entertain and develop specific skills. Which traditional childhood activity/game is easily and effectively integrated into an educational setting to develop bodily awareness?

a. any card game
b. Simon Says
c. Operation®
d. jump-roping

Chapter Summary

- The early years are a critical time in a child's development and can avert or reduce later failure.
- The Individuals With Disabilities Education Improvement Act (IDEA-2004) incorporates provisions for two age groups: preschool children (ages 3 to 6) and for infants and toddlers (ages birth to 3).

- Motor learning is a developmental skill, and it is considered a key curriculum activity in the general education setting for young children.
- Perception is an important domain for young children with disabilities.
- Consideration should be given to auditory and visual processing.

Questions for Discussion and Reflection

1. Why are the early years so important? What are some of the benefits of early intervention?
2. What are the developmental indicators of disabilities found in young children? How can early intervention practices help young children with special needs?
3. Describe the two early childhood age groups covered in the Individuals With Disabilities

Education Improvement Act (IDEA-2004). Compare and contrast the effect of the law for these two age groups.

4. What are some educational settings for young children with disabilities?

Key Terms

at risk (p. 217)

child-find (p. 237)

developmental delay (p. 237)

developmental indicators (p. 225)

educational environments (p. 222)

Head Start (p. 223)

individualized family service
   plan (IFSP) (p. 221)

kinesthetic perception (p. 236)

occupational therapist (OT) (p. 227)

perception (p. 231)

perceptual motor learning (p. 229)

perceptual processing concept (p. 231)

phonological awareness (p. 233)

screening (p. 237)

sensory integration (SI) (p. 230)

tactile perception (p. 236)

visual perception (p. 234)

Steve Debenport/iStockphoto.com

Adolescents and Adults With Learning Disabilities and Related Disabilities

LEARNING OBJECTIVES

After reading this chapter, you should be able to:

9.1 Describe the characteristics of adolescents with learning problems

9.2 List effective inclusionary strategies at the secondary level

9.3 Describe the required components of a transition plan

9.4 List the approaches to effectively teach adolescents with learning problems

9.5 Describe the components of learning strategies instruction

9.6 Describe the characteristics of postsecondary programs

9.7 Discuss the characteristics of adults with learning problems

If you give a starving man a fish, you feed him for a day. But if you teach the man how to fish, you feed him for a lifetime. If you teach a student with learning disabilities a fact, you help the student for the moment. But if you teach that student how to learn, you help the student for a lifetime.

—Deshler, Ellis, and Lenz (1996)

STANDARDS Addressed in This Chapter:

CEC Initial Level Special Educator Preparation Standards as approved by the National Council for the Accreditation of Teacher Education

CEC Initial Preparation Standard 1: Learner Development and Individual Learning Differences

- 1.0—Beginning special education professionals understand how exceptionalities may interact with development and learning and use this knowledge to provide meaningful and challenging learning experiences for individuals with exceptionalities.

- 1.1—Beginning special education professionals understand how language, culture, and family background influence the learning of individuals with exceptionalities.

- 1.2—Beginning special education professionals use understanding of development and individual differences to respond to the needs of individuals with exceptionalities.

CEC Initial Preparation Standard 2: Learning Environments

- 2.0—Beginning special education professionals create safe, inclusive, culturally responsive learning environments so that individuals with exceptionalities become active and effective learners and develop emotional well-being, positive social interactions, and self-determination.

- 2.1—Beginning special education professionals through collaboration with general educators and other colleagues create safe, inclusive, culturally responsive learning environments to engage individuals with exceptionalities in meaningful learning activities and social interactions.

- 2.2—Beginning special education professionals use motivational and instructional interventions to teach individuals with exceptionalities how to adapt to different environments.

CEC Initial Preparation Standard 4: Assessment

- 4.0—Beginning special education professionals use multiple methods of assessment and data-sources in making educational decisions.

- 4.1—Beginning special education professionals select and use technically sound formal and informal assessments that minimize bias.

- 4.3—Beginning special education professionals in collaboration with colleagues and families use multiple types of assessment information in making decisions about individuals with exceptionalities.

- 4.4—Beginning special education professionals engage individuals with exceptionalities to work toward quality learning and performance and provide feedback to guide them.

CEC Initial Preparation Standard 5: Instructional Planning and Strategies

- 5.0—Beginning special education professionals select, adapt, and use a repertoire of evidence-based instructional strategies to advance learning of individuals with exceptionalities.

- 5.1—Beginning special education professionals consider an individual's abilities, interests, learning environments, and cultural and linguistic factors in the selection, development, and adaptation of learning experiences for individuals with exceptionalities.

- 5.4—Beginning special education professionals use strategies to enhance language development and communication skills of individuals with exceptionalities.

- 5.5—Beginning special education professionals develop and implement a variety of education and transition plans for individuals with exceptionalities across a wide range of settings and different learning experiences in collaboration with individuals, families, and teams.

- 5.6—Beginning special education professionals teach to mastery and promote generalization of learning.

- 5.7—Beginning special education professionals teach cross-disciplinary knowledge and skills such as critical thinking and problem solving to individuals with exceptionalities.

CEC Initial Preparation Standard 6: Professional Learning and Ethical Practice

- 6.2—Beginning special education professionals understand how foundational knowledge and current issues influence professional practice.

- 6.3—Beginning special education professionals understand that diversity is a part of families, cultures, and schools, and that complex human issues can interact with the delivery of special education services.

CEC Initial Preparation Standard 7: Collaboration

- 7.0—Beginning special education professionals collaborate with families, other educators, related service providers, individuals with exceptionalities, and personnel from community agencies in culturally responsive ways to address the needs of individuals with exceptionalities across a range of learning experiences.

- 7.1—Beginning special education professionals use the theory and elements of effective collaboration.

- 7.2—Beginning special education professionals serve as a collaborative resource to colleagues.

- 7.3—Beginning special education professionals use collaboration to promote the well-being of individuals with exceptionalities across a wide range of settings and collaboration.

For many individuals, learning difficulties are lifelong problems that continue into the adolescent and adult years. In this chapter, we discuss (1) adolescents and adults with learning disabilities and other related disabilities, (2) special issues at the middle school and secondary levels, (3) approaches to teaching adolescents with learning disabilities and related mild disabilities, (4) learning strategies instruction, (5) postsecondary programs, and (6) the adult years.

9.1 Adolescents With Learning Disabilities and Other Related Disabilities

The period of adolescence is well documented as a stage of turmoil and difficult adjustment. The physical, mental, and emotional adjustments that characterize adolescents in middle school and high school affect many dimensions of the adolescent's life. In addition to facing difficulties in school and in their social life, teenagers with learning disabilities and other related disabilities must also cope with the normal challenges and adjustments of adolescence. Because many characteristics of learning difficulties and adolescence overlap, it is hard to know whether a particular behavior stems from a learning disability or from normal adolescent development. In many cases, the challenges stem from both, thus complicating the student's learning, social, and behavioral problems.

9.1a Characteristics of Adolescence

The period of adolescence is marked by conflicting feelings about (1) freedom and independence versus security and dependence, (2) rapid physical changes, (3) developing sexuality, (4) peer pressure, (5) illegal drugs, and (6) self-consciousness. Many of the characteristics of adolescence can affect the processes of learning (Snowman & McCown, 2013).

Freedom and Independence Versus Security and Dependence Adolescents want to become independent and separate themselves from their families; however, at the same time, they also need to keep these ties. According to Erikson's (1968) psychosocial model of development, adolescents must resolve a conflict between their desire for freedom and independence and their desire for security and dependence.

Rapid Physical Changes Adolescence is a period of rapid changes in physical growth and in appearance, including dramatic changes in facial and body structure. Adolescents must develop a new self-image and learn to cope with a different physical appearance, as well as new psychological and biological drives.

Developing Sexuality The adolescent period is also one of developing sexuality—another change to which the adolescent must learn to adjust. The sexual dimensions of adolescence may be very demanding in terms of time, energy, and worry.

Peer Pressure Adolescents are greatly influenced by peer pressure and peer values. When the values of friends differ from those of parents, family confrontation and conflict may result.

Easy Access to Illegal Drugs In today's society, students have easy access to drugs and may be tempted to experiment to discover the feeling of being "high" on drugs.

Self-Consciousness Teenagers tend to be very conscious of themselves, of how they look, and of how they compare with group norms. This self-consciousness can lead to feelings of inferiority and withdrawal.

9.1b Characteristics of Adolescents With Learning Disabilities

For adolescents with learning disabilities and other related disabilities, the problems of adolescence are compounded by their learning difficulties. As illustrated in Student Stories 9.1, "Tim, an Adolescent With Learning Disabilities," the adolescent can find it devastating to cope with learning disabilities, in addition to the difficulties created by normal adolescent development.

Tim is a 14-year-old freshman at Washington High School who has learning disabilities. His first-semester grades confirmed what he had feared: He failed three subjects—English, algebra, and history. He made only a *D* in general science, and he received a *C* in physical education and mechanical drawing.

Tim finds that he cannot cope with the assignments, the workload, and the demands of his courses. Even worse, he cannot read the textbooks, and he does not understand all that goes on in his classes. Tim also does poorly on the written exams. He feels as though he is drowning, and he knows he needs help.

When Tim was in elementary school, he received intermittent help from the learning disabilities resource teacher. Last year, in eighth grade, Tim was placed in general education content-area classes, and he received no resource help or direct special education services. The special education teacher, his eighth-grade homeroom teacher, and his other subject-area teachers informally discussed Tim's academic progress and planned his program. Tim was very involved in these planning sessions. In general, he had a successful year in eighth grade, passing all his subjects with above-average grades, although he had to work hard to accomplish this.

Over the summer, Tim grew so rapidly that he had to buy a complete set of new clothes. His voice changed, and he found that he must now shave the dark hair sprouting over his upper lip about once a week. Tim has made new friends at the high school and has kept many of his old friends from eighth grade. However, he has not told any of them about his grades. In fact, he is so embarrassed about his grades that he has started to stop seeing his friends.

At this point, Tim does not know where to turn. In a conference that the school counselor held with Tim and his parents, they were told that the tests show he has the ability and that he should try harder. His parents are disappointed and angry. Tim is discouraged and depressed. Since the grades were mailed to his parents, he has cut a number of classes. Clearly, without help, there is danger that Tim will become another dropout statistic.

REFLECTIVE QUESTION

1. How can Tim go about getting help at the high school?

It is critical to know the characteristics of adolescents with learning disabilities and other disabilities, but it is equally important to recognize the demands of the setting within which the adolescent lives and learns (Harris et al., 2011; Deshler et al., 2008; Lenz & Deshler, 2003). The characteristics of students with learning problems vary. Many students with learning disabilities show evidence of higher rates of absenteeism, lower grade point averages, higher course failure rates, feelings of low self-esteem, and more inappropriate social behaviors than their peers without disabilities (Deshler, 2008, 2009). Many adolescents do not display the characteristics described here, and they may even excel and possess strengths in some of these areas. Nevertheless, when one considers the combination of academic difficulties, the traits of adolescents, and the characteristics of learning disabilities and related mild disabilities, it is small wonder that these years are often trying. The following characteristics are seen in some, but certainly not in all, adolescents with learning disabilities:

 Cultural and Linguistic Diversity Learning difficulties can be related to the adolescent's cultural and language background. The family's cultural views about school, academic performance, reading, studying, and test taking can shape the student's attitude. Some families will not acknowledge any failure or disability and refuse to seek help for their student. In some cultures, adolescents are expected to take on many family responsibilities, and therefore, they have less time for schoolwork. Some cultures are not as time oriented as the mainstream American culture, and they may not see the importance of being on time or turning in work at a specified time. Many classes stress competition, while the adolescent's culture may reward group or teamwork, rather than individual accomplishment.

English-language learners (ELL) are adolescents whose first language is not English and may lack English proficiency, which leads to obstacles in many academic subjects. In addition, the testing demands of the school can be particularly challenging for ELL students. It is important for secondary teachers to recognize the impact of cultural and linguistic differences and to understand the hurdles that these adolescents face (Klingner, Artiles, & Barletta, 2006). A website that is designed to help teachers with special students who have cultural and linguistic differences is the IRIS Center, *http://iris.peabody .vanderbilt.edu/CLDE/chalcycle.htm.*

Passive Learning Many adolescents with learning disabilities and other related disabilities become *passive learners.* In response to many failure-producing experiences, they develop an attitude of *learned helplessness.* They learn to be passive instead of active learners. Instead of trying to solve a problem, passive learners tend to wait until the teacher directs them and tells them what to do. In an academic task, they fail to associate new information with what they already know, and they do not elaborate in their thinking (Deshler, Ellis, & Lenz, 1996; Lenz & Deshler, 2003). In addition, adolescents who experience repeated failures may also begin to exhibit acting-out behaviors or other types of behavioral reactions.

Poor Self-Concept Poor self-concept and low self-esteem result from years of failure and frustration. These students do not have opportunities to develop confidence in their ability to learn and achieve. Often, emotional problems also develop from their lack of successful experiences. Thus, they often have low self-esteem and little self-confidence (Deshler et al., 2008, 2009; Deshler et al., 1996; Lenz & Deshler, 2003; Silver, 2006).

Social and Behavioral Problems During these critical adolescent years, when friendships and peer approval are so important, struggles with social skills create another impediment for adolescents with learning disabilities and related mild disabilities. Characteristics of social ineptitude lead to difficulty making and keeping friends. In fact, the social and behavioral difficulties become even more troublesome than the academic problems. Years of failure, low self-esteem, poor motivation, inadequate peer acceptance, and disruptive and maladaptive behavior take their toll. Disproportionately high rates of incarcerated juveniles are identified with learning disabilities and learning disabilities is the second most common disability that is seen among incarcerated juveniles (Cortiella, 2011). Students with learning disabilities accounted for 52% of all students with disabilities who experienced disciplinary actions during the 2007–2008 year (Cortiella, 2011).

Difficulty with social interactions and nonverbal communication are also characteristic of adolescents with nonverbal learning disorders and Asperger's syndrome (Baker & Welkowitz, 2005; Thompson, 1997) (see Chapter 7, which discusses attention deficit hyperactivity disorder). Websites for these 2 social conditions are *http://www.NLDline.org*, from the Nonverbal Learning Disorders Association, and The Source: Autism Asperger Syndrome, at *http://www.asperger.org*.

Attentional Difficulties Many adolescents with learning disabilities and related mild disabilities do not have the attentional capacity to meet the demands of secondary school. High school heightens the demand for students to sustain cognitive effort and to concentrate for extended periods. The requirements of the secondary curriculum can place a strain on the adolescent's capacity to attend to the varied sources of input from teachers, instructional materials, and peers. Given the long periods of concentration needed for studying and listening in class, difficulty with attention can seriously impede progress (Barkley, 2005; Lerner, Lowenthal, & Lerner, 1995).

One 14-year-old described his attention problem as follows:

> I'll tell you just what my head is like. It's like a television set. Only one thing, it's got no channel selector. You see, all the programs keep coming over my screen at the same time (Levine, 1988).

This student had difficulty maintaining attention, which kept interfering with his ability to focus. The websites Children and Adults with Attention-Deficit/Hyperactivity Disorder, *http://www.chadd.org*, and ADD/ADHD, *http://www.adders.org*, offer information about attention deficit hyperactivity disorders.

Language Difficulties Some adolescents with learning disabilities and emotional/behavioral disorders have language deficits. They may exhibit pragmatic language difficulties, and they may not understand the type of information that should be shared or how much information should be shared. Negative social interactions related to the inability to initiate, develop, and maintain social relationships, can be the result of poor pragmatic language skills. Students with disabilities earn lower vocabulary scores than other struggling readers (Harris et al., 2011). Effective language-based interventions should include teaching students how to use mnemonics and other learning strategies, bibliotherapy, self-monitoring, and problem solving (Getty & Summy, 2006).

attribution theory
A person's ideas concerning the causes of his or her successes and failures.

The problems of adolescence are compounded by learning disabilities.

Lack of Motivation By the time students with learning disabilities and related mild disabilities reach secondary school, many have experienced years of school failure. Many begin to doubt their intellectual abilities. They lack resiliency and come to believe that their efforts to achieve are futile. These feelings, in turn, lead to a low persistence level; these adolescents give up quickly as soon as something appears to be difficult (Lavoie, 2007; Brooks & Goldstein, 2002).

Attribution theory suggests that even when these adolescents do have successes, they do not believe that they were responsible for the achievement. Instead, they attribute their success to some outside force, such as luck, something the teacher did, or an easy task (Yasutake & Bryan, 1995). Therefore, even success does not bring much satisfaction or raise their confidence level. It is difficult to motivate such students to exert the effort needed to learn. Yet, the best-made decisions about what to teach and the most skillful applications of how to teach will be successful only if students are motivated to learn and can attribute success to their own efforts (Lenz & Deshler, 2003; Zigmond, 1997, 2007) (see Chapter 6, "Social, Emotional, and Behavioral Challenges" for a further discussion of motivation).

Did You Get It?

_____ theory states that when students who are not used to achieving success do experience it, they are quick to disregard their own role in the success, preferring instead to "blame" something or someone else, or just sheer luck.

- **a.** Attribution
- **b.** Acknowledgement
- **c.** Incrimination
- **d.** Distribution

9.2 Special Issues at the Secondary Level (Middle School and High School)

According to the U.S. Department of Education (2012), from 1997 through 2006, the percentage of the general population ages 12 through 17 served under *IDEA, Part B,* increased from 10.2% to 11.6%. This was the largest increase among the age groups. The special challenges for these adolescents include placement in inclusive classes, dealing with Common Core Standards and high-stakes testing for secondary school students, and adapting to content-area secondary teachers.

9.2a Challenges for Adolescents With Learning Disabilities and Other Related Disabilities

The demands of secondary school differ significantly from those of elementary school. Students move from a pupil-oriented elementary-school environment to a content-driven secondary school setting. Often, the secondary students with learning disabilities or other related disabilities lack the requisite skills needed to meet high school academic expectations. If methods used to teach content areas are not suited to the adolescent's particular learning strengths and interests, the prospect of graduating with a high school diploma becomes increasingly problematic (Deshler et al., 2008; Deshler et al., 2001; Wagner, Cameto, & Newman, 2003).

Adolescents can experience numerous problems, ranging from mild to severe, that interfere with mastering many of the subjects of the secondary curriculum. In addition to academic problems, these students may have difficulties

TABLE 9.1

- Severe deficits in basic academic skills, such as reading, spelling, language, and math
- Generalized failure and below-average performance in content-area courses, such as science, social studies, and health
- Deficient work-related skills, such as listening well in class, taking notes, and studying for and taking tests
- Passive academic involvement and a pervasive lack of motivation
- Inadequate interpersonal skills
- Difficulty with executive function and self-determination

© Cengage Learning

with cognitive skills, social behaviors, and emotional stability. Many adolescents who received special education services at the elementary level continue to need help when they reach middle school and high school. In some cases, problems are not identified until the adolescent enters the secondary school because of the subtle nature of the problem and the increased demands of the secondary curriculum.

Almost one of every three youths with learning disabilities fails content-area, general education high school courses (Cowan, 2006; Getzel & Thoma, 2006; Blackorby & Wagner, 1997; Reith & Posgrove, 1996). In reading and math, at least 20% of students with learning disabilities are five or more grade levels behind their enrolled grade (Cortiella, 2011). Table 9.1 summarizes the problems faced by adolescents with disabilities.

9.2b Educational Settings in Middle School and High School

The inclusion movement is growing at the middle school and high school level, as more adolescents with learning disabilities and related mild disabilities are placed in general education, content-area classes for instruction. More than one-quarter (27%) of secondary school students with disabilities spent all of their instruction time in general education courses and earned all their credits there. In contrast, 3% of students with disabilities earned all their credits in a special education setting and none in a general education setting (National Longitudinal Transition Study 2, (2011). Table 9.2 shows the educational settings for students with learning disabilities. The percentage of students with learning disabilities who spent 80% or more of their school day in general education has increased, between 2000 and 2008, from 40% to 62%. No other category of special education students except students with speech-language impairments had higher percentages spending more time in general education (Cortiela, 2011).

9.2c Inclusion at the Secondary Level

Even though there has been a significant increase in the students at the secondary level who spend their time in general education classes, it has been reported that only 60% of students with learning disabilities have general

TABLE 9.2

Number of Secondary School Students With Disabilities, Ages 12–17, Receiving Special Education and Related Services in Different Educational Environments as of 2004 as Compared With 1995

	1995	2004
Outside the regular class less than 21% of the school day	793,324	1,335,713
Outside the regular class 21–60% of the school day	755,875	951,201
Outside the regular class more than 60% of the school day	541,250	584,600

Source: From U.S. Department of Education, Office of Special Education Programs, Data Analysis System (DANS) "Part B, Individuals with Disabilities Education Act implementation of FAPE requirements," 2004. Data updated as of July 30, 2005.

education teachers who receive any information about the needs of these students. Approximately half of all students have teachers who receive advice from special educators or other staff on how the needs of the students can be met (Cortiela, 2011).

Secondary schools face several obstacles in providing inclusion programs, including (1) the complex content-area curriculum; (2) the large gap between student skill levels and classroom demands; (3) content-area secondary school teachers not trained to meet the needs of students with learning disabilities; and (4) the standards-based, high-stakes testing movement (Beckman, 2001; Cole & McLeskey, 1997; Deshler, 2003; Friend & Cook, 2003; Lenz & Deshler, 2003; Orkwis, 2003). Including Students in General Education 9.1, "The Middle School and Secondary Classroom," lists strategies for including students in general education classrooms.

9.2d Effective Inclusion Practices for Secondary Teachers

To make *inclusion* work at the secondary level, it is necessary to establish partnerships between the content-area teachers, who are high school teachers that specialize in a content area, and special education teachers. Special educators must realize that the content-area teachers deal with many students throughout a school day and may feel pressured by time and the many other demands facing them. Special educators should be available to work with classroom teachers on understanding the specific needs of individual students, on differentiating instruction, and on making reasonable accommodations. Some schools provide the content-area teachers with a list of accommodations that the student needs but don't provide an explanation of those accommodations and don't explain why the student needs the accommodations. At times the classroom teacher then wonders why the student needs the accommodation and the teacher may not know how to provide the accommodation. Classroom teachers can benefit not only from a list of accommodations needed, what those accommodations mean, and how to provide those

content-area teachers
High school teachers whose primary orientation and expertise is the subject matter of their specialty. In contrast, elementary teachers tend to have an orientation and more expertise in child development.

The Secondary Classroom

- Establish partnerships between content-area teachers and special educators. Two or more professionals work together to plan and deliver instruction.

- Use collaborative teams. In this ongoing process of collaborative teaming, teachers with different areas of expertise work together to develop creative solutions to problems that may be impeding a student's progress. Collaborative team members develop supportive and mutually beneficial relationships and share their resources.

- Special educators should provide specialized instruction to secondary students that is based on their individual needs.

- Special educators should work together with content-area teachers to provide accommodations to students and to enhance instructional techniques that will assist the student with a disability.

- If utilizing coteaching, ensure that it is being implemented with fidelity. The content-area teacher and the special education teacher instruct students in the classroom jointly. Ingredients for successful coteaching include:

a. Determining each teacher's strengths and preferences
b. Developing trust and respect
c. Receiving strong administrative support
d. Providing adequate communication and time

- Provide differentiated instruction. Individualized instruction is given to *all* students in the classroom; both students who do not have disabilities and students who have special needs. According to Beckman (2001), the principles for differentiated instruction include:

a. Content-area teacher and special educator should share responsibility
b. Content-area teacher and special educator should be familiar with the student's IEP
c. Content-area teacher and special educator should be aware of the student's strengths and weaknesses
d. Sufficient coplanning time should be built into the day
e. Student expectations should be set by student abilities, not by classification

Professional Resource Download

---

collaborative teaming
Teachers working together. Partnerships between the general education teachers and special education teachers.

accommodations. The classroom teacher can also benefit from a brief summary of the student's particular disability and how it impacts the student's classroom performance. As an example, if the teacher knows the student has a problem in the area of auditory memory, it will help in understanding that the student will have difficulty listening to long periods of lecture and will need visual cues during the lecture.

Special educators must also provide students with specially designed instruction that is unique to the student and is based on how the student's disability adversely impacts their performance. At the secondary level, focus for the special educator may be on teaching the student how to utilize mnemonic devices to memorize key content material, strategies for completing math problems or writing essays, teaching time management, and specifically teaching reading or math utilizing a method that is appropriate for the student.

Special educators may coteach a specific class with a general educator. Partnerships consist of two or more professionals working together to plan and deliver instruction in general education classes that include adolescents with disabilities (Friend & Cook, 2003; Gately & Gately, 2001; McLeskey, Hoppery, Williamson, & Rentz, 2004; Murawski & Dieker, 2004). One example of successful inclusion at the secondary level is presented in Student Stories 9.2, "Tracy —Trusting One's Strengths."

9.2e Performance Standards and High-Stakes Testing

Accountability has become the watchword in education. Common core standards have been adopted in the majority of states across the country and are an influential force in our secondary schools today, with directives about academic levels coming from national, state, and local sources. Secondary schools have established common core standards in the high school content areas, which are standards that all students are expected to meet. In addition, states have developed assessment tests to determine whether students meet these set academic standards. Statewide assessment tests are given to all students. These statewide assessment tests are often called high-stakes testing because so many critical decisions are based on the test results. There are rewards and punishments for students, teachers, administrators, and schools.

Holding students responsible for their performance on state and district tests is increasing in popularity among governors and legislators. When tests are used to make high-stakes decisions, such as whether a student will graduate or be promoted to the next grade level, dropout rates often increase. Many educators are concerned about the large number of

▶ ❚❚ **TeachSource** Video Case Activity

© Cengage Learning 2015.

Watch the TeachSource Video Case entitled "Motivating Adolescent Learners: Curriculum Based on Real Life." A sixth-grade teacher uses a store in the classroom to teach the math curriculum of fractions, decimals, percent, taxes, discounts. The teacher found that working in the store made the math concepts come alive and become more relevant. Discuss these questions after you view the video.

QUESTIONS

1. How does the store make the concepts more relevant for the math curriculum?
2. What teaching strategy from this chapter does this video illustrate?
3. What responsibilities did the students learn to take?

STUDENT STORIES 9.2

Trusting One's Strengths

For Tracy, inclusion worked very well. Tracy's learning disability was detected in first grade. When his first-grade teacher asked the students to copy words from the blackboard, he was unable to do so. Tracy could not recognize words, and he still has significant reading problems. However, Tracy learned to trust his strengths. He had many friends and good social skills. He was good in sports. His learning disability in reading was identified in early elementary school. He was placed in the general education class. Although he continued to have reading problems, he had many strengths. Tracy was elected president of his class in high school, and he was a winning member of the basketball team. He also was on the debate team. With the school's support, he slowly improved. After high school, Tracy went to college where he played on the college basketball team. In thinking about his learning disabilities, Tracy thought it was important to know and trust his strengths.

REFLECTIVE QUESTIONS

1. How did Tracy's strengths assist him in high school?
2. What skills do you believe his teachers taught him that resulted in his success?

---

high-stakes testing
Statewide tests given to all students that result in critical decisions for the child.

students with learning disabilities who are not passing these assessment tests. They frequently drop out of school and, consequently, these students have poor prospects for employment and postsecondary education (Thurlow, 2000; Ysseldyke, 2001).

In the past, students with disabilities were excluded from such statewide and districtwide assessments. All of this changed with the IDEA-1997. The current laws, the Individuals With Disabilities Education Improvement Act (IDEA-2004) and the No Child Left Behind Act (NCLB-2001), require that students with disabilities be included in statewide and districtwide assessments and that the results be reported.

IDEA-2004 also requires that states develop alternate assessment guidelines and policies on accommodations for students with disabilities. The law outlines several requirements for including students with disabilities in the statewide or districtwide assessments. Each student's IEP must include a plan that details how the student will be assessed and what accommodations the student will need for assessment (Thurlow, 2000; Individuals With Disabilities Education Improvement Act, 2004).

accommodations
Refers to adjustments within a general education program to meet the needs of students with disabilities. Required under Section 504 of the Rehabilitation Act and IDEA.

The goal for standards-based testing is the desire to improve teaching and learning so that all students can demonstrate their mastery of the knowledge and skills needed to participate in the global economy of today and the future. We should not lose sight of these goals. Assessment is only one part of the picture. The most critical piece is providing all students with the chance to learn. Unless students are given adequate opportunities to learn, holding them to higher standards will only further victimize those students already being harmed by gross inequities in the educational system (Kauffman & Wiley, 2004; Lenz & Deshler, 2003; Thurlow, 2000; Salvia, Ysseldyke, and Bolt, 2013).

In addition to meeting these Common Core Standards, problems for adolescents with learning disabilities are magnified by the complex set of curriculum demands in high school. At the high school level, students are faced with a larger, more impersonal, and competitive school environment (Mcintosh, Flannery, Sugai, Braun, & Cochrane, 2008). When adolescents with learning disabilities or mild disabilities are in general education content-area classes for four periods a day, they are expected to meet the same requirements that all other students meet. There are heavy expectations of reading proficiency that many adolescents cannot meet. There is an increase in the new vocabulary words that students are expected to know in the content areas. In spite of their learning problems, they are expected to learn, integrate, manage, and express large amounts of information (Deshler et al., 2008; Deshler et al., 1996, 2001; Kauffman & Wiley, 2004).

Students with disabilities may be eligible for accommodations in taking high-stakes tests. The Educational Testing Service (ETS) offers information on obtaining accommodations. The website for ETS is at *http://www.ets.org/disability*. Teaching Tips 9.1, "Test-Taking Tips for Students With Learning Challenges," offers some helpful advice for taking tests.

TEACHING TIPS 9.1

Test-Taking Tips for Students With Learning Challenges

- Get enough sleep and try to remain calm.
- Look over the entire test and read the directions carefully.
- Read each question carefully and note key words and phrases.
- Read each question all the way through. Do not read into the question what is not there.
- If you are unsure about a question, reread it and try to eliminate one or two of the answers.
- Budget the time allotted for the test and do not waste time by getting stuck on one question.
- Take all authorized breaks. Also, periodically take a few breaks by stopping for a moment, shutting your eyes, and taking some deep breaths.
- Have a sheet of scrap paper to help track lines of print.
- Allow time at the end to look over the test and make sure that you did not skip any questions.

Professional Resource Download

9.2f Content-Area Secondary Teachers

Many content-area secondary teachers are not prepared to work with students with disabilities. Their training is in their content specialization, be it mathematics, French, physics, or English literature, and they are considered "highly qualified teachers" under the NCLB law. Schools should promote a shared responsibility for students with disabilities among special educators and general educators. That shared responsibility must include instructionally focused collaboration. All teachers must have the opportunities for professional development adequate planning time, and manageable caseloads (Eisenman et al., 2011). An important collaborative role for the special educator in the high school is to work with content-area teachers to help them develop a sensitivity to the needs of students with disabilities and to provide subject-matter teachers with strategies for teaching these students. Collaboration involves helping the high school, content-area teacher understand the nature of a specific student's problem and how to make the needed accommodations for that student. For example, if the student has a severe reading disability, that student may be helped by recording the lesson or using digitized text. Recording for the Blind and Dyslexics, now called Learning Ally (http://www.learningally.org), provides books on audiotapes and CDs that are accessible to students with learning disabilities. In fact, about 75% of those who use recordings for the blind and dyslexics are individuals with learning disabilities. An increasing number of books are available in digital versions and those versions then allow the student to have additional supports through universal design.

More schools are making iPads available to students so that they have easy access to digitized texts. During examinations, the student with a severe writing problem might be allowed to give answers orally, to tape answers, or to dictate answers to someone else. Students who process information very slowly could be allowed additional time.

> **Did You Get It?**
>
> Most recent statistics from the U.S. Department of Education (2006) show that approximately ___% of the teen/adolescent population is receiving disability-related services under IDEA.
>
> **a.** 5
> **b.** 12
> **c.** 18
> **d.** 30

The IEP team discusses transition for a student.

9.3 Transition Legislation for Secondary Students

transition

The process of moving from one type of program to another. In early childhood programs it can be from the birth-through-2 program to the ages 3–5 program, or from the ages 3–5 program to another educational placement. For adolescents, transition refers to the passage from school to the adult world.

transition planning

Planning for making the change from being a student to being an adult. Students with learning disabilities need help with this process.

Transition refers to a change in status from behaving primarily as a student to assuming emerging adult roles. These new roles include employment, becoming a student in postsecondary school, maintaining a home, and experiencing satisfactory personal and social relationships. Research shows that adolescents receive inadequate transition planning, which does not help them in seeking employment (Brown, 2000). Adolescents are most likely to find a job on their own, with little support from schools or adult agencies. Relatively few adolescents with learning disabilities and related disabilities go to college. Only 5% of students with learning disabilities are enrolled in postsecondary education only (Corteilla, 2011). Adolescents need training in self-advocacy because they are expected to take increasingly more responsibility for their own decisions and lives.

The Individuals With Disabilities Education Improvement Act (IDEA-2004) contains requirements in regard to transition (IDEA-2004, 2004). Beginning not later than the first IEP to be in effect when the student is 16, and then updated annually, IDEA-2004 requires

1. Appropriate measurable postsecondary goals based upon age-appropriate transition assessments related to training, education, employment, and, where appropriate, living skills
2. The transition services (including courses of study) needed to assist the student in reaching those goals
3. Beginning not later than one year before the student reaches the age of majority under state law, a statement that the student has been informed of the student's rights under this title, if any, that will transfer to the student on reaching the age of majority

Transition focuses on improving academic and functional achievement, facilitating movement from school to postschool activities, such as postsecondary education, vocational education, employment (including supported employment), continuing and adult education, adult services, independent living, and community participation. It must be based on the individual needs of the student, taking into account the child's strengths, preferences, and interests. It includes instruction, related services, community experiences, the development of employment and other postschool adult living objectives, and if appropriate, acquisition of daily living skills and a functional vocational evaluation (IDEA-2004). Even though IDEA 2004 requires transition planning at the age of 16 it should begin long before that time. Cohen and Spenciner (2009) recommend that it begin 4 to 5 years before leaving school. Skills such as social skills, self-advocacy, work habits, decision-making skills, participation in community activities, identifying interests and building on those interests must begin early. Some states recognize this and require that transition planning start earlier.

Some examples of transition goals might include:

- Nathan will be able to articulate three key points about how his disability impacts his academic work with 90% accuracy. (Note: Nathan is an 11th-grader with ADHD and he is planning to attend a four-year college. Nathan will need to advocate for himself in the postsecondary world and this goal helps him do that.

- When confronted with an angry customer at the grocery store, Jeffrey will be able to retain a calm tone of voice and refer the customer to the manager. (Jeffrey receives services for his emotional/behavioral disorders and has a job in a grocery store after school and has had difficulties in the past remaining calm in a potentially difficult situation.)
- Given a job application, Jessica will proofread the application after she completes it using a proofreading checklist. (Jessica has a learning disability and exhibits difficulty with written expression and tends to rush through writing assignments without checking her work. Her teacher wants to work with her to proofread job applications before giving them to an employer.)
- When given a list of custodial work that needs to be completed, Josh will be able to complete the work within the given period of time allowed and will also be able to look at the environment and determine one other job that needs to be done and will complete that job also. (Josh has mild intellectual disabilities and has been assigned to work with a custodian. He can complete work that he is told to complete but there is a problem because when he completes the tasks on the list, he then sits and does nothing. When other people observe this, they believe he isn't doing his work. His supervisor wants him to also be able to engage in self-starting behavior—seeing what else needs to be done and completing it.
- When asked by an adult, Beth Ann will be able to articulate at least two of her strengths. (Beth Ann focuses on what she can't do and about 50% of the time makes negative statements about herself.)
- Given Eric's interest in becoming an automotive mechanic, Eric be able to articulate the definitions of 10 vocabulary words related to this field with 70% accuracy. (Eric, a student who has behavioral problems, has shown interest in becoming an automotive mechanic but currently does not understand the words that are utilized in the field today. Using picture cues paired with the vocabulary word and the meaning of the word, Eric will be specifically taught the vocabulary.)

The law views *transition* as a set of activities that is based on the needs of the individual student and that is designed to prepare the student for the years beyond secondary school. To ensure that the student completes secondary school prepared for employment or postsecondary education, as well as for independent living, the law requires that an *individualized transition plan (ITP)* be written for students with disabilities, beginning at age 16, as part of the IEP. Many school districts use an attachment to the student's IEP to indicate transition goals and activities designed to meet those goals. Other schools develop a separate ITP. The special education teacher may need to take the lead in developing the ITP.

9.3a Content of the Transition Plan

The transition plan (IEP/ITP) should include the following (Mazzotti et al., 2009; Hartmann, 2009; Ankeny, Wilkins, & Spain, 2009; Brown, 2000; NICHCY, 1999; Obiakor & Wilder, 2010):

1. **Current levels of academic achievement and functional performance.** The transition plan should document the student's current levels of achievement so that the transition team knows where to begin.

2. **Interests and aptitude.** The plan should take into account the student's interests, aptitudes, potential, and vision for the future.
3. **Background.** For students who are culturally and linguistically diverse, the transition plan must consider the student's culture, which includes the student's beliefs, values, customs, perceptions, and family expectations.
4. **Postschool goals.** The plan should define and project desired postschool goals as identified by the student, parents, and transition teams for community living, employment, postsecondary education, and/or training.
5. **Transition activities.** The plan should include specific transition activities in areas such as vocational and career education, work experience, and community-based instruction.
6. **Designate responsible persons.** The plan should designate a person or agency that is responsible for the continuation of the transition after the student's high school years.
7. **Review.** The transition plan should be reviewed and revised as necessary.

Teaching Tips 9.2, "Guidelines for Developing Transition Plans for Secondary Students With Disabilities," provides guidelines for preparing transition plans for secondary students.

TEACHING TIPS 9.2

Guidelines for Developing Transition Plans for Secondary Students With Disabilities

- Form an individual transition team for each student to develop the individual transition plan (ITP). Identify resources that are available to meet the goals of the plan. Include all agencies that may be able to provide support systems for the student when the student exits the high school program.

- Work with business and industry representatives and build relationships for students to meet the goals of the transition plan.

- Develop a transition curriculum. Include communication skills, self-esteem development, decision-making skills, career exploration, community-living skills, and time-management skills to help students during the transition.

- Teach self-advocacy skills. Help students understand the legislative mandates that support requests for accommodations, both in the classroom and on the job. Adolescents can use this information in making decisions about their futures. Teach students to advocate for themselves. Many of their interactions require a constructive request for accommodations and services. Students must interact with teachers in high school, in postsecondary school, and with employers. They may need to get services from other agencies. By learning to speak for themselves and to bear the consequences of their actions or inactions, students learn the skills necessary for adulthood.

- Build competencies in academic skills. Ensure that students have competencies in reading, writing, mathematics, and computer usage.

- Teach study skills. Adolescents need help in test preparation, test-taking strategies, and learning strategies.

- Teach students to use accommodations and modifications appropriately and effectively.

- Teach social skills and interpersonal communication skills.

- Teach students to advocate for themselves so that when they exit the secondary system they are able to explain their disability, their specific needs, and how their disability may impact their future study or work.

Professional Resource Download

9.3b Summary of Performance

The Individuals With Disabilities Education Act of 2004 regulations require that secondary school staff complete a Summary of Performance (SOP) when a student is going to exit the school system. The local education agency is to provide the student with a summary of the student's academic achievement and functional performance, which is to include recommendation on how to assist the student in meeting postsecondary goals. The idea of this document is to assist the student as he or she transitions from the secondary setting to higher education, employment, or another postsecondary option. It also provides the necessary documentation that the student has a disability and may need accommodations under Section 504 of the Rehabilitation Plan and the Americans With Disabilities Act. Postsecondary settings can then make eligibility decisions.

Summary of Performance (SOP) When students are going to exit the school system, the local educational agency provides the student with a summary of the student's academic achievement and functional performance which includes recommendations on how to assist the student in meeting postsecondary goals.

The SOP is to be completed during the final year of high school. When completing the SOP, the student should be involved and the document should include pertinent background information, postsecondary goals for the student, summary of academic achievement and functional performance, recommendations that assist the student in meeting postsecondary goals, and the student's input.

9.3c Developing Transition Plans

The goals for transition planning for adolescents with learning disabilities and other related disabilities follow several paths.

Competitive Employment   Fifty-five percent of adults with learning disabilities were employed compared to 76% of those without learning disabilities (Cortiela, 2011). As of February 2012, the employment rate for young adults ages 20–24 with disabilities was less that half of the rate of those without disabilities within that same age range (GAO report, July 2012). Vocational educators need to be an integral part of the transition team to help these students explore occupations and to gain at least a basic knowledge within the various fields. Parents and educators must work together to help students identify areas of interest and potential fields of employment and to determine how the students can meet the entry-level requirements of those fields. Students will benefit from job experience by participating in a *co-op* project (Brown, 2000; Gerber & Brown, 1997).

Career-Training and Apprenticeship Programs Some students prepare for a trade after high school by going to a career-training program or by entering an apprenticeship program.

Postsecondary and College Attendance In the past, many students with learning disabilities did not consider postsecondary education options. Twenty-two percent of students with learning disabilities are engaged in both work and some type of postsecondary education (Cortiella, 2011). However, meeting these goals requires transition plans that are carefully laid out and that include significant encouragement toward college. The transition to postsecondary services can be difficult and overwhelming to students and their families because students are moving from all services provided through the high school to services delivered by multiple programs and agencies (GAO report, July 2012).

Supported Employment Some transition programs offer a bridge from school to work through supported employment. In this type of program, transition educators seek potential employers to hire special education students. In some cases, a job coach works at the employment site, supervising and helping the students over the inevitable rough spots. Job coaches work for the business that employs the student and for the school or agency.

The National Longitudinal Transition Study The National Longitudinal Transition Study recommends transition planning activities that are more heavily influenced by the students themselves and better connected to the skills that are needed to realize postschool goals (Cortiella, 2009). Few adults with learning disabilities are accessing workplace accommodations and do not understand their rights (Cortiella, 2011). It is critical that educational programs teach students about their disabilities and teach them to advocate for their specific needs.

Did You Get It?

In the context of both general and special needs education, the terms "transition" and "transition planning" refer to which of the following passages?

a. That of student to real-world adult
b. That of high school to college
c. That of middle school to high school
d. That of "normal" to "disabled"

9.4 Approaches to Teaching Adolescents With Learning Disabilities and Related Disabilities

Several different instructional approaches and curriculum models are used with students with learning disabilities and related mild disabilities in secondary schools (Cole & McLeskey, 1997; Sitlington, 1996; Swanson & Hoskyn, 2001).

9.4a Features of Effective Secondary Programs

According to Zigmond (1997, 2003, 2007), essential features of effective secondary programs for students with learning disabilities include the following components.

- **Intensive Instruction in Reading and Mathematics.** Many students with learning disabilities receive failing grades in general education courses because of their poor skills in reading, writing, and mathematics. Sixty-five percent of eighth-graders with disabilities scored below the basic level on the 2007 National Assessment of Educational Progress measure of reading achievement (Morgan et al., 2012; U.S. Department of Education, 2009). These students still require basic instruction in reading, writing, vocabulary development, and mathematics (Fuchs & Fuchs, 2001a).

- **Instruction in Survival Skills.** Several functional skills or survival skills that are needed for successful functioning in a high school include (1) strategies to help students stay out of trouble in school; (2) skills to help students acquire behavioral patterns that will make teachers consider them in a positive light; and (3) study and test-taking skills, such as organizing time, approaching a textbook, taking notes from a lecture or text, organizing information, studying for tests, and taking tests (Zigmond, 1990).

functional skills or survival skills
Teaching survival skills to enable students to get along in the outside world.

9.4b Curriculum Models for Serving Adolescents With Learning Disabilities and Mild Disabilities at the Secondary Level

A range of curriculum models are used with adolescents with learning disabilities in junior and senior high schools (Cole & McLeskey, 1997; Deshler et al., 1996; Lenz & Deshler, 2003; Sitlington, 1996). These include (1) basic academic skills instruction, (2) strategies instruction, (3) tutorial instruction, (4) functional skills or survival skills instruction, and (5) work-study programs. More high schools are allowing alternative learning models such as taking some classes online or taking community college classes while still in high school. Alternative modes for receiving high school credits are important for students who exhibit emotional or behavioral challenges (Chaney, 2010).

Basic Academic Skills Instruction The objective of teaching basic skills is to remediate the student's academic deficits. It has been estimated that more than 8 million middle and high school students are struggling readers (Joseph & Schisler, 2009; Grigg et al., 2003). Basic academic skills instruction usually focuses on improving the student's abilities through direct teaching, especially in reading and mathematics. Students receive instruction at a level that approximates their achievement or instructional level. For example, if a 16-year-old student is reading at the fifth-grade level, reading instruction for that student would be geared to the fifth-grade level (Fuchs & Fuchs, 2001b). Adolescence is not too late for targeted interventions and those interventions that focus on word study, developing word meanings and word concepts, and comprehension strategies. Struggling readers can improve their ability to decode words when provided appropriate instruction. Interventions such as repeated reading have been demonstrated to be an effective strategy for adolescent readers (Malmgren & Trezek, 2009).

basic academic skills instruction
Instruction focusing on direct teaching, especially in reading and mathematics. Students receive instruction at a level that approximates their achievement or instructional level.

Tutorial Programs The objective of tutorial instruction is to help students in their specific academic-content subjects and to achieve success in the regular curriculum. For example, if Alex experiences failure or difficulty in his American history class, his instruction will focus on the specific history material he is studying. This instruction will be based on the individual needs of the student and the general curriculum content will be utilized to strengthen the skills of the student. As an example, if the student has a significant visual memory problem, Alex will be taught history in a way that compensates for his visual memory skill deficit, and at the same time, the American history content will be utilized to build Alex's visual memory skills. The goal is to help Alex succeed in the general

tutorial instruction
Teaching designed to help students meet requirements in their specific academic-content subjects and to achieve success in the regular curriculum. This teaching is usually accomplished through one-to-one instruction or in small groups.

education curriculum. The special education resource teacher must know the requirements of all academic subjects in which students may have difficulty. Instruction should include the model:

1. **I do**—the teacher does the expected task for the student so the student observes how the teacher approaches the task and completes it correctly.
2. **We do**—the teacher and the student work together on the expected task so the student has the additional assistance of the teacher and has another opportunity to model and practice.
3. **You do together**—Two students work on the task together while the teacher observes the students working to check to make sure the task is being completed correctly.
4. **You do**—The student is then ready to complete the task independently after the opportunities to model and practice.

Students need to have multiple opportunities for modeling and practice before they are expected to do a task independently. This procedure provides those opportunities.

Functional Skills or Survival Skills Instruction The objective of the functional skills instruction model is to equip students to function in society. Survival skills enable adolescents to get along in the world outside of school. The curriculum includes such subjects as consumer information; the completion of application forms, such as job applications; banking and money skills, such as understanding interest rates and installment purchases; life-care skills, such as grooming; and computer literacy. Academic content is geared to the students' careers and life needs. For example, reading is directed toward relevant areas, such as directions, want ads, or a driver's instruction manual. Guidance and counseling for self-identity and career planning are also often part of the curriculum.

work-study program
A high school program in which students work on a job for a portion of the day and go to school for a portion of the day.

Work-Study Programs The objective of a work-study program is to provide adolescents with job- and career-related skills, as well as actual on-the-job experience. Students in work-study programs typically spend half the day on the job and the remainder of the day in school. While in school, they may study materials that are compatible with their jobs. Sometimes these students take general education courses and also work with a special education teacher. The work-study approach is particularly successful for students who are not motivated by the high school environment. The special education teacher serves as a coordinator who integrates education with desired job skills and supervises students on the work site.

High school curricula can incorporate work-study and vocational programs to teach job skills.

Bob Daemmrich/The Image Works

9.4c Assistive and Instructional Computer Technology

The ability to use common computer applications has become an absolute necessity. Students who have difficulty with reading, writing, and spelling often excel with the aid of computer applications. Adolescents with learning disabilities and related mild disabilities should learn basic computer technologies, such as e-mail, word processing, graphic organizers, spreadsheets, and presentation software (e.g., PowerPoint) (Belson, 2003; Raskind, 1998a). Experience with computers helps students develop the essential technological skills needed for many types of jobs. However, according to the National Longitudinal Study 2 in 2003, only 6% of students with learning disabilities were using a computer for activities (NLTS2, 2003). It has also been found that an estimated 25%–35% of students with learning disabilities are being provided assistive technology to support their instruction (Cortiella, 2011).

Because technology is in such a continual state of change, it has been difficult for researchers to conduct appropriate experimental testing of interventions before they become outdated. However, principles that apply to effective instruction should be utilized when using multimedia. Specifically, it should explicitly help students build skills necessary for literacy, limit extraneous processing, foster active learning, and match individual student needs (Kennedy & Deshler, 2010). Technology should be used systematically and strategically in instruction and should incorporate effective instructional design principles (Maccini, Gagnon, & Hughes, 2002). Student Stories 9.3, "Richard—How Computers Changed My Life," presents the story of an individual with learning disabilities who believes computers changed his life.

9.4d What Happens to High School Students With Learning Disabilities

Cortiella (2011) reported data on the status of high school students with learning disabilities as they leave school.

- 64% graduate with a diploma
- 22% drop out of school

STUDENT STORIES 9.3

Richard—How Computers Changed My Life

Computers changed my experience of being dyslexic and dysgraphic. Computers allow me to compensate (some might say overcompensate) for my writing and organizational problems so well that, aside from the few times when people see my handwriting, my dyslexia and dysgraphia are not evident in my daily life. Further, I've been lucky enough to actually build a career out of talking about this with audiences all over the world. The very tools that I talk about are those that allow me to organize and give these presentations.

Source: From "Tools and dyslexia," by Richard Wanderman, 2003, *Perspectives*, 29(4), 5–9.

REFLECTIVE QUESTION

1. In what way did computers change Richard's life?

In addition, the U.S. Department of Education (2002) notes that schools offer several different types of diplomas or certificates:

1. **Standard diploma.** Students must meet the same criteria as all general education students, including adequate performance on tests.
2. **Standard diploma with multiple criteria for earning the diploma.** Students can earn the diploma by meeting different criteria, such as completing IEP goals.
3. **Certificate of attendance, completion, or achievement.** Students with IEPs may be allowed to meet the criteria in different ways.
4. **Special education certificate.** Available only to students with IEPs.

The fact that 22% of students with learning disabilities drop out of school suggests that schools are failing to serve these students appropriately. Students with learning disabilities and related mild disabilities who stay in school and graduate fare much better than those who leave. Those who drop out of school face an uncertain and grim future. Some individuals, however, earn a high school certificate—a General Education Degree (GED), which is a high school equivalency degree—after they leave school.

Many students with learning disabilities and related mild disabilities do well after receiving special instruction in elementary and secondary school, and they graduate from high school and go to college. Student Stories 9.4, "Dawn and Teach for America," presents the story of a successful student with learning disabilities.

Did You Get It?

Which of the following "Survival Skills" would be taught to Desiree, a 15-year-old student with a learning disability who is attending high school in Milwaukee, Wisconsin?
a. How to endear yourself to teachers with great behavior
b. How to stand up to a workplace bully
c. How to survive an atomic explosion
d. How to budget your paycheck effectively

STUDENT STORIES 9.4
Dawn and Teach for America

Dawn had learning disabilities as a student, with particular difficulties in reading, attention, focus, and organizational issues. She worked hard and received excellent instruction geared to her learning disabilities at her elementary and secondary schools. Dawn was able to go on to college and do well in her college studies. During her senior year, she heard about the Teach for America program. The idea of being a special education teacher—after being a special education student—struck a chord within her. Dawn was accepted in the Teach for America program.

In teaching her special education students, she tells them, "You can achieve. You may have to do it in a different way, but you can achieve. I know what it is like to struggle" (Montes, 2007).

REFLECTIVE QUESTION

1. How did Dawn's learning disability make her able to work with students with disabilities in the Teach for America program?

9.5 Learning Strategies Instruction

Learning strategies instruction offers a viable and promising approach to help adolescents with learning disabilities learn to take control of their own learning. The focus of this instruction is to teach students how to learn, rather than teach what is contained in a specific curriculum. Effective learning strategy instruction involves helping students learn and use procedures that will empower them to accomplish important academic tasks, to solve problems, and to complete work independently. With proficiency in learning strategies, students can overcome or lessen the effects of learning disabilities. Learning strategies are tools that students can use to approach tasks in content-area classes or other learning situations. In effect, the teacher helps students learn how to learn (Deshler et al., 1996, 2001; Lenz & Deshler, 2003).

A *learning strategy* is an individual's approach to a task that includes how a person thinks and acts when planning, executing, and evaluating performance on a task and its outcome. It includes both cognitive (thinking processes) and behavioral (overt actions) elements that guide the student's planning, performance, and evaluation of strategy engagement (Lenz, Ellis, & Scanlon, 1996).

Learning strategies research shows that adolescents with learning disabilities are *inefficient learners* (DLD and DR, 2012). These adolescents do not lack the ability to learn, but, rather they go about learning in an inefficient manner. For example, Maria's memory may be adequate for remembering the facts in a history lesson, but she has to put the right kind of learning effort into remembering those facts. For Sam, who is having difficulty in science, learning strategies instruction would teach some techniques for organizing his materials for learning, rather than teach him the content of the subject. Thus, the emphasis is on teaching students how to adapt and cope with the changing world; that is, the emphasis is on how to learn how to learn. The opening quotation for this chapter embodies the goal of learning strategies instruction: "If you give a starving man a fish, you feed him for a day. But if you teach the man *how* to fish, you feed him for a lifetime. If you teach an adolescent with learning disabilities a fact, you help the adolescent for the moment. But if you teach this adolescent *how* to learn, you help the adolescent for a lifetime" (Deshler, Ellis, & Lenz, 1996).

Instruction in learning strategies is particularly effective with adolescents with learning disabilities who are above third-grade reading level, are able to deal with symbolic as well as concrete learning tasks, and have an average intellectual ability (Deshler et al., 1996, 2001; Lenz & Deshler, 2003). Learning strategies can be applied to all academic areas of the secondary curriculum, as well as to social and behavioral learning.

As an example with the focus on high-stakes test, it is critical to teach students strategies on how to take a test. One such strategy that is well researched is PIRATES (Hughes, 1996). In this strategy, the mnemonic to be taught to the student is as follows:

P—Prepare to succeed
I—Inspect instructions
R—Read, remember, reduce
A—Answer or abandon
T—Turn back

learning strategies instruction
A series of methods to help students direct their own learning, focusing on how students learn rather than on what they learn.

E—Estimate-teaching students valuable guessing and estimating techniques. Within the E, students are taught ACE (Hughes, 1996; Holzer, Madaus, Bray, & Kehle, 2009)

S—SURVEY

    A—Avoid absolute words in answers

    C—Choose the longest most detailed choice

    E—Eliminate similar or absurd choices

9.5a Guidelines for Teaching Learning Strategies

The intense interest in learning strategies instruction has generated a significant amount of research (DLD & DR, 2012; Schumaker & Deshler, 2009; Deshler et al., 1996; Lenz & Deshler, 2003; Slavin, 2006). Teaching Tips 9.3, "Teaching Learning Strategies," gives some practical guidelines for putting learning strategies instruction into practice.

background knowledge Information and experiences that are gained about the topic of instruction or about a reading selection.

TEACHING TIPS 9.3

Teaching Learning Strategies

- **Use background knowledge.** Students get more from instruction when their background knowledge, which is defined as information or experiences that are gained about the topic of instruction or about a reading selection, is activated or when the teacher elicits, builds, and focuses on appropriate background knowledge. Background knowledge is the strongest predictor of a student's ability to learn new material. The more students know about a topic, the better they comprehend and learn about the topic from the text.

- **Monitor progress.** Successful learners monitor their own progress. They have an idea of how they are doing. In reading, for example, they use their knowledge of text features and appropriate strategies to monitor their own learning.

- **Teach generalization.** Successful learners use skills and knowledge in new situations, adapting it to particular contexts. Providing students with direct instruction about situations when a skill will be useful and monitoring their implementation can improve their generalization.

- **Create active learners.** Students who are actively involved in their learning are more successful than students who play a more passive role. Effective learners generate questions, make summaries, and help determine the direction of the lesson.

- **Enhance self-concept.** There is a strong correlation between successful learning and the student's self-concept and positive attitude. Students with high levels of achievement tend to have high self-concepts, while low achievers have poor self-concepts. Success in learning enhances self-concept.

- **Use memory strategies.** Successful learners use effective memory strategies. Memory is related to background; those who know more are able to remember more. Short-term memory is limited in capacity. Most of what is learned is forgotten quickly if it is not acted upon or linked with previous learning.

- **Use interactive learning.** The opportunity for students to interact with other students is important. Cooperative learning and peer tutoring increase achievement and motivation, as well as improve interpersonal relationships. When one student teaches another student, the achievement of both students can improve.

- **Develop questions.** Questioning helps comprehension. Students learn more effectively when they generate their own questions. Students exposed to higher order questions understand more than students who are exposed only to lower order questions. They tend to give more thoughtful, reflective responses to questions when teachers allow more time for responses and encourage follow-up.

Professional Resource Download

9.5b Strategies Intervention Model

One widely used model of strategy instruction, the strategies intervention model (SIM), was developed and validated through many years of programmatic research with adolescents with learning disabilities by Deshler and colleagues (2001) at the Kansas Center for Research on Learning. SIM is a recognized, fully developed procedure for teaching learning strategies to adolescents with learning disabilities (Deshler et al., 1996; Ellis et al., 1991; Lenz & Deshler, 2003; Lenz et al., 1996; Oas, Schumaker, & Deshler, 1995). This practical and useful model has two phases for helping students cope with the demands of the high school curriculum: (1) teachers must identify the curriculum demands of their students and (2) teachers must match these school demands with specific learning strategies.

strategies intervention model (SIM)
An instructional method for teaching learning strategies to adolescents with learning disabilities.

9.5c Steps for Teaching Learning Strategies

Central to the SIM model is a series of eight instructional stages (Schumaker & Deshler, 2009; Clark, 2000; Deshler et al., 1996; Lenz & Deshler, 2003). The integrated series of overt acts and cognitive behaviors enables students to solve a problem or to complete a task. Table 9.3 summarizes the steps for teaching a learning strategy. In the following steps, the process of teaching a learning strategy is applied to a specific situation.

Step 1: Elena Martinez (the teacher) pretests Andrew Fleming (the student) to determine his current learning habits, and she obtains a commitment from him to learn Andrew is asked to perform a task that requires the target learning strategy. For example, for the strategy of self-questioning, Ms. Martinez asks Andrew to read a passage and answer the comprehension questions. Ms. Martinez and Andrew discuss the results of his performance and she helps him see his need for acquiring the learning strategy. Seeing the benefit, Andrew readily commits to learning the new strategy.

Step 2: Ms. Martinez describes the new learning strategy Next, Ms. Martinez explains to Andrew the steps and behaviors involved in performing the learning strategy: "First, Andrew, you will read a paragraph. Then you will stop reading and ask yourself some questions. As you think of a question, you will either answer it yourself or go back to the paragraph to find the answer. After you have answered all the questions you can think of, you will read the next paragraph." She also explains to Andrew the situations in which the strategy will be useful.

Step 3: Ms. Martinez models the new learning strategy She demonstrates all the steps described in Step 2. While doing so, Ms. Martinez *thinks aloud* so that Andrew can witness the entire process. In subsequent modeling, Ms. Martinez includes Andrew by asking appropriate questions.

Step 4: Andrew verbally rehearses the steps of the learning strategy Andrew rehearses the steps by talking aloud until he reaches the goal of 100% correct without prompting from Ms. Martinez. Andrew becomes familiar with the steps through a self-instruction procedure.

Step 5: Andrew practices with controlled materials and obtains feedback Elena Martinez provides materials for Andrew to practice the new

TABLE 9.3

Steps for Teaching a Learning Strategy

Stage 1. Teacher pretests students and obtains a commitment
Phase 1. Orientation and pretest
Phase 2. Awareness and commitment

Stage 2. Teacher describes the learning strategy
Phase 1. Orientation and overview
Phase 2. Presentation of strategy and system for remembering

Stage 3. Teacher models the strategy
Phase 1. Orientation
Phase 2. Presentation
Phase 3. Student enlistment

Stage 4. Students verbally practice the strategy
Phase 1. Verbal elaboration
Phase 2. Verbal rehearsal

Stage 5. Students have controlled practice and feedback
Phase 1. Orientation and overview
Phase 2. Guided practice
Phase 3. Independent practice

Stage 6. Students have advanced practice and feedback
Phase 1. Orientation and overview
Phase 2. Guided practice
Phase 3. Independent practice

Stage 7. Teacher posttests students and obtains a commitment
Phase 1. Confirmation and celebration
Phase 2. Forecast and commitment to generalize

Stage 8. Students generalize the learning strategy
Phase 1. Orientation
Phase 2. Activation
Phase 3. Adaptation
Phase 4. Maintenance

Source: Adapted from "An instructional model for teaching learning strategies" by E. Ellis, D. Deshler, B. Lenz, J. Schumaker, & F. Clark, 1991, *Focus on Exceptional Children*, 23(6), 11. Reprinted by permission of Love Publishing Company, Denver.

learning strategy. By carefully selecting practice materials, she keeps other intervening problems to a minimum. For example, to practice the strategy of self-questioning in reading material, she selects material that is easy enough for Andrew to practice the target strategy without being bogged down in very difficult vocabulary.

Step 6: Andrew practices with classroom materials and obtains feedback Once Andrew has gained proficiency in the strategy with controlled materials, Ms. Martinez applies the strategy to materials used in his general education classroom. This step is a stage in developing an application and generalization of the learning strategy. After using the strategy successfully in the resource room, Andrew must learn to generalize the technique to broader learning situations.

Step 7: Ms. Martinez post tests to determine Andrew's progress, and she obtains his permission to generalize Instruction is successful if Andrew has progressed sufficiently to cope with curricular demands in the target area.

Step 8: Andrew generalizes the learning strategy The real measure of effective strategy instruction is the degree to which students generalize the acquired strategy to the real world and maintain its use in new settings and situations. Ms. Martinez assists Andrew in generalization by monitoring his performance of the strategy in other settings, reviewing the steps as necessary, helping him brainstorm appropriate adaptations to the strategy, and encouraging him in its use.

In summary, the goal of the learning strategies approach is to teach adolescents with disabilities to become involved, active, and independent learners. Research shows that learning strategies instruction is effective because students "learn how to learn." For additional information about the strategies intervention model, contact the Center for Research on Learning (University of Kansas, 3061 Dole Human Development Center, Lawrence, KS 66045; phone (785) 864-4780; website *http://www.ku-crl.org*).

Did You Get It?

Ruth, a student with a mild learning disability, is having difficulty in algebra class, specifically in understanding the concept and function of the quadratic equation. The tutorial instruction she is given will focus on

a. algebra
b. her entire course-load
c. the quadratic equation
d. mathematics in general

9.6 Postsecondary Programs

Postsecondary education is becoming the new academic frontier for individuals with learning disabilities and related disabilities. Postsecondary education includes community colleges, vocational-educational training, nondegree postsecondary programs, and four-year colleges (Cook & Rumrill, 2006; Cowan, 2006). An increasing number of high schools are now allowing students to participate in college classes while still in high school.

9.6a College Programs

Some years ago, attending college was out of the question for most adults with learning disabilities and related mild disabilities. Today, however, the prospects for getting a college education have brightened considerably, and there are now many college opportunities for such young adults. Many individuals with learning disabilities and related mild disabilities can look forward to enrolling at a college and being better prepared for their future (Cook & Rumrill, 2006; Vogel, 1998; Vogel & Adelman, 2000). Community colleges are often a good choice for young adults. They bridge the gap between high school and college and may offer special programs and services. Student Stories 9.5, "Darlene, a College Student With Learning Disabilities" presents the story of a college student with learning disabilities.

Darlene was the youngest of three children. Her older sister and brother were model students—they received good grades in school with little effort. For Darlene, however, school was difficult. At first her parents would say, "Why can't you get As like your brother and sister?" Finally, in sixth grade, her parents realized that Darlene had learning disabilities. She received help during her middle school years, and her grades improved. During her high school years, Darlene, her parents, and the transition team developed a transition plan for college. She wanted to major in art, an area in which she excelled. She worked with her high school counselor and selected a college with a good arts curriculum and a supportive learning disabilities program. Darlene requested special accommodations for the college entrance examinations, and she was admitted to the college of her choice. At the college, she worked with the learning disabilities staff in planning her courses. When she needed any special accommodations in her courses, she knew her rights under the law and was able to advocate for herself. She decided to take three courses each semester instead of four so that she would graduate in five years instead of four years. Darlene is now a college senior, and she looks forward to her graduation. With careful planning and preparation, her college education has been a challenging, but happy, experience.

REFLECTIVE QUESTION

1. What accommodations did Darlene request to help her during her college education?

9.6b Legislation for Students With Disabilities in College Programs

The protections of the Individuals With Disabilities Education Improvement Act (IDEA-2004) end when the student graduates from high school or when the student has reached the maximum age of 22. Two other laws explained in more detail in Chapter 10 come into play for protection of adults with disabilities: (1) the Americans With Disabilities Act (ADA) and (2) Section 504 of the Rehabilitation Act. The Americans With Disabilities Act Amendments is a federal law that was first passed in 1990 and reauthorized in 2008 to ensure the rights of individuals with disabilities to nondiscriminatory treatment. ADAA provides protections of civil rights in the specific areas of employment, transportation, public accommodations, state and local government, and telecommunications. It also can protect the rights of adults with disabilities in educational settings. This law has been used to provide accommodations for individuals with disabilities taking licensing exams.

Section 504 of the Rehabilitation Act of 1973 largely triggered the proliferation of postsecondary and college programs. Section 794 of the Rehabilitation Act of 1973 states:

> No otherwise qualified individual with a disability . . . shall, solely, by reasons of his/her disability, be excluded from participation in, be denied the benefits of, or be subject to discrimination under any program or activity receiving federal financial assistance . . . .

Case law further clarifies the interpretation of Section 504 with regard to the requirements of schools and educational institutions. Because most colleges receive some federal financial assistance, they are subject to the Section 504 regulations (Weber, 2006; Rothstein, 1998).

Learning disabilities and students with other mild disabilities are recognized as a disability under both ADAA and Section 504. As this legislation is increasingly being implemented at educational institutions, adults with learning

Americans With Disabilities Act (ADA)
A federal law passed in 1990 to protect the rights of individuals with disabilities. The ADA was updated in 2008 as the *Americans With Disabilities Act Amendments* (ADAA).

Section 504 of the Rehabilitation Act of 1973
Federal law that covers all agencies and institutions receiving financial assistance and that requires that no otherwise qualified handicapped individual shall be excluded from participation.

TEACHING TIPS 9.4

Guidelines for Helping College Students With Learning Disabilities

1. Make the syllabus available 4 to 6 weeks before the beginning of the class and, when possible, be available to discuss it with students with learning disabilities who are considering taking the course.

2. Begin lectures and discussions with reviews and overviews of the topics to be covered.

3. Utilize graphic organizers or outlines as an introduction to the lecture or discussion.

4. Use PowerPoint slides to outline lecture material, reading what is written or what is on previously prepared slides to highlight key concepts, unusual terminology, or foreign words (being mindful of legibility and of the necessity to read what is written).

5. Emphasize important points, main ideas, and key concepts orally in lecture.

6. Give assignments in writing, as well as orally, and be available for further clarification.

7. Provide clear deadlines and reminders about when assignments are due.

8. Provide opportunities for student participation, question periods, and/or discussion.

9. Provide time for individual discussion of assignments and questions about lectures and readings.

10. Provide study guides for the text, study questions, framed outlines, and review sessions to aid in mastering material and preparing for exams.

11. Allow oral presentations or tape-recorded assignments instead of a written format.

12. Modify evaluation procedures. For example, permit untimed tests and oral, taped, or typed exams instead of written exams. Allow alternative methods to demonstrate course mastery and provide adequate scratch and lined paper for students with overly large or poor handwriting. Offer alternatives to computer-scored answer sheets.

13. Assist students in obtaining e-books or audio books. A valuable resource is http://www.learningally.org, which replaces the previous Recording for the Blind and Dyslexic.

Professional Resource Download

disabilities and related disabilities are able to enroll at colleges and postsecondary schools in steadily growing numbers, and they are eligible to receive a variety of services there (Weber, 2006). Teaching Tips 9.4 provides a whole array of ways that educators within the college/university setting can assist students in being successful in learning.

9.6c Accommodations in College Programs

Compliance with the regulations of Section 504 and ADAA (Americans With Disabilities Act Amendments) require that colleges make reasonable accommodations. Including Students in General Education 9.2, "Suggested Accommodations in College Programs," offers some common accommodations in college programs (Bursuck et al., 1989; Vogel, 1998). The Association on Higher Education and Disability (AHEAD) (2012) stresses that postsecondary level institutions may request a reasonable level of documentation for students to receive accommodations. However it does not require extensive medical and scientific evidence that there is a disability. Discussed are three types of documentation:

1. Primary documentation, which is the student's self report.
2. Secondary documentation, which comes from observation and interaction by higher education disability professionals during interviews and conversations.

reasonable accommodations
The phrase used in Section 504 of the Rehabilitation Act to describe what can fairly easily be done in a setting to make adjustments for an individual with a disability.

Including Students in GENERAL EDUCATION 9.2

Suggested Accommodations in College Programs

- Extending the time allowed to complete a program
- Adapting the method of instruction
- Substituting an alternative course for a required course
- Modifying or substituting courses for the foreign language requirements
- Allowing for part-time, rather than full-time, study
- Modifying examination procedures to measure achievement without contamination from areas of deficit

- Providing e-texts or audiobooks
- Providing note takers to help students with lectures
- Offering counseling services and other necessary support services to the students
- Developing accommodation plans for students
- Developing IEPs for the students
- Providing basic skills instruction in areas of reading, mathematics, and language

Professional Resource Download

3. Tertiary documentation, which includes external or third-party information such as medical records, previous testing, or discussions with the high school system (AHEAD, 2012).

College Entrance Testing for Individuals With Learning Disabilities Special accommodations are also available for students with learning disabilities who are taking college entrance examinations. Information on accommodations for the Scholastic Aptitude Test (SAT) can be obtained at the College Board website, *http://www.collegeboard.org*, and for the ORE and the GMAT from the Educational Testing Service (ETS) (Rosedale Road, Princeton, NJ, 08541; phone 609-921-9000; fax 609-734-5410; website *http://www.ets.org*). Information on special accommodations on the American College Test (ACT) is provided in the ACT Assessment Special Testing Guide (available from ACT Universal Testing Special Testing: 61, P.O. Box 4028, Iowa City, IA, 52243-4028; phone 319-337-1332; fax 319-337-1285; website *http://www.act.org*). A resource for college programs can be found in *The K & W Guide for Students with Learning Disabilities or Attention Deficit Disorder* (Kravetz & Wax, 2003). Teaching Tips 9.4, "Guidelines for Helping College Students With Learning Disabilities," offers ways to help college students with learning disabilities.

9.6d Professional Licensing and Learning Disabilities

Individuals entering professions such as law, medicine, and optometry must pass licensing examinations. Under the 2008 ADAA, individuals with learning disabilities may receive accommodations when taking these exams. A frequently requested accommodation is an extension of time on the exam. Research shows that extended time is beneficial to such people (Weaver, 2000). Unfortunately, individuals with learning disabilities trying to enter professions are too often denied the opportunity for accommodations (Hagin & Simon, 2000).

Such barriers are all the more cruel because these young adults are usually among the most promising graduates. They are individuals whose intelligence, motivation, and perseverance, together with the supports and accommodations supplied by families and teachers, have enabled them to succeed in higher education and in their professional education despite the vicissitudes of a learning disability. Given the opportunity to serve society as professionals, they could make substantial contributions (Hagin & Simon, 2000).

9.6e Nondegree Postsecondary Programs

Some young adults with learning disabilities may not be eligible for college programs, yet they will benefit from postsecondary transitional programs that will provide them with opportunities to learn independence; social experiences; practical activities, such as budgeting; computer skills; life experiences; and work experiences. A few colleges have developed such programs for these students. One is the PACE program, located at National-Louis University in Skokie, Illinois. Another is the Threshold Program, which is part of Lesley University in Cambridge, Massachusetts. Both are two-year programs that provide students with a college-like experience of living in dormitories. Students take classes in consumer math, problem solving, health and wellness, human development, music and art appreciation, social strategies, assertiveness training, independent living, and computer technology. They also gain experience working at jobs throughout their two-year program, with the support of a job coach. The Threshold Program conducted a follow-up study of its graduates for the past twelve years and found that 69% were living independently in apartments and 82% were employed (Yuan & Reisman, 2000). A study of graduates of the PACE program showed that 82% were employed, a figure that is much higher than that for other adults with learning disabilities (Harth & Burns, 2004). The PACE program website can be found at *http://www.nl.edu /academics/pace*.

Other postsecondary programs are Elmhurst Life Skills Academy (ELSA) located at Elmhurst College, Elmhurst, Illinois (*http://public.elmhvirst.edu*), and the College Living Experience (CLE) with several locations in the United States (*http://www.cleinc.net*).

Did You Get It?

Which of the following legislative acts provides "coverage" for the student with a learning and/or related disability once he or she graduates from high school or reaches the age of 22?
  a. The Individuals With Disabilities Education Improvement Act (IDEA-2004)
  b. The Americans With Disabilities Act (ADA)
  c. No Child Left Behind
  d. Head-Start Adult

9.7 Adults With Learning Disabilities and Related Disabilities

Learning disabilities do not disappear when individuals leave school. For many, difficulties continue throughout their lives. Oftentimes the postschool outcomes that students with learning disabilities anticipate differ from the postschool results they experiences. They may be satisfied with their position but not receive raises or get promotions (Daviso et al., 2011). Adults with learning disabilities and related mild disabilities need support and assistance to successfully make the transition to the adult world. Through public awareness programs about learning disabilities, as seen on television and reported in newspapers and magazine articles, many adults come to recognize that their problems are related to learning disabilities. For example, an article in *Newsweek* brought information about learning disabilities to the general public (Wingert & Kantrovitz, 1997).

What is the life of Frank, an adult with learning disabilities, like? These adults may have difficulty finding their niche in the world. They have trouble finding and keeping a job, developing a satisfying social life, and even coping with individual daily living. Many adults with learning disabilities have developed amazing strategies for avoiding, hiding, and dealing with their problems. Such a situation is described in Student Stories 9.6, "Frank, an Adult With a Learning Disability."

Surveys of adults with learning disabilities indicate that their major needs are in the areas of (1) social relationships and skills; (2) career counseling; (3) developing self-esteem and confidence; (4) overcoming dependence; (5) survival skills; (6) vocational training; (7) job procurement and retention; and (8) reading, spelling, management of personal finances, and organizational skills. When these adults lose a job, they are uncertain about what has gone wrong (Gerber & Brown, 1997). The Ohio Longitudinal Transtion Study indicates that students with learning disabilities have better employment outcomes when they are involved career and technical education, work-study opportunities, and paid employment prior to leaving secondary education. They also have minimal contact with social and vocational rehabilitative agencies after graduation, so providing these transition services when students are in secondary education is very important (Daviso et al., 2011).

STUDENT STORIES 9.6
Frank, an Adult With a Learning Disability

Frank is a 36-year-old man with a learning disability. He is of average intelligence, but he has great difficulty with reading. Employed as a journeyman painter, and supporting his wife and two children, he has learned to cope with many daily situations that required reading skills. Although he was unable to read the color labels on paint cans, and he could not decipher street and road signs, nor find streets, addresses, or use a city map to find the locations of his house-painting jobs, Frank had learned to manage by compensating for his inability to read. He visually memorized the color codes on paint cans to determine their color. He tried to limit his work to a specific area of the city because he could not read street signs. When he was sent into an unfamiliar area, he would ask a fellow worker to provide directions and accompany him, or he would request help from residents of the area

to reach his destination. He watched television to keep abreast of current affairs, and his wife read and answered his correspondence. However, Frank finally realized that advancement was not possible unless he learned to read. Moreover, his children were rapidly acquiring the reading skills that he did not possess. His disability was a continual threat to him and finally led him to seek help at a university learning disabilities clinic. It is remarkable that after so many years of failure and frustration, Frank recognized that his problem is a learning disability and that he had the fortitude and motivation to attempt once again the formidable task of learning to read.

REFLECTIVE QUESTION

1. What prompted Frank to seek help?

What is unique about adults with learning disabilities? They are usually self-identified and self-referred. To succeed, they must be intimately involved in both the diagnosis and the remediation process. They are likely to be highly motivated to learn the skills they know they need in life. They want to know what test results mean and the goals and purposes of the remediation program. It is their commitment to the remediation program that enables them to succeed. Adults with learning disabilities should learn about their rights under the law (Latham & Latham, 1997).

9.7a Literacy Organizations for Adults

Often adults are motivated to seek instruction in learning to read. The problem is that after individuals with learning disabilities leave school, there are fewer educational options open to them. Some literacy programs designed for adults include:

- **Literacy Volunteers of America.** Literacy Volunteers of America (LVA) is a national, nonprofit organization that has a network of volunteer tutors to teach reading, writing, and English-speaking skills to adults. (LVA can be contacted at 1320 Jamesville Ave., Syracuse, NY 13210; phone 800-448-8878; websites *http://www.literacyvolunteers.org*; *http://www.proliteracy.org*).
- **The Laubach program.** The objective of this private organization is to teach literacy to people around the world. (Write to Laubach Literacy Action, P.O. Box 131, 1320 Jamesville Ave., Syracuse, NY 13210; phone 800-528-2224; website *http://www.laubach.org*).
- **Adult Basic Education (ABE) and General Education Degree (GED).** These government-sponsored programs offer education for adults. A person passing the GED examination is awarded a high school equivalency degree.

I Have a Kid Who...

ELLIE: *A Student With Social Interaction Difficulties*

Ellie is 14 years old and in ninth grade. She has just moved to the community from another city. Ellie's mother said that Ellie's previous school reported that Ellie had learning disabilities. Ellie is quiet, withdrawn, and doesn't appear to have made many new friends. She often sits alone in the back of the classroom and doesn't volunteer responses, ideas, or engage in class discussions. While she does most, if not all, of the independent work required of her, she does not actively participate in any partner or cooperative activities. Ellie avoids group contact by reading or drawing quietly, or asking to be excused to go to the rest-room, locker, or office. From all the information the teachers have gathered and their observations, Ellie appears to be able to read and write on grade level.

Mr. Salinas, Ellie's English teacher, is concerned because her nonparticipation in group activities is beginning to cause some resentment from her peers. Some students have stated they don't want to be placed in a group with Ellie because, "She won't help out and it just drags us down. It's like she doesn't even know we're there." Academically, this is also impacting Ellie's grade in English class because several of the semester competencies and assignments require peer and group interaction. There are upcoming small-group literature-discussion activities and peer editing/writing support groups.

QUESTIONS

1. What strategies could be used to help Ellie participate with the class?

2. How can Ellie be taught specifically the skills to work with others?

Source: The Iris Center, *http://iris.peabody.vanderbilt.edu*.

Did You Get It?

The Ohio Longitudinal Transition Study found that those students with learning disabilities who experienced certain settings/scenarios had more-positive vocational outcomes than those who did not. Which of the following is not one of the settings pointed to in this study?

a. Career and technical education
b. Work-study
c. Paid employment during high school
d. Experiences with a mentor

Chapter Summary

- Adolescents with learning disabilities and related disabilities must cope with the dramatic changes in their lives caused by puberty, conflicting feelings, physical changes, peer pressure, illegal drugs, and self-consciousness, as well as with problems related to their disabilities.
- Characteristics of adolescents with learning problems include: cultural and linguistic diversity, poor self-concept, social and behavioral issues, attentional and language difficulties, and lack of motivation.
- The required components of the transition plan include current levels of academic achievement and functional performance including interests and aptitudes, measurable postsecondary goals and the services to meet those goals, and connections to those agencies available to provide services during and after the student's school career.
- Important features for success in high school include intensive instruction in reading and mathematics, explicit instruction

in survival skills, and completion of all required high school courses for graduation. Curriculum models for learning disabilities in the secondary schools include basic skills instruction, tutorial instruction, functional skills instruction, and work-study programs.

- Learning strategies instruction helps adolescents with learning disabilities learn how to learn and become active, efficient learners. The learning strategies approach teaches students how to learn rather than what to learn. Students can apply learning strategies to all areas of the secondary curriculum.
- Postsecondary and college programs for young adults with learning disabilities are growing, and an increasing number of colleges have developed special services for college students with learning disabilities and related mild disabilities. The Americans With Disabilities Act Amendments and Section 504 of the Rehabilitation Act provide protection for college students with disabilities.

Questions for Discussion and Reflection

1. Describe three characteristics of adolescents with learning disabilities and related disabilities and discuss how these characteristics affect high school achievement.
2. What special problems occur at the secondary level that differ from the those at the elementary level?
3. More secondary students with learning disabilities and other related disabilities are

in general education content-area classes. How can content-area teachers and special education teachers work together? When they don't agree on what should be covered in class, what steps should be taken to resolve their differences?
4. What is a transition plan for secondary students with disabilities? What are some of the possible goals for such a transition plan?

5. Several different curriculum models are used for teaching adolescents with learning disabilities. Describe three of these approaches and provide the advantages and disadvantages of each.

6. What is the purpose of using learning strategies instruction for adolescents with learning disabilities? Describe each of the eight steps in learning strategies instruction.

7. How does Section 504 of the Rehabilitation Act affect the education of college students with disabilities? Describe three accommodations for college students.

Key Terms

accommodations (p. 258)

Americans With Disabilities Act (ADA) (p. 274)

attribution theory (p. 252)

background knowledge (p. 270)

basic academic skills instruction (p. 265)

collaborative teaming (p. 256)

content-area teachers (p. 255)

functional skills or survival skills (p. 265)

high-stakes testing (p. 258)

learning strategies instruction (p. 269)

reasonable accommodations (p. 275)

Section 504 of the Rehabilitation Act of 1973 (p. 274)

strategies intervention model (SIM) (p. 271)

Summary of Performance (SOP) (p. 263)

transition (p. 260)

transition planning (p. 260)

tutorial instruction (p. 265)

work-study program (p. 266)

Spencer Grant/PhotoEdit

10

Understanding the Laws Related to Students With Disabilities

You get justice in the next world, in this world you have the law.

—William Gaddis

LEARNING OBJECTIVES

After reading this chapter, you should be able to:

10.1 Explain the reasons that laws are so important

10.2 Describe the history of special education law

10.3 Explain the key provisions of Special Education Law

10.4 Describe other laws that affect students with disabilities

10.5 Describe the key concepts that have been determined by the U.S. Supreme Court.

STANDARDS Addressed in This Chapter:

Council for Exceptional Children Initial Level Special Educator Preparation Standards as approved by the National Council for the Accreditation of Teacher Education

CEC Initial Preparation Standard 6: Professional Learning and Ethical Practice

- 6.0—Beginning special education professionals use foundational knowledge of the field and their professional ethical principles and practice standards to inform special education practice, to engage in lifelong learning, and to advance the profession.

- 6.1—Beginning special education professionals use professional ethical principles and professional practice standards to guide their practice.

- 6.2—Beginning special education professionals understand how foundational knowledge and current issues influence professional practice.

- 6.3—Beginning special education professionals understand that diversity is a part of families, cultures, and schools, and that complex human issues can interact with the delivery of special education services.

- 6.4—Beginning special education professionals understand the significance of lifelong learning and participate in professional activities and learning communities.

- 6.5—Beginning special education professionals advance the profession by engaging in activities such as advocacy and mentoring.

Teachers may think that it is not important for them to pay attention to laws that govern special education or court cases that clarify the intent of those laws. This is a myth that must be dispelled. Educators are responsible for translating the law, the regulations that implement those laws, and the court case law. Educators must have the background and the knowledge to translate the law into their work with students with disabilities and their families.

Laws and regulations are designed to protect the rights of students; if educators do not understand those rights they cannot protect the students they serve. Imagine the teacher who does not understand the protections of the Family Educational Rights and Privacy Act (FERPA) and gives students' records to someone who should not have those records. That teacher has violated the law and failed to protect the rights of the student. Imagine the teacher who is continuing to have behavioral problems with a student but does not relay that information at the Individual Education Program (IEP) meeting and therefore no functional assessment is conducted and no behavioral intervention plan is written to address the needs of the student. The parent would have the right to a call for a due process hearing because of the teacher's failure to do what was required for the child.

In this chapter we describe the laws that govern education and special education. This chapter (a) provides an historical perspective of federal special education laws, (b) describes important features of special education laws, and (c) describes the implications of several other federal laws that affect children and teachers.

10.1 Special Education Laws: Why Are They So Important?

Many families and educators erroneously take for granted that special education services have always been available for students with disabilities. This is not the case. There was a relatively recent time in our history when students with disabilities did not have the right to go to school—when there was no mandate for special education services. Children with disabilities were either ignored or excluded from attending public schools. It was only through the persistence of many dedicated advocates that laws were passed to provide education for children with disabilities. These advocates can be credited for working with policy-makers to create the mandate for special education.

The important federal laws, regulations, and court cases that pertain to students with disabilities are discussed in this chapter. However, it is also paramount for teachers to know the specific laws and regulations that govern special education in their states. Teachers can find that information through their State Department of Education website and through their professional organizations.

Student Stories 10.1 exemplifies the state of education before the Education for All Handicapped Children Act. Three decades ago, children with disabilities were neglected or ignored and their education was out of the realm of possibility.

Let us now look at the basic laws that protect the rights of students with disabilities and investigate the key concepts associated with those laws.

Laws and regulations provide protections to students with disabilities.

Paul Doyle/Alamy

Did You Get It?

In describing the steps necessary in getting legislation passed to include students with disabilities in a system that not so long ago shunned and excluded them, your authors use which word(s) to describe the efforts of the advocates who took on this fight?

a. "Persistent"
b. "Shocking, militant, and at times violent"
c. "Stoic"
d. "Unpretentious and fatalistic"

STUDENT STORIES 10.1
Before There Was a Special Education Law

Sally was a 10-year-old student enrolling in school for the first time. Sally had been diagnosed with severe behavioral disorders, significant intellectual development disabilities, and cerebral palsy. She had an unrepaired cleft palate and virtually no speech or language skills. Grunting was her chief form of communication. Every year from the time that Sally was 5 years old, her mother attempted to register her for school. Year after year, the principal said the school could not accommodate a special needs student like Sally.

Until Sally was 10, there was no law that said that she had the right to a free, appropriate public education.

Many formative years for Sally's education were lost—Sally would have had a much better chance for some educational success if she could have been enrolled at school when she was 3 years of age.

REFLECTIVE QUESTIONS

1. Do you believe that what happened to Sally could happen in today's schools—why or why not?

2. How would Sally have benefited from receiving special education services when she was 3 years old?

10.2 History of Special Education Legislation

A series of 5 special education laws were passed over a period of almost 40 years to ensure the education of students with disabilities.

1. The Education for All Handicapped Children Act of 1975 (PL 94-142)
2. Early Childhood Amendments of 1986 (PL 99-457)
3. The Individuals with Disabilities Education Act of 1990 (PL 101-476)
4. The Individuals with Disabilities Education Act of 1997 (PL 105-17)
5. The Individuals With Disabilities Education Improvement Act of 2004 (PL 108-456)

individualized education program (IEP)
The written plan for the education of an individual student with learning disabilities. The plan must meet requirements specified in the rules and regulations of IDEA.

related services
Those services that are designed to supplement the special education program designed to meet the needs of the student.

The first special education law was passed, and it is considered a landmark legislation. The Education for All Handicapped Children's Education Act gave students with disabilities the right to a free appropriate public education (FAPE). Prior to the passage of the first special education law in 1975, children with disabilities were largely ignored or were excluded from attending public school. This law also required that schools develop individualized education program (IEP) to plan for the instruction of each child identified with a disability. The IEP became the determinant document for what specific educational programs and related services were needed for that child. Placement was to be based on a thorough analysis of the child's levels of performance. From those levels of performance, the goals and objectives were determined for the child. The IEP was done yearly and a thorough reevaluation of the student's ability and achievement is conducted every three years.

Related services are services delivered by specially trained professionals and are needed for the student with disability to benefit from special education. Such services include speech-language services and auditory services, psychological services, physical and occupational therapy, social worker services, counseling services, travel training instruction (or orientation and mobility services), and medical services for diagnostic and evaluation purposes.

10.2a Early Childhood Amendments of 1986 (PL 99-457)

In 1986, the Education for All Handicapped Children Act was amended with Early Childhood Amendment (Public Law 99-457). This amendment was significant because it extended the provisions of the law to young children with disabilities, ages 3 through 5 years of age. Whereas PL 94-142 focused on the individual child with a disability, this latest set of amendments also focused on family needs and interventions. Programming for infants and toddlers also became a reality. While not a mandate that schools must provide services to children birth through 2, states must establish an interagency coordinating council to determine how services will be

Children ages 3 through 5 have the right to a free, appropriate public education. Programming for infants and toddlers is available for many students with disabilities.

Barros & Barros/The Image Bank/Getty Images

provided, and the coordinating council must specify the statewide system that includes definitions for children with disabilities who are eligible, individualized family service plans that are required for young children receiving services, and Child Find that requires that babies who may be eligible for services are sought, and a lead agency in each state must be designated.

10.2b The Individuals With Disabilities Education Act of 1990 (PL 101-476)

In 1990, the Education for All Handicapped Children Act was renamed and became the Individuals with Disabilities Education Act (IDEA) (PL 101-476). Two new categories of students with disabilities—autism and traumatic brain injury—were added. This revision also began the era of transition services— to prepare students from school to the world of work and independent living. The 1990 revision also began the provisions of assistive technology devices and services.

transition
The process of moving from one type of program to another. In early childhood programs, it can be from the birth-through-2 program to the ages 3–5 program, or from the ages 3–5 program to another educational placement. For adolescents, transition refers to the passage from school to the adult world.

10.2c The Individuals With Disabilities Education Act of 1997 (PL 105-17)

In 1997, there was a major revision to the IDEA, which became known as the Individuals with Disabilities Act of 1997 (IDEA-1997). The purpose of the law was to broaden the 1997 revision. Beyond the purpose of a FAPE emphasizing special education and related services designed to meet the student's individual needs, the 1997 revision added that it also must be designed to prepare students for employment and independent living, including students who have been suspended or expelled from school. New protections were also provided for students with behavioral challenges. Although those protections were maintained in the 1997 revision of the law, they were modified in IDEA-2004.

In IDEA-1997, many new requirements were added to the IEP process in order to more thoroughly address the needs of students with disabilities. The IEP feature called the *present levels of performance* included how the disability affects the child's involvement and progress in the general curriculum. In addition, the IEP team had to consider the participation of students with disabilities in statewide and local assessment and the accommodations that were be needed for taking those tests. If a student could not take the statewide and local assessment, the IEP team needed to specify why the assessment was not appropriate and had to determine an alternate method of assessment.

In IDEA-1997, for the first time, the general education teacher was required to be a participant in the IEP process. Teachers' organizations had voiced serious concerns that, with the movement toward inclusion, they were being expected to provide significant services and accommodations for students with disabilities within their classroom yet were not involved in the decision-making process. There was also an addition in the focus of the IEP process. Previously the IEP team addressed the needs of the student alone. With IDEA-1997, language was added to support school personnel. Consequently, if teachers stated, within the IEP process, that they needed additional training to meet the needs of the student, then the training had to be addressed within the IEP process (Johns, 1998).

IDEA-1997 also required that the IEP team consider the strengths of the student and the concerns of the parents for enhancing the education of the child. Additional requirements in the IEP process included addressing special factors, such as: positive behavioral interventions when the student's behavior impeded learning; the language needs of students with limited English proficiency; instruction in Braille and the use of Braille unless the IEP team determined otherwise; communication needs of the student; and the provision of assistive technology devices and services.

10.2d The Individuals With Disabilities Education Improvement Act of 2004 (PL 108-456)

In 2004 President George W. Bush signed the most recent version of the law, the Individuals With Disabilities Education Improvement Act of 2004 (IDEA-2004), or Public Act 108-446. The Final Regulations for IDEA-2004 were issued by the U.S. Department of Education in 2006. IDEA-2004, the current revision of the law (as did the original law) assures that all students with disabilities are provided FAPE based on their individual needs. IDEA is based on the premise that there is zero reject (i.e., all students have the right to go to school regardless of the severity of their disability).

zero reject
No student can be rejected from attending school because of his or her disability. All students, regardless of the severity of their disability, have the right to go to school.

Remember also that in IDEA-97 and continuing in IDEA-2004, a FAPE is provided to all students—even those students who are suspended or expelled from school. Students who are suspended from school for any more than 10 days per year must have access and reach progress in the general curriculum and their IEP services. Also they should receive a functional behavioral assessment, behavioral intervention services, and modifications that are designed to address the behavior violation so that it does not recur (IDEA-2004, Section 615, 34 C.F.R. 300.530–300.536).

> **Did You Get It?**
>
> The key right granted to students with disabilities as a result of The Education for All Handicapped Children's Education Act is "FAPE," otherwise known as Free _____ Public Education.
> a. Accessible
> b. Applicable
> c. Acceptable
> d. Appropriate

10.3 Key Provisions of Special Education Law

10.3a Individualized Education Program (IEP)

IEP is a mandate of the IDEA. The IEP is a written statement for a child with a disability. A student's IEP is developed, reviewed, and revised in accordance with the law (IDEA-2004). Educational services and settings for students with disabilities are based on the individual needs of the student as determined by the IEP team. The IEP is the hallmark of good planning for students and has been in existence since the inception of the special education mandate in 1975.

The IEP is developed at least yearly and addresses the educational implications of the evaluations. The IEP includes the child's levels of academic achievement, the child's functional performance, the annual goals for the child, and the placement and services where those goals can be met and where the student can receive meaningful benefit. IDEA-2004 allows 15 states to apply for waivers to do students' IEPs, with parental consent, every three years at key transition points for the student. Figure 10.1 shows the first page of a sample IEP.

Special Considerations in the IEP Figure 10.2 lists a number of special factors that must also be considered within the IEP process.

IEP Planning Team *There is no such thing as unilateral action in special education.* This is a theme that should govern actions of school personnel in special education. This concept, however, is very difficult for school personnel to understand because school officials in general education are able to make unilateral decisions about general education students. In special education, however, it is the IEP team that determines the needs of the student and the placement of that student. In the evaluation process, there must be a multidisciplinary

---

FIGURE **10.1**
Sample IEP

SAMPLE IEP

Please note that this sample includes some of the components for a particular child. It does not constitute all of the components that might be required in individual states. States have developed their own recommended IEP forms and readers should visit the websites of their state departments of education to review the specific forms and the requirements based on that state. This is just to give you an example of some of the material that will be required in an IEP. This is a fictitious student.

IEP for Betty Lou Holden

Date of Conference: May 15, 2012

Date of Recent Evaluation: May 21, 2011   Date of Next Reevaluation: May 21, 2014

Purpose of Conference: IEP Review/Revision

Student Identification Information:

Name: Betty Lou Holden   Date of Birth: November 6, 2002   ID number: 55015

Student Address: 106 East Maple Court, Clarksville, Indiana 47130

Female

Ethnicity: Caucasian

Language/Mode of Communication Used by Student: English

Current Grade: fourth grade

Disability: Learning Disability—Auditory Memory Deficits and Fine-Motor Deficits

Resident District: Clark County Schools   Serving District: same

Resident School: Gurnsee School

Parent/Guardian Information:

Parents' name: James and Martha Holden

Parents' address: 106 East Maple Court, Clarksville, Indiana 47130

Parents' telephone number: 812-546-6789

Language/Mode of Communication Used by Parents: English

© Cengage Learning 2015

Download the complete IEP from CourseMate.

FIGURE **10.2**
Special Considerations in
the IEP

Special Considerations in the IEP

- *Positive behavioral interventions and supports.* In the case of a child whose behavior impedes the child's learning or that of others, consider the use of positive behavioral interventions and supports.

- *English-Language Learners (ELL).* In the case of a child with limited English proficiency, consider the language needs of the child as such needs relate to the child's IEP.

- *Visual Impairment.* In the case of a student with visual impairment, provide for instruction in Braille and the use of Braille unless the IEP team determines it is not needed.

- *Hearing Impairment.* In the case of a student with specific communication needs, consider those needs.

- *Assistive Technology.* In the case of a child who may need assistive technology, consider those needs.

ELL

© Cengage Learning 2015

Professional Resource Download

evaluation that is conducted by a group of individuals. No one individual within the educational system determines that the student has a disability which adversely impacts educational performance. Instead, a group of individuals must conduct a variety of assessments and then as a team with the parent determine the disability of the student, whether that disability results in an adverse effect on educational performance, and what the needs of the student are. For example, if the student has speech/language problems, it is critical that an individual who has expertise and certification or licensure in speech/language be part of the evaluation team.

Figure 10.3 shows the IEP team members as specified within IDEA-2004.

FIGURE **10.3**
The IEP Team Members

The IEP Team Members

- *A parent.* The parent of a child with a disability;

- *An education teacher.* Not less than one regular education teacher of such child (if the child is, or may be, participating in the regular education environment);

- *A special education teacher.* Not less than one special education teacher, or where appropriate, not less than one special education provider of such child;

- *A person who is knowledgeable about special education and the general education curriculum.* A representative of the local educational agency who is qualified to provide, or supervise the provision of, *specially designed instruction* to meet the unique needs of children with disabilities, is knowledgeable about the general education curriculum, and is knowledgeable about the availability of resources of the local educational agency;

- *A person who can interpret the evaluation.* An individual who can interpret the instructional implications of evaluation results, who may be a member of the team described in the other sections;

- *Other individuals.* At the discretion of the parent or the agency, other individuals who have knowledge or special expertise regarding the child, including related services personnel as appropriate; and whenever appropriate, the child with a disability (IDEA Section 614, 34 C.F.R. 300.321).

© Cengage Learning 2015

Professional Resource Download

Thus, the IEP team is charged with examining the needs of the student, planning goals, and then determining how and where those goals can be met. It is critical for the IEP team to consider the whole range of student needs:

- Students who have a disability that results in an adverse effect on educational performance require specialized instruction to meet those needs.
- They also require sufficient accommodations in assessment and instruction.
- They may require specific modifications to the general curriculum.
- They may also require related services coordinated with their special education program and placement.

The IEP team is charged with examining the needs of the student, planning goals, and then determining how and where those goals can be met. Figure 10.4 represents a flow chart of how the IEP team should proceed in determining the individualized needs of the child.

After the IEP meeting is over, the team members' responsibilities continue every day. The IEP team members are responsible for implementing the IEP and monitoring whether the student is making progress. Progress reports must be provided to the family in accordance with the school district's reporting system. When the student is not making progress it is up to the team members to call a new IEP team meeting to determine what needs to be changed.

Review of educational implications of the evaluation

Concerns of parents

Levels of student's achievement and functional performance

Goals and short-term objectives

Placement, accommodations, aids and services, technology, etc.

© Cengage Learning 2015

FIGURE **10.4**
What the IEP Team Should Consider

STUDENT STORIES 10.2

Teacher's Role in an IEP

Mrs. Johns, the special education teacher, has been working with Jonathan, a fifth-grade student with significant learning disabilities, and he has made good progress. His reading comprehension has increased from a 1.3 grade level to a 2.6 grade level, as measured on an individualized achievement test. Each day Jonathan receives 90 minutes of specialized instruction—one-on-one with Mrs. Johns and peer-to-peer collaboration.

Jonathan's IEP includes his progress based on Mrs. Johns's observations and curriculum-based assessment. Going into the IEP meeting, Mrs. Johns believes Jonathan should continue to receive the same amount of instructional time in the learning disabilities resource class. When the administrator talks about placement recommendations, he announces that the school district is going to cut back on services and wants to provide more time for the special education students in the regular classroom. He explains that rather than receive pullout special services, those services will be provided in the general education classroom. Jonathan's parents are upset because they want him to receive the same amount of services as in the past. The general education classroom teacher, Ms. Lee, also agrees with the parents; however she is afraid to speak up and voice her opinion because she does not yet have tenure. She knows that she should have a voice in the decision-making process. She also knows that the decision should be based on the individual needs of Jonathan and not the convenience of the school district. However Ms. Lee is torn between the needs of the student and the opinion of the school administrator.

REFLECTIVE QUESTIONS

1. What could Mrs. Johns have done to prevent this dilemma from occurring?

2. What is Mrs. Johns's obligation as an active participant in this IEP?

3. What is the responsibility of Ms. Lee as an active IEP participant?

© Cengage Learning 2015

TeachSource Video Case Activity

Watch the TeachSource Video Case entitled "Foundations: Aligning Instruction With Federal Legislation." In this video a teacher, a specialist, an intern, and the principal discuss the federal laws of the Individuals With Disabilities Education Act (IDEA) and No Child Left Behind Act (NCLB), and the implementation of these laws and the implications of the law for special educators:

QUESTIONS

1. What will you do when you begin teaching to ensure that you are following the laws that govern children with disabilities?

2. What will you do when you disagree with another IEP team member about what the least restrictive environment should be for the student?

3. What role do you believe that state testing should play in evaluating students with disabilities and in evaluating the teacher's performance?

10.3b Nondiscriminatory Evaluation Procedures

Each school district is responsible for assuring that no one single measure or assessment is utilized as the sole criterion for determining whether a child has a disability. Further, the school district must assure that, within the evaluation process, only technically sound instruments are utilized. Criteria established in IDEA-2004 require that school districts ensure that:

- Assessments and other evaluation materials are selected and administered so as not to be discriminatory on a racial or cultural basis.
- Assessments are provided and administered in the language and form most likely to yield accurate information on what the child knows and can do academically, developmentally, and functionally, unless it is not feasible to do so.
- Assessments are used for purposes for which the assessments or measures are valid and reliable.
- Assessments are administered by trained and knowledgeable personnel.
- Assessments are administered in accordance with any instructions provided by the producer of such assessments.
- Assessments are provided to the child in all areas of suspected disability (Individuals With Disabilities Education Improvement Act 2004, Section 614).

Assessments and other evaluations are to be tailored to assess specific areas of educational need and are not merely those that are designed to provide a single general intelligence quotient (34 C.F.R. 300.304). Assessments are also to be selected and administered, so as to ensure that if an assessment is administered to a child with impaired sensory, manual, or speaking skills, the assessment results accurately reflect the child's aptitude or achievement level or whatever other factors the test purports to measure, rather than reflecting the child's impaired sensory, manual, or speaking skills (unless those skills are the factors that the test purports to measure) (IDEA Regulations Section 300.304).

We know that students and their needs change, and therefore IDEA-2004 requires an evaluation at least every three years or more often as determined by the parent and school district personnel. Parental consent must be given for the evaluation. A team meeting is held after the evaluation occurs to review the results of the evaluation with the parent. No one person is responsible for all components of the evaluation; rather, it is a multidisciplinary process.

10.3c Least Restrictive Environment

The least restrictive environment (LRE) provisions of the IDEA provide that, to the maximum extent appropriate, students with disabilities are educated with their peers without disabilities. The premise of the LRE is that placement decisions about the student's educational setting should be based on each student's individual needs.

IEP teams must consider the student's level of academic achievement and functional performance and then develop goals to address the individual needs of the student. Based on that information, the IEP team must determine where those goals can be met—in what specific educational setting is the student likely to gain *meaningful benefit*?

Some educators interpret the LRE feature of the law to mean that students should always be educated within the general education classroom. Some individuals and organizations go further, advocating the philosophy of full inclusion.

Actually the word *inclusion* does not appear anywhere in the law. The concept of *full inclusion* is a philosophy that goes further, proposing that all children, regardless of the severity of their disability, are to be educated within the general education classroom. Criteria for determining the LRE were established in the Rachel Holland case. Rachel Holland was a child with intellectual disabilities and went to school in the Sacramento Unified School District. Rachel's parents wanted her to be educated within the regular classroom setting but the school district believed that it was more appropriate to educate her in a special education classroom. The school district lost the case. The criteria established were as follows:

1. Will the student derive educational benefit from the placement considered?
2. Will the student derive noneducational benefit from the placement? The examples used within the case were friendships, improved self-confidence, and excitement for learning.
3. Will there be detriment because the student is disruptive, distracting or unruly, and would the student take up so much of the teacher's time that the other students would suffer from lack of attention?
4. What is the cost of the proposed placement? Will the placement burden the school district's funds or adversely impact services available to other children?

Sacramento City Unified School District Board of Education v. Rachel H., 20 IDELR 182 (9th Cir., 1994).

Later the year that *Holland* was decided, the same circuit ruled differently with another student while applying this 4-prong test. (*Clyde K. and Sheila K. individually and as guardians for Ryan K. v. Puyallup School District*, 21 IDELR 664, September 13, 1994). Ryan K. was a 15-year-old with Tourette's Syndrome and ADHD who had also engaged in incidents of sexual harassment. Because of escalations in his behavior,

least restrictive environment (LRE)
To the maximum extent appropriate, students are educated with their nondisabled peers.

TEACHING TIPS 10.1
Preparing for an IEP

- As an IEP participant, you are part of a decision-making process that will impact a student's life. Take that responsibility very seriously.
- Be well prepared by reviewing the student's previous IEP and evaluations.
- Be prepared to talk about the student's strengths and interests.
- Be prepared to share factual information about your work with the student.
- Remain objective in the information that you provide. During the discussion of the present levels of academic achievement and functional performance, reveal information that is based on assessment information and your observations.
- Suggest goals that are measurable, observable, and objective.
- Engage the parent actively in the discussion by asking specific questions about what the student does well at home.
- Participate actively in the decision-making process. Use data to justify your recommendations.

Professional Resource Download

including an assault on a staff member, the district recommended that Ryan be placed in STARS—Students Temporarily Away from Regular School. That program provided a more structured environment and provided more individualized attention. Parents originally agreed but then changed their minds and filed a lawsuit alleging violation of his rights to due process. The parents believed that Ryan could be educated in a mainstream setting if the school provided a personal aide for him.

The court determined that the STARS program was the least restrictive environment for Ryan, applying the *Holland* test as follows:

a. Ryan's disruptive behavior kept him from learning.
b. He derived at best only minimal nonacademic benefits from his previous general education placement.
c. The record indicated that his presence in classes in the regular school building had an "overwhelmingly negative effect on teachers and other students."
d. He was dangerously aggressive. Schools have a special obligation to ensure that students in their care are kept out of harm's way.
e. Ryan's sexual harassment was also problematic. Public officials have a compelling duty not to tolerate it in classrooms and hallways. School officials should be concerned about liability for failing to remedy peer sexual harassment that exposes students to a hostile educational environment.

The court said that disruptive behavior that significantly impairs the education of other students strongly suggests that a mainstream placement is not appropriate. School officials have a duty to ensure that students with disabilities receive an appropriate education but they are "not required to sit on their hands when a disabled student's behavioral problems prevent both him and those around him from learning."

10.3d Procedural Safeguards

A cornerstone of IDEA is the right of the parent or the school district to disagree with decisions that might be made by the IEP planning team. School districts and parents all want the same thing for children, but sometimes they may not agree on how to achieve these goals. There are safeguards to protect the rights of the students. School personnel and parents are always encouraged to resolve their differences through informal measures. Under IDEA-2004 *mediation* is provided. Mediation is more informal and less legalistic procedure than going to a due process hearing and requires an impartial individual, who is not an employee of the school district, to listen to both sides of the issue and render a decision. Mediation is provided at no cost to the parents. In addition, IDEA-2004 designates a requirement that prior to a due process hearing, the school district will convene a meeting with the parents and the relevant member or members of the IEP team to resolve differences. If informal procedures and mediation still fail to resolve the issue, then the due process system is provided and specific procedures are outlined for it in IDEA-2004 and its accompanying regulations (34 C.F.R. 300.500–300.518). States then determine the specific procedure for who is a hearing officer and how the due process hearings are conducted. Figure 10.5 summarizes the list of procedures from least to most formal.

When there is a dispute between the parent and the school district—:

1. Parents and school district meet with each other to attempt to resolve differences. If that is unsuccessful,
2. Parent can file a complaint with the appropriate State Department of Education. If that is unsuccessful,
3. Parent can request mediation where a neutral third party is appointed by the State Department of Education to listen to both sides of the story and render a decision. If that is unsuccessful,
4. Parent can request a due process hearing and prior to that hearing, the school district must convene a meeting with the parents and the relevant member or members of the IEP. If the district has not resolved the complaint to the satisfaction of the parent, the due process hearing occurs.

© Cengage Learning 2015

Professional Resource Download

10.3e Contentious Issues Surrounding IDEA

However, IDEA-2004 is very contentious on several issues.

- *Rights of Parents.* For the first time in a reauthorization, the rights of parents and students were reduced, particularly in the areas of transition, due process rights, and discipline issues (Johns, 2005).
- *Transition.* Transition planning had previously been required at the age of 14, but in IDEA-2004, it is not required until the age of 16.
- *Attorney's fees.* Within due process rights, if a parent files a hearing that could be construed as frivolous, the parent's attorney or the parent will be required to not only pay their own attorney's fees but also the fees of the school district.
- *Discipline.* In the area of discipline, if the behavior is not a manifestation of the disability, the school district may move the child to the recommended disciplinary setting regardless of whether the parent agrees. The parents' recourse is to file for a due process hearing, but in the meantime, the student's placement is the recommended disciplinary setting.
- *Response-to-Intervention.* Another change was in the evaluation procedures for students with learning disabilities. IDEA-2004 provides that a local school district may use a *response-to-intervention* model in determining whether a student has a learning disability. The Regulations for IDEA-2004 (34 C.F.R. 300.307) permits the process of response-to-intervention, but it does not require its use. The district may choose not to use a discrepancy between ability and achievement model for identification purposes. Many families of children with learning disabilities, as well as educators, fear that the lack of a research base for response-to-intervention may result in delays in case study evaluations for those students who need such evaluations. Response-to-Intervention is discussed earlier in this book.

10-3f Specific Legal Protections for Students With ADHD

- **Special education services.** Children with ADHD may be eligible for special education services under the category of "other health impaired" in IDEA-2004. The law describes other health impaired, when applied to children with ADHD, as heightened alertness to environmental stimuli that results in limited alertness with respect to the educational environment.

A child with ADHD may also be eligible for special education services under other existing categories of special education, in addition to other health impaired, such as the categories of learning disabilities or emotional disturbance.

- **Section 504 services.** A child with ADHD may be eligible for services under the legislation of Section 504 of the Rehabilitation Act of 1973, even if that child is not eligible for special education services. Section 504 mandates that any agency receiving federal funds must provide reasonable accommodations for people with disabilities.

According to Section 504, if the child is found to have a physical or mental impairment that substantially limits a major life activity, such as learning, the school must make an individualized determination of the child's educational needs, and reasonable accommodations must be provided within the general education classroom (Section 504 of the Rehabilitation Act). Students who are eligible for Section 504 have a disability but the disability does not adversely impact educational performance. As an example, a student with ADHD would be eligible for a Section 504 plan if there is no adverse effect on educational performance; if there is an adverse effect, however, then the student would have an IEP. Students who have IEPs have a disability that impacts educational performance.

Did You Get It?

IDEA-2004 placed the onus on which of the following in ensuring that neither assessments nor any other form of evaluation contained any aspects at all which could be considered discriminatory in nature?
  a. Local school districts
  b. State governments
  c. The federal government
  d. Both states and the federal government

10.4 Other Laws Impacting Students With Disabilities

10.4a No Child Left Behind Act of 2001

Educators must not only focus on the laws that govern the rights of students with disabilities, they must also be cognizant of how laws governing all students impact on students with disabilities. The most important law governing all students is No Child Left Behind (NCLB) Act of 2001, the latest reauthorization of the Elementary and Secondary Education Act. NCLB resulted in massive changes to the entire field of education, including special education. School personnel struggle to meet the requirements of NCLB, which looks at all students and at what level they achieve as compared to their grade level peers, while at the same time it also addresses the individual needs of the student as the cornerstone of the IDEA-2004. NCLB focuses on these major requirements: highly qualified personnel and accountability for results for all students,

Highly Qualified Personnel What are the implications of NCLB for special education teachers? NCLB requires that all teachers be highly qualified to teach the students within their classroom. This law requires that special education teachers not only have certification in special education, but also are highly qualified in the core academic subjects if they are the sole provider of that instruction. If the teacher is providing consultation/collaboration to the classroom teacher regarding appropriate accommodations to the classroom curriculum, the teacher must possess certification in special education. If the special education teacher provides the instruction for students who take alternate assessment with alternate achievement standards, then the teacher must be qualified as an elementary-school teacher. Each state must establish certification standards for teachers and, therefore, must establish a mechanism to assure that all teachers are highly qualified for their positions. If a student in a Title I school is being taught for more than 4 weeks by a teacher who is not considered highly qualified, then the school district must notify the parents of the student that the student has a teacher who does not meet the standard.

The provisions for highly qualified teachers do not apply to teachers hired by or working in private elementary schools and private secondary schools (34 C.F.R. 300.18).

Accountability for Results for All Students Special educators have long been responsible for assuring that students with disabilities gain meaningful benefits as a result of their special education and related services. Since NCLB, accountability is the expectation for all students. All students must make adequate yearly progress (AYP) in reading, math, and science. Scores are disaggregated or separated for specific groups of students—students with disabilities may be a disaggregated group of students depending upon the number of students that the state has determined as the minimum size of a disaggregated group. Data is disaggregated for students by poverty levels, race ethnicities, disabilities, and English-Language Learners (*Office of the Undersecretary of Education, 2002*). The data is reported according to each of these groups separately.

Students must take a state-determined assessment and then each State Department of Education compiles the results of the tests. With the latest adoption of the Common Core Standards in the majority of states, schools are revising their tests to measure the common core.

Each state must report the information back to the school district, while also reporting the school and district results to the public via newspaper and the Internet. For students with disabilities, the IEP team determines whether the student takes the state assessment with or without *accommodations*. If the student takes the test with accommodations, the IEP team determines the specific accommodations that should mirror the accommodations made within instruction. No more than 1% of students with the most significant cognitive disabilities may take an alternate assessment based on alternate achievement standards.

The U.S. Department of Education is also allowing an additional 2% of students with disabilities to take a modified assessment based on modified achievement standards. The 2% subgroup (about 20% of students with disabilities)

ELL

adequate yearly progress (AYP) Progress of schools that is determined by the state in accordance with No Child Left Behind Act requirements and that must result in continuous and substantial academic improvement for all students. The term that refers to the results of statewide tests and how those results meet the threshold of the state's requirement for a specific score.

Students participating in assessment.

would be in addition to the separate 1% group of students (about 10% of students with disabilities), with the most significant intellectual disabilities who are permitted to take alternate assessments aligned to alternate achievement standards. Therefore, about 30% of students with disabilities could take either the alternate assessment based on alternate achievement standards or a modified assessment based on modified achievement standards.

The final regulations that govern how states can measure the students in the 2% group (34 C.F.R. Parts 200 and 300) are as follows:

- States may develop modified achievement standards and give assessments to qualified students based on those standards.
- States must develop, disseminate information on, and promote the use of appropriate accommodations to increase the number of students with disabilities who are tested against academic achievement standards for the grade in which a student is enrolled.
- Standards must continue to hold students to high expectations; modified standards must be aligned with grade level curriculum.
- Students assessed under modified achievement standards must receive grade level instruction in the relevant subjects.
- Students who are eligible to be assessed based on alternate or modified academic achievement standards may be from any of the disability categories listed in IDEA.
- Out-of-level testing is not permitted: a student who is in fifth grade, for example, cannot take the test at the third-grade level.
- If the student's IEP includes goals for a subject that is assessed at the grade level in which the student is enrolled, the goals must be based on the academic-content standards for the grade in which the student is enrolled.
- Modified achievement standards may not preclude a student from earning a regular high school diploma (34 C.F.R. Parts 200 and 300).

NCLB also holds schools accountable to ensure that students attend schools that are safe. Each state shall establish and implement a policy that a student attending a persistently dangerous school or who becomes a victim of a violent criminal offense is allowed to attend a safe school.

10.4b Section 504 of the Rehabilitation Act of 1973

Section 504 of the Rehabilitation Act of 1973 prohibits *discrimination* on the basis of a disability. Section 504 also provides reasonable accommodations to students with disabilities and those accommodations are to be determined within the scope of a Section 504 accommodation plan for the student who has a disability but may not be eligible for special education.

The ADA Amendments Act of 2008 amended the definition of a disability. The term disability means a physical or mental impairment that substantially limits one or more major life activities of the individual. Major life activities include but are not limited to: caring for oneself, performing manual tasks, seeing, hearing, eating, sleeping, walking, standing, lifting, bending, speaking, breathing, learning, reading, concentrating, thinking, communicating, and working. An individual meets the requirements of having an impairment if the individual establishes that he or she has a disability even if the disability can be corrected. The exception is for a person who has a vision problem that can be corrected with eye glasses (ADA Amendments Act of 2008).

Under Section 504, an appropriate education means an education comparable to the education of other students without disabilities, unlike IDEA that defines an appropriate education as one that meets the individualized needs of the student. A student with a disability may be eligible for the provisions of Section 504, yet not eligible for services under the IDEA. In order for a student to be eligible for services under IDEA, the student must exhibit a disability that results in an adverse effect on educational performance. First, the evaluation team determines whether there is a disability. If there is a disability determination, then the team determines whether there is an adverse effect on educational performance. If there is not an adverse effect, then the student may need accommodations for his or her disability and will need an accommodation plan under Section 504 of the Rehabilitation Act of 1973. If there were an adverse effect, then the student would need an IEP.

Section 504 provides that the student have the same access as other students such as physical accessibility to the building and accommodations in instruction and assessment so the student has access to the same curriculum and instruction. IDEA provides that the student's education be individualized to meet his or her special needs.

10.4c The Americans With Disabilities Amendments Act (ADAA)

School personnel must also be aware of the laws that govern the rights of any individual who comes in to the school setting. Physical and program accessibility must be available to all individuals who need access to the school. The Americans With Disabilities Act (ADA) of 1990 broadened the scope of services to individuals with disabilities throughout their lifetime and in multiple settings. This legislation prohibits employers from discriminating against a person with a disability who is able to perform the essential functions of the job. Employers must make reasonable accommodations for employees with disabilities unless it would create an undue hardship. The law applies to businesses that employ 15 or more workers. The law also requires that public transportation must be accessible and local areas must provide alternative transportation if persons with disabilities are unable to use the fixed route service. New buildings must be accessible. Telephone companies must also have relay assistance to telephones for those who are hard of hearing or have speech impediments (Wood, 1992).

10.4d Family Educational Rights and Privacy Act (FERPA)

The Family Educational Rights and Privacy Act (FERPA) is a critical law that protects students' records. It is important that all educators understand how the records of each of their students are handled and with whom records can be shared. This law is also known as the *Buckley Amendment* and it applies to all educational agencies that receive funds administered by the U.S. Secretary of Education. Educational records are those that are specific to the student and are maintained by an educational agency. They may include handwritten or print materials, computer media, video or audiotape, film, microfilm and microfiche, and e-mail. Exceptions to those records include records that are maintained by educational personnel that are not revealed to anyone else—these records are known as *sole possession records*. Examples of sole possession include records created and kept by a law enforcement unit, employment records, medical records, and alumni records (Allen, 2003).

FERPA requires that school personnel must obtain written permission from a parent/guardian prior to disclosing the records to a third party outside of a public school. There are exceptions to the rule. Specifically, schools can disclose information:

- To appropriate authorities in the event of an emergency to protect the health and safety of a student.
- To comply with a lawfully issued subpoena or court order.
- To comply with requests of local law enforcement information that is based on an official's personal knowledge or observation.
- To comply with an audit or evaluation of federal or state supported education programs.

Teachers will generate information for a student's record—most of it will be considered a temporary record but some part may be a student's permanent record. Temporary records are records that are only kept until the student is out of school for a designated period of time (usually five years). Permanent records are maintained within the district for many years. Special education records are considered temporary records (Johns & Crowley, 2003).

Did You Get It?

In terms of accountability, states are required by No Child Left Behind Act to report the results of statewide assessments to both the school district in question and the
- **a.** federal government
- **b.** Attorney General
- **c.** U.S. Senate
- **d.** public-at-large

10.5 The Court System: Case Law

When laws and regulations are ambiguous on specific issues (and this is the case in a number of areas), the courts become involved. You have learned earlier that both parents and school district personnel may go to due process on specific issues. When a decision is rendered, one party will have been deemed to have "won" the case. The other party will be dissatisfied and will have to decide whether they wish to appeal the case to a higher level. Ultimately, a case may move through the system and a very few will go as far as the U.S. Supreme Court. Relatively speaking, few cases pertaining to special education have been heard by the Supreme Court. Those cases however have become the law of the land. Table 10.1 lists key cases in education that have been decided by the Supreme Court.

It is important that educators be lifelong learners. This is especially true in the arena of special education laws and regulations. These laws and regulations and court interpretations of these laws are changing continually.

Educators must work to have their voice heard in the development of such laws and regulations and should grab every opportunity possible to provide input. Internet access makes it easier for educators to provide input into the development of future policies. It is also critical for educators to be active in their professional organizations, so that they can stay abreast of the latest policy issues. Policy issues drive what happens to students and to the educators providing services to the students—educators must be active in those policy issues.

The Supreme Court building.

Orhan Cam/Shutterstock.com

TABLE 10.1

Key Cases in Education Decided by the Supreme Court

Brown v. Board of Education of Topeka (1954)

The U.S. Supreme Court rules that school segregation based on race was prohibited by Fourteenth Amendment of the U.S. Constitution. Such case law raised the question that if schools could not discriminate based on race, then they should not be able to discriminate based on disability. Oliver Brown and a group of other parents took their children to schools in their neighborhood in Topeka, Kansas, and were denied entrance and told that their children had to attend schools that were designated for African American students. As a result the local chapter of the NAACP filed the suit on behalf of these families.

Brown v. Board of Education of Topeka, 347 U.S. 483, 74 S. Ct. 686, 98 L. Ed. 873 (1954).

Board of Education of the Hendrick Hudson Central School District v. Rowley (1982)

Amy Rowley was a deaf student who needed an interpreter. The U.S. Supreme Court determined that her school district was not required to provide a sign language interpreter. The Court ruled that schools must offer personalized instruction with sufficient support services to permit the child with a disability to benefit educationally from that instruction. They do not have to ensure that the student reaches his or her full potential. Since that ruling, the law has changed to require interpreters for students who need them.

Bd. Ed. Hendrick Hudson Sch. Dist. v. Amy Rowley (458 U.S. 176)

Irving Independent School District v. Tatro (1984)

The student had spina bifida and required intermittent catheterization. The Supreme Court ruled that a Texas school district must provide sterile, intermittent catheterization as a related service.

Irving Indep. Sch. Dist. v. Amber Tatro, 468 U.S. 883 (1984)

School Committee of the Town of Burlington v. Department of Education of the Commonwealth of Massachusetts (1985)

The student from Massachusetts was placed in a private school without the approval of public school officials. The Supreme Court decided that the parents of the student should be reimbursed for tuition even though they took their son out of a public school and placed him in a private school without the approval of public school officials. The Supreme Court also stated that the parents can be reimbursed in such situations if hearing officers or judges subsequently rule that the move was in the child's best interest. The Supreme Court did warn that parents are not entitled to such payments if hearing officers or judges rule that the student's public school placement was "appropriate" under the law.

Burlington Sch. Comm. v. Mass. Dept Ed., 471 U.S. 359 (1985)

Honig v. Doe (1988)

The Supreme Court ruled that when students pose an immediate threat to the safety of others, officials might temporarily suspend the student for only up to 10 school days. Schools cannot permanently and unilaterally exclude disabled children by means of indefinite suspensions and expulsions.

Honig v. Doe (484 U.S. 305)

(Continued)

Bowen v. Massachusetts (1988)

The Supreme Court ruled that services provided under a student's individualized education program could not be excluded from Medicaid reimbursement just because the services were characterized as partly "educational" (Illinois Alliance for Exceptional Children and Adults, 1990). Bowen v. Massachusetts, 487 U.S. 879 (1988)

Bowen v. Massachusetts, 487 U.S. 879 (1988)

Zobrest v. Catalina Foothills School District (1993)

The Supreme Court ruled that the provision of a publicly paid sign language interpreter for a deaf student on the grounds of the student's parochial school did not violate the Establishment Clause of the First Amendment to the Constitution (Maloney and Pitasky, 1995).

Zobrest v. Catalina Foothills School Dist., 509 US 1 - Supreme Court 1993

Cedar Rapids v. Garret F. (1999)

Garret Fry was a teenaged quadriplegic who required intensive medical services within the school. The district believed it was not responsible for such complex services under the definition of IDEA's related services. The Supreme Court ruled that the school district is responsible for services other than what would need to be performed by a physician. This is known as the "bright line" rule (Lake and Pitasky, 2000).

Cedar Rapids Community School Dist. v. Garret F., 526 US 66 - Supreme Court 1999

Brian Schaffer v. Jerry Weast, Superintendent of Montgomery County Schools 04-698 (2005)

The Supreme Court ruled that parents who want better special education programs for their children and challenge the school district would have the burden of proof, if the state does not specify who has the burden of proof. The case involved a Maryland family that challenged the school district's special education program designed for their son with ADHD.

Schaffer v. Weast, 546 US 49 - Supreme Court 2005

Arlington Central School District v. Murphy 05-18 (2006)

The Supreme Court ruled 6–3 that the IDEA does not authorize the courts to reimburse parents for the fees of experts (including consultants) when parents prevail in a hearing.

Arlington Central School District Board of Education v. Murphy, 548 U.S. 291 (2006)

Winkelman by Winkelman v. Parma City School District 5-983 (2007)

The Supreme Court ruled that a parent of a child with a disability could pursue a case involving IDEA in federal court without hiring an attorney.

Jacob Winkelman v. Parma City School District (No. 05-983)

Forest Grove School District v. T.A. 08-305 (2009)

The Supreme Court ruled that parents in a special education dispute with a school district may be reimbursed for "unilaterally" placing their child in a private school when the child has never received special education services from the district.

Forest Grove School District v. T. A., 129 S.Ct. 2484 (2009)

© Cengage Learning

10.5a Application of the Law: You Be the Judge

You have read throughout this chapter about the students and their guardians' legal rights. You may be wondering whether you as a teacher have any rights when you advocate for the rights of the child. How would you rule in this case shown in Figure 10.6?

In *Sturm v. Rocky Hill Board of Education*, 43 IDELR 36 (D. Conn. 2005), the U.S. District Court in Connecticut ruled that the teacher had standing to assert a claim because Section 504 does extend its protections to those who advocate on behalf of those individuals with disabilities. The court ruled that individuals with disabilities might need assistance in vindicating their rights from those

TEACHING TIPS 10.2

Ways to Keep Up With Current Laws

- Become active in your special education professional organization, such as the Council for Exceptional Children or the Learning Disabilities Association of America.
- Attend local and statewide workshops on legal issues impacting special education.
- Download your own copy of the federal and state special education laws and keep those in a binder for your reference.
- Familiarize yourself with your state's Department of Education's website.
- Become familiar with this compilation of websites related to Special Education:

Council for Exceptional Children *www.cec.sped.org*

Learning Disabilities Association of America *www.ldaamerica.org*

Department of Education *www.ed.gov/nclb/landing .jhtml*

Wrights Law *www.wrightslaw.com*

LD Online *www.ldonline.org*

Council for Exceptional Children *www.cec.sped.org*

U.S. Department of Education *www.ed.gov*

Our Children Left Behind *www.ourchildrenleftbehind .com*

Autism Society of America *www.autism-society.org*

The ARC *www.thearc.org*

National Association of Special Education Teachers *www.naset.org*

National Information Center for Children and Youth with Disabilities *www.nichcy.org*

Disability Rights Education and Defense Fun *www.dredf.org*

Council of Parent Attorneys and Advocates *www.copaa.org*

National Down Syndrome Society *www.ndss.org*

National Association of Protection and Advocacy Systems *www.napas.org*

TASH *www.TASH.org*

Americans With Disabilities Act *www.ada.gov*

Professional Resource Download

individuals who have their own claim to relief under Section 504 of the Rehabilitation Act (Norlin, 2006). Therefore, the court ruling was B.

It is important that teachers advocate for the needs of their students. To do so, teachers should follow the appropriate chain of command within the school system. When a teacher is concerned that a student may not be getting what he or she needs, the teacher should go to his or her immediate supervisor and talk with that individual. It is important that the teacher go to the supervisor with factual information about the student's progress or lack of progress. It is always important for the teacher to collect data about how the student is doing.

A Court Case: *Sturm v. Rocky Hill Board of Education*

A teacher advocated on behalf of the students with disabilities in the district's special education programs. Because of her advocacy on behalf of the children, she suffered from retaliation in the school district. She decided to assert retaliation within the protections of Section 504 of the Rehabilitation Act.

You be the judge for this case. Which of the following was the court's ruling? Select A or B.

A. The court ruled that Section 504 did not protect her right to advocate for her students.

B. The court ruled that, because of her advocacy efforts, she had the right to claim retaliation under Section 504.

FIGURE **10.6**
A Court Case: *Sturm v. Rocky Hill Board of Education*

© Cengage Learning 2015

TeachSource Video Case Activity

Watch the TeachSource Video Case entitled "Legal and Ethical Dimensions of Teaching: Reflections from Today's Educators." In this video, you will hear several educators discuss the daily ethical issues that they face and how they resolve those issues acting responsibly and in the best interests of the students.

QUESTIONS

1. After watching this video, what do you believe are the major ethical issues that might be seen within the IEP process and why?

2. What will you do if you observe a teacher not following an IEP? What steps will you take?

3. How do you express your opinion when you see that a student is not getting the services that are outlined in the student's IEP?

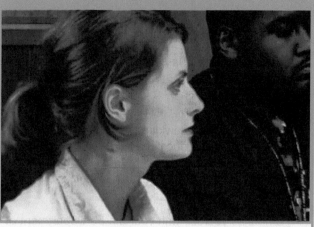

© Cengage Learning 2015.

4. How can you be proactive in learning information about special education laws?

As an important member of the IEP team, the teacher should ask for a new IEP if he or she believes that the student is not making progress. Within the IEP meeting, the teacher should present the relevant information to substantiate his or her beliefs that changes need to be made. If the team does not agree with this information and consensus is reached that is not in accord with the teacher's belief, then the teacher has an obligation to file a *minority report*. Such a report allows the teacher to voice his or her beliefs about the needs of the student.

I Have a Kid Who...

What About Jesse?

When Jesse enrolled in kindergarten, his mother told the principal and his kindergarten teacher that she had obtained an evaluation for Jesse. Jesse had been diagnosed with ADHD and was on medication that was administered at home. She offered to provide a copy of the evaluation to the school. The principal told her the school didn't need to have the information. Jesse had problems focusing in kindergarten and his teacher recommended that he be retained. The parent was upset and requested that Jesse have an evaluation by the school. The kindergarten teacher thought that would be a good idea but the principal thought that another year in kindergarten would make a positive difference, so Jesse repeated kindergarten.

Jesse had a different teacher his second year in kindergarten and he continued to have difficulty staying on task. His mother again asked for another evaluation and the new kindergarten teacher thought that would be a good idea. The principal told the mother to take Jesse back to the doctor to evaluate his medication. Jesse's mother did that and his medication was changed. Jesse began to do

better and went on to the first grade. In first grade, Jesse struggled with reading. By the end of the first semester, Jesse was behind his peers. His mother again asked for an evaluation and the first-grade teacher and principal told the mother it was not necessary; they wanted to wait to see if he would catch up. He ended his first-grade year not reading at all but went to second grade.

In second grade Jesse struggled more with his reading and his mother got an attorney and requested that he be evaluated. The evaluation was finally done, and it was determined that Jesse had a significant learning disability. The mother, together with the attorney, took the school district to a due process hearing.

QUESTIONS

1. What were the legal responsibilities of each of Jesse's teachers and the building principal at the school?

2. How do you think the due process hearing officer ruled in this case and why?

Did You Get It?

An 8-year-old Texas girl with spina bifida required intermittent catheterization every few hours, including in school, in order to avoid kidney damage. The Supreme Court ruled that the school district had to include this procedure as a related service. This case was

   a. *School Committee of the Town of Burlington v. Department of Education of the Commonwealth of Massachusetts* (1985)

   b. *Zobrest v. Catalina Foothills Sch. Dist.* (1993)

   c. *Irving Independent School District v. Tatro* (1984)

   d. *Arlington Central School District v. Murphy 05-18* (2006)

Chapter Summary

1. Public Law 94-142 was the first federal special education law in the United States. This law provided for a free, appropriate public education. This law has had several revisions since its passage in 1975 and is now the Individuals with Disabilities Education Act (IDEA 2004).

2. Laws protect the rights of students with disabilities to have an education and without those laws some children might not receive an education or would not receive an appropriate education. Laws mandate that all school districts provide an appropriate education in the least restrictive environment to all students with disabilities regardless of the severity of the disability.

3. Key requirements of the Individuals with Disabilities Education Act of 2004 include an individualized educational program for all students whose disability has an adverse impact on their educational performance. That IEP must be reviewed at least once a year. Students have the right to a free appropriate public education in the least restrictive environment. Parental participation is required.

4. There are other laws that impact the education of students with disabilities. Those laws include Section 504 of the Rehabilitation Act of 1973, the Americans with Disabilities Act, FERPA, and No Child Left Behind.

5. Over the years, the Supreme Court has defined what is an appropriate education, what is a free education, what specific related services must be provided, and what disciplinary measures are appropriate for students with disabilities.

Questions for Discussion and Reflection

1. Why is it so important to have laws and regulations that protect the rights of students with disabilities?

2. Do you believe that school districts would provide services if they were not mandated to do so? Why or why not?

3. What are the laws that protect the rights of students with disabilities?

4. What is the major difference between Section 504 of the Rehabilitation Act of 1973 and the Individuals with Disabilities Education Act—2004?

5. What is the 4-prong test established to determine least restrictive environment?

6. Which of the Supreme Court cases do you believe has had the most impact on students with disabilities and why?

Key Terms

adequate yearly progress (AYP) (p. 297)
individualized education program (IEP) (p. 286)
least restrictive environment (LRE) (p. 293)

related services (p. 286)
transition (p. 287)
zero reject (p. 288)

Bolot/iStockphoto.com

11

Spoken Language Difficulties: Listening and Speaking

Language shapes the way we think, and determines what we can think about.

—Benjamin Lee Whorf

LEARNING OBJECTIVES

After reading this chapter, you should be able to:

11.1 Explain theories describing spoken language difficulties

11.2 Describe the components of the language system

11.3 Outline the challenges of teaching language in the general education classroom

11.4 List components of the language system

11.5 Identify types of language problems

11.6 Explain the difficulties of students who are English-Language Learners (ELL)

11.7 Define early literacy and oral language

11.8 Discuss how to assess oral language

11.9 List teaching strategies to improve spoken language difficulties

11.10 Describe problems in listening

11.11 Describe problems in speaking

11.12 Identify computer technology to help teach speaking

P art IV considers the major areas of learning that affect children and youth with learning disabilities and related mild disabilities: (1) spoken language (Chapter 11), (2) reading (Chapter 12), (3) written language (Chapter 13), and (4) mathematics (Chapter 14). In each of these chapters, there are 2 major sections: the "Theories" section describes the concepts underlying the chapter's area of learning, and

STANDARDS Addressed in This Chapter:

CEC

Council for Exceptional Children Initial Level Special Educator Preparation Standards as approved by the National Council for the Accreditation of Teacher Education

CEC Initial Preparation Standard 1: Learner Development and Individual Learning Differences

- 1.0—Beginning special education professionals understand how exceptionalities may interact with development and learning and use this knowledge to provide meaningful and challenging learning experiences for individuals with exceptionalities.
- 1.1—Beginning special education professionals understand how language, culture, and family background influence the learning of individuals with exceptionalities.
- 1.2—Beginning special education professionals use understanding of development and individual differences to respond to the needs of individuals with exceptionalities.

CEC Initial Preparation Standard 3: Curricular Content Knowledge

- 3.0—Beginning special education professionals use knowledge of general and specialized curricula to individualize learning for individuals with exceptionalities.
- 3.1—Beginning special education professionals understand the central concepts, structures of the discipline, and tools of inquiry of the content areas they teach and can organize this knowledge, integrate cross-disciplinary skills and develop meaningful learning progressions for individuals with exceptionalities.
- 3.2—Beginning special education professionals understand and use general and specialized content knowledge for teaching across curricular content areas to individualize learning for individuals with exceptionalities.
- 3.3—Beginning special education professionals modify general and specialized curricula to make them accessible to individuals with exceptionalities.

CEC Initial Preparation Standard 4: Assessment

- 4.0—Beginning special education professionals use multiple methods of assessment and data-sources in making educational decisions.

- 4.1—Beginning special education professionals select and use technically sound formal and informal assessments that minimize bias.
- 4.2—Beginning special education professionals use knowledge of measurement principles and practices to interpret assessment results and guide educational decisions for individuals with exceptionalities.
- 4.3—Beginning special education professionals in collaboration with colleagues and families use multiple types of assessment information in making decisions about individuals with exceptionalities.
- 4.4—Beginning special education professionals engage individuals with exceptionalities to work toward quality learning and performance and provide feedback to guide them.

CEC Initial Preparation Standard 5: Instructional Planning and Strategies

- 5.0—Beginning special education professionals select, adapt, and use a repertoire of evidence-based instructional strategies to advance learning of individuals with exceptionalities.
- 5.1—Beginning special education professionals consider an individual's abilities, interests, learning environments, and cultural and linguistic factors in

the selection, development, and adaptation of learning experiences for individuals with exceptionalities.

- 5.2—Beginning special education professionals use technologies to support instructional assessment, planning, and delivery for individuals with exceptionalities.
- 5.3—Beginning special education professionals are familiar with augmentative and alternative communication systems and a variety of assistive technologies to support the communication and learning of individuals with exceptionalities.
- 5.4—Beginning special education professionals use strategies to enhance language development and communication skills of individuals with exceptionalities.
- 5.6—Beginning special education professionals teach to mastery and promote generalization of learning.
- 5.7—Beginning special education professionals teach cross-disciplinary knowledge and skills such as critical thinking and problem solving to individuals with exceptionalities.

For students, Common Core Standards for English Language Arts and Literacy in History/Social Studies, Science, and Technical Subjects can be found at: *www.corestandards.org.*

COMMON CO STATE STAND

the "Teaching Strategies" section describes methods for improving skills in that area of learning.

The three chapters on language constitute an integrated segment. Each chapter focuses on a different form of language, from spoken language (Chapter 11) to reading (Chapter 12) to written language (Chapter 13). Their organic unity comes from the underlying integrated language system.

This chapter highlights spoken language, which includes listening and speaking. In the "Theories" section, we review (1) the integrated language system; (2) language as a communication process; (3) how children acquire language; (4) the components of the language system; (5) types of language problems; (6) English-language learners; (7) early literacy and oral language; and (8) assessing oral language.

11.1 Theories Describing Spoken Language Difficulties

Language is recognized as one of the greatest of human achievements—more important than all the physical tools invented in the past 2,000 years. The acquisition of language is unique to human beings. Although other animals have communication systems, only humans have attained the most highly developed system of communication—speech. Language fulfills several very human functions: It provides a means of communicating and socializing with other human beings, it enables the culture to be transmitted from generation to generation, and it is a vehicle of thought.

Understanding language learning is critical for understanding learning disabilities and related mild disabilities. We know that language is essential for development, thinking, and human relationships; yet many aspects of language remain mysterious. How is language acquired by the child? What are the links between language, reading, and cognitive and social learning? How does a language impairment affect learning? Language researchers continue to investigate these complicated issues (Stone & Carlisle, 2006; Stillman & Scott, 2006).

Did You Get It?

The power of speech and language are, comparatively speaking, greater than _____.
   a. the wheel
   b. the automobile and Internet
   c. the four greatest physical inventions in history: the wheel, the plow, the printing press, and the telephone
   d. all human inventions of the past two millennia combined

11.2 Spoken Language, Reading, and Writing: An Integrated Language System

Language appears in several forms: (1) *spoken language* (listening and speaking), (2) *reading,* and (3) *writing.* These forms of language are linked through an underlying integrated language system. The interrelationships of spoken language, reading, and writing serve to build the core of the language system. As children gain competence and intimacy with language in one form, they also build knowledge and experience with the underlying language core, which are then carried into learning language in another form. What the child learns about the language system through oral language provides a knowledge base for reading and writing, and what the child learns about language through writing improves reading and spoken language. Further, when a child exhibits language difficulty in one form, the underlying language deficit often reappears in other forms. For example, a child who has a language delay at age 3 may have a reading disorder at age 8 and a writing disorder at age 14 (Mather & Goldstein, 2008; Tomblin, 2006; Lyytinen, Ekland, & Lyytinen, 2005).

Early experiences in listening and talking provide the foundation for reading and writing. Through experience with oral language, children learn the linguistic structures of language, expand their vocabularies (or semantic knowledge), and become familiar with different types of sentences (syntactic knowledge). Examples include oral language experiences of hearing stories, songs, and rhymes, and recognizing repeated refrains in books. The knowledge of sentence sequences or the formation of plurals carries over to reading and writing (Jennings, Caldwell, & Lerner, 2010; Adams Foorman, Lundberg, and Beeler, 1998).

By becoming familiar with the sounds of language, children develop a language base for reading. Poor readers often lack an awareness of the sounds of language and they will need specific practice with phonological awareness to establish the basis for word-recognition skills in reading (Adams et al., 1998; Blachman, Tagel, & Ball, 2004; Moats, 2000).

In summary, language is an integrated system, and many areas of learning depend upon mastery of language. As the child matures, language plays an increasingly important part in the development of the thinking processes and in the ability to grasp abstract concepts. Words become symbols for objects, groups of objects, and ideas. Language permits human beings to speak of things unseen, of the past, and of the future.

11.2a Forms of the Language System

The language system encompasses the language forms of listening, speaking, reading, and writing. The acquisition of these language skills follows a general sequence of development: (1) listening, (2) speaking, (3) reading, and (4) writing. As shown in Figure 11.1, the different language forms have an underlying language core that integrates the four forms of language. Moreover, experiences with each form of language strengthen the underlying language core, which in turn improves the individual's facility in other language forms.

Historically, as civilization evolved, oral language systems for listening and speaking developed hundreds of thousands of years before the creation of written systems for reading and writing. In fact, in historical terms, the written form of language is relatively recent; even today, many societies in the world have only a spoken language and no written language.

Because the oral skills of listening and speaking are developed first, they are considered the primary language system. Reading and writing are considered the secondary language system because we are dealing with a symbol of a symbol. Whereas the spoken word is a symbol of an idea or a concrete experience, the written word is a symbol of the spoken word. Helen Keller's primary language system was finger spelling because she learned it first, and Braille was her secondary system. Student Stories 11.1, "Language and Learning," illustrates Helen Keller's first experiences in language learning.

Two of the four forms of the language system can be categorized as input or *receptive language modes,* and the other 2 are output or

primary language system
The child's first language, usually oral language. In relation to bilingual students it can refer to the student's native language.

secondary language system
A student's second language, not the student's native language.

FIGURE **11.1**
Language Forms and the Integrated Language Core

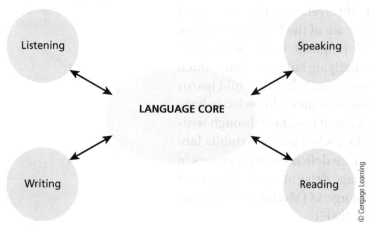

© Cengage Learning

One of the most dramatic illustrations of the dependency of thought on language is the experience of Helen Keller as she became aware that things have symbolic names that represent them. The impact of this discovery, made at age 7, changed her behavior from that of an intractable, undisciplined, animal-like child to that of a thinking, language-oriented human being.

Her teacher, Anne Sullivan, described the events (Keller, 1961):

> I made Helen hold her mug under the spout while pumped. As the cold water gushed forth, filling the mug, I spelled "w-a-t-e-r" in Helen's free hand. The word coming so close upon the sensation of cold water rushing over her hand seemed to startle her. She dropped the mug and stood as one transfixed. A new light came into her face. She spelled "water" several times. Then she dropped to the ground and asked for its name and pointed to the pump and the trellis and suddenly turning around she asked for my name. . . . All the way back to the house she was highly excited, and learned the name of every object she touched, so that in a few hours she had added 30 new words to her vocabulary (pp. 273–274).

Helen Keller also described the transformation caused by her own awareness of language:

> As the cool water gushed over one hand she spelled into the other the word *water*, first slowly, then rapidly. I stood still, my whole attention fixed upon the motion of her fingers.
>
> Suddenly I felt a misty consciousness as of something forgotten—a thrill of returning thought; and somehow the mystery of language was revealed to me. I knew then that "w-a-t-e-r" meant the wonderful, cool something that was flowing over my hand. That living word awakened my soul, gave it light, hope, joy, set it free. . . . I left the wellhouse eager to learn. Everything had a name, and each name gave birth to a new thought, (p. 34).

Helen Keller had learned that a word can be used to signify objects and to order the events, ideas, and meaning of the world about her. Language had become a tool for her to use.

REFLECTIVE QUESTION

1. For Helen, what was the importance of learning that words signify objects?

---

expressive language modes. Listening and reading are input or *receptive* skills, feeding information into the central nervous system. Speaking and writing are output or *expressive* skills in which ideas originate in the brain and are sent outward.

One implication for teaching is that abundant quantities of input experience and information are needed before output skills can be effectively executed. This principle has been concisely stated as "*intake* before *outgo.*" Students should not be assigned to produce output, such as a written theme or an oral report, before they have been exposed to adequate input experiences, such as discussions, graphic organizers, field trips, or reading. These experiences will enhance the productivity of the output. The integrating mechanism between the input and the output is the brain, or the central nervous system. Figure 11.2 shows the relationship between the four language forms.

11.2b **Language as a Communication Process**

Language provides a way for people to communicate with one another. There are also other methods of communication, such as gesturing, using body language, and using sign language. The communication process between two people consists of sending a message (*expressive language*) and receiving a message (*receptive language*). As Figure 11.3 illustrates, Person A, who is transmitting an idea to Person B, must convert her idea into language symbols.

FIGURE **11.2**
Relationship of the Four Forms
of Language

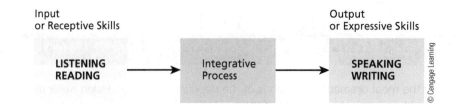

Input
or Receptive Skills

Output
or Expressive Skills

LISTENING
READING
→
Integrative
Process
→
SPEAKING
WRITING

© Cengage Learning

She encodes (or converts) the message into either sound symbols (speaking) or visual graphic symbols (writing). Person B, who receives the message, must then convert the symbols back into an idea. He decodes (converts) either the sound symbols (listening) or the visual graphic symbols (reading).

A breakdown can occur anywhere in this process. For example, in the expressive portion of the communication process, the impairment could be in formulating the idea, in coding it into spoken and written language symbols, or in remembering the sequences of previous speaking or writing. In the receptive portion of the communication process, the impairment could be in the reception and perception of the symbols through the eye or ear, in the integration of these stimuli in the brain, or in the recall or memory as it affects the ability to translate the sensory images into an idea. Understanding the communication process helps teachers deal with the communication problems of students with language disabilities.

Did You Get It?

What is the sequence of language acquisition and skill development for all children, in all societies and cultures?
   a. speaking to listening to writing to reading
   b. speaking to listening to reading to writing
   c. listening to speaking to reading to writing
   d. listening to speaking to writing to reading

FIGURE **11.3**
Model of the Communication
Process

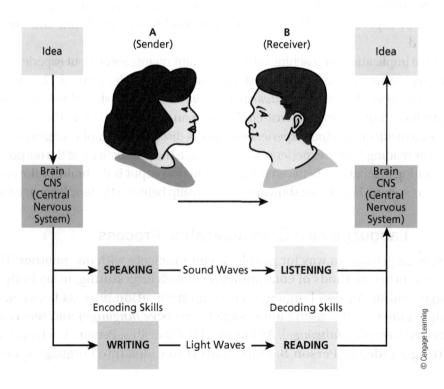

Idea

A
(Sender)

B
(Receiver)

Idea

Brain
CNS
(Central
Nervous
System)

Brain
CNS
(Central
Nervous
System)

SPEAKING — Sound Waves → LISTENING

Encoding Skills

Decoding Skills

WRITING — Light Waves → READING

© Cengage Learning

11.3 Teaching Language in the General Education Classroom

Many children in general education classrooms have problems with spoken language. Students with learning disabilities and other related disabilities often have coexisting language difficulties. General education and special education teachers can assist these students in general education classrooms. Including Students in General Education 11.1, "Teaching Language," provides some ideas for helping students with language.

11.3a How Do Children Acquire Language?

Most children acquire language before they reach school age; they understand and respond to the language of others in a meaningful way. However, up to 8% of children exhibit deviations and delays in language development and require additional time and teaching to internalize the language system (Tallal, 2000; Tallal et al., 1997). Several different views of how children learn language are (1) imitation and reinforcement (2) innate factors, and (3) social factors.

- **Imitation and reinforcement.** This is a behavioral view of language learning, which suggests that young children try to imitate the sounds they hear in their environment and they are reinforced for their language attempts. Children begin to learn language when adults reward the child for their language attempts with attention and praise. Student Stories 11.2, "Peter's First Word," describes how Peter learned his first word.
- **Innate factors.** The innate view of language learning is that the task of learning human language is so complex that some important aspects of language cannot be learned but are innate within the brain and that children are biologically predisposed to learn and use language. In all cultures, children have the ability to perform this feat in their native language at about the same chronological and developmental stage. The innate view

Including Students in GENERAL EDUCATION 11.1

Teaching Language

- Encourage students to use spoken language during the class session. Provide students with many opportunities for speaking, explaining, and giving their own points of view.

- Find areas of interest that students want to talk about. Promote discussion groups on topics of interest.

- Students can explain to classmates the steps in an activity. Have students explain how to do something or demonstrate how to make something.

- Students have many interests that they like to talk about. Provide opportunities for students to talk about themselves and their interests.

- Teach vocabulary that is related to an area of study. Have students talk about the meaning of words in a content area.

- Provide good language models. The teacher should encourage a give-and-take discussion about a topic of interest.

- Use role-playing and acting out of stories. Often areas of the curriculum provide opportunities to role play and act out stories. For example, what might a character in history say about some topic?

- Encourage students to talk about their interests, such as movies, television shows, books, sports, music, or hobbies.

Professional Resource Download

Peter's mother was worried about her 22-month-old son who was not, as yet, saying words.

During a Thanksgiving dinner, Peter was sitting in a high chair at the family gathering of about 25 people. When Peter gestured that he wanted to get up, his mother said the word *up,* and Peter tried to imitate the sound. When Peter attempted to utter the sound, the group decided to encourage his vocalizations, so all 25 people stood up and in unison said "up." Peter looked around and was delighted with the response he had generated. He uttered the sound "up" again and again, each time eliciting the same response from the group. By the end of the Thanksgiving meal, Peter had learned his first word, "up."

REFLECTIVE QUESTION

1. How did positive reinforcement help Peter learn his first word?

suggests that in learning language, the child does not merely learn a set of sentences, but rather internalizes the total language system (Tomasello, 2003; Chomsky, 1965). In terms of teaching, the innate view implies that a child's language will naturally develop and flourish if the child is given a stimulating language environment.

- **Social factors.** Another perspective of the way in which children acquire language is through social interactions within interpersonal relationships with more knowledgeable language users. The reciprocal interactions between the child and the parent and between the child and other people are essential for language learning. The acquisition of language is promoted in a natural environment where human relationships help the child become an active processor of language (Vygotsky, 1997).

In terms of teaching, the social factors involved in language learning are emphasized as the child and adult develop a reciprocal relationship, influencing each other in the communication process. In terms of teaching, the adult plays a mediating role, shaping learning opportunities to bring them to the attention of the young child. For example, 18-month-old Sarah knew the word *plane* and the phrase *all gone.* While Sarah was sitting at the kitchen table with her mother, an airplane flew over the house. Her mother, initiating a conversation, pointed up questioningly as the plane flew overhead, and Sarah said, "Plane." When the noise disappeared, her mother continued the conversation, asking, "What happened?" Sarah replied, "Plane all gone," along with a gesture of extended hands to show "all gone." With her mother's guidance, Sarah produced her first sentence.

Did You Get It?

Having _____ would not be considered an effective way to teach and/or promote spoken language in a general education classroom.
- **a.** a student explain the steps needed to hang a picture on a wall
- **b.** a student tell the class what she did over the weekend
- **c.** a student speak about his favorite topic and refraining from giving his own opinions and views
- **d.** two students act out the words to a song they know as they sing

11.4 Components of the Language System

Basic linguistic concepts and terms comprise the components of language. They include (1) phonology, (2) morphology, (3) syntax, (4) semantics, and (5) pragmatics. In this section, we discuss each of these language components and how they affect language learning and language difficulties.

components of language
The language system includes phonology, morphology, syntax, semantics, and pragmatics.

11.4a Phonology

Phonology refers to the speech sounds in a language. The smallest unit of sound in a language system is a phoneme. Different languages and dialects use different phonemes. The word *cat* contains three phonemes: *k-a-t*. Phoneme recognition is extremely important in oral language and reading. Phonics is the recognition, analysis, and synthesis of phoneme elements in written words. Learning phonics is difficult for some children because they have poor phonological awareness or recognition of phoneme sounds.

phonology
The linguistic system of speech sounds in a particular language. The word *cat*, for example, has three sounds (or phonemes).

phoneme
The smallest sound unit of a language system.

phonics
An application of phonetics to the teaching of reading in which the sound (or phoneme) of a language is related to the equivalent written symbol (or grapheme).

11.4b Morphology

Morphology refers to the meaning units in language. The smallest unit of meaning is a morpheme. Different languages indicate meaning changes through different morphological forms. For example, in Standard English, the word *boy* is one morpheme or meaning unit; and the word *boys* contains two morphemes or meaning units (*boy* plus plurality). A child who has not internalized the morphemic structure of Standard English—for example, a student whose native language is Spanish—might say, "There are three boy."

Children who are unaware of exceptions to morphemic rule may overgeneralize. For example, they might formulate the past tense *of fight* and *go* as *fighted* and *goed*. Typical preschool and first-grade children have well-established rules of morphology and can apply their morphological rules to nonsense words. For example, researcher Berko (1958) showed each child a drawing of a birdlike creature and said, "This is a *wug*." Next, she pointed to a drawing with two of these creatures and asked each child to complete the sentence, "There are two _____." By applying the morphological rule for plurals, typical children were able to give the answer of *wugs* by adding the phoneme /z/.

morphology
The linguistic system of meaning units in any particular language; for example, the word *played* contains two meaning units (or morphemes): play + ed (past tense).

morpheme
The smallest meaning unit of a language system.

Standard English
The linguistic system of English recognized by the literate culture and used in school.

11.4c Syntax

Syntax is the grammar system of a language—the way the words are strung together to form sentences. Different languages have different syntactic or grammatical systems. In the English language, unlike some other languages, word order is extremely important to convey meaning. Thus, "John pushes a car" differs in meaning from "A car pushes John." A child with a syntactic language disorder may not have learned how to order words in a sentence. Further, in English, we can transform the order of the words—still keeping the same subject—to generate a new meaning. The sentence "Mother is working" can be transformed to generate "Is Mother working?" A child with a syntactic language difficulty may be unable to generate such sentence transformations. For example, when children with language disorders are asked to repeat the question form of "Is the boy running?" many simply repeat the simple declarative form "The boy is running."

The active form of a sentence—"Mother bakes cookies"—is easier to comprehend than the passive form, "The cookies are baked by Mother." Children

syntax
The grammar system of a language; the linguistic rules of word order; the function of words in a sentence.

with language disabilities may not understand a passive sentence. To illustrate, when first graders are shown two pictures, one of a cat chasing a dog and the other of a dog chasing a cat, and are asked to point to the picture called "The cat is chased by the dog," many children choose the incorrect picture because they do not understand the passive form of the sentence.

11.4d Semantics

semantics
A linguistic term referring to the vocabulary system of language.

Semantics refers to the vocabulary system or word meanings in a language. Pupils who have meager vocabulary understanding or usage and those who have difficulty relating a string of words to a meaningful association may have a semantic language disorder. While morphology, phonology, and syntax components normally become firmly established during the preschool years, the development of vocabulary (the semantic component) continues throughout life.

A student with a semantic disorder may understand a concept but may not possess the appropriate word to express it. For example, referring to twins, one boy with language problems talked about the "two girls with the same face." He did not know the word *twin* to communicate his idea.

11.4e Pragmatics

pragmatics
The social side of language; the social context and social customs surrounding language.

Pragmatics refers to the social side of language, how the speaker uses language in his or her environment. Pragmatics takes into account factors such as the relationship between speaker and listener; the speaker's assessment of the listener's degree of knowledge about the subject; behaviors, such as taking turns in conversation, staying on topic, and asking pertinent questions; the individual's involvement in the conversation; and eye contact. Some students have more difficulty in the social use of language and are less effective in their communication attempts. They may interrupt the speaker more frequently in order to insert their own ideas in the conversation (Orlich et al., 2013; Wong and Donahue, 2002).

Another element of the language system is *intonation,* or the sound patterns of spoken language, including *pitch* (melody), *stress* (accent), and *juncture* (pauses). The intonation system of each language is different.

When listening to the intonation pattern of infants, one cannot distinguish the babbling of a 3-month-old Chinese baby from that of a Dutch or an American baby of the same age. By the age of 6 months, however, the intonation of the babbling is similar to the intonation of the language in the infant's immediate environment; the babbling is in Chinese, Dutch, or English. The "native language" of a 6-month-old baby can be identified through tape recordings of the baby's babbling. The baby's babble consists of the intonation patterns and the phonemes of the native language.

Did You Get It?

According to the _____ view of language acquisition and development, language is such a complex undertaking that specific aspects of language must be preprogrammed in the brain rather than being learned.
   a. innate
   b. wired
   c. naturalistic
   d. extrinsic

11.5 Types of Language Problems

Many children with learning disabilities and related mild disabilities have speech and/or language difficulties. They do not do well in situations that require extensive language interactions and conversations, and they are also less skillful in maintaining a conversation. About 88% of preschool children (ages 3 through 5) who receive special education services are classified with speech or language impairment (U.S. Department of Education, 2012). In addition, speech and/or language disorders are a common co-occurring condition for older students with disabilities. Adolescents and adults with learning disabilities often continue to have poor oral language and communication skills (Vogel & Reder, 1998).

In this section, we discuss (1) language disorders versus speech disorders, (2) delayed speech, (3) problems with phonological awareness, (4) temporal acoustical processing, (5) rapid automatized naming and word finding, and (6) language disorders. The National Dissemination Center for Children with Disabilities, a website that describes spoken language problems, can be found at *http://www.nichcy.org*.

11.5a Language Disorders Versus Speech Disorders

Language disorders differ from speech disorders. Speech disorders are abnormalities of producing sounds, such as (1) articulation difficulties (e.g., the child who cannot produce the *r* sound and says "wabbit"), (2) voice disorders (e.g., a very hoarse voice), or (3) fluency difficulty (e.g., stuttering). Language disorders are much broader and encompass the entire spectrum of communication. Types of language disorders are described in the following sections.

speech disorders
Disorders of articulation, fluency, or voice.

language disorders
The term that refers to children with a language delay or language disabilities.

11.5b Delayed Speech

Children with a language delay may not speak at all, or they may use very little language at an age when language normally develops. For example, the 4-year-old child who has not yet learned to talk has a language delay. At least 8% of children fail to develop speech and language at or near the expected age (Tallal, 2000; Tallal et al., 1997). Examples of a speech delay can be found in Student Stories 11.3, "Marsha: A Child With a Language Delay" and in "I Have a Kid Who..." at the end of this chapter.

Otitis media is a relatively common childhood condition that can seriously impair language learning in children. Otitis media involves an infection of the middle ear that can cause temporary hearing loss. Even if the hearing loss is temporary and mild, it can lead to language delay if it occurs at stages that are critical to language learning in young children.

language delay
Slowness in the acquisition of language. The child with a language delay may not be talking at all or may be using very little language at an age when language normally develops.

otitis media
Middle-ear infection that may cause temporary hearing loss and may impede language development.

11.5c Poor Phonological Awareness

Phonological awareness refers to the child's ability to focus on and manipulate phonemes (or the sounds of language) in spoken words. As noted earlier, phonemes are abstract units of language, the smallest units constituting spoken language. Learning to reflect about the phoneme sounds of language is different from learning to understand and use language. Many children who have difficulty in learning to read are not sensitive to the phoneme sounds of language

Marsha is 4 years old and has a language delay.

Marsha's early development was typical in terms of motor development. She walked at 11 months old, she learned to ride her tricycle early, and she enjoys playing with her dolls, blocks, and puzzles. Marsha's language development, however, has been very slow. She did not use single words until age 3. Her speech now consists of one- or two-word phrases. Marsha understands the speech of others, she can follow directions that are given to her, and her receptive language is good—she understands the language of others. Her parents enrolled her in the school's special early childhood program. The speech/language therapist, the preschool teacher, and her parents are collaborating using a technique called *naturalistic language teaching*. When Marsha says, "Go" and points to the door, her teacher expands her language by asking, "Go out now?" Marsha repeats the expanded phrase, saying, "Go out now."

REFLECTIVE QUESTION

1. What kind of language problem does Marsha have? What strengths does Marsha have?

and words (Blachman, Tangel, & Ball, 2004; Mann & Foy, 2003; Lyon, Shaywitz, & Shaywitz, 2003). Table 11.1 illustrates the number of phonemes in several common words.

Successful beginning readers must be aware of phoneme sounds within words to appreciate that the words *cat* and *bat* differ in a single phoneme sound. Children with poor phonological abilities are unable to tap out the number of sounds within a word, such as *mop.* As children become aware of the phonological system, they can gain entry into the alphabetic system, in which letters of the alphabet represent speech sounds. Written English is an alphabetic system. Research shows that there is a link between the lack of phonological awareness and poor reading in alphabetic languages, such as English, Swedish, Spanish, French, Italian, Portuguese, and others (Lundberg, 2002). (Some written languages, such as Chinese, are pictorial—the printed characters reflect ideas, not sounds.)

The National Reading Panel is a research group that was established by the National Institute of Child Health and Human Development to assess the status of research-based knowledge on the effectiveness of teaching children to read. The website for the National Reading Panel report is *http://www .nationalreadingpanel.org.*

TABLE 11.1

Number of Phonemes in Several Common Words

Word	Number of Phonemes
Oh	one
Go	two
Check	three
Stop	four
Checkers	five
Shaque	three

© Cengage Learning

TABLE 11.2

Phonological Awareness Tasks

Task*	Activity
1. Phoneme segmentation	How many phonemes are in the word *ship?*
2. Phoneme isolation	Tell me the first sound in *paste.*
3. Phoneme blending	What word is *s/k/u/i?*
4. Phoneme identity	Tell me the sound that is the same in *bike, boy, bell.*
5. Phoneme categorization	Which word does not belong: *bus, bun, rat?*
6. Rhyming	Did you ever see a fly kissing a *tie?*
7. Phoneme deletion	Say *smile* without the s.

*Listed from the easiest to the most difficult.

© Cengage Learning

After an exhaustive search of over 100,000 research-based studies, the National Reading Panel (2000) reached the following conclusions about phonological awareness. Phonological awareness

- can be taught and helps in reading,
- is effective in kindergarten and first grade,
- helps older students, all socioeconomic status (SES) groups, and bilingual students,
- can be successfully taught by many different methods,
- is usually used for an average instructional session of 25 minutes,
- can be taught by classroom teachers, and
- can be used along with printed letters.

Table 11.2 shows examples of several phonological awareness tasks that teachers can use in instruction (Adams et al., 1998; Blachman et al., 2004; Coyne, Kame'enui, & Simmons, 2001). An informal test of phonological awareness is provided in Table 11.3.

For formal tests of phonological awareness, see Table 11.4.

11.5d Temporal Acoustical Processing

Temporal acoustical processing offers an explanation for why some children do not develop speech and language at or near the expected ages. Some children find it difficult to process sounds quickly enough to distinguish rapid acoustical change in speech. During the course of normal language, the speech sounds come in too fast for these children to recognize and decipher. A series of studies conducted by Paula Tallal and her colleagues over many years suggests that children who have delays in speech and language development may have difficulty with rapid temporal integration of acoustically varying signals and serial memory. These deficits impact central auditory processing in the millisecond time range (Hall et al., 2002; Tallal, 2000; Tallal et al., 1997).

temporal acoustical processing
The ability to process sounds of language rapidly enough to distinguish speech sounds and words.

11.5e Rapid Automatized Naming (RAN) and Word Finding

Some children with a language delay have difficulty with rapid automatized naming (RAN) and word finding . These children cannot quickly and automatically name objects and are slow at recalling the correct words. For example, when given the task of naming pictures as they are shown, these children cannot

rapid automatized naming (RAN)
The ability to quickly and automatically name objects and pictures of objects.

word finding
Recalling the correct words.

TABLE 11.3

Informal Test of Phonological Awareness

Give the child two demonstration items to help the child understand that task. For example, say the word *playground*. Then ask the child to say the word. Then ask the child to say the word again, but not to say *play*.

Then give the child the word *snowflake*. Then ask the child to say the word. Then ask the child to say the word again, but not to say *snow*. Then give the child the following test.

Item	Question	Correct Response
1. Say the word *toolbox*	Now say it again but do not say /box/	tool
2. Say the word *compute*	Now say it again but do not say /com/	pute
3. Say the word *telephone*	Now say it again but do not say /tele/	fone
4. Say the word *surface*	Now say it again but do not say /sur/	face
5. Say the word *boat*	Now say it again but do not say /b/	oat
6. Say the word *feet*	Now say it again but do not say / f/	eat
7. Say the word *make*	Now say it again but do not say / m/	ache
8. Say the word *start*	Now say it again but do not say / s/	tart
9. Say the word *please*	Now say it again but do not say /p/	lease
10. Say the word *clean*	Now say it again but do not say /k/	lean
11. Say the word *sting*	Now say it again but do not *say /t/*	sing
12. Say the word *play*	Now say it again but do not say (l)	pay
13. Say the word *stock*	Now say it again but do not say /t/	sock

Scoring: Give one point for each correct answer.

Score	Expected Level
1–3	kindergarten
4–9	Grade 1
10–11	Grade 2
12–13	Grade 3

© Cengage Learning 2015

rapidly say the names of the pictures. Slowness in word finding and naming is an accurate predictor of later reading and learning disabilities. Slowness in naming is probably caused by memory retrieval problems, which make it difficult to access verbal information (Dejong & Vrielink, 2004; Catts, 1993; German, 2001).

Problems with naming and slow word retrieval affect adolescents and adults with learning disabilities and related mild disabilities, as well as children. Word-finding problems can be lifelong sources of difficulty in reading, learning, and using expressive language.

There are various resources that address word-finding problems. In a study published in 1998, Meyer and colleagues described useful instructional methods for dealing with word-finding problems in children. Word-finding strategies for adults can be found in the book *It's on the Tip of My Tongue* by Diane German (2001). The Word Finding Intervention Program (German, 1993) is a word-finding teaching program for children. Additional information is available at the Word Finding website at *http://www.wordfinding.com*. (See Table 11.4.)

11.5f Language Disorders

Language disorders are sometimes referred to as *acquired aphasia* or *developmental aphasia*. The term *acquired aphasia* is a medical term used to identify adults who lose the ability to speak because of brain damage from a stroke, disease, or accident. In contrast, the term developmental aphasia is used to describe children who have severe difficulty in acquiring oral language (Kuder, 2003). Children can have difficulty with (1) receptive language disorders or (2) expressive language disorders.

Receptive language disorders refers to difficulty in understanding language. Receptive language is a prerequisite for the development of expressive language. A child with receptive language problems may be able to understand single words, such as *sit, chair, eat,* and *candy,* but will have difficulty understanding a sentence using those words, such as "Sit on the chair after you eat the candy." Some children understand a word in one context, but they are unable to relate it to another context. The word *run* may be understood as a method of locomotion, but the child may not understand the meaning when the word is used in reference to baseball, a faucet, a woman's stocking, or a river.

Expressive language disorders refers to difficulty in producing spoken language. Children with expressive language disorders may depend on pointing and gesturing to make their wants known. These children can understand speech and language produced by others, they do not have a muscular paralysis that prevents them from talking, and they do well on nonverbal tasks. Yet these children have difficulty in producing speech or in talking.

Several clinical conditions are related to expressive language. One such condition is dysnomia, a word-finding problem or a deficiency in remembering and expressing words. Children with dysnomia may substitute a word, such as *thing,* for every object they cannot remember, or they may attempt to use other expressions to talk around the subject. For example, when asked to list the foods she ate for lunch, one 10-year-old girl used circumlocution in describing a tomato as a "round red thing that rhymed with potato," but she was unable to remember the word *tomato.*

developmental aphasia
The term used to describe a child who has severe difficulty in acquiring oral language. This term implies that the disorder is related to a central nervous system dysfunction.

receptive language disorders
Difficulty understanding oral language or listening.

expressive language disorders
Difficulties in using language (or speaking).

dysnomia
A deficiency in remembering and expressing words. Children with dysnomia may substitute a word like *thing* for many objects when they cannot remember the name of the object. They may attempt to use other expressions to talk around the subject.

Did You Get It?

According to the U.S. Department of Education (2012), approximately _____ in ten of all preschool-aged children who are receiving special education services have at least some form of speech impairment.
- **a.** 2
- **b.** 4
- **c.** 7
- **d.** 9

11.6 English-Language Learners (ELL)

English-language learners (ELLs) are students for whom English is not their primary language. ELL students are not proficient in English, and they use their native language. They encounter many difficulties in classes taught entirely in English. In today's diverse society, an increasing number of students come from homes in which a language other than English is spoken. In fact, ELL students

ELL

represent one of the fastest growing groups among the school-age population (Samson & Lesaux, 2009). ELL students speak over 350 different languages, but Spanish is the language spoken by nearly 77% of ELL students, or approximately 3 million students (Samson & Lesaux, 2009).

These children are sometimes referred to as bilingual students, but children who are truly *bilingual* understand and use 2 languages well, both their native language and their second language. In fact, research shows that true bilingual abilities are associated with a higher level of cognitive attainment. Bilingual acquisition involves a process that builds on an underlying base for both languages. The duality of languages does not hamper overall language proficiency or cognitive development for bilingual children (Miller, Heilmann, & Nockerts, 2006; Hakuta, 1990; Jiménez, 2002).

The problem for many ELLs is that they have limited English proficiency and they have difficulty understanding and using English. Some ELL students speak only in their native language; others use both English and their native language but still have considerable difficulty with English. A child's native language provides the foundation upon which English-language skills are built. Students who use their native language effectively are likely to acquire and use English appropriately, but students who have problems in their native language also experience problems in English as a second language (Miller et al., 2006; Lundberg, 2002). Research shows that a student may acquire conversational English in six months but may not have the language proficiency to support the complex demands of academic development in English. Reaching that proficiency level may take up to two years or more (Jiménez, 2002; Ortiz, 1997).

Some students who are ELLs also have learning disabilities or related disabilities. These students must cope not only with learning English, but also with their underlying disabilities. When students have a language disorder in their primary language, the language problem will also be reflected in the second language (Samson & Lesaux, 2009; Miller et al., 2006).

Teachers must be particularly sensitive to the needs of English-language learners and recognize that achieving proficiency in English requires time. These teachers need competencies in both special education and in teaching students with limited English proficiency. Teaching Tips 11.1, "Effective Practices for Supporting English-Language Learners," provides some suggestions for ELLs who have learning disabilities.

11.6a Learning a Second Language

There are four methods for teaching a second language: *ESL, bilingual, sheltered English,* and *immersion* methods.

▶❚❚ TeachSource Video Case Activity

© Cengage Learning 2015

Watch the TeachSource Video Case entitled "Culturally Responsive Teaching: A Multicultural Lesson for Elementary Students." In this video, the teacher leads the class in talking about their diverse multicultural backgrounds. They talk about the countries they came from, the food in their culture, the people, and the language they spoke in their country. The multicultural discussion is then woven into a writing lesson on coming to America.

QUESTIONS

1. How can a discussion about multicultural backgrounds of children in the class be used to teach language skills?

2. What subjects could students from diverse cultures talk about?

- The English as a Second Language (ESL) method is used in classes that have students who come from many different language backgrounds. Students learn through carefully controlled oral repetitions of selected second-language patterns.

- Bilingual instruction is used when all of the students are from one language background. Students use their native language for part of the school day and use the second language (English) for the other portion of the school day. Instruction is provided in 2 languages. Academic subjects are often taught in the native language and the student receives oral practice in English. The objective of the bilingual program is to strengthen school learning through the native language and gradually to add the secondary language. An underlying philosophy is that students will recognize and respect the importance of their native culture and language in American society.

- Sheltered English is a method of teaching children who have some proficiency in English by having students learn English more rapidly through instruction with printed materials that are written in English, typically used for a content-area subject. The rationale for this approach is that spoken language is fleeting and inconsistent over time. In written language, the text is stable and does not pass the learner by. With written text, students can reread and reconsider what is being learned. For children whose native language is Spanish, the students continue to use Spanish for part of the day, while English is used in teaching certain subjects with written materials, such as reading or social studies. Wide reading of high-interest stories in English helps develop English-language competence.

- Immersion instruction is a method in which students are *immersed* in, or receive extensive exposure to, the second language. In fact, where there is no formal instruction for a person learning a second language, this is essentially what occurs. Individuals learn through this type of repeated exposure as they live daily in the mainstream of the dominant-language society. Immersion is the instructional method for schoolchildren in Canada, where it is used to teach French to English-speaking children by enrolling them in French-speaking immersion schools (Fortin & Crago, 1999).

TEACHING TIPS 11.1 ELL

Effective Practices for Supporting English-Language Learners

- Be responsive to cultural and individual diversity.
- Teach English-language reading to develop English-language competence.
- Become familiar with assessment tools, and acceptable accommodations.
- Encourage collaboration between home and school.
- Develop cooperation between general educators and special education teachers.

Professional Resource Download

English as a Second Language (ESL) method
A method of teaching English to students whose native language is not English.

bilingual instruction
A teaching approach in which students use their native language for one part of the instructional day and English for the other part of the instructional day.

sheltered English
A method of teaching children who have some proficiency in English to learn English more rapidly by having them use materials written in English.

immersion instruction
An approach to teaching a second language in which students receive extensive exposure to a second language.

11.6b Disproportionality

The disproportionate representation of English-language learners has long been a concern in discussions of educational equity. The issue is that culturally and linguistically diverse students are disproportionately enrolled in special education. Research shows that ELL students have a greater chance of being identified as a student with a disability, often within the category of learning disabilities (De Valenzuela, Copeland, Huaqing, & Park, 2006). To form a more just and equitable society for all students, it is important for the educational system to correct the inequities of ELL students.

 ELL

Did You Get It?

Three students whose primary languages are Spanish, Vietnamese, and Igbo, respectively, and who now live and learn in the United States are _____ students.
  a. ELL
  b. ELF
  c. LEFL
  d. SLE

11.7 Early Literacy and Oral Language

early literacy
The child's early entrance into the world of words, language, and stories. Literacy emerges in children through simultaneous experiences with oral language, reading, and writing.

Early literacy refers to the child's early entrance into the comprehensive world of words, language, books, poetry, and stories. The importance of providing young children with a rich literary environment and helping children become aware of print, words, and the sounds of language is essential to the world of language. The early literacy philosophy encourages young children to enjoy experiences with stories and books, and it encourages early writing (Strickland & Shanaham, 2004). It is especially important that children with learning disabilities and related mild disabilities be given an abundant and rich literature environment. From an early age, they should hear stories, tell stories, and even write journals and stories. Story reading helps build oral language experiences. Predictable books that have a pattern or refrain should be used and children should be encouraged to repeat the predictable elements. It is also important to read and reread favorite stories and have the children listen to them on CDs or tapes while following along in their books. Teaching Tips 11.2, "Activities to Promote Early Literacy," describes methods that foster early literacy.

TEACHING **TIPS 11.2**

Activities to Promote Early Literacy

- **Promote Oral Language Activities.** Give children many opportunities to talk and use language.

- **Surround children with a Literacy Environment.** Have many books, stories and poems for the child and discuss them.

- **Concepts about print.** Show the children that print has meaning, that it is read left to right, top to bottom, and that words are separated by white spaces.

- **Use word and sound games.** Teach rhyming games. Use nursery rhymes, poetry.

- **Build alphabet knowledge.** Help children to recognize letters of the alphabet. Have children write letters of the alphabet.

- **Help children to recognize letter-sound correspondence.** Help children know the relationship between letters and sounds.

- **Encourage early writing.** Have writing materials available. Let children scribble, draw pictures, or write letters.

- **Help children build a reading vocabulary.** Compile a collection of their favorite words.

Professional Resource Download

Did You Get It?

The early literacy philosophy stresses which aspect of the use of stories and books?

a. lenience

b. stringency

c. rigor

d. enjoyment

11.8 Assessing Oral Language

The purpose of assessing oral language is to determine what language abilities the child has acquired, what language problems the child exhibits, and how well the child uses language functionally. Assessment information should be a guide in planning the teaching. Assessment should consider the two sides of oral language: listening and speaking. Language assessment measures include (1) informal measures and (2) formal tests.

11.8a Informal Measures

Often the most valuable information is obtained by observing as the child uses language functionally in a real environment, such as a class or recreational setting. When rating scales are used in assessment, an informant (usually a parent) provides information about the child's language development and usage. Informal assessment measures are not standardized but offer valuable information about the child's language ability.

An informal measure of listening can be obtained by assessing the child's ability to understand a story that the teacher reads aloud. This listening test is often used as part of an informal reading inventory (IRI) (see Chapter 12, "Reading Difficulties"). The procedure requires the teacher to read aloud stories that are graded for difficulty level. Then the child is asked comprehension questions to determine how well he or she understands this material (Jennings et al., 2010; Spinelli, 2006).

Early literacy refers to the child's entrance into the world of words.

Robert Berner/Photo Edit Inc.

11.8b Formal Tests

Formal tests are standardized instruments for gathering information about oral language development. Formal test results are often included in the child's individualized education program (IEP). Table 11.4 lists some examples of formal language tests.

TABLE 11.4

Oral Language Tests

Test	Age or Grade Tested	Publisher
General Oral Language Tests		
• Clinical Evaluation of Language Fundamentals—Revised (CELF-R)	Grades K–12	Harcourt Brace *http://www.harcourt.com*
• Detroit Tests of Learning Aptitude—4 (DTLA-4)	Ages 6–17	Pro-Ed *http://www.proedinc.com*
• Oral and Written Language Scales (OWLS)	Ages 3–21	AGS *http://pearsonassessments.com*
• Test of Adolescent Language—3 (TOAL-3)	Ages 12–18	Pro-Ed *http://www.proedinc.com*
• Test of Language Development—3: Intermediate (TOLD-3: Intermediate)	Ages 8.5–12.1	Pro-Ed *http://www.proedinc.com*
• Test of Language Development—3 (TOLD-3: Primary)	Ages 8–11	Pro-Ed *http://www.proedinc.com*
Listening Tests		
• Listening Comprehension Scales—Oral, Written, and Language Scales (OWLS)	Ages 5–21	AGS *http://www.pearsonassessments.com*
• Peabody Picture Vocabulary Test—II	Ages 2–18	AGS *http://www.pearsonassessments.com*
• Test de Vocabulario en Images Peabody (Spanish version of the Peabody Picture Vocabulary Test—III)	Ages 2.5–18	AGS *http://www.pearsonassessments.com*
Phonological Awareness Tests		
• Comprehensive Test of Phonological Processing	Ages 5–21	Pro-Ed *http://www.proedinc.com*
• Lindamood Auditory Conceptualization Test	Preschool–adult	Riverside *http://www.riverpub.com*
• Phonological Awareness Test	Ages 5–9	http://
• Test of Phonological Awareness	Grades K–2	Pro-Ed *http://www.proedinc.com*
Word-Finding Tests		
• Test of Word Finding—2	Ages 6.5–13	Pro-Ed *http://www.proedinc.com*
• Test of Adolescent and Adult Word Finding	Ages 12–80	Riverside *http://www.riverpub.com*

© Cengage Learning

Did You Get It?

The Peabody Picture Vocabulary Test—II is an assessment battery that tests and evaluates abilities in which context?
a. writing
b. listening
c. reading
d. memorization

11.9 Teaching Strategies to Improve Spoken Language Difficulties

In this section, we focus on strategies for listening and speaking. Oral language has two contrasting sides: understanding oral language (listening) and producing oral language (speaking).

> **Did You Get It?**
>
> Oral language has two distinct and contrasting components. One of these components, the understanding of oral language, focuses on
>
> **a.** listening.
> **b.** interpreting.
> **c.** processing.
> **d.** filtering.

11.10 Listening

Listening is an often-neglected element of language learning. Students are typically expected to acquire the ability to listen without special instruction. However, many students do not acquire functional skills in listening by themselves. Over half the people referred to medical hearing specialists for suspected deafness have no defect in hearing acuity and no organic pathology that would cause their seeming hearing impairment. In this section, we suggest some strategies for listening in the areas of (1) listening comprehension, (2) phonological awareness of language sounds, (3) understanding words and building a listening vocabulary, (4) understanding sentences, (5) listening comprehension, (6) critical listening, and (7) listening to stories.

11.10a Listening Means Comprehension

Listening is a basic skill that can be improved through practice. An explanation for poor listening is that students today are so bombarded with constant sound that they learn to "tune out." Students who are skillful at not listening should be taught to "tune in."

Listening differs from hearing, which is a physiological process that does not involve interpretation. One can *hear* a foreign language with good auditory acuity but be unable to *listen* to what is being said. In contrast to hearing, listening demands that one select appropriate meanings and organize ideas according to their relationships. In addition, listening calls for evaluation, acceptance or rejection, internalization, and, at times, appreciation of the ideas expressed. Listening is the foundation of all language growth, and the child with a deficit in listening skills will have difficulty with all the communication skills.

There are significant differences between listening and reading. The reader can reread and study the material, but the listener hears the material only once and then it is gone. (Of course, using a recording device modifies this difference.) Readers can regulate their own speed, going slower or faster as their purpose and the difficulty of the material dictate, but the listener's speed of listening is set by the speaker. The listener has additional clues from the speaker's voice, gesture, appearance, and emphasis, but the reader cannot derive such supporting information from the printed page. The listener–speaker combination also offers more opportunity for feedback, questioning, and a two-way discussion than reading offers.

When teachers ask students to *listen,* they do not want them simply to *hear* or to recognize the words being spoken. Students who are directed to listen are expected to comprehend the communication message being sent.

Teaching strategies for each of the following listening skills are described in the next sections.

- Phonological awareness of language sounds
- Understanding words and building a listening vocabulary
- Understanding sentences
- Listening comprehension
- Critical listening
- Listening to stories

11.10b Phonological Awareness of Language Sounds

Precursors for learning to read include recognizing phonemes, which are the sounds of our language. To be successful during the beginning stages of reading, children must hear individual phoneme sounds of the language and be aware that the words they are hearing are composed of individual sounds. Abilities in phoneme awareness prepare children for learning phonics.

1. **Nonsense.** Have children listen to and detect the slight change in the name of a familiar story or poem, such as "Baa, Baa, Purple Sheep" or "Twinkle, Twinkle, Little Car."
2. **Clapping names.** Ask children to clap out syllables in names and words. For example, clap "Jenn-if-er" (three claps) or "Zip-pi-ty-doo-dah" (five claps).
3. **Finding things: Initial phonemes.** Use real objects or pictures of objects. Say the name of the object and ask children which picture or object begins with the same sound. For example, the initial consonant *m* may be presented with *milk, money, moon, man,* and *monkey.*
4. **Take away a sound.** Have children say their names or a word without the initial sound. For example, say, "_____enjamin." Children in the group must identify the whole word.
5. **Troll talk: Blending games.** The troll talks funny, saying the sounds of words separately. The children must guess the word by blending the sounds. For example, the troll utters the phonemes "ch-ee-z," "p-e-n," "f-u-n," or "What is your n-a-m?" The children blend the sounds and identify the word.
6. **Nursery rhymes.** Read nursery rhymes or Dr. Seuss books to children. Look at the pictures and emphasize the rhyming elements. Children enjoy the many repetitions of nursery rhymes. Occasionally leave off the word that is the rhyming element and have the child say the word: "Jack and Jill went up the _____."
7. **Using visual cues to segment speech sounds.** To help children recognize the speech sounds in words, put a picture representing a short word on a card. Draw a rectangle underneath the picture and divide it into the number of phonemes in the word. Have the child say the word slowly, putting a counter in each square as each sound is articulated. Figure 11.4

FIGURE **11.4**
A Segmenting Card for
Speech Sounds

© Cengage Learning

Professional Resource Download

illustrates a segmenting card for the word *sun.* To use a segmenting card, obtain counters such as buttons or pennies. Place a picture with a short word on a card. Use words with the same number of letters as sounds (e.g., *cap, run,* and *lamp*). For sound counting, say the word slowly and have the child put down a counter for each sound. One set of cards can have both pictures and words, and another can have only the pictures (Blachman, 1997; Blachman et al., 2004).

8. **Rhyming riddles and games.** The teacher selects a group of words, one to rhyme with *head* and the other to rhyme with *feet.* Then the teacher asks a riddle so that the answer rhymes with either *head* or *feet.* The children then point to the part of their body that has a name that rhymes with *head* or *feet* to answer the riddle. For example, "When you are hungry, you want to _____." The children point to their *feet* because *eat* rhymes with it. Repeat by naming other parts of the body to elicit words that rhyme with *hand* or *knee* or with *arm* or *leg* (Jennings, Caldwell, & Lerner, 2010). Make up riddle rhymes and encourage students to make up others. One such example is, "I rhyme with *look.* You read me. What am I?" Have students listen to a series of three words, such as *ball, sit,* and *wall* or *hit, pie,* and *tie,* and tell which two words rhyme.

9. **Deleting sounds.** In this activity, children learn to take a word apart, remove one sound, and pronounce the word without that sound. For example, to remove a syllable: "Say *playground.* Now say it without *play.*" It is more difficult to remove a phoneme: "Say *ball.* Now say it without the *b.*" "Say *stack.* Now say it without the *t.*"

10. **Beginning sounds.** Give three words like *astronaut, mountain,* and *bicycle.* Have the students tell which word begins like *milk.* Ask the children to think of words that begin like *Tom,* to find pictures of words that begin like *Tom,* or to find pictures of words that begin with the sound *T.* Show them three pictures of different objects (for example, a pear, a table, and a car) and ask the students to select the picture of an object with a name that begins like *Tom.*

11. **Beating out names.** Beat the syllables in the rhythm and accent of names of the children in the group. For example, for a name like *Marilyn McPhergeson,* you might beat out the following pattern:

Drumbeat: LOUD-soft-soft   soft-LOUD-soft-soft
         1   2   3   4   1   2   3

12. **Consonant-blend bingo.** Make bingo cards with consonant blends and consonant digraphs in the squares. Read words and ask the students to cover the blend that begins each word.

13. **Substitutions.** Help the students learn to substitute one initial sound for another to make a new word. For example: "Take the end of the word *book* and put in the beginning of the word *hand,* and get something you hang coats on." (The word would be *hook.*)

11.10c Building a Listening Vocabulary

Listening requires that students acquire a listening vocabulary. Students must understand the names of objects, actions, qualities, and more abstract concepts. It is easier to teach words that carry primary lexical meaning (such as nouns, verbs, adjectives, and adverbs) than to teach structure or function words (such as prepositions and articles) that indicate relationships within sentences.

1. **Names of objects.** To help students understand names, use actual objects, such as a ball, pencil, or doll. Sometimes you will have to add exaggeration and gestures to help the student with a severe receptive disorder understand the meaning of the word that symbolizes the object.

2. **Verb meanings.** It is more difficult to teach the concept of a verb than the name of an object. You can illustrate verbs such as *hop, sit,* and *walk* by performing the activity.

3. **Pictures.** Pictures are useful in reinforcing and reviewing the vocabulary that has been taught. Short clips from television shows or DVDs can also be utilized to reinforce vocabulary.

4. **Concepts of attributes.** Words that describe the attributes of objects can be taught by providing contrasting sets of experiences that illustrate the attributes. Examples of such sets are *rough-smooth, pretty-ugly, little-big,* and *hot-cold.* Both concrete objects and pictures are useful in teaching attributes.

5. **Classes of objects.** A broader classification of objects must be made and labeled with a word. For example, the word *food* refers not to any single type of food, but to all foods. The students, therefore, could be taught objects that "are food" and could be asked to remove from a display any objects that "are not food."

11.10d Understanding Sentences

It is more difficult to understand sentences than single words. Some students with language disabilities need structured practice in understanding sentences.

1. **Directions.** Give simple directions in sentences to provide the students with needed experiences in understanding sentences. For example, you can say, "Give me the blue truck" or "Put the book on the table."

2. **Finding the picture.** Line up several pictures. State a sentence describing one of them and ask the students to point to the correct picture. You can make this exercise harder by adding more sentences to your description of the picture.

3. **Function words.** Function or structure words establish structural relationships between parts of a sentence and grammatical meaning. They include noun determiners, auxiliary verbal forms, subordinators, prepositions, connectors, and question words. These words cannot be taught in isolation; they must be taught within a sentence or phrase. You might, for example, teach words such as *on, over, under, behind, in front of, beneath, inside,* and *in* by placing objects *in* a box or *under* a chair while saying the entire phrase to convey the meaning.

4. **Riddles.** Have students listen to a sentence and fill in the word that fits. For example, for the word *sled,* you might say, "I am thinking of a word that tells what you use to go down a snowy hill."

11.10e Listening Comprehension

Listening comprehension is similar to reading comprehension, but the information is received by hearing rather than by reading language.

1. **Following directions.** Students listen to a set of directions for making something. Have the materials ready and ask students to follow the directions step by step.

2. **Understanding a sequence of events.** Students listen to a story and are then asked to picture the different events in the order in which they happened. Pictorial series, such as comic strips, can help illustrate the events of the story, and you can mix the pictures and ask the students to place the series in the proper chronological order.

3. **Listening for details.** The teacher can read a story aloud and ask detailed questions about it. Phrase questions to ask *who, what, when, where,* and *how.* The teacher can also read aloud an instructional manual on a subject, such as how to care for a new pet, and then ask students to list all the things that should be done.

4. **Getting the main idea.** The teacher reads aloud a short but unfamiliar story and asks the students to make up a good title for the story. The teacher also reads aloud a story and asks the students to choose the main idea from 3 choices.

5. **Making inferences and drawing conclusions.** The teacher reads part of a story that the students do not know and stops at an exciting point to ask the students to guess what happens next.

11.10f Critical Listening

Good listening means not only understanding what is said, but also being able to listen critically and to judge and evaluate what is being said.

1. **Recognizing absurdities.** Tell a short story with a word or phrase that does not fit the story. Ask the students to discover what is funny or foolish about the story. For example, you could say, "It rained all night in the middle of the day," or "The sun was shining brightly in the middle of the night."

2. **Listening to advertisements.** Have the students listen to advertisements and determine *how* the advertiser is trying to get the listener to buy the products. Adolescents enjoy detecting propaganda techniques.

11.10g Listening to Stories

Story reading is a useful strategy for building oral language experiences. Frequently reading stories to small groups of children with language problems helps them to acquire language, figure out grammar, and learn the structure of stories (Jennings et al., 2010). Read stories frequently (at least once each day) to small groups of five to seven children. Involve all the children in the story by asking questions appropriate to their individual levels of language acquisition. Select predictable books (ones that have a pattern, refrain, or sequence) to read aloud, encouraging the children to repeat the predictable element. Select well-illustrated books (ones with many illustrations closely tied to the text) to read aloud. Throughout the story, ask the children thought-provoking questions. Read and reread favorite stories and let the children listen to them on CDs or tapes while following along in their books. Children can also watch a DVD of some stories.

Did You Get It?

What skill is frequently overlooked and neglected because a young child is "expected" to acquire it without the need for formal instruction?
- **a.** reading comprehension
- **b.** dictation
- **c.** listening
- **d.** imitating

11.11 Speaking

The activities in this section focus on speaking and include (1) stages of oral language development, (2) activities for natural language stimulation, (3) activities for teaching oral language, and (4) activities for improving the oral language of adolescents.

11.11a Stages of Oral Language Development

A general overview of a child's oral language development provides a perspective for viewing language deviations. A child's first attempt to use vocal mechanisms is the birth cry. In the short span of time from the birth cry to the full acquisition of speech, the child goes through several stages. Visit the student website for this text to see speech and language milestones for ages 1–6.

Babbling Vocalization during the first nine months of life is called *babbling*. During this stage, children produce many sounds, those in their native language as well as those found in other languages. Infants derive pleasure from hearing the sounds they make, and making such sounds gives them the opportunity to use the tongue, larynx, and other vocal apparatuses and to respond orally to others. Children who are deaf begin the babbling stage but soon stop because they receive no satisfaction from hearing the sounds they produce. Parents of children with language disorders often report that their child does not engage in the activities of babbling, gurgling, or blowing bubbles. These children should be encouraged to engage in such oral play to help them have the normal experiences of language acquisition.

Jargon By about 9 months, the babbling softens and becomes *jargon*. Children retain the phoneme sounds that are used in the language they hear. Their vocalizations reflect the rhythm and melody of the oral speaking patterns of others around them. Although their intonational patterns may be similar to those of adults, children do not yet use words at this stage; it is as though they are pretending to talk. The parents of children who are diagnosed as having language disabilities often report that their children missed this stage of development.

Chinese children have been observed to have a mastery of basic Chinese intonation patterns by 20 months of age, a feat that is very difficult for an English-speaking adult to accomplish. Yi was a baby from China who was adopted at 10 months of age. Her adoptive parents became concerned about a possible language disorder because she displayed no signs of language play and did not engage in jargon. The problem was happily solved when the family had lunch at a Chinese restaurant. As soon as Yi heard people talking in Chinese, she spontaneously began "talking" in jargon, using Chinese sounds and intonational patterns.

Single Words Single words, such as *mama* and *dada,* normally develop between 12 and 18 months of age. The ability to *imitate* is evident at this stage, and children may well imitate sounds or words that they hear others say or that they themselves produce. Parents often report that their child with language disabilities did not engage in verbal imitation and repetition activities.

Two- and Three-Word Sentences Two- and three-word sentences, such as *Baby eat, Daddy home,* and *Coat off,* mark the next stage and follow the use of single words. Once children begin to use language, their skill in producing speech increases at a remarkably rapid pace.

Between 18 months, when a toddler first produces a two-word utterance, and age 3, many children learn the essentials of English grammar and can produce all linguistic types of sentences. The child's oral language development at age 3 appears to be almost abrupt; the child has an extensive vocabulary and uses fairly complex sentence structures. During this stage, reports become rather hazy—partly because things develop so rapidly and partly because as observers, we do not understand the underlying mechanism of language acquisition. By the time children enter school at age 6, they are fairly sophisticated users of the grammar of their native language.

11.11b Problems in Language Acquisition

Most children acquire spoken language in a relatively natural and easy manner, without a need for direct teaching. Many children with learning disabilities and related mild disabilities, however, do not go through the typical developmental stages of language acquisition and exhibit difficulty in acquiring one or several properties of language. Some have difficulty with the phonology of language—differentiating and producing the appropriate sounds. Others have difficulty remembering words or structuring morphological rules. Some have difficulty with grammar or syntax and in putting words together to formulate sentences. Still others have a semantic difficulty in vocabulary development.

11.11c Activities for Natural Language Stimulation

Teachers, parents, and family members can take advantage of many opportunities in the daily life of a child in school or at home to provide natural language stimulation (Lerner, Lowenthal, & Egan, 2003).

1. **Expansion.** This is a technique to enlarge and enhance the child's language. In the conversation that follows, the adult expands a child's limited utterance.
   Child: "Cookie."
   Teacher or parent: "'Cookie? I want cookie.' Well, here it is!"

2. **Parallel talk.** In this technique, the adult tries to help language development by supplying language stimulation, even when no speech is heard. As the child plays, the teacher or parent guesses what the child is thinking and supplies short phrases describing the actions, thereby placing words and sentences in the child's mind for future reference. For example, if the child is banging a block on the floor, the teacher might say, "There's a block. If I hit the block on the floor, it makes a noise. A big noise. Bang, bang, bang. Block. My block. Bang the block."

3. **Self-talk.** In this technique, teachers model language by engaging in activities that do not directly involve the child. As teachers complete their own tasks and work in close proximity to the child, they can capitalize on opportunities to use meaningful language stimulation that the child can hear. For example, while cutting some paper, the teacher might say, "I have to cut the paper. Cut the paper. I need scissors. My scissors. Open, shut the scissors. Open, shut. I can cut, cut, cut."

11.11d Activities for Teaching Spoken Language

Activities for teaching spoken language skills include (1) building a speaking vocabulary, (2) learning language patterns, (3) formulating sentences, and (4) practicing spoken language skills.

Building a Speaking Vocabulary Some children with language disorders have an extremely limited vocabulary and a very specific, narrow, and concrete sense of the meaning of words. Throughout their lives, people have a much larger listening vocabulary than speaking vocabulary. Young children are able to understand words long before they are able to produce and use them. Children with a language disorder may be able to recognize words when they hear them, but they may be unable to use those words. Adults with known brain injuries may lose their ability to remember words easily as a result of damage to the language area of the brain. This condition, as noted earlier, is *dysnomia,* meaning the inability to remember the names of objects. Children may substitute another referent like *thing, whatsit,* or *that,* or a gesture or pantomime for the word they cannot bring to mind. The following activities can help children use words and build an accessible speaking vocabulary.

1. **Naming.** Have the children name common objects in or outside the room (chair, door, table, tree, or stone). Have a collection of objects in a box or bag. As each is removed, have the children name it. Have the children name colors, animals, shapes, and so forth. A collection or a file of good pictures of objects provides excellent teaching material. You can make pictures more durable and washable by backing them with cardboard and covering them with a self-adhesive transparent covering.

2. **Department store.** The game of department store (or hardware store, supermarket, restaurant, shoe store, etc.) gives the children an opportunity to use naming words. One child plays the role of the customer and gives orders to another, who is the clerk. The clerk collects pictures of the ordered items and names the items while giving them to the customer.

3. **Rapid naming.** Give the students a specified length of time, such as 60 seconds, to name all the objects in the room. Keep a record of the number of words named to note improvement. You can also ask the students to rapidly name objects in pictures. Another variation could be related to sports, the outdoors, pets, and so forth.

4. **Missing words.** Have the students say the word that finishes a riddle. For example: "Who delivers the mail? *(mail carrier).* I bounce a _____. *(ball)*" Read a story to the children, pausing at certain places to leave out words. Have the children supply the missing word. The use of pictures helps in recalling and naming the object.

5. **Word combinations.** Some words can best be learned as part of a group. When one member of the group is named, the children may be helped to remember the second; for example, *paper-pencil, boy-girl, hat-coat,* and *cats-dogs.* Series such as days of the week and months of the year may also be learned in this fashion.

6. **Troublesome words.** Be alert for troublesome words. When you note such a word, you may be able to give an immediate lesson on it and then plan for future exercises using that word.

Children with problems with spoken language need intervention to build their facility with spoken language.

Nick White/Photodisc/Getty Images

Formulating Sentences   Some children are able to use single words or short phrases but are unable to generate longer syntactic units or sentences. In acquiring language, children must learn to internalize sentence patterns so that they can generate new sentences. Some linguists have said that the child becomes a sentence-producing machine. To achieve this state, the child needs many skills, including the ability to understand language, to remember word sequences, and to formulate complex rules of grammar.

1. **Provide experiences with many kinds of sentences.** Start with the basic simple sentence and help the child generate transformations. For example, 2 basic sentences can be combined in various ways:

Basic sentence:	"The children play games."
Basic sentence:	"The children are tired."
Combined sentences:	"The children who are tired play games."
	"The children who play games are tired."

   Sentence pattern variations can also be practiced:

Statements	*Questions*
Children play games.	Do children play games?
Games are played by children.	Are games played by children?

2. **Demonstrate structure words.** As mentioned earlier, words such as *on, in, under,* and *who,* which show the relationship among parts of the sentence, are best taught within the sentence. Close observation reveals that many children have hazy concepts of the meanings of such words. You can help students understand these concepts if you ask them to put blocks *in, on,* or *under* a table or chair, and then ask them to explain what they did.

Words such as *yet, but, never,* and *which* often need clarification. Give a sentence with only the key or class words and then ask the students to add the structure words, as in this example:

"Jack—went—school—late."
"Jack went to school, but he was late."

3. **Substitute words to form sentences.** Have students form new sentences by substituting a single word in an existing kernel sentence. For example:

"I took my *coat* off. I took my *boots* off."
"The child is *reading*. The child is *running*. The child is *jumping*."

4. **Play a detective game.** To help students learn to formulate questions, hide an object and have students ask questions concerning its location until it is found.

Practicing Spoken Language Skills Students with a deficiency in spoken language need practice and many opportunities to use words and formulate sentences. The following activities can help students to practice their speaking skills.

1. **Use spoken language activities.** A number of activities can be used to practice spoken language, such as conversations; discussions; radio or television broadcasts; show-and-tell sessions; puppetry; dramatic play; telephoning; choral speaking; reporting; interviewing; telling stories, riddles, or jokes; giving book reports; and role-playing.

2. **Discuss objects.** Help the students tell about the attributes of an object—its color, size, shape, composition, and major parts—and to compare it with other objects.

3. **Use categories.** Place items in a box that can be grouped to teach categories, such as toys, clothes, animals, vehicles, furniture, and fruit. Ask the students to find the ones that go together and tell what they are. You can vary this activity by naming the category and asking the students to find and name the items or by putting items together and asking which do not belong.

4. **Finish stories.** Begin a story and let the students finish it. For example: "Betty went to visit her aunt in a strange city. When the plane landed, Betty could not see her aunt at the airport _____."

11.11e Activities for Improving the Oral Language of Adolescents

Direct instruction in language also helps improve the communication skills of adolescents. Sometimes students at the middle school or high school levels appear, at first, to have adequate oral language skills, so their true needs are often overlooked. In addition, the secondary school curriculum emphasizes performance in written language more than in oral language, so their deficiencies may go undetected. On closer observation, however, we find that the spoken language of many secondary students is meager. Many of the methods described earlier work for adolescents, and the following methods are also useful.

1. **Learning strategies.** Instruction in learning strategies is particularly useful for adolescents. They should be involved in setting the goals they are trying to reach and in selecting learning strategies to reach these goals. Self-monitoring, verbal rehearsal, and error analysis are the kinds of strategies that have been helpful in reading, and they can also be used for improving their spoken language.

2. **Building vocabulary.** Adolescents can expand their oral vocabularies by classifying and organizing words. For example, they can build lists or hierarchies of words on a topic. For example, for the topic of space exploration, they might use words that classify space vehicles, space inventions, first events that occurred in space, and so on. There are several approaches to this activity. The teacher can supply the words for classifying, the students can supply the words, or the teacher can provide a partial classification system and the students can complete it.

3. **Reciprocal questioning.** This is a variation of reciprocal teaching. Instead of the teacher asking the questions, the students ask the questions. The technique encourages the development of questioning skills.

4. **Sentence combining.** Say 2 short sentences aloud and ask students to think of all the ways in which the sentences can be combined into one sentence.

5. **Reviewing a group discussion.** Have students hold a short discussion on an assigned topic. After the discussion, ask them to analyze the effectiveness of the discussion. Did they stay on the topic? Did they allow others to talk? Did they direct the conversation to the right people? Did they follow through when a point was made?

6. **Explaining how to play a game.** Many students with learning disabilities have difficulty giving explanations and need practice in this activity. Such practice could consist of having students explain to another person how to play a game, how to make something, or how to do something. The recipient of the explanation can be a peer or a younger child. The students could first engage in verbal rehearsal to practice the explanation and then try to be sensitive to whether the listener understands and is able to respond to questions. Examples of subjects for explanation include the rules of a video game, how to cook and peel a hard-boiled egg, or how to play checkers or bingo.

> **Did You Get It?**
>
> At approximately 9 months, children are expected to progress out of the "babbling" stage. If they are displaying age and developmentally appropriate levels and skills, they should begin replacing babble with
>   **a.** syntax
>   **b.** chatter
>   **c.** jargon
>   **d.** vernacular

11.12 Assistive and Instructional Computer Technology for Oral Language

Computer technology can be helpful in teaching oral language skills. A few select computer software programs are described in this section. Before using these in the classroom, you may wish to review the National Educational Technology Standards for Students to determine how they can best be incorporated into your teaching. These standards were developed by the International Society for Technology in Education, *http://www.iste.org*.

- **Earobics.** This educational software program teaches auditory and phonological awareness skills. It uses a CD-ROM and six interactive games that teach oral language skills. Earobics has small positive effects on alphabetics and potentially positive effect on reading fluency, according to the What Works Clearinghouse. (*http://ies.ed.gov/ncee/wwclintervention* report), Publisher: Cognitive Concepts, Inc., *http://www.cogcon.com*.

Did You Get It?

An effective computer-based learning program that presents six interactive games designed to teach oral language skills, focusing primarily on the development of auditory and phonological awareness, is

- **a.** Earobics
- **b.** Auditory Olympics
- **c.** Run, Jump, and Listen
- **d.** Ear I Am

I Have a Kid Who...

NOAH: *A Child With a Language Delay*

Noah G., age 5 years 6 months, was in kindergarten when his parents were contacted about problems he was having in school. The kindergarten teacher said that Noah did not seem to get along with the other children in class. He had no friends, would often strike out and hit his classmates, and was especially disruptive during the conversation time and story periods. He refused to participate in class activities, such as the puppet show that was being prepared for presentation to the parents. The kindergarten teacher said that when she did not know what Noah wanted, this situation often provoked a tantrum.

Mrs. G. said that Noah does not want to go to school and that it is sometimes difficult to get him to go to his class. In describing his developmental history, Mrs. G. said that Noah was born 6 weeks prematurely, weighing 4 lb 5 oz., and that he had been placed in an incubator for a short period. He was a colicky baby and had difficulty nursing. His motor development was average; he crawled at 8 months and walked alone at 12 months. Language development, however, was slow. He spoke his first word at 24 months and did not begin speaking in sentences until age 4. Because he could not communicate with others, he often resorted to pointing and grunting to make his desires known, and frequently Noah had temper tantrums when others did not understand what he wanted. Noah does not get along well with his 2 older sisters. Both sisters are very verbal and do not give Noah much chance to talk. When Noah is asked a question, his sisters answer before he can respond. Mrs. G. said that the doctor suspected a hearing loss when Noah was younger. He had many colds as a toddler and had a condition the doctor called *otitis media*, with fluid behind the

eardrums. The doctor put tubes in Noah's ears when he was 4, and his hearing tested normal after this procedure.

The speech teacher observed Noah during class and reported that he played alone most of the time. During the storytelling period and show-and-tell time, he wandered about the room. Often, when another child was playing with a toy, Noah would grab it. If the other child did not give the toy up readily, Noah would hit his classmate until he got it. He listened very little and did not talk to other children in the class. He seemed to tire of one activity very quickly, and would move on to another.

During the multidisciplinary evaluation, the speech teacher checked Noah's hearing with an audiometer, and his auditory acuity was normal. The school psychologist tested Noah with an IQ test, the Wechsler Preschool and Primary Scale of Intelligence-Revised. His full-scale IQ score was in the normal range (FSIQ 101), with his performance IQ score (PIQ 119) substantially higher than his verbal IQ score (VIQ 84). The IEP team identified Noah with a speech delay.

The case conference team recommended that Noah be placed in a developmental kindergarten and receive language therapy from the speech-language pathologist in the school, who would also collaborate with Noah's parents and kindergarten teacher to develop language activities for the home and the developmental kindergarten.

QUESTIONS

1. Why do you think Noah had temper tantrums?
2. What were Noah's strengths?
3. What were Noah's weaknesses?

Chapter Summary

- Components of the language system include phonology, morphology, syntax, semantics, and pragmatics.
- English-language learners are students whose first language is not English and who exhibit limited English proficiency. Some children are both English-language learners and also have a learning disability or a related disability.
- Many children have problems in listening and understanding what they hear.
- Problems in listening include phonological awareness of language sounds, understanding words, and building a listening vocabulary, understanding sentences, critical listening, and listening to stories.
- Problems in speaking involve delayed speech, lack of phonological awareness, problems with temporal or acoustical processing, receptive language disorders, and expressive language disorders.
- Computer technology can be helpful in teaching oral language skills.

Questions for Discussion and Reflection

1. Describe the communication process. Discuss the kinds of problems that a student may encounter in communicating.
2. What are the components of language? Give an example of each. What kinds of problems can a student with learning disabilities or related mild disabilities encounter with each component of language?
3. Describe a few of the problems faced by students who are English-language learners. Describe a few practices that have been shown to be helpful for English-language learners.
4. What is meant by the term *early literacy*? Describe a few methods that foster early literacy.
5. What is phonological awareness? Why is it important for young children to develop skills in phonological awareness?

Key Terms

bilingual instruction (p. 323)
components of language (p. 315)
developmental aphasia (p. 321)
dysnomia (p. 321)
early literacy (p. 324)
English as a second language (ESL) method (p. 323)
expressive language disorders (p. 321)
immersion instruction (p. 323)
language delay (p. 317)
language disorders (p. 317)
morpheme (p. 315)
morphology (p. 315)
otitis media (p. 317)
phoneme (p. 315)

phonics (p. 315)
phonology (p. 315)
pragmatics (p. 316)
primary language system (p. 310)
rapid automatized naming (RAN) (p. 319)
receptive language disorders (p. 321)
secondary language system (p. 310)
semantics (p. 316)
sheltered English (p. 323)
speech disorders (p. 317)
Standard English (p. 315)
syntax (p. 315)
temporal acoustical processing (p. 319)
word finding (p. 319)

Maria Uspenskaya/Shutterstock.com

CHAPTER 12

Reading Difficulties

I don't believe in the kind of magic in my books. But I do believe something very magical can happen when you read a good book.

—J. K. ROWLING, Author of the Harry Potter Books

LEARNING OBJECTIVES

After reading this chapter, you should be able to:

12.1 Explain theories describing the consequences of reading difficulties

12.2 Describe reading strategies for the general education classroom

12.3 List the elements of reading

12.4 Explain the connection between reading and writing

12.5 Explain the literature-based approach to teaching reading

12.6 Discuss the challenges faced by ELL students and reading

12.7 Discuss methods to assess reading

12.8 List teaching strategies to improve reading difficulties

12.9 Describe strategies to improve word recognition

12.10 List strategies to improve reading fluency

12.11 List strategies to improve reading comprehension

12.12 Explain the importance of reading enjoyment and appreciation

12.13 Describe assistive technology to promote reading

STANDARDS Addressed in This Chapter:

Council for Exceptional Children Initial Level Special Educator Preparation Standards as approved by the National Council for the Accreditation of Teacher Education

CEC Initial Preparation Standard 1: Learner Development and Individual Learning Differences

- 1.0—Beginning special education professionals understand how exceptionalities may interact with development and learning and use this knowledge to provide meaningful and challenging learning experiences for individuals with exceptionalities.

- 1.1—Beginning special education professionals understand how language, culture, and family background influence the learning of individuals with exceptionalities.

- 1.2—Beginning special education professionals use understanding of development and individual differences to respond to the needs of individuals with exceptionalities.

CEC Initial Preparation Standard 3: Curricular Content Knowledge

- 3.0—Beginning special education professionals use knowledge of general and specialized curricula to individualize learning for individuals with exceptionalities.

- 3.1—Beginning special education professionals understand the central concepts, structures of the discipline, and tools of inquiry of the content areas they teach and can organize this knowledge, integrate cross-disciplinary skills and develop meaningful learning progressions for individuals with exceptionalities.

- 3.2—Beginning special education professionals understand and use general and specialized content knowledge for teaching across curricular content areas to individualize learning for individuals with exceptionalities.

- 3.3—Beginning special education professionals modify general and specialized curricula to make them accessible to individuals with exceptionalities.

CEC Initial Preparation Standard 4: Assessment

- 4.0—Beginning special education professionals use multiple methods of assessment and data-sources in making educational decisions.

- 4.1—Beginning special education professionals select and use technically sound formal and informal assessments that minimize bias.

- 4.2—Beginning special education professionals use knowledge of measurement principles and practices to interpret assessment results and guide educational decisions for individuals with exceptionalities.

- 4.3—Beginning special education professionals in collaboration with colleagues and families use multiple types of assessment information in making decisions about individuals with exceptionalities.

- 4.4—Beginning special education professionals engage individuals with exceptionalities to work toward quality learning and performance and provide feedback to guide them.

CEC Initial Preparation Standard 5: Instructional Planning and Strategies

- 5.0—Beginning special education professionals select, adapt, and use a repertoire of evidence-based instructional strategies to advance learning of individuals with exceptionalities.

- 5.1—Beginning special education professionals consider an individual's abilities, interests, learning environments, and cultural and linguistic factors in the selection, development, and adaptation of learning experiences for individuals with exceptionalities.

- 5.2—Beginning special education professionals use technologies to support instructional assessment, planning, and delivery for individuals with exceptionalities.

- 5.3—Beginning special education professionals are familiar with augmentative and alternative communication systems and a variety of assistive technologies to support the communication and learning of individuals with exceptionalities.

- 5.4—Beginning special education professionals use strategies to enhance language development and communication skills of individuals with exceptionalities.

- 5.6—Beginning special education professionals teach to mastery and promote generalization of learning.

- 5.7—Beginning special education professionals teach cross-disciplinary knowledge and skills such as critical thinking and problem solving to individuals with exceptionalities.

For students, Common Core Standards for English Language Arts and Literacy in History/Social Studies, Science, and Technical Subjects can be found at: *www.corestandards.org*.

This chapter focuses on reading and is the second of 3 chapters on the integrated language system. Reading is an integral part of the language system and is closely linked to both spoken language and writing.

In the first half of this chapter, the "Theories" section, we discuss several topics about reading: (1) the consequences of reading disabilities, (2) dyslexia, (3) the elements of reading, (4) phonemic awareness, (5) phonics and word-recognition clues, (6) fluency, (7) vocabulary, (8) comprehension, (9) the reading-writing connection, (10) literature-based reading instruction (whole language), (11) reading instruction for English-language learners (ELL), and (12) assessing reading. In the "Teaching Strategies" section, we review methods for teaching reading.

12.1 Theories Describing the Consequences of Reading Disabilities

If our children do not learn to read, they cannot succeed in life. Without the ability to read, the opportunities for academic and occupational success are limited. Unfortunately, over 80% of students with learning disabilities and related disabilities encounter difficulties in reading (Lerner & Johns, 2012). In fact, the reading of books is on a decline, with only 57% of adults reported to have read a book in 2002 (National Endowment for the Arts, 2004).

It is critical to identify children with reading problems early and provide them with appropriate early instruction. More than 17.5% of the nation's school children—about 1 million children—encounter reading problems during the crucial first 3 years of schooling (National Reading Panel, 2000). Moreover, 74% of children who are unsuccessful in reading in third grade are still unsuccessful in ninth grade (National Institute for Child Health and Human Development, 1999). The reading problems of adolescents and adults reflect reading difficulties that were not resolved during their early years. The *wait-and-fail method* refers to the policy of not promptly addressing the reading difficulties of young children but, instead, waiting to do so when they are older. Research supported by the National Institute of Child Health and Human Development resulted in some key findings about reading disorders (Dunn, 2010; Mazzocco & Meyers, 2003; Lyon, 2003):

- Reading is so critical to success in our society that reading failure not only constitutes an educational problem, but it also rises to the level of a major public health problem.
- Characteristics of children who are most at risk for reading failure are:
  - They lack phonemic awareness (or sensitivity to the sounds of language).
  - They are not familiar with the letters of the alphabet.
  - They may not understand the purpose of print.
  - They often lack sufficient oral language and verbal skills and have meager vocabularies.
- Children may also be at risk for reading failure because of their linguistic and cultural backgrounds and their limited exposure to the English language.
- Early identification of young children who are at risk for reading failure and timely intervention to assist them are essential for maximizing treatment success.

Because reading is the basic skill for all academic subjects, failure in school can be traced to inadequate reading skills. Students today face more mandatory tests than ever before, and they need to earn diplomas and degrees to obtain jobs. Overcoming these hurdles, as well as facing the necessity of filling out application forms and taking licensing examinations, makes life for poor readers difficult and full of impassible barriers. In today's world, high technology and automation have created a demand for highly trained people. Telecommunications, e-mail, and the Internet all require users to read and comprehend written electronic information on a computer screen.

The development of reading skills serves as the major academic foundation for all school-based learning. Workers in every occupation now have to retrain themselves to prepare for new jobs many times during their work/careers. Efficient reading is a key skill for maintaining employment or retraining for another job. Poor reading skills cause many problems for individuals in the world of work. Fewer jobs are available for unskilled and semiskilled workers, and these individuals are likely to end up being chronically unemployed. Opportunities for gainful employment decrease for youth who drop out of school. Dropouts

Children should be surrounded by the world of books and have many experiences listening to stories, reading books, and writing.

have twice the unemployment rate that high school graduates do, so they have fewer opportunities for continued training. Further, they lack the qualifications to attend postsecondary school or college (National Joint Committee and Learning Disabilities, 2008; Wagner et al., 2006; Gerber et al., 2004; Hennesy, Rosenberg, & Tramaglini, 2003).

Reading is not a natural process. In contrast to other developmental achievements, such as learning to walk or to talk, learning to read requires careful instruction. Learning to read is also a relatively lengthy process. It takes several years, and the learner must persevere over a long period of time. Moreover, the process of recognizing words is complex; readers must use a variety of strategies to accomplish this task. Children must first learn to read so that later they can *read to learn*. Current information and research about reading can be found at the Reading Rockets website at *http://www.readingrockets.org*.

Did You Get It?

According to statistics compiled by the National Institute for Child Health and Human Development (1999), approximately _____% of students who experienced reading deficits in third grade still had related deficits by the ninth grade.
   a. 15
   b. 45
   c. 5 to 8
   d. 75

12.2 Reading Strategies for the General Education Classroom

Many children with learning disabilities and related disabilities who have reading problems receive their instruction in general education classrooms. Throughout this chapter, we present many reading strategies for students in general education classrooms. Including Students in General Education 12.1, "Reading Strategies," gives some overall suggestions for students with reading disabilities in general education classrooms.

12.2a Response-to-Intervention (RTI)

Response-to-intervention (RTI) is a process for *all* students in general education. RTI uses evidence-based instruction, and its purpose is to resolve reading

Reading Strategies

General Modifications and Accommodations

- Increase the amount of repetition and review.
- Allot more time for completing work.
- Provide more examples and activities.
- Introduce the work more slowly.

Phonics

- Play word and rhyming games.
- Analyze the phoneme elements that make up a word.
- Build word families.

Fluency

- Help students recognize sight words.
- Find opportunities for students to reread passages aloud.
- Use predictable books.
- Use read-along methods.
- Use the language experience method to let the children read their own language.

Vocabulary

- Teach content vocabulary before reading a chapter in a science or social studies text.
- Find words in the student's areas of interest (sports, movies, television shows, current events) and use these words for study.
- Use word webs to study vocabulary words.

Reading Comprehension

- Provide students with background knowledge about a story or content-area reading.
- Have students predict what will happen next in a story.
- Use graphic organizers to visualize the reading passage.
- Show movies or videos about a book to enhance interest.
- Have students act out passages in a story.

Professional Resource Download

problems by using tiers of instruction. (See Chapter 2 "Assessment and the IEP Process," for an extensive description of RTI.)

Next we will discuss dyslexia, which is a severe reading challenge faced by many students.

12.2b Dyslexia

The condition known as *dyslexia* is an unusual type of severe reading disorder that has puzzled the educational and medical communities for many years. Actually, dyslexia is one type of learning disability that affects some children, adolescents, and adults. People with this baffling disorder find it extremely difficult to recognize letters and words and to interpret information that is presented in print form. People with dyslexia are intelligent and may have very strong mathematics or spatial skills. Student Stories 12.1, "People With Dyslexia," offers the reflections of well-known individuals with dyslexia about how this reading problem affected their lives.

Although there are several different definitions of dyslexia there is general agreement on several points (Rosen, 2010; Shaywitz, 2003):

1. Dyslexia has a biological basis and is caused by a disruption in the neural circuits in the brain.
2. Dyslexic problems persist into adolescence and adulthood.
3. Dyslexia has perceptual, cognitive, and language dimensions.
4. Dyslexia leads to difficulties in many areas of life as the individual matures.
5. Many individuals with dyslexia excel in other facets of life.

Individuals with dyslexia who are successful adults possess the quality of resilience and a strong desire to succeed. Bob exemplifies these qualities. Bob's problems with reading began in the first grade. He developed a school phobia and refused to go to school. At age 12, his parents sent him to a private residential school, where he was diagnosed with dyslexia. He developed a resilience to cope with his reading failure and he also learned how to advocate for his rights under the law. His poor working memory meant that he read very slowly and could not complete examinations during a time limit. He was able to take entrance examinations with extended time, and he completed an engineering degree at a major university, using the accommodations he needed under the law. Bob really wanted to be a physician. He had to take the MCAT exams many times until he was finally admitted to a medical school. When he failed a class, he managed to retake it. He failed the Medical Boards several times before he passed this test. Bob failed the Boards for his specialty several times before he passed this Board exam, with the accommodation of extended time. Today Bob is a successful physician, with outstanding clinical skills and a thriving practice.

REFLECTIVE QUESTION

1. What is a major characteristic that permitted Bob to succeed?

The life stories of corporate CEOs with dyslexia show their remarkable skills in the business world (Morris, 2002). People with dyslexia tend to find ingenious ways to hide their disability. For example, a widowed gentleman caught in the social dating whirl routinely handled the problem of dining in restaurants by putting down his menu and saying to his companion, "Why don't you order for both of us, dear? Your selections are always so delicious." This man hired professionals to handle his reading and writing matters. His friends attributed his actions to wealth, never suspecting his inability to read.

For many years, scholars strongly suspected that dyslexia had a neurobiological basis; however, they lacked the scientific evidence to support this belief. Today, the cognitive neurosciences research provides strong evidence that dyslexia is caused by variant in brain structure, a difference in brain function, or genetic factors (Rosen, 2010; Pugh, 2010; Shaywitz, 2003; Gilger, 2010; Shaywitz & Shaywitz, 1998, 1999). The brain research studies on dyslexia and the new technologies for assessing the link between brain function and learning are fascinating. While neuroscientists continue their search for the causes of dyslexia, however, teachers must provide the instruction to teach these individuals how to read.

We will now discuss elements of effective reading instruction for all children.

Did You Get It?

Which alteration or modification can be made to a general education reading program to help students overcome reading difficulties?
   a. providing few informal and enjoyable activities and sticking with the basics and fundamentals
   b. deescalating review and repetition when the student is making mistakes
   c. rapid introduction of new concepts and exercises
   d. providing additional time for task completion

12.3 Elements of Reading

The National Reading Panel (2000) is a commission of reading scholars that was assigned by the U.S. Congress to conduct an evidence-based assessment of the research literature on reading and its implications for reading instruction. Finding that over 100,000 research studies on reading had been published since 1966, the National Reading Panel established stringent criteria for the inclusion of research studies in their evidence-based assessment. (More information about their findings is available at the National Reading Panel website at *http://www.nationalreadingpanel.org.*)

The conclusions of the National Reading Panel (2000) included a list of key reading components in which effective readers need to be competent.

1. Phonemic awareness (discussed in Chapter 11, "Spoken Language Difficulties: Listening and Speaking")
2. Phonics (discussed in this chapter)
3. Fluency (discussed in this chapter)
4. Vocabulary (discussed in this chapter)
5. Text comprehension (discussed in this chapter)

Each of these elements is described in the following sections.

12.3a Phonemic Awareness

Phonemic awareness is the ability to notice, think about, and work with the individual sounds in spoken words. Before children learn to read print, they need to become aware of how the sounds work in words. They must understand that words are made of speech sounds, or phonemes. The term phonological awareness is broad and includes the ability to identify and manipulate larger parts of spoken language, such as words, syllables, and rhymes, as well as phonemes. Phonemic awareness is a part of phonological awareness. Phonological awareness focuses on children's hearing and using the sounds of language. You can find more information on the National Institute for Literacy's website at *http://www.nifl.gov*. (See Chapter 11, "Spoken Language Difficulties: Listening and Speaking," for more information about phonological awareness.)

phonemic awareness
An awareness of the sounds in words and language.

phonological awareness
A child's recognition of the sounds of language. The child must understand that speech can be segmented into syllables and phonemic units.

12.3b Phonics and Word-Recognition Skills

Reading requires the reader to recognize words. Once readers develop a facility in word recognition, they can concentrate on the meaning of the text. Without these lower-level reading skills, the higher cognitive skills cannot function. When readers exert so much effort into recognizing words, they will have little processing capacity remaining for comprehension.

Early attention to word-recognition skills is important because this early ability accurately predicts later skill in reading comprehension. Children who get off to a slow start rarely become strong readers (National Reading Panel, 2000). Learning word-recognition skills early leads to wider reading abilities in and out of school. Reading a wide variety of material provides opportunities to increase the student's vocabulary, increase the student's interest in books, and foster the student's general reading growth (Moats, 2000; Henry, 2003; Lyon, 2003).

word-recognition procedures
Strategies for recognizing words, including phonics, sight words, context clues, structural analysis, and combinations of these strategies.

Readers use several word-recognition procedures to identify words, including (1) phonics, (2) sight words, (3) context clues, and (4) structural analysis. The "Teaching Strategies" section of this chapter suggests methods for teaching each of these word-recognition skills.

12.3c Phonics

phonics
An application of phonetics to the teaching of reading in which the sound (or phoneme) of a language is related to the equivalent written symbol (or grapheme).

Phonics refers to the relationship between printed letters (graphemes) and the sounds (phonemes) in language. As an essential word-recognition skill, phonics involves learning the correspondence of language sounds to written letters and applying that knowledge in recognizing words and reading. Children must learn to decode printed language and translate print into sounds through the alphabetic principle of the symbol–sound relationship, a process known as *breaking the code.*

decode
The process of unlocking words into component sounds.

Children with reading disabilities require systematic phonics instruction. A systematic phonics program is a planned, sequential set of phonics elements that is taught explicitly and systematically. Research shows that children who learn the sound-symbol system of English read better than children who have not mastered this skill (Chall, 1967, 1983; Lyon, 2003; Moats, 2000; National Reading Panel, 2000). As noted, learning phonics requires that the child has competencies in phonological awareness and the ability to recognize that speech can be segmented into sounds. (See Chapter 11, "Spoken Language Difficulties: Listening and Speaking.")

Understanding phonics helps children break the code so that they can recognize words quickly and easily. In a written alphabet language, such as English, the code involves a system of mapping, or seeing the correspondences between letters and sounds. Once a child learns these mappings, the child has broken the code and can then apply this knowledge to figure out plausible pronunciations of printed words (Adams, 1990; Moats, 2000).

Children with reading disabilities need direct instruction in phonics and decoding that makes the relationship between printed letters and sounds explicit. Explicit code-emphasis instruction helps children develop a basis for remembering the relationship of sounds to the printed letters and for deriving the meanings of printed words. (See "Teaching Strategies" section later in this chapter for phonics instruction.)

explicit code-emphasis instruction
Systematic and direct teaching of decoding and phonics skills.

Findings of the National Reading Panel on the Effectiveness of Phonics Instruction The National Reading Panel (2000) reached the following conclusions about the effectiveness of phonics instruction:

1. Systematic phonics instruction makes a bigger contribution to children's growth in reading than other programs that provide unsystematic or no phonics instruction.
2. All systematic phonics programs are effective in promoting reading achievement, and they do not appear to differ significantly from one another.
3. Systematic phonics instruction is effective when delivered through tutoring, through small groups, or through teaching classes of students.
4. Systematic phonics instruction is effective when taught in kindergarten. It must be appropriately designed for young learners and must begin with foundational knowledge involving letters and phonemic awareness.

5. Phonics instruction is effective in helping to prevent reading difficulties among at-risk students and in helping to remediate reading difficulties in students with reading disabilities.
6. Systematic phonics instruction is beneficial to students regardless of their socioeconomic status (SES).

Teacher Knowledge About Phonics Children who are taught phonics directly and systematically in the early grades receive higher scores on reading achievement tests during their primary years than children who do not receive this instruction (Chall, 1991; Lyon & Moats, 1997; Moats, 2000; National Reading Panel, 2000). Many teachers, however, lack a firm grounding in phonics and phonics generalizations (Horne, 1978; Moats, 2000). Some teachers do not remember learning phonics themselves, and many do not receive adequate phonics instruction during their teacher training. (The reader may wish to take the *Foniks Kwiz* in "Phonics Quiz and Review" on the student website that accompanies this book. A brief review of phonics generalizations follows the quiz.)

Types of Phonics Approaches There are several different types of phonics instructional approaches (Jennings, Caldwell, & Lerner, 2010). Table 12.1 lists types of phonics approaches, with an explanation and examples of each approach.

Sight Words Sight words are words that are recognized instantly, without hesitation or further analysis. Unlike some other languages, written English has an inconsistent phoneme–grapheme relationship, or spelling pattern. The relationship

sight words
Words that a student recognizes instantly, without hesitation or further analysis.

TABLE 12.1

Different Types of Phonics Approaches

Phonics Approach	Explanation	Example
Synthetic phonics	Teaching students explicitly to convert letters into sounds (or phonemes) and then blend the sounds to form recognizable words	Take the word *stop*. Break it into sounds: *s/t/o/p*. Then blend the sounds into the word.
Analytic phonics	Teaching students to analyze letter–sound relations in previously learned words to avoid pronouncing sounds in isolation	Analyze the sounds in the whole word *making*.
Analogy phonics	Recognizing that a rhyme segment of an unfamiliar word is identical to that of a familiar word	Known word *kick* New word *brick* Known word *sing* New word *ring*.
Embedded phonics	Teaching students phonics skills by embedding phonics instruction in text reading; this is a more implicit approach that relies on incidental learning	Instruction in phonics skills is incidental and is taught during the reading of a text.
Phonics through spelling	Teaching students phonics through spelling instruction and to segment words into phonemes	Students are instructed to spell words phonemically.

Source: From *Teaching children to read: An evidence-based assessment of the scientific research literature on reading and its implications for reading instruction*, p. 8, Report of the National Reading Panel, 2000, Washington, DC: National Institute of Child Health and Human Development.

TABLE 12.2

Typical First-Grade Sight Words

English Spelling	Phonic Spelling
of	uv
laugh	laf
was	wuz
is	IZ
come	kum
said	sed
what	wut
from	frum
one	wun
night	nite
know	noe
they	thai

© Cengage Learning

between the letter and its sound equivalent is not always predictable. The letter *a*, for example, is given a different sound in each of the following typical first-grade words: *at, Jane, ball, father, was, saw,* and *are.* Another example of this complexity is the phoneme of the long *i*, which has a different spelling pattern in each of the following words: *aisle, aye, I, eye, ice, tie, high, buy, sky, rye, pine,* and *type.* To further complicate the problem of learning to read English, many of the most frequently used sight words in first-grade books have irregular spelling patterns. A few of these words are shown in the first column of Table 12.2; the second column shows the way they would be spelled with a dependable phoneme–grapheme relationship so that readers could "sound them out." These irregular spelling pattern words must thus be learned as sight words (Jennings et al., 2010).

The problems caused by the undependable written form of English can be approached in 2 ways:

1. **Introduce only a small number of words at a time, selecting words on the basis of frequency of use.** Some beginning reading words have regular spellings, whereas others have irregular spellings. Sight words are learned visually through extensive review and through context, meaning, and language. Basal readers, for example, rely on a controlled introduction of a small number of new words.

2. **Simplify the initial learning phase by selecting only words that have a consistent sound–symbol spelling relationship.** With this approach, students learn phonics and are exposed to carefully selected words with dependable spellings. Eventually, of course, the child must learn about the undependable spelling of many common English words. Through careful selection of the words for reading, students are kept from learning the awful truth about spelling until second grade or later. Inevitably, however, the reader must confront the undependable written form of English.

Context Clues Context clues help a student recognize a word through the meaning, or context, of a sentence or paragraph in which the word appears. There are many redundancies in our language, which occur when information from one source repeats or supports information from another source. These language redundancies provide hints about unknown words from the meaning of the surrounding text, which helps readers make conjectures and guesses about unfamiliar words.

Instruction in recognizing words through context is best done by actual reading. When students with reading disabilities have consistent practice in reading stories and books, they naturally learn to use context clues. The meaning of the sentence plus the initial sounds in the word may provide enough clues for the reader to recognize the word.

context clues
Clues that help readers recognize words through the meaning or context of the sentence or paragraph in which the words appear.

Structural Analysis Structural analysis refers to the recognition of words through the analysis of meaningful word units such as prefixes, suffixes, root words, compound words, and syllables. Structural elements include compound words (*cowboy*), contractions (*can't*), word endings or inflectional suffixes (*s, -ed, -er, -est, -ing*), word beginnings or prefixes (*in-, pre-, un-, re-, ex-*), roots (*play* in *replaying*), and syllables (i.e., breaking multisyllabic words into smaller units).

A reader may recognize structural elements of a word (e.g., the prefix *re-* and the suffix *-tion* in *repetition*). These clues, combined with the context of the sentence, may be sufficient for recognizing the word.

structural analysis
The recognition of words through the analysis of meaningful word units, such as prefixes, suffixes, root words, compound words, and syllables.

Combining Word-Recognition Clues Readers should be encouraged to use all of the word-recognition clues (phonics, sight words, context clues, and structural analysis). However, they will need these strategies only when an unknown word stops the reading process. Readers usually use several clues together until they recognize the unknown word. Students with learning disabilities and related mild disabilities need instruction and practice in each of these word-recognition clues to achieve independence and flexibility and to gain fluency.

12.3d Fluency

Reading fluency is the ability to read connected text rapidly, effortlessly, and automatically (Hook & Jones, 2004; Meyer, 2002; National Reading Panel, 2000). Readers must develop fluency to make the bridge from word recognition to reading comprehension (Jenkins et al., 2003). In this section, we describe (1) building sight vocabulary, (2) automaticity, (3) repeated reading, and (4) other methods to improve reading fluency. The "Teaching Strategies" section of this chapter offers additional strategies to improve fluency.

reading fluency
The ability to recognize words and passages readily and smoothly.

Building a Sight Vocabulary Many poor readers have difficulty reading fluently because they do not possess an adequate sight vocabulary and must labor to decode many of the words in the reading passages. With their energies focused on recognizing words, their oral reading is filled with long pauses and many repetitions, and may be characterized by monotonous expression. Fluent reading requires that most of the words in a selection be recognized as sight words. When a selection contains too many difficult (nonsight) words, the reading material will be too arduous and frustrating for the reader (Jennings, Caldwell, & Lerner, 2010). Table 12.3 shows the 100 most common sight words.

TABLE 12.3

100 Common Words

1 the	21 this	41 so	61 people	81 back
2 be	22 but	42 up	62 into	82 after
3 to	23 his	43 out	63 year	83 use
4 of	24 by	44 if	64 your	84 two
5 and	25 from	45 about	65 good	85 how
6 a	26 they	46 who	66 some	86 our
7 in	27 we	47 get	67 could	87 work
8 that	28 say	48 which	68 them	88 first
9 have	29 her	49 go	69 see	89 well
10 I	30 she	50 me	70 other	90 way
11 it	31 or	51 when	71 than	91 even
12 for	32 an	52 make	72 then	92 new
13 not	33 will	53 can	73 now	93 want
14 on	34 my	54 like	74 look	94 because
15 with	35 one	55 time	75 only	95 any
16 he	36 all	56 no	76 come	96 these
17 as	37 would	57 just	77 its	97 give
18 you	38 there	58 him	78 over	98 day
19 do	39 their	59 know	79 think	99 most
20 at	40 what	60 take	80 also	100 us

© Cengage Learning 2015

Professional Resource Download

Table 12.3 illustrates common sight words that students should know by the end of third grade. One of the best and certainly most natural ways to learn sight words is by actually reading stories. Sight words appear many times in context. A natural way to expose children to sight words is through language experience stories, which contain many sight words. Students with reading disabilities need other direct approaches to strengthen their sight vocabulary. Some methods for teaching sight vocabulary are presented in the "Teaching Strategies" section of this chapter.

automaticity
In cognitive learning theory, the condition in which learning has become almost subconscious and therefore requires little processing effort.

Automaticity Automaticity is the fast, accurate, and effortless word identification at the single word level. The speed and accuracy with which single words are identified is a key predictor of reading comprehension. The range of children's skill in recognizing words is large. One research study reported that in a first-grade class, the number of words that children recognized ranged from 15 words to 1,933 words. The average skilled reader reads three times as many words as the average less skilled reader (Compton & Appleton, 2004).

Recognizing Syllables A powerful tool to develop automatic word recognition is to teach students the visual patterns in the 6 syllable types, which are shown in Table 12.4.

352 CHAPTER 12 Reading Difficulties

TABLE 12.4

Syllable Types

Syllable Types	Examples
Closed (closed with a consonant, vowel takes its short sound)	peg, big
Open (ends in a vowel, vowel makes its long sound)	we, go
Silent _e_ (ends in vowel consonant _e_, makes the long sound)	make, ride
Vowel combination (2 vowels together make a sound	boat, fried
Controlled _r_ (Contains a vowel plus _r_, vowel sign is changed)	card, corn
Consonant + _le_ (at end of a word)	ta/ble, fa/ble

© Cengage Learning 2015

Repeated Reading Repeated reading is an instructional strategy in which students read a passage aloud several times. The repeated reading method is simple and straightforward, emphasizing practice and repetition. Repeated reading improves fluency, comprehension, and overall reading achievement (Jennings et al., 2010; National Reading Panel, 2000). Research shows that repeated reading improves reading fluency for both elementary students and secondary students (Nelson, Alber, & Gordy, 2004). The "Strategies" section in this chapter describes strategies to improve reading fluency through repeated reading.

repeated reading
Having children reread material aloud to build fluency.

Other Methods to Improve Reading Fluency Fluency occurs when students begin to read easily instead of laboring through reading material. Students need many opportunities to read if they are to gain fluency. The books or passages that children read have to be at the appropriate difficulty level—not too hard, but not too easy. The following strategies are additional methods to improve reading fluency:

- **Read-along method.** The teacher and one student read a passage together orally.
- **Paired reading.** Two students read in pairs, alternating pages; paired reading provides extensive reading practice for both students.
- **Echo reading.** First, the teacher models an oral reading passage; the student is then asked to imitate the teacher's reading.
- **Reading aloud to other audiences.** Children can read aloud to willing listeners, such as grandparents, other family members, or even the dog.

12.3e Vocabulary

vocabulary occupies a central position in learning to read. The student's vocabulary has a significant effect on reading achievement and is strongly related to reading comprehension (Jennings et al., 2010; National Reading Panel, 2000).

vocabulary
Recognition and knowledge of words. Consists of oral vocabulary and reading vocabulary.

Vocabulary knowledge requires the reader to not only know the word, but also to apply it appropriately in context. For example, when 2 boys tried to make cookies, they were puzzled when their cookies stuck to the pan. They had followed the directions in the recipe and greased the bottom of the pan. Their vocabulary problem was they thought the meaning of the word *bottom* referred to the underside of the pan. The part on which they had been told to place the cookies seemed to them to be the top of the pan.

Some important facets of teaching vocabulary are

- **Differences between oral vocabulary and reading vocabulary.** (1) *Oral vocabulary*—the words the child uses in speaking and in listening—and (2) *reading vocabulary*—the words the reader recognizes in print. Children enter school with a large oral vocabulary, estimated to be about 6,000 words. The average high school senior knows about 45,000 words (Stahl, 2004). Many of these words are in the student's reading vocabulary.

- **Indirect instruction and direct instruction.** Students build their vocabulary knowledge both indirectly and directly. Methods for indirect instruction include the expansive use of oral language and students reading extensively on their own. In direct instruction, words are explicitly taught using word-learning strategies.

- **Stages of learning words.** It is important to recognize that students learn words gradually. Most words require 20 exposures in context before an adequate grasp of their meanings is acquired (McKenna, 2004).

indirect instruction
Instruction that is incidental.

direct instruction
A method associated with behavioral theories of instruction. The focus is directly on the curriculum or task to be taught and the steps needed to learn that task.

The National Reading Panel (2000) summarized its findings about vocabulary instruction, noting that

- Instruction in vocabulary leads to gains in comprehension and the method must be appropriate for the age and ability of the reader.
- Computer programs are helpful in teaching vocabulary.
- Vocabulary can be learned incidentally in the context of storybook reading or by listening to others.
- The instructional procedure of teaching vocabulary before reading a text is helpful.

The "Teaching Strategies" section of this chapter offers some specific strategies to improve students' vocabulary.

12.3f Comprehension

comprehension
The purpose of reading—gathering meaning from the printed page.

The purpose of reading is comprehension, that is, gathering meaning from the printed page. All reading instruction should provide for the development of reading comprehension. Reading comprehension is the major problem for many students with reading disabilities. Comprehension skills do not automatically evolve after word-recognition skills have been learned. Although most students with reading disabilities eventually learn the basics of word-recognition skills, many continue to have great difficulty with tasks that require comprehension of complex passages. These students need to learn strategies that will help them become active readers who understand the text. In this section, we describe (1) different views of reading comprehension, (2) strategies to promote reading comprehension, and (3) comprehension of narrative and informational materials.

Views of Reading Comprehension Reading comprehension is an active process that requires an intentional and thoughtful interaction between the reader and the text. As readers try to comprehend the material they read, they must bridge the gap between the information presented in the written text and the knowledge they possess. Reading comprehension thus involves thinking. The reader's background knowledge, interest, and the reading situation all affect comprehension of the material. Each person's integration of the new information in the text with what is already known will yield unique information (Jennings et al., 2010; National Reading Panel, 2000).

reading comprehension
Understanding of the meaning of printed text.

Reading Comprehension Depends on What the Reader Brings to the Written Material Reading comprehension depends on the reader's experience, knowledge of language, and recognition of syntactic structure, as well as on the redundancy of the printed passage (Jennings et al., 2010).

When a reader is faced with text that is about something the reader knows nothing about yet is able to read the individual words, the individual will not be able to comprehend the text. The implication for teaching is that when a reader has limited knowledge to relate to text content, no amount of rereading will increase comprehension. What students with learning disabilities and related disabilities need in many cases is more background knowledge to improve their comprehension.

Reading Comprehension Is a Thinking Process The relationship between reading and thinking has been noted for a long time. In 1917, Thorndike likened the thinking process used in mathematics to that of reading:

According to Thorndike, understanding a paragraph is like solving a problem in mathematics. It consists of selecting the right elements of the situation and putting them together in the right relations, and also with the right amount of weight or influence or force for each . . . all under the influence of the right mental set or purpose or demands.

Reading can be viewed as thinking or as something akin to problem solving. As in problem solving, the reader must employ concepts, develop and test hypotheses, and modify those concepts. Thus, reading comprehension is a mode of inquiry, and methods that employ discovery techniques should be used in the teaching of reading. The key to teaching from this perspective is to guide students to set up their own questions and purposes for reading. Students then read to solve problems that they have devised for themselves. Students can be encouraged first to guess what will happen next in a story, for example, and then to read to determine the accuracy of those predictions (Stauffer, 1975). This approach, which is called a directed reading-thinking activity (DRTA), is described in the "Teaching Strategies" section of this chapter.

directed reading-thinking activity (DRTA)
A guided method of teaching reading comprehension in which readers first read a section of text, then predict what will happen next, and then read to verify the accuracy of the predictions.

© Cengage Learning 2015

TeachSource Video Case Activity

Watch the TeachSource Video Case entitled "Reading Comprehension Strategies for the Elementary School: Questioning Techniques." In this video, the teacher, Liz Page, instructs students on how to understand the text, read between the lines, and interpret texts at multiple levels, then leads a discussion with the group on interpretation questions.

QUESTIONS

1. How does the teacher model the reading strategy?
2. How does an interpretation comprehension question differ from a factual comprehension question?

Reading Comprehension Requires Active Interaction with the Text Readers must be active participants, interacting with the text material. They must actively combine their existing knowledge with the new information of the printed text.

There is evidence that good readers generally do not read every word of a passage; instead, they "sample" certain words to determine the meaning and skip many others. They go back and read every word only when they encounter something unexpected. For example, when people in love are reading a love letter, they read for all they are worth. They read every word three ways; they read the whole in terms of the parts, and each part in terms of the whole; they grow sensitive to context and ambiguity, to insinuation and implication; they perceive the color of words, the order of phrases, and the weight of sentences. They may even take punctuation into account (Adler, 1956).

Strategies to Promote Reading Comprehension In its review of reading comprehension, the National Reading Panel (2000) recognized several strategies that have a solid scientific basis of instruction for improving reading comprehension.

1. **Comprehension monitoring.** Students learn how to be aware of their understanding of the material.
2. **Cooperative learning.** Students learn reading strategies together.
3. **Using graphic and semantic organizers, including story maps.** Students make graphic representations of the material to assist their comprehension.
4. **Question answering.** Students answer questions posed by the teacher and receive immediate feedback.
5. **Question generation.** Students ask themselves questions about various aspects of the story.
6. **Story structure.** Students are taught how to use the structure of the story as a means of helping them recall story content in order to answer questions about what they have read.
7. **Summarization.** Students are taught to integrate ideas and to generalize from the text information.

Students with reading disabilities often require a different type of comprehension instruction. Just as students with reading disabilities need explicit structured instruction to learn word-recognition skills, they need explicit, highly structured instruction to learn reading comprehension skills. Incidental, literature-based instruction may be successful to teach reading comprehension to typical learners but such instruction is not sufficient for students with reading disabilities. Joanna Williams (1998) taught comprehension to students with reading disabilities through a "Themes Instruction Program," which consists of a series of twelve 40-minute lessons. Each lesson is organized around a single story and is composed of five parts:

1. Prereading discussion on the purpose of the lesson and the topic of the story that will be read.
2. Reading the story.
3. Discussion of important story information using organized (schema) questions as a guide.
4. Identification of a theme for the story, stating it in general terms so that it is relevant to a variety of stories and situations.
5. Practice in applying the generalized theme to real-life experiences.

Comprehension Activities Before, During, and After Reading Reading comprehension can be taught before reading, during reading, and after reading, as indicated in Teaching Tips 12.1, "Strategies to Promote Reading Comprehension."

Before reading a story, teachers should motivate and interest students in the reading selection, review the vocabulary, build background information, and have the students predict what the story will be about. *During reading*, the teacher should direct the students' attention to the difficult or subtle dimensions of the story, anticipate difficult words and ideas, talk about problems and solutions, encourage silent reading, as well as encourage students to monitor their own comprehension. *After reading*, comprehension strategies can include

TEACHING TIPS 12.1

Strategies To Promote Reading Comprehension

Before Reading	During Reading	After Reading
Establish a purpose for reading.	Direct attention to difficult or subtle dimensions of the text.	Ask students to retell or summarize the story.
Review vocabulary.	Point out difficult words and ideas.	Create graphic organizers (e.g., webs, cause-and-effect charts, outlines).
Build background knowledge.	Ask students to identify problems and solutions.	Put pictures of story events in order.
Relate background knowledge and information to the story.	Encourage silent reading.	Link background information.
Encourage children to predict what the story will be about.	Encourage students to monitor their own comprehension while reading.	Generate questions for other children.
Discuss the author if such knowledge helps to set up the story.	Insert author information in the story.	Have students write their own reactions to stories and factual material.

Professional Resource Download

having the readers summarize or retell the story, talk about what they liked and what they wished had been different in the story, create graphic organizers, put pictures of story events in order, link background information, and talk about the characters in the story (Jennings et al., 2010).

Comprehension of Narrative and Informational Text Two types of reading comprehension materials are narrative materials and informational materials. *Narrative* materials are stories that are usually fiction. *Informational* materials are nonfictional materials that provide new knowledge about a subject.

Narrative Materials Narratives have characters, a plot, and a sequence of events. To read narrative materials effectively, students must be able to identify the following:

- Important characters
- Setting, time, and place
- Major events in sequence
- Problems that the characters had to solve and how those problems were resolved

Sometimes narratives are inspirational. Readers can leave the limits of their everyday lives and travel to other parts of the world, to space, and to other time periods. Poor readers often respond negatively to narrative materials and have to be strongly encouraged to read stories. It is important to ask students for their reactions and to find narrative materials that meet their interests. Different varieties of narrative reading materials are called *genres*. To become good readers, students need to have experiences with a variety of narrative materials, such as realistic fiction; fantasy fiction (such as books with talking animals); science fiction; fairy tales, folktales, and tall tales; fables; mysteries; historical fiction set in a period in the past; plays; and narrative poetry (poems that tell stories).

informational materials
Reading text material that is about subject matter. Usually nonfiction.

Comprehension of Informational Materials Informational materials include subject-matter materials, such as textbooks used in social studies or science content areas. As students move through the grades, the reading tasks they confront change dramatically. Reading assignments in content-area textbooks take the place of narrative stories. Students are often assigned to read textbooks independently, without supervision or help. They may be required to read a chapter, complete a written assignment on the chapter, prepare for a class activity based on the chapter, and take a test on the content of the chapter. It is not surprising that many students with learning disabilities and related mild disabilities cannot complete such assignments. A student whose reading has been limited to narrative stories will lack experience with, and the ability to do, the kind of reading that informational, content-area textbooks require.

Instruction at the secondary level places heavy demands on reading proficiency and provides little teacher direction. Major problems in content-area reading for students with learning disabilities and related disabilities include the following:

1. **There is a heavy emphasis on reading to obtain information.** Content-area instruction is based on presumed proficiency in reading. Students are expected to read, comprehend, and retain large amounts of information—up

to 50 pages a week for each general education content class. Furthermore, students may be required to take four content-area classes (e.g., English, science, mathematics, and history). For students with reading disabilities, the reading demand can become overwhelming.

2. **Content textbooks are generally written above the grade level in which they are used.** The textbook could be extremely difficult for the student with reading disabilities to understand. For example, if a tenth-grade student is at a fifth-grade reading level and the social studies textbook is written at an eleventh-grade level, there will be a 6-year discrepancy between the student's reading level and the reading level of the textbook.

3. **Content-area teachers often assume that students have adequate reading ability, and they do not teach reading skills.** At the secondary level, there is little time spent on teaching reading skills, such as organizing or studying an outline. Teachers can help students read content books by making the reading meaningful, connecting it to other material that the students have covered, and encouraging students to review the material to get an orientation to the text as a whole. Teachers can also introduce difficult or technical words before reading the text and alert students to monitor for comprehension as they are reading.

The "Teaching Strategies" section of this chapter provides some suggestions to help students read informational materials when using content-area textbooks.

Did You Get It?

In 2000, the National Reading Panel published a list of 5 categories in which every child should/must be able to display specific levels of reading competency. The list did not include which category?

a. test comprehension
b. literary critique
c. phonemic awareness
d. fluency

12.4 The Reading-Writing Connection

Strong ties exist between reading and writing. As students write, their reading skills improve. Both readers and writers construct meaning. Readers construct meaning from the author's text; writers compose or construct meaning as they write.

12.4a Early Literacy and Writing

Young children begin to grasp the insight that alphabet letters represent abstract speech segments. At a very early stage of literacy development, young children begin to write letters for words. For example, a child might write *KR* for *car*, *TRKE* for *turkey*, or *PTZU* for *pizza*. Children should be encouraged to write. Acceptance of "invented spelling" encourages children's writing. Figure 12.1 shows the writing of a young child who uses the alphabetic principle.

© Cengage Learning

With the early literacy emphasis, sometimes children learn to write before they learn to read. Student Stories 12.2, "Writing Before Reading," tells the story of a kindergartner who learned to write before learning to read.

Did You Get It?

A very young child wrote a new word he heard, "bicycle," as "bykicl." This to-be-accepted form of early writing is referred to as "_____ spelling."
  a. invented
  b. ventured
  c. gambled
  d. aspiration

STUDENT STORIES 12.2
Writing Before Reading

The following example describes an incident involving a kindergartner who confidently used writing before learning to read. A business call was made to a client's home and the client's 5-year-old child answered the phone. The caller's side of the telephone conversation was overheard and went as follows:

"Hello, I want to speak to Mr. John Walsh. . . Oh, he's in the shower? Well, would you please write a message for him?. . . Good. Please write that. . . What? You haven't any paper?. . . Okay, I'll wait until you get a piece of paper. . . You got the paper? Good. Please write that. . . What?

You haven't got a pencil?. . . Okay, I'll wait. . . Good. You found a pencil. Please write that Eugene Lerner called. I'll spell that— *E-U-G-E-N-E L-E-R-N-E-R.* My phone number is 708-555-1437. Did you write that down?. . . Good. Now would you read the message back to me?. . . What's that? You can write, but you haven't learned to read?"

REFLECTIVE QUESTION

1. What kind of early childhood curriculum do you think this child was in?

12.5 Literature-Based Reading Instruction/ Whole-Language Reading Instruction

A contentious issue regarding approaches for teaching reading involves the controversy between whole-language reading instruction and skills-based reading instruction that includes phonics. The concept of whole-language reading instruction was first introduced by Kenneth Goodman (1967). The underlying philosophy of this approach was that children should learn to read in the same way they learned to talk. By being involved in numerous books and stories and having many experiences listening to stories, they can learn to read in a natural way. The whole-language approach quickly rose in popularity in the schools during the late 1980s and the 1990s and was used in many schools throughout the country. The popularity of whole language has waned with the current emphasis on skills and phonics, but there are still many proponents of whole-language reading instruction (Flurkey & Yu, 2003).

The literature-based approach to teaching reading promotes a number of sound principles for reading instruction:

1. **There are strong interrelationships among the various language systems: oral language, reading, and writing.** The links between reading and oral language and writing should be strengthened. Active experiences with writing and oral language will improve a child's reading. The early literacy curriculum focuses on the links between oral and written language and encourages children to write as early as kindergarten and even before learning to read.

2. **Young children should be immersed in language and books from infancy.** Children need much exposure to language, books, and stories. The value of using stories has been part of our culture from Mother Goose to Dr. Seuss. It is essential that books, stories, and poems become an integral part of a child's life. Children benefit greatly from sharing books and hearing stories. (See Chapter 11, "Spoken Language Difficulties: Listening and Speaking.")

3. **Children should be given many experiences with writing.** Children need opportunities to engage in abundant writing and to express their thoughts and ideas in writing and in journals. Figure 12.2 shows the written journal entry of a 5-year-old kindergarten student.

4. **Children need time for independent reading.** Children need opportunities to engage in reading for enjoyment when they are not under the supervision of a teacher.

Did You Get It?

Children should be presented with opportunities for language and book-related activities from infancy on in a manner that constitutes _____.
   a. superficial exposure
   b. familiarity
   c. empiricism
   d. immersion

FIGURE **12.2**
Journal of a Kindergarten
Student

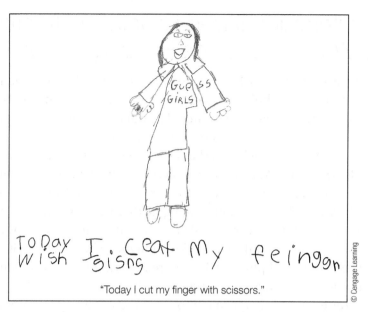

"Today I cut my finger with scissors."

© Cengage Learning

12.6 English-Language Learners (ELL) and Reading

ELL

English-language learners (ELL) are students who are not yet proficient with the English language, and their native language is not English. An increasing number of students come from homes in which a language other than English is spoken. For over 77% of ELL students in the United States, Spanish is the native language, but over 350 languages are used by ELL students in U.S. schools (Samson & Lesaux, 2009; McCardle, 2005). Chapter 11, "Spoken Language Difficulties: Listening and Speaking," provides additional information about English-language learners. Many students who are English-language learners have much difficulty learning to read in English.

The following methods for teaching reading to ELL students are recommended by Hudson and Smith (2001):

- **Build reading fluency.** Have students reread orally two familiar books in English from previous lessons.
- **Keep a running record of errors.** The teacher has a duplicate copy of the text the student is reading aloud and marks errors that the student makes in the oral reading. The teacher and student discuss these errors.
- **Incorporate writing into the lesson.** The student writes the story that has been read.
- **Cut up the written story into sentences.** The student reassembles the sentences, and rereads it several times.
- **Write a new story.** The student reads a new book and then writes a new story about what has been read.

Did You Get It?

How many primary languages other than English are spoken by students in schools in the United States?
  a. 25–50
  b. 100–150
  c. 200–300
  d. well over 300

12.7 Assessing Reading

There are many more measures and tests for assessing reading than for other areas of the curriculum. Reading can be assessed through (1) *informal measures,* such as the informal reading inventory and portfolio assessment or (2) *formal tests,* such as survey tests, diagnostic tests, and comprehensive batteries.

12.7a Informal Measures

One of the simplest methods of assessing reading is to observe informally as the student reads aloud. The teacher can readily detect the student's general reading level, word-recognition abilities, types of errors, and understanding of the material. This method is very practical and can be as informative as elaborate test batteries.

Informal Reading Inventory The informal reading inventory (IRI), which can be administered quickly and easily, provides a wealth of information concerning the student's reading skills, reading levels, types of errors, techniques of attacking unknown words, and related behavioral characteristics (Jennings et al., 2010; Johnson, Kress, & Pikulski, 1987).

> **informal reading inventory (IRI)**
> An informal method of assessing the reading level of a student by having the student orally read successively more difficult passages.

   The informal reading inventory procedure requires the examiner to choose selections of approximately 100 words in length from a series of graded reading levels. The student reads aloud from several graded levels while the teacher systematically records the errors. If the student makes more than 5 errors per 100 words, the student is given progressively easier selections until a level is found at which there are no more than 2 errors per 100 words. To check comprehension, the teacher asks the student 4 to 10 questions about each selection. By means of the following criteria, an informal reading inventory can determine 3 reading levels:

1. **Independent reading level.** The student is able to recognize about 95% of the words and to answer about 90% of the comprehension questions correctly. (This is the level at which the student is able to read library books or do reading work independently.)
2. **Instructional reading level.** The student is able to recognize about 90% of the words in the selection, with a comprehension score of about 70%. (This is the level at which the student will profit from teacher-directed reading instruction.)
3. **Frustration reading level.** The student is able to recognize fewer than 90% of the words, with a comprehension score of less than 70%. (If the student does not understand the material, this level is too difficult and should not be used for instruction.)

   In addition to informal reading inventories developed by teachers, several standard commercial inventories are available, and they offer a convenient way to administer the reading inventory.

The IOTA Informal Word-Reading Test The IOTA test is an informal test for word-reading skills in the public domain. This means it is no longer under copyright law. It was originally published by M. Monroe (1932). (See the Student Website for information about how to administer the IOTA informal reading test.)

Portfolio Assessment of Reading Portfolio assessment is an alternative to traditional, standardized reading assessment tests. The problem with standardized reading tests is that they do not measure what students are actually doing in the reading classroom and do not closely link the assessment to the reading curriculum. Proponents of portfolio assessment propose that learning is too complex and assessment too imperfect to rely on any single index of achievement.

Specifically, *portfolio assessment* consists of keeping samples of the students' reading and writing work. It is relatively easy to collect samples of students' writing during the school year. For reading, the teacher keeps a reflective log, recording the students' reactions to books they read, along with the teacher's own reactions. The log shows the growth of each student in reading comprehension. Samples of language experience stories can be kept in the portfolio. Other assessment methods of this type are observations of students ("kid watching"), checklists, interviews with students, and collections of student work. By reviewing the students' work over a period of time, teachers, parents, and students themselves are able to evaluate progress (Jennings et al., 2010).

12.7b Formal Tests

Formal reading tests can be classified as survey tests, diagnostic tests, or comprehensive batteries. *Survey tests* are group tests that give an overall reading achievement level. These tests generally give at least 2 scores: word recognition and reading comprehension. *Diagnostic tests* are individual tests that provide more in-depth information about the student's strengths and weaknesses in reading. *Comprehensive batteries* are tests with components that measure several academic areas, including reading. Table 12.5 lists some of the widely used formal reading tests in each of these categories.

Did You Get It?

_____ level is an assessment result used to determine the level of reading at which a student is not able to perform adequately—a level considered beyond optimal for him or her.
  a. Frustration
  b. Antagonistic
  c. Vexation
  d. Apprehension

12.8 Teaching Strategies to Improve Reading Difficulties

The "Teaching Strategies" section presents approaches, methods, and materials to teach reading to students with learning disabilities and related disabilities. It is organized by the following strategies: (1) strategies to improve word recognition, (2) strategies to improve fluency, (3) strategies to improve reading comprehension, (4) enjoyment and appreciation of reading, (5) multisensory methods, and (6) assistive and instructional technology for reading.

TABLE 12.5

Commonly Used Formal Reading Tests

Test	Grade or Age Assessed
Survey tests	
• Gates-MacGinitie Reading Tests (4th ed.), Riverside Publishing *http://www.riverpub.com*	Grades 1–12
• Metropolitan Achievement Tests, Harcourt *http://www.harcourtassessment.com*	Grades K–12
• Wide-Range Achievement Test—4 (WRAT-4), Ann Arbor *http://www.annarbor.co.uk*	Ages 5–adult
Diagnostic tests	
• Stanford Diagnostic Reading Test (4th ed.), Harcourt *http://www.harcourtassessment.com*	Grades 1–12
• Woodcock Reading Mastery Test—Revised Normative Updates (WRMT-R), AGS *http://ags.pearsonassessments.com*	Ages 5–adult
Comprehensive batteries	
• Brigance Comprehension Inventory of Basic Skills—Revised Curriculum Associates *http://www.curriculumassociates.com*	Grades K–9
• Kaufman Test of Educational Achievement, 2nd ed. (KTEA-2), AGS *http://ags.pearsonassessments.com*	
• PIAT-R/NL Peabody Individual Achievement Test—Revised Normative Update, AGS *http://ags.pearsonassessments.com*	Grades K–12
• Woodcock-Johnson Tests of Achievement III, Riverside Publishing *http://www.riverpub.com*	Preschool–adult

© Cengage Learning

Did You Get It?

Phoneme awareness is considered an inextricable link in the process of teaching/improving word recognition. Which strategy is not used to build phoneme awareness?

    a. segmenting the sounds and syllables in words
    b. learning to recognize and assess rhyming patterns
    c. learning to recognize basic aspects of word-origin
    d. learning to properly count the sounds within a word

12.9 Strategies to Improve Word Recognition

12.9a Building Phoneme Awareness

A child who is learning to read must first become aware of the sounds in words and language. Strategies for teaching children to become aware of the phonemes, or sounds, in language include (1) learning to count the sounds in words, (2) learning to segment the sounds and syllables in words, and (3) learning to recognize rhyming words. These strategies are presented in Chapter 11, "Spoken Language Difficulties: Listening and Speaking."

12.9b Dynamic Indicators of Basic Early Literacy Skills (DIBELS)

DIBELS

A measurement system to assess early reading skills of young children, including phonological awareness, alphabetic principles, and oral reading fluency.

Some schools are using a measurement system called DIBELS to assess the early reading skills of young children in grades K-2. DIBELS stands for *Dynamic Indicators of Basic Early Literacy Skills*. DIBELS measures are designed to assess the young child's skills in phonological awareness (initial sound fluency and phonemic segmentation fluency), alphabetic principles (nonsense word fluency), and oral reading fluency. The intent of DIBELS is to monitor the early reading skills of young children frequently to identify young children who are likely to have difficulty in learning to read and to provide the appropriate intervention. More information about DIBELS can be found at the DIBELS website at *http://dibels.uoregon.edu.*

12.9c Phonics Methods

Phonics systems and phonics books have been on the market for over 70 years. Many phonics programs today are repackaged as preprinted masters for duplication or as CDs, recordings, audiotapes, videotapes, computer software programs, and multimedia packages. Two phonics approaches are (1) synthetic and (2) analytic. *Synthetic phonics* methods first teach students isolated letters and their sound equivalents. Then they teach students to synthesize or blend these individual phoneme elements into whole words. *Analytic phonics* methods teach students whole words that have a consistent sound-spelling pattern, and they then teach students to analyze the phoneme elements that make up the words. A typical exercise in phonics materials appears in Figure 12.3.

The Dollar Store Many useful reading games and materials can be found by browsing through a dollar store. These bargain items include phonics games, alphabet letters, sight word cards, and other reading-related materials. Teachers can develop a collection of these items that can be placed in an activity center or used to reinforce a reading lesson. Dollar store items can also be purchased through the Internet. The URL for one such dollar store, Oriental Trading, is *http://www.OrientalTrading.com.* Figure 12.4 provides you with a menu of some reading activities you can plan using low cost materials.

Did You Get It?

Repetition is a very effective strategy for improving fluency. The basic length of a standard passage meant for repetition should be
- **a.** 10 to 15 words—a standard sentence.
- **b.** 30 to 45 words—a short paragraph.
- **c.** 50 to 200 words—a half-page of text.
- **d.** 1,200–1,500 words—a short chapter.

FIGURE **12.3**
Examples of Phonics Exercises

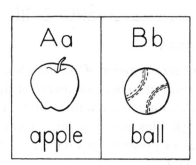
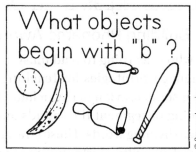

© Cengage Learning

12.10 Strategies to Improve Fluency

In addition to recognizing words accurately, readers must read the words quickly and fluently. Otherwise, reading is labored and not enjoyable, and the reader loses meaning. Some strategies to improve fluency include (1) repeated reading, (2) predictable books, and (3) the neurological impress method.

12.10a Repeated Reading

Repeated reading is a strategy used to give the student repeated practice to improve his or her oral reading fluency. It is especially useful with slow, halting readers who accurately identify most words in a passage but have not developed fluency. The method involves the selection of passages that are 50 to 200 words long and at a difficulty level that enables the student to recognize most of the words. The student then reads the selection orally three or four times before proceeding to a new passage. Word-accuracy rates and reading speed are usually reported to the student after each reading, and daily practice is recommended (Jennings et al., 2010). Some students particularly enjoy repeated reading when the passages are displayed on a computer screen. *Read Naturally* is a commercial fluency and training program that focuses on fluency development. Its website is at *http://www.readnaturally.com.*

12.10b Predictable Books

Predictable books contain patterns or refrains that are repeated over and over. Many are based on folktales and fairy tales. For example, in *The Three Billy Goats Gruff,* the question "Who is that trip-trapping over my bridge?" is asked by the troll as each Billy goat goes over the bridge. Another favorite predictable book is *Brown Bear, Brown Bear.* After the book has been read to young children several times, they are able to predict the wording and begin saying the refrain along with the storyteller. Using predictable books is an excellent way to actively involve children in a story even before they can read. They begin to develop language knowledge and anticipate what will be said. This experience helps develop support for word recognition when they do read the story (Jennings et al., 2010).

12.10c Neurological Impress Method

Another approach to improving fluency for students with severe reading disabilities is the *neurological impress method* (Heckelman, 1969; Langford, Slade, & Barnett, 1974). It is a system of rapid-unison reading by the student and teacher. The student sits slightly in front of the teacher, and both read together out of one book. The voice of the teacher is directed into the ear of the student at a fairly close range. The student or the teacher places a finger on the word as it is read. At times, the teacher's voice may be louder and faster than the student's, and at other times the teacher may read more slowly than the student, who may lag slightly behind. No preliminary preparations are made with the reading material before the student sees it. The goal is simply to cover as many pages as possible within the time available without tiring the student. The theory underlying this method is that the auditory process of feedback from the reader's own voice and from the voice of someone else reading the same material strengthens the reading process.

In the *read-along method,* a similar process occurs. In this method, children listen to a CD or a tape recording of a story as they read along with the text. In the classroom, headphones may be used so that the tape recording does not disturb other children. There are many commercial stories and tapes available for this purpose.

Did You Get It?

The fundamental aspect of the structure of a basal reading series is its _____ nature of difficulty levels as the series progresses.
a. escalating
b. deescalating
c. stable
d. random

12.11 Strategies to Improve Reading Comprehension

This section describes strategies to improve reading comprehension. Comprehension is the essence of the reading act. Students must understand and interact with the text. The section discusses (1) basal readers, (2) activating background knowledge, (3) language experience method, (4) the K-W-L technique, (5) building meaning with vocabulary and concepts, (6) the reading-writing connection, (7) thinking strategies, and (8) cognitive learning strategies for reading.

12.11a Using Basal Readers

basal reading series
A sequential and interrelated set of books and supportive material intended to provide the basic material for the development of fundamental reading skills.

Basal readers are a sequential and interrelated set of books and supportive materials intended to provide the basic material for the development of fundamental reading skills. A basal reading series consists of graded readers that gradually increase in difficulty, typically beginning with very simple readiness and first-grade books and going through the sixth- or eighth-grade level. The books increase in difficulty in vocabulary, story content, and skill development. Auxiliary material, such as teacher's manuals and activity books, often accompanies the books. Most basal reading series incorporate an eclectic approach to the teaching of reading, using many procedures to teach readiness, vocabulary, word recognition, comprehension, and the enjoyment of literature.

As the major tool of reading instruction for the past 40 years, the basal reader has been the target of continual criticism from diverse groups, including some educators, scholars from other academic disciplines, the popular press, parent groups, political observers, moralists, and, recently, ethnic and women's groups. Critics have scoffed at and satirized the language, phonics presentation, story content, class appeal, pictures, qualities, and environment of the characters of the basal reader. In spite of this highly vocal and severe criticism, basal readers continue to be the major tool for reading instruction in elementary classrooms throughout the country.

Because most basal readers are not committed to any one teaching procedure, publishers are continually modifying them in response to the demands of the times and the consumer market. For example, more phonics and decoding activities are currently being added to basal readers. Other recent basal reader modifications have more literature-based materials and language activities in the early grades. The modifications have also made stories longer and more sophisticated and added stories that are culturally and ethnically diverse. There are also series of readers produced especially for slow readers.

12.11b Activating Background Knowledge

The following strategies alert the student to the background knowledge needed for reading comprehension and build on student experiences.

Language Experience Method The language experience method is well accepted as a method that builds on the student's knowledge and language base, linking the different forms of language—listening, speaking, reading, and writing. This method uses the student's own experiences and language as the raw material. Students begin by dictating stories to the teacher (or writing stories by themselves). These stories then become the basis of their reading instruction. Through the language experience approach, students conceptualize written material as follows:

> What I can think about, I can talk about.
>
> What I can say, I can write (or someone can write for me).
>
> What I can write, I can read.
>
> I can read what others write for me to read.

There is no predetermined, rigid control over vocabulary, syntax, or content. The teacher uses the text or stories that the student composes to develop reading skills. The language experience approach to reading has a vitality and immediacy, as well as an element of creativity. The method is effective both in the beginning-to-read stage with young children and in corrective instruction with older pupils. The interest of the student is high because the emphasis is on reading material that grows out of the student's personal experiences and natural language in expressing these experiences. Figure 12.4 shows an example of a language experience story. (Language experience is also discussed as a writing strategy in Chapter 13, "Written Language Difficulties: Written Expression, Spelling, and Handwriting.")

The K-W-L Technique K-W-L is a technique for reading and studying content-area textbooks (Ogle, 1986). The letters represent 3 questions in 3 steps of a lesson:

1. **What I know.** Students think of and state all the knowledge they have on a subject. A group of students can pool their knowledge.
2. **What I want to find out.** Each student thinks of and writes on a sheet of paper what he or she wants to (or expects to) learn from the reading. Students can then compare their answers to this question.
3. **What I learned.** Students read the lesson silently and write what they have learned from the reading. Answers to this question can be shared by the group.

language experience method
A method of teaching reading based on the experiences and language of the reader. The method involves the generation of experience-based materials that are dictated by the student, written by the teacher, and then used as the material for teaching reading.

FIGURE **12.4**
Sample Page from Phonics
Remedial Reading Lessons

10 WAYS TO USE LOW COST MATERIALS TO BUILD READING SKILLS

1. Purchase three hula hoops and put three different letters that make a word in each hula hoop. Have the student jump in the hoops in sequence as they say the sounds of the letter and then put them together in the last hoop to make a word.

2. Purchase a shower curtain or a plastic tablecloth and write words that you are working on with the students on the curtain or cloth and tape to the floor. Say the word and have the student jump to the correct word.

3. Purchase a large plain ball where you have written in permanent marker key words that you want to review with your students or where you have written key letters. You throw the ball to the student and wherever the student's left thumb lands, the student has to read the word or give the sound of the letter closest to where the student's left thumb landed.

4. Purchase hand clappers for each student. Students get to clap for each sound they hear in the words they say.

5. Purchase sand paper and cut out letters in sand paper so students are able to feel the letters as they say them and provide the sound.

6. Purchase flash cards that have a picture and the matching word.

7. Purchase sheets of foam and make puzzles with letters that make words and have the students put together the puzzle to make a word.

8. Purchase a plastic bucket and scoop and place various words in the bucket and have students read those words as they scoop the letters one at a time from the bucket.

9. Purchase blank name tags. Give 3 or 4 or 5 students a nametag with a letter on it and have students put themselves together and in order to make a word.

10. Purchase a dot to dot book with letters. In order for a student to connect the dot, he or she has to say a word that begins with the letter. You can also make your own dot to dots.

© Cengage Learning 2015

Professional Resource Download

Figure 12.5 provides a chart that shows the importance of passage review. To increase comprehension, the teacher must build on prior knowledge, review key vocabulary words in the passage, review the big ideas, review what students want to learn about the passage, how they want to learn about the passage, and then review what they learned that can then provide a basis for new passages.

12.11c Building Meaning With Vocabulary and Concepts

To read effectively, readers need to have knowledge of word meanings and of the concepts underlying the words. The more students read, the more word meanings and language they will acquire. It is important to use strategies that will build the student's vocabulary and understanding of words.

Knowledge of vocabulary and the ability to understand the concepts of words are closely related to reading achievement. Limited vocabulary knowledge can seriously hamper reading comprehension. Further, as words become more abstract, the concepts become more difficult to grasp.

Concepts are commonly explained as ideas, abstractions, or the essence of things. For example, the concept of *chair* refers to an idea, an abstraction, or a symbol of concrete experiences. A person's experiences may have included exposure to a specific rocking chair, an upholstered chair, and a baby's highchair, but the concept *chair* symbolizes a set of attributes about "chairness." The word *chair* allows a person to make an inference about new experiences with chairs, such as a lawn chair observed for the first time. The word or concept of *chair* by itself does not have an empirical reference point.

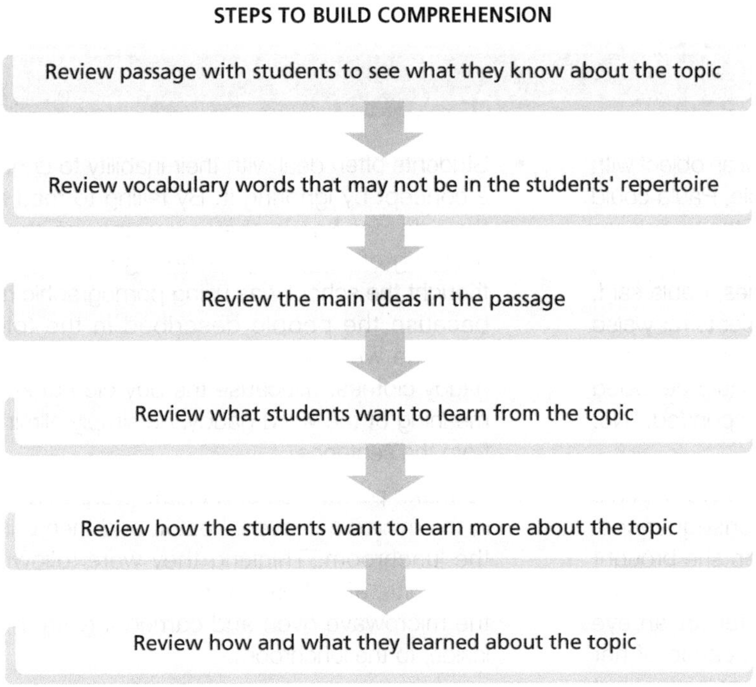

STEPS TO BUILD COMPREHENSION

FIGURE **12.5**
Steps to Build Comprehension

Review passage with students to see what they know about the topic

Review vocabulary words that may not be in the students' repertoire

Review the main ideas in the passage

Review what students want to learn from the topic

Review how the students want to learn more about the topic

Review how and what they learned about the topic

© Cengage Learning 2015

At a still more abstract level, words become further removed from concrete referents. The concept *chair* is part of a broader concept *of furniture*. Concepts even more removed from the sensory world are ideas, such as *democracy, loyalty, fairness,* and *freedom.*

A further confusion in school learning is related to the fact that textbooks present important concepts as technical terms, such as *plateau, continental divide, density of population, pollution, the law of gravity,* or *space exploration.* Problems in reading in the content areas are frequently due not to the difficulty of the words, but to the concentration and compactness of the presentation of the concepts.

Because language plays a key role in concept development, language problems are likely to be reflected in faulty conceptual abilities and limited vocabulary development. Students who have meager, imprecise, or inaccurate concepts will have difficulties understanding a reading passage. Student Stories 12.3, "Misunderstanding of Concepts," illustrates the consequences of imprecise concept development.

Expanding Vocabulary The following activities are designed to expand and build vocabulary:

1. **Highlighting multiple word meanings.** Multiple meanings of words often cause confusion in reading. For example, there are many meanings of the word *note.* In music, *note* means the elliptical character in a certain position on the music staff. In arithmetic or business, a *note* might mean a written promise to pay. In English or study hall, a *note* might refer to an informal written communication. In social studies, a *note* might refer to a formal communiqué between the heads of two nations. In science, one might be able to *note* the results of an experiment, meaning to observe them. In English class, the selection of literature might discuss an individual who was a person of great *note,* or importance, in the community. In any lesson, the student could be asked to make *note* of an examination date, meaning to remember it. The teacher could make a *note,* meaning a remark, in the margin of the paper.

- Some students confuse one attribute of an object with the concept of the object. For example, Paula could not understand the circular concept of the roundness of a plate. When told that the plate was "round" and asked to draw a circle around its edges, Paula said, "That's not round; that's a dish." Students may also confuse the concept of an object with its name. When Paula was asked if the moon could be called by another name, such as cow, she responded, "No, because the moon doesn't give milk."

- Misunderstanding a symbol that conveys multiple concepts may have unexpected consequences. Nine-year-old Susie was in tears when she brought home a medical form from the school nurse advising Susie's parents to take their daughter for an eye examination. Susie sobbed that the cause of her anguish was not that she needed eyeglasses, but that the nurse had filled in an *F* in the blank next to the word sex on the examination form. That symbol *F* conveyed the concept of a grade, and Susie feared she had "failed sex."

- Students often deal with their inability to understand a concept by ignoring it. By failing to read a word they do not know, they may change the entire meaning of a passage. One high school student thought the school was using pornographic material because the people described in the following passage were nude: "The pilgrims did not wear gaudy clothes." Because the boy did not know the meaning of the word gaudy, he simply eliminated it from the sentence.

- To make pizza, Lisa and Jaime were told to put it in the microwave oven, heat it, and then bring it to the lunchroom. Thinking they were following the directions, after heating the pizza, they unplugged the microwave oven and carried it (with the pizza inside) to the lunchroom.

REFLECTIVE QUESTION

1. How can a student's lack of understanding vocabulary affect reading comprehension?

In material on England, paper money may be called a *bank note*. The student who cannot hold the various concepts of this word in mind will have trouble understanding many areas of the curriculum. By highlighting multiple meanings—through dictionary games, sentence-completion exercises, and class discussion—teachers can offer important help to students who must develop an awareness of one word's different meanings.

2. **Providing concrete experiences.** To build vocabulary and develop concepts for reading, students need concrete experiences with words. A first step is to provide students with primary experiences with the word or concept. The next step is to encourage and assist students to draw conclusions from their experiences. As students progress to more advanced stages, teachers can foster skills of classifying, summarizing, and generalizing.

3. **Exploring sources of vocabulary.** Because vocabulary is woven into every phase of our lives, new words can be drawn from any aspect of a student's experience: television, sports, newspapers, advertising, science, and so on. Many students enjoy keeping lists of new words and developing word books.

4. **Expanding vocabulary through classification.** Another way to learn new words is to attach them to known words. Much vocabulary growth takes place in this manner. Vertical vocabulary expansion involves taking a known word and breaking it down into categories. For example, students take the concept *dog* and break it into many species (*collie, terrier, cocker spaniel*). Horizontal vocabulary growth refers to enrichment and differentiation. Children may first call all animals *dogs*. Then they learn to distinguish cats, horses, and other creatures.

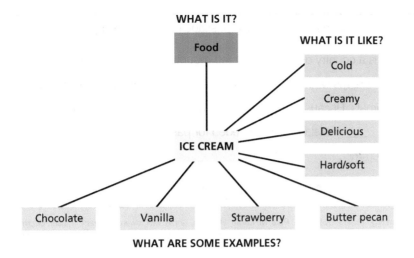

WHAT IS IT?

Food

WHAT IS IT LIKE?

Cold

Creamy

Delicious

Hard/soft

ICE CREAM

Chocolate   Vanilla   Strawberry   Butter pecan

WHAT ARE SOME EXAMPLES?

FIGURE **12.6**
Word Web

Source: From Cook, D. M (Ed.). *Strategic learning in the content area*, 1989, Madison, WI: Department of Public Instruction. Reprinted with the permission of the Wisconsin Department of Public Instruction, 125 South Webster Street, Madison, WI 53702, 800-243-8782.

Word Webs A word web is a type of graphic organizer, which is a strategy for helping build vocabulary and making information easier to understand and learn. Word webs enrich associations with a word and deepen a student's understanding of important concepts. Figure 12.6 shows an example of a word web for *ice cream.* A group of students developed the word web by answering 3 questions: "What is it?" "What is it like?" and "What are some examples?" Research shows that graphic organizers help students with learning disabilities and related mild disabilities understand reading material and improve their comprehension (Fisher et al., 1995; Sabbatino, 2004). A computer program that produces many types of graphic organizers is Inspiration (Inspiration Software, *http://www.inspiration.com*).

word web
A type of graphic organizer. It helps students learn words, build vocabulary, and makes information about the word easier to understand and learn.

Cloze Procedure The cloze procedure is a useful technique for building comprehension and language skills. It is based on a person's impulse to provide closure, or complete a structure and make it whole by supplying a missing element. When the cloze procedure is applied to the reading process, the following steps are used:

1. Select a passage of reading material.
2. Rewrite the material and delete every *x*th word (e.g., every fifth word or every tenth word). Replace the deleted word with a blank line; all lines should be the same length.
3. Ask students to fill in each blank by writing the word they think was deleted.

cloze procedure
A technique that is useful in testing, in teaching reading comprehension, and in determining readability (or difficulty level of the material). The cloze procedure involves deleting words from the text and inserting underlined blank spaces. Measurement is made by counting the number of blanks that students can correctly fill.

One advantage of the cloze test over the conventional reading test or other fill-in-the-blank tests is that because words are deleted at random, both *lexical* words and *structural* words are omitted. Lexical words carry primary meaning and are roughly similar to verbs, nouns, adjectives, and adverbs. Relationships are indicated by structural words, such as articles, prepositions, conjunctions, and auxiliary verbs. What the reader supplies provides clues to his or her underlying language processes.

The cloze procedure may be modified and used for a variety of purposes. To teach vocabulary, for example, only the words of the vocabulary lesson can be deleted. In content areas, such as social studies, technical words can be deleted.

FIGURE **12.7**
Sample Cloze Exercise

Fill in the deleted words in the following passage entitled "Farming in Switzerland":

Switzerland is a country of very high, steep mountains _____ narrow valleys. In the

valleys are the farms where _____ farmers raise much of the food they need for _____

and their animals. Because the valleys are tiny, the _____ are small. There is no room

on them for _____ grassland that is needed for pasturing cows or goats _____ sheep

during the summer.

Answers: *and, the, themselves, farms, the, or*

Source: From *High Roads*, by McKee Paul, M. Lucile Harrison, Annie McCowen, & Elizabeth Lehr. Copyright 1962, renewed 1990 by Beverly McKee Eaton, Paul E. Harrison, and Gloria Royer. Reprinted with the permission of Houghton Mifflin Company. All rights reserved.

Or the teacher can delete other selected categories, such as adjectives, adverbs, or prepositions. For students who have difficulty in writing, the cloze words can be printed on cards backed with felt or Velcro, which students place on the appropriate blank space in the written passage.

In the sample cloze exercise shown in Figure 12.7, the reading material was retyped with every tenth word deleted and replaced by a standard-size line. Students supply the missing words.

12.11d The Reading–Writing Connection

The following strategies connect reading with writing.

Dialogue Journals Dialogue journals are a personal way to integrate reading and writing. To initiate this activity, the teacher gives each student a notebook, and teachers and students write personal messages to one another through the notebook. A variety of topics can be addressed; teachers may ask students how they liked a story or ask them about their pets, birthdays, holidays, or something that happened to them. Some teachers paste a picture, a cartoon, or a Polaroid photograph of the student in the journal and ask for student comments. After the student writes something, the teacher responds in the journal. The response may provide some personal information and then ask for more information or may start another topic. Typically, as students get used to the journal, they begin to write more and look forward to a regular interchange through the journal.

Materials Without Words To foster reading comprehension, the teacher can use materials that do not have words, such as comic books without captions, silent films, and books of photographs. The students first figure out the story content from the pictures; then they make the transition to printed words. Once the students understand the material, words become meaningful. The students can even write their own dialogue.

Written Conversations Instead of saying what they wish to communicate to the teacher or to friends, students can write the message and give it to their teacher or to other students. The teacher's (or classmates') responses should also be written (Jennings et al., 2010). Students in middle school often surreptitiously send small folded notes to their friends. This activity legitimizes the note exchange ventures.

12.11e Cognitive Learning Strategies for Reading

Learning strategies are discussed in greater detail in Chapter 5, "Theories of Learning," and Chapter 9, "Adolescents and Adults With Learning Disabilities and Related Mild Disabilities." A major reading comprehension problem for students with reading disabilities is that they tend to be passive and to wait for teacher direction. They do not know how to interact effectively with the text or to merge the information with what they already know. They often read reluctantly, hesitating to ask questions and focusing solely on what they think the teacher wants them to remember. These students may not monitor their reading comprehension. When they are not sure of the meaning of a passage they are reading, they do not take action by going back and trying to understand. Instead, they continue to read and lose even more of the meaning. Often, they are unaware that something is wrong.

Young children should be immersed in language and books from infancy.

Students who have difficulty with reading comprehension need instruction that helps them become actively involved in the reading and in trying to reconstruct the author's message. They need to develop metacognitive abilities by learning to recognize their loss of comprehension when it occurs and employing "fix-up" strategies. Learning strategies for improving reading comprehension help students become active, involved learners who are able to direct their own learning (Lenz & Deshler, 2003; Deshler et al., 2001).

12.11f Multisensory Methods

A collection of programs that are based on the Orton-Gillingham Method comprise the multisensory methods for students with severe reading and learning disabilities (Birsh, 2005). They include the Orton-Gillingham Method, Project READ, the Wilson Reading System, Alphabetic Phonics, the Herman Method, and the Spalding Method (Birsh, 2005; Henry, 1998). These multisensory groups have formed an umbrella organization called the International Multisensory Structured Language Council (McIntyre & Pickering, 1995). The multisensory methods have the following similar characteristics (Oakland et al., 1998):

multisensory methods
A collection of programs based on the Orton-Gillingham Method that use several sensory avenues to teaching reading.

- Help anchor verbal information by providing links with the visual, auditory, tactile, and kinesthetic pathways for learning.
- Use highly structured phonics instruction with an emphasis on the alphabetic system.
- Include abundant drill, practice, and repetition.
- Have carefully planned sequential lessons.
- Emphasize explicit instruction in the language rule systems to guide reading and spelling.

VAKT

The abbreviation for *visual, auditory, kinesthetic,* and *tactile* learning, a multisensory approach to teaching reading that stimulates all avenues of sensory input simultaneously.

The multisensory methods use several senses to reinforce learning, as indicated in the acronym VAKT, which is formed from the first letter of the words *visual, auditory, kinesthetic,* and *tactile.* To stimulate all of these senses, students hear the teacher say the word, say the word to themselves, hear themselves say the word, feel the muscle movement as they trace the word, feel the tactile surface under their fingertips, see their hands move as they trace the word, and hear themselves say the word as they trace it. Several of the multisensory methods are described in this section.

The Orton-Gillingham Method The *Orton-Gillingham Method* is an outgrowth of the Orton theory of reading disability (Orton, 1937, 1976). This method focuses on a multisensory, systematic, structured language procedure for reading-decoding and spelling instruction. Initial activities focus on learning individual letter sounds and blending. The student uses a tracing technique to learn single letters and their sound equivalents. These single sounds are later combined into larger groupings and then into short words (Gillingham & Stillman, 1970; Orton, 1976).

Simultaneous spelling tasks are also part of the Orton-Gillingham Method. While writing the letters, the students say both the sounds of the letters in sequence and the letter names. The method emphasizes phonics and depends on a formal sequence of learning. Independent reading is delayed until the major part of the phonics program has been covered.

There are a number of extensions and applications of the Orton-Gillingham Method. Project READ, an adaptation of the Orton-Gillingham Method in the public schools of Minnesota, reported significant gains in reading achievement (Enfield, 1988). A variation of the Orton-Gillingham Method was developed by Slingerland (1976), who offered an extensive set of materials. Another adaptation is the *Recipe for Reading* (Traub & Bloom, 1978), which is accompanied by 21 supplementary readers.

The Wilson Reading System *The Wilson Reading System* (Wilson, 1988) is a multisensory, structured language program based on the Orton-Gillingham philosophy. It provides a step-by-step method for teachers working with students who require direct, multisensory, structured language teaching. The Wilson Reading System targets students who have difficulty decoding independently, reading with fluency, or spelling words, even with the help of a spell checker or dictionary. The program teaches students the structure of words and language through a carefully sequenced 12-step program that helps them master decoding and improve encoding in English. It directly teaches phonological awareness, phonology, and total word structure, and it takes one to three years to complete. The Wilson program is also used for adults with dyslexia.

The Fernald Method Grace Fernald (1988) developed an approach to reading that uses visual, auditory, kinesthetic, and tactile senses, but it differs from the other multisensory programs in that it teaches a whole word (rather than single sounds). The student traces the entire word, thereby strengthening the memory and visualization of the entire word. Teaching Tips 12.2, "The Fernald Method for Learning Words," describes a method used by Grace Fernald. It consists of four stages, but its uniqueness is most evident in Stage 1. The Fernald Method is also effective for teaching spelling. (See Chapter 13, "Written

TEACHING TIPS 12.2
The Fernald Method For Learning Words

Stage 1
It is essential that the student select the word to be learned. The teacher writes the student's word on paper with a crayon. The student then traces the word with his or her fingers, making contact with the paper, thus using both tactile and kinesthetic senses. As the student traces it, the teacher says the word so that the student hears it (using the auditory sense). This process is repeated until the student can write the word correctly without looking at the sample. Once the student learns the word, the sample is placed in a file box. The words accumulate in the box until there are enough words for the student to write a story by using them. The story is then typed so that the student can read his or her own story.

Stage 2
The student is no longer required to trace each word, but rather learns each new word by looking at the teacher's written copy of the word and saying it to himself or herself while writing it.

Stage 3
The student learns new words by looking at a printed word and repeating it to himself or herself before writing it. At this point, the student may begin reading from books.

Stage 4
The student is able to recognize new words from their similarity to printed words or to parts of words previously learned. The student now can generalize the knowledge he or she has acquired through the reading skills.

Professional Resource Download

Language Difficulties: Written Expression, Spelling, and Handwriting.") *A Multisensory Teaching of Basic Language Skills: Activity Book* (Carreker & Birsh, 2005) provides activities for multisensory teaching.

Did You Get It?

In the K-W-L model of reading comprehension, "W" represents
   a. goals and expectations of new knowledge to be acquired.
   b. previous knowledge pertaining to a subject.
   c. what was learned from a given written passage.
   d. what students found confusing.

12.12 Enjoyment and Appreciation of Reading

The man who does not read good books has no advantage over the man who cannot read them.

—Mark Twain

An important goal for reading instruction is for students to enjoy reading. Students enjoy reading series books, such as the *Magic Tree House* series. They also enjoy books about horses, animals, sports figures, and books that hook them into reading independently. The Harry Potter series is a remarkable example of books that students like to read.

Unfortunately, because of stringent curriculum demands, less skilled readers often find themselves reading materials that are too difficult to enjoy or to be helpful in building their fluency. As a consequence, poor readers do not have the opportunities to read books and stories at their reading level and to practice newly acquired skills. All children should be provided with as many reading experiences as possible, regardless of their achievement levels. In fact, frequent reading not only improves reading fluency and reading skills, but it also improves verbal abilities and thinking abilities (Cunningham & Stanovich, 1998; Nelson et al., 2004).

The greatest reward for any teacher is to see a child engrossed in a book and developing a love of reading. This experience vividly came home to all teachers and parents on July 16, 2005, when the seventh of the wildly popular series of Harry Potter books went on sale. Harry Potter book lovers anxiously awaited the moment and a record 8 million copies of this book were sold to ardent Harry Potter fans on the first day after the book was released, a record for book sales.

The Harry Potter series appeals to many different readers. Children who are good readers; children who are struggling readers; younger children, adolescents, and adults; and children from diverse cultures are all captured by the tale of Harry Potter and his friends and their adventures at a boarding school for wizards in England. Taking a cold, calculating look at this book, we can conjure up many reasons why children would not like it. It takes place at a boarding school in England, a locale that is not familiar to children in America. There are many difficult words and names in the book and one would think this would keep poor readers away from this book. Not so. Children are willing to envision this strange place and struggle to read through the difficult words because the story line and the presentation are so intriguing. J. K. Rowling, the author of the Harry Potter books, has the wizardry to capture the hearts and minds of young readers. (See the author's website at *http://www.jkrowling.com*.)

Many other books have captured children's attention over the years, for example, *A Wrinkle in Time* by Madeline L'Engle, *The Wind in the Willows* by Kenneth Grahame, *Charlotte's Web* by E. B. White, and *Little House on the Prairie* by Laura Ingalls Wilder. Teachers often have fond memories of their own favorites that turned them on to reading. Teachers have to cherish their own experiences when children show a love for reading.

Did You Get It?

In a standard school curriculum, _____ exists between the levels of reading difficulty typically presented and the inability to derive pleasure from the reading material.
   a. no correlation
   b. an inconclusive correlation
   c. a negative correlation
   d. a positive correlation

12.13 Assistive and Instructional Technology and Reading

New technology is changing the way that students with learning disabilities and related mild disabilities communicate. Social networking websites have rocketed from a niche activity into a phenomenon that engages tens of millions of youths, ages 12 through 17. Over 55% of online teens use social networking sites, such as Facebook, MySpace, and YouTube (Roe, Stoodt-Hill, Burns, 2010; Lenhart & Madden, 2008).

Computers also offer many instructional advantages for students with reading difficulties. Computer programs are motivating, they provide time for learning on a one-to-one basis, they help develop automaticity, and they offer time to think about reading passages. Computer reading programs are available for the prereading, elementary, secondary, and adult levels. Computer programs can teach literacy, sight words, phonics skills, vocabulary, reading comprehension, and they improve reading rate (Belson, 2003).

- Reading Blaster (Knowledge Adventure). A skill-and-drill software application that allows students to practice spelling and letter-sound relationships
- The Living Books Series (The Learning Company). CD-based books that read stories to children in a normal (human) voice
- Earobics (Cognitive Concepts). A software application designed to teach phonemic awareness through a series of activities and games
- Inspiration and Kidspiration (Inspiration Software). This software provides a graphic organizer to help students organize their ideas about stories and words. The Inspiration website is at *http://www.inspiration.com.*

12.13a Text-to-Speech Programs

There are several computer programs that are designed to read text aloud. These programs are designed for very poor readers and for individuals with visual disabilities. Several of these programs are described in the following list.

- Recording for the Blind and Dyslexic (RFBD) provides information on their program at *http://www.rfbd.org.* This organization is dedicated to providing books, including textbooks, for individuals who are dyslexic or blind. Material is available in two formats: (1) *RFBD Classic Cassettes* are audio recordings that are played on cassette players, and (2) *RFBD AudioPlus* are digital recordings that are played on CD players.
- Kurzweil Educational Systems provides software programs that read text aloud. Information about Kurzweil can be viewed at *http://www.kurzweiledu.com.* With these programs, text can be scanned, and there are several electronic voices that can be chosen.
- Read Please (free) and Read Please Plus (shareware) read any electronic text. Their website is *http://www.readplease.com.* The program is available in several languages, which users can download to their computers.
- E-Text Reader currently allows its material to be downloaded without charge. The website is *http://www.readingmadeeasy.com.* E-Text Reader will read any electronic or scanned text. There are three excellent voice choices. It comes from Premier Assistive Technology, which also sells a more robust text-to-speech program.

12.13b Recorded Textbooks and Digital CD-ROMs

There are several sources for obtaining recorded books on tape or on digital CD-ROMs that are available to students with disabilities. Students who are identified as having learning disabilities are eligible to obtain, at no cost, books recorded for the blind. In addition, new titles can be recorded if needed. For students with severe reading problems, recorded textbooks can be a real boon; using recorded books allows them to keep up with content while continuing to improve their reading skills. The website for Reading for the Blind and Dyslexic is at *http://www.rfbd.org*.

Did You Get It?

Computer programs that read passages aloud to the student are called _____ programs.

a. visual-to-auditory
b. text-to-speech
c. eye-to-ear
d. difficult-to-easy

I Have a Kid Who...

PABLO: *A Child With Reading Comprehension Difficulties*

Pablo is 10 years 3 months and is in fifth grade. Pablo has been identified as having learning disabilities, and his major reading difficulty is with reading comprehension. Pablo's reading strengths include a strong vocabulary, average decoding skills, and average fluency. He has built these strengths across the past 3 years working with the special education teacher, Mr. Trout. Pablo enjoys reading but still has difficulty comprehending what he reads. Pablo's comprehension difficulties are in reading narrative stories. Pablo has difficulty identifying the main components of a story. As the end of the school year approaches, Pablo's classroom teacher has become concerned about his lack of progress in reading comprehension. A collaboration meeting was held with his classroom teacher, with the reading specialist, and the special education teacher, Mr. Trout. They discussed Pablo's reading strengths, his reading difficulties, and possible instructional strategies.

Source: Adapted from The Iris Center for Faculty Enhancement: Comprehension, *http://iris.peabody.vanderbilt.edu.*

QUESTIONS

1. What are Pablo's strengths in reading?
2. What are Pablo's difficulties in reading?
3. The team recommended using graphic organizers to improve his reading of narrative text. How could graphic organizers be used for narrative stories?

Chapter Summary

- Reading is part of the language system and is closely linked to the other forms of language—oral language and writing.
- Reading is a major academic difficulty for students with learning disabilities and related mild disabilities. The detrimental effects of reading disabilities have serious consequences in terms of academic achievement, employment, and success in life.
- Many students with learning disabilities and related mild disabilities have reading problems and are in general education classrooms.

- Dyslexia is a learning disability in which the individual has extreme difficulty in learning to read. Dyslexia is associated with neurological dysfunction.
- Major elements of reading are phonemic awareness, phonics and word-recognition skills, fluency, vocabulary, and comprehension.
- Readers need skills in word recognition to develop fluency in reading. Word recognition takes place through phonics, sight words, context clues, and structural analysis.

- Reading fluency refers to the reader's ability to recognize words quickly and read text with speed, accuracy, and proper expression.
- The purpose of reading is comprehension, which is the active understanding and involvement with the written material.
- Narrative text is the reading of stories. Informational text is the reading of subject-matter material, such as textbooks.
- There are many ways to assess reading ability. Informal measures include informal reading

inventories and portfolio assessment. Formal tests include survey tests, diagnostic tests, and comprehensive batteries.
- The "Teaching Strategies" section of this chapter presents strategies for teaching reading to students with reading disabilities. It includes methods for improving word recognition, improving fluency, and improving reading comprehension.
- Assistive and instructional technology can be useful in teaching reading.

Questions for Discussion and Reflection

1. Describe the elements of reading. What does each element contribute to learning to read?
2. Readers use a variety of methods to recognize words. Describe the different methods of word recognition. What method(s) do you think good readers rely upon?
3. Describe reading fluency. Why is it important to teach fluency?
4. What is reading comprehension? Identify a few strategies used to promote reading comprehension. Describe how students might respond to these strategies.
5. What are the differences between informal and formal methods for assessing reading achievement?

Key Terms

automaticity (p. 353)
basal reading series (p. 368)
cloze procedure (p. 373)
comprehension (p. 354)
context clues (p. 351)
decode (p. 348)
DIBELS (p. 366)
direct instruction (p. 354)
directed reading-thinking activity (DRTA) (p. 356)
explicit code-emphasis instruction (p. 348)
indirect instruction (p. 354)
informal reading inventory (IRI) (p. 363)
Informational materials (p. 358)
phonemic awareness (p. 347)

language experience method (p. 369)
multisensory methods (p. 375)
phonics (p. 348)
phonological awareness (p. 347)
reading comprehension (p. 355)
reading fluency (p. 351)
repeated reading (p. 353)
sight words (p. 349)
structural analysis (p. 351)
VAKT (p. 376)
vocabulary (p. 353)
word web (p. 372)
word-recognition procedures (p. 348)

Tom Odulate/Cultura/Getty Images

Written Language Difficulties: Written Expression, Spelling, and Handwriting

What is the most frightening thing you ever encountered? —A blank sheet of paper.

—Ernest Hemingway

STANDARDS Addressed in This Chapter:

Council for Exceptional Children Initial Level Special Educator Preparation Standards as approved by the National Council for the Accreditation of Teacher Education

CEC Initial Preparation Standard 1: Learner Development and Individual Learning Differences

- 1.0—Beginning special education professionals understand how exceptionalities may interact with development and learning and use this knowledge to provide meaningful and challenging learning experiences for individuals with exceptionalities.

- 1.1—Beginning special education professionals understand how language, culture, and family background influence the learning of individuals with exceptionalities.

- 1.2—Beginning special education professionals use understanding of development and individual differences to respond to the needs of individuals with exceptionalities.

CEC Initial Preparation Standard 3: Curricular Content Knowledge

- 3.0—Beginning special education professionals use knowledge of general and specialized curricula to individualize learning for individuals with exceptionalities.

- 3.1—Beginning special education professionals understand the central concepts, structures of the discipline, and tools of inquiry of the content areas they teach and can organize this knowledge, integrate cross-disciplinary skills and develop meaningful learning progressions for individuals with exceptionalities.

- 3.2—Beginning special education professionals understand and use general and specialized content knowledge for teaching across curricular content areas to individualize learning for individuals with exceptionalities.

- 3.3—Beginning special education professionals modify general and specialized curricula to make them accessible to individuals with exceptionalities.

CEC Initial Preparation Standard 4: Assessment

- 4.0—Beginning special education professionals use multiple methods of assessment and data-sources in making educational decisions.

- 4.1—Beginning special education professionals select and use technically sound formal and informal assessments that minimize bias.

- 4.2—Beginning special education professionals use knowledge of measurement principles and practices to interpret assessment results and guide educational decisions for individuals with exceptionalities.

- 4.3—Beginning special education professionals in collaboration with colleagues and families use multiple types of assessment information in making decisions about individuals with exceptionalities.

- 4.4—Beginning special education professionals engage individuals with exceptionalities to work toward quality learning and performance and provide feedback to guide them.

CEC Initial Preparation Standard 5: Instructional Planning and Strategies

- 5.0—Beginning special education professionals select, adapt, and use a repertoire of evidence-based instructional strategies to advance learning of individuals with exceptionalities.

- 5.1—Beginning special education professionals consider an individual's abilities, interests, learning environments, and cultural and linguistic factors in the selection, development, and adaptation of learning experiences for individuals with exceptionalities.

- 5.2—Beginning special education professionals use technologies to support instructional assessment, planning, and delivery for individuals with exceptionalities.

- 5.3—Beginning special education professionals are familiar with augmentative and alternative communication systems and a variety of assistive technologies to support the communication and learning of individuals with exceptionalities.

- 5.4—Beginning special education professionals use strategies to enhance language development and communication skills of individuals with exceptionalities.

- 5.6—Beginning special education professionals teach to mastery and promote generalization of learning.

- 5.7—Beginning special education professionals teach cross-disciplinary knowledge and skills such as critical thinking and problem solving to individuals with exceptionalities.

For students, Common Core Standards for English Language Arts and Literacy in History/Social Studies, Science, and Technical Subjects can be found at: *http://www.corestandards.org*

Written language is the third form of the integrated language system. In the "Theories" section of this chapter, we consider three areas of written language: (1) written expression, (2) spelling, and (3) handwriting. In the "Teaching Strategies" section of this chapter, we present specific instructional strategies for (1) written expression, (2) word processing, (3) spelling, and (4) handwriting to help students with writing difficulties develop their written language skills.

13.1 Theories Describing Written Language Difficulties

Many people dislike writing and try to avoid writing. Their disdainful attitude is depicted in the story of the New York City taxicab driver who skillfully guided his cab past a pedestrian. The cabby then explained to his passenger why he was so careful: "I always try to avoid hittin' 'em because every time ya hit one, ya gotta write out a long report about it."

Words are the primary means of communication for human beings. Using words is the way we tell one another what we want, what we do not want, what we think, and how we feel. When words are spoken, they are a wonderful asset—quick, direct, and easy. But when words must be written, they can become burdensome, part of a slow and laborious task. Many students with learning disabilities and related mild disabilities have difficulty writing. Some of these students also have underlying language problems, including difficulty with spoken language. Many students, however, do well with oral language but encounter significant problems in the acquisition and use of written language. Moreover, written language difficulties often continue to adversely affect their lives as adults (Linstrom, 2007; Harris, Graham, & Mason, 2003; Lenz & Deshler, 2003; Adelman & Vogel, 2003; Vogel & Adelman, 2000).

Writing is the most sophisticated and complex achievement of the language system. In the sequence of language development, writing is typically the last to be learned, although the early literacy approach encourages children to write even before they learn to read. Through writing, we integrate previous learning and experiences in listening, speaking, and reading. Proficiency in written language requires an adequate basis of oral language skills, as well as many other competencies. The writer must be able to keep one idea in mind while formulating the idea into words and sentences, and the writer must also be skilled in planning the correct graphic form for each letter and word while manipulating the writing instrument. In addition, the writer must also possess sufficient visual and motor memory to integrate complex eye–hand relationships.

The instructional concept of "writing across the curriculum" has become a persuasive force in the teaching of writing. This implies that writing should be taught in all subjects of the curriculum, not only those in which written language is the center of instruction. Three components of writing are addressed in this chapter: (1) written expression, (2) spelling, and (3) handwriting.

Did You Get It?

There are a myriad of tasks, processes, and expectations that go into the learning and mastery of our language system. In that regard, experts deem which of the following as being both the most complex and most sophisticated?

a. speaking
b. writing
c. reading
d. processing

13.2 Written Expression

Success as a writer is intimately tied to the quality of writing instruction the student receives. Writing requires many related abilities, including facility in spoken language, the ability to read, skills in spelling, legible handwriting or skill with computer keyboarding, knowledge of the rules of written usage, and cognitive strategies to organize and plan the writing (Bashir & Singer, 2009).

Written language skills are required in most occupations today—even to be a successful bank robber. The following news story from Miami illustrates the importance of writing skills for successful communication. In an attempted burglary, a would-be robber handed this handwritten note to the bank teller:

A GOT A BUM. I ALSO HAVE A CONTOUR. I'M GOING TO BLOW YOU SKY HEIGHT. I'M NO KILLEN. THIS IS A HELD UP.

Unable to decipher the note, the teller asked the robber for help in reading the message. By the time the robber deciphered the words for the teller, the police had arrived and arrested the robber. To make matters worse for the robber, the police were able to trace him to other bank holdups in which the same spelling and writing errors were made in the burglary notes (*Miami Herald*, 1980).

(Possible translation: I got a bomb. I also have a control. I'm going to blow you sky high. I'm no killer. This is a holdup.)

REFLECTIVE QUESTION

1. Analyze the would-be bank robber's note. Do you think the bank robber's note displayed difficulty with phonics or visual memory of sight words? Why?

Many students with learning disabilities and related mild disabilities may lack many of these critical writing-related abilities and therefore find communicating through writing very challenging. The writing of these students is often replete with errors in spelling, punctuation, capitalization, handwriting, and grammar. Their written products tend to be short, poorly organized, and impoverished in terms of development of ideas.

Poor skills in written communication and difficulty in sharing thoughts through writing can persist over time and into the adult years (Harris et al., 2003; Lenz & Deshler, 2003). Student Stories 13.1, "Written Language Problems," provides one account of an individual with writing difficulties.

13.2a The Writing Connection in the Integrated Language System

The links among the elements of language connect the language forms with one another and also strengthen the underlying language system. Extensive oral language experiences promote reading. In turn, instruction in reading improves performance in writing. Further, experiences with writing and composing improve one's knowledge of language and skills in speaking and reading. All of these language experiences strengthen the underlying language system (Jennings, Caldwell, & Lerner, 2010).

There are many similarities in the processes used in spoken language, reading, and writing. In both reading and writing, people set and revise goals, refining and reconstructing meaning as they go through the material. They develop expectations about what they will read or write next, form attitudes about the text, and they monitor the information they wish to remember or convey (Mason, 2009; Harris et al., 2003).

By its very nature, writing is an active process. The physical aspect of writing literally forces active involvement upon the writers. Writers perform the actions of picking up a pen or pencil (or using a computer keyboard) and recording their thoughts. While people write, they must actively work at producing something that did not exist before by using their own background knowledge and integrating their language skills. The process of revising requires rethinking and reconstruction. Much reading also occurs during the process of writing. When adults write, over half of the writing time is actually devoted to reading. As soon as good writers complete a section of writing, they reread it. They also reread to see how to connect a previously written section to one they are about to write. When writers complete an entire text, they reread it again immediately and then reread it a short time later. The kind of reading that takes place during writing is intensive and involves much critical analysis (Mason, 2009; Berry, 2006; Graham & Harris, 2005; Graham, Harris, & Mason, 2005).

13.2b Early Literacy and Writing

The term early literacy refers to a young child's early entrance into the world of words, language, and stories. The concept of early literacy emphasizes the interrelatedness of the various forms of language in the child's development. Children develop literacy through simultaneous experiences with language, reading, and writing.

The philosophy of early literacy instruction suggests that writing may be easier than reading and may actually develop earlier than reading (Snow, Burns, & Griffin, 1998). Writing is a more self-involving task than reading because the meaning of a writer's message originates from within the writer and is known to the writer in advance. In contrast, reading requires that the reader be able to interpret someone else's ideas and use of language, which is a more difficult task for the beginner.

The early literacy curriculum emphasizes that writing is beneficial, even for primary-age children, and should be encouraged (CIERA, 1998; Snow et al., 1998). When young children write, they directly explore both the functions and the forms of written language. Writing helps children understand that, in English, print progresses from left to right. Many young children who have not yet learned this rule of written English reverse this process, writing from right to left, as shown in Figure 13.1.

In their early writing experiences, young children should not be required to adhere to criteria of proper form or correct spelling; they should simply be encouraged to explore and to play with writing. Young children are encouraged to use invented spelling , which means they follow their own spelling rules. Early writing also increases the child's awareness of the phonological properties of language. When children attempt to put their ideas into print, they explore and learn about the alphabetic nature of written English. As they begin to realize that words can be segmented into sounds, they acquire important skills for the early stages of reading. Figure 13.2 shows an example of a child's writing.

early literacy
The child's early entrance into the world of words, language, and stories. Literacy emerges in children through simultaneous experiences with oral language, reading, and writing.

invented spelling
The beginning writer's attempt to write words. The young writer attends to the sound units and associates letters with them in a systematic, although unconventional, way.

FIGURE **13.1**
Children Must Learn That Writing in English Goes from Left to Right

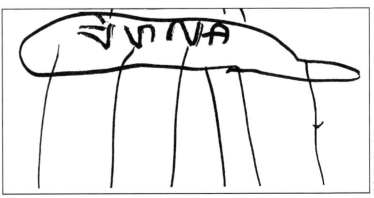

© Cengage Learning

FIGURE **13.2**
Example of a Child's Writing in a Kindergarten Early Literacy Class

---

writing product
A method of teaching writing that focuses on the final written document.

---

writing process
The process whereby writers go through a series of stages during writing. The 4 stages of the writing process are (1) prewriting, (2) drafting, (3) revising, and (4) sharing with an audience.

13.2c The Writing Process

Current theories on the teaching of writing call for a major shift in instructional emphasis to the *writing process* instead of the *writing product* (Harris, Grahm, & Mason, 2008; Graves, 1994; Harris et al., 2003). The traditional writing product approach to writing emphasized the written assignment (or product) created by the writer. In contrast, the writing process approach to writing focuses on the entire process that writers use in developing a written document.

In the traditional writing product approach, the teacher's checking and grading of the written product is based on certain expectations of perfection. Students are expected to spell correctly, to use adjectives, and to compose topic sentences. Their written papers are graded on word choice, grammar, organization, and ideas. The graded papers are then returned to the students with corrections (often in red ink), and students are expected to learn and improve their writing skills from these grades and teacher corrections. The more conscientious the teacher, the more conscientiously the corrections fill student papers. Too often, the result of applying the writing product approach to writing instruction is that people learn to dislike writing.

The writing process approach to writing is different; it emphasizes the thinking that goes on during writing. Teachers are encouraged to understand the complexity of the writing process as they help students think about, select, and organize tasks. Students are encouraged to ask themselves questions such as: What is the purpose of my writing? How can I get ideas? How can I develop and organize the ideas? How can I translate and revise the ideas so that the reader will understand them? Who is the intended audience?

Writing is a learned skill that can be taught in a school setting as a thinking-learning activity, with emphasis on the writing process. As a cognitive process, writing requires both backward and forward thinking. Good writers do not simply sit down and produce a text. Rather, they go through several stages of the writing process—prewriting, drafting, revising, and sharing with an audience, as shown in Figure 13.3 (Graham et al., 2002; Graves, 1994).

Stage 1: Prewriting During this first stage, the writer gathers ideas and refines them before beginning formal writing. Prewriting involves a type

FIGURE **13.3**
Stages of the Writing Process

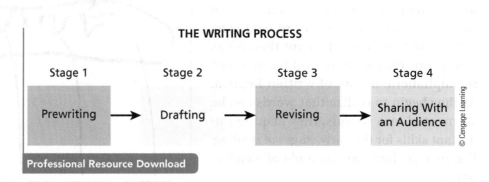

of brainstorming, such as talking through some thoughts and ideas, jotting a few notes in a margin, or developing a graphic organizer or list of the main points. During this time, the writer also identifies an intended audience. Students are more willing to write if they choose the topic. They may write about someone they know, a special event, or themselves. Teachers can help by asking students to make a list of people who are special to them or to list activities they did during a holiday break.

Stage 2: Drafting In the second stage of the writing process, the writer records ideas on paper. Although many people think of this stage as "writing," it actually is only one step in the process. The term drafting is used instead of *writing* to emphasize that this is one version of what eventually will be written and that it will be changed. The first draft of a piece of writing is not for the reader, but for the writer. As the writer jots down words, sentences, and paragraphs, these give rise to new ideas or ways to revise ideas already written. At this stage, there may be an overflow of ideas, with little organization or consideration of prose, grammar, and spelling.

Stage 3: Revising Having completed the prewriting and drafting stages, the writer then refines the draft version of the text by revising and editing. Mature writers take the ideas of the first draft, and then reorganize and polish them. There may be several revisions, with different kinds of changes made in each, such as in content, the way of expressing the ideas, the vocabulary, the sentence structure, and the sequence of ideas. The last revision is editing, which includes checking for grammatical, punctuation, and spelling errors. This stage requires a very critical view of one's own work.

Students who have writing difficulties are often reluctant to revise. Just writing the draft requires extensive effort, and making revisions can seem overwhelming. Rewriting of earlier drafts is greatly facilitated by using computers and word-processing software programs.

To help writers learn to revise, teachers can model revisions in dictated stories or in their own work. They can have students make suggestions for revising some of the teacher's writing, make the revisions, and share the revised version. Students can also make suggestions for revising the drafts of their classmates. It is important to make this a positive experience. Be sure to note some good features of a student's work before making suggestions for revision.

Stage 4: Sharing With an Audience This stage is important because it gives value and worth to the entire writing process. It provides students with the opportunity to receive feedback and to perceive themselves as authors who are

▶❚❚ **TeachSource** Video Case Activity

© Cengage Learning 2015

Visit the Education CourseMate website and watch the TeachSource Video Case entitled "Elementary Writing Instruction: Process Writing." In this video, the classroom teacher and the literacy coordinator work together to help students at various stages of the writing process. The students get ideas from social studies and history to develop stories of historical fiction.

QUESTIONS

1. How do the students in this video get their ideas for writing?

2. What are the stages of the writing process shown in this video?

prewriting
The first step of the writing process, in which writers evoke and gather ideas for writing.

drafting
A stage in the writing process in which a preliminary version of the written product is developed.

revising
A stage of the writing process in which the writer reworks a draft of a written product.

responding to an audience. In this final stage, the writer considers the audience for whom the material is intended and whether the ideas will be well communicated to the reader. The amount of rewriting will depend on the intended audience. The audience could be the teacher, other students in the class, or a larger audience that is reached through publication (Harris, Graham, & Mason, 2005; Graham et al., 2002; Graves, 1994).

Sharing with an audience can occur in a number of ways: A written document can be published and bound and shared with a class or placed in a classroom library. Students can share their work through a presentation, a bulletin board display, a newsletter, or a puppet show.

sharing with an audience
A stage of the writing process in which the final written product is read by others.

13.2d Principles for Teaching the Writing Process

The following principles apply to planning instruction for the writing process (Harris et al., 2003).

1. During the prewriting stage, the writing process requires much time, input, and attention. Writers need something to write about. They need sufficient prior experiences to create and stimulate ideas for a good written production. When teachers give a written assignment (such as "write a 100-word theme on spring") without first supplying a prewriting buildup, the process will not produce a rich written product. Teachers can provide necessary input experiences through activities, such as trips, stories, discussions, and oral language activities. Sources of inspiration for writing include reading, art, content-area activities, films, television, newspapers, trips and field experiences, brainstorming, and Internet searches. Devote as much time to the prewriting stage as to the writing stage.

2. The drafting stage frees students from undue concentration on the mechanics of writing. Students should realize that all writers make errors in spelling and grammar in the first draft. Although such mistakes should *eventually* be corrected, they need not be fixed immediately. Instead, the student should focus on the content during the drafting stage and later clean up the work through editing.

3. The revising stage helps students edit their work. Students often think that their writing is finished when they have completed their first draft. When they realize that they must go through the revising stage before their work will be complete, they begin to think of writing as a process instead of a product. A teacher can demonstrate the imperfections of a first draft by exhibiting first drafts of his or her own writing to show the students that all writing needs to be edited. Students can form small groups to review and edit one another's work.

4. Avoid excessive corrections of students' written work. Students are discouraged from trying if their attempts to express ideas are met by having their papers returned full of grammatical, spelling, punctuation, and handwriting corrections in red ink, with heavy penalties for mistakes. As one pupil remarked, "An *F* looks so much worse in red ink."

When students receive negative reinforcements, they soon learn to beat the game. They will limit their writing vocabulary to words they know how to spell, to keeping their sentences simple, to avoid complex and creative ideas, and to keep their compositions short.

13.2e The Learning Strategy Approach to Writing

A learning strategy approach called *self-regulated strategy development (SRSD)* is an explicit, structured approach to teaching writing (Graham & Harris, 2005; Graham, Harris, & Larsen, 2001; Harris et al., 2003). Students who have difficulty with writing need structure and direction to acquire writing strategies. The goals of SRSD are (1) to help students develop a knowledge of writing and the strategies involved in the writing process, (2) to support students in the ongoing development of the abilities needed to monitor and manage their writing, and (3) to promote students' development of positive attitudes about writing and about themselves as writers.

By its very nature, writing is an active process. When people write, they must actively work at producing something that did not exist before by using their own background knowledge and integrating that with their language skills.

The six stages of the SRSD model of writing are (Mason, 2009; Harris et al., 2003):

1. **Develop background knowledge.** Working within a group, students think about what is known about the topic and find additional information from a variety of sources.
2. **Discuss it.** The students talk about and discuss what they have learned with one another and with their teacher. They then discuss a specific writing strategy that they plan to use. For example, they may decide to use the strategy of semantic mapping.
3. **Model it.** The students model how to use a writing strategy, thinking aloud as they work.
4. **Memorize it.** Students review and say aloud the parts of the writing strategy.
5. **Support it.** Students begin to write a story by using the writing strategy.
6. **Independent performance.** Students now use the writing strategy independently.

13.2f Strategies for Writing

For students who find writing tasks overwhelming, teachers must provide adequate structure to help students carry out a writing assignment. Support students in finding ideas for writing, sharing ideas on paper, and finding interesting and descriptive vocabulary. Use a variety of writing strategies, such as (1) personal journals, (2) written conversations, (3) patterned writing, (4) graphic organizers, and (5) drawing pictures (Graham et al., 2001; Harris et al., 2003; Jennings et al., 2010).

Personal Journals In a personal journal, students record personal events or experiences in writing. They practice writing by recording day-to-day accounts of events in their lives and their feelings about these experiences, which they can read later. Each student needs a journal, usually a notebook of lined paper.

FIGURE **13.4**
An Example of a Journal Entry

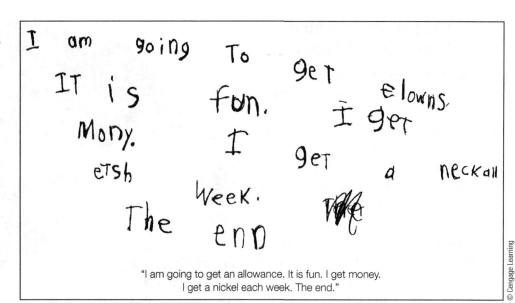

"I am going to get an allowance. It is fun. I get money.
I get a nickel each week. The end."

© Cengage Learning

Students often create titles for their journals and decorate the cover or title page. Set aside time (usually at least a few periods a week) to record personal thoughts in journals. It is easier for students to read and write if they use only one side of a page.

Students may choose to share some of their journal entries, but they should have the choice of not doing so. If a student does not want the teacher to read a journal entry, the student can fold a page in half lengthwise, and the teacher will then not read the folded pages. Teachers should also be careful not to correct grammatical errors or spelling errors because this practice undermines the student's confidence and may decrease the amount of writing.

Some students with writing difficulties lack the confidence to maintain a journal. Teachers can help students overcome this problem by modeling journal writing and help students who cannot think of journal topics with suggestions, such as favorite places, special people, favorite stories, things I like to do, things I don't like to do, things that make me angry, and things I do well. When one parent asked for permission to take a student out of school for a special family trip, the teacher asked that the student keep a journal about the trip. A list of "Ideas for Writing" could be put on a chart in the room or placed in the student's journal on an "Ideas" page. An example of a journal entry is shown in Figure 13.4

Written Conversations Written conversations or dialogue journals are written interactions between teacher and student or between 2 students. Students write their thoughts or questions to the teacher, and the teacher writes a response. Students keep their journal during the day and then give it to the teacher at the end of the school day. The teacher responds to the student's thoughts. A student and teacher can also use e-mail to communicate with each other. For example, the teacher can ask the student in writing how things are going. Or the teacher can write a greeting and message, and the student can answer. For this exchange, each writer can use a different-colored pen or pencil (Jennings et al., 2010). Figure 13.5 shows an example of a written conversation.

Patterned Writing In this strategy, the students use a favorite predictable book with a patterned writing, and then they write their own version. This method

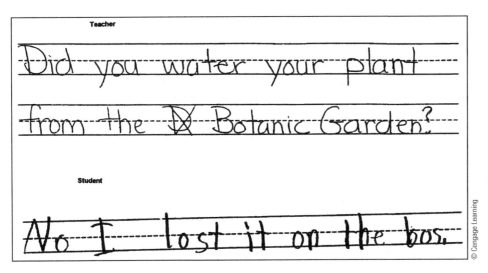

FIGURE **13.5**
An Example of Written
Conversation

gives students the security of a "frame" to use to write a personalized response. For example, "Black Dog, Black Dog, What do you see? I see a red bird looking at me." Students make up their own refrain and illustrate it. The finished writing of several students can be put together into a book and placed on the library table for others to read.

Graphic Organizers Graphic organizers are visual displays that organize and structure ideas and concepts. In the context of reading, graphic organizers help students understand the reading material. Research shows that reading comprehension improves when students use graphic organizers. In the context of writing, graphic organizers can help students generate and organize ideas as they prepare for a writing assignment (Lenz & Deshler, 2003; Sabbatino, 2004).

graphic organizers
Visual representations of concepts, knowledge, or information that incorporate both text and pictures to make the material easier to understand.

The Venn diagram is one graphic organizer in which there are 2 intersecting circles. This graphic is useful for preparing for a "compare and contrast" writing assignment. For example, in comparing 2 people in history, one puts the descriptors of one person in one circle, the characteristics of the other person in the second circle, and the common characteristics in the intersecting section. Figure 13.6 shows a Venn diagram comparing oranges and apples.

Inspiration is a software program that makes it easy for students to develop graphic organizers to plan, develop, organize, or summarize a writing project.

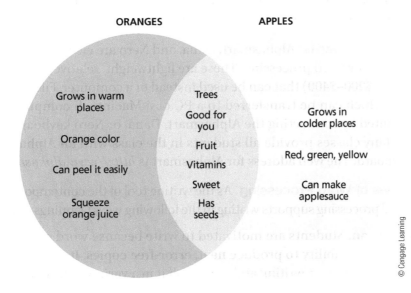

ORANGES **APPLES**

Grows in warm places

Orange color

Can peel it easily

Squeeze orange juice

Trees
Good for you
Fruit
Vitamins
Sweet
Has seeds

Grows in colder places

Red, green, yellow

Can make applesauce

FIGURE **13.6**
Venn Diagram
Comparing Oranges
and Apples

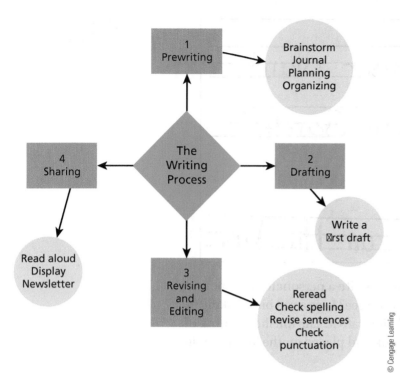

The website for Inspiration Software, Inc. is at *http://www inspiration.com*. Users can download or request trial versions of this software. Students find it easier to tackle a writing assignment if they begin to organize their ideas in the prewriting stage using this graphic organizer program. Kidspiration is a version of this software for younger children. Figure 13.7 displays a graphic organizer of the writing process that was accomplished using Inspiration software.

Drawing Pictures An important communication method for children with writing difficulties is the drawing of pictures. Children with learning disabilities and related mild disabilities often excel at expressing their ideas in pictures. The visual areas of learning are often an area of strength and should be encouraged (Smith, 2001, 2005; West, 1997).

© Cengage Learning

FIGURE **13.7**
Graphic Organizer for the Writing Process

13.2g Assistive and Instructional Technology for Struggling Writers

Technology offers a wide range of applications to support struggling writers (MacArthur, 2009; Roe, Stoodt-Hill, & Burns, 2011). In this section, we discuss word processing, electronic keyboards, keyboarding, talking word programs, word-prediction programs, voice-recognition systems, e-mail, and presentation software.

word processing
Writing with a computer (as contrasted with writing by hand or on a conventional typewriter).

Computers and Word Processing One of the most widely used computer applications, word processing offers an excellent means of teaching writing and integrating the language systems. With this effective tool, writing can become a less arduous task for many individuals with writing difficulties. With a computer, students can write without worrying about handwriting and can revise without making a mess of the written document. In Figure 13.8, a fourth-grade student uses a word-processing program to describe his invention for a science project.

Electronic Keyboards Alphasmart, Dana, and Nero are electronic keyboards that are used for word processing. These are lightweight, relatively low-cost devices (about $200–$400) that can be used instead of a computer. Files are stored on a disk, which can be transferred to a PC or a Macintosh computer. Pages can be printed by connecting the Alphasmart, Dana, or Nero keyboards to any printer. Many classes provide all students in the class with an Alphasmart or Dana keyboard. The web address for Alphasmart is *http://www.alphasmart.com*.

Advantages of Word Processing As the writing tool of the contemporary classroom, word processing supports writing in the following ways (Jennings et al., 2010):

- **Motivation.** Students are motivated to write because word processing increases their ability to produce neat, error-free copies. It also encourages them to share their writing and to publish it in a variety of formats.

- **Collaboration** Students learn to collaborate in the writing process with teachers and peers because of the visibility of the screen and the anonymity of the printed text.
- **Ease of revision.** The editing power of the computer eases the physical burden of revising, making it easier to correct, revise, and rewrite a text. The writer can readily add, correct, delete, and revise and can freely experiment until the display screen shows exactly what the writer wants to say. The writer can also work with the printed copy to make further changes, if desired, and then enter those changes into the computer.
- **Help with fine-motor problems.** Typing is inherently easier and neater than handwriting, especially for students with fine-motor problems. At any point, by clicking "print," the writer can obtain a printed copy. Word processing eliminates the difficult task of recopying or retyping and encourages the student to expend energy on the important part of the writing process—thinking about content, editing, and revising.
- **Special features.** Many word-processing software programs have special features, such as spell checkers, a thesaurus, grammar checkers, and speech synthesis programs, that make the process of writing easier.

Keyboarding To use a word processor for writing, students must learn typing or keyboarding skills. Keyboarding is discussed in this chapter, in the section on handwriting instruction.

Talking Word-Processing Programs Talking word-processing programs are text-to-speech programs that allow users to hear electronic text. These programs are helpful for people who have difficulty reading print. Several text-to-speech programs are listed in Table 13.1.

Word-Prediction Programs Word-prediction programs can be very helpful for poor writers. Word-prediction programs work together with a word processor to *predict* the word the user wants to enter into the computer. When the user types the first one or 2 letters of a word, the word-prediction software offers a list of words beginning with that letter. The user simply selects the desired word. The word-prediction software can also predict the next word in a sentence, even before the letters of the next word are entered. The prediction is based on syntax, spelling rules, word frequency, redundancy, and repetitive factors. The word-prediction software is helpful for students with learning disabilities and related mild disabilities who have difficulty in writing (MacArthur, 2009; Belson, 2003; Lewis, 1998; Raskind & Higgins, 1998a; Roe, Stoodt-Hill, & Burns, 2011). A popular word-prediction program is Co:Writer (see Table 13.1).

Voice-Recognition Systems Voice-recognition systems are dictation programs that allow a person to operate a computer by speaking to it. Using it in combination with a word processor, the user dictates to the system through a microphone, and the spoken words are converted to text on the computer screen. The computer learns to recognize the speech of the individual using it. The more the system is used, the more accurate it becomes in recognizing the

The Sanitary Sleeve

I invented the sanitary sleeve so people could wipe their nose on their sleeve and not ruin their shirt. You make a sanitary sleeve by gluing Velcro on the sleeve of your shirt (glue the Velcro on the left sleeve if you are a lefty and on the right sleeve if you are a righty). You'll also need special Kleenex with Velcro on it. This is an invention that your Mom will like because your shirt will stay clean even when you have a cold.

© Cengage Learning

FIGURE **13.8**
The Sanitary Sleeve

© Cengage Learning

TABLE 13.1

Computers and Writing

Type of Computer Program	Name	Company and Web Address
Talking word-processing programs	Write: OutLoud	Don Johnston, http://www.donjohnston.com
	Kurzweil 3000	Kurzweil Education Systems, http://www.kurzweiledu.com
	WYNN 5.1	Freedom Scientific, http://www.freedomscientific.com
Word-prediction programs	Co:Writer	Don Johnston, http://www.donjohnston.com
Word-processing software	Microsoft Works	Microsoft, http://www.microsoft.com
	Microsoft Word	Microsoft, http://www.microsoft.com
	WordPerfect	Corel, http://www.wordperfect.com
Voice-recognition programs	Type to Learn Dragon	Sunburst, http://www.sunburst.com
	NaturallySpeaking	Nuance, http://www.Nuance.com

user's spoken language. Voice-recognition systems may be particularly helpful for those individuals who have oral language abilities that are superior to their written language abilities. Voice-recognition programs are especially useful for individuals with dyslexia (MacArthur, 2009; Belson, 2003; Raskind & Higgins, 1998a). Some voice-recognition systems are listed in Table 13.1.

Word-Processing Software Many excellent word-processing programs are available for students at all levels. Table 13.1 lists some of the programs used in schools.

Writing E-mail Messages A widely used and exciting method for encouraging writing and sharing written messages with an audience is through e-mail. Many classes are linking up with other classes through the Internet, providing children with the opportunity to write to one another. Many students with learning disabilities and related mild disabilities use social networking websites, such as Facebook and MySpace.

Using Presentation Software Software that allows users to develop presentation slides (such as Microsoft PowerPoint) provides an excellent way for students to engage in writing. Students with writing difficulties often struggle with writing, a skill that taps into many of their most severe disability areas. Secondary students with severe writing disabilities often master presentation software very quickly.

Students might develop, for example, a PowerPoint slide presentation about what they did during their winter break, recalling an experience that was recent and vivid. Presentations can be augmented with color, a variety of fonts, background colors, animations, graphics, and photos. Students can then present their PowerPoint shows to the class.

Many students with writing difficulties are enthusiastic about using Power-Point and about making PowerPoint presentations in lieu of writing compositions. They explain that it is easier to write in short phrases rather than in long sentences; it is fun; and, most important, it is easy to share their work with an audience. Creating a presentation slide project seems to call upon the students' visual skills, an area of strength for many students with learning disabilities.

Making a Web Page Wikispaces is a program that allows classes or groups of students to easily develop websites. The address for Wikispaces is *http://www .wikispaces.com*.

13.2h Assessment of Written Expression

The assessment of writing usually focuses on the written product. As with other areas of instruction, both informal and formal measures can be used to assess writing. Some of these measures are listed in Table 13.2. Written language tests usually require students to first write a passage, which is then evaluated.

Did You Get It?

The authors of your text describe success and achievement in writing as being "intimately tied" to something else specifically, that tangible something which allows students to hone their skills now and for the future. To what are the authors referring?

a. Proper instruction
b. Inherent, nonteachable factors
c. Inner drive and motivation
d. A high intelligence quotient

TABLE 13.2

Tests of Written Expression

Test	Age or Grade Assessed
• OWLS: Written Language Scales, AGS *http://ags.pearsonassessments.com*	Ages 3–21
• Test of Adolescent Language—3 (TOAL-3), Pro-Ed *http://www.proedinc.com*	Ages 12–19
• Test of Written Expression (TOWE), Pro-Ed *http://www.proedinc.com*	Ages 5–17
• Test of Written Language—3 (TOWL-3), Pro-Ed *http://www.proedinc.com*	Ages 7–18
• Woodcock-Johnson Psychoeducational Battery—III, Tests of Achievement, Riverside Publishers *http://www.riverpub.com*	Grades K–17

© Cengage Learning

13.3 Spelling

Spelling has been called "the invention of the devil." Continuing this spiritual analogy, someone has quipped that the ability to spell well is "a gift from God." Spelling is one curriculum area in which neither creativity nor divergent thinking is encouraged. Only one pattern or arrangement of letters can be accepted as correct; no compromise is possible. What makes spelling so difficult is that the written form of the English language has an inconsistent pattern; there is not a dependable one-to-one correspondence between the spoken sounds of English and the written form of the language. Therefore, spelling is not an easy task, even for people who do not have learning disabilities and related mild disabilities.

Spelling a word is much more difficult than reading a word. In reading, there are several clues—context, phonics, structural analysis, and configuration—that help the reader recognize a word in print. Spelling offers no such opportunities to draw on peripheral clues. Many individuals who have trouble spelling words are skilled in recognizing words in reading. However, individuals who are poor in decoding words in reading are almost always poor in spelling as well.

13.3a Developmental Stages of Learning to Spell

Children go through several distinct stages of spelling development, following a general progression of spelling knowledge. The rate of progression differs among children with different spelling abilities, but all children pass through the stages in order. Moreover, the spelling errors that children make reflect their current developmental stage of spelling. There are overlaps in the ages at which children pass through each developmental stage of spelling. The stages and their accompanying ages and characteristics follow:

Stage 1: Developing Prephonetic Writing, Ages 1–7 Children scribble, identify pictures, draw, imitate writing, and learn to make letters, as shown in Figure 13.9.

Stage 2: Using Letter Names and Beginning Phonetic Strategies, Ages 5–9 Children attempt to use phoneme representations but exhibit limited knowledge. They use invented spelling by letter name (e.g., *HIKT* for *hiked, LRN* for *learn,* or *TRKE* for *turkey).* Children may be able to spell some sight words correctly, as shown in Figure 13.10.

Stage 3: Using Written Word Patterns, Ages 6–12 Spelling attempts are readable, pronounceable, and recognizable, and they approximate conventional spelling, even though they are not precise (e.g., *offis* for *office* or *alavater* for *elevator).* The child's invented spellings follow rules of short vowel and long vowel markers. Many sight words are spelled correctly, as shown in Figure 13.11.

Stage 4: Using Syllable Junctures and Multisyllabic Words, Ages 8–18 Students display errors in multisyllabic words. Invented spelling errors occur at syllable juncture and *schwa* positions and follow

FIGURE **13.9**
Developing Prephonetic Writing: Making Letters

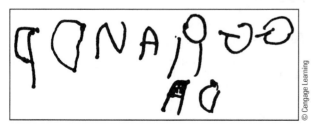

© Cengage Learning

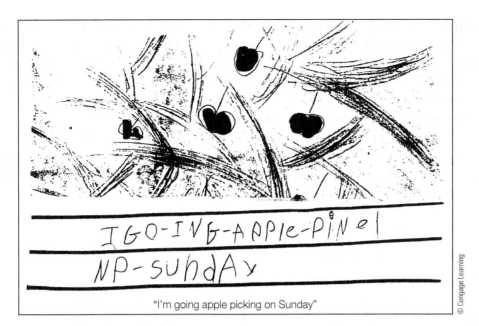

FIGURE **13.10**
Pictures and Beginning
Phonetic Stages

© Cengage Learning

"I'm going apple picking on Sunday"

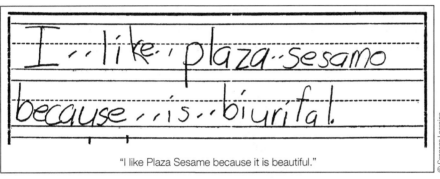

FIGURE **13.11**
Witten Word Patterns

© Cengage Learning

"I like Plaza Sesame because it is beautiful."

deviational rules (e.g., *useage* for *usage;* the term *schwa* refers to unaccented syllables and reflects common spelling errors, such as *cottin* for *cotton*). Multisyllabic sight words may or may not be transferred to spelling performance.

Stage 5: Developing a Mature Spelling Perspective, Ages 10–Adult At this stage, previously acceptable invented spellings are now viewed as errors. Many individuals continue to have great difficulty with spelling, even if they follow the rules. Because of the many exceptions in English, individuals should learn to rely on backup sources, such as dictionaries, computer spelling checks, and electronic spellers. (Franklin Electronics offers many handheld electronic spelling devices, *http://www.franklin.com.*)

13.3b Problems Related to Spelling

Spelling requires many different abilities. For example, a child who lacks phonological awareness will not recognize that there are phonemes or sounds within spoken words and will have difficulty with the spelling-to-sound linkages that are necessary in spelling (Torgesen, 1998). Some children are initially unable to read a spelling word. Other children do not know how to apply phonics and structural analysis to spell a word. Still others are poor at visualizing the appearance of the word. Some children have poor motor facility and physical difficulty writing words.

To spell a word correctly, an individual must not only have stored the word in memory, but must also be able to completely retrieve it from memory without the help from visual clues. Poor spellers who cannot remember or visualize the letters and the order of the letters in words benefit from activities to help strengthen and reinforce the visual memory of the spelling words. Fernald (1988), for example, developed a tracing technique to teach spelling by reinforcing the visual image of the word, drawing on the tactile and kinesthetic senses. (The Fernald Method is described in the "Teaching Strategies" section of this chapter.)

Some poor spellers have difficulty with auditory memory and cannot hold the sounds or syllables in their minds. These students need instruction that will help them recognize the sounds of words and build phonological skills. Motor memory is also a factor in spelling because the speller must remember how the word "felt" or recall the motor movement when the word was previously written.

13.3c Invented Spelling

Invented spelling is the beginning writer's attempt to write words by attending to their sound units and associating letters with them in a systematic, although unconventional, way (Jennings, Caldwell, & Lerner, 2010). Examples of invented spellings used by young children are *evry budy* for *everybody, na-bor* for *neighbor, ez* for *easy, neck all* for *nickel,* and *1000ilnd* for *thousand island.* Examples of writing with invented spelling are shown in Figures 13.12 and 13.13.

FIGURE **13.12**
Example of Invented Spelling

SuuMENN Poo
I AMMGO ENN

"Swimming pool. I am going in."

© Cengage Learning

Children who are encouraged to use invented spelling and to write anything they want in whatever way they can are much more willing to write. They learn to take risks in a failure-free environment, and they come to understand that writing is a pleasurable form of communication in which thoughts are translated into symbols that mean something to other people. Figure 13.13 illustrates the writing of a second-grade student who was able to express her deep emotional feelings about a ladybug. Research shows that children who were allowed to invent their own spelling at an early age tend to spell as well as, or better than, children who were not given this instruction (Sipe, 2001).

It is important that teachers who use invented spelling as an instructional technique make sure that parents understand the philosophy and purpose of the method. Student Stories 13.2, "Learning the Awful Truth About Spelling," relates the tale of Brian, who happily used invented spelling in first and second grade and was shocked when told that spelling has rules.

A critical factor in using invented spelling is the child's phonological awareness of the sounds of language. Young children who have acquired phonemic awareness of the sounds of language have proficiency in invented spelling and tend to write more.

13.3d Multisensory Approaches to Spelling

We discussed multisensory approaches for reading in Chapter 12, "Reading Difficulties." Multisensory techniques are also useful for teaching spelling. Using several senses helps to reinforce the learning of spelling words. Multisensory learning involves learning spelling through

"From Karla to my mom. It's no fair that you made me let my ladybug go. What if I was your mom and I made you take your ladybug. I am sure you would be sad like me. That ladybug might have been an orphan. So you should have let me have it anyway."

FIGURE **13.13**

A Second-Grade Student's Note to Her Mother Using Invented Spelling

---

STUDENT STORIES 13.2

Learning the Awful Truth About Spelling

Sometimes children who freely use invented spelling in first and second grades are jolted when they realize that there are strict rules about correct spelling. Brian had been in third grade for two weeks in the fall semester when he asked his mother to transfer him to a different third-grade class. When his mother asked Brian about why he wanted to change teachers, Brian explained that the reason was that his current third-grade teacher was not a very good teacher. When his mother probed further, Brian confided that his third-grade teacher thought there was only one way to spell a word.

REFLECTIVE QUESTION

1. Do you think children should be encouraged to use invented spelling?

the visual, auditory, kinesthetic, and tactile senses. The multisensory spelling approaches include the *multisensory method* and the *Fernald Method,* which are described in detail in the "Teaching Strategies" section of this chapter.

13.3e Two Theories of Word Selection for Teaching Spelling

In selecting words for teaching spelling, there are two alternative approaches: (1) the *word-pattern approach* and (2) the *word-frequency approach.*

word-pattern approach to spelling
A theory of word selection and instruction in spelling. It is based on the belief that the spelling of English is sufficiently rule-covered to warrant a method of selection and instruction that stresses phonological, morphological, and syntactic rules or word patterns.

Word-Pattern Approach to Spelling The word-pattern approach to spelling is based on the contention that the spelling of American English is sufficiently rule-covered to warrant an instructional method that stresses phonological, morphological, and syntactic rules or word patterns. This word-pattern approach capitalizes on the underlying regularity between the phonological and morphological elements in oral language and their graphic representations in written language.

In spite of the seemingly numerous exceptions to the rules of spelling, research demonstrates that American English spelling does have predictable patterns and an underlying system of phonological and morphological regularity. Teachers can help students discover underlying linguistic patterns by selecting certain words for spelling instruction. For example, when teaching the spelling pattern of the phoneme *oy,* the teacher should include words such as *boy, joy, Roy,* and *toy* to help students form a phonics generalization. The teaching of spelling can be merged with phonics instruction so that phonics and word-analysis skills are practiced during the spelling lesson.

word-frequency approach to spelling
A method of word selection and instruction for spelling. Words are selected for spelling instruction on the basis of how frequently they are used in writing.

Word-Frequency Approach to Spelling In the word-frequency approach to spelling, words for spelling instruction are chosen on the basis of frequency of use, rather than on phonological patterns.

A core of spelling words that are most frequently used in writing was determined through extensive investigations of the writing of children and adults (Fitzgerald, 1951). A few words in our language are used over and over. In fact, only 2,650 words and their derivative repetitions make up about 95% of the writing of elementary-school children. A basic list of 3,500 words covers the needs of children in elementary school (Fitzgerald, 1955), and 60% of our writing consists of the 100 words shown in Table 13.3.

The word-frequency approach to spelling is based on the contention that so many exceptions to spelling rules occur in the most frequently used words that it is difficult to convey patterns and rules to beginning spellers. Examples of the irregular relationship between phonemes (the spoken sounds) and graphemes (the written symbols) are easy to cite. George Bernard Shaw, an advocate of spelling reform, is credited with the suggestion that the word *fish* be spelled *ghoti: gh* as in cough, *o* as in *women, ti* as in *nation.* Following phonic generalizations, the word *natural* could be spelled *pnatchurile.*

One teacher found that students' spelling of the word *awful* was varied and included *offul, awfull, offel,* and *offle.* Each is an accurate phonetic transcription of the oral sounds of the word.

TABLE 13.3

The 100 Most Common Words in Written Language

a	eat	in	our	there
all	for	it	out	they
am	girl	it	over	this
and	go	just	play	time
are	going	know	pretty	to
at	good	like	put	too
baby	got	little	red	tree
ball	had	look	run	two
be	has	made	said	up
big	have	make	saw	want
boy	he	man	school	was
but	her	me	see	we
can	here	mother	she	went
Christmas	him	my	so	what
come	his	name	some	when
did	home	not	take	will
do	house	now	that	with
dog	how	of	the	would
doll	I	on	them	you
down	I'm	one	then	your

© Cengage Learning

Professional Resource Download

13.3f Assessment of Spelling

Informal Tests Informal and teacher-constructed spelling tests are particularly useful. Curriculum-based assessment also offers a way to obtain information on spelling that is directly linked to instruction (Spinelli, 2006).

A short informal spelling test, as shown in Table 13.4, was developed by selecting 10 words from a frequency-of-use word list. The student is asked to spell on paper words from each grade list until 3 words in a grade list are missed. The student's spelling level can be estimated as that at which only 2 words are missed.

Formal Tests Some formal tests of spelling are individual spelling tests, and others are part of a comprehensive academic achievement battery. Table 13.5 shows some commonly used spelling tests.

TABLE 13.4

Informal Spelling Test

Grade 1	Grade 2	Grade 3	Grade 4	Grade 5	Grade 6	Grade 7
all	be	after	because	bread	build	although
at	come	before	dinner	don't	hair	amount
for	give	brown	few	floor	music	business
his	house	dog	light	beautiful	eight	excuse
it	long	never	place	money	brought	receive
not	must	in	sent	minute	except	measure
see	ran	gray	table	ready	suit	telephone
up	some	hope	town	snow	whose	station
me	want	live	only	through	yesterday	possible
go	your	mother	farm	bright	instead	straight

© Cengage Learning

Professional Resource Download

TABLE 13.5

Tests of Spelling

Test	Type	Age or Grade Assessed
Brigance Comprehensive Inventory of Basic Skills—Revised, Curriculum Associates *http://www.curriculumassociates.com*	Battery	Grades K–9
Peabody Individual Achievement Test—Revised (PIAT-R), AGS Pearson *http://ags.pearsonassessments.com*	Battery	Grades K–12
Test of Written Spelling—3 (TOWS-3), Pro-Ed *http://www.proedinc.com*	Spelling	Grades 1–12
Wide-Range Achievement Test—4 (WRAT-4), PAR Psychological Assessment Resources *http://www3.parinc.com*	Battery	Ages 5–adult

© Cengage Learning

Did You Get It?

Mr. Kelvin and Ms. Santiago are parallel teachers of a class of young students. These students are today working on spelling-related tasks, such as basic letter-writing, imitation of writing, and simple pictures and sketches, which run the gamut from scribbling to basic drawing. This class is at which level of writing?
  a. Syllable junctures
  b. Prephonetic
  c. Phonetic
  d. Written word patterns

13.4 Handwriting

Three different ways to produce writing are currently taught in schools: (1) manuscript writing (a version of printing), (2) cursive writing (sometimes called *script*), and (3) keyboarding (or typing).

Even though computer word processing is becoming more common in our schools, handwriting remains a necessary competency. Handwriting is still the major means by which students convey to teachers what they have learned. In many life situations, adults find handwriting an unavoidable necessity.

Handwriting is the most concrete of the communication skills. It can be directly observed, evaluated, and preserved, providing a permanent record of the output. The process of handwriting is intricate and depends on many different skills and abilities. Handwriting requires accurate perception of the graphic symbol patterns. The act of writing entails keen visual and motor skills that depend on the visual function of the eye, the coordination of eye movements, smooth motor coordination of eye and hand, and control of arm, hand, and finger muscles. Writing also requires accurate visual and kinesthetic memory of the written letters and words.

Extremely poor handwriting is sometimes called dysgraphia, and this condition may reflect other underlying neurological conditions. Poor handwriting may be a manifestation of fine-motor difficulties because the student is unable to execute efficiently the motor movements required to write or to copy written letters or forms. Students may be unable to transfer the input of visual information to the output of fine-motor movement, or they may have difficulty in activities that require motor and spatial judgments. Some students exhibit dystrophic problems when they cannot go from a far-point visual task of seeing a letter or word on a chalkboard to then copying that form on a piece of paper, a near-point visual task. Other underlying shortcomings that interfere with handwriting performance are poor motor skills, faulty visual perception of letters and words, and difficulty in remembering visual impressions.

Figure 13.14 illustrates the attempts of two 10-year-old boys with learning disabilities and handwriting difficulty to copy some writing materials.

dysgraphia
Extremely poor handwriting or the inability to perform the motor movements required for handwriting. The condition is associated with neurological dysfunction.

13.4a Manuscript Writing

Handwriting instruction usually begins with manuscript writing in kindergarten, where children begin to write letters of the alphabet. Manuscript writing usually continues in first, second, and third grade.

Manuscript writing has certain advantages: It is easy to learn because it consists of only circles and straight lines, and the letter forms are closer to the printed form used in reading. Some educators believe it is not essential to transfer to cursive writing at all because the manuscript form is legal, legible, and probably just as rapid. Many children with learning disabilities and related mild disabilities find manuscript writing easier than cursive writing. The manuscript letters are shown in Figure 13.15.

manuscript writing
The form of handwriting sometimes called *printing*. This form of writing, closer to the printed form, is easier to learn than cursive writing because it consists of only circles and straight lines.

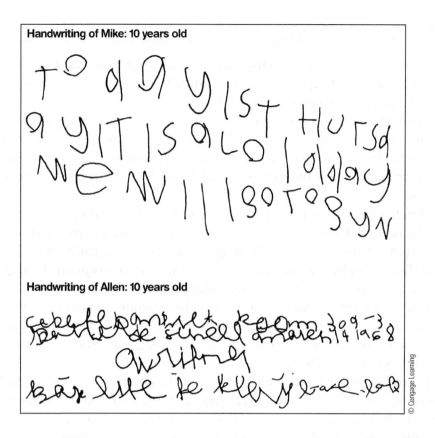

Handwriting of Mike: 10 years old

Handwriting of Allen: 10 years old

© Cengage Learning

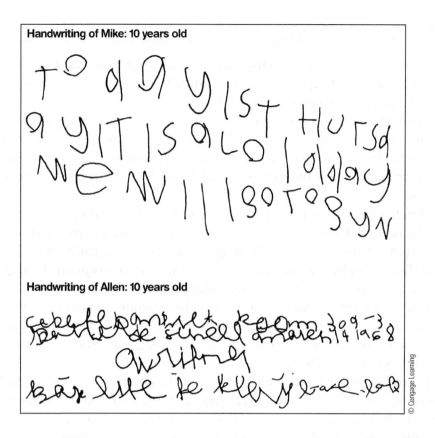

FIGURE **13.15**
Manuscript Letters

© Cengage Learning 2015

cursive writing
The style of writing sometimes called script. The individual letters are joined in writing a word. Children typically learn cursive writing in third grade.

13.4b Cursive Writing

In cursive writing (sometimes called *script),* the letters are connected. The transfer to cursive writing is typically made somewhere in the third grade, although schools teach cursive writing as late as fifth grade. In an earlier era, writing instruction emphasized the flourishes of cursive writing, but today the goal is to teach functional handwriting. Cursive writing has certain advantages: (1) it minimizes spatial judgment problems for the student and (2) it has a rhythmic continuity and wholeness that are missing from manuscript writing. In addition, errors of reversals are virtually eliminated with cursive writing. However, many students with learning disabilities and related mild disabilities find it difficult to make the transfer to cursive writing after they have learned manuscript writing. Samples of cursive letters are shown in Figure 13.16.

Another handwriting form is the *D'Nealian* writing system. This system helps students make the transition to cursive writing more easily. The D'Nealian system is a simplified cursive writing style in which manuscript letters have the basic forms of the corresponding cursive letters. Most of the manuscript letters are made with a continuous stroke that produces a kind of connected manuscript writing, and the student does not have to lift the pencil. Some students can more easily transfer from manuscript writing to this modified form of cursive writing. A website for D'Nealian writing can be found at *http://www.dnealian.com/lessons.html.*

13.4c The Left-Handed Student

Left-handed people encounter a special handwriting problem because their natural tendency is to write from right to left on the page. In writing from left to right, left-handers have difficulty seeing what they have written. Their hand covers up the writing and tends to smudge the writing as it moves over the paper. To avoid the smudging, some left-handed students begin "hooking" their hand when they start using pens. Left-handedness today is accepted as natural. Students who have not yet stabilized handedness should be encouraged to write with their right hand, unless it is observed that the student has great difficulty doing so.

Students with a strong preference for the left hand should be permitted to write as a lefty, although this creates some special problems in writing and requires special instruction. Research shows that left-handers can learn to write just as quickly as right-handers. For manuscript writing, the paper should be placed directly in front of the left-handed student, without a slant. For cursive writing, the top of the paper should be slanted north-northeast, opposite to the slant used by the right-handed student. The pencil should be long, gripped about 1 inch from the tip, with the eraser pointing to the left shoulder. The position of the hand should be curved, with the weight resting on the outside of the little finger, and hooking should be avoided.

Many word-processing programs include adjustments to change the mouse to a left-handed clicking position. The teacher must observe closely the preference of the student since some left-handed individuals do not want to use a left-handed clicking position.

FIGURE **13.16**
Cursive Letters

© Cengage Learning 2015

13.4d Keyboarding or Typing Skills

The skills needed to use a computer keyboard are referred to as keyboarding or *typing* skills. Students with learning disabilities and related mild disabilities who have handwriting difficulties often find that word-processing programs offer a very welcome and feasible solution to their handwriting difficulties. The motor skills required for keyboarding are easier than the motor skills required for cursive writing, and the output is certainly more legible for the reader. However, simply putting a student in front of a computer is not enough; it is essential to provide explicit and consistent instruction in keyboarding. Teaching students the correct finger positions initially is far superior to allowing them to develop the bad habits of a hunt-and-peck method.

keyboarding
The process of typing on a computer keyboard.

Learning to type is hard work and requires direct and regular instruction over an extended period of time, with ample opportunities for drill and practice. Sufficient time must be provided in the schedule for keyboarding instruction and for the student to practice the skills.

Good keyboarding software programs for students, such as Type to Learn (*http://www.K12software.com*) and Mavis Beacon Teaches Typing (The Learning Company at *http://www.learningco.com*), are based on sound instructional principles. They begin by demonstrating how each new key should be pressed, showing a keyboard on the screen and demonstrating key strokes by highlighting specific keys. As students practice using the new keys, they receive feedback on their accuracy. There are frequent opportunities for practice, and the programs contain drills emphasizing both accuracy and speed. Good typing instructional programs keep a running record of the students' proficiency level so that students can keep track of how fast they type (in words per minute) and how many errors they make. Students enjoy computer typing games that are provided in these keyboarding programs.

Did You Get It?

Handwriting is considered to be a necessary and useful form of communication; it is considered the most concrete of all forms of communication. Why, and in what aspect is it deemed such a critical and necessary task?

a. It leaves a permanent record of production.
b. Because of its history and tradition.
c. It is mandated to be part of every curriculum.
d. Actually, in light of technology, it is no longer considered critical or as necessary.

13.5 Teaching Strategies to Improve Written Language Difficulties

The balance of this chapter presents specific instructional strategies for teaching written language in the areas of (1) writing strategies for the general education classroom, (2) written expression, (3) word processing, (4) spelling, and (5) handwriting.

13.6 Writing Strategies for the General Education Classroom

Most students with learning disabilities and related mild disabilities who have writing difficulties receive their writing instruction in the general education classroom.

13.6a Instruction for Essay Writing Tests

Often the statewide assessment tests include a writing sample. These writing tests are usually graded by a trained writing evaluator, using a specific framework for the evaluation. To produce an acceptable written essay, students in general education need specific instruction in the scoring framework. The components of a writing framework to teach students how to develop a brief informational written product are described by Jennings and Haynes (2006).

Topic sentence

It is important to follow basic safety rules when enjoying an outdoor activity. When you do an outdoor activity, you should wear pads and a helmet at the appropriate time. You should also carry a first-aid kit with you when you go hiking or when you swim. You should do it with a buddy.

Supporting sentence

First of all, when you are hiking or skateboarding, you should wear a helmet or other protection. The helmet may save your life if you fall and other pads could prevent other injuries. If a person fell off their bike or skateboard, then there is a chance that they could get hurt. For example, when I first started to learn to ride a two-wheeled bike, I would always fall. Each day I would come in with cuts and scrapes. If I had not worn my helmet, then I could have gotten large cuts on my head. Thankfully, I am a quick learner.

Supporting sentence

Secondly, when someone hikes, he or she should carry a first-aid kit with them. When someone hikes, there is always a chance of him or her getting hurt. If someone got hurt when he or she was hiking, then there would most likely be no one around to help him or her. For example, whenever I hike somewhere, I always carry a first-aid kit. The reason I do this is that I have gotten hurt while hiking. I was by myself and I sprained my ankle. With my first-aid kit, I was able to wrap my ankle.

Supporting sentence

Thirdly, swimming with a buddy is a safe thing to do. Swimming is not always a safe thing to do by yourself. There is always a risk that someone may drown. If you were swimming by yourself, you should tell someone where you are going. For example, my friend decided that he was hot and wanted to go for a swim. His mom and dad were not at home, so he decided to go anyway. The problem was that he forgot to leave a note for his parents. His parents were worried sick. He likes to go to a pond in Topsfield. The pond is not open this time of year so his parents started to think he might have drowned, but he was only taking a walk around the pond.

Conclusion

In conclusion, following safety rules when doing an activity is important. Many bad things could happen to someone if they did not follow the rules.

Source: From "Essay writing: An attainable goal for students with dyslexia," by Terrill M . Jennings & Charles W. Haynes, 2006, *Perspectives: The International Dyslexia Assoc, 32(2),* 36–39.

1. **Topic sentence.** The topic sentence tells what this essay is about.
2. **Develop 3 sentences that support the topic.**
   a. **Supporting sentence 1.** The student might start out with the introductory words, "First of all."
   b. **Supporting sentence 2.** The student might start with the word, "Secondly."
   c. **Supporting sentence 3.** The student might start with the word, "Thirdly," or "Finally."
3. **Provide an example of each supporting sentence.** This can be a specific fact or a supporting sentence to back up the supporting topic sentence.
4. **Concluding sentence.** The student could start out with the words, "In conclusion." This sums up what has been presented in the essay.

Teaching Tips 13.1, "A Writing Framework," gives an example of an essay that follows this writing framework.

Most students with learning disabilities and related mild disabilities receive their writing instruction in the general education classroom. General education teachers need to be familiar with strategies for teaching writing to all students. Some writing strategies for the general education classroom teacher are given in Including Students in General Education 13.1, "Writing Strategies."

Writing Strategies

Written Expression

- Allocate sufficient time for writing. Students learn to write by writing; therefore, have students write four times per week.

- Encourage students in the primary grades to use invented spelling.

- Use brainstorming to create ideas about writing topics.

- Give students a range of writing tasks, including both creative writing and functional writing. Creative writing is personal writing, while functional writing conveys information about a subject.

- Teach students the stages of the writing process: prewriting, drafting, revising, sharing.

- Use a graphic organizer, such as Inspiration (*http://www.inspiration.com*), to plan a story.

- Use a presentation program, such as Microsoft PowerPoint, to develop a story.

- Use the Internet to conduct research on a topic.

Spelling

- Limit the number of spelling words to be learned at one time.

- Analyze the phonemes of new words.

- Point out the syllables in multisyllabic words.

- Teach word families (e.g., *at, sat, rat, mat*).

- Provide periodic retesting and review.

- Use multisensory strategies (e.g., see the word, say the word, write the word in the air, see the word in your mind's eye, write the word on paper, and compare the word to the model).

- Use games to motivate students to learn their spelling words. For example, Wheel of Fortune is an enjoyable game that reinforces the learning of particular spelling words.

Handwriting

- Begin with manuscript writing and explain that it consists of lines and circles.

- The teacher says the name of the letter to be written.

- Have the students trace the letter with their finger.

- Use dotted lines for a letter and have the students trace the dots with a pencil.

- The teacher gives stroke directions to the students (e.g., first we go down, then we go up).

- Have the students copy a letter (or word) on paper while looking at a model.

- The students write the letter from memory while saying the name of the letter.

Professional Resource Download

Did You Get It?

Within a formatted essay, a student typically writes two or three sentences or short paragraphs beginning—optionally—with the words "firstly," "secondly," or some approximation thereof. These critical sentences are composed in order to do what, in relation to the argument posited by the essay?
  a. Open
  b. Close
  c. Support
  d. Dispel

13.7 Strategies for Teaching Written Expression

Many students with learning disabilities and related mild disabilities reach upper elementary or secondary levels with little exposure to, and little experience with, written expression. There is so much effort and intense instruction to improve poor reading skills that it often overshadows instruction in writing.

- **Provide opportunities for extensive writing.** Student writers need sufficient time to think, reflect, write, and rewrite. Many students with writing difficulties spend less than 10 minutes per day composing. It is recommended that composing time be extended to 50 minutes each day, 4 days each week. Break the writing time into several smaller segments for students who need a shorter period of writing concentration.

- **Establish a writing environment.** The atmosphere of the writing classroom should foster writing activities and encourage cooperative writing work. Teachers can use individual writing folders containing the students' current writing projects, a list of finished pieces, ideas for future topics, and writing assistance materials, such as individual spelling dictionaries. Keep materials and books in one place, so that students can begin their writing without having to request teacher assistance.

- **Allow students to select their own topics.** Writing projects are most successful when students have a personal interest in the subject. If they need more information, reading other source materials and facilities to use the Internet should be readily available.

- **Model the writing process and thinking aloud.** The act of writing is encouraged when teachers and classmates model the cognitive processes involved in writing. For example, the teacher could model the writing stages by thinking aloud: "I want to plan a mysterious setting for my story. What about a haunted house? Next, I must decide on the characters in this story . . ." (Graham & Harris, 2005).

- **Develop a sense of audience.** In the traditional writing curriculum, students write for the teacher and think they must *match the teacher's* standards of correctness. Expand the students' sense of audience by having them engage in peer collaboration, consulting, group sharing, and publication. Provide opportunities to discuss their writing progress with classmates who are not writing experts. When the writing projects are finished, students can read their material to an audience of peers and discuss their work.

- **Transfer ownership and control of the writing to the students.** A goal of the writing process is to transfer ownership and control to the writer. As students learn to internalize the strategies that are being taught, they should gradually take more responsibility for their writing and be able to work without teacher direction.

- **Capitalize on students' interests.** Learn about the students' interests and be alert for relevant events that can become the subject for writing. Interests in sports, school, music, movies, local and national news, trips, family vacations, or holidays offer subjects for writing. One teacher found that trolls (the little dolls with the homely, elf-like features and colorful hair) were reemerging as a popular toy. So many students were bringing them to school that the teacher had to limit students to one troll guest a day. Capitalizing on their interest, the teacher had students design their own trolls in drawings and write stories telling why the manufacturer should adopt their troll designs.

- **Avoid punitive grading.** Do not allow grading practices to discourage students. Consider grading only ideas, not the technical form, for some assignments, or give 2 grades—one for ideas and one for technical skills. If a student makes errors in many areas, correct only one skill, such as capitalization. When the student masters that skill, concentrate on another area.

- **Differentiate between creative and functional writing.** Creative and functional writing lessons have different goals, and students should understand that different skills are required for each. In creative writing, the goal is to develop ideas and express them in written form, and there is less need for technical perfection. In contrast, functional writing may require students to learn specific formats. For example, if the final product is a business letter, the writer must adhere to certain standards and forms.

- **Provide abundant input.** Students need something to write about. Before asking students to write, make sure that they have enough firsthand experiences, such as trips, creative activities, viewing a television show, movies, or sports events that can be drawn upon for writing. Talk about these experiences.

- **Schedule frequent writing.** Students need frequent writing experiences to develop skills in writing. An assignment to write a certain number of pages per week in a personal journal that will not be corrected (or perhaps even read) by the teacher is an excellent technique for providing necessary practice and improving the quality of writing.

- **Teach how to combine sentences.** This approach is especially useful for adolescents and adults. The teacher writes several separate kernel sentences. Students must combine those sentences into a more complex sentence by adding clauses and connectors.

Professional Resource Download

Learning to write requires abundant time and opportunities for various kinds of writing.

Some guides for the teaching of writing are given in Teaching Tips 13.2, "Teaching the Writing Process."

Did You Get It?

There are a myriad of suitable strategies that can be implemented with the goal of improving written expression. One of these is to develop a class-wide sense of what the authors of your text refer to as "audience." What is the primary reason for implementing this strategy?

a. To teach social skills in addition to writing skills
b. To break the shackles of students writing for teacher alone
c. To create a sense of unity and brotherhood
d. To provide upper-level students with a venue to showcase their work

13.8 Strategies for Using Word Processing

The following list suggests some activities for using computer word processing to teach writing:

- **Expanding vocabulary.** Using a word-processing program, write a sentence or short paragraph on the computer. Use the computer thesaurus to find synonyms for several words.
- **Learning story sequence.** Place several sentences about a series of events in incorrect order. Have the students use the "cut" and "paste" functions to put them in the proper sequence.
- **Beginning a story.** Put the beginning of a story on a disk and have each student continue the narrative. Each student's story can be compared with others'. In another variation, begin a story on a disk and then have one student write the next segment, another student write the following segment, and so on.
- **Keeping an electronic diary or journal.** Keeping a journal of daily events has proved to be an effective technique for improving reading and writing skills. Instead of writing on paper, the student can use a computer with word-processing software.
- **Sending e-mail.** Students can use e-mail to send messages. The messages can be sent between students in the class, between the teacher and the students, or between the students and students in other classes throughout the world.
- **Writing book reports.** To make writing a book report on the computer easier, develop a template with key topics, such as title of the book, author, type of book, summary, and the student's name. To write the book report, the student simply loads the template and fills out the information next to each topic.
- **Writing a class newsletter.** A newsletter can be written with any word-processing program. Several commercial programs allow users to write, illustrate, paste up, and print pages that resemble a newspaper or newsletter. Microsoft Word allows users to set up two columns.

- **Using graphics.** Graphics can easily be added to a word-processing document. Graphics can be found on Internet sites, or photos can be taken with a digital camera. Clipart often comes with word-processing software programs. Graphics can be scanned in with a scanner, or students can create their own art graphics. The search engine Google has a collection of images that can be accessed at *http://www.google.com* (click on "images").
- **Using the Internet.** Students who have access to the Internet can find a wealth of information (such as text, pictures, photographs, and charts) about a topic of their interest. Topics such as dinosaurs, baseball, sports figures, or the history of Canada can be investigated through a search engine. With material gathered from their searches, the students can develop stories and reports or develop PowerPoint presentations to share their reports with others.

Did You Get It?

As a teacher and staff member at Minnesota's Jules Verne high school, you know how absolutely annoying and distracting it is when a student or teacher uses any device to send an e-mail or text during school. Why not just place a sign that says "Forbidden!"
  a. No—students need to be able to communicate with loved ones regularly
  b. No—contextually, e-mailing can be a useful processing tool
  c. Yes—in most school districts this is now mandated
  d. Yes—this is recommended

13.9 Strategies for Teaching Spelling

The following list provides strategies for teaching spelling:

1. **Auditory perception and memory of letter sounds.** Provide practice in auditory perception of letter sounds, strengthen knowledge of phonics and structural analysis, and develop skills in applying phonic generalizations. (See Chapter 11, "Spoken Language Difficulties: Listening and Speaking.")
2. **Visual memory of words.** Help the students strengthen visual images of each word. Flash cards and computer spelling software can also be used to develop speed and strengthen memory of spelling words. (See Chapter 8, "Young Children With Disabilities," for specific strategies for developing visual perception and memory.)
3. **Multisensory methods in spelling.** Students who are told to study spelling lessons are frequently at a loss as to what to do. The following describes a multisensory approach for learning spelling that engages the visual, auditory, kinesthetic, and tactile senses:
   a. **Meaning and pronunciation.** Have the students look at the word, pronounce it correctly, and use it in a sentence.
   b. **Imagery.** Ask students to "see" the word and say it. Have students say each syllable of the word, say the word syllable by syllable, spell the word orally, and then use one finger to trace the word, either in the air or by touching the word itself.

TEACHING TIPS 13.3

The Fernald Method for Teaching Spelling

a. Students are told that they are going to learn words in a new way that has proved to be very successful. They are encouraged to select a word that they wish to learn.

b. The teacher writes that word on a sheet of paper, as the students watch and as the teacher says the word.

c. The students trace the word, saying it several times, and then write it on a separate piece of paper while saying the word.

d. The students write the word from memory without looking at the original copy. If the word is incorrect,

students repeat Step C. If the word is correct, it is put in a file box. The words in the file box are used later in writing stories.

e. At later stages, this painstaking tracing method for learning words is not needed. Students learn a word by *looking* as the teacher writes it, *saying* it, and *writing* it. At a still later stage, the students can learn by only looking at a word in print and writing it. Finally, they learn by merely looking at the word.

Professional Resource Download

c. **Recall.** Ask students to look at the word and then close their eyes and see it in their mind's eye. Have them spell the word orally. Then ask them to open their eyes and look at the word to see if they were correct. (If they make an error, they should repeat the process.)

d. **Writing the word.** Ask the students to write the word correctly from memory, check the spelling against the original, and then check the writing to make sure that every letter is legible.

e. **Mastery.** Have the students cover the word and write it. If they are correct, they should cover and write it two more times.

4. **The Fernald method.** This method is a multisensory approach, and it is used to teach reading and writing as well as spelling (Fernald, 1988). The Fernald method for teaching spelling is shown in Teaching Tips 13.3, "The Fernald Method for Teaching Spelling."

5. **The "test-study-test" method versus the "study-test" method.** There are 2 common approaches to teaching spelling in the classroom: the "test-study-test" and the "study-test" plans. The test-study-test method uses a pretest, which is usually given at the beginning of the week. The students then study only those words that were missed on the pretest. This method is better for older students who have fairly good spelling abilities because they do not need to study words they already know. The study-test method is better for young students and for those with poor spelling abilities who would miss too many words on a pretest. The study-test method permits them to study a few well-selected words before the test is given.

6. **Listening centers, audiotapes, and CDs.** Spelling lessons can easily be put on audiotapes or CDs. After students have advanced to a level that enables them to work by themselves, they can complete their spelling lessons in a listening laboratory. Earphones allow for individualized instruction and help many students to block out distracting auditory stimuli.

7. **Electronic spellers and computer spell checkers.** Students should learn how to use these spelling devices as an aid in spelling. Franklin Learning (*http://www.franklin.com*) is one manufacturer of electronic spellers.

Did You Get It?

One method of testing for spelling adds an additional "test" to the traditional "study-test" method used in many classrooms. What purpose does this additional test serve?

a. It is a pretest
b. It is an additional posttest
c. It is an adjunct, informal essay test
d. It is an additional role-play test

13.10 Strategies for Teaching Handwriting

The following are useful activities for teaching handwriting:

1. **Chalkboard activities.** These activities provide practice before writing instruction is begun. Circles, lines, geometric shapes, letters, and numbers can be made with large, free movements using the muscles of the shoulders, arms, hands, and fingers. (For additional suggestions, see Chapter 8, "Young Children With Disabilities.")

2. **Position.** Have the students prepare for writing by sitting in comfortable chairs at a table that is at the proper height. Be sure that the students' feet are flat on the floor and both forearms are on the writing surface. Each student's nonwriting hand should hold the paper at the top. Have students stand and work at a chalkboard for the initial writing activities.

3. **Paper.** For manuscript writing, the paper should be placed without a slant, parallel with the lower edge of the desk. For cursive writing, the paper is tilted at an angle—approximately 60 degrees from vertical—to the left for right-handed students and to the right for left-handed students. To help the student remember the correct slant, place a strip of tape parallel to the top of the paper at the top of the desk. It may be necessary to attach the paper to the desk with masking tape to keep it from sliding.

4. **Holding the pencil.** Many students with writing disorders do not know how or are unable to hold a pencil properly between their thumb and middle finger, with the index finger riding the pencil. They should grasp the pencil above the sharpened point. A piece of tape or a rubber band placed around the pencil can help the student hold it at the right place.

   If a student has difficulty grasping the pencil, the pencil can be put through a practice golf ball (the kind with many holes). Have the student place the middle finger and thumb around the ball to practice the right grip. Large, primary-size pencils, large crayons, and felt-tip pens are useful for the beginning stages of writing. Clay might also be placed around the pencil to help the student grasp it. Short pencils should be avoided because it is impossible to grip them correctly. There are also a number of types of pencil grips that can be purchased.

5. **Stencils and templates.** Make cardboard or plastic stencils of geometric forms, letters, and numbers. Have the students trace the form with one finger, a pencil, or a crayon. (Clip the stencil to the paper to prevent it from moving.) Then remove the stencil and reveal the figure that has been made. The stencil can be cut so that the hole creates the shape or, in reverse, so that the outer edges of the stencil create the shape.

6. **Tracing.** Make heavy black figures on white paper and clip a sheet of onion skin or transparent paper over the letters. Have the students trace the forms and letters. Start with diagonal lines and circles, then horizontal and vertical lines, geometric shapes, and finally, letters and numbers. The students may also trace a black letter on paper with a crayon or felt-tip pen or they may use a transparent sheet. Another idea is to put letters on transparencies and project the images onto a chalkboard or a large sheet of paper. Students can then trace over the images.

7. **Drawing between the lines.** Have the students practice making "roads" between double lines in a variety of widths and shapes. Then ask the students to write letters by going between the double lines of outlined letters. Use arrows and numbers to show the direction and sequence of the lines (Figure 13.17).

FIGURE **13.17**

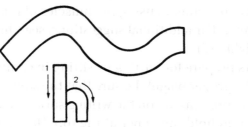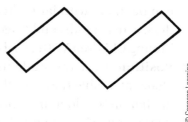

8. **Dot-to-dot.** Draw a complete figure and then draw an outline of the same figure by using dots. Ask the students to make the figure by connecting the dots (Figure 13.18).

FIGURE **13.18**

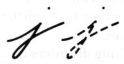

9. **Tracing with reducing cues.** Write a complete letter or word and have the students trace it. Then write the first part of the letter or word and have the students trace your part and then complete the letter or word. Finally, reduce the cue to only the upstroke and have the students write the entire letter or word (Figure 13.19).

FIGURE **13.19**

10. **Lined paper.** Begin by having students use unlined paper. Later, have them use lined paper with wide lines to help them with the placement of letters. It may be helpful to use specially lined paper that is color cued to aid in letter placement. Regular lined paper can also be color cued to help students make letters (Figure 13.20).

Red

Green

Green

Red

© Cengage Learning

FIGURE **13.20**

11. **Template lines.** For students who need additional help in stopping at lines, tape can be placed at bottom and top lines. Windows can be cut out of cardboard to give further guidance for spacing letters. The following figure shows a template made from a piece of cardboard with 3 windows for one-line, two-line, and three-line letters. One-line letters are those that fit in a single-line space: *a, c, e, i, m, n.* Two-line letters are those with ascenders only: *b, d, h, k, I, t.* Three-line letters are those with descenders: *f g j p q z y* (Figure 13.21).

FIGURE **13.21**

© Cengage Learning

12. **Letter difficulty.** In terms of ease, cursive letters are introduced in the following order: beginning letters—*m, n, t, i, u, w, r, s, l,* and *e;* more difficult letters—*x, z, y, j, p, h, b, k, f, g,* and *q;* and combinations of letters—*me, be, go, it, no,* and so forth.

13. **Verbal cues.** Students are helped in the motor act of writing by hearing the directions for forming letters—for example, "down-up-and-around." When using this technique, teachers must take care not to distract the students with these verbal instructions.

14. **Words and sentences.** After the students learn to write single letters, instruction should proceed to writing words and sentences. Spacing, size, and slant are additional factors to consider at this stage.

I Have a Kid Who...

ROSIE: *A Student Who Struggles With Handwriting*

Rosie is a 12-year-old girl in the seventh grade at the Rosa Parks Middle School. Her seventh-grade teacher, Mr. Trump, complained that Rosie never turns in her written assignments. When asked to write a story or write a report for a subject-area assignment, Rosie does not complete the project and does not turn in her assignments. Mr. Trump observed that during the class writing assignment, Rosie just looks up at the ceiling as though she was trying to think of something to write about, but she never gets any ideas down on paper.

Rosie has many strengths. She does very well in oral language activities, and she enjoys giving oral presentations. Her reading skills are above average. She also likes mathematics and does well on her math assignments. Rosie has many friends and gets along well socially with her peers.

In terms of writing, Rosie's handwriting is so illegible that even she cannot read what she has written. Rosie still uses manuscript writing and refuses to shift to cursive writing. She says that it is too hard to connect all the letters the right way.

The occupational therapist, Ms. Walters, provides related services to children at the school. Ms. Walters observed Rosie as she tries to write and noted that her writing was painstakingly slow and very laborious. Some informal evaluations showed that Rosie has difficulty with several fine-motor tasks, such as copying shapes and designs.

The occupational therapist, Mr. Trump, and Ms. Joseph, the special education teacher, met as a team to discuss Rosie's handwriting difficulties. The team recommended that Rosie learn keyboarding skills so she could use a computer and word processing for her written assignments. The special education teacher will take the lead for teaching keyboarding skills to Rosie.

QUESTIONS

1. What alternatives are available for handwriting for students who have very poor motor skills?
2. What are important strategies for teaching a student keyboarding or typing skills?
3. Do you think keyboarding can be taught to a small group or must it be taught individually?

Did You Get It?

"Drawing outside of the lines"—proverbially thought of as "thinking outside of the box"—is something that experts emphatically state fosters creativity. Drawing inside of the lines should not be used in teaching handwriting.

a. True—the same principle applies
b. Yes and no—children should be taught both formal and more haphazard expressive handwriting
c. No—students need to learn to stay within parameters with regards to handwriting
d. Probably false—experts are divided on this issue

Chapter Summary

- Written language includes: written expression, spelling, and handwriting.
- Spelling is particularly difficult in English because of their regularity between the spoken and written forms of the language.

- Manuscript writing is the first type of writing most children learn. It is similar to print.
- Cursive writing is more complex and is difficult for many children.
- Word processing is the ability to type with a computer.

Questions for Discussion and Reflection

1. What are the differences between instruction for the writing process and the writing product?
2. Describe the stages of the writing process.
3. How can graphic organizers be used in writing?
4. Discuss the advantages of computer word processing for writing.
5. What is invented spelling? How does invented spelling influence a young child's writing?
6. What kinds of problems do students with learning disabilities and related mild disabilities have in written language?

Key Terms

cursive writing (p. 405)
drafting (p. 389)
dysgraphia (p. 405)
early literacy (p. 387)
graphic organizers (p. 393)
invented spelling (p. 387)
keyboarding (p. 407)
manuscript writing (p. 405)

prewriting (p. 389)
revising (p. 389)
sharing with an audience (p. 390)
word-frequency approach to spelling (p. 402)
word-pattern approach to spelling (p. 402)
word processing (p. 394)
writing process (p. 388)
writing product (p. 388)

Courtesy of Elizabeth Crews Photography

14

Mathematics Difficulties

I hear and I forget.
I see and I remember.
I do and I understand.

—Chinese Proverb

STANDARDS Addressed in This Chapter:

Council for Exceptional Children Initial Level Special Educator Preparation Standards as approved by the National Council for the Accreditation of Teacher Education

CEC Initial Preparation Standard 1: Learner Development and Individual Learning Differences

- 1.0—Beginning special education professionals understand how exceptionalities may interact with development and learning and use this knowledge to provide meaningful and challenging learning experiences for individuals with exceptionalities.

- 1.1—Beginning special education professionals understand how language, culture, and family background influence the learning of individuals with exceptionalities.

- 1.2—Beginning special education professionals use understanding of development and individual differences to respond to the needs of individuals with exceptionalities.

CEC Initial Preparation Standard 3: Curricular Content Knowledge

- 3.0—Beginning special education professionals use knowledge of general and specialized curricula to individualize learning for individuals with exceptionalities.

- 3.1—Beginning special education professionals understand the central concepts, structures of the discipline, and tools of inquiry of the content areas they teach and can organize this knowledge, integrate cross-disciplinary skills, and develop meaningful learning progressions for individuals with exceptionalities.

- 3.2—Beginning special education professionals understand and use general and specialized content knowledge for teaching across curricular content areas to individualize learning for individuals with exceptionalities.

- 3.3—Beginning special education professionals modify general and specialized curricula to make them accessible to individuals with exceptionalities.

CEC Initial Preparation Standard 4: Assessment

- 4.0—Beginning special education professionals use multiple methods of assessment and data-sources in making educational decisions.

- 4.1—Beginning special education professionals select and use technically sound formal and informal assessments that minimize bias.

- 4.2—Beginning special education professionals use knowledge of measurement principles and practices to interpret assessment results and guide educational decisions for individuals with exceptionalities.

- 4.3—Beginning special education professionals in collaboration with colleagues and families use multiple types of assessment information in making decisions about individuals with exceptionalities.

- 4.4—Beginning special education professionals engage individuals with exceptionalities to work toward quality learning and performance and provide feedback to guide them.

CEC Initial Preparation Standard 5: Instructional Planning and Strategies

- 5.0—Beginning special education professionals select, adapt, and use a repertoire of evidence-based instructional strategies to advance learning of individuals with exceptionalities.

- 5.1—Beginning special education professionals consider an individual's abilities, interests, learning environments, and cultural and linguistic factors in the selection, development, and adaptation of learning experiences for individuals with exceptionalities.

- 5.2—Beginning special education professionals use technologies to support instructional assessment, planning, and delivery for individuals with exceptionalities.

- 5.3—Beginning special education professionals are familiar with augmentative and alternative communication systems and a variety of assistive technologies to support the communication and learning of individuals with exceptionalities.

- 5.4—Beginning special education professionals use strategies to enhance language development and communication skills of individuals with exceptionalities.

- 5.6—Beginning special education professionals teach to mastery and promote generalization of learning.

- 5.7—Beginning special education professionals teach cross-disciplinary knowledge and skills such as critical thinking and problem solving to individuals with exceptionalities.

For students, the Common Core Standards for Math can be found at: *www.corestandards.org*

Some individuals with learning disabilities and related disabilities do well in language and reading, but their nemesis is with mathematics and quantitative learning. Two mathematics problem areas for students with learning disabilities are identified in the law through the Individuals With Disabilities Education Improvement Act of 2004 (IDEA-2004) are: (1) mathematics calculation and (2) mathematics reasoning. Difficulties in either of these areas of mathematics can interfere with mathematics achievement in school and with success in later life.

In the "Theories" section of this chapter, we examine (1) mathematics as a universal language, (2) mathematics difficulties, (3) early number concepts and number sense, (4) characteristics of mathematics disabilities, (5) mathematics disabilities at the secondary level, (6) mathematics standards, (7) learning theories for mathematics instruction, and (8) assessing mathematics skills.

In the "Teaching Strategies" section of this chapter, we discuss strategies and methods for teaching mathematics.

14.1 Theories Describing Difficulties With Mathematics

We live in a mathematical world. Every culture and language group uses concepts involved in quantity and math. Mathematics is a symbolic language, which enables human beings to think about, record, and communicate ideas about the elements and relationships of quantity. Mathematics is also a universal language because it has meaning for all cultures and civilizations. In every culture, social class, language, and ethnic group, children live in a natural environment that is rich in quantitative information and events. Human beings in all cultures, languages, social classes, and ethnic groups think about, record, and communicate ideas through quantity. Children in some cultures count blocks; children in other cultures count stones. Students rely on mathematical concepts when they think about the scores of their favorite baseball team, compare player standings, plan to purchase a CD, or pay for a movie ticket. When adolescents and adults plan their budget, balance a checkbook, or use a spreadsheet, they are using mathematics. The level of mathematical thinking and problem solving needed in the workplace and in day-to-day living has increased dramatically (National Council of Teachers of Mathematics, 2000, 2006).

problem solving
The kind of thinking needed to work out mathematics word problems.

> ## Did You Get It?
>
> Given that mathematics is universal in its scope, meaning, and use across all geographical areas and cultures, the statement that mathematics is _____ is inaccurate.
> **a.** used for problem solving
> **b.** a language based on symbols
> **c.** considered the language of the intelligent but typically too difficult for a majority of the masses
> **d.** used to explain and quantify

14.2 Students With Mathematics Difficulties and Students With Mathematics Learning Disabilities

Many students have difficulty in acquiring and using mathematics skills. Researchers differentiate 2 different groups: (1) students with math difficulties and (2) students with mathematics learning disabilities. In this book, we offer strategies for teaching both groups. Students with math difficulties perform poorly in mathematics achievement tests. Over 30% of eighth-grade students score below basic math performance on the National Assessment of Educational Progress (NAEP) (Maccini, et al., 2008; Mazzocco, 2007).

mathematics learning disabilities
Students whose learning disability is in the area of mathematics.

In contrast, students with mathematics learning disabilities comprise about 6% of the general population (Mazzocco, 2007). Mathematics learning disabilities is a biologically based disorder and is related to difficulties in cognitive processing and brain functioning. Research with functional Magnetic Resonance

Imaging (fMRI) shows these cognitive processing dysfunctions (Mazzoco, 2007; Gersten, Clarke, & Mazzocco, 2007).

Approximately 26% of students with learning disabilities exhibit problems in the area of mathematics. Over 50% of students with disabilities have mathematics goals written into their individualized education programs (IEPs) (Kunsch, Jitendra, & Sood, 2007; Miller & Hudson, 2007; Cass et al., 2003).

dyscalculia
A medical term indicating lack of ability to perform mathematical functions. The condition is associated with neurological dysfunction.

The term dyscalculia is a medically oriented term that describes a severe disability in mathematics with medical connotations. When an adult suffers a brain injury and loses abilities in arithmetic, medical professionals identify the loss of math skills related to the neurological impairment as dyscalculia. An analogous term in reading is *dyslexia*, the loss of reading skills that has medical and cognitive connotations.

Both mathematics difficulties and mathematics learning disabilities that emerge in elementary school often continue through the secondary school years. Not only is a mathematics disability a debilitating problem for individuals during school years, but it also continues to impair them as adults in their daily lives (Maccini, Mulcahy, & Wilson, 2007; Adelman & Vogel, 2003; Cass et al., 2003). Almost one-half of the children who are identified with severe mathematics difficulties in the fourth grade are still classified as having serious mathematics difficulties three years later (Gersten & Jordan, 2005; National Center for Learning Disabilities, 2006; Swanson, 2007).

It should be emphasized that not all students with learning disabilities or related disabilities encounter difficulty with number concepts. In fact, some individuals with severe reading disabilities do well in mathematics and exhibit a strong aptitude in quantitative thinking.

The identification and treatment of mathematics disabilities have received much less attention than problems associated with reading disabilities (Fuchs, Fuchs, & Hollenbeck, 2007; Gersten, Clarke, & Mazzocco, 2007). For students with mathematics difficulties, the mathematics curriculum in most general education classrooms does not pay sufficient attention to learning differences in mathematics among students. Moreover, the general education mathematics curriculum does not allot sufficient time for instruction, for guided practice, or for practical applications. Further, mathematical concepts are introduced at too rapid a rate for students who have difficulty with math. If students do not have sufficient time to fully grasp a mathematical concept and to practice it before another mathematical concept is introduced, they feel overwhelmed and become confused (Cawley & Foley, 2001; Butler et al., 2003).

14.2a Early Number Concepts and Number Sense

Number sense refers to the facility to think about quantity. Examples of number sense for young children include the ability to count, match and sort objects, and understand one-to-one correspondence. For some children, difficulties with number sense begin at an early age. Number sense hinges on the child's experience in manipulating objects. A child with unstable perceptual skills, attention problems, or difficulties in motor development may have insufficient experiences with the activities of manipulation that serve to pave the way for understanding quantity, space, order, time, or distance (Berch & Mazzocco, 2007; Kephart, 1971).

one-to-one correspondence
A relationship in which one element of a set is paired with one and only one element of a second set.

When children are expected to perform mathematics assignments, they may not have yet acquired the early skills needed for mathematics learning.

If these children are introduced to a number concept before they have the necessary prerequisite experiences, they will not understand, and they will be confused. Learning mathematics is a sequential process, and children must acquire skills at an earlier stage before going on to the next stage (Jordan et al., 2007).

Early number learning and number sense include skills in (1) one-to-one correspondence, (2) counting, (3) spatial relationships, (4) visual-motor and visual-perception skills, and (5) concepts of time and direction.

One-to-One Correspondence This refers to the ability to pair one element of a set to another element of a second set. For example, the child is able to place one cookie on a table for each child in a group.

Counting Counting entails the ability to count objects by numbers. Children may first have to point to objects in a set and then count each object verbally. Some children are unable to see objects in groups (or sets)—an ability needed to identify the number of objects quickly. Two developmental counting procedures are called *counting-all* and *counting-on*. With counting-all, when children count the objects in 2 groups, they count each object starting with number 1. With counting-on, children start with the number in the larger group and the count-on each number in the smaller group. Even when adding a group of 3 with a group of 4, some young children with mathematics difficulties persist in counting the objects starting with the number 1, instead of adding onto the number of the larger group (Bley & Thornton, 2001; Van de Walle, Karp, & Bay-Williams, 2010).

Spatial Relationships Typically, young children learn by playing with objects such as pots and pans, boxes that fit into each other, and objects that can be put into containers. These play activities help develop a sense of space, sequence, and order. Parents of children with mathematics difficulties often report that their child did not enjoy or play with blocks, puzzles, models, or construction-type toys as preschoolers. These children may have missed these early number-learning experiences.

Many concepts of spatial relationships are normally acquired at the preschool age. Children destined to have mathematics disabilities are baffled by such concepts as up-down, over-under, top-bottom, high-low, near-far, front-back, beginning-end, and across. The child may be unable to perceive distances between numbers on number lines or rulers and may not know whether the number 3 is closer to 4 or to 6.

Visual-Motor and Visual-Perception Abilities Children with mathematics difficulties may have trouble with activities requiring visual-motor abilities and visual-perception abilities. Visual-motor abilities combine motor movement with what one sees, such as copying a figure or shape. Visual perception refers to the ability to interpret what one sees, for example, the ability visually to perceive a geometric shape as a complete and integrated entity. For a child with difficulty with visual perception, a square may not appear as a square shape, but rather as 4 unrelated lines. Some children may be unable to count objects in a series by pointing to each of them and saying, "1, 2, 3, 4, 5." These children must first learn to count by physically grasping and manipulating objects. Some children have difficulty in learning to perceive number symbols visually. They might confuse the vertical strokes of the number 1 and the number 4, or they may confuse the upper half of the number 2 with portions of the number 3.

early number learning
The young child's early learning of quantitative concepts.

spatial relationships
Concepts such as up-down, over-under, top-bottom, high-low, near-far, beginning-end, and across. A disturbance in spatial relationship can interfere with the visualization of the entire number system.

number lines
A sequence of numbers forming a straight line that allows the student to manipulate computation directly. Number lines help students develop an understanding of number symbols and their relationship to each other.

Other children are unable to see objects in groups (or sets)—an ability needed to identify the number of objects quickly. Even when adding a group of 3 with a group of 4, some young children with mathematics difficulties persist in counting the objects starting with the number 1 to determine the total number in the groups instead of using the counting-on strategy. With the counting-on strategy, children learn to add onto the number of the larger group (Bley & Thornton, 2001; Van de Walle, Karp, & Bay-Williams, 2010).

Children with inadequate mathematics abilities often do poorly in visual-motor tasks. Because of their difficulties in perceiving shapes, recognizing spatial relationships, and making spatial judgments, they are unable to copy geometric forms, shapes, numbers, or letters. These children are likely to struggle with handwriting, as well as in arithmetic. When children cannot write numbers easily, they cannot properly align the numbers that they write, which leads to computation errors (Bley & Thornton, 2001).

Concepts of Time and Direction Basic concepts of time are typically acquired during the preschool years. For example, a 4-year-old counted the time until his grandmother would come to visit in terms of "sleeps" (e.g., Grandma will be here after three sleeps). Expressions such as "10 minutes ago," "in a half hour," and "later" are usually part of the preschooler's understanding and speaking vocabulary. By the end of first grade, children are expected to tell time to the half hour, and by the middle grades to the nearest minute.

Many students with mathematics difficulties have a poor sense of time and direction. They become lost easily and cannot find their way to a friend's house or to their own home from school. They sometimes forget whether it is morning or afternoon and may even go home during the recess period, thinking the school day has ended. Because they have difficulty estimating the time span of an hour, a minute, several hours, or a week, they cannot estimate how long a task will take. They may not be able to judge and allocate the time needed to complete an assignment.

Did You Get It?

While math disability affects approximately 6% of the general population, math difficulty affects approximately _____ out of 10 students.
  a. 1
  b. 3
  c. 5
  d. 7

14.3 Characteristics of Students With Mathematics Disabilities

A number of characteristics of students with learning disabilities and related disabilities affect quantitative learning. However, each student who encounters difficulties in mathematics is unique; not all exhibit the same traits. In this section, we discuss the following characteristics of students who have

TABLE 14.1

Information Processing and Problems in Mathematics

Information-Processing Problems	Effects on Mathematics Functioning
Motor problems	• Problems in writing numbers, illegible, slow, and inaccurate • Difficulty writing numbers in small spaces
Attention problems	• Poor attention doing the steps of mathematics in calculation • Poor attention during mathematics instruction
Problems in memory and retrieval	• Cannot remember math facts • Forgets the sequence of steps • Forgets the multiple steps in word problems
Problems in visual-spatial processing	• Difficulty in visual • Problems aligning numbers
Problems with auditory processing	• Difficulty with remembering auditory arithmetic facts • Difficulty with "counting-on"

© Cengage Learning

mathematics difficulties or mathematics learning disabilities: (1) information-processing difficulties, (2) language and reading abilities, and (3) math anxiety.

14.3a Information-Processing Difficulties

The information-processing model of learning is discussed in Chapter 5. Briefly, information processing traces the flow of information during learning. Many of the elements of information processing are linked to mathematics learning, such as paying attention, visual-spatial processing, auditory processing, long-term memory and retrieval, working memory, and motor skills (Geary et al., 2007; Cirino et al., 2007; Wilson & Swanson, 2001). Table 14.1 shows how problems with elements of information processing affect mathematics.

14.3b Language and Mathematics Abilities

Early concepts of quantity are evidenced by the child's use of language, such as *all gone, that's all, more, big,* and *little.* Although some children with mathematics disabilities have superior verbal language skills and may even be excellent readers, for many children the mathematics disability is compounded by oral language and reading deficiencies. Their language problems may cause them to confuse mathematics terms such as *plus, take away, minus, carrying, borrowing,* and place value. Mathematics word problems are particularly difficult for students with reading disabilities. If they are unable to read or do not understand the underlying language structure of the mathematics problem, they cannot plan and perform the tasks required to solve the problem (Bley & Thornton, 2001).

place value
The aspect of the number system that assigns specific significance to the position a digit holds in a numeral.

14.3c Math Anxiety

Math anxiety is an emotion-based reaction to mathematics that causes individuals to freeze up when they confront math problems or when they take

math anxiety
Refers to a debilitating emotional reaction to mathematics situations.

math tests. The anxiety may stem from the fear of school failure and the loss of self-esteem. Brain research using brain imaging (functional Magnetic Resonance Imaging—fMRI) shows that triggers for stress and anxiety are actually located in specific areas of the brain (Lytle & Todd, 2009). Anxiety has many repercussions. It can block the school performance of students with mathematics disabilities by making it difficult for them to initially learn the mathematics, it impedes their ability to use or transfer the mathematics knowledge they do have, and it becomes an obstacle when they try to demonstrate their knowledge on tests (Ashcraft, Krause, & Hopko, 2007; Barkley, 2005; Slavin, 2009).

Many students and adults with learning disabilities and related mild disabilities report that anxiety is a constant companion. One individual said that she sprinkled anxiety wherever she went, making calm people nervous and nervous people fall apart. She described how she couldn't get out the right words and how she trembled. Teaching Tips 14.1, "Guidelines for Dealing With Math Anxiety," gives suggestions for dealing with math anxiety.

Did You Get It?

According to the information-processing model, a 6-year-old student who has difficulty writing numbers legibly and coherently, probably has a deficit in

   a. attention
   b. visual-spatial ability
   c. motor control
   d. memory

TEACHING TIPS 14.1

Guidelines for Dealing With Math Anxiety

- Use competition carefully. Have students compete with themselves rather than with others in the class or school. In a competitive situation, make sure that students have a good *chance* of succeeding.

- Provide abundant practice with similar tests. Students become familiar with the test procedure.

- Use clear instructions. Make sure that students understand what they are to *do* in math assignments. Ask students to work sample problems and be sure that they understand the assignment. When doing a new math procedure, give students plenty of practice and examples or models to show how the work is done.

- Avoid unnecessary time pressures. Give students ample time to complete math assignments in the class period. Give occasional take-home tests. If necessary, reduce the number of problems to be completed.

- Try to remove pressure from test-taking situations. Teach students test-taking strategies. Give practice tests. Make sure that the test format is clear and that students are familiar with the format. For example, a student may be familiar with the problem in the following format:

$$7$$
$$+\ 3$$

The same child may be unfamiliar with a test format that presents the same problem in a different form:

$$7 + 3$$

Professional Resource Download

14.4 Students With Mathematics Disabilities at the Secondary Level

The mathematics problems of students with learning disabilities and related mild disabilities in middle school and high school differ from those at the elementary level. The secondary mathematics curriculum becomes increasingly more sophisticated and abstract and it is based on the presumption that the basic skills have been learned. The increased mathematics requirements at the high school level and the pressure of more testing are likely to adversely affect students with mathematics difficulties (Maccini & Gagnon, 2006; Deshler et al., 2001).

In the United States, high school mathematics requirements for graduation are becoming more rigorous. In most states, high school graduation is contingent upon passing mathematics courses, such as algebra, that previously were required only of students in a college preparatory curriculum. Many states now include algebra as a graduation requirement for all students (National Council of Teachers of Mathematics, 2000, 2006; Witzel, Mercer, & Miller, 2003).

Many secondary students with mathematics difficulties are able to be successful in advanced mathematics courses, but others shy away from geometry, statistics, and calculus. In the past, students with learning disabilities who faced mathematics disabilities were advised to continue remedial or basic mathematics courses. However, because algebra is now required for a high school diploma in most states, we must consider how to teach algebra to students with learning disabilities and related mild disabilities.

Common mathematics problems at the secondary level include basic operations (including fractions), decimals and percentages, fraction terminology, multiplication of whole numbers, place value, measurement skills, and division (Cass et al., 2003). Adolescents with learning disabilities and related mild disabilities continue to have memory deficits that interfere with the automatic learning of computation facts. These adolescents appreciate techniques that will help them learn and remember calculation facts. Students with severe problems in mathematics need direct instruction, with emphasis on learning basic skills to help them acquire functional abilities for successful living.

direct instruction
A method associated with behavioral theories of instruction. The focus is directly on the curriculum or task to be taught and the steps needed to learn that task.

Many students with learning disabilities and related disabilities can succeed in advanced mathematics courses. Many of these students will be going on to postsecondary education and college, and many will enter professions such as engineering or computer science that require competencies in advanced mathematics.

Effective instructional strategies in mathematics for secondary students include the following (Maccini & Gagnon, 2006; Cass et al., 2003; Witzel et al., 2003):

- **Provide many examples.** Students need to have many examples that illustrate the concept being taught. Teachers often provide too few examples.
- **Provide practice in discriminating various problem types.** Secondary students with mathematics disabilities have problems with discrimination. They ignore the operation sign and add instead of subtract. Once a skill is learned, the mathematics problem should be placed with different problems so that the student will learn to discriminate and generalize.
- **Provide explicit instruction.** Students with mathematics disabilities need direct instruction that is organized with step-by-step presentations.

Did You Get It?

The sophistication and _____ nature of the secondary mathematics curriculum increases.
  a. concrete
  b. anxiety-producing
  c. abstract
  d. hypothetical

14.5 Mathematics Standards

14.5a High Standards and Annual Testing

Federal and state governments now require the establishment of high mathematics standards and annual testing that uses those standards as a measure of achievement. Under the No Child Left Behind Act of 2002, schools are accountable for results, and schools are punished or rewarded on the basis of students' test results. The scores that students receive on these mathematics tests affect high-stakes decisions, such as whether the student will be promoted to the next grade or will receive a high school diploma. Garrison Keillor, the satirist, describes Lake Wobegon as where "all the women are strong, all the men are good looking, and all the children are above average." Schools in high socioeconomic areas tend to have students who do well under high-stakes mathematics assessment, while schools in impoverished areas struggle to have their students perform at the expected levels. In general, students with mathematics disabilities do not fare well under the high-stakes assessment approach to mathematics education without special considerations and accommodations (Witzel et al., 2003; Ysseldyke et al., 2001). (See more information on high-stakes testing in Chapter 2, "Assessment and the IEP Process.")

The Obama administration's Department of Education proposes to continue promoting high-stakes testing. Federal incentive grants were awarded to states and districts that have set high standards for the students they serve. The majority of states have now adopted the Common Core Standards for math, and students will be tested based on the Common Core Standards, which are described further in this chapter.

14.5b Common Core State Standards for Mathematics

The Common Core State Standards for math define what students should understand and what students should be able to do in their study of math. There are standards for practice and for content.

In math there are eight standards for mathematical practice.

1. Make sense of problems and persevere in solving them.
2. Reason abstractly and quantitatively.
3. Construct viable arguments and critique the reasoning of others.
4. Model with mathematics.

At grade 5, the following math content standard areas are:

Operations and Algebraic Thinking
Number and Operations in Base Ten
Number and Operations-Fractions
Measurement and Data
Geometry (Common Core Standards, 2010)

© Cengage Learning 2015.

FIGURE **14.1**
Fifth Grade Areas/Domains for Common Core State Standards for Mathematics

5. Use appropriate tools strategically.
6. Attend to precision.
7. Look for and make use of structure.
8. Look for and express regularity in repeated reasoning. (Common Core State Standards Initiative, 2010)

These eight practices describe the ways in which students should engage with the subject matter as they grow in mathematical maturity. The content standards are a combination of procedure and understanding. Students who do not understand have difficulty engaging in the mathematical practices. The content standards then at each grade level set an expectation of understanding (Common Core State Standards for Mathematics, 2010). There are standards for kindergarten through 8. Domains are the broad areas. Then there are clusters of standards that are related and there are the individual standards.

The areas for the Common Core Content Standards (domains) at Grade 5 are listed in Figure 14.1.

At each grade level, within each domain there are specific clusters and individual standards. A complete set of the standards is available at *http://www .corestandards.org*. A free app is available to download for your iPhone or iPad and is known as Common Core.

Did You Get It?

Annual mathematics assessments, comprehensive standards, and a system of reward and punishment for educational institutions dependent on student grades are hallmarks of which piece of educational legislation?
  a. No Child Left Behind Act
  b. IDEA
  c. Section 504 of the Rehabilitation Act
  d. Elementary and Secondary Education Act

14.6 Learning Theories for Mathematics Instruction

14.6a Active Involvement

Learning mathematics should be an active process that involves doing. Use of hands-on learning materials allows students to explore ideas for themselves. Manipulative materials enable students to see, to touch, and to move objects. As students become actively involved in mathematics, they should be encouraged to use mathematics for solving real-life problems. This active view of

The following examples illustrate how a young child uses estimation skills.

- Four-year-old Lee had just had his first experience sleeping overnight in a tent. Lee, his brother and his grandparents put up their tent, in which they place 4 sleeping bags for their overnight campout. After Lee excitedly described the experience to his parents the next day, they asked if they could come along next time. Lee did not answer immediately but spent some time considering the question. After estimating the space, he responded to his parents, "No you cannot come with us because the tent is not big enough to hold 2 more sleeping bags."

- The following problems show how young children construct solutions to subtraction problems.

  Problem A: Jane had 8 trucks. She gave 3 to Ben. How many trucks does she have left?

Problem B: Jane has 8 trucks. Ben has 6 trucks. How many more trucks does Jane have than Ben?

In problem A, a young child counts out 8 trucks and gives 3 away. Then the child counts the trucks that are left. In Problem B, the child counts out 8 trucks for Jane and a set of 6 trucks for Ben. The child then matches Jane's trucks to Ben's. Finally the child counts to see how many more trucks Jane has than Ben. The child has constructed meaning and does not need to ask, "Should I add or subtract?"

REFLECTIVE QUESTION

1. What process did Lee use to estimate how many sleeping bags would fit into the tent? Draw a picture to show the solution of problem A or problem B.

---

mathematics learning is epitomized in the following Chinese proverb: "I hear and I forget. I see and I remember. I do and I understand."

Student Stories 14.1, "Active Involvement in Mathematics," illustrates the active process approach to mathematics.

14.6b Progression From Concrete Learning to Abstract Learning

COMMON CORE
STATE STANDARDS

The learning of mathematics is a gradual process. It is not a matter of either knowing it or not knowing it. Instead, the learning of mathematics follows a continuum that gradually increases in strength. The Common Core Standards reflect this progression. As mathematics learning progresses, knowledge slowly builds from concrete to abstract learning, from incomplete to complete knowledge, and from unsystematic to systematic thinking. To help students progress from concrete to abstract learning, three sequential levels of mathematics instruction are suggested (Mercer & Pullen, 2009; Miller & Hudson, 2007; Cass et al., 2003).

The three levels from concrete thinking to abstract thinking are shown in Figure 14.2.

FIGURE **14.2**
Concrete to Abstract Learning

Concrete Level	Semiconcrete Level	Abstract Level

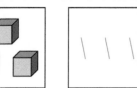

© Cengage Learning

1. **The concrete level.** At this level, students manipulate actual materials such as blocks, cubes, marbles, plastic pieces, poker chips, or place-value sticks. Students can physically touch, move, and manipulate these objects as they work out solutions to number problems.

2. **The semiconcrete level (or the representational level).** Once the students master the skill on the concrete level, instruction progresses to the semiconcrete

or representational level. Students use pictures or tallies (i.e., marks on the paper) to represent the concrete objects as they work on mathematics problems.

3. **The abstract level.** At this level, students use only the numbers to solve mathematics problems without the help of semiconcrete pictures or tallies.

14.6c Direct Instruction of Mathematics

Direct instruction is a method of mathematics teaching that helps students achieve mastery of mathematics skills through instruction that is explicit, carefully structured, and planned. It is a comprehensive system that integrates curriculum design with teaching techniques to produce instructional programs in mathematics (Miller & Hudson, 2007; Marchand-Marella, Slocum, & Martella 2004; Kroesbergan & Van Luit, 2003; Swanson & Hoskyn, 2001). The sequential nature of mathematics makes the direct instruction approach particularly adaptable to the content of mathematics.

Mathematics programs that are based on direct instruction are highly organized and carefully sequenced. Instruction follows an ordered plan. Teachers determine the objectives of the teaching, plan the teaching through task analysis, provide explicit instruction, and plan for continuous testing. Direct instruction has been shown to be very effective for students with learning disabilities and related mild disabilities (Miller & Hudson, 2007; Marchand-Marella et al., 2004; Jones & Southern, 2003). To use direct instruction, teachers do the following:

1. Break tasks into small steps
2. Administer probes to determine whether the students are learning
3. Supply immediate feedback
4. Provide diagrams and pictures to enhance student understanding
5. Give ample independent practice

14.6d Learning Strategies Instruction

Learning strategies instruction helps students with mathematics disabilities acquire specific procedures for meeting the challenges of mathematics in their curriculum and to take control of their own mathematics learning (Deshler, 2003). Intervention practices that use learning strategy instruction are effective in increasing achievement. Teachers who implement a learning strategies instruction model perform the following (Deshler, 2003; Mainzer et al., 2003):

1. Provide elaborate explanations to model learning processes
2. Provide prompts to use strategies
3. Engage in teacher–student dialogues
4. Ask processing questions

See Chapter 9, "Adolescents and Adults With Learning Disabilities and Related Disabilities," for more information about learning strategies instruction.

14.6e Problem Solving

Problem solving was identified as the top priority for the mathematics curriculum by the National Council of Teachers of Mathematics (NCTM, 2000) and is reflected in the Common Core Standards. Moreover, problem solving is rapidly assuming a larger part of the curriculum in both general education and special education (Cawley & Foley, 2001; NCTM, 2000; Van de Walle, Karp, & Bay-Williams, 2010). Mathematics problem solving involves the kind of thinking needed to work out mathematics word problems. In addition, a current view of mathematics expands the perspective of problem solving to the processes by which a student resolves unfamiliar situations. Implicit in the teaching of problem solving are the following underlying beliefs about mathematics: (1) there is no single way to do mathematics, (2) there is no single way to organize mathematics for instructional purposes, and (3) important mathematical concepts are actually learned through problem solving (Van de Walle, Karp, & Bay-Williams 2010).

An example of a problem-solving task is to ask students to think about the number 8 and to draw a picture of how the number 8 can be broken in two different amounts. Then ask the students to tell a story to go with their pictures (Van de Walle, Karp, & Bay-Williams, 2010).

Problem solving is the most difficult area of mathematics for many students with mathematics difficulties. Students with math difficulties need extensive guidance and practice to learn to combine thinking and language with the calculation skills and concepts required to solve mathematics problems. To solve mathematics problems, students must analyze and interpret information so that they can make selections and decisions. Problem solving requires that students know how to apply mathematics concepts and how to use computation skills in new or different settings.

How do students go about solving problems in mathematics? Research shows that first and second graders readily invent their own ways to solve simple word problems. However, by the middle grades, they stop their personal problem-solving attempts and begin to rely on rote procedures they have learned in school. Middle-grade students should be encouraged to continue to create and use their own ways to solve mathematics problems, as illustrated in Student Stories 14.2, "Encouraging a Problem-Solving Attitude."

Middle-grade students tend to automatically compute with whatever numbers are in the problems. To encourage a problem-solving attitude, teachers should help structure the students' responses to problems by talking with them about those responses. Encouraging such a discussion raises the reasoning level

STUDENT STORIES 14.2

Encouraging a Problem-Solving Attitude

The following example of a word problem illustrates how teachers can encourage an inventive, problem-solving attitude (Lindquist, 1987).

Problem: Rebecca wants to sell 30 boxes of Girl Scout cookies. She has sold 25. How many more must she sell? The teacher asks if anyone can draw a picture to show this problem.

One student drew the figure at right to solve this problem.

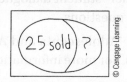

REFLECTIVE QUESTION

1. How does drawing a picture help the student with problem solving?

of the students' answers. Teachers can help by listening to the students as they think aloud about the word problems. It is also important to encourage the use of different strategies to solve mathematics problems and to ask students, "How did you get your answer?"

Many of the mathematics textbooks that are used in general education classrooms today use a problem-solving approach. Because problem solving is often difficult for students with learning disabilities and related mild disabilities, they need extensive guidance and practice to learn to combine thinking and language with the calculation skills and concepts required in mathematics problem solving. To solve mathematics problems, students must analyze and interpret information so that they can make selections and decisions. The following 3 steps can help structure mathematics problem-solving lessons (Van de Walle, Karp, & Bay-Williams, 2010):

Step 1. Getting ready First, students attend to the problem and translate the problem into their own experiences and language. The teacher makes sure they understand what is expected.

Step 2. Students work It is at this stage that students have a chance to work without constant guidance. The teacher lets go, listens carefully, and provides hints.

Step 3. Class discussion In the final step, there is a discussion of the solutions. The teacher accepts student solutions without evaluation. Students justify and evaluate their results and methods. Teaching Tips 14.2 provides some problem-solving examples.

TEACHING TIPS 14.2
Some Problem-Solving Examples

1. Ask the students to view a pair of items, such as $5 - 2 = 3$ and $8 - 5 = 3$. Next, ask the students to explain how 2 different number combinations result in the same answer. For example, you arrived at the same answer because the answer represents the difference between the numbers in each combination (Cawley & Foley, 2001).

2. Ask students to compare the fractions $\frac{6}{8}$ and $\frac{4}{5}$. Then ask which fraction is larger. (Assume that the students have not been taught about common denominators.) One student answered, "I know that $\frac{4}{5}$ is the same as $\frac{8}{10}$ and that is $\frac{2}{10}$ *away from a whole*. Because tenths are smaller than eighths, $\frac{8}{10}$ must be closer to a whole, so $\frac{4}{5}$ is larger" (Van de Walle, 2004).

3. Ask students how the number 7 can be broken into different amounts. Then ask the students to draw pictures showing ways in which the number 7 can be broken into different amounts (Van de Walle, 2004).

Professional Resource Download

Did You Get It?

Which strategy is not recommended in a comprehensive, instructive mathematics curriculum?
- **a.** theory trumping actuality
- **b.** real-life application
- **c.** much manipulation
- **d.** action oriented

14.7 Assessing Mathematics Achievement

Information about a student's proficiency in mathematics can be gathered through (1) formal tests and (2) informal measures. Formal tests include standardized survey tests, group survey tests, individually administered achievement tests, and diagnostic math tests. Informal measures include informal inventories, analyzing mathematics errors, and curriculum-based assessment.

14.7a Formal Tests

Formal mathematics tests include standardized survey tests; some are designed for group administration, and some are individually administered achievement tests. There are also diagnostic mathematics tests. It is important to check the validity, reliability, and standardization procedures of tests before using them (Salvia, Ysseldyke, & Bolt, 2013).

Standardized Survey Tests Survey tests provide information on the general level of a student's mathematics performance.

Group Survey Tests Group survey tests are designed for group administration. Usually, data are available on a test's reliability, validity, and standardization procedures. Often there are accompanying manuals with tables for various kinds of score interpretations, including grade scores, age scores, standard scores, and percentiles. Most survey tests in mathematics are part of a general achievement test battery. Some of the most widely used tests are listed in Table 14.2.

TABLE 14.2

Formal Tests of Mathematics

Test	Grade or Age
Group Standardized Survey Tests	
• California Achievement Tests, CTB/McGraw-Hill *http://www.ctb.com*	Grades K–12
• Iowa Tests of Basic Skills, Riverside Publishing *http://www.riverpub.com*	Grades K–12
• Metropolitan Achievement Tests, Harcourt Assessment *http://www.harcourtassessment.com*	Grades K–12
Individually Administered Achievement Tests	
• Brigance Comprehensive Inventory of Basic Skills—Revised, Curriculum Associates *http://www.curriculumassociates.com*	Grades K–9
• Brigance Diagnostic Inventory of Essential Skills, Curriculum Associates *http://www.curriculumassociates.com*	Grades 6–Adult
• Kaufman Test of Educational Achievement—Normative Upgrade (K-TEA-NU), AGS *http://ags.pearsonassessments.com*	Grades K–12
• Peabody Individual Achievement Test—Revised (PIAT-R), AGS *http://ags.pearsonassessments.com*	Grades K–12
• Wide-Range Achievement Test—4(WRAT-4), PAR Inc. *http://www3.parinc.com*	Age 5–Adult
• Woodcock-Johnson Psychoeducational Battery—III, Riverside Publishing *http://www.riverpub.com*	Grades K–12
Diagnostic Math Tests	
• Key Math-Revised: A Diagnostic Inventory of Essential Mathematics, AGS *http://ags.pearsonassessments.com*	Grades K–6
• Stanford Diagnostic Mathematics Test 4, Harcourt Assessment *http://www.harcourtassessment.com*	Grades K–12
• Test of Mathematical Abilities—2, Pro-Ed *http://www.proedinc.com*	Grades 3–12

© Cengage Learning

The standardized achievement tests are useful as screening instruments because they identify those students whose performance scores are below expected levels (Salvia, Ysseldyke, & Bolt, 2013). The major test batteries are well constructed, generally have excellent technical characteristics, and cover most items in the mathematics curriculum. However, because they are paper-and-pencil tests that rely on multiple-choice responses, the diagnostic information that can be obtained from them is limited. The group survey tests can also be given to individuals.

Individually Administered Achievement Tests These tests are designed for individual assessment. They can yield more diagnostic information than the group survey tests, providing information on specific areas of mathematics difficulty and more clues for planning instruction.

In addition, a number of commonly used criterion-referenced measures are available, such as the Brigance Comprehensive Inventory of Basic Skills—Revised, which provides extensive information about math achievement patterns. Table 14.2 lists some of the widely used individual tests.

Diagnostic Math Tests Diagnostic math tests are available for both group and individual administration. Group tests serve 2 purposes: (1) to provide diagnostic information for student program planning and (2) to assist in program evaluation for administrative purposes. Individual tests generally are used to evaluate patterns of strength and weakness or skills in mathematics that have been mastered and skills that have not been mastered.

14.7b Informal Measures

Informal measures offer another option for obtaining information about a student's performance and abilities in mathematics. Observations of a student's daily behavior in mathematics class and performance on homework assignments and on teacher-made tests or tests that accompany the textbook can provide information about the student's mathematics skills (Spinelli, 2006). Informal measures to assess mathematics include: (1) informal inventories, (2) analysis of mathematics errors, and (3) curriculum-based assessment.

Informal Inventories Informal tests can be devised by teachers to assess the student's mathematics skills (Bryant & Rivera, 1997). Once the general area of difficulty is determined, a more extensive diagnostic test of that area can be given. A sample informal arithmetic test appears in Figure 14.3. Teachers can easily construct informal tests to assess the student's achievement in a specific mathematics skill or in a sequence of mathematics skills. The informal test can be tailored for an individual student.

Analyzing Mathematics Errors Teachers should be able to detect the types of errors a student with mathematics difficulty is making so that instruction can be directed toward correcting those errors (Ashlock, 2006). This information is obtained by examining the students' work or by asking the student to explain how he or she went about solving a problem. When teachers observe the methods used by a student, they can deduce the thought processes the student is using. The four most common types of calculation errors are

FIGURE **14.3**
Informal Inventory of Arithmetic
Skills

Addition

3	8	25	20	15	77	5
+5	+0	+71	+49	+ 7	+29	2
						+7

5 + 7 = ☐   3 + ☐ = 12   ☐ + 7 = 15

233	879	648
+ 45	+ 48	745
		+286

Subtraction

7	25	78	72	546	6762
−5	− 9	− 23	− 49	− 222	− 4859

5 − 2 = ☐   7 − ☐ = 4   ☐ − 3 = 5

Multiplication

5	6	24	86	59	25
×3	×7	× 2	× 7	×34	×79

6 × 3 = ☐   7 × ☐ = 56   ☐ × 5 = 20

Division

2⟌10   4⟌16   8⟌125   11⟌121   12⟌108

12 ÷ 4 = ☐   24 ÷ ☐ = 6   ☐ ÷ 9 = 6

© Cengage Learning

(1) place value, (2) computation facts, (3) using the wrong process, and (4) working from left to right. The following list shows examples of these common errors.

- **Place value.** Place value is the aspect of the number system that assigns specific significance to the position a digit holds in a numeral. Students who make this error do not understand the concepts of place value, regrouping, carrying, or borrowing and might make errors such as those shown here.

$$
\begin{array}{r} 75 \\ -27 \\ \hline 58 \end{array}
\qquad
\begin{array}{r} 63 \\ +18 \\ \hline 71 \end{array}
$$

These students need concrete practice in the place value of 1s, 10s, 100s, and 1,000s. Effective tools for such practice are an abacus and a place-value box or chart with compartments. Students can sort objects such as sticks, straws, or chips into compartments to show place value.

- **Computation facts.** Students who make errors in basic adding, subtracting, multiplying, and dividing need more practice and drill. For example:

$$
\begin{array}{r} 6 \\ \times 8 \\ \hline 46 \end{array}
\qquad
\begin{array}{r} 9 \\ \times 7 \\ \hline 62 \end{array}
$$

A handy multiplication chart, like the one shown in Figure 14.4, might be useful in checking their work.

1	2	3	4	5	6	7	8	9	10	11	12
2	4	6	8	10	12	14	16	18	20	22	24
3	6	9	12	15	18	21	24	27	30	33	36
4	8	12	16	20	24	28	32	36	40	44	48
5	10	15	20	25	30	35	40	45	50	55	60
6	12	18	24	30	36	42	48	54	60	66	72
7	14	21	28	35	42	49	56	63	70	77	84
8	16	24	32	40	48	56	64	72	80	88	96
9	18	27	36	45	54	63	72	81	90	99	108
10	20	30	40	50	60	70	80	90	100	110	120
11	22	33	44	55	66	77	88	99	110	121	132
12	24	36	48	60	72	84	96	108	120	132	144

FIGURE **14.4**
Multiplication Chart

© Cengage Learning

Professional Resource Download

- **Using the wrong process.** Some students make errors because they use the wrong mathematical process. For example:

$$\begin{array}{r} 6 \\ \times 2 \\ \hline 8 \end{array} \qquad \begin{array}{r} 15 \\ -3 \\ \hline 18 \end{array}$$

These students need work in recognizing symbols and signs.
- **Working from left to right.** Some students reverse the direction of calculations and work from left to right. For example:

$$\begin{array}{r} 35 \\ +81 \\ \hline 17 \end{array} \qquad \begin{array}{r} 56 \\ +71 \\ \hline 28 \end{array}$$

These students need work in place value.

In addition, poor writing skills cause many math errors. When students cannot read their own writing or fail to align their numbers in columns, they may not understand what to do.

Curriculum-Based Assessment The procedure of curriculum-based assessment or progress monitoring (see Chapter 2, "Assessment and the IEP Process") provides a useful way to measure mathematics progress. Curriculum-based assessment closely links assessment to the material that is being taught in the mathematics curriculum. The procedure may involve teacher-constructed tests that measure student progress on curricular objectives. In relation to mathematics, curriculum-based assessment consists of four steps (Baroody & Ginsburg, 1991; Shinn & Hubbard, 1992):

1. **Identify target skills.** For example, the skill might be math computation, such as adding two-digit numbers.
2. **Determine the objectives to be met.** For example, in a period of 4 weeks, the student will be able to write the answers to 20 two-digit addition problems correctly in 5 minutes.

3. **Develop test items to sample each skill.** Assemble a collection of two-digit number problems.

4. **Develop criteria to measure achievement.** The student will write answers without errors to 20 randomly selected two-digit math problems in a 5-minute period.

Did You Get It?

A teacher who is paying particular attention to a student's homework, a quiz he just took, and his behaviors and performance as he works through several assigned problems in class is conducting what form of testing?

a. informal measures

b. an informal inventory test

c. an individually administered achievement test

d. a standardized survey test

14.8 Teaching Strategies to Improve Mathematics Difficulties

The "Teaching Strategies" section of this chapter highlights: (1) mathematics strategies for the general education classroom, (2) the mathematics curriculum, (3) principles of instruction for students with mathematics difficulties, (4) activities for teaching mathematics, and (5) assistive and instructional technology for mathematics instruction.

14.9 Mathematics Strategies for the General Education Classroom

Many students with learning disabilities and related mild disabilities who have mathematics difficulties receive their instruction in general education classrooms. General education teachers are therefore responsible for their instruction. General education teachers may not have enough training or background to address the mathematics difficulties of these students. Including Students in General Education 14.1, "Mathematics Strategies," provides several strategies for teaching mathematics to students with mathematics difficulties in the general education classroom.

Additional math strategies for teaching students with math difficulties in the general education classroom can be found on the following websites:

- Schrockguide, *http://www.school.discoveryeducation.com/schrockguide /math.html*
- PBS Teacher Source, *http://www.pbs.org/teachers*
- Illuminations, National Council of Teachers of Mathematics, *http://www .illuminations.nctm.org*
- Teacher Resources for the Classroom, *http://www.mathgoodies.com*
- Stuart Murphy *http://www.stuartmurphy.com*
- K-3 Teaching Resources, *http://www.k-3teachingresources.com*

Mathematics Strategies

- Determine the students' basic computational skills in addition, subtraction, multiplication, and division.
- Have students use manipulatives to help them understand a concept.
- Teach the students mathematics vocabulary.
- Use visuals and graphics to illustrate concepts to the students.
- Have students make up their own word story problems.

- Teach students how to use a calculator.
- Teach money concepts by using either real money or play money.
- Teach time by using manipulative clocks.
- Provide many opportunities for practice and review.

(For additional information on teaching students with math difficulties in the general education classroom, see LD Online at *http://www.ldonline.org/indepth/math*.)

Professional Resource Download

- National Literacy of Virtual Manipulatives, *http://www.nationalibraryofvirtualmanipulatives.com*
- Cool Math 4 Kids, *http://www.coolmath4kids.com*

Did You Get It?

What is not a legitimate practice in a general education classroom?
a. the use of calculators
b. teaching about time constraints and limitations
c. the use of visuals to teach and reinforce concepts
d. performing work for a frustrated student

14.10 The Mathematics Curriculum

Both general education teachers and special education teachers should have a basic picture of the overall mathematics curriculum. It is important to know what the student has already learned in the mathematics curriculum and what mathematics learning lies ahead.

14.10a The Sequence of Mathematics: Grades K–8

Mathematics is a naturally cumulative subject typically taught in a sequence that introduces certain skills at each grade level. For example, learning multiplication depends on knowing addition. The major topics that are covered in the mathematics curriculum from kindergarten through grade 8 include numbers and numeration; whole numbers—addition and subtraction; whole numbers—multiplication and division; decimals; fractions; measurement; geometry; and computer education, a subject that is beginning to show up in many mathematics programs.

Although the sequence may vary somewhat in different programs, the general timetables of instruction are as follows:

Kindergarten Basic number meanings, counting, classification, seriation or order, recognition of numerals, and the writing of numbers

Grade 1 Addition through 20, subtraction through 20, place value of 1s and 10s, time to the half hour, money, and simple measurement

Grade 2 Addition through 100, subtraction through 100, counting from 0 to 100, skip-counting by 2s, place value of 100, and regrouping for adding and subtracting

Grade 3 Multiplication through 9s, odd or even skip-counting, place value of 1,000s, two- and three-place numbers for addition and subtraction, and telling time

Grade 4 Division facts, extended use of multiplication facts and related division facts through 9s, and two-place multipliers

Grade 5 Fractions, addition and subtraction of fractions, mixed numbers, long division, two-place division, and decimals

Grade 6 Percentages, three-place multipliers, two-place division, addition and subtraction of decimals and mixed decimals, multiplication and division of decimals, and mixed decimals by whole numbers

Grade 7 Geometry, rounding, ratios, and simple probability

Grade 8 Scientific notation, using graphs, complex fractions, complex applications, and word problems

14.10b The Secondary Mathematics Curriculum

The Common Core Standards at the secondary level (Grades 9 through 12) include these areas. (Common Core State Standards Initiative, 2010). These can be found at: *http://www.corestandards.org*.

- Number and Quantity
- Algebra
- Functions
- Modeling
- Geometry
- Statistics and Probability

Remember that the mathematical practices that were discussed earlier in the elementary standards are also in place in the secondary set of standards. (Common Core State Standards Initiative, 2010).

Did You Get It?

The math curriculum is heavily standardized, cumulative, and age specific concerning the grade when concepts are introduced, when assessment is done, and when students are expected to complete objectives. Multiplication through the "9s" is a task that your mathematics students should be tackling, and hopefully mastering, in which grade?

a. first
b. third
c. fourth
d. seventh

14.11 Principles of Instruction for Students With Mathematics Disabilities

Several principles of mathematics learning offer a guide for effective mathematics instruction. The principles discussed here include (1) early number learning, (2) progressing from the concrete to the abstract, (3) providing opportunity for practice and review, (4) generalizing the concepts and skills that have been learned, and (5) teaching mathematics vocabulary.

14.11a Early Number Learning

It is important to check into the previously acquired early number learning to ensure that the student is ready for what needs to be learned. Time and effort invested in building a firm foundation can prevent many later difficulties as the student tries to move on to more advanced and more abstract mathematics processes (Jordan et al., 2007). Table 14.3 gives descriptions of the essential basic early number-learning abilities. If they are lacking, they must be taught.

14.11b Progressing From the Concrete to the Abstract

Pupils can best understand a mathematics concept when teaching progresses from the concrete to the abstract. A teacher should plan three instructional stages: concrete, semiconcrete, and abstract (Miller & Hudson, 2007; Cass et al., 2003; Witzel et al., 2003).

1. In the concrete instruction stage, the student manipulates real objects in learning the skill. For example, the student could see, hold, and move 2 blocks and 3 blocks to learn that they equal 5 blocks.

$$\square\square + \square\square\square = 5$$

concrete instruction
Students manipulate actual materials for mathematics learning, such as blocks, cubes, and marbles.

TABLE 14.3

Early Number Learning

Ability	Description
Matching	Grouping similar objects together
Recognizing groups of objects	Recognizing a group of 3 objects without counting
Counting	Matching numerals to objects
Naming a number that comes after a given number	Stating what number comes after 7
Writing numerals from 0 to 10	Knowing the right sequence
Measuring and pairing	One-to-one correspondence, estimating, fitting objects
Sequential values	Arranging like objects in order by quantitative differences (e.g., by size)
Operations	Manipulation of the number facts to 10 without reference to concrete objects

© Cengage Learning

Professional Resource Download

semiconcrete instruction
The level of mathematics instruction in which the students use representational objects to refer to math concepts, such as tallies, pictures, or marks, instead of the actual objects.

abstract instruction
At this level of mathematics instruction, students manipulate symbols without the help of concrete objects or representational pictures or tallies.

2. In the semiconcrete instruction stage, a graphic representation is substituted for actual objects. In the following example, circles represent objects in an illustration from a worksheet:

$$\bigcirc\bigcirc + \bigcirc\bigcirc\bigcirc = 5$$

3. At the abstract instruction stage, numerals finally replace the graphic symbols:

$$2 + 3 = 5$$

14.11c Provide Opportunity for Practice and Review

Students need many opportunities for review, drill, and practice to over-learn the math concepts because they must be able to use computation facts almost automatically. There are many ways to provide this practice, and teachers should vary the method as often as possible. Such techniques can include worksheets, flash cards, games, behavior management techniques (such as rewards for work completed), and computer practice (special software programs that give immediate feedback).

14.11d Teach Students to Generalize to New Situations

Students must learn to generalize a skill to many situations. For example, students can practice computation facts with many story problems that the teacher or students create and then exchange with each other. The goal is to gain skill in recognizing computational operations and applying them to various new situations.

14.11e Teach Mathematics Vocabulary

The vocabulary and concepts of mathematics are new to students and must be learned. The student may know the operation, but may not know the precise term applied to the operation. Table 14.4 shows the vocabulary for basic mathematics operations.

TABLE 14.4

Mathematics Vocabulary for Basic Operations

Operation		Terms
Addition	3 →	addend
	+5 →	addend
	8 →	sum
Subtraction	9 →	minuend
	−3 →	subtrahend
	6 →	difference
Multiplication	7 →	multiplicand
	×5 →	multiplier
	35 →	product
Division	7 →	quotient
	$6\sqrt{42}$	
	↑_____Divisor	

© Cengage Learning

If a teacher substitutes sticks for numbers to illustrate the process of addition, she is providing _____ instruction.
   a. semiconcrete
   b. semiabstract
   c. abstract
   d. quasi-inferential

14.12 Activities for Teaching Mathematics

The instruction activities in this section are grouped into three areas: (1) teaching early number skills, (2) teaching computation skills, and (3) teaching word story problems.

14.12a Teaching Early Number Skills

Classification and Grouping

1. **Sorting games.** Give students objects that differ in only one attribute, such as color or texture, and ask them to sort the objects into two different boxes. For example, if the objects differ by color, have students put red items in one box and blue items in another box. At a more advanced level, increase the complexity of the classification of the attributes, asking students to sort, for example, movable objects from stationary objects. Another variation is to use objects that have several overlapping attributes, such as shape, color, and size. You might present the students with cutouts of triangles, circles, and squares in three colors (e.g., blue, yellow, and red) and two sizes (e.g., small and large). Ask the students to sort them according to shape and then according to color. Then ask the students to discover a third way of sorting.

2. **Matching and sorting.** A first step in the development of number concepts is the ability to focus on and to recognize a single object or shape. Have the student search through a collection of assorted objects to find a particular type of object. For example, the student might look in a box of colored beads or blocks for a red one, search through a collection of various kinds of coins for all the pennies, choose the forks from a box of silverware, look in a box of buttons for the oval ones, sort a bagful of cardboard shapes to pick out the circles, or look in a container of nuts and bolts for the square pieces.

3. **Recognition of groups of objects.** Domino games, playing cards, concrete objects, felt boards, magnetic boards, and cards with colored disks all provide excellent materials for developing concepts of groups.

Ordering

1. **Serial order and relationships.** When teaching the concept of ordering, ask the student to tell the number that comes after 6 or before 5 or between 2 and 4. Also, ask the student to indicate the first, last, or third of a series of objects. Other measured quantities can be arranged by other dimensions, such as size, weight, intensity, color, or volume.

2. **Number lines.** A number line is a sequence of numbers forming a straight line that allows the student to manipulate computation directly. Number lines

and number blocks for the students to walk on are helpful in understanding the symbols and their relationships to one another.

```
 •    •    •    •    •    •    •
├────┼────┼────┼────┼────┼────┤
 0    1    2    3    4    5    6
```

3. **Arranging by size and length.** Have the student compare and contrast objects of different size, formulating concepts of smaller, bigger, taller, and shorter. Make cardboard objects, such as circles, trees, houses, and so forth; or collect objects, such as washers, paper clips, and screws. Have the student arrange the objects by size and then estimate the size of the objects by guessing whether certain objects would fit into certain spaces.

4. **One-to-one correspondence: Pairing.** One-to-one correspondence is a relationship in which one element of a set is paired with one, and only one, element of a second set. Pairing provides a foundation for counting. Activities designed to match or align one object with another are useful. Have the student arrange a row of pegs in a Peg-Board to match a prearranged row, or set a table and place one cookie on each dish, or plan the allocation of materials to the group so that each person receives one object.

Counting

1. **Motor activities for counting.** Some students learn to count verbally, but they do not attain the concept that each number corresponds to one object. Such students are helped by making strong motor and tactile responses along with the counting. Looking at visual stimuli or pointing to the objects may not be enough because such students will count erratically, skipping objects or saying 2 numbers for one object. Motor activities to help students establish the counting principle include placing a peg in a hole, clipping clothespins on a line, stringing beads onto a pipe cleaner, clapping 3 times, jumping 4 times, and tapping on the table 2 times. Use the auditory modality to reinforce visual counting by having students listen to the counts of a drumbeat with their eyes closed. The students may make a mark for each sound and then count the marks.

2. **Counting cups.** Take a set of containers, such as cups, and designate each with a numeral. Have the students fill each container with the correct number of items, using objects such as bottle caps, chips, buttons, screws, or washers.

Recognition of Numbers

1. **Visual recognition of numbers.** Students must learn to recognize both the printed numbers (7, 8, 3) and the words expressing these numbers (seven, eight, three). They must also learn to integrate the written forms with the spoken symbols. If students confuse one written number with another, color cues may help them to recognize the symbol. You might make, for example, the top of the number 3 green and the bottom of the number 3 red. Another activity is to have the students match the correct number with the correct set of objects; felt, cardboard, or sandpaper symbols or groups of objects can be used.

2. **Parking lot poster.** Draw a "parking lot" on a poster, numbering parking spaces with dots instead of numerals. Paint numerals on small cars and have the students park the cars in the correct spaces.

14.12b Teaching Computation Skills

The following list gives some strategies for teaching computation skills.

1. **Part–whole concepts.** The "big concept" idea is that addition and subtraction have a part–whole relationship; you add to find the whole or total of two or more parts, and you subtract from the whole to find the missing part. Use Figure 14.5 to help students see the part–whole relationship. Use counters or put the figure on an overhead projector to demonstrate the part–whole relationship to the entire group. Students can use counters to demonstrate the part–whole relationship.

2. **Basic computation skills.** Many problems in mathematics are due to deficiencies in basic computation skills. To help students to overcome these deficiencies, teach the basic mathematics computation skills that the students lack: addition, subtraction, multiplication, division, fractions, decimals, and percentages. An inexpensive way to teach many mathematics computation skills is to obtain mathematics games and materials from a dollar store. Online dollar stores also can be a good source. At a dollar store, you can often get large stickers of multiplication tables. Students can put them on their file folder for math. (The online dollar store, Oriental Trading, is at *http://www .OrientalTrading.com.*) Mathematics games on CDs are also helpful for teaching computation skills. (Some games and CDs can be found at Planet CD Rom at *http://www.planetcdrom.com.*) A collection of these games and activities can be placed on a mathematics activities table.

3. **Addition.** Knowledge of addition facts provides the foundation for all other computational skills. Addition is a short method of counting, and students should know that they can resort to counting when all else fails. Addition can be thought of as "part plus part equals whole." Important symbols to learn are $+$ (plus, or "put together") and $=$ (equals, or "the same as"). As with the other areas, begin by using concrete objects, then use cards with sets that represent numbers, and finally use the number sentence with the numbers alone: $3 + 2 = \square$. From this, the students can also learn that $2 + 3 = \square$; $\square + 2 = 5$; and $3 + \square = 5$.

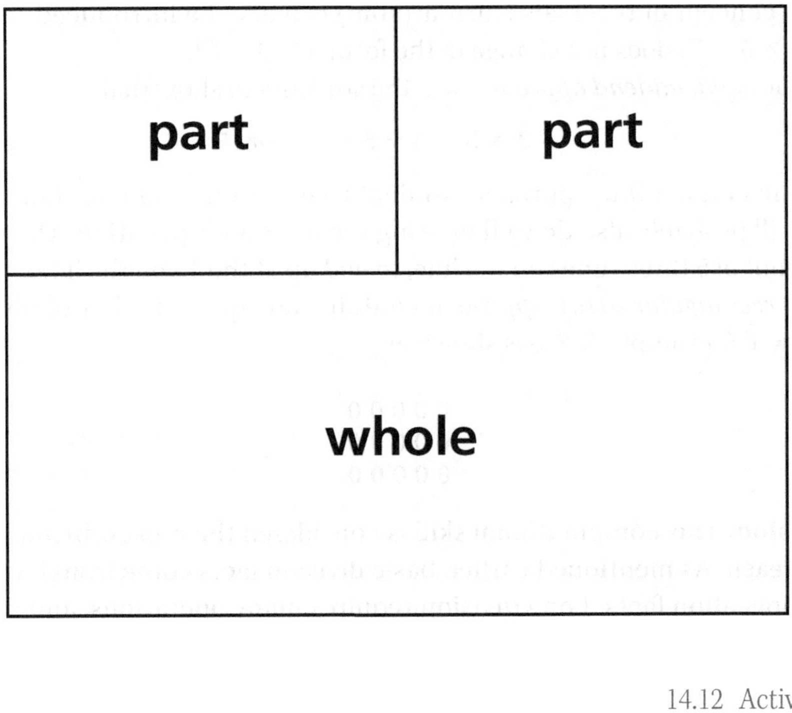

part–whole relationship
Addition and subtraction have a part-whole relationship. Add to the whole or total of 2 parts; and you subtract from the whole to find the missing part.

mathematics computation
The basic mathematical operations, consisting of addition, subtraction, multiplication, division, fractions, decimals, and percentages.

FIGURE **14.5**
Part–Whole Relationships

© Cengage Learning

Teaching addition using sums between 10 and 20 is more difficult. There are several approaches. It is easier to start with doubles, such as $8 + 8 = 16$. Then ask what $9 + 8$ equals: one more than 16.

Another way is to "make a 10." For example, in $7 + 5$, the pupil takes 3 of the 5, and adds the 3 to the 7 to make 10. Now the students can see that $10 +$ the remaining $2 = 12$. Use movable objects so that the students can actually experience the process:

$$
\begin{array}{l}
\text{O O O O O O O} \bullet \bullet \bullet \\
\text{O O} \bullet \bullet \bullet
\end{array}
\qquad
\begin{array}{l}
7 + 3 = 10 \\
10 + 2 = 12
\end{array}
$$

The number line provides another way to teach addition. With a number line, the students can visually perceive the addition process.

4. Subtraction. After the students have a firm basis in addition, introduce subtraction. An important new symbol is $-$ (minus, or "take away"). A student places a set of objects on the desk and then takes away certain objects. How many are left? $6 - 2 = \square$. Then use cards with sets on them. Find 6 by using a card with a set of 2 and a card with a set of 4. Tell the students you have a set of 6 when the cards are joined. Take away the set of 2 and ask the students what is left.

The number line is also useful in subtraction.

Regrouping is an important concept that is introduced in subtraction, along with the ideas of "1s," "10s," and "100s."

5. Multiplication. Many students with a mathematics disability do not know multiplication facts (refer to Figure 14.4). Those students will be unable to learn division until they master multiplication facts.

Multiplication is a short method of adding. Instead of adding $2 + 2 + 2 + 2$, the students can learn $2 \times 4 = 8$. Subtraction is not a prerequisite of multiplication, and a student having difficulty with subtraction may do better with multiplication. The symbol to learn is x (times).

There are several ways of explaining multiplication. One way is the multiplication sentence. How much are 3 sets of 2? Using sets of objects, the students can find the total either by counting objects or by adding equal addends.

The concept of reversals (turn-around) can also be introduced. The sentence $3 \times 5 = \square$ does not change in the form $5 \times 3 = \square$.

In the *equal addend approach,* ask the students to show that

$$3 \times 5 = 5 + 5 + 5, \quad \text{or } 15$$

In the number line approach, students who can use number lines for addition will probably also do well in using them for multiplication. The student adds a unit of 5 three times on the line, to end up at the 15 on the line.

The *rectangular array approach* contains an equal number of objects in each row. For example, 3×5 is shown as

$$
\begin{array}{l}
\text{O O O O O} \\
\text{O O O O O} \\
\text{O O O O O}
\end{array}
$$

6. Division. This computational skill is considered the most difficult to learn and to teach. As mentioned earlier, basic division facts come from knowledge of multiplication facts. Long division requires many operations, and students must be able to do all the steps before they can put them together. The new symbol is ÷ (divide).

There are a number of ways to approach division. Sets can be used: $6 \div 3 = \square$. Draw a set of 6 and enclose 3 equal sets. The missing factor is seen as 2:

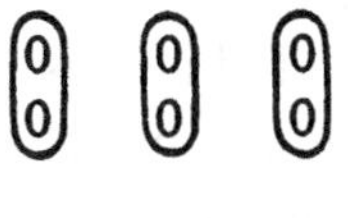

How many subsets are there? How many objects are there in each set? The number line can also be used. By jumping back a unit of 3, how many jumps are needed?

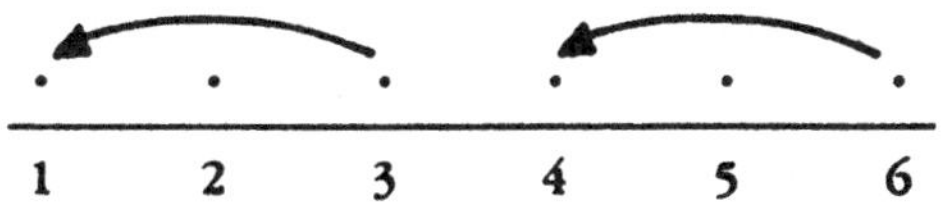

The missing factors approach uses known multiplication facts and reverses the process: $3 \times \square = 12$. Then change to a division sentence: $12 \div 3 = \square$.

7. **Fractions.** Geometric shapes are commonly used to introduce fractional numbers. The new symbol is shown next:

$$\frac{1}{2} \begin{array}{l} \rightarrow \text{number of special parts} \\ \rightarrow \text{total number of equal parts} \end{array}$$

Start with halves, then with quarters and then eighths. Cut shapes out of flannel or paper plates. Figure 14.6 illustrates common fractions.

8. **Learning the computational facts.** Once the concepts behind the facts are known, the students must memorize the facts themselves. Many different learning opportunities are needed. Students can write the facts, say them, play games with facts, take speed tests, and so forth. Also helpful are flash cards, rolling dice, playing cards, or learning a fact a day. A wide variety of methods should be used.

To learn computational skills, students with mathematics difficulties require much experience with concrete and manipulative materials before moving to the abstract and symbolic level of numbers. Objects and materials that can be physically taken apart and put back together help the students to observe visually the relationship of the fractional parts of the whole.

There are 56 basic number facts to be mastered in each mode of arithmetic computation (addition, subtraction, multiplication, and division), if the facts involving the 1s $(3 + 1 = 4)$ and doubles $(3 \times 3 = 9)$ are not included. Examples of number facts are $3 + 4 = 7$; $9 - 5 = 4$; $3 \times 7 = 21$; $18 \div 6 = 3$. In the computational skill of addition, for example, there are 81 separate facts involved in the span from $1 + 1 = 2$ to $9 + 9 = 18$.

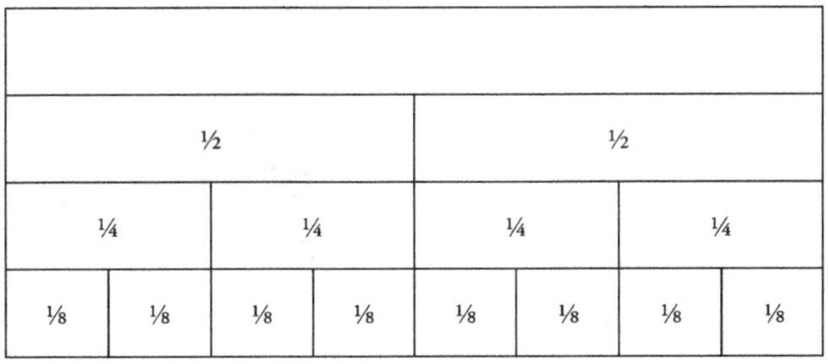

FIGURE **14.6**
Some Common Fractions

© Cengage Learning

FIGURE **14.7**
Calendar for Learning Facts

Sun	Mon	Tue	Wed	Thur	Fri	Sat
1	2	3	4	5	6	7
8	9	10	11	12	13	14
15	16	17	18	19	20	21
22	23	24	25	26	27	28

Few students have trouble with the 1s $(5 + 1 = 6)$ or with the doubles $(2 + 2 = 4)$. Therefore, if these facts are omitted, there are 56 basic addition facts to be mastered. Similarly, without the 1s and doubles, there are 56 facts to be mastered in each of the other computation areas—subtraction, multiplication, and division.

9. **The 2-weeks facts:** $7 + 7$. Students circle 2 full calendar weeks and count the number of days in each week, as shown in Figure 14.7, to learn that $7 + 7 = 14$.

10. **Subtraction of 9s from teen numbers.** One useful technique to help students learn subtraction of 9s from the teen numbers is to have students consider the following problem: $16 - 9 = \square$. Adding the 1 and 6 gives the correct answer of 7. This technique works with subtracting 9s from all teen numbers.

11. **Arrangements.** Present students with arrangement problems. For example, give students the numbers 1, 2, 3. Ask them in how many ways they can be arranged: 1-2-3; 1-3-2; 2-1-3; 2-3-1; 3-1-2; 3-2-1 (or $3 \times 2 \times 1 = 6$). Another example: If 4 children sit around a square table, in how many ways can they arrange themselves? $(4 \times 3 \times 2 \times 1 = 24)$.

12. **Puzzle cards of combinations.** Make cardboard cards on which problems of addition, subtraction, multiplication, and division are worked. Cut each card in 2 so that the problem is on one part and the answer is on the other. Each card must be cut uniquely so that when the students try to assemble the puzzle, only the correct answer will fit.

13. **Playing cards.** An ordinary deck of cards becomes a versatile tool for teaching number concepts. Some activities are arranging suits in sequential order by number, matching sets of numbers, adding and subtracting with individual cards, and quickly recognizing the number in a set.

Computer spreadsheets and charts are an essential part of the mathematics curriculum, and the National Council of Teachers of Mathematics recommends their use.

14.12c Teaching Word Story Problems

The goal of mathematics instruction is to apply the concepts and skills in problem solving. The National Council of Teachers of Mathematics (2000) calls for more emphasis on problem solving at all levels. Some suggestions for teaching word story problems are provided in the following list.

1. **Word story problems.** Use word story problems that are of interest to the students and within their experience.
2. **Posing problems orally.** This method is especially important for students with reading problems.
3. **Visual reinforcements.** Use concrete objects, drawings, graphs, or other visual reinforcements to clarify the problem, demonstrate solutions, and verify the answers. Have students act out the problem.
4. **Simplifying.** Have students substitute smaller and easier numbers for problems with larger or more complex numbers so that they can understand the problems and verify the solutions more readily.
5. **Restating.** Have students restate the problems in their own words. This verbalization helps the students to structure the problems for themselves and also shows whether they understand the problems.
6. **Supplementary problems.** Supplement textbook problems with your own, which could deal with classroom experiences. Including students' names makes the problem more realistic.
7. **Time for thinking.** Allow students enough time to think. Ask for alternative methods for solving the problems. Try to understand how the students thought about the problem and went about solving the problem.
8. **Steps in solving word problems.** Many students with learning disabilities have difficulty with word problems. Although problems in reading may be a factor, the difficulty is often in thinking through the math problems. Students tend to begin doing computations as soon as they see the numbers in the problems. The following steps are helpful in teaching word problem applications:

   a. **Seeing the situations.** Have the students first read the word problem and then relate the setting of the problem. The students do not need paper and pencil for this task. They should simply describe the setting or situation.
   b. **Determining the question.** Have the students decide what is to be discovered—What is the problem to be solved?
   c. **Gathering data.** The word problem often gives much data—some relevant, some not relevant to the solution. Ask the students to read the problem aloud, or silently, and then list the relevant and irrelevant data.
   d. **Analyzing relationships.** Help the students analyze the relationships among the data. For example, if the problem states that the down payment on an automobile costing $2,000 is 25%, the students must see the relationship between these two facts. Seeing relationships is a reasoning skill that students with mathematics disabilities often find difficult.
   e. **Deciding on a process.** Students must decide which computational process should be used to solve the problem. Students should be alert to key words, such as total or in all, which suggest addition, and is left or remains, which suggest subtraction. They should next put the problem into mathematical sentences.

f. **Estimating answers.** Have the students practice estimating what a reasonable answer might be. If the students understand the reasoning behind the problem, they should be able to estimate answers.

g. **Practice and generalization.** After students have thought through and worked out one type of problem, the teacher can give similar problems with different numbers.

time concepts
The sense of time, which is not easily comprehended by some students with learning disabilities, who may be poor at estimating the span of an hour, a minute, several hours, or a weekend and may have difficulty estimating how long a task will take. Trouble with time concepts characterizes students with mathematics disabilities.

9. **Time.** Time concepts involve a difficult dimension for many students with mathematics disabilities to grasp, so they may require specific instructions to learn how to tell time. Real clocks or teacher-made clocks are needed to teach this skill. A teacher-made clock can be created by using a paper fastener to attach cardboard hands to a paper plate. A sequence for teaching time might be the hour (1:00), the half hour (4:30), the quarter hour (7:15), 5-minute intervals (2:25), before and after the hour, minute intervals, and seconds. Use television schedules of programs or classroom activities and relate them to clock time.

10. **Money.** The use of real money and lifelike situations is an effective way to teach number facts to some students. Have them play store, make change, or order a meal from a restaurant menu and then add up the cost and pay for it. All of these situations provide concrete and meaningful practice for learning arithmetic.

14.12d Secondary Mathematics Strategies

Teaching Algebra Through Active Learning High school students used algebra to analyze variable pricing of local cell phone plans. They used advertisements from cell phone companies to sell monthly charges and they also looked at additional charges, such as texting charges, to fund the real cost of the phone plan. They created an algebraic equation to reflect the real cost. They then compared various cell phone costs. They created electronic presentations, using charts, graphs, and PowerPoint to show their results to parents and fellow students (Boss, 2009).

Word Problems STAR is a strategy for word problems for students with learning disabilities and related mild disabilities (Maccini & Hughes, 2000).

S- Search the word problem. Read the problem, ask yourself questions, and write down facts.

T- Translate the words into an equation. For example, identify the operation, representing the equation through manipulative objects or drawings.

A- Answer the problem.

R- Review the solution and check that the solution is reasonable.

Order of Operations Strategy Knowing the order of operations is an important prerequisite for learning algebra. The ORDER strategy helps students with learning disabilities and related mild disabilities remember the order of operations (Minskoff & Allsopp, 2003).

O- Observe the problem. Read the problem and look for multiple operation signs.

R- Read the signs. Look at each sign and identify the operation it represents.

D- Decide which operation to do first. Operations must be performed in a particular order.

E- Execute the rules of order. The phrase "many Dogs are Smelly" reminds students that multiplication and division come before addition and subtraction.

R- Relax. You are done.

Did You Get It?

What basic skillset serves as the foundation for all other mathematical computational skills?
  a. ordering
  b. sorting
  c. addition
  d. matching

14.13 Using Technology for Mathematics Instruction

14.13a Calculators

Students must be required to learn the computation facts, but there are times for using the calculator as well. Calculators are available as stand alone low cost products but are also a part of an iPhone, iPad, or computers. Students in school should be taught how to make efficient use of the calculator. In doing a mathematics-reasoning problem, students often become so bogged down in computation that they never get to the reasoning aspects of the lesson. By using calculators, students can put their energies into understanding the mathematical concept rather than on performing the underlying calculation process (Center for Implementing Technology in Education, 2007).

A low-cost pocket calculator is easily accessible and handy. It can be used to compute basic facts, as well as more complicated math processes, and it is also useful for self-checking. Because it is more socially acceptable than other counting systems, it is particularly helpful for adults who have not memorized basic computation facts. Students do need instruction in the proper way to use a calculator, so lessons must be designed to teach calculation skills.

Students with mathematics difficulties may find talking calculators useful. The talking calculator is a calculator with a speech synthesizer. When a number, symbol, or operation is pressed, it is vocalized by the speech synthesizer. The user gets auditory feedback and can double-check the answers.

mathematics difficulties
Difficulty using quantitative and number concepts.

Secondary students and adults are likely to need programmable calculators to perform more complex math functions.

14.13b Computers

The rapid pace of change in computer applications has made computer technology especially useful for teaching mathematics.

Beyond calculators and computer games, teachers today have the opportunity to utilize virtual manipulatives as discussed previously. Interactive whiteboards are also found in many of today's schools and can be used very effectively to build math skills.

© Cengage Learning 2015

TeachSource Video Case Activity

Watch the TeachSource Video Case entitled "Using Technology to Promote Discovery Learning: High School Geometry Class."

In this video, Gary Simons, the geometry teacher, uses "discovery learning" to help students learn how to make conjectures in geometry class. They use a technology tool called "sketchpad" to study angles in geometry. The geometry teacher explains that discovery learning is an essential part of the teacher's repertoire. He also points out that "traditional mathematics" teaching is also a part of the teacher's repertoire.

QUESTIONS

1. What is "discovery learning" in geometry?

2. How does "traditional mathematics" teaching differ from "discovery learning"?

There are a number of math apps that are available for the iPad. Aronin and Floyd (2013) provide some examples of apps for preschoolers.

Monkey Math School Sunshine
My First Tangrams

When selecting apps for math, it is important to match children's preferences, strengths, specific needs, and developmental levels with appropriate levels (Aronin and Floyd, 2013).

Now there is increased emphasis on STEM (science, technology, engineering, and mathematics). The National Aeronautics and Space Administration (*http://www.nasa.gov/*) has many resources available for free. These lesson plans and resources provide an array of integrated activities for science, technology, engineering, and math. Other websites that might be helpful include:

Math Fact Fluency—*www.reflexmath.com*
Online Math Learning—*www.onlinemathlearning
.com*

Many mathematics software programs, although not specifically designed for students with mathematics disabilities, may be useful. Computers motivate students, and the mathematics software programs can individualize, provide feedback, and offer repetition (Belson, 2003; Lewis, 1998; Raskind & Higgins, 1998a). These programs should have as little clutter as possible and should offer concise, clear directions, moving from simple and concrete directions to longer and more complex ones. The programs should question the student frequently (asking, for example, "Are you sure? Do you want to change your answer?"). They should also provide immediate feedback to the student.

Mathematics programs range from drill-and-practice programs to problem-solving programs. A good source for mathematics software programs for students with learning disabilities is Closing the Gap's Resource Directory. The website for Closing the Gap is at *http://www.closingthegap.com*.

14.13c Spreadsheets

Computer spreadsheets are an essential part of the mathematics curriculum, and their use is recommended by the National Council of Teachers of Mathematics (2000). Moreover, students with learning disabilities often do very well with spreadsheet applications, possibly because spreadsheets are a visual task, rather than a linguistic task. A spreadsheet displays numeric information through a grid of columns and rows. The intersection of a column and a row is called a cell. When numbers are placed in the cells, they can be used in mathematics computations or in mathematics formulas, such as averages. Charts and

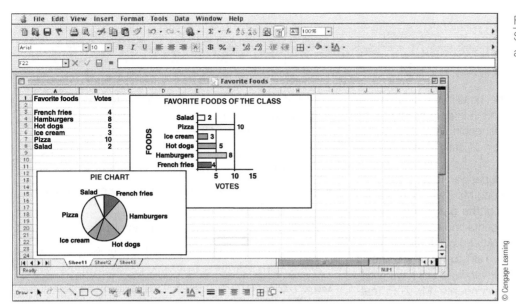

FIGURE **14.8**
Spreadsheet, Pie Chart, and Bar Graph

graphs, such as pie charts, bar graphs, or line graphs, are electronically made, based on the numbers in the spreadsheets (see Figure 14.8).

A pie chart is a circular chart cut into segments illustrating magnitudes or frequencies. A bar graph is a type of chart in which different values are represented by rectangular bars. A wide variety of student activities can be accomplished with spreadsheets, such as planning a budget, keeping records of grades, compiling an inventory of items used in a hobby, or tracking election results.

In one activity, students noted their favorite foods. These foods were then listed on a chalkboard and each student voted for his or her favorite food. The class votes were tallied (e.g., pizza, 10 votes; hot dogs, 5 votes). The favorite foods and votes were then put into Columns A and B on a spreadsheet, and the students made pie charts and bar graphs from their spreadsheets. Figure 14.8 shows the spreadsheet, pie chart, and bar graph that resulted from this activity.

pie chart
A circular chart showing segments that illustrate magnitude or frequencies.

bar graph
A type of chart in which different values are represented by rectangular bars.

spreadsheets
A display of numeric information through rows and columns, usually used in a computer program.

Did You Get It?

Spreadsheets, a valuable and effective tool for teaching mathematical computation, are helpful because they are visual. The use of spreadsheets in mathematics is

a. mandated by CORE.

b. recommended by the National Council of Teachers of Mathematics.

c. frowned upon by the National Education Association.

d. mandated by No Child Left Behind Act.

I Have a Kid Who...

SAM: *A Student Who Has Difficulty in Algebra*

Sam is age 14 years 8 months, he is in the ninth grade, and he is identified through his IEP as a student with learning disabilities. Sam enjoys reading and does well in English, but he has encountered difficulty in mathematics since his elementary years.

Sam is in the general education algebra class. At the beginning of the school year, Mr. Zero, Sam's algebra teacher, reviewed some of the basic concepts of basic pre-algebra that the students had been taught the previous year in eighth grade. After a quick review, most students were ready to move on to more advanced algebra concepts. Sam, however, was still having difficulty with the basic algebra concepts. Mr. Zero realizes these early algebra concepts must be mastered before moving on to more advanced concepts. He collaborates with the special education teacher and they both work with Sam to teach him basic pre-algebra skills. They will teach Sam to solve the following types of algebra problems:

- Addition, subtraction, multiplication, and division problems involving integers. For example: $4 + 6$; $4 + -6$; 4×5; $-18 \div -3$.
- Simplify addition, subtraction, and division equations. For example: $(2x + 6) + (4x + 7) = 6x + 13$.
- Solve expressions with variables. For example: $3x = -24$.
- Solve two-step equations. For example: $3x - 4 = 2$.
- Solve multi-step equations. For example: $5x - 4 = 2x + 5$.

Source: Adapted from The Iris Center for Faculty Enhancement, Case Study Unit, Algebra (Part 1), *http://www.iris.peabody.vanderbilt.edu.*

QUESTIONS

1. How is the strategy of collaboration being used for Sam?

2. Do you think that other students in the algebra class would benefit from this collaborative teaching?

Chapter Summary

- Some students with learning disabilities and related mild disabilities have severe difficulty in learning mathematics. For others, mathematics seems to be an area of strength.
- Dyscalculia is a severe disability in learning and using mathematics that is associated with a neurological dysfunction.
- Early number learning in young children includes abilities in spatial relations, visual-motor and visual-perception processing, and concepts of time and direction.
- Characteristics of mathematics disabilities are related to information-processing difficulties, language and reading abilities, and math anxiety.
- Views about teaching mathematics have changed over the years in response to national concerns. Today's approach is to require high standards and annual testing.
- There are several learning theories of mathematics instruction for students with mathematics disabilities, which include the progression from concrete learning to abstract learning, direct instruction, learning strategies instruction, and problem-solving approaches.
- Students' mathematics skills can be assessed through formal tests and informal measures. Each provides a different kind of information about mathematics performance.
- The content of the mathematics curriculum is sequential and cumulative. Different elements of mathematics are taught at different grade levels.
- Principles of instruction in mathematics stress that the students should have early number learning. Instruction should progress from the concrete to the abstract, with ample opportunity for practice and review. The students must learn to generalize concepts that have been learned, and they should also know the vocabulary for basic mathematics operations.

- Students should learn basic computational facts, but they should be allowed to use calculators for some purposes in the classroom. Calculator use should be part of the mathematics curriculum.

- Computers have many useful applications in teaching mathematics to students with learning disabilities and related mild disabilities.

Questions for Discussion and Reflection

1. The Individuals With Disabilities Education Improvement Act (IDEA-2004) recognizes 2 areas in which students can have mathematics disabilities. Identify these 2 areas and discuss the implications for services.
2. Characteristics of learning disabilities and related mild disabilities can affect the learning of mathematics. Select two characteristics of students with mathematics disabilities, and describe how these characteristics can affect mathematics learning.
3. Do you think calculators should be used in mathematics instruction? Why or why not? Discuss how they could be used.
4. How can computers be used in the teaching of mathematics?
5. Describe how students can be instructed to go from concrete learning to abstract learning.

Key Terms

abstract instruction (p. 444)
bar graph (p. 455)
concrete instruction (p. 443)
direct instruction (p. 429)
dyscalculia (p. 424)
early number learning (p. 425)
math anxiety (p. 427)
mathematics computation (p. 447)
mathematics difficulties (p. 453)
mathematics learning disabilities (p. 423)

number lines (p. 425)
one-to-one correspondence (p. 424)
part–whole relationship (p. 447)
pie chart (p. 455)
place value (p. 427)
problem solving (p. 423)
semiconcrete instruction (p. 444)
spatial relationships (p. 425)
spreadsheet (p. 455)
time concepts (p. 452)

GLOSSARY

abstract instruction At this level of mathematics instruction, students manipulate symbols without the help of concrete objects or representational pictures or tallies.

accommodations Refers to adjustments within a general education program to meet the needs of students with disabilities. Required under Section 504 of the Rehabilitation Act and IDEA.

accommodations for assessment Accommodations that do not change the content and that are made in testing students with disabilities.

active learners Students who are involved with their learning and contribute to the learning process.

active learning Dynamic involvement in the learning process.

adaptive behavior Skills that people need to function in their everyday lives, such as independent skills and social responsibility. Part of the definition of mental retardation.

adaptive behavior scales A rating scale of information provided by an informant who knows the child (such as the parent). It is usually obtained during an interview with the parent and provides information about the student's self-help skills, communication skills, daily living skills, socialization, and motor skills.

adequate yearly progress (AYP) Progress of schools that is determined by the state in accordance with No Child Left Behind Act requirements and that must result in continuous and substantial academic improvement for all students. The term that refers to the results of statewide tests and how those results meet the threshold of the state's requirement for a specific score.

alternate assessments A different test based on alternate achievement standards as determined by the state for no more than 1% of the total population of students. The students must be those with the most significant cognitive disabilities.

Americans With Disabilities Act Amendments (ADAA) A federal law passed in 1990 to protect the rights of individuals with disabilities. The ADA was updated in 2008 as the *Americans with Disabilities Act Amendments* (ADAA).

annual goals General estimates of what the student will achieve in one year. These goals should represent the most essential needs of the student. Annual goals are part of the written individualized education program.

antecedent event In behavioral psychology, the situation that precedes the target behavior.

Asperger's syndrome (or Asperger syndrome) (AS) Qualitative impairment in social interactions, impulse control, and self-motivation. Included in the disability category of autism.

assessment The process of collecting information about a student to form a judgment and make decisions about the student.

assessment stages This is the stage during which tests are given (multidisciplinary evaluation) and decisions are made (the case conference or IEP meeting).

assistive technology Any technology that enables an individual with a disability to compensate for specific deficits. It includes low-tech or high-tech equipment.

at risk Children who are at risk have factors that lead to poor general development and learning failure.

attention deficit disorder (ADD) Difficulty in concentrating and staying on a task. It may or may not be accompanied by hyperactivity. Used by the U.S. Department of Education.

attention deficit hyperactivity disorder (ADHD) Difficulty in concentrating and staying on a task. Accompanied by hyperactivity. The condition of ADHD is identified and defined by the American Psychiatric Association's *Diagnostic and Statistical Manual of Mental Disorders,* Fourth Edition.

attribution *See* attribution theory.

attribution theory A person's ideas concerning the causes of his or her successes and failures.

auditory blending The ability to synthesize the phonemes of a word in recognizing the entire word. In an auditory blending test, the individual sounds of a word are pronounced with separations between each phoneme sound. The child must combine the individual sounds to say and recognize the word.

auditory discrimination The ability to recognize a difference between phoneme sounds; also the ability to identify words that are the same and words that are different when the difference is a single phoneme element (for example, *big-pig).*

autism Lifelong developmental disability that is best described as a collection of behavioral systems that affect verbal communication, nonverbal communication, and social interactions.

autism spectrum disorder (ASD) A range of disorders that are included within the category of autism, including autism and Asperger's syndrome.

automaticity In cognitive learning theory, the condition in which learning has become almost subconscious and therefore requires little processing effort.

background knowledge Information and experiences that are gained about the topic of instruction or about a reading selection.

backward chaining The teacher constructs a backward chain, which is a chain for the task in a reverse order from that in which the chain is performed. The last step in backward chaining is established first, then the next to the last step is taught and linked to the last step. The last step is taught first and then the teacher works backwards in teaching the skill.

bar graph A type of chart in which different values are represented by rectangular bars.

basal reader *See* basal reading series.

basal reading series A sequential and interrelated set of books and supportive material intended to provide the basic material for the development of fundamental reading skills.

basic academic skills instruction Instruction focusing on direct teaching, especially in reading and mathematics. Students receive instruction at a level that approximates their achievement or instructional level.

behavior management Using behavioral strategies to direct an individual's activity in an appropriate manner.

behavior momentum Student can gain momentum to do a more difficult task by first doing a simpler task. This one could be eliminated since it is covered in the behavioral momentum definition.

behavioral analysis The process of determining the subskills or steps needed to accomplish a task.

behavioral disorders Disabilities that result in an adverse effect on educational performance and are characterized by one or more of these problems: an inability to build or maintain satisfactory interpersonal relationships with peers and teachers; inappropriate types of behaviors or feelings under normal circumstances; general pervasive mood of unhappiness or depression; or a tendency to develop physical symptoms or fears associated with personal or school problems.

behavioral momentum Before giving a student a difficult task, give the student an easy task. The student gains confidence by completing an easy task and gains momentum to accomplish a more difficult task.

behavioral unit In behavioral psychology, the core unit that constitutes an action and its environment. It consists of the antecedent event, the target behavior, and the consequent event.

bibliotherapy A technique of using characters in books to help children work through personal problems.

bilingual instruction A teaching approach in which students use their native language for one part of the instructional day and English for the other part of the instructional day.

brain injured child A child who before, during, or after birth has received an injury to or suffered an infection of the brain. As a result of such organic impairment, there are disturbances that prevent or impede the normal learning process.

case history A compilation of the student's background, development, and other information. Case-history information is usually obtained from parents and from the student's school and medical histories. Often this information is obtained by interview.

central nervous system The organic system comprising the brain and the spinal cord.

cerebral hemisphere One of the two halves (the right hemisphere and the left hemisphere) that constitute the human brain.

child-find Ways of locating young children with disabilities in the community.

clinical teaching Teaching that tailors learning experiences to the unique needs of an individual learner.

cloze procedure A technique that is useful in testing, in teaching reading comprehension, and in determining readability (or difficulty level of the material). The cloze procedure involves deleting words from the text and inserting underlined blank spaces. Measurement is made by counting the number of blanks that students can correctly fill.

cognitive abilities Clusters of human abilities that enable one to know, be aware, think, conceptualize, reason, criticize, and use abstractions.

cognitive behavior modification A self-instructional approach to learning. It requires individuals to talk to themselves out loud, give themselves instruction on what they should be doing, and reward themselves verbally for accomplishments.

cognitive processing The mental processes involved in thinking and learning, such as perception, memory, language, attention, concept formation, and problem solving.

cognitive strategies A method of learning that incorporates the individual's mental processes.

collaboration Teachers working together to plan and teach a child, usually a general education teacher and a special education teacher.

collaborative teaming Teachers working together. Partnerships between the general education teachers and special education teachers.

components of language The language system includes phonology, morphology, syntax, semantics, and pragmatics.

comprehension The purpose of reading—gathering meaning from the printed page.

comprehensive evaluation Entails collecting information about an individual student that can be used to form judgments and make critical decisions about the student and to plan appropriate instruction.

concrete instruction Students manipulate actual materials for mathematics learning, such as blocks, cubes, and marbles.

concrete operations stage In Piaget's theory, the stage at which children can systematize and organize thoughts on the basis of past sensual experience.

consequent event In behavioral psychology, the reinforcement that follows the behavior.

content-area teachers High school teachers whose primary orientation and expertise is the subject matter of their specialty. In contrast, elementary teachers tend to have an orientation and more expertise in child development.

context clues Clues that help readers recognize words through the meaning or context of the sentence or paragraph in which the words appear.

contingency contracting A behavioral management strategy that entails a written agreement between the student and the teacher stating that the student will be able to do something he or she wants if he or she first completes a specified task.

continuum of alternative placements An array of different settings that should be available in a school system to meet the varied needs of students with disabilities.

co-occurring conditions A term used to describe conditions that exist along with an attention deficit disorder. Also called *comorbidity*.

coteaching The process of two professionals working together to seek a joint solution. Often refers to the joint efforts of the special education teacher and the general education classroom teacher.

criterion-referenced tests Tests that measure the student's abilities in specific skills (rather than tests that compare a student to others in a norm group).

cultural and linguistic diversity Representation by many different cultures and language groups.

current achievement level A student's present stage of performance in an academic area.

curriculum-based measurement (CBM) Assessment designed to measure student performance on the student's curriculum activities and materials. The student's performance on an academic task is repeatedly measured and charted to assess changes in learning performance.

cursive writing The style of writing sometimes called script. The individual letters are joined in writing a word. Children typically learn cursive writing in third grade.

decode The process of unlocking words into component sounds.

developmental aphasia The term used to describe a child who has severe difficulty in acquiring oral language. This term implies that the disorder is related to a central nervous system dysfunction.

developmental delay A term designating that a child is slow in a specific aspect of development, such as in cognitive, physical, communication, social/emotional, or adaptive development. It is considered a noncategorical label for identifying a young child for services.

developmental indicators Early precursors or signs of learning disabilities.

developmental variations Differences in rate of development in different areas of learning within an individual.

DIBELS (Dynamic Indicators of Basic Early Literacy Skills) A measurement system to assess early reading skills of young children, including phonological awareness, alphabetic principles, and oral reading fluency.

differentiated instruction Teaching that seeks to find that special method will be successful for an individual student to help that student learn.

direct instruction A method associated with behavioral theories of instruction. The focus is directly on the curriculum or task to be taught and the steps needed to learn that task.

directed reading-thinking activity (DRTA) A guided method of teaching reading comprehension in which readers first read a section of text, then predict what will happen next, and then read to verify the accuracy of the predictions.

discrepancy between achievement and intellectual ability The student's achievement is compared to the student's intellectual ability. A significant difference between these two scores indicates a learning disability.

discrepancy score A mathematical calculation for quantifying the discrepancy between the student's current achievement and his or her potential.

drafting A stage in the writing process in which a preliminary version of the written product is developed.

dyscalculia A medical term indicating lack of ability to perform mathematical functions. The condition is associated with neurological dysfunction.

dysgraphia Extremely poor handwriting or the inability to perform the motor movements required for handwriting. The condition is associated with neurological dysfunction.

dyslexia A severe reading disorder in which the individual cannot learn to read or does not acquire fluent and efficient reading skills. Research suggests that there is a connection between dyslexia and neurological dysfunction.

dysnomia A deficiency in remembering and expressing words. Children with dysnomia may substitute a word like *thing* for many objects when they cannot remember the name of the object. They may attempt to use other expressions to talk around the subject.

early literacy The child's early entrance into the world of words, language, and stories. Literacy emerges in children through simultaneous experiences with oral language, reading, and writing.

early number learning The young child's early learning of quantitative concepts.

ecological system The several environments within which an individual lives and grows, including home and school, as well as social and cultural environments.

educational environments *See* educational setting.

educational setting The student's placement for instruction.

Elkonin card A method of teaching phonemic awareness.

emotional/behavioral disorders (EBD) Students who have emotional disorders or behavioral disturbances. Many states use the designation EBD to refer to both conditions.

emotional disorders Involves feelings about oneself, such as depression or low self-esteem, that can interfere with a person's outlook on life and the ability to learn.

English as a second language (ESL) method A method of teaching English to students whose native language is not English.

English-language learners (ELL) Students who speak a language other than English and have a limited proficiency with English.

evidence-based intervention Scientific, research-based instruction.

executive control A component in the information-processing model that refers to the ability to control and direct one's own learning. It is also referred to as *metacognition*.

explicit code-emphasis instruction Systematic and direct teaching of decoding and phonics skills.

explicit teaching Teachers provide the student with a clear explanation of the skills to be taught and then precisely teach each step or skill rather than relying on the student to make inferences from the student's experiences.

expressive language disorders Difficulties in using language (or speaking).

externalizing Conduct disorders that encompass a broad range of antisocial behaviors such as aggressive acts, theft, vandalism, arson, lying, truancy, and running away.

fading A gradual removal of supports.

Feingold diet A diet that eliminates artificial flavors, artificial preservatives, and artificial colors in an attempt to control hyperactivity in children.

formal operations stage In Piaget's theory, the stage at which children can work with abstractions.

formal standardized tests Commercially prepared tests that have been used with and standardized on large groups of students. Manuals that accompany the tests provide derived scores on student performance, such as grade scores, age scores, percentiles, and standard scores.

functional behavioral assessment (FBA) Evaluating a child's behavior problems by analyzing the behavioral unit.

functional magnetic resonance imaging (fMRI) The fMRI is used to study the live human brain at work.

functional skills or survival skills Teaching survival skills to enable students to get along in the outside world.

general education classroom The regular class, in which most students in school receive instruction.

genetics of dyslexia The inheritability of dyslexia.

genetics of learning disabilities The study of the inheritability of learning disabilities.

grapheme The written representation of a phoneme sound.

goal setting The teacher models setting a goal. Teacher helps student in setting a goal. Students set the goal and monitor progress toward the goal.

graphic organizers Visual representations of concepts, knowledge, or information that incorporate both text and pictures to make the material easier to understand.

Head Start A preschool program intended to provide compensatory educational experiences for children from low-income families who might otherwise come to school unprepared and unmotivated to learn. Head Start is sponsored by the Office of Child Development.

high-incidence categories Categories of disabilities that include many children.

high-stakes testing State-wide tests given to all students that result in critical decisions for the child.

home-school coordination A behavior management strategy for helping a child learn. Progress at school is reinforced at home.

hyperactivity A condition characterized by uncontrollable, haphazard, and poorly organized motor behavior. In young children, excessive gross-motor activity makes them appear to be on the go, and they have difficulty sitting still. Older children may be extremely restless or fidgety, may talk too much in class, or may constantly fight with friends, siblings, and classmates.

IEP meeting A meeting attended by parents, school staff, and sometimes the student to make decisions about the individualized education plan (IEP).

individualized education program (IEP) The hallmark of special education that requires that an individualized program be developed by a team of individuals and that program delineate the present levels of academic achievement and functional performance, the strengths of the students, goals for the student, and the special education and related services designed to meet those goals.

immersion instruction An approach to teaching a second language in which students receive extensive exposure to a second language.

impulsiveness A characteristic of attention deficit disorder, in which the child reacts quickly without careful thought.

inattention Not concentrating on a task.

indirect instruction Instruction that is incidental.

individualized education program (IEP) The written plan for the education of an individual student with learning disabilities. The plan must meet requirements specified in the rules and regulations of IDEA. Redundant with previous definition.

individualized family service plan (IFSP) A plan for young children that includes the family as well as the child.

informal assessment measures Ways of evaluating performance that are not formal standardized tests. These can include teacher-made tests, diagnostic teaching, commercial nonstandardized tests, curriculum-based assessment, and so on.

informal reading inventory (IRI) An informal method of assessing the reading level of a student by having the student orally read successively more difficult passages.

informational materials Reading text material that is about subject matter. Usually nonfiction.

information-processing model A systems approach to cognitive processing. The information processing model emphasizes the flow of information, the memory system, and the interrelationships among the elements of cognitive processes.

instruction stages This stage is part of the IEP process and includes implementing a teaching plan, and reviewing and reevaluating the student's progress.

instructional support team A teacher-assistive team that develops prereferral activities for a student before a referral is made.

instructional technology Use of technology, such as computers, for teaching.

intellectual disabilities The term that has replaced cognitive disabilities and mental retardation. Significantly subaverage general intellectual functioning existing concurrently with deficits in adaptive behavior and manifested during the developmental period.

interactive dialogues Discussions between the teacher and children in the class.

Interagency Committee on Learning Disabilities (ICLD) A committee commissioned by the U.S. Congress and made up of representatives from 12 agencies of the Department of Health and Human Services and the Department of Education to develop a federal definition of learning disabilities.

internalizing Disorders that are inward, such as refusal to learn, resistance to pressure, withdrawal, clinging to dependency, or sadness.

invented spelling The beginning writer's attempt to write words. The young writer attends to the sound units and associates letters with them in a systematic, although unconventional, way.

keyboarding The process of typing on a computer keyboard.

kinesthetic perception Perception obtained through body movements and muscle feeling, such as the awareness of positions taken by different parts of the body and bodily feelings of muscular contraction, tension, and relaxation.

language delay Slowness in the acquisition of language. The child with a language delay may not be talking at all or may be using very little language at an age when language normally develops.

language disorders The term that refers to children with a language delay or language disabilities.

language experience method A method of teaching reading based on the experiences and language of the reader. The method involves the generation of experience-based materials that are dictated by the student, written by the teacher, and then used as the material for teaching reading.

lateral preference A tendency to use either the right or left side of the body or to favor using the hand, foot, eye, or ear of one side of the body.

learned helplessness A trait of students with learning disabilities in which they exhibit passiveness and do not take on the responsibility for their own learning.

learning differences The concept that all individuals have variations in learning abilities in various areas.

learning disabilities A disorder in one or more of the basic processes involved in understanding spoken or written language. It may show up as a problem in listening, thinking, speaking, reading, writing, or spelling or in a person's ability to do math, despite at least average intelligence. The term does not include children who have learning problems that are primarily the result of visual, hearing, or physical handicaps, mental retardation, or emotional disturbance, or of environmental, cultural, or economic disadvantage. Individuals with learning disabilities encounter difficulty in one or more of seven areas: (1) receptive language, (2) expressive language, (3) basic reading skill, (4) reading comprehension, (5) written expression, (6) mathematics calculations, or (7) mathematics reasoning.

learning strategies approach *See* learning strategies instruction.

learning strategies instruction A series of methods to help students direct their own learning, focusing on how students learn rather than on what they learn.

least restrictive environment (LRE) To the maximum extent appropriate, students are educated with their nondisabled peers.

long-term memory Permanent memory storage that retains information for an extended period of time.

low-incidence categories Categories of disabilities that include few children.

manifestation determination The process that the IEP undertakes in order to determine whether a student's behavior is the result of a disability.

manuscript writing The form of handwriting sometimes called *printing*. This form of writing, closer to the printed form, is easier to learn than cursive writing because it consists of only circles and straight lines.

mastery learning The steps of a subject are put in sequential order. Mastery learning determines if the child has learned (or mastered) each step.

math anxiety Refers to a debilitating emotional reaction to mathematics situations.

mathematics computation The basic mathematical operations, consisting of addition, subtraction, multiplication, division, fractions, decimals, and percentages.

mathematics difficulties Difficulty using quantitative and number concepts.

mathematics learning disabilities Students whose learning disability is in the area of mathematics.

mediation A process of resolving disputes between the parent and the school in a nonadversarial fashion.

mental retardation Significantly subaverage general intellectual functioning existing concurrently with deficits in adaptive behavior and manifested during the developmental period. The correct term now is Intellectual disabilities.

metacognition The ability to facilitate learning by taking control and directing one's own thinking process.

mild disabilities A grouping of students with different disabilities for instruction, such as learning disabilities, mild mental retardation, emotional disturbances, and other disabilities.

mild/moderate disabilities A term that includes both students with mild disabilities and students with moderate disabilities.

mind mapping A technique that employs a pictorial method to transfer ideas from a student's mind onto a piece of paper.

minimal brain dysfunction (MBD) A term that refers to mild or minimal neurological abnormality that causes learning difficulties.

morpheme The smallest meaning unit of a language system.

morphology The linguistic system of meaning units in any particular language; for example, the word *played* contains two meaning units (or morphemes): play + ed (past tense).

multidisciplinary evaluation The assessment process in which specialists from several disciplines evaluate a child and coordinate their findings.

multimodal treatment plan Combines several approaches to treating children with ADD/ADHD, which refers both to attention deficit disorders and attention deficit hyperactivity disorder.

multiple intelligences Many different talents or intelligences, such as verbal or linguistic intelligence and visual or spatial intelligence.

multisensory methods A collection of programs based on the Orton-Gillingham method that use several sensory avenues to teaching reading.

multistore memory system The central idea in the information-processing model of learning. Information is seen as flowing among three types of memory: the sensory register, short-term memory, and long-term memory.

narrative text Reading text material that tells a story—usually fiction.

National Joint Committee on Learning Disabilities (NJCLD) An organization of representatives from several professional organizations and disciplines involved with learning disabilities.

neurobiological disorder A category under which some exceptionalities are grouped, such as Asperger's syndrome and autism spectrum disorders.

neurology The medical specialty that deals with the functioning and development of the central nervous system.

neurons Nerves within the brain.

neuropsychology A discipline that combines neurology and psychology and studies the relationship between brain function and behavior.

neurosciences Disciplines that are involved with the study of the brain and its functions.

neurotransmitter The chemicals that transmit messages from one cell to another across the synapse (a microscopic space between nerve cells).

No Child Left Behind Act (NCLB) Act The 2001 revision of the Elementary and Secondary Education Act of 2001. Public Law 107-110.

nonverbal learning disorders (NVLD) Poor skills in nonacademic areas of learning, such as poor social skills.

norm-referenced tests Standardized tests that compare a child's performance to that of other children of the same age.

number line A sequence of numbers forming a straight line that allows the student to manipulate computation directly. Number lines help students develop an understanding of number symbols and their relationship to each other.

observation Careful watching of a student's behavior, usually in the classroom setting.

occupational therapist (OT) A therapist who is trained in brain physiology and function and who prescribes exercises to improve motor and sensory integration.

one-to-one correspondence A relationship in which one element of a set is paired with one and only one element of a second set.

one-to-one instruction Teaching with one teacher and one student.

ophthalmologist A medical specialist concerned with the physiology of the eye, its organic aspects, diseases, and structure.

otitis media Middle-ear infection that may cause temporary hearing loss and may impede language development.

otology The medical specialty that deals with auditory or hearing disorders.

parent support groups Small groups of parents who meet to obtain information about their children with disabilities and to discuss common problems.

parents' rights Used in IDEA-2004 for procedural safeguards to protect the rights of parents.

Part B of IDEA-2004 The part of the law (IDEA) that refers to regulations for children with disabilities. In reference to early childhood, Part B covers preschoolers with disabilities ages 3 through 5.

Part C of IDEA-2004 The part of the law (IDEA) that covers infants and toddlers from birth through age 2.

part–whole relationship Addition and subtraction have a part–whole relationship. Add to the whole or total of two parts; and you subtract from the whole to find the missing part.

passive-aggressive behavior A student shows aggression by refusing to do something.

passive learners Adolescents with learning disabilities who tend to wait for teacher direction instead of being actively involved in the learning situation.

peer tutoring A method of instruction in which the student is taught by a peer or classmate.

perception The process of recognizing and interpreting information received through the senses.

perceptual disorder A disturbance in the ability to perceive objects, relations, or qualities—a difficulty in the interpretation of sensory stimulation.

perceptual motor learning The integration of motor learning and visual perceptual learning.

perceptual processing concept A theory that learning problems are related to difficulty in mental processes.

performance standards Academic levels set by national, state, and local bodies that students should achieve on achievement tests.

phoneme The smallest sound unit of a language system.

phonemic awareness An awareness of the sounds in words and language.

phonics An application of phonetics to the teaching of reading in which the sound (or phoneme) of a language is related to the equivalent written symbol (or grapheme).

phonological awareness A child's recognition of the sounds of language. The child must understand that speech can be segmented into syllables and phonemic units.

phonology The linguistic system of speech sounds in a particular language. The word *cat,* for example, has three sounds (or phonemes).

pie chart A circular chart showing segments that illustrate magnitude or frequencies.

place value The aspect of the number system that assigns specific significance to the position a digit holds in a numeral.

placement The selection of the appropriate setting for teaching a child.

portfolio assessment A method of evaluating student progress by analyzing samples of the student's classroom work.

positive behavioral supports Methods that assist as the child learns new ways of behaving.

positron emission tomography (PET) A procedure that permits one to measure metabolism within the brain.

postmortem anatomical studies Autopsy studies of the brain of persons with a history of dyslexia.

pragmatics The social side of language; the social context and social customs surrounding language.

Premack principle A preferred activity is earned after a non-preferred activity is completed.

preoperational stage One of Piaget's developmental stages of learning. During this stage, children make intuitive judgments about relationships and also begin to think with symbols.

prereferral activities Preventive procedures taken prior to referral for special education evaluation and intended to help regular teachers work more successfully with the child in the regular classroom.

prewriting The first step of the writing process, in which writers evoke and gather ideas for writing.

primary language system The child's first language, usually oral language. In relation to bilingual students, it can refer to the student's native language.

problem solving The kind of thinking needed to work out mathematics word problems.

problem-solving model to RTI Focuses on individualized intervention for one student.

problem-solving approach An approach to learning that uses problem solving.

procedural safeguards Regulations in federal law that are designed to protect the rights of students with learning disabilities and their parents.

progress monitoring Assessment procedures to measure the student's academic performance and evaluate the effectiveness of instruction.

psychiatrist The medical specialist who deals with emotional problems and mental health issues.

psychological processing A phrase used in the definition of learning disabilities in the Individuals with Disabilities Education Improvement Act of 2004, which refers to abilities in visual or auditory perception, memory, or language.

psychological processing disorders A phrase in the federal definition of learning disabilities that refers to disabilities in visual or auditory perception, memory, or language.

psychostimulant medications Medications, including Ritalin, that are initially prescribed for a child with attention deficit disorder.

psychotherapeutic teaching An approach to teaching that concentrates on the student's feelings and relationship with the teacher.

Public Law 94-142 The Education for All Handicapped Children Act, Public Law 94-142, was passed by Congress in 1975. The law guarantees a free and appropriate public education to children with disabilities. This law was reauthorized in 1990 and 1997 as the Individuals with Disabilities Education Act (IDEA). The most recent version is the 2004 Individuals with Disabilities Education Improvement Act (IDEA-2004).

Public Law 101-476 This is the Individuals with Disabilities Education Act (IDEA) passed by Congress in 1990. It updated PL 94-142, the Education for All Handicapped Children Act.

Public Law 105-17 The 1997 Individuals with Disabilities Education Act that was passed by Congress in 1997.

Public Law 108-364, Assistive Technology Act (2004) The federal law related to using assistive technology.

Public Law 108-446 The most recent federal special education law. The Individuals with Disabilities Education Improvement Act of 2004 (IDEA-2004).

rapid automatized naming (RAN) The ability to quickly and automatically name objects and pictures of objects.

rapport A close relationship between teacher and child that is based on total acceptance of the child as a human being worthy of respect.

rating scales A ranking of student behavior as judged by a parent, teacher, or other informant.

readiness The state of maturational development that is necessary before a skill can be learned.

reading comprehension Understanding of the meaning of printed text.

reading fluency The ability to recognize words and passages readily and smoothly.

Reading Recovery A reading program first used in New Zealand in which first graders who rank very low in reading are selected for a period of intensive reading instruction.

reasonable accommodations The phrase used in Section 504 of the Rehabilitation Act to describe what can fairly easily be done in a setting to make adjustments for an individual with a disability.

receptive language disorders Difficulty understanding oral language or listening.

reciprocal teaching A method of teaching through a social interactive dialogue between teacher and student that emphasizes the development of thinking processes.

referral The initial request to consider a student for a special education evaluation.

referral stages The initial stages of the IEP process. They include the prereferral activities and the referral activities.

reinforcement An event following a response that increases the likelihood that the person will make a similar response in similar situations in the future.

reinforcement theory A behavioral concept of learning based on using rewards or reinforcement.

related services Those services that are designed to supplement the special education program designed to meet the needs of the student.

repeated reading Having children reread material aloud to build fluency.

residential facilities Educational institutions in which students live away from home and receive their education. A residential facility may be sponsored by a government agency or may be privately managed.

resource room A special instructional setting, usually a room within a school. In this room, small groups of children meet with a special education teacher for special instruction for a portion of the day. Children spend the remainder of the day in the general education classrooms.

response-to-intervention (RTI) The Individuals with Disabilities Education Improvement Act of 2004 advocates the procedure of teaching all students with evidence-based instructional materials through general education in order to judge the students' response to this intervention. RTI is also identified as a procedure for assessing children with learning disabilities.

retrieval Recalling information from long-term memory.

revising A stage of the writing process in which the writer reworks a draft of a written product.

scaffolded instruction Teacher supports for the student, particularly at the initial stage of learning a task.

school-wide positive behavior support (SWPBS) A system approach for establishing a positive whole school climate and individualized behavior supports to create an accepting environment for students.

screening A type of assessment using ways to survey many children quickly to identify those who may need special services.

secondary language system A student's second language, not the student's native language.

Section 504 of the Rehabilitation Act of 1973 Federal law that covers all agencies and institutions receiving financial assistance and that requires that no otherwise qualified handicapped individual shall be excluded from participation.

self-esteem Feelings of self-worth, self-confidence, and self-concept that provide an experience of success.

self-management Using behavior strategies to take charge of one's own activities.

self-questioning A strategy of building comprehension through asking questions.

semantics A linguistic term referring to the vocabulary system of language.

semiconcrete instruction The level of mathematics instruction in which the students use representational objects to refer to math concepts, such as tallies, pictures, or marks, instead of the actual objects.

sensorimotor stage One of Piaget's developmental stages of learning. During this stage, children learn through senses and movements and by interacting with the physical environment.

sensory integration (SI) A theory stemming from the field of occupational therapy that physical exercises can modify the brain.

sensory register The first memory system in the information-processing model that interprets and maintains memory information long enough for it to be perceived and analyzed.

separate class A special class for children with disabilities taught by a teacher with special training. Children in a separate class usually spend most of the day in this setting.

separate schools Schools for students with learning disabilities that students attend during the day. They return home after school.

severe discrepancy A significant difference between a child's current achievement and intellectual potential.

sharing with an audience A stage of the writing process in which the final written product is read by others.

sheltered English A method of teaching children who have some proficiency in English to learn English more rapidly by having them use materials written in English.

short-term memory A second memory storage within the information-processing model. It is a temporary storage facility serving as working memory as a problem receives one's conscious attention.

sight words Words that a student recognizes instantly, without hesitation or further analysis.

social maturity The development of social aspects of life.

social perception The ability to understand social situations, as well as sensitivity to the feelings of others.

social skills Skills necessary for meeting the basic social demands of everyday life.

soft neurological signs Minimal or subtle neurological deviations that some neurologists use as indicators of mild neurological dysfunction.

spatial relationships Concepts such as up-down, over-under, top-bottom, high-low, near-far, beginning-end, and across. A disturbance in spatial relationship can interfere with the visualization of the entire number system.

specialized instruction Instruction that is specially designed to meet the needs of the individual student and that instruction is based on the specific strengths and deficits that the student exhibits.

speech disorders Disorders of articulation, fluency, or voice.

spreadsheet A display of numeric information through rows and columns, usually used in a computer program.

stages of acceptance The different emotions parents go through when they learn they have a child with disabilities.

stages of learning The stages a person goes through in mastering material, such as acquisition, proficiency, maintenance, and generalization.

Standard English The linguistic system of English recognized by the literate culture and used in school.

standards Specific expectations for what students will learn at given grade levels.

statewide standards Standards that are set by individual states for what students are expected to learn at given grade levels. Many states have now adopted the Common Core Standards.

strategies intervention model (SIM) An instructional method for teaching learning strategies to adolescents with learning disabilities.

structural analysis The recognition of words through the analysis of meaningful word units, such as prefixes, suffixes, root words, compound words, and syllables.

Summary of Performance (SOP) When students are going to exit the school system, the local educational agency provides the student with a summary of the student's academic achievement and functional performance, which includes recommendations on how to assist the student in meeting postsecondary goals.

syntax The grammar system of a language; the linguistic rules of word order; the function of words in a sentence.

tactile perception Perception obtained through the sense of touch via the fingers and skin surfaces.

target behavior In the behavioral unit, A-B-C, the target behavior is "B," the actual behavior of the student.

task analysis A teaching approach that analyzes an activity by breaking it down into a sequence of steps.

team teaching A method of collaboration by which two or more teachers work together.

temporal acoustical processing The ability to process sounds of language rapidly enough to distinguish speech sounds and words.

theories The purpose of theory is to bring form and coherence, and meaning, to what is observed in the real world. Underlying concepts explaining what is observed.

time concepts The sense of time, which is not easily comprehended by some students with learning disabilities, who may be poor at estimating the span of an hour, a minute, several hours, or a weekend and may have difficulty estimating how long a task will take. Trouble with time concepts characterizes students with mathematics disabilities.

time-out A behavior management method in which a child is removed from a group for a short period of time.

transition The process of moving from one type of program to another. In early childhood programs it can be from the birth-through-2 program to the ages

3-through-5 program, or from the ages 3-through-5 program to another educational placement. For adolescents transition refers to the passage from school to the adult world.

transition planning Planning for making the change from being a student to being an adult. Students with learning disabilities need help with this process.

tutorial instruction Teaching designed to help students meet requirements in their specific academic-content subjects and to achieve success in the regular curriculum. This teaching is usually accomplished through one-to-one instruction or in small groups.

Universal Design for Learning (UDL) A policy of designing solutions for people with disabilities that are useful for others in the general population.

VAKT The abbreviation for *visual, auditory, kinesthetic,* and *tactile* learning, a multisensory approach to teaching reading that stimulates all avenues of sensory input simultaneously.

visual discrimination The ability to note visual differences or similarities between objects, including letters and words.

visual perception The identification, organization, and interpretation of sensory data received by the individual through the eye.

vocabulary Recognition and knowledge of words. Consists of oral vocabulary and reading vocabulary.

whole language reading A method of teaching reading based on using literature, stories, and books.

word finding Recalling the correct words.

word-frequency approach to spelling A method of word selection and instruction for spelling. Words are selected for spelling instruction on the basis of how frequently they are used in writing.

word-pattern approach to spelling A theory of word selection and instruction in spelling. It is based on the belief that the spelling of English is sufficiently rule-covered to warrant a method of selection and instruction that stresses phonological, morphological, and syntactic rules or word patterns.

word processing Writing with a computer (as contrasted with writing by hand or on a conventional typewriter).

word-recognition procedures Strategies for recognizing words, including phonics, sight words, context clues, structural analysis, and combinations of these strategies.

word web A type of graphic organizer. It helps students learn words, build vocabulary, and makes information about the word easier to understand and learn.

working memory *See* short-term memory.

work-study program A high school program in which students work on a job for a portion of the day and go to school for a portion of the day.

writing process The process whereby writers go through a series of stages during writing. The four stages of the writing process are (1) prewriting, (2) drafting, (3) revising, and (4) sharing with an audience.

writing product A method of teaching writing that focuses on the final written document.

zero reject All children regardless of the severity of their disability have a right to a free and appropriate public education and cannot be denied the right to go to school.

zone of proximal development (ZPD) A term, used by Vygotsky, envisioning a range of levels of difficulty for a student. The lower end is very easy, the upper end beyond the student's capacity. The ZPD is the midpoint and is an appropriate level for learning.

Accardo, P., & Blondis, T. (2000). Pediatric management of ADHD medication. In P. Accardo, T. Blondis, B. Whitman, & M. Stein (Eds.), *Attention deficits and hyperactivity in children and adults* (2nd ed., pp. 513–534). New York: Marcel Dekker.

Accardo, P., Blondis, T., Whitman, B., & Stein, M. (2000). *Attention deficits and hyperactivity in children and adults* (2nd ed.). New York: Marcel Dekker.

Adams, A., Foorman, B., Lundberg, I., & Beeler, T. (1998). The elusive phoneme. *American Educator, 22*(1&2), 18–31.

Adams, M. J. (1990). *Beginning to read.* Cambridge, MA: MIT Press.

Adelman, P. B., & Vogel, S. A. (2003). Life-style issues of adults with learning disabilities. In S. A. Vogel, G. Vogel, V. Sharoni, & O. Dahan (Eds.), *Adults with learning disabilities in higher education and beyond: An international perspective* (pp. 315–337). Baltimore, MD: York Press.

Adler, M. (1956). *How to read a book.* New York: Simon & Schuster.

Administration for Children and Families. (2001, January 25). *Fact sheet.* Washington, DC: U.S. Department of Health and Human Services.

Alberto, P., & Troutman, A. (1995, 1998, 2003). *Applied behavior analysis for teachers.* Columbus, OH: Merrill.

Algozzine, B. (1991). Curriculum-based assessment. In B. Wong (Ed.), *Learning about learning disabilities* (pp. 40–59). San Diego: Academic Press.

Allen, G. (2003). *The section 504 guide to a successful school-level program: A handbook for principals including charts, forms and sample procedures.* Horsham, PA: LRP Publications.

Allen J. E., & Cowdrey, G. E. (2009). *The exceptional child: Inclusion in early childhood education.* Clifton Park, NY: Cengage Learning/Delmar.

American Academy of Pediatrics. (2001). Clinical practice guideline: Treatment of the school-age child with attention deficit hyperactivity disorder. *Pediatrics, 108*(4), 1033–1044.

American Association on Mental Retardation. (2002). *Mental retardation: Classification, definitions, and systems of supports.* Washington, DC: Author.

American Guidance Services. http://www.pearsonassessments.com.

American Psychiatric Association. (2004). *Diagnostic and statistical manual of mental disorders* (4th ed. rev.). Washington, DC: Author.

American Psychiatric Association. (2013). *Diagnostic and statistical manual of mental disorders* (5th ed.) Washington, DC: Author.

Ankeny, E., Wilkins, J., & Spain, J. (2009). Mothers' experiences of transition planning for their children with disabilities. *Teaching Exceptional Children, 41*(6), 28–36.

Aronin, S., & Floyd, K. (2013). Using an iPad in inclusive preschool classrooms to introduce STEM concepts. *Teaching Exceptional Children, 45*(4), 34–39.

Ashcraft, M., Krause, J., & Hopko, D. (2007). Is math anxiety a mathematical learning disability? In D. Berch & M. Mazzocco (Eds.), *Why is math so hard for some children? The nature and origins of mathematical learning difficulties and disabilities* (pp. 329–348). Baltimore, MD: Paul H. Brooks.

Ashlock, R. (2006). *Error patterns in computation.* Englewood Cliffs, NJ: Prentice-Hall.

Association for Persons with Severe Handicaps (TASH). (1995). Resolution on inclusive education. In J. Kauffman & D. Hallahan (Eds.), *The illusion of full inclusion* (pp. 314–316). Austin, TX: Pro-Ed.

Association on Higher Education and Disability. (2012). *Supporting accommodation requests: Guidance on documentation practices, April 2012.* Huntersville, NC: Author.

Atkinson, R., & Shiffrin, R. (1968). Human memory: A proposed system and its control processes. In K. Spence & J. Spence (Eds.), *The psychology of learning and motivation: Advances in theory and research* (Vol. 2, pp. 89–195). New York: Academic Press.

Aylward, E. H., Richards, T. L., Berninger, V. W., Nagy, W. E., Field, K. M., Grimme, A. C., et al. (2003). Instructional treatment associated with changes in brain activation in children with dyslexia. *Neurology, 61,* 212–219.

Ayres, J. (1994). *Sensory integration and learning disorders.* Los Angeles: Western Psychological Services.

Baker, L., & Welkowitz, L. (2005). *Asperger's syndrome: Intervening in schools, clinics, and communities.* Mahwah, NJ: Lawrence Erlbaum.

Ball, E. W., & Blachman, B. A. (1991). Does phoneme awareness training in kindergarten make a difference in early word recognition and spelling? *Reading Research Quarterly, 26*(1), 49–66.

Barbetta, P., Norona, K., & Bicard, D. (2005). Classroom behavior management: A dozen common mistakes and what to do instead. *Preventing School Failure, 49*(3), 11–19.

Barkley, R. (2001). The executive functions and self-regulation: An evolutionary neuropsychological perspective. *Neuropsychology Review, 11*(1), 1–29.

Barkley, R. (2005). *Attention-deficit hyperactivity disorder: A handbook for diagnosis and treatment.* New York: Guilford Press.

Baroody, A., & Ginsburg, H. (1991). A cognitive approach to assessing the mathematical difficulties of children labeled "learning disabled." In H. L. Swanson (Ed.), *Handbook on the assessment of learning disabilities* (pp. 117–228). Austin, TX: Pro-Ed.

Bashir, A., & Singer, B. (2009). Assessment, instruction, and intervention for the struggling writer. *Perspectives on Language and Literacy. International Dyslexia Association, 35*(3), 7–10.

Batsche, G., Kavale, K., & Kovaleski, J. (2009). Competing views: A dialogue on response to intervention. *Assessment for Effective Intervention, 32*(1), pp. 6–19.

Bauer, A., Keefe, C., & Shea, T. (2001). *Students with learning disabilities or emotional/behavioral disorders.* Columbus, OH: Merrill/Prentice Hall.

Baxendell, B. (2003). Consistent, coherent, creative: The three C's graphic organizers. *Teaching Exceptional Children, 35*(3), 46–53.

Beckman, P. (2001). *Access to the general education curriculum for students with disabilities* (Report No. EC308681). Arlington, VA: ERIC Clearinghouse on Disabilities and Gifted Education. (ERIC Document Reproduction Service No. ED458735)

Belson, S. (2003). *Technology for exceptional learners.* Boston: Houghton Mifflin Co.

Bender, L. (1957). Specific reading disability as maturational lag. *Bulletin of the Orton Society, 7*, 9–18.

Bender, W. (2006). *Differentiating instruction for students with learning disabilities.* Arlington, VA: Council for Exceptional Children.

Berko, J. (1958). The child's learning of English morphology. *Word, 14*, 15–17.

Berch, D., & Mazzocco, M. (2007). *Why is math so hard for some children? The nature and origins of mathematical learning difficulties and disabilities.* Baltimore: Brookes Publishing.

Berry, R. (2006). Beyond strategies: Teacher beliefs and writing instruction in two primary inclusion classrooms. *Journal of Learning Disabilities, 39*(1), 11–24.

Biegler, E. (1987). Acquired cerebral trauma, neuropsychiatric and psychoneurological assessment and cognitive retraining issues. *Journal of Learning Disabilities, 20*, 579–580.

Birsh, J. (2005). *Multisensory teaching of basic skills.* Baltimore: Brookes.

Blachman, B. (Ed.). (1997). *Foundations of reading acquisition and dyslexia: Implications for early instruction.* Mahwah, NJ: Erlbaum.

Blachman, B., Tangel, D., & Ball, E. (2004). Combining phonological awareness and word recognition instruction. *Perspectives on Language and Literacy. The International Dyslexia Association, 24*(9), 12–14.

Blackorby, J., & Wagner, M. (1997). The employment outcomes of youth with learning disabilities: A review of findings from the NLTS. In P. Gerber & D. Brown (Eds.), *Learning disabilities and employment* (pp. 57–76). Austin, TX: Pro-Ed.

Bley, N., & Thornton, C. (2001). *Teaching mathematics to students with learning disabilities.* Austin, TX: Pro-Ed.

Blood, E. (2010). Effects of student response systems on participation and learning of students with emotional and behavioral disorders. *Behavioral Disorders, 35*(3), 214–228.

Boyle, J., & Scanlon, D. (2010). *Methods and strategies for teaching students with mild disabilities.* Belmont, CA: Cengage Learning/Wadsworth.

Bolton, P. (2007). Early childhood education offers opportunity to build a better future. *EdLine, 11*(2), 2–3.

Boss, S. (2009, September). When the money isn't there. *Edutopia Magazine.* Retrieved 8/10/2009. http://www.edutopia.org/economic-stimulus-education-technology-oklahoma.

Bowe, F. G. (2007). *Early childhood special education: Birth to eight.* Clifton Park, NY: Cengage Learning/Delmar.

Boyle, J., & Scanlon, D. (2010). *Methods and strategies for teaching students with mild disabilities.* Clifton Park, NY: Cengage Learning/Wadsworth.

Bradley, C. (1937). The behavior of children receiving benzedrine. *American Journal of Psychiatry, 94,* 577–585.

Bradley, R., Danielson, L., & Doolittle, J. (2005). Response to Intervention. *Journal of Learning Disabilities, 38*(6), 485–487.

Brainerd, C. J. (2003). Jean Piaget, learning research, and American education. In B. J. Zimmerman & D. H. Schunk (Eds.), *Educational psychology: A century of contributions* (pp. 251–287). Mahwah, NJ: Erlbaum.

Bransford, J., & Johnson, M. (1972). Contextual prerequisites for understanding: Some investigations of comprehension and recall. *Journal of Verbal Learning and Verbal Behavior, 11,* 726–727.

Bravo-Valdivieso, L., & Müller, N. (2001). Learning disabilities studies in South America. In D. Hallahan & B. Keogh (Eds.), *Research and global perspectives in learning disabilities: Essays in honor of William M. Cruickshank* (pp. 309–326). Mahwah, NJ: Erlbaum.

Broadbent, D. (1958). *Perception and communication.* London: Pergamon Press.

Brooks, R., & Goldstein, S. (2002). *Raising resilient children.* Baltimore: Paul H. Brookes.

Brooks, R., & Goldstein, S. (2004). *The power of resilience.* Chicago: Contemporary Books.

Brown, D. (2000). *Educate yourself for the world of work.* New York: Woodbine House.

Bryan, T. (1997). Assessing the personal and social status of students with learning disabilities. *Learning Disabilities Research and Practice, 12*(1), 63–76.

Bryant, B., & Rivera, D. (1997). Educational assessment of mathematics skills and abilities. *Journal of Learning Disabilities, 30,* 57–68.

Buck, J., Palloway, E., Kirkpatrick, M., Patton J., & McConnell, K. (2000). Developing behavioral intervention plans: A sequential approach. *Intervention in School and Clinic, 36*(1), 3–9.

Burns, M., Ardoin, S., Parker, D., Hodgson, J., Klingbeil, D., & Scholin, S. (2009). Interspersal technique and behavioral momentum for reading word lists. *School Psychology Review, 38*(3), 428–434.

Bursuck, W. D., Rose, E., Cowen, S., & Yahaya, M. (1989). Nationwide survey of postsecondary education services for students with learning disabilities. *Exceptional Children, 56,* 236–254.

Butler, F., Miller, S., Crehan, K., Babbitt, B., & Pierce, T. (2003). Fraction instruction for students with mathematics disabilities: Comparing two teaching sequences. *Learning Disabilities Research & Practice, 18*(2), 91–111.

Carnine, D., Silbert, J., Kame'enui, E., & Tarver, S. (2004), *Direct instruction in reading instruction. Reading* (4th ed.). Upper Saddle River, NJ: Pearson Education.

Carr, G. (2006, December 23). Who do you think you are? *Economist*, 79–86.

Carreker, S., & Birsh, J. (2005). *Multisensory teaching of basic language skills activity book.* Baltimore: Brookes.

Cass, M., Cates, D., Smith, M., & Jackson, C. (2003). Effects of manipulative instruction: Solving area and perimeter problems by students with learning disabilities. *Learning Disabilities Research & Practice, 18*(2), 112–120.

Catts, H. W. (1993). The relationship between speech-language impairments and reading disabilities. *Journal of Speech and Hearing Research, 36*(5), 948–958.

Cawley, J., & Foley, T. (2001). Enhancing the quality of mathematics for students with learning disabilities: Illustrations from subtraction. *Learning Disabilities: A Multidisciplinary Journal, 11*(2), 47–60.

Cawley, J., Hayden, S., Cade, E., & Baker-Kroczynski, S. (2002). Including students with disabilities in the general education science classroom. *Exceptional Children, 68,* 423–435.

Centers for Disease Control and Prevention (CDC). (2003, 2005). *Mental health in the United States: Prevalence of diagnosis and medication treatment for attention-deficit/hyperactivity disorder.* United States 2003. *Morbidity and Mortality Weekly Report, 54*(34), 842–847.

Centers for Disease Control and Prevention (CDC). (2009). *Facts about ASDs.* http://www.cdc.gov/ncbddd/autism/facts.html.

Centers for Disease Control and Prevention (CDC). (2012, March 29). *New estimates find 1 in 88 U.S. children has autism.*

Center for Effective Collaboration and Practice. (1998). *An IEP team's introduction to functional behavior assessment and behavior intervention plans.* Washington, DC: Author.

Center for Implementing Technology in Education, www.cited.org/index.aspx?page_id=48. Retrieved 6-21-2013.

Center for the Improvement of Early Reading Achievement (CIERA). (1998). *Improving the reading achievement of America's children: Ten research-based principles.* Washington, DC: Department of Education.

Chalfant, J., & Pysh, M. (1993). Teacher assistance teams: Implications for the gifted. In C. J. Maker (Ed.), *Critical issues in gifted education: Vol. 888. Gifted students in the regular classroom* (pp. 32–48). Austin, TX: Pro-Ed.

Chalfant, J. C. (1989). Diagnostic criteria for entry and exit from services: A national problem. In L. Silver (Ed.), *The assessment of learning disabilities* (pp. 1–26). Boston: College Hill Press.

Chall, J. (1967, 1983). *Learning to read: The great debate.* New York: McGraw-Hill.

Chapman, J. (1992). Learning disabilities in New Zealand: Where kiwis and kids with LD can't fly. *Journal of Learning Disabilities, 26*(6), 363–370.

Cheney, D. (2010). An overview of transition issues, approaches, and recommendations for youth with emotional or behavioral disorders. In D. Cheney (Ed.), *Transition of secondary students with emotional or behavioral disorders: Current approaches for positive outcomes* (pp. 1–19). Champaign, IL: Research Press.

Cheung, N., & Cohn, S. (2005). *Neuroblastoma.* Berlin Heidelberg: Springer Verlag.

Chomsky, N. (1965). *Aspects of the theory of syntax.* Cambridge, MA: MIT Press.

Cirino, P., Fletcher, J., Ewing-Cobbs, L., Barnes, M., & Fuchs, L. (2007). Cognitive arithmetic differences in learning difficulty groups and the role of behavioral inattention. *Learning Disabilities Research and Practice, 22*(1), 25–35.

Clark, F. (2000). The strategies intervention model: A research-validated intervention for students with learning disabilities. *Learning Disabilities: An Interdisciplinary Journal, 10*(4), 209–217.

Clark, F., Mailloux, Z., & Parham, D. (1989). Sensory integration and children with learning disabilities. In P. N. Pratt & A. S. Allen (Eds.), *Occupational therapy for children* (pp. 457–507). St. Louis: C. V. Mosby.

Clements, S. (1966). Minimal brain dysfunction in children: Terminology and identification (NINDS. Monograph No. 3 Public Health Services. Publication No. 1415). Washington, DC: U.S. Department of Health, Education, and Welfare.

Clyde K. and Sheila K. individually and as guardians for Ryan K. v. Puyallup School District, 21 IDELR 664, September 13, 1994.

Cohen, L., & Spenciner, L. (2009). *Teaching students with mild and moderate disabilities; research-based practices.* Upper Saddle River, NJ: Pearson.

Cohen, M. (2009). Recent Supreme Court decision sends a message to schools: Timely and appropriate evaluations and eligibility decisions are required by IDEA. *Scope. Learning Disabilities Association of Illinois, Inc., 43*(1), 6.

Cole, C., Davenport, T., Bambara, L., & Ager, C. (1997). Effects of choice and task preference on the work performance of students with behavior problems. *Behavioral Disorders, 22*(2), 65–74.

Cole, C., & McLeskey, J. (1997). Secondary inclusion programs for students with mild disabilities. *Focus on Exceptional Children, 29*(6), 1–15.

Common Core State Standards Initiative. (2010). *Common Core State Standards.* www.corestandards.org.

Compton, D., & Appleton, A. (2004). Exploring the relationship between text-leveling systems and reading accuracy and fluency in second-grade students who are average and poor decoders. *Learning Disabilities Research and Practice, 19*(3), 176–184.

Cook, B., & Rumrill, P. (2006). Introduction to post secondary education and students with learning disabilities. *Learning Disabilities: A Multidisciplinary Journal, 14*(1), 1–4.

Cook, R., Klein, M., & Tessier, A. (2008). *Adaptive early childhood curricula for children with special needs.* Englewood Cliffs, NJ: Prentice Hall.

Cortiella, C. (2011). *The state of learning disabilities.* New York: National Center for Learning Disabilities.

Council for Exceptional Children. (1987). *Academy for effective instruction: Working with mildly handicapped children.* Reston, VA: Author.

Council for Exceptional Children. (2004). Student progress monitoring gains supporters. *Today, 10*(7), 1, 9, 17, 19, 25.

Cowan, R. (2006). Preparing high school students with learning disabilities for success in college: Implications for students, parents, and educators. *Learning Disabilities: A Multidisciplinary Journal, 14*(1), 5–14

Coyne, M., Kame'enui, E., & Simmons, D. (2001). Prevention and intervention in beginning reading: Two complex systems. *Learning Disabilities Research and Practice, 16*(2), 62–73.

Cratty, B. (2004). Adapted physical education: Self-control and attention. *Focus on Exceptional Children, 37*(3), 1–8.

Creel, C., Fore, C., Boon, R., & Bender, W. (2006). Effects of self-monitoring on classroom preparedness skills of middle school students with attention deficit hyperactivity disorder. *Learning Disabilities: A Multidisciplinary Journal, 14*(2), 105–114.

Crockett, J., & Kauffman, J. (2001). The concept of the least restrictive environment and learning disabilities? Least restrictive of what? Reflections on Cruickshank's 1997 Guest Editorial for the *Journal of Learning Disabilities.* In D. Hallahan & B. Keogh (Eds.), *Research and global perspectives in learning disabilities: Essays in honor of William M. Cruickshank* (pp. 147–161). Mahwah, NJ: Erlbaum.

Cruickshank, W., Bentzen, F., Ratzeburgh, F., & Tannhauser, M. (1961). *Teaching methods for brain-injured and hyperactive children.* Syracuse, NY: Syracuse University Press.

Cunningham, A., & Stanovich, K. (1998). What reading does for the mind. *American Educator, 22*(1&2), 8–17.

da Fonseca, V. (1996). Assessment and treatment of learning disabilities in Portugal. *Journal of Learning Disabilities, 29*(2), 114–117.

Daviso, A., Denney, S., Baer, R., & Flexer, R. (2011). Postschool goals and transition services for students with learning disabilities. *American Secondary Education, 39*(2), 77–93.

deBettencourt, L. (2002). Understanding the differences between IDEA and Section 504. *Teaching Exceptional Children, 34*(3), 16–23.

Dehaene, S. (2009). *Reading in the brain: The science and evolution of human invention.* New York: Viking: The Penquin Group.

de Hirsch, I., Jansky, J., & Langford, W. (1966). *Predicting reading failure.* New York: Harper & Row.

DeJong, P., & Vrielink, L. (2004). Rapid automatic naming: Easy to measure hard to prove (quickly). *Annals of Dyslexia, 54*(1), 39–64.

Deno, S. (2003). Developments in curriculum-based measurement. *Journal of Special Education, 37*(3), 184–192.

Denton, C. (2006). Responsiveness to intervention as an indication of learning disability. *Perspectives on Language and Literacy. The International Dyslexia Association, 31*(4), 4–7.

Denton, C. (2012). Response to Intervention for reading difficulties in the primary grades: Some answers and lingering questions. *Journal of Learning Disabilities, 45*(3), 232–245.

Deshler, D. (2003). A time for modern-day pioneers. *Learning Disabilities Association Newsbriefs, 38*(3), 3–10, 24.

Deshler, D., Ellis, E. S., & Lenz, B. K. (1996). *Teaching adolescents with learning disabilities: Strategies and methods.* Denver: Love Publishing.

Deshler, D., Milland, D., Tollefson, J., & Bryd, S. (2005). Research topics to responsiveness to intervention: Introduction to the special series. *Journal of Learning Disabilities, 38*(6), 483–485.

Deshler, D., Schumaker, J., Lenz, B., Bulgren, J., Hock, M., Knight, J., et al. (2001). Ensuring content-area learning by secondary students with learning disabilities. *Learning Disabilities Research & Practice, 16*(2), 96–108.

Deshler, D., Schumaker, J., Lenz, B. K., Bulgren, J., Hock, M., Knight, J., et al. (2008, 2009). Ensuring content-area learning by secondary students with learning disabilities. *Journal of Education, 189*(1/2), 6.

De Valenzuela, J., Copeland, S., Huaqing, C., & Park, M. (2006). Examining educational equity: Revisiting the disproportionate representation of minority students in special education. *Exceptional Children, 72*(4), 421–425.

Dewey, J. (1946). *The public and its problems.* Chicago: Gateway.

Dewey, J. (1998). *How we think.* Boston: Houghton Mifflin.

Diamond, G. (1983). The birth date effect: A maturational effect? *Journal of Learning Disabilities, 16,* 161–164.

Dimitrovsky, L., Spector, H., Levy-Shiff, R., & Vakil, E. (1998). Interpretation of facial expressions of affect in children with learning disabilities with verbal or nonverbal deficits. *Journal of Learning Disabilities, 31*(3), 286–292, 312.

Di Pasquale, G., Moule, A., & Flewelling, R. (1980). The birth date effect. *Journal of Learning Disabilities, 13,* 234–238.

Division for Learning Disabilities. (2007). *Thinking about response to intervention and learning disabilities: A teacher's guide.* Arlington, VA: Author.

Division for Learning Disabilities & Division for Research of the Council for Exceptional Children. (2012). *Current practice alerts: A focus on cognitive strategy instruction, Spring 2012,* (19), 1–4.

Doe v. Withers, 20 IDELR 422 (W.Va. Cir. Ct. 1993).

Duncan, A. (2009). *Reauthorization of ESEA: Why we can't wait. Secretary Arne Duncan's remarks at the monthly stake holders meeting.* Retrieved 5-19-2010. http://www.ed.gov/news/speeches/2009/09/09242009.html.

Dunn, M. (2010). Defining learning disability: Does IQ have anything significant to say? *Learning Disabilities: A Multidisciplinary Journal, 16*(1), 31–40.

Eisenman, L., Pleet, A., Wandry, D., & McGinley, V. (2011). Voices of special education teachers in an inclusive high school: Redefining responsibilities. *Remedial and Special Education, 32*(2), 91–104.

Elbaum, B. (2002). The self-concept of students with learning disabilities. A meta-analysis of comparisons across different placements. *Learning Disabilities Research and Practice, 17,* 216–226.

Elison, P. (2006). Positive psychology: Hope, strength, and optimism. *Attention!, 13*(3), 19–20.

Elkins, J. (2001). Learning disabilities in Australia. In D. Hallahan & B. Keogh (Eds.), *Research and global perspectives in learning disabilities: Essays in honor of William M. Cruickshank* (pp. 181–196). Mahwah, NJ: Erlbaum.

Elkonin, D. B. (1973). U.S.S.R. In J. Downing (Ed.), *Comparative reading* (pp. 551–580). New York: MacMillan.

Elksnin, L., & Elksnin, N. (2004). The social-emotional side of learning disabilities. *Learning Disability Quarterly, 27*(1), 3–8.

Elliott, L. (2012). *Accidental techie to the rescue.* Peterborough, NH: Crystal Springs Books.

Ellis, E., Deshler, D., Lenz, K., Schumaker, J., & Clark, F. (1991). An instructional model for teaching learning strategies. *Focus on Exceptional Children, 23*(6), 1–23.

Enfield, M. (1988). The quest for literacy. *Annals of Dyslexia, 38,* 8–21.

Englemann S., & Bruner, E. (1974). *Reading mastery series.* Worthington, OH: SRA Macmillan/McGraw-Hill.

Erikson, E. H. (1968). *Identity: Youth and crisis.* New York: Norton.

Eunice Kennedy Shriver National Institute of Child Health and Human Development. (2008). *Autism spectrum disorders.* http://www.nichd.nih.gov/health/topics/asd.cfm

Fabbro, F., & Masutto, C. (1994). An Italian perspective on learning disabilities. *Journal of Learning Disabilities, 27*(3), 139–141.

Fabelo, T., Thompson, M., Plotkin, M., Carmichael, D., Marchbanks, M., & Booth, E. (2011). *Breaking schools' rules: A statewide study of how school discipline relates to students' success and juvenile justice involvement.* New York: Council of State Governments Justice Center.

Farley, C., Torres, C., Wailehua, C., & Cook, L. (2012). Evidence-based practices for students with emotional and behavioral disorders: Improving academic achievement. *Beyond Behavior, 21*(2), 37–42.

Fennel, E. B. (1995). The role of neuropsychological assessment in learning disabilities. *Journal of Child Neurology, 10*(Suppl. 1), S36–S41.

Fernald, G. (1988). *Remedial techniques in basic school subjects.* Austin, TX: Pro-Ed. (Original work published 1943)

Fisher, S., & DeFries, J. (2002). Developmental dyslexia: Genetic dissection of a complex cognitive trait. *Nature Reviews Neuroscience, 10,* 767–780.

Fitzgerald, J. (1951). *A basic life spelling vocabulary.* Milwaukee: Bruce.

Fitzgerald, J. (1955). Children's experiences in spelling. In V. Herrick & L. Jacobs (Eds.), *Children and the language arts* (Chapter 11). Englewood Cliffs, NJ: Prentice-Hall.

Fitzpatrick, M., & Knowlton, E. (2009). Bringing evidence-based self-directed intervention practices to the trenches for students with emotional and behavioral disorders. *Preventing School Failure, 53*(4), 253–266.

Flannagan, D., Ortiz, S., Alfonso, V., & Mascolo, J. (2006). *The achievement test desk reference: A guide to learning disability identification.* New York: John Wiley & Sons.

Flannery, K., Sugai, G., & Anderson, C. (2009). School-wide positive behavior support in high school. *Journal of Positive Behavioral Interventions, 11*(3), 177–185.

Fletcher, J., Aram, D., Shaywitz, S., & Shaywitz, B. (2000). Learning, language, and attention deficit disorders in children: Comorbidity, assessment and intervention. In P. Accardo, T. Blondis, B. Whitman, & M. Stein (Eds.), *Attention deficits and hyperactivity in children and adults* (2nd ed., pp. 241–257). New York: Marcel Dekker.

Fletcher, J., Coulter, W., Reschly, D., & Vaughn, S. (2004). Alternative approaches to the definition and identification of learning disabilities: Some questions and answers. *Annals of Dyslexia, 54*(2), 304–331.

Fletcher, T. V., & DeLopez, C. (1995). A Mexican perspective on learning disabilities. *Journal of Learning Disabilities, 28*(9), 530–534, 544.

Flurkey, A., & Yu, J. (2003). *In the revolution of reading: Selected writings of Kenneth S. Goodman.* Portsmouth, NH: Heinemann.

Foorman, B., & Torgesen, J. (2001). Critical elements of classroom and small-group instruction promote reading success in all children. *Learning Disabilities Research & Practice, 16*(4), 203–212.

Forness, S., & Knitzer J. (1992). A new proposed definition and terminology to replace "serious emotional disturbance" in Individuals with Disabilities Education Act. *School Psychology Review, 21,* 12–20.

Fortin, J., & Crago, M. (1999). French language acquisition in North America. In O. L. Taylor & L. Leonard (Eds.), *Language acquisition across North America: Cross cultural and cross linguistic perspectives* (pp. 209–244). San Diego: Singular Publishing Co.

Fox, J., & Gable, R. (2004). Functional behavioral assessment. In R. Rutherford, M. Quinn, & S. Mathur (Eds.), *Handbook of research in emotional and behavioral disorders* (pp. 143–162). New York: The Guilford Press.

Francks, C., Fisher, S., Marlow, A., MacPhie, L., Taylor, K., Richardson, A., et al. (2003). Familial and genetic effects on motor coordination, laterality, and reading-related cognition. *American Journal of Psychiatry, 160,* 1970–1977.

Freiberg, H. J. (1993). A school that fosters resiliency in inner-city youth. *Journal of Negro Education, 62,* 364–376.

Friend, M., & Bursuck, W. (1996, 2002). *Including students with special needs: A practical guide for classroom teachers* (3rd ed.). Boston: Allyn & Bacon.

Friend, M., & Bursuck, W. (2006). *Including students with special needs: A practical guide for classroom teachers.* Boston: Allyn & Bacon.

Friend, M., & Cook, L. (2003). *Interactions: Collaborative skills for school professionals* (4th ed.). New York: Longman.

Friend, M., & Cook, L. (2010). *Interactions: Collaboration skills for school professionals.* Columbus, OH: Merrill.

Fuchs, D., & Deshler, D. (2007). What we need to know about responsiveness to intervention (and shouldn't be afraid to ask). *Learning Disabilities Research and Practice, 22*(2), 129–136.

Fuchs, L., & Fuchs, D. (2001). Principles for the prevention and intervention of mathematics difficulties. *Learning Disabilities Research & Practice, 6*(2), 85–95.

Fuchs, L., & Fuchs, D. (2006). Identifying learning disabilities with RTI. *Perspectives on Language and Literacy. The International Dyslexia Association, 32*(1), 39–43.

Fuchs, L., Fuchs, D., & Hollenbeck, K. (2007). Extending responsiveness to intervention to mathematics in first and third grades. *Learning Disabilities Research & Practice, 22*(1), 13–25.

Fuchs, L., & Vaughn, S. (2012). Responsiveness-to-Intervention: A decade later. *Journal of Learning Disabilities, 45*(3), 195–203.

Gage, N., Lewis, T., & Stichter, J. (2012). Functional behavioral assessment-based interventions for students with or at risk for emotional and/or behavioral disorders in school: A hierarchical linear modeling meta-analysis. *Behavioral Disorders, 37*(2), 55–77.

Galaburda, A. (1990). The testosterone hypothesis: Assessment since Geschwind and Behan, 1982. *Annals of Dyslexia, 40,* 18–38.

Galaburda, A., LoTurco, J., Ramus, F., Fitch, R., & Rosen, G. (2006). The response of left temporal cortex to sentences. *Journal of Cognitive Neuoroscience, 14*(4), 550–560.

Gardner, H. (1983). *Frames of mind.* New York: Basic Books.

Gardner, H. (1993). *Multiple intelligences: The theory in practice.* New York: Wiley.

Gardner, H. (1999). *Intelligence reformed: Multiple intelligences for the twenty-first century.* New York: Basic Books.

Gargiulo, R., & Kilgo, J. (2005). *Young children with special needs.* New York: Cengage Learning.

Gargiulo, R. M., & Metcalf, D. J. (2010). *Teaching in today's inclusive classrooms.* New York: Wadsworth/Cengage Learning.

Gately, S., & Gately, F. (2001). Understanding coteaching components. *Teaching Exceptional Children, 33*(4), 40–47.

Geary, D., Hoard, M., Nugent, L., & Byrd-Craven, J. (2007). In D. Berch & M. Mazzocco (Eds.), Strategy use, long-term memory, and working memory capacity. *Why is math so hard for some children? The nature and origins of mathematical learning difficulties and disabilities* (pp. 83–105). Baltimore, MD: Paul H. Brooks.

George, C. (2010). Effects of response cards on performance and participation in social studies for middle school students with emotional and behavioral disorders. *Behavioral Disorders, 35*(3),200–213.

Gerber, M. (2005). Teachers are still the test: Limitations to response to instruction strategies for identifying children with learning disabilities. *Journal of Learning Disabilities, 38*(6), 516–524.

Gerber, P. (1997). Life after school: Challenges in the workplace. In P. Gerber & D. Brown (Eds.), *Learning disabilities and employment* (pp. 3–18). Austin, TX: Pro-Ed.

Gerber, P., & Brown, D. (Eds.). (1997). *Learning disabilities and employment.* Austin, TX: Pro-Ed.

Gerber, P., Price, L. Mulligan, R., & Shessel, I. (2004). Beyond transition: A comparison of the employment and experiences of American and Canadian adults with LD. *Journal of Learning Disabilities, 37,* 283–291.

Gerber, P. J., & Reiff, H. B. (1991). *Speaking for themselves: Ethnographic interviews with adults with learning disabilities.* Ann Arbor: University of Michigan Press.

German, D. (1993). *Word finding interactive programs.* Itasca, IL: Riverside Publishing.

German, D. (2001). *It's on the tip of my tongue.* Chicago: Word Finding Materials.

Gersten, R. (1998). Recent advances in instructional research for students with learning disabilities: An overview. *Learning Disabilities Research & Practice, 13*(3), 162–170.

Gersten, R., Brengelman, S., & Jiménez, R. (1994). Effective instruction for culturally and linguistically diverse students: A reconceptualization. *Focus on Exceptional Children, 27*(1), 1–16.

Gersten, R., Clarke, B., & Mazzocco, M. (2007). Historical and contemporary perspectives on mathematical learning disabilities. In D. Berch & M. Mazzocco (Eds.), *Why is math so hard for some children? The nature and origins of mathematical learning difficulties and disabilities* (pp. 7–28). Baltimore, MD: Paul H. Brooks.

Gersten, R., & Jordan, N. (2005). Early screening and intervention in mathematics difficulties: The need for action: Introduction to the special series. *Journal of Learning Disabilities, 38*(4), 291–292.

Getty, L., & Summy, S. (2006). Language deficits in students with emotional and behavioral disorders: Practical applications for teachers. *Beyond Behavior, 15*(3), 15–22.

Getzel, E., & Thoma, C. (2006). Voice of experience: What college students with learning disabilities and attention deficit/hyperactivity disorders tell us are important: Self-determination skills for success. *Learning Disabilities: A Multidisciplinary Journal, 14*(1), 33–40.

Gilger, J. (2010). Dyslexics are more than people with reading problems. Genes, brains, and treatment predictions for the future. *Perspectives on Language and Literacy. International Dyslexia Association, 36*(1), 33–39.

Gillingham, A., & Stillman, B. (1970). *Remedial training for children with specific difficulty in reading, spelling, and penmanship.* Cambridge, MA: Educators Publishing Service.

Goldey, E. (1998). New angles on motor and sensory coordination in learning disabilities: A report on the 1998 LDA medical symposium. *Learning Disabilities: A Multidisciplinary Journal, 9*(2), 65–72.

Goldstein, S. (2007). Understanding AD/HD and co-occurring conditions. *Attention!, 13*(6), 42–44.

Goldstein, S., & Brooks, R. (2005). *Handbook of resilience in children.* New York: Kluwer Academic/ Plenum Publishers.

Goldstein, S., Naglieri, J., & Ozonoff, S. (2008). *Assessment of autism spectrum disorders.* New York: Guilford Press.

Goodman, K. (1967). Reading: A psycholinguistic guessing game. *Journal of the Reading Specialist, 6,* 126–133.

Gopnick, A., Meltzoff, A., & Kuhl, P. (1999). *The scientist in the crib: Minds, brains, and how children learn.* New York: William Morrow.

Gorman, C. (2003). The new science of dyslexia. *Time, 162*(4), 52–59.

Gorman, J. (1999). Understanding children's hearts and minds: Emotional functioning and learning disabilities. *Teaching Exceptional Children, 31*(3), 72–77.

Government Accountability Office. (2012). *Students with disabilities: Better federal coordination could lessen challenges in the transition from high school.* Washington, DC. GAO report to the Ranking Member, Committee on Education and the Workforce, House of Representatives.

Graham, S., & Harris, K. (2005). Improving the writing performance of young struggling writers. Theoretical and programmatic research from the center to accelerate student learning. *Journal of Special Education, 39,* 19–33.

Graham, S., Harris, K., & Larsen, L. (2001). Prevention and intervention of writing difficulties for students with learning disabilities. *Learning Disabilities Research & Practice, 16*(2), 62–73.

Graham, S., Harris, K., & Mason, L. (2005). Improving the writing performance, knowledge, and self-efficacy of struggling young writers: The effect of self-regulated writing development. *Contemporary Educational Psychology, 30,* 207–241.

Graham, S., Harris, K., McArthur, C., & Fink, B. (2002). Primary grade teachers' theoretical orientations concerning writing instruction. *Contemporary Educational Psychology, 27,* 147–166.

Graves, D. H. (1994). *A fresh look at writing.* Portsmouth, NH: Heinemann.

Greeno, J., Collins, A., & Resnick, L. (1996). Cognition and learning. In B. Berliner & R. Calfee (Eds.), *Handbook of educational psychology* (pp. 15–46). New York: Macmillan.

Gresham, F., Shaughnessy, M., Escajeda, T., & Greathouse, D. (2006). An interview with Frank Gresham. *North American Journal of Psychology, 8*(3), 533–540.

Grigg, W. S., Daane, M., Jin, Y., & Campbell, J. (2003) *The nation's report card: Reading 2002.* Washington, DC: U.S. Department of Education. National Center for Education Statistics, Institute of Education Sciences.

Grossman, H. (1983). *Classification in Mental Retardation.* Washington, DC: American Association on Mental Deficiency.

Groteluschen, A., Borkowski, J., & Hale, C. (1990). Strategy instruction is often insufficient: Addressing the interdependency of executive and attributional processes. In T. Scruggs & B. Wong (Eds.), *Intervention research in learning disabilities* (pp. 81–101). New York: Springer-Verlag.

Guralnick, M. J. (Ed.). (1997). *The effectiveness of early intervention.* Baltimore: Paul H. Brookes.

Guralnick, M. J. (Ed.). (2005). *The developmental systems approach to early intervention.* Baltimore: Paul H. Brookes.

Haager, D., & Vaughn, S. (1997). Assessment of social competence in students with learning disabilities. In J. Lloyd, E. Kame'enui, & D. Chard (Eds.), *Issues in educating students with disabilities* (pp. 129–152). Mahwah, NJ: Erlbaum.

Haber, J. (2000). *The great misdiagnosis: ADHD.* Dallas: Taylor Trade Publishing.

Hagin, R., & Simon, J. (Eds.). (2000). Adults with learning disabilities enter the professions: Issues of diagnosis, education, accommodations, and licensing. *Learning Disabilities: A Multidisciplinary Journal, 10*(2), 35–106.

Hakuta, K. (1990). Language and cognition in bilingual children. In A. M. Padilla, H. H. Fairchild, & C. Valadez (Eds.), *Bilingual education: Issues and strategies* (pp. 47–59). Newbury Park, CA: Sage.

Hall, D., Johnsrude, I., Haggard, M., Palmer, A., Akeroyd, M., & Summerfield, A. (2002). Spectral and temporal processing in human auditory cortex. *Cerebral Cortex, 12*(2), 140–149.

Hall, R., Strangman, N., & Meyer, A. (2011). *Differentiated instruction and implications UDL implementation.*

National Center on Assessable Instructional Materials. NIMAS in www.ed.gov.

Hallahan, D. (2007). Learning disabilities: Whatever happened to intensive instruction? *LDA Newsbriefs, 42,* 1, 3, 5, 24.

Hallahan, D., & Cohen, S. (2008). Many students with learning disabilities are not receiving special education. *Learning Disabilities: A Multidisciplinary Journal, 15*(1), 3–10.

Hallahan, D., Keller, C., Martinez, E., Byrd, E., Gelman, J., & Fan, X. (2007). How variable are interstate prevalence rates of learning disabilities and other special education categories? A longitudinal comparison. *Exceptional Children, 73*(2), 136–146.

Hallgren, B. (1950). Specific dyslexia (congenital word-blindness): A clinical and genetic study. *Acta Psychiatrica Scandinavica Supplementum, 65,* 1–287.

Hambrick, D., & Engle, R. (2003). The role of working memory in problem solving. In J. Davidson & R. Sternberg (Eds.), *The psychology of problem solving* (pp. 176–205). Cambridge, England: Cambridge University Press.

Harris, K., Graham, S., & Mason, L. (2003). Self-regulated strategy development in the classroom: Part of a balanced approach to writing instruction for students with disabilities. *Focus on Exceptional Children, 35*(7), 1–16.

Harris, K., Graham, S., & Mason, L. (2008). *Powerful writing strategies for all students.* Baltimore: Brooks Publishing.

Harris, M., Schumaker, J., & Deshler, D. (2011). The effects of strategic morphological analysis instruction on the vocabulary performance of secondary students with and without disabilities. *Learning Disabilities Quarterly, 34*(1), 17–33.

Hart, E. (2009). Learning disability forum. *LDNews.* Learning Disabilities News and Advocacy. Retrieved 9-16-2009. http://www.learnngdisabilityforum.com.

Harth, R., & Burns, C. (2004). Vocational outcomes for young adults with multiple learning disabilities. *Learning Disabilities: A Multidisciplinary Journal, 13*(2), 49–54.

Hartman, M. (2009). Step by step: creating a community-based transition program for students with intellectual disabilities. *Teaching Exceptional Children, 41*(6), 6–11.

Hasselbring, T., & Glaser, C. (2000). Use of computer technology to help students with special needs. *The Future of Children: Children and Computer Technology, 10*(2), 102–122.

Hauser, P., Zametkin, A. J., Martinez, P., Vitiello, B., Matochik, J. A., Mixson, J. A., et al. (1993). Attention deficit-hyperactivity disorder in people with generalized resistance to thyroid hormone. *New England Journal of Medicine, 328*(14), 997–1001.

Haydon, T., Borders, C., Embury, D., & Clarke, L. (2009). Using effective instructional delivery as a classwide management tool. *Beyond Behavior, 18*(2), 12–17.

Head Start Bureau. (1993). *Head Start performance standards on services for children with disabilities.* Office of Human Development: Administration on Children, Youth, and Families. Washington, DC: U.S. Government Printing Office.

Heckelman, R. (1969). A neurological impress method of reading instruction. *Academic Therapy, 4,* 277–282.

Heiman, T., & Shemesh, D. (2012). Students with LD in higher education: Use and contribution of assisted technology and website courses and their correlation to students' hope and well-being. *Journal of Learning Disabilities, 45*(4), 308–319,

Hennesy, N., Rosenberg, D., & Tramaglini, S. (2003). A high school model for students with dyslexia: Remediation to accommodation. *International Dyslexia Association, 29*(2), 38–40.

Henry, M. (1998). Structured, sequential, multisensory teaching: The Orton legacy. *Annals of Dyslexia, 48,* 3–26.

Henry, M. (2003). *Unlocking literacy: Effective decoding and spelling instruction.* Baltimore, MD: Brookes.

Hernandez, H. (2002). *Multicultural education.* Upper Saddle River, NJ: Prentice-Hall.

Hervey, A., Epstein, J., Curry, J., Tonev, S., Arnold, E., Conners, K., et al. (2006). Reaction time distribution analysis of neuropsychological performance in an ADHD sample. *Child Neuropsychology, 12,* 125–140.

Hiscock, M., & Kinsbourne, M. (1987). Specialization of the cerebral hemispheres: Implications for learning. *Journal of Learning Disabilities, 20*(3), 130–143.

Hodge, J., Riccomini, P., Buford, R., & Herbst, M. (2006). A review of instructional interventions in mathematics for students with emotional and behavioral disorders. *Behavioral Disorders, 31*(3), 297–311.

Hollenbeck, A. (2007). From IDEA to implementation: A discussion of foundational and future response-to-intervention research. *Learning Disabilities Research & Practice, 22*(2), 137–146.

Holloway, J. (2001). Inclusion and students with learning disabilities. *Educational Leadership, 57*(6), 86–118.

Holzer, M., Madaus, J., Bray, M., & Kehle, T. (2009). The test-taking strategy intervention for college students with learning disabilities. *Learning Disabilities Research and Practice, 24*(1), 44–56.

Hook, P., & Jones, S. (2004). The importance of automaticity and fluency for efficient reading comprehension. *Perspectives on Language and Literacy. International Dyslexia Association, 24*(2), 16–21.

Horne, M. (1978). Do learning disabilities specialists know their phonics? *Journal of Learning Disabilities, 11,* 580–582.

Hsu, C. (1988). Correlates of reading success and failure in a logographic writing system. *Thalmus, 6*(1), 33–59.

Hudson, R., & Smith, S. (2001). Effective reading instruction for struggling Spanish-speaking readers: A combination of two literatures. *Intervention in School and Clinic, 37*(1), 36–40.

Hughes, C. (1996). Memory and test-taking strategies. In D. Deshler, E. Ellis, & B. Lenz (Eds.), *Teaching adolescents with learning disabilities: Strategies and methods.* (pp. 209–266). Denver, CO: Love Publishing.

Hund, A., & Landau, S. (2012). You never get a second chance to make a first impression: Social competence of boys with ADHD. In Barkley & Associates. *The ADHD report, 20*(3), 1–4, 16.

Hunt, N., & Marshall, K. (2013). *Exceptional children and youth.* Belmont, CA: Wadsworth/Cengage Learning.

Huttenlocher, P. (1991, September 26). *Neural plasticity.* Paper presented at the Brain Research Foundation Women's Council, University of Chicago, Chicago.

Hutton U., & Towse, J. (2001). Short-term memory and working memory as indices of children's cognitive skills. *Memory, 9,* 382–394.

IDEA–2004. Individuals with Disabilities Education Improvement Act of 2004. Public Law 108–446, 108th Cong., 2nd sess. (December 3, 2004).

Institute of Educational Sciences. *What works clearinghouse.* Retrieved 8-29-2012. http://ies.ed.gov/ncee/wwclinterventionreport.

Interagency Committee on Learning Disabilities (Ed.). (1988). *Learning disabilities: A report to the U.S. Congress.* Washington, DC: U.S. Government Printing Office.

Isaacson, W. (2007). *Einstein: His life and theories.* New York: Simon & Schuster.

Itard, J. (1962). *The wild boy of Aveyron* (G. Humphrey & M. Humphrey, Trans.). New York: Appleton-Century-Crofts. (Original work published 1801).

Jenkins, J., Fuchs, L., Van den Broek, P., Epsin, C., & Deno, S. (2003). Accuracy and fluency in list and context reading of skilled and RD groups: Absolute & relative performance levels. *Learning Disabilities Research & Practice, 18*(4), 237–245.

Jennings, J., Caldwell, J., & Lerner, J. (2010). *Reading problems: Assessment and teaching strategies.* Boston: Allyn & Bacon.

Jennings, T., & Haynes, C. (2006). Essay writing: An attainable goal for students with dyslexia. *Perspectives on Language and Literacy. The International Dyslexia Association, 32*(2), 36–39.

Jiménez, R. (2002). Fostering the literacy development of Latino students. *Focus on Exceptional Children, 34*(6), 1–10.

Johns, B. (1990). *Special education from the parents' point of view.* Springfield, IL: Illinois Alliance for Exceptional Children and Adults.

Johns, B. (1998a). Approaching the millennium for students with disabilities: Implementing IDEA 97 and its accompanying regulations. *Learning Disabilities: A Multidisciplinary Journal, 9*(3), 75–79.

Johns, B. (1998b). What the new Individuals with Disabilities Education Act (IDEA) means for students who exhibit aggressive or violent behavior. *Preventing School Failure, 42*(3), 102–105.

Johns, B. (2003). NCLB and IDEA: Never the twain should meet. *Learning Disabilities: A Multidisciplinary Journal, 12*(3), 89–92.

Johns, B. (2004). Practical behavioral strategies for students with autism. *Journal of Safe Management of Disruptive and Assaultive Behavior, 12*(2), 6–11.

Johns, B. (2005). Congress dramatically changes IDEA. *Learning Disabilities: A Multidisciplinary Journal, 13*(3), 81–86.

Johns, B., & Carr, V. (2007). *Reduction of school violence: Alternatives to suspension* (4th ed.). Horsham, PA: LRP Publications.

Johns, B., & Carr, V. (2009). *Techniques for managing verbally and physically aggressive students* (3rd ed.). Denver: Love Publishing.

Johns, B., & Carr, V. (2012). *Reduction of school violence: Alternatives to suspension.* Palm Beach Gardens, FL: LRP Publications.

Johns, B., & Crowley, E. (2003). *Students with disabilities and general education: A desktop reference for school personnel.* Horsham, PA: LRP Publications.

Johns, B., & Kauffman, J. (2009). Caution: Response to Intervention (RtI). *Learning Disabilities: A Multidisciplinary Journal, 15*(4), 157–161.

Johnson, D. D. (1971). The Dolch list reexamined. *Reading Teacher, 24*(5), 455–456. Reprinted with permission of Dale D. Johnson and the International Reading Association. All rights reserved.

Johnson, E., Kimball, K., & Brown, S. (2001). A statewide review of the use of accommodations in large-scale, high stakes assessments. *Exceptional Children, 67*(2), 261–264.

Johnson, M., Kress, K., & Pikulski, J. (1987). *Informal reading inventories.* Newark, DE: International Reading Association.

Jolivette, K., Peck-Stichter, J., Scott, T., Ridgley, R., & Siblinsky, S. (2002). Naturally occurring opportunities for preschool children with or at-risk for disabilities to make choices. *Education and Treatment of Children, 25,* 396–414.

Jones, E., & Southern, W. (2003). Balancing perspectives on mathematics instruction. *Focus on Exceptional Children, 35*(9), 1–16.

Jordan, N. M., Kaplan, D., Locuniar, M., & Ramineni, C. (2007). Predicting first-grade math achievement from developmental number sense trajectories. *Learning Disabilities Research & Practice, 22*(1), 36–46.

Joseph, L., & Schisler, R. (2009). Should adolescents go *back* to the basics: A review of teaching word reading skills to middle and high school students. *Remedial and Special Education, 30*(3), 131–147.

Kantrowitz, B., & Scelfo. J. (2006, November 27). What happens when they grow up. *Newsweek,* 46–53.

Kantrowitz, B., & Underwood, A. (1999, November 2). Dyslexia and the new science of reading. *Newsweek,* 72–80.

Kauffman, J. (2005). *Special education: What it is and why we need it.* Boston: Pearson.

Kauffman, J. (2007). Labels and the nature of special education: We need to face realities. *Learning Disabilities: A Multidisciplinary Journal, 14*(4), 1–9.

Kauffman, J., & Hallahan, D. (1997). A diversity of restrictive environments: Placement as a problem of social ecology. In J. Lloyd, E. Kame'enui, & D. Chard (Eds.), *Issues in educating students with disabilities* (pp. 325–342). Mahwah, NJ: Erlbaum.

Kauffman, J., & Landrum, T. (2009). *Characteristics of emotional and behavioral disorders of children and youth* (9th ed.) Upper Saddle River, New Jersey: Pearson.

Kauffman, J., & Wiley, A. (2004). How the president's commission on excellence in special education devalues special education. *Learning Disabilities: A Multidisciplinary Journal, 13*(1), 3–6.

Kavale, K. (2005). Identifying specific learning disability: Is responsiveness to intervention the answer? *Journal of Learning Disabilities, 38*(6), 553–562.

Kavale, K., Holdnack, J., & Mostert, M. (2005). Responsiveness to intervention and the identification of specific learning disability. A critique and alternative proposal. *Learning Disability Quarterly, 28*, 2–16.

Keller, H. (1961). *The story of my life*. New York: Dell.

Kennedy, M., & Deshler, D. (2010). Literacy instruction, technology, and students with learning disabilities: Research we have, research we need. *Learning Disability Quarterly, 33*(4), 289–298.

Keogh, B. (2000). Risk, families, and schools. *Focus on Exceptional Children, 33*(4), 1–11.

Kephart, N. (1963). *The brain-injured child in the classroom*. National Society for Crippled Children and Adults: Chicago.

Kephart, N. (1967). Perceptual-motor aspects of learning disabilities. In E. Frierson & W. Barbe (Eds.), *Educating children with learning disabilities* (pp. 405–413). New York: Appleton-Century-Crofts.

Kephart, N. (1971). *The slow learner in the classroom*. Columbus, OH: Charles E. Merrill.

Kibby, M., & Hynd, G. (2001). Neurological basis of learning disabilities. In D. Hallahan & B. Keogh (Eds.), *Research and global perspectives in learning disabilities: Essays in honor of William A. Cruickshank* (pp. 25–42). Mahwah, NJ: Erlbaum.

Kim, B., Rhee, K., Burns, C., & Lerner, J. (2009). Special education in South Korea: Daegu University. *Learning Disabilities: A Multidisciplinary Journal, 15*(4), 179–183,

Kirk, S. (1987). The learning-disabled preschool child. *Teaching Exceptional Children, 19*(2), 78–80.

Kirk, S., & Chalfant, J. (1984). *Academic and developmental learning disabilities*. Denver: Love Publishing.

Kirk, S., Gallagher, J., Coleman, M., & Anastasiow, N. (2009). *Educating exceptional children*. Boston: Houghton-Mifflin.

Kirk, S., Kirk, W., & Minskoff, E. (1985). *Phonic Remedial Reading Drills*. Novato, CA: Academic Therapy Publications.

Klingner, J., Artiles, A., & Barletta, L. (2006). English language learners who struggle with reading: Language acquisition or LD? *Journal of Learning Disabilities, 39*(2), 108–128.

Kluwe, R. (1987). Executive decisions and regulation of problem solving behavior. In F. Weinert & R. Kluwe (Eds.), *Metacognition, motivation and understanding* (pp. 31–64). Hillsdale, NJ: Erlbaum.

Kohn, A. (1995). *Punished by rewards: The trouble with gold stars, incentive plans, As, praise, and other bribes*. Boston: Houghton Mifflin.

Kolb, B., & Wishaw, I. (2009). *Fundamentals of human neuropsychology*. New York: Worth.

Korkunov, V., Nigayev, A., Reynolds, L., & Lerner, J. (1998). Special education in Russia: History, reality, and prospects. *Journal of Learning Disabilities, 31*(2), 186–192.

Kotulak, R. (2004, May 2). Scientists offer hope for poor readers. *Chicago Tribune*, Section 1, pp. 1, 10.

Kranowitz, C. (2006). *The out-of-sync child: Recognizing and coping with sensory integration dysfunction*. London: The Penguin Group.

Kratochvil, C., Heiligenstein, J., Dittmann, R., Spencer, T., Biederman, J., Wernicke, J., et al. (2002). Atomoxetine and methyiphenidate treatment in children with ADHD: A prospective, randomized, open-label trial. *Journal of the American Academy of Child and Adolescent Psychiatry, 41*, 1–9.

Kravetz, M., & Wax, I. (2003). *The K & W guide to colleges for students with learning disabilities or attention deficit disorder*. New York: Princeton Review.

Krezmien, M., Leone, P., & Achilles, G. (2006). Suspension, race, and disability: Analysis of statewide practices and reporting. *Journal of Emotional and Behavioral Disorders, 14*(4), 217–226.

Kroesbergen, E., & Van Luit, J. (2003). Mathematics interventions for children with special educational needs. *Remedial and Special Education, 24*, 97–114.

Kuder, S. (2003). *Teaching students with language and communication disorders*. Boston: Allyn & Bacon.

Kunsch, C., Jitendra, A., & Sood, S. (2007). The effects of peer-mediated instruction in mathematics for students with learning problems: A research synthesis. *Learning Disabilities Research & Practice, 22*(1), 1–12.

Lahey, B., Pelham, W., Loney, J., Lee, S., & Willcutt, E. (2005). Instability of the DSM-IV subtypes of ADHD from preschool through elementary school. *Archives of General Psychiatry, 62*, 896–902.

Lake, S., & Norlin, J. (2004). *You be the judge: Test your section 504 IQ*. Horsham: PA: LRP Publications.

Lake, S., & Pitasky, V. (2000). *The special educator 2000 desk book*. Horsham, PA: LRP Publications.

Lambert, M., Cartledge, G., Heward, W., & Lo, Y. (2006). Effects of response cards on disruptive behavior and academic responding during math lessons by fourth-grade urban students. *Journal of Positive Behavior Interventions, 8*(2), 88–99.

Lambie, R. (2006). At-risk students and environmental factors. *Focus on Exceptional Children, 38*(4), 1–16.

Lane, K. L., & Beebe-Frankenberger, M. (2004). *School-based interventions: The tools you need to succeed*. Boston: Pearson Education, Inc.

Lane, K. L., Weisenbach, J., Little, M., Phillips, A., & Wehby, J. (2006). Illustrations of function-based interventions implemented by general education teachers: Building capacity at the school site. *Education and treatment of children, 29*(4), 549–571.

Langford, K., Slade, K., & Barnett, A. (1974). An explanation of impress techniques in remedial reading. *Academic Therapy, 9,* 309–319.

Latham, P., & Latham, P. (1997). Legal rights of adults with learning disabilities in employment. In P. Gerber & D. Brown (Eds.), *Learning disabilities and employment* (pp. 39–58). Austin, TX: Pro-Ed.

Lavoie, R. (2005). *It's so much work to be your friend: Helping the child with learning disabilities find social success.* New York: A Touchstone Book, Simon & Schuster.

Lavoie, R. (2006). Reading, writing, 'rithmetic: Teaching the fourth "R" relationships. *Attention!, 13*(2), 23–28.

Lavoie, R. (2007). *The Motivaton Breakthrough.* New York: Simon & Schuster

Lavoie, R. D. (1995). Life on the waterbed: Mainstreaming on the homefront. *Attention!, 2*(1), 25–29.

Lazar, I., & Darlington, R. (Eds.). (1982). Lasting effects of early education: A report from the Consortium for Longitudinal Studies. *Monographs of the Society for Research in Child Development*, 27(2–3, Serial No. 195) (Summary Report, DHEW Publication No. OHDS 80–30/79).

Learning Disabilities Association of America. (1995). *Secondary education and beyond: Providing opportunities for students with learning disabilities.* Pittsburgh: Author.

Learning Disabilities Association of America. (2006a). *LDA position statement on response to intervention.* http://www.ldaamerica.org/about/position/rti.asp.

Learning Disabilities Association of America. (2006b). What is response to intervention of RTI? *LDA Newsbriefs, 41*(1), 10. http://www.ldaamerica.org.

Learning Disabilities Association of America. (2009). http://www.ldaamerica.org

Lee, C., & Jackson, R. (1992), *Faking it: A look into the mind of a creative learner.* Portsmouth, NJ: Heinemann

Lenhart, A., & Madden, M. (2008). *Social networking websites and teens: An overview.* Washington, DC: Pew Internet & American Life Project.

Lenz, B., & Deshler, D. (2001). *Teaching content to all: Evidenced-based inclusive practice in middle and secondary schools.* Boston: Pearson.

Lenz, B. K., & Deshler, D. D. with (Kissam, B.). (2003). *Teaching content to all: Evidence-based inclusive practice in middle and secondary schools.* Boston: Pearson.

Lenz, B. K., Ellis, E. S., & Scanlon, D. (1996). *Teaching learning strategies to adolescents and adults with learning disabilities.* Austin, TX: Pro-Ed.

Lerner, J. (1990). Phonological awareness: A critical element in learning to read. *Learning Disabilities: A Multidisciplinary Journal, 1,* 50–54.

Lerner, J., & Johns. B. (2011). *Learning disabilities and related mild disabilities.* Minneapolis: Cengage Learning. http://www.ldonline.org/njcld.

Lerner, J., Lowenthal, B., & Egan, R. (2003). *Preschool children with special needs: Children at-risk and children with disabilities.* Boston: Allyn & Bacon.

Lerner, J., Lowenthal, B., & Lerner, S. (1995). *Attention deficit disorders: Assessment and teaching.* Pacific Grove, CA: Brooks/Cole.

Lerner, J. W., & Chen, A. (1992). The cross-cultural nature of learning disabilities: A profile in perseverance. *Learning Disabilities Research and Practice, 8,* 147–149.

Levine, M. (1988). Learning disability: What is it? *ACLD Newsbriefs, 173,* 1–2.

Levine, M. (1994). *Educational care: A system for understanding and helping children with learning problems at home and in school.* Cambridge, MA: Educators Publishing Services.

Levine, M. (2002). *A mind at a time.* New York: Simon & Schuster.

Lewin, T. (2012, March 6). Black students face more discipline, data suggests. *New York Times.*

Lewis, M., Church, R., & Tsantis, L. (2006). Technology and young children. *Learning Disabilities: A Multidisciplinary Journal, 14*(2), 115–122.

Lewis, R. (1998). Assistive technology and learning disabilities: Today's realities and tomorrow's promises. *Journal of Learning Disabilities, 31*(1), 16–26.

Lewis, T., & Sugai, G. (1999). Effective behavior support: A systems approach to proactive schoolwide management. *Focus on Exceptional Children, 31*(6), 1–24.

Liaupsin, C., Umbreit, J., Ferro, J., Urso, A., & Upreti, G. (2006). Improving academic engagement through systematic, function-based interventions. *Education and Treatment of Children, 29*(4), 573–591.

Liberman, I., & Liberman, A. (1990). Whole language vs. code emphasis: Underlying assumptions and their implications for reading instruction. *Annals of Dyslexia, 40,* 51–78.

Lindquist, M. (1987). Strategic teaching in mathematics. In B. F. Jones et al. (Eds.), *Strategic teaching and learning: Cognitive instruction in the content areas* (pp. 11–134). Washington, DC: Association for Supervision and Curriculum Development.

Linstrom, J. (2007). Determining appropriate accommodations for postsecondary students with reading and written expression disorders. *Learning Disabilities Research and Practice, 22*(4), 229–236.

Little, M. (2000). Reframing challenging behaviors by meeting basic needs. *Reaching Today's Youth: The Community Circle of Caring Journal, 4*(2), 21–26.

Long, N., & Long, J. (2002). *Managing passive-aggressive behavior of children and youth at school and home.* Austin, TX: Pro-Ed.

Losen, D., & Skiba, R. (2012). *Suspended education: Urban middle schools in crisis.* Southern Poverty Law Center.

Lovett, B., & Lewandowski, L. (2005). Gifted students with learning disabilities: Who are they? *Journal of Learning Disabilities, 39*(6), 515–527.

Lundberg, I. (2002). Second language learning and reading with the additional load of dyslexia. *Annals of Dyslexia, 52,* 165–188.

Lundberg, I., & Höien, T. (2001). Learning disabilities in Scandinavia. In D. Hallahan & B. Keogh (Eds.),

Research and global perspectives in learning disabilities: Essays in honor of William M. Cruickshank (pp. 291–308). Mahwah, NJ: Erlbaum.

Lyon, G. R. (1996). Learning disabilities. *The Future of Children, 6*(1), 54–76.

Lyon, G. R. (1998). Why reading is not a natural process. *Educational Leadership, 55*(6), 14–18.

Lyon, G. R. (2003). Reading disabilities: Why do some children have difficulty learning to read? What can be done about it? *Perspectives on Language and Literacy. International Dyslexia Association, 29*(2), 17–19.

Lyon, G. R., Alexander, D., & Yaffee, S. (1997). Programs, promise, and research in learning disabilities. *Learning Disabilities: A Multidisciplinary Journal, 8,* 1–6.

Lyon, G. R., Fletcher, J. M., Shaywitz, S. E., Shaywitz, B. A., Torgesen, J. K., Wood, F. B., et al. (2001). Rethinking learning disabilities. In C. E. Finn, Jr., A. J. Rotherham, & C. R. Hokanson, Jr. (Eds.), *Rethinking special education for a new century* (pp. 259–288). Washington, DC: Thomas B. Fordham Foundation. www.edexcellence. net/library/special_ed/index.html.

Lyon, G. R., & Krasnegor, N. (Eds.). (1996). *Attention, memory, and executive function.* Baltimore: Paul H. Brookes.

Lyon, G. R., & Moats, L. C. (1997). Critical conceptual and methodological considerations in reading intervention research. *Journal of Learning Disabilities, 30*(6), 578–588.

Lyon, G. R., Shaywitz, S., & Shaywitz, B. (2003). Defining dyslexia, comorbidity, teachers' knowledge of language and reading. *Annals of Dyslexia, 53,* 1–14.

Lytle, R., & Todd, T. (2009), Stress and the student with autism and enhanced learning. *Teaching Exceptional Children, 41*(4), 36–42.

Lyytinen, P., Ekland, K., & Lyytinen, H. (2005). Language development and literacy skills in late-talking toddlers with and without familiar risk for dyslexia. *Annals of Dyslexia, 55*(2), 151–165.

MacArthur, C. (2009). Assistive technology for struggling writers. *Perspectives on Language and Literacy. International Dyslexia Association, 35*(3) 31–33.

Maccini, P., & Gagnon, J. (2006). Mathematics instructional practices and assessment accommodations by secondary special and general educators. *Exceptional Children, 72*(2), 217–234.

Maccini, P., Gagnon, J., & Hughes, C. (2002). Technology-based practices for secondary students with learning disabilities. *Learning Disabilities Quarterly, 25,* 247–261.

Maccini, P., & Hughes, C. (2000). The effects of an instructional strategy incorporating concrete representation on the introductory algebra performance of secondary students with learning disabilities. *Learning Disabilities Research and Practice, 15,* 10–21.

Maccini, P., Mulcahy, C., & Wilson, M. (2007). A follow-up of mathematics interventions for secondary students with learning disabilities. *Learning Disabilities Research and Practice, 2*(1), 58–74.

Maccini, P., Strickland, T., Gagnon, J., & Malmgren, K. (2008). Assessing the general education math curriculum for secondary students with high-incidence disabilities. *Focus on Exceptional Children, 40*(8), 1–32.

Maccini, P., & Ruhl, K. (2000). Effects of a graduated instructional sequence on the alegebraic subntraction of integers by secondry students with learning disabilites. *Education and Treatment of Chldren, 23,* 465–489.

Mainzer, R., Deshler, D., Coleman, M., Kozleski, M., & Rodriguez-Walling, E. (2003). To ensure the learning of every child with a disability. *Focus on Exceptional Children, 35*(5), 1–12.

Malmgren, K., & Trezek, B. (2009). Literacy instruction for secondary students with disabilities. *Focus on Exceptional Children, 41*(6), 1–12.

Maloney, M., & Pitasky, V. (1995). *The special educator 1995 desk book.* Horsham: PA: LRP Publications.

Mann, V., & Foy, J. (2003). Phonological awareness, speech development, and letter knowledge in preschool children. *Annals of Dyslexia, 53,* 149–173.

Marchand-Marella, N. E., Slocum, T. A., & Marcella, R. C. (Eds.). (2004). *Introduction to direct instruction.* Boston: Pearson.

Martin, B. (1992). *Brown bear, brown bear, what do you see?* New York: Holt, Rinehart, & Winston.

Martin, G., & Pear, J. (2003). *Behavior modification: What it is and how to do it.* Upper Saddle River, NJ: Prentice Hall.

Martin, M. (2004). *Helping children with nonverbal learning disabilities flourish: A guide for parents and professionals.* London: Jessica Kingley Publishers.

Mason, L. (2009). Effective instruction for written expression. *Perspectives on language and literacy. International Dyslexia Association, 35*(3), 21–24.

Mastropieri, M. (1987). Statistical and psychometric issues surrounding severe discrepancy: A discussion. *Learning Disabilities Research, 3*(1), 29–31.

Mastropieri, M., & Scruggs, T. (1998). Constructing more meaningful relationships in the classroom: Mnemonic research into practice. *Learning Disabilities Research & Practice, 13*(3), 138–145.

Mastropieri, M., & Scruggs, T. (2005). Feasibility and consequences of response to intervention: Examination of the issues and scientific evidence as a model for the identification of individuals with learning disabilities. *Learning Disabilities Research and Practice, 15*(6), 525–531.

Mastropieri, M., & Scruggs, T. (2010). *Inclusive Classroom: The Strategies of Effective Instruction.* Columbus, OH: Merrill.

Mather, N., & Goldstein, S. (2008). *Learning disabilities and challenging behaviors: A guide to intervention and classroom management.* Baltimore: Brookes Publishing.

Mayers, S., Calhoun, S., & Crowell, E. (2000). Learning disabilities and ADHD: Overlapping spectrum disorders. *Journal of Learning Disabilities, 33,* 417–424.

Mayes, S., Calhoun, S.L., Mayes, R. D., & Molitoris, S. (2012). Autism and ADHD: Overlapping and discriminating symptoms. *Research in Autism Spectrum Disorders, 6,* 277–285.

Mazzoco, M. (2007). Defining and differentiating mathematical learning disabilities and difficulties. In D. Berch & M. Mazzocco (Eds.), *Why is math so hard for some children? The nature and origins of mathematical learning difficulties and disabilities* (pp. 29–48). Baltimore, MD: Paul H. Brooks

Mazzocco, M., & Meyers, G. (2003). Complexities in identifying and defining mathematics learning disability in the primary school-age years. *Annals of Dyslexia, 53,* 218–253.

Mazzotti, V., Rowe, D., Kelley, K., Test, D., Fowler, C., Kohler, P., et al. (2009). Linking transition assessment and postsecondary goals: Key elements in the secondary transition planning process. *Teaching Exceptional Children, 42*(2), 44–51.

McCardle, P. (2005). Bilingual literacy research. The DELSS Research Network and beyond. *International Dyslexia Association Perspectives, 31*(2), 1–5.

McGough, R. (2004, September 2). Dyslexia manifests differently for Chinese readers. *Wall Street Journal,* Section D4, p. 3.

McGrady, H., Lerner, J., & Boscardin, M. (2001). The educational lives of students with learning disabilities. In P. Rodis, A. Garrod, & M. L. Boscardin (Eds.), *Learning disabilities and life stories* (pp. 177–193). Boston: Allyn & Bacon.

McIntosh, K., Flannery, K., Sugai, G., Braun, D., & Cochrane, K. (2008). Relationship between academics and problem behavior with transition from middle school to high school. *Journal of Positive Behavioral Interventions. 10*(4), 243–255.

McIntyre, C., & Pickering, J. (1995). *Clinical studies of multisensory structured language education for students with dyslexia and related disorders.* Salem, OR: International Multisensory Structured Language Education Council.

McKee, P., Harrison, M., McCowen, A., & Lehr, E. (1962, 1990). *High Roads.* Boston: Houghton Mifflin Co.

McKenna, M. (2004). Teaching vocabulary to struggling older readers. *Perspectives on Language and Literacy. International Dyslexia Association, 30*(1), 13–16.

McLeskey, J., Hoppery, D., Williamson, P., & Rentz, T. (2004). Is inclusion an allusion? An examination of the national and state trends toward the education of students with learning disabilities in general education classrooms. *Learning Disabilities Research and Practice, 19*(2), 109–115.

McMaster, K., Funchs, D., Fuchs, L., & Compton, D. (2005). Responding to nonresponders: An experimental field trial of identification and intervention methods. *Exceptional Children, 72*(4), 445–463.

Meece, J. L. (2002). *Child and adolescent development for educators* (2nd ed.). New York: McGraw-Hill.

Meichenbaum, D. (1977). *Cognitive behavior modification.* New York: Plenum.

Meltzer, L., & Montague, M. (2001). Strategic learning in students with learning disabilities: What have we learned? In D. Hallahan & B. Keogh (Eds.), *Research and global perspectives in learning disabilities: Essays in honor of William M. Cruickshank* (pp. 111–130). Mahwah, NJ: Lawrence Erlbaum.

Mercer, C., & Miller, S. (1992). Teching students with learning problems in math to acquire, understand, and apply basic math facts. *Remedial and Special Education, 13*(3), 78–82.

Mercer, C., & Pullen, P. (2009). *Students with learning disabilities. 7th edition.* Pearson.

Merzenich, M. M., Jenkins, W. M., & Tallal, P. (1996). Temporal processing deficits of language-learning impaired children ameliorated by training. *Science, 271*(5245), 77–80.

Meyer, M. (2002). Repeated reading: An old standard is revisited and renovated. *Perspectives on Language and Literacy. International Dyslexia Association, 28*(1), 15–18.

Mihalas, S., Morse, W., Allsopp, D., & McHatton, P. (2009). Cultivating caring relationships between teachers and secondary students with emotional and behavioral disorders: Implications for research and practice. *Remedial and Special Education, 30*(2), 108–125.

Miller, J., Heilmann, J., & Nockerts, A. (2006). Oral language and reading in bilingual children. *Learning Disabilities Research and Practice, 21*(1), 30–43.

Miller, S., & Hudson, P. (2007). Using evidence-based practices to build mathematics competence related to conceptual, procedural, and declarative knowledge. *Learning Disabilities Research & Practice, 22*(1), 47–57.

Minskoff, E. (1998). Sam Kirk: The man who made special education special. *Learning Disabilities Research and Practice, 13*(1), 15–21.

Minskoff, E. (2005). *Teaching reading to struggling learners.* Baltimore, MD: Brookes.

Minskoff, E., & Allsopp, D. (2003). *Academic success strategies for adolescents with learning disabilities and ADHD.* Baltimore: Brookes Publishing.

M.L. by C.D. and S.L. v. Federal Way Sch. Dist., 42 IDELR 57 (9th Circuit, 2004).

Moats, L. (2000). *Speech to print: Language essentials for teachers.* Baltimore, MD: Brookes.

Molfese, D., & Molfese, V. (Eds). (2002). *Developmental variations in learning: Applications to social, executive function, language, and reading skills.* Mahwah, NJ: Lawrence Erlbaum.

Monroe, M. (1932). *Children who cannot read: The analysis of reading disabilities and the use of diagnostic tests in instruction of retarded readers.* Chicago: University of Chicago Press.

Montes, S. (2007, April 23). Education "Peace Corps" expanding area presence. *Washington Post,* B–2.

Montessori, M. (1912). *The Montessori method* (A. E. George, Trans.). New York: Frederick Stokes.

Morgan, P., Sideridis, G., & Hua, Y. (2012). Initial and over-time effects of fluency interventions for students with or at risk for disabilities. *Journal of Special Education, 46*(2), 94–116.

Morris, B., Munoz, L., & Neering, P (2002, May 13). In Fortune R. Kirkland (Ed.), *Overcoming Dyslexia.* Retrieved from http://money.cnn.com/magazines/fortune/fortune_archive/2002/5/13/322876/index.htm. Pages 1–5. Retrieved 6-22-2013.

Murawski, W., & Dieker, L. (2004). Tips and strategies for coteaching at the secondary level. *Teaching Exceptional Children, 36*(5), 52–58.

Murawski, W., & Swanson, H. (2002). A meta-analysis of coteaching research: Where are the data? *Remedial and Special Education, 22,* 258–267.

Musgrove, M. (2011, January 21). *Memorandum to State Directors of Special Education (OSEP 11-07).* U.S. Department of Education Office of Special Education and Rehabilitative Services.

Myklebust, H., & Boshes, B. (1969). *Minimal brain damage in children* (final report, U.S. Public Health Service Contract 108–65–142). Evanston, IL: Northwestern University Publications.

Myles, B., Adreon, D., & Gitlitz, D. (2006). *Simple strategies that work.* Shawnee Mission, KS: Autism Asperger Publishing Co.

Myles, B. S., Cook, K. T., Miller, N. E., Rinner, L., & Robbins, L. A. (2000). *Asperger's syndrome and sensory issues: Practical solutions for making sense of the world.* Shawnee Mission, KS: American Academy of Professional Coders.

Myles, B. S., Hagiwara, T., Dunn, W., Rinner, L., Reese, M., Huggins, A., & Becker, S. (2004). Sensory issues in children with Asperger syndrome and autism. *Education and Training in Developmental Disabilities, 39*(4), 283–290.

National Center for Learning Disabilities. (2006). *Dyscalculia: A quick look.* http://www.ncld.org.

National Center for Learning Disabilities. (2009). *2009 the state of learning disabilities.* New York: NCLD.

National Council of Teachers of Mathematics (NCTM). (2000). *Principles and standards for school mathematics.* Reston, VA: Author.

National Council of Teachers of Mathematics (NCTM). (2006). *Curriculum focal points; prekindergarten to grade 8.* Reston, VA: Author.

National Endowment for the Arts. (2004). *Reading at risk: A survey of literacy reading in America.* Washington, DC: Author.

National Governors Association Center for Best Practices, Council of Chief State School Officers. (2010). *Common Core State Standard, 2010.*

National Information Center for Children and Youth (NICHCY). (1999). *P.O. Box 492.* Washington, DC: Author.

National Institute for Child Health and Human Development. (1999). *Keys to successful learning* (pp. 1–3). Washington, DC: Author.

National Joint Committee and Learning Disabilities (NJCLD). (2008). *Executive summary of adolescent literacy and older students with learning disabilities.*

National Reading Panel. (2000). *Teaching children to read: An evidence-based assessment of the scientific research literature on reading and implications for reading instruction.* Washington, DC: National Institute of Child Health and Human Development. http://www.nichd.nih.gov/publications/nrp/smallbook.htm.

National Research Council. (1998). *Preventing reading difficulties in young children.* Washington, DC: National Academy of Sciences.

Nelson, J., Alber, S., & Gordy, A. (2004). Effects of systematic error correction and repeated readings on the reading accuracy and proficiency of second graders with disabilities. *Education and Treatment of Children, 27,* 186–198.

Nelson, J., Benner, G., & Mooney, P. (2008). *Instructional practices for students with behavioral disorders: Strategies for reading, writing, and math.* New York: Guilford Press.

Newman, L., Wagner, M., Huang, T., Shaver, D., Knokey, A.-M., Yu, J., et al. (2011). *Secondary school programs and performance of students with disabilities: A special topic report of findings from the National Longitudinal Transition Study-2 (NLTS2) (NCSER 2012-3000).* U.S. Department of Education. Washington, DC: National Center for Special Education Research. Menlo Park, CA: SRI International. www.nlts2.org/reports/2011_11/nlts2_report_2011_11_complete.pdf.

Nichell, G., Pederson, K., & Rossow, C. (2003). The birthdate effect: An extension of the mere ownship effect. *Psychological Reports, 92,* 1 161–163.

Norlin, J. (2005). *The special education 2005 desk book.* Horsham, PA: LRP Publications.

Oakland, T., Black, J., Stanford, G., Nussbaum, N., & Balise, R. (1998). An evaluation of the dyslexia training program: A multisensory method for promoting reading in students with reading disabilities. *Journal of Learning Disabilities, 31,* 14–147.

Oas, B. K., Schumaker, J. B., & Deshler, D. D. (1995). In P. Adelman (Ed.), Learning strategies: Tools for learning to learn in middle and high schools. In *Secondary education and beyond: Providing opportunities for students with learning disabilities* (pp. 90–100). Pittsburgh: Learning Disabilities Association of America.

Obiakor, F., & Wilder, L. (2010) Transitioning culturally and linguistically diverse learners with emotional or behavioral disorders. In D. Cheney (Ed.), *Transition of secondary students with emotional or behavioral disorders: current approaches for positive outcomes* (pp. 23–49). Champaign, IL: Research Press.

Obrzut, J., & Boliek, C. (1991). Neuropsychological assessment of childhood learning disabilities. In H. Swanson (Ed.), *Handbook on the assessment of learning disabilities* (pp. 121–145). Austin, TX: Pro-Ed.

O'Conner, R. (2007). *Division for learning disabilities. thinking about response to intervention and learning disabilities: A teachers guide.* Arlington, VA: Author.

Office of the Undersecretary of Education. (2002). *No child left behind: A desktop reference* (p. 9). Washington, DC: U.S. Department of Education.

O'Neill, R., Horner, R., Albin, R., Storey, K., Sprague, J., & Newton, J. (1997). *Functional analysis of problem behavior: A practical assessment guide* (2nd ed.). Pacific Grove, CA: Brooks/Cole.

Opp, G. (2001). Learning disabilities in Germany: A retrospective analysis, current status, and future trends. In D. Hallahan & B. Keogh (Eds.), *Research and global per spectives in learning disabilities: Essays in honor of William M. Cruickshank* (pp. 217–238). Mahwah, NJ: Erlbaum.

Orkwis, R. (2003). *Universally designed instruction* (Report No. EC309565). Arlington, VA: ERIC Clearinghouse on Disabilities and Gifted Education. (ERIC Document Reproduction Service No. E641).

Orlich, D., Harder, R., Callahan, R., Trevisan, M., Brown, A., & Miller, D. (2013). *Teaching strategies: A guide to effective instruction.* Belmont, CA: Wadsworth/Cengage Learning.

Ortiz, A. (1997). Learning disabilities occurring concomitantly with linguistic differences. *Journal of Learning Disabilities, 30*(3), 321–332.

Orton, J. (1976). *A guide to teaching phonics.* Cambridge, MA: Educators Publishing Service.

Orton, S. (1937). *Reading, writing and speech problems in children.* New York: Norton.

P.L. 94-142. (1975). All Handicapped Children's Act. Washington, DC: U.S. Department of Education.

P.L. 108-446. (2004). Individuals With Disabilities Education Improvement Act of 2004.

Palinscar, A., Brown, A., & Campione, J. (1991). Dynamic assessment. In H. L. Swanson (Ed.), *Handbook on the assessment of learning disabilities* (pp. 75–94). Austin, TX: Pro-Ed.

Patten, B. (1973). Visually mediated thinking: A report of the case of Albert Einstein. *Journal of Learning Disabilities, 6,* 415–420.

Pennington, B. (1995). Genetics of learning disabilities. *Journal of Child Neurology, 10*(Suppl. 1), S69–S77.

Piaget, J. (1952). *The origins of intelligence in children* (M. Cook, Trans.). New York: International University Press. (Original work published in 1936).

Piaget, J. (1970). *The science of education and psychology of the child.* New York: Grossman.

Polloway, E., Patton, J., & Serna, L. (2001). *Strategies for teaching learners with special needs.* Columbus, OH: Merrill/Prentice-Hall.

Powers, C. A. (2000). The pharmacology of drugs used for the treatment of attention deficit hyperactivity disorder. In P. Accardo, T. Blondis, B. Whitman, & M. Stein (Eds.), *Attention deficits and hyperactivity in children and adults: Diagnosis, treatment, management* (pp. 477–512). New York: Marcel Dekker.

Price, L. (1997). Psychosocial issues of workplace adjustment. In P. Gerber & D. Brown (Eds.), *Learning disabilities and employment* (pp. 275–306). Austin, TX: Pro-Ed.

Pugh, K. (2010). New directions in the cognitive neuroscience of reading development and disability. *Perspectives on Language and Literacy. International Dyslexia Association, 36*(1), 22–25.

Pugh, K., Sandak, R., Frost, S., Moore, D., & Mencl, W. (2005). Examining reading development and reading disability in English language learners: Potential contributions from functional neuroimaging. *Learning Disabilities Research & Practice, 20*(1), 24–30.

Quinn, M., Rutherford, M., & Leone, P. (2001). The relationship between *learning disability* and *juvenile delinquency*: Current state of knowledge. *Journal of Special Education, 7,* 18–26.

Rapkin, I. (1995). Physician's testing of children with developmental disabilities. *Journal of Child Neurology, 10* (Suppl. 1), S11–S15.

Rappley, M. (2004). Attention deficit–hyperactivity disorder. *New England Journal of Medicine, 352,* 165–173.

Raskind, M., & Higgins, E. (1998a). Assistive technology for postsecondary students with learning disabilities: An overview. *Journal of Learning Disabilities, 30*(1), 27–40.

Raskind, M., & Higgins, E. (1998b). Technology and learning disabilities: What do we know and where should we go? *Perspectives on Language and Literacy. The International Dyslexia Association, 24*(2), 1.

Raymond, E. (2004). *Learners with mild disabilities: A characteristics approach.* Boston: Allyn & Bacon.

Regulations for the Individuals with Disabilities Education Improvement Act of 2004. (2006). U.S. Department of Education, Federal Register, August 14, 2006.

Regulations for the Individuals with Disabilities Education Improvement Act. (2006). 34 CFR 300.115.

Regulations for Title I—Improving the Academic Achievement of the Disadvantaged; Individuals with Disabilities Education Act (IDEA); Final Rule. (2007). 34 CFR Parts 200 and 300.

Renaissance Learning. (2009). *Making RTI Work: A practical guide to using data for successful "Response to Intervention" program.* Wisconsin Rapids, WI: Renaissance.

Robinson, T. (2007). Cognitive behavioral interventions: Strategies to help students make wide behavioral choices. *Beyond Behavior, 17*(1), 7–13.

Rockefeller, N. (1976, October 16). *TV Guide,* pp. 12–14.

Roe, B., Stoodt-Hill, B., & Burns, P. (2010). Secondary School Literacy Instruction. Belmont, California: Wadsworth.

Roman, M. A. (1998). The syndrome of nonverbal learning disabilities: Clinical description and applied aspects. *Current Issues in Education, 1*(1), 1–21.

Rosen, G. (2010). Dyslexia, genes, and the brain: 10 Years and beyond. *Perspectives on Language and Literacy. International Dyslexia Association, 36*(1), 18–21.

Rosenshine, B., & Stevens, R. (1986). Teaching functions. In M. Wittock (Ed.), *Handbook of research on teaching* (3rd ed., pp. 376–391). New York: Macmillan.

Rosenthal, D. (2003). Atomoxetine (Strattera) in the treatment of ADHD. *The ADHD Challenge, XVII*(2), 1–3.

Rothstein, L. (1998). Americans with Disabilities Act, Section 504, and adults with learning disabilities in adult education and transition to employment. In S. Vogel & S. Reder (Eds.), *Learning disabilities, literacy, and adult education* (pp. 29–43). Baltimore: Paul H. Brookes.

Rourke, B. P. (1995). *Syndrome of nonverbal learning disabilities: Neurodevelopmental manifestations*. New York: Guilford Press.

Rutter, M. (2003). Commentary; causal processes leading to anti-social behavior. *Developmental Psychology, 39,* 372–378.

Sabbatino, E. (2004). Students with learning disabilities construct meaning through graphic organizers: Strategies for achievement in inclusive classrooms. *Learning Disabilities: A Multidisciplinary Journal, 13*(2), 69–74.

Sacramento City Unified Sch. Dist. Bd. of Educ. v. Rachel H., 20 IDELR 182 (9th Cir. 1994).

Safran, J. (2002). Supporting students with Asperger's syndrome in general education. *Teaching Exceptional Children, 34*(5), 60–66.

Salend, S. (2008). *Creating inclusive classrooms*. Upper Saddle River, NJ: Pearson Education.

Salvia, J., Ysseldyke, J., & Bolt, S. (2013). *Assessment in special and inclusive education*. Belmont, CA: Wadsworth/Cengage Learning.

Samson, J., & Lesaux, N., (2009). Language-minority learners in special education: Rates and predictors of identification for services. *Journal of Learning Disabilities, 42*(2), 148–162.

Scheffler, R., Brown, T., Fulton, B., Hinshaw, S., Levine, P., & Stone, S. (2009). Positive association between attention-deficit/hyperactivity disorder medication use and academic achievement during elementary school. *Pediatrics, 123*(5), 1273–1279.

Scherer, M. (2006). Celebrate strengths, nurture affinities: A conversation with Mel Levine. *Educational Leadership, 64*(1), 8–15.

Schultz, E. (2009). SLD Evaluation: Linking cognitive assessment data to learning disabilities. *LDA Newsbriefs, 44*(3), 1, 8–9.

Schumaker, J., & Deshler, D. (1995, March–April). Social skills and learning disabilities. *Learning Disabilities Association of America Newsbriefs*. Retrieved from LD OnLine, 9-1-2009. http://www.ldonline.org/article/Social_Skills_and_Learning_Disabilities.

Schumaker, J., & Deshler, D. (2009). Adolescents with learning disabilities as writers: Are we selling them short? *Learning Disabilities Research and Practice, 24*(2), 81–92.

Schwarz, P. (2006). *From disability to possibility: The power of inclusive classrooms*. Portsmouth, NH: Heinemann.

Schweinhart, L. J., Barnes, H. V., & Weikart, D. B. (1993). *Significant benefits: The High/Scope Perry Preschool study through age 27* (Monographs of the High/Scope Educational Research Foundation, No. 10). Ypsilanti, MI: High Scope Press.

Scott, T. (2003). Making behavior intervention planning decisions in a schoolwide system of positive behavior support. *Focus on Exceptional Children, 36*(1), 1–18.

Scotti, J., & Meyer, L. (1999). *Behavioral intervention: Principles, models and practices*. Baltimore: Paul H. Brookes.

Section 504 of the Rehabilitation Act of 1973. (PL 93-112).

Semb, G., & Ellis, J. (1994). Knowledge taught in school: What is remembered? *Review of Educational Research, 64*(2), 253–286.

Semrud-Clikeman, M. (2005). Neuropsychological aspects for evaluating learning disabilities. *Journal of Learning Disabilities, 38*(6), 561–568.

Sequin, E. (1970). *Idiocy and its treatment by the physiological method*. New York: Columbia University Press. (Original work published 1866).

Shalev, R., Manor, O., Auerbach, J., & Grodd-Tour, V. (1998). Persistence of developmental dyscalculia: What counts. *Journal of Pediatrics, 133*(3), 358–362.

Shaywitz, B., Fletcher, J., & Shaywitz, S. (1995). Defining and classifying learning disabilities and attention deficit hyperactivity disorder. *Journal of Child Neurology, 10*(Suppl. 1), S50–S57.

Shaywitz, B., Shaywitz, S., Pugh, K., Fulbright, R., Constable, T., & Mencl, E., et al. (1998). Functional disruption in the organization of the brain for reading in dyslexia. *Proceedings of the National Academy of Sciences, 95*(5), 2636–2641.

Shaywitz, B., & Shaywitz, S. (1999, May). *Brain research and reading: Lecture at Schwab learning*. San Mateo, CA. www.schwablearning.com.

Shaywitz, B., Shaywitz, S., Blachman, B., Pugh, K., Fulbright, R., Skudlarki, P., et al. (2004). Development of left occipitotemporal systems for skills reading in children after a phonologically-based intervention. *Journal of Biological Psychiatry, 55*(9), 926–933.

Shaywitz, B., Shaywitz, S., Pugh, K., Mensi, W., Fulbright, R., Skudlarski, P., et al. (2002). Disruption of the posterior brain systems for reading in children with developmental dyslexia. *Biological Psychiatry, 52*(2), 101–110.

Shaywitz, S. (2003). *Overcoming dyslexia: A new and complete science-based program for reading problems at any level*. New York: Alfred A. Knopf.

Shinn, M. R., & Hubbard, D. (1992). Curriculum-based measurement and problem-solving assessment: Basic procedures and outcomes. *Focus on Exceptional Children, 24*(5), 1–20.

Siegel, L., & Smythe, I. (2006). Reflection on research on reading disability with special attention to gender issues. *Journal of Learning Disabilities, 38*(5), 473–478.

Silver, A., & Hagin, R. (1966). Maturation of perceptual functions in children with specific reading disabilities. *Reading Teacher, 19,* 253–259.

Silver, A., & Hagin, R. (1990). *Disorders of learning in childhood.* New York: Wiley.

Silver, L. (2004). *Attention deficit/Hyperactivity disorder: A clinical guide to diagnosis and treatment for health and mental health professionals.* Washington, DC: American Psychiatric Association.

Silver, L. (2006). *The misunderstood child.* New York: Three Rivers Press.

Silver, L. (2010). Why are there so many different medications to treat ADHD? *LD Online.* http://www.ldonline.org.

Simos, P., Fletcher, J., Skart, S., Billingsly-Marshall, R., Denton, C., & Papancicolaou, A. (2007). Intensive instruction affects brain magnetic activity associated with oral word reading in children with persistent reading disabilities. *Journal of Learning Disabilities, 29*(1), 37–48.

Sipe, L. (2001). Invention, convention, and intervention: Invented spelling and the teacher. *Reading Teacher, 55*(3), 264–273.

Sitlington, P. H. (1996). Transition to learning: The neglected component of transition programming for individuals with learning disabilities. *Journal of Learning Disabilities, 29*(1), 31–39.

Slavin, R. (2009). *Educational psychology: Theory and practice.* Boston: Allyn & Bacon.

Slingerland, B. (1976). *A multisensory program for language arts for specific language disability children: A guide for primary teachers.* Cambridge, MA: Educators Publishing Service.

Smith, C. (2000). Behavioral and discipline provisions of IDEA '97: Implicit competencies yet to be confirmed. *Exceptional Children, 66,* 403–412.

Smith, S. (2005). *Live it, learn it. The Academic Club methodology for students with learning disabilities and ADHD.* Baltimore: Paul H. Brookes.

Smith, S. L. (1991). *Succeeding against the odds: Strategies and insights from the learning disabled.* Los Angeles: Jeremy P. Tarcher.

Smith, S. L. (2001). *The power of the arts: Creative strategies for teaching exceptional learners.* Baltimore: Paul H. Brookes.

Smith, T. (2002). *The section 504 trainer's manual: A step-by-step guide for in-service and staff development.* Horsham, PA: LRP Publications.

Smith, T., Polloway, E., Patton, R., & Dowdy, C. (2002). *Teaching children with special needs in inclusive settings.* Boston: Allyn & Bacon.

Snow, C., Burns, M., & Griffin, P. (Eds.). (1998). *Report of the committee on the prevention of reading difficulties in young children.* Washington, DC: National Research Council, National Academy of Sciences.

Snowling, S., Gallagher, A., & Frith, U. (2003). Family risk of dyslexia is continuous: Individual differences with the precursors of reading skill. *Child Development, 74*(7), 358–373.

Snowman, J., & Biehler, R. (2006). *Psychology applied to teaching.* Boston: Houghton Mifflin.

Snowman, J., & McCown, R. (2013). *Ed psych.* Belmont, CA: Wadsworth/Cengage Learning.

Sorensen, L. G., Forbes, P. W., Bernstein, J. H., Weiler, M. D., Mitchell, W. M., & Waber, D. P. (2003). Psychosocial adjustment over a two-year period in children referred for learning problems: Risk resilience, and adaptation. *Learning Disabilities Research & Practice, 18*(1), 10–24.

Sousa, D. (2001). *How the Brain Learns.* Thousand Oaks, CA: Corwin Press.

Speece, D. (2005). Hitting the moving target known as reading development. Some thoughts on screening children for secondary intervention. *Journal of Learning Disabilities, 38*(6), 487–493.

Spinelli, C. (2006). *Classroom assessment for students in special and general education.* Columbus, OH: Pearson Merrill/Prentice Hall.

Squire, J., & Bricker, D. (2007). *An activity-based approach to developing young children's social emotional competencies.* Baltimore, MD: Paul H. Brookes.

Sridhar, D., & Vaughn, S. (2001). Social functioning of students with learning disabilities. In D. Hallahan & B. Keogh (Eds.), *Research and global perspectives in learning disabilities: Essays in honor of William M. Cruickshank* (pp. 65–92). Mahwah, NJ: Erlbaum.

Stahl, S. (2004). Scaly? Audacious? Debris? Salubrious?: Vocabulary learning and the child with learning disabilities. *Perspectives on Language and Literacy. International Dyslexia Association, 30*(1), 5–12.

Stahl, S. A., & Murray, B. A. (1994). Defining phonological awareness and its relationship to early reading. *Journal of Educational Psychology, 86,* 221–234.

Stauffer, R. G. (1975). *Directing the reading-thinking process.* New York: Harper & Row.

Stevens, L., & Werkhoven, W. (2001). Learning disabilities in the Netherlands. In D. Hallahan & B. Keogh (Eds.), *Research and global perspectives in learning disabilities: Essays in honor of William M. Cruickshank* (pp. 273–291). Mahwah, NJ: Erlbaum.

Stichter, J., Conrty, M., & Kauffman, J. (2008). *An introduction to students with high-incidence disabilities.* Upper Saddle River, NJ: Pearson/Merrill/Prentice Hall.

Stillman, E., & Scott, C. (2006). Language impairment and reading disability: Connections and complexities. *Learning Disabilities Research and Practice, 21*(1), 1–7.

Stone, C., & Carlisle, J. (2006). From the outgoing editors. *Learning Disabilities Research and Practice, 21*(1), v.

Strauss, A., & Lehtinen, L. (1947). *Psychopathology and education of the brain-injured child.* New York: Grune & Stratton.

Strout, M. (2005). Positive behavioral support at the classroom level: Considerations and strategies. *Beyond Behavior, 14*(2), 3–8.

Stuebing, K., Barth, A., Molfese, P., Weiss, B., & Fletcher, J. (2009). IQ is not strongly related to response to reading instruction: A meta-analytic interpretation. *Exceptional Children, 76*(1), 31–51.

Sugai, G., & Homer, R. (1999). Discipline and behavioral support: Preferred processes and practices. *Effective School Practice, 17,* 10–22.

Sutherland, K., Alder, N., & Gunter, R. (2003). The effect of varying rates of opportunity to respond to academic requests on the classroom behavior of students with e/bd. *Journal of Emotional and Behavioral Disorders, 11*(4), 230–248.

Swanson, H. (1996). Informational processing: An introduction. In D. Reid, W. Hresko, & H. Swanson (Eds.), *Cognitive approaches to learning disabilities* (pp. 251–286). Austin, TX: Pro-Ed.

Swanson, H. L. (2007). Commentary on Part I, Section II: Cognitive aspects of math disabilities. In D. Berch & M. Mazzocco (Eds.), *Why is math so hard for some children?The nature and origins of mathematical learning difficulties and disabilities* (pp. 133–146). Baltimore, MD: Paul H. Brooks.

Swanson, H. L., & Deshler, D. (2003). Instructing adolescents with learning disabilities. Converting a meta-analysis to practice. *Journal of Learning Disabilities, 36*(2), 124–135.

Swanson, H. L., Harris, K., & Graham, S. (2003). Overview of foundations, causes, instruction, and methodology in the field of learning disabilities. In H. L Swanson, K. Harris, & S. Graham (Eds). *Handbook of learning disabilities* (pp. 3–15). New York: Guilford Press.

Swanson, H. L., & Hoskyn, M. (2001). Instructing adolescents with learning disabilities: A component and composite analysis. *Learning Disabilities Research & Practice, 16*(2), 109–119.

Swanson, H. L., & O'Conner, R. (2009). The role of working memory and fluency practice on the reading comprehension of students who are dysfluent readers. *Journal of Learning Disabilities, 42*(6), 548–575.

Swanson, H. L., Zheng, X., & Jerman, O. (2009). Working memory, short-term memory, and reading disabilities: A selective meta-analysis of the literature, *Journal of Learning Disabilities, 24*(3), 260–287.

Tallal, P. (2000). The science of literacy: From the laboratory to the classroom. *Proceedings of the National Academic of Sciences. USA, 97,* 2402–2404.

Tallal, P., Allard, L., Miller, S., & Curtiss, S. (1997). Academic outcomes of language impaired children. In C. Hulme & M. Snowling (Eds.), *Dyslexia: Biology, cognition, and intervention* (pp. 167–179). London: Whurt, British Dyslexia Association.

Tallal, P., Miller, S. L., Jenkins, W., & Merzenich, M. (1997). The role of temporal processing in developmental language-based learning disorders: Research and clinical implications. In B. Blachman (Ed.), *Foundations of reading acquisition and dyslexia* (pp. 49–66). Mahwah, NJ: Erlbaum.

Tallal, P., Miller, S. L., & Merzenich, M. M. (1996). Language comprehension in language-learning impaired children improved with acoustically modified speech. *Science, 271*(5245), 81–83.

Test, D., Toms, O., & Scroggins, L. (2011a). *Tool for what secondary special education teachers need to know.* Charlotte, NC: National Secondary Transition Technical Assistance Center, University of North Carolina.

Test, D., Toms, O., & Scroggins, L. (2011b). *Tool for what transition specialists need to know.* Charlotte, NC: National Secondary Transition Technical Assistance Center, University of North Carolina.

Thompson, L. (1971). Language disabilities in men of eminence. *Journal of Learning Disabilities, 4,* 34–45.

Thompson, S. (1997). *The source for nonverbal learning disabilities.* East Moline, IL: LinguiSystems.

Thurlow, M. (2000). Standards-based reform and students with disabilities: Reflections on a decade of change. *Focus on Exceptional Children, 33*(3), 1–16.

Tomasello, M. (2003) *Constructing a language: A usage based theory of language acquisition.* Cambridge: Harvard University Press.

Tomblin, J. (2006). A normativist account of language-based learning disability. *Learning Disabilities Research and Practice, 21*(1), 8–18.

Tomlinson, Brimijoin, K., & Narvaez, L. (2008), *The differentiated school: Making revolutionary changes in teaching and learning.* Alexandria: VA: American Association for Curriculum Development.

Torgesen, J. (1998). Catch them before they fall. *American Educator, 22*(1&2), 32–39.

Torriero, E.A. & Gowler, V. (1980, October 11). Illiterate bank robber shamed into second try. *Miami Herald-Palm Beach News,* pp. B1.

Traub, N., & Bloom, F. (1978). *Recipe for reading.* Cambridge, MA: Educators Publishing Service.

Tsatsanis, K., Fuerst, D., & Rourke, B. (1997). Psychosocial dimensions of learning disabilities: External validation and relationship with age and academic functioning. *Journal of Learning Disabilities, 30*(5), 490–502.

Tsuge, M. (2001). Learning disabilities in Japan. In D. Hallahan & B. Keogh (Eds.), *Research and global perspectives in learning disabilities: Essays in honor of William M. Cruickshank* (pp. 255–272). Mahwah, NJ: Erlbaum.

Tuckman, B., & Monetti, D. (2013), *Educational Psychology.* Belmont, CA: Wadsworth/Cengage.

Turnbull, A., Turnbull, H., Shank, M., & Smith, S. (2004). *Exceptional lives: Special education in today's schools.* Englewood Cliffs, NJ: Prentice-Hall.

U. S. Department of Education. (2012). *30th Annual Report to Congress on the Implementation of the Individuals with Disabilities Education Act.* Washington, DC: Government Printing Office.

U.S. Department of Education, Institute of Education Sciences. (2008). *IES Practice Guide: Reducing behavior problems in the elementary school classroom.* Washington, DC: Government Printing Office.

U.S. Department of Education, Institute of Education Sciences, National Center for Education Statistics. (2009). *The nation's report card.* http://nationsreportcard.gov/reading_2007.

U.S. Department of Education, Office of Special Education Programs, Data Analysis System (DANS). (2004). *Part B, Individuals with Disabilities Education Act implementation of FAPE requirements, 2004.* Data updated as of July 30, 2005.

Vail, P. (1992). *Learning styles.* Rosemont, NJ: Modern Learning Press.

Van der Lief, A., & Morfidi, E. (2006). Core deficits and variable differences in Dutch poor readers learning English. *Journal of Learning Disabilities, 39*(1), 74–91.

Van de Walle, J. (2004). *Elementary and middle school mathematics: Teaching developmentally.* Boston: Allyn & Bacon.

Van de Walle, J., Karp, K., & Bay-Williams, J. (2010). *Elementary and middle school mathematics: Teaching developmentally.* Boston: Allyn & Bacon.

Vaughn, S. (2006). A few remarks on response to intervention. *New Times for DLD, 24*(1), 1–2.

Vaughn, S., Elbaum, B., & Boardsman, A. (2001). The social functions of students with learning disabilities: Implications for inclusion. *Exceptionality, 9,* 47–65.

Vaughn, S., Gersten, R., & Chard, D. (2000). The underlying message in LD intervention research: Findings from research syntheses. *Exceptional Children, 67*(1), 99–114.

Vaughn, S., Wanzek, J., & Fletcher, J. (2007). Multiple tiers of intervention: A framework for prevention and identification of students with reading/learning disabilities. In B. M. Taylor & J. E. Ysseldyke (Eds.). *Effective instruction for struggling readers, K–6* (pp. 173–195). New York: Teachers College Press.

Vellutino, F., Scanlon, D., & Lyon, G. R. (2000). Differentiating between difficult-to-remediate and readily remediated poor readers. More evidence against the IQ-achievement discrepancy definition of reading disabilities. *Journal of Learning Disabilities, 33*(3), 223–238.

Villa, R., Thousand, J., Meyers, H., & Nevin, A. (1996). Teacher and administrator perceptions of heterogenous education. *Focus on Exceptional Children, 63,* 29–45.

Voeller, K. (1994). Techniques for measuring social competence in children. In G. R. Lyon (Ed.), *Frames of reference for the assessment of learning disabilities: New views of measurement issues* (pp. 525–554). Baltimore: Paul H. Brookes.

Vogel, S. (1998). Adults with learning disabilities. In S. Vogel & S. Reder (Eds.), *Learning disabilities, literacy, and adult education* (pp. 5–8). Baltimore: Paul H. Brookes.

Vogel, S., & Adelman, P. (2000). Adults with learning disabilities, 8–15 years after college. *Learning Disabilities: A Multidisciplinary Journal, 10*(3), 165–182.

Vogel, S., & Reder, S. (1998). Educational attainments of adults with learning disabilities. In S. Vogel & S. Reder (Eds.), *Learning disabilities, literacy, and adult education* (pp. 43–68). Baltimore: Paul H. Brookes.

Von Mizener, B., & Williams, R. (2009). The effects of student choices on academic performance. *Journal of Positive Behavior Interventions, 11*(2), 110–128.

Vukovic. R., & Siegel, L. (2006). The double-deficit hypothesis: A comprehensive analysis of the evidence. *Journal of Learning Disabilities, 39*(1), 25–47.

Vygotsky. L. S. (1997). Development of speech and thinking. In R.W. Rieber (Ed). *Collected works of L.S. Vygotsky: Vol. 4. (the history of development of the higher mental functions.)* (pp. 191–2005). New York: Plenum. Original work published 1982–1984.

Wagner, M., Cameto, R., & Newman, L. (2003). *Youth with disabilities: A changing population.* A report of findings from the National Longitudinal Transition Study (NTLS) and the National Longitudinal Transition Study-2 (NLTS2). Menlo Park, CA: SRI International.

Wagner, M., Marder, C., Blackorby, J. Cameto, R., Newman, L., Levine, P., et al. (2003). *The achievements of youth with disabilities during seconedary school.* A report from the National Longitudinal Transition Study-2 (NLTS2). Menlo Park, CA: SRI.

Wagner, M., Newman, L., Cameto, R., Levine, P., & Garza, N. (2006). *An overview of findings from Wave 2 of the National Longitudinal Transition Study-2.* National Center for Special Education Research. Menlo Park, CA: SRI International.

Walther-Thomas, C., Korinek, L., & McLaughlin, V. (2000). *Collaboration for inclusive education: Developing successful programs.* Boston: Allyn & Bacon.

Wanzek, J., & Vaughn, S. (2009). Students demonstrating persistent low response to reading intervention: Three case studies. *Learning Disabilities Research and Practice, 24*(3), 151–163.

Warner-Rogers, J., Taylor, A., Taylor, E., & Sandberg, S. (2000). Inattentive behavior in childhood: Epidemiology and implications for development. *Journal of Learning Disabilities, 18*(4), 520–536.

Weaver, S. M. (2000). The efficacy of extended time for post-secondary students with learning disabilities. *Learning Disabilities: A Multidisciplinary Journal, 10*(2), 47–56.

Weber, M. (2006). Legal protections against discrimination for students in higher education: Four leading issues. *Learning Disabilities: A Multidisciplinary Journal, 14*(1), 15–20.

Wedell, K. (2001). British orientations to specific learning difficulties. In D. Hallahan & B. Keogh (Eds.), *Research and global perspectives in learning disabilities: Essays in honor of William M. Cruickshank* (pp. 239–254). Mahwah, NJ: Erlbaum.

West, T. (1997). Slow words, quick images—Dyslexia as an advantage in tomorrow's workplace. In P. Gerber & D. Brown (Eds.), *Learning disabilities and employment* (pp. 334–370). Austin, TX: Pro-Ed.

West, T. (2003). Secret of the super successful...they're dyslexic. *Thalmus, 21*(1), 48–52.

West, T. G. (1997). *In the mind's eye: Visual thinkers, dyslexia and other learning difficulties, computer imaging, and the ironies of creativity.* New York: Prometheus Books.

Whitby, P., Leinger, M., & Grillo, K. (2012). Tips for using interactive whiteboards to increase participation of students with disabilities. *Teaching Exceptional Children, 44*(6), 50–58.

Williams, J. P. (1998). Improving comprehension of disabled readers. *Annals of Dyslexia, 48,* 213–238.

Williamson, G., & Anzalone, M. (1997, April/May). Sensory integration: A key component of the evaluation and treatment of young children with severe difficulty with relating and communication. *Zero to Three, 17,* 29–36.

Williamson, P., McLeskey, J., Hoppey, D., & Rentz, T. (2006). Educating students with mental retardation in general education classrooms. *Exceptional Children, 72*(3), 347–362.

Willingham, E. (2013, March 20). Autism prevalence is now at 1 in 50 children. *Forbes Magazine.* http://www.forbes.com/emilywillingham/2013.

Wilson, B. A. (1988). *Wilson reading system.* Millbury, MA: Wilson Language Training.

Wilson, K., & Swanson, H. L. (2001). Are mathematics disabilities due to a domain-general or a domain-specific working memory deficit? *Journal of Learning Disabilities, 34*(3), 237–248.

Wingert, P., & Kantrovitz, B. (1997, October 27). Why Andy couldn't read. *Newsweek,* 56–64.

Witzel, B., Mercer, C., & Miller, M. (2003). Teaching algebra to students with learning difficulties: An investigation of an explicit instructional model. *Learning Disabilities Research & Practice, 18*(2), 121–131.

Wood, J. (1992). *Adapting instruction for mainstreamed and at-risk students.* New York: Macmillan Publishing Co.

Wolery, M., & Bailey, D., Jr. (2003). Early childhood special education research. *Journal of Early Intervention, 25*(2), 88–99.

Wolery, M., & Bailey, D. (2004). *Assessing infants and preschoolers with special needs.* Upper Saddle River, NJ: Merrill/Prentice Hall.

Wong, B. (1999). Metacognition in writing. In R. Gallimore, L. Bernheimer, D. McMillan, D. Speece, & S. Vaughn (Eds.), *Developmental perspectives on children with high-incidence disabilities* (pp. 183–198). Mahwah, NJ: Erlbaum.

Wong, B., & Donahue, M. (2002). *The social dimensions of learning disabilities: Essays in honor of Tanis Bryan.* Mahwah, NJ: Lawrence Erlbaum.

Wong, B., & Hutchinson, N. (2001). Learning disabilities in Canada. In D. Hallahan & B. Keogh (Eds.), *Research and global perspectives in learning disabilities: Essays in honor of William M. Cruickshank* (pp. 197–216). Mahwah, NJ: Erlbaum.

Wood, J. (1992). *Adapting instruction for mainstreamed and at-risk students.* New York: Macmillan Publishing Co.

Wright P., & Wright P. (2009). *Supreme Court issues pro-child decision in Forest Grove School Dist v. T.A.* http://www.wrightslaw.com.

Yasutake, D., & Bryan, T. (1995). The influence of induced positive affect on middle school children with and without learning disabilities. *Learning Disabilities Research and Practice, 10*(1), 38–45.

Yell, M. (1997). Education and the law. *Preventing School Failure, 41*(4), 185–187.

Yell, M., Rozalski, M., & Drasgrow, E. (2001). Disciplining students with disabilities. *Focus on Exceptional Children, 33*(9), 1–20.

Yell, M., Shriner, J., & Katsiyannis, A. (2006). Individuals with Disabilities Education Improvement Act of 2004 and IDEA Regulations of 2006: Implications for educators, administrators, and teacher trainers. *Focus on Exceptional Children, 39*(1), 1–24.

Ysseldyke, J. (2001). Reflections on a research career: Generalizations from 25 years of research on assessment and instructional decision making. *Exceptional Children, 67*(3), 295–308.

Ysseldyke, J., Thurlow, M., Bielinski, J., House, A., & Moody, M. (2001). The relationship between institutional and assessment accommodations in an inclusive state accountability system. *Journal of Learning Disabilities, 34*(3), 212–220.

Yuan, F., & Reisman, E. (2000). Transition to adulthood: Outcomes for graduates of a non-degree, post-secondary program for young adults with severe learning disabilities. *Learning Disabilities: A Multidisciplinary Journal, 10*(3), 153–164.

Zeffrino, T., & Eden, G. (2000). The neural basis of developmental dyslexia. *Annals of Dyslexia, 50,* 3–30.

Zigmond, N. (1990). Rethinking secondary school programs for students with learning disabilities. *Focus on Exceptional Children, 23,* 1–22.

Zigmond, N. (1997). Educating students with disabilities: The future of special education. In J. Lloyd, E. Kame'enui, & D. Chard (Eds.), *Issues in educating students with disabilities* (pp. 275–304, 377–391). Mahwah, NJ: Erlbaum.

Zigmond, N. (2003a). Search for the most effective service delivery model for students with learning disabilities. In H. Swanson, K. Harris, & S. Graham (Eds.), *Handbook of learning disabilities* (pp. 110–124). New York: Guilford Press.

Zigmond, N. (2003b). Where should students with disabilities receive special education services? Is one place better than another? *Journal of Special Education, 37*(3), 193–199.

Zigmond, N. (2007, February 14). *The special education teaching in the twenty-first century: A call for unconventional thinking.* Presentation at the Learning Disabilities Association Conference, Pittsburgh, PA.

Zirkel, P. (1994, April). Costly lack of accommodations. *Phi Delta Kappan,* 652–653.

Zirkel, P. (2007). What does the law say IV? *Teaching Exceptional Children, 39*(3), 61–63.

Zirkel, P. (2009). What does the law say? New Section 504 student eligibility standards. *Teaching Exceptional Children, 4*(4), 68–75.

NAME INDEX

A

Accardo, P., 197, 206
Achilles, G., 165
Adams, A., 310
Adams, H., 3
Adams, M. J., 348
Adelman, P., 273, 385
Adelman, P. B., 386, 424
Adler, M., 356
Adreon, D., 170
Ager, C., 178
Akeroyd, M., 319
Alber, S., 353, 378
Alberto, P., 181
Albin, R., 167
Alder, N., 178
Alfonso, V., 83
Algozzine, B., 138
Allen, G., 300
Allen J., E., 217, 223, 224
Allsopp, D., 176, 452
Anastasiow, N., 6
Anderson, C., 168
Ankeny, E., 261
Anzalone, M., 230
Appleton, A., 352
Aram, D., 196
Ardoin, S., 165
Arnold, E., 206
Aronin, S., 454
Artiles, A., 251
Ashcraft, M., 428
Ashlock, R., 437
Asperger, H., 192
Atkinson, R., 142
Auerbach, J., 20
Aylward, E. H., 28
Ayres, J., 230

B

Babbitt, B., 424
Baer, R., 277, 278
Bailey, D., Jr., 217, 218
Baker-Kroczynski, S., 29
Baker, L., 192, 193, 251
Balise, R., 375
Ball, E., 310, 318
Ball, E. W., 233
Bambara, L., 178
Barbetta, P., 176

Barkley, R., 97, 197, 200, 206, 207, 208, 252, 428
Barletta, L., 251
Barnes, H. V., 218
Barnes, M., 427
Barnett, A., 367
Baroody, A., 439
Barth, A., 47
Bashir, A., 385
Batsche, G., 46
Baxendell, B., 148
Bay-Williams, J., 425, 426, 434, 435
Becker, S., 170
Beckman, P., 255
Beebe-Frankenberger, M., 159
Beeler, T., 310
Belson, S., 31, 267, 379, 395, 396, 454
Bender, L., 131
Bender, W., 81, 149
Benner, G., 159
Bentzen, F., 22
Berko, J., 315
Berninger, V. W., 28
Bernstein, J. H., 163
Berry, R., 387
Bicard, D., 176
Biederman, J., 207
Biegler, E., 25
Biehler, R., 249
Bielinski, J., 430
Billingsly-Marshall, R., 28
Birsh, J., 375
Blachman, B., 28, 142, 310, 318, 329
Blachman, B. A., 233
Black, J., 375
Blackorby, J., 254
Bley, N., 425, 426, 427
Blondis, T., 197, 206
Bloom, F., 376
Boardsman, A., 110
Boliek, C., 25
Bolton, P., 224
Bolt, S., 258, 436, 437
Boon, R., 149
Booth, E., 166
Borders, C., 165, 178
Borkowski, J., 181
Boscardin, M., 26, 181
Boshes, B., 202
Boss, S., 452
Bowe, F. G., 217, 239

Boyle, J., 107, 195
Bradley, C., 206
Bradley, R., 41
Brainerd, C. J., 132
Braun, D., 258
Bravo-Valdivieso, L., 20
Bray, M., 270
Bricker, D., 229
Brimijoin, K., 80
Broadbent, D., 142
Brooks, R., 86, 163, 164, 252
Brown, A., 152, 316
Brown, D., 164, 260, 261, 263, 278
Brown, S., 64
Brown, T., 197, 205
Bruner, E., 138
Bryan, T., 160, 161, 253
Bryant, B., 437
Buck, J., 165, 168
Buford, R., 178
Bulgren, J., 151, 250, 251, 253, 258, 269, 271, 375, 429
Burns, C., 20, 277
Burns, M., 115, 165, 387
Bursuck, W., 108, 119
Bursuck, W. D., 275
Butler, F., 424
Byrd-Craven, J., 427
Byrd, E., 204

C

Cade, E., 29
Caldwell, J., 233, 310, 329, 349, 351, 386, 391, 392, 394, 400
Calhoun, S. L., 199
Callahan, R., 316
Cameto, R., 253, 344
Campbell, J., 265
Campione, J., 152
Camus, A., 105
Carlisle, J., 309
Carmichael, D., 166
Carnine, D., 138
Carr, G., 29
Carr, V., 165, 166, 176, 181, 182
Cartledge, G., 178
Cass, M., 424, 429, 432, 443
Cates, D., 424, 429, 432, 443
Catts, H. W., 320
Cawley, J., 29, 424, 434, 435

489

Grahame, K., 378
Graham, S., 147, 383, 385, 386, 387, 388, 390, 391, 411
Graves, D. H., 388, 390
Greathouse, D., 160, 161
Greeno, J., 142
Gresham, F., 160, 161
Griffin, P., 115, 387
Grigg, W. S., 265
Grillo, K., 239
Grimme, A. C., 28
Grodd-Tour, V., 20
Groteluschen, A., 181
Gunter, R., 178
Guralnick, M. J., 217, 218

Holdnack, J., 83
Hollenbeck, K., 31, 424
Holloway, J., 110
Holzer, M., 270
Homer, R., 166
Hook, P., 351
Hopko, D., 428
Hoppery, D., 110, 256
Horne, M., 349
Horner, R., 167
Hoskyn, M., 264
House, A., 430
Hsu, C., 20
Huaqing, C., 323
Hua, Y., 264
Hubbard, D., 439
Hudson, P., 424, 432, 433, 443
Hudson, R., 362
Huggins, A., 170
Hughes, C., 267, 269, 270
Hund, A., 197
Hunt, N., 6
Hutchinson, N., 20
Huttenlocher, P., 219
Hutton U., 144
Hynd, G., 24

Katsiyannis, A., 64
Kauffman, J., 8, 42, 109, 111, 157, 163, 258
Kavale, K., 46, 83
Kehle, T., 270
Keillor, G., 37
Keller, C., 204
Keller, H., 310, 311
Kelley, K., 261
Kennedy, M., 267
Keogh, B., 163, 219
Kephart, N., 229, 424
Kibby, M., 24
Kilgo, J., 216, 217, 219, 237
Kim, B., 20
Kimball, K., 64
Kinsbourne, M., 24
Kirkpatrick, M., 165, 168
Kirk, S., 6, 76, 225
Kissam, B., 386, 393
Klein, M., 228
Kliebhan, J. M., 215
Klingbeil, D., 165
Klingner, J., 251
Kluwe, R., 149
Knight, J., 151, 250, 251, 253, 258, 269, 271, 375, 429
Knitzer J., 8
Knowlton, E., 183
Kohler, P., 261
Kohn, A., 137
Korinek, L., 116
Korkunov, V., 20
Kotulak, R., 27
Kovaleski, J., 46
Kozleski, M., 83, 98, 151, 433
Kranowitz, C., 230
Krasnegor, N., 142, 146
Kratochvil, C., 207
Krause, J., 428
Kravetz, M., 276
Kress, K., 363
Krezmien, M., 165
Kroesbergen, E., 433
Kuder, S., 321
Kuhl, P., 219
Kunsch, C., 424

Todd, T., 428
Tomasello, M., 314
Tomblin, J., 309
Tomlinson, 80
Tonev, S., 206
Torgesen, J., 111, 399
Torgesen, J. K., 95
Torres, C., 159, 165
Towse, J., 144
Tramaglini, S., 344
Traub, N., 376
Trevisan, M., 316
Trezek, B., 265
Troutman, A., 181
Tsantis, L., 239
Tsatsanis, K., 196
Tsuge, M., 20
Tuckman, B., 136
Turnbull, A., 121
Turnbull, H., 121

Vaughn, S., 30, 40, 41, 42, 47, 85, 110, 161
Vellutino, F., 132
Vitiello, B., 27
Voeller, K., 160
Vogel, S., 273, 275, 317, 385
Vogel, S. A., 386, 424
Von Mizener, B., 178
Vrielink, L., 320
Vukovic. R., 15

Whorf, B. L., 307
Wilder, L., 261
Wilder, L. I., 378
Wiley, A., 258
Wilkins, J., 261
Williams, J., 357
Williams, J. P., 357
Williamson, G., 230
Williamson, P., 110
Williams, R., 178
Wilson, B. A., 376
Wilson, K., 427
Wilson, M., 424
Wingert, P., 278
Witzel, B., 429, 430, 443
Wolery, M., 217, 218
Wong, B., 20, 152, 161, 316
Wood, F. B., 95
Wood, J., 299
Wright, P., 45

behavior analysis, implications for learning disabilities, 139–140
behavior management strategies, 181–186
  cognitive behavior modification, 183
  contingency contracting, 181
  home-school coordination, 184–185
  reinforcement theory, 183–184
  time-outs, 181–182
behavior momentum, 180
bibliotherapy, 89
bilingual instruction, 323
birth-date effect, 135
blending games, 328
bodily/kinesthetic intelligence, 81
Braille, 310
brain
  early development of, 219
  early research on, 21–22
  minimal brain dysfunction (MBD), 22
  neurochemistry of psychostimulant medications and, 207–208
  neurons, 207
  perceptual processing concept, 231–232
  role of neurotransmitters and ADHD in, 207
  traumatic brain injury, 9, 10
brain, structure and functions, 23–25
  cerebral dominance, 24
  cerebral hemisphere, 24
  lateral preference, 25
  right/left, differences in function, 24
brain-injured child, 20–22
brain research, 25–27
  computed tomography (CT), 27
  dyslexia, 25
  genetics studies, 26–27
  positron-emission tomography (PET), 27
  postmortem anatomical studies, 25–26
breaking the code, 348
Brigance Diagnostic Comprehensive Inventory of Basic Skills, 68
Broca's area, 27
Brown Bear, Brown Bear, What Do You See? (Martin), 367
Buckley Amendment, 300

C

calculators, 453
career-training, 263
case history, 57–58
catching activities, 241
Centers for Disease Control and Prevention, 190

central nervous system dysfunction, 13, 14
cerebral dominance, 24
cerebral hemisphere, 24
CHADD (Children and Adults With Attention Deficit Disorder), 197
chalkboard activities, for handwriting, 415
Charlotte's Web (White), 378
charts and graphs, 454–455
checking, as metacognitive strategy, 149
cherish stage, 125
child-find phase, 237
child-initiated activities, 239
children
  at-risk, 217
  clinical studies of, 21–22
  developmental stages of, 134–135
  See also adolescents; elementary-age children; preschool children; young children
chunking, for improving memory, 145
circle of friends strategy, 194
circle time activity, 173
classification
  of assessment information, 38
  in early number learning, 445
  expanding vocabulary through, 372
  as metacognitive strategy, 149
class newsletters, 412
classroom environment
  creating positive, 175–177
  reduced class size, 117
  for writing, 408–410
classwide peer tutoring, 95
clinical teacher, remembrance of, 79–80
clinical teaching, 76–78
  assessment, 78
  cycle, stages of, 77–78
  evaluation of student performance, 78
  examples of, 78
  goal of, 77
  implementation of teaching plan, 78
  planning of teaching task, 78
  qualities of, 78–80
  See also specialized instruction
closing the gap, 454
cloze procedure, 373–374
coaching strategies, in inclusive classrooms, 120
cognitive abilities, 140
cognitive abilities tests, 66–67
cognitive behavior modification, 183
cognitive development, assessment of, 237

cognitive learning theories, 147
  apprenticeships, 147–148
  automaticity, 141
  concept maps, 148
  graphic organizers, 148
  metacognition, 149–150
  mind mapping, 148
  social challenges and, 172
  See also learning strategies instruction
cognitive processing, 82–83
  psychological processing disorders in, 141
cognitive psychology, 140–141
  basic concepts of, 140–141
  cognitive abilities, 140
  cognitive processing, 140–142
  implications of, 150
  information-processing model, 142–147
  psychological processing disorders, 141
  as strategy for teaching, 150
  See also cognitive learning theories
collaborations
  education/content-area teachers, 259
  family-school, 121
  principles of effective, 118
  special education/general education, 116–120
  in writing process, 395
collaborative teaching, 259
collaborative teaming, 256
college entrance testing, 276
College Living Experience (CLE), 277
college students
  accommodations, 275–276
  legislation for, 274–275
common core standards, 23
communication
  components of language, 315–316
  development, assessment of, 238
  language and, 311–312
  model for process of, 312
  nonverbal communication, improving, 171
components of language, 315–316
comprehension
  listening, 331
  monitoring, 356
  reading, 368–377
comprehensive evaluation, 45–47
  achievement-intellectual ability discrepancies in, 46–47
  information obtained in, 45–46
computational facts, learning, 449–450
computation skills, 447–450
computed tomography (CT), 27

computer technology
  applications for, 33
  electronic keyboards, 394
  electronic spellers, 415
  e-mail, 396
  in IEP, 56
  for individualized teaching, 115
  for mathematics, 453–454
  for oral language, 337–338
  PowerPoint, 396–397
  presentation software,
    396–397
  reading strategies and use of, 389
  recorded textbooks and digital
    CD-ROMs, 379–380
  secondary school students
    and, 267
  spell checkers, 415
  spreadsheets, 454–455
  text-to-speech programs, 33, 379
  types of computer programs, 396
  use by students with learning
    disabilities, 33
  voice-recognition systems,
    395–396
  Web pages, 397
  word-prediction programs, 395
  word processing programs, 395
  young children and, 239
  See also word processing
concept maps, 148
concepts, 370–374
concerta, 206
concrete level
  in math instruction, 432
  in vocabulary building, 357
concrete operations stage, 133
conferences, parent-teacher, 126
confidentiality, in IEP process, 48
consequent event, 137
consonant-blend bingo, 330
content-area reading
    problems, 358
content-area teachers
  collaborations with special
    educators, 259
  inclusion practices for, 255
  teaching reading skills and, 359
  See also general education
    teachers
context clues, 351
contingency contract, 181
continuum of alternative placements
    in, 109–111
continuum of alternative services
    in, 110
controlling instructional variables
  difficulty level, 84–85
  language, 85–86
  space, 85
  time, 85
conversation skills, 172

cooperative learning, of reading
    strategies, 356
coteaching, 119–120
  in general education
    classroom, 109
  for secondary classroom, 256
  strategies for, 120
  types of, 119
Council for Exceptional Children
    (CEC), 31, 216
  assessment, 38, 74, 158, 190, 216,
    248, 308, 342, 384, 422
  collaboration, 106, 216, 248
  curricular content knowledge, 74,
    190, 308, 342, 384, 422
  initial level special educator
    preparation standards, 38,
    74, 130, 248, 284, 308, 342,
    384, 422
  instructional planning and
    strategies, 38, 74, 106, 158,
    190, 216, 248, 308, 342,
    384, 422
  learner development and
    individual learning
    differences, 4, 38, 74, 106,
    158, 190, 216, 248, 308, 342,
    384, 422
  learning environments, 74, 106,
    158, 190, 216, 248
  National Council for
    Accreditation of Teacher
    Education, 158, 190, 216,
    342, 384
  professional learning and ethical
    practice, 4, 106, 158, 216,
    248, 284
counting, in early number learning,
    425, 443, 446
court system, case law, 300–304
  law, application of, 302–304
  Section 504 of the Rehabilitation
    Act, 303
criterion-referenced tests, 63
critical listening, 331
cross-age peer tutoring, 94
crystallized intelligence, 83
cultural and linguistic diversity
  of adolescents, 250–251
  disproportionality and, 323
  English-language learners (ELL)
    and, 323
  IEP process and, 48, 50, 60
  learning disabilities, 250–251
  learning second language, 323
  reading problems and, 343
  of young children, 218, 221
culturally responsive teachers, 91
curriculum
  mathematics, 441–442
  models for secondary level,
    265–266

curriculum-based assessment
    (CBA), 439–440
curriculum-based measurement
    (CBM), 44–45
cursive writing, 406

D

Dana keyboard, 394
decode, 348
delayed speech, 317
demonstrate structure words, 335–336
denial stage, 125
department store game, 334
depression, 163
detective game, 336
Detroit Tests of Learning
    Aptitude, 67
developmental aphasia, 321
developmental delay, 221, 237
  diagnosing, 237
  evaluating, 237
  in preschool children, 244
developmental indicators, in young
    children, 225, 226
developmental psychology, 131–136
  developmental variations in,
    131–132
  implications for learning
    disabilities, 135–136
  Piaget's maturational stages of
    development, 132–134
  stages of learning in, 134–135
  zone of proximal development
    (ZPD) in, 132
develop questions, 270
Dexedrine, 206
Diagnostic and Statistical Manual
    of Mental Disorders, IV-TR
    (APA), 191, 192, 196, 211, 227
diagnostic tests
  for mathematics, 437
  for reading, 364, 365
dialogue journals, 374, 392
dialogues, interactive, 152
DIBELS. *See* Dynamic Indicators of
    Basic Early Literacy Skills
    (DIBELS)
differentiated instruction, 30, 80–81
  multiple intelligences, 81
  for secondary classroom, 256
  and teaching approaches, 82–84
Digital Download
  Early Number Learning, 443
  100 Common Words, 352
  100 Most Common Words in
    Written Language, 403
  Including Students in
    General Education:
    Accommodations for
    the General Education
    Classroom, 92

Kurzweil Educational Systems, 379
K & W Guide for Students with Learning Disabilities or Attention Deficit Disorder, The (Kravetz & Wax), 276
K-W-L technique, 369–370

L

Lab School of Washington, DC, 142
language
    acquisition of, 313–314
    behavioral view of, 313
    as communication process, 311–312
    components of, 315–316
    forms of, 310–311
    as integrated system, 309–312
    language experience method, 369
    and mathematics abilities, 427
    in preoperational stage, 132–133
    primary *vs.* secondary systems of, 310
    receptive *vs.* expressive modes of, 310–311
    social factors of, 314
    teaching in general education classroom, 313–314
    teaching strategies, 327–337
language delay, 317
language disorders, 317
language experience method, 386
language problems
    delayed speech, 317
    as developmental indicator, 225–226
    language disorders, 321
    language disorders *vs.* speech disorders, 317
    poor phonological awareness, 317–319
    rapid automatized naming, 319–320
    temporal acoustical processing, 319
    types of, 317–321
    word finding, 319–320
lateral preference, 25
Laubach Program, 115, 279
learned helplessness, 151, 251
learning, information-processing model of, 142–147
learning conversation skills, 172
learning difficulties
    emotional challenges and, 162–163
    financial success and, 16
learning disabilities, 10–23
    academic and learning tasks, 14
    characteristics of, 16–19
    cognitive processing factors of, 14
    cross-cultural nature of, 20
    in different life stages, 16–19
    eminent people with, 19

emotional/behavioral disorders, 7–9
    exclusion of other causes in, 15
    federal definition of, 12–13
    gender differences in, 16
    gifted and talented children with, 15–16
    history of field of, 20–22
    neurological factors of, 14
    new issues and directions, 29–34
    origin of term, 20
    other significant definitions of, 13
    potential-achievement discrepancies in, 14–15
    prevalence of, 11–12
Learning Disabilities Association of America (LDAA), 10, 20, 126
learning strategies instruction, 97–98, 151–153, 336
    approach to writing, 391
    definition of, 269
    guidelines for, 270
    implications of, 153
    interactive dialogues, 152
    for secondary students, 269–273
    social influences and, 152
    social interactions and, 152
    steps for teaching, 271–273
    strategies intervention model (SIM), 271
least restrictive environment (LRE), 54, 107–109, 293–294
left-handed students, 407
left interior front gyrus, 27
left occipitotemporal area, 27
left parietotemporal area, 27
legislation
    for ADHD special services, 203
    for college students, 274–275
    for determining eligibility, 39
    Education for All Handicapped Children Act (Public Law 94-142), 10, 12, 22
    Individuals with Disabilities Education Improvement Act of 2004 (IDEA-2004, Public Law 107-476), 12–13
    No Child Left Behind Act (NCLB), 8, 63
    transition planning for secondary students, 260–264
    for young children, 220–223
Lesley University, 277
letter difficulty, 417
lexical words, 373
linguistic diversity
    of adolescents, 250–251
    oral language and, 323
listening, 327–332
    comprehension and, 327–328, 331
    as primary language system, 310
    as receptive skill, 311
    strategies for improving, 210
    vs. reading, 327–328

listening skills
    assessment of, 325
    building listening vocabulary, 330
    critical listening, 331
    improving, 210
    listening comprehension, 327–328, 331
    listening to stories, 331–332
    phonological awareness of language sounds, 328–330
    teaching strategies for, 327–337
    understanding sentences, 330–331
literacy organizations, for adults, 359–360
Literacy Volunteers of America (LVA), 115, 279
literature-based reading instruction, 361
Little House on the Prairie (Wilder), 378
local education agency (LEA), 48
logical/mathematical intelligence, 81
long-term memory, 145

M

Magic Tree House series, 377
mainstreaming, 108
manifestation determination, 165, 166
manuscript writing, 405, 406
mastery learning, 84
materials without words, 374
math anxiety, 427–428
mathematics
    analyzing errors, 437–439
    assessment, 435–440
    common core standards for, 430–431
    curriculum-based assessment, 439–440
    formal tests, 436–437
    informal measures, 437–440
    intensive instruction in, 264
    language and, 427
    standards and annual testing, 430
mathematics computation skills, 447–450
mathematics difficulties, 421–457
    characteristics of students with, 426–428
    common calculation errors, 437–439
    information-processing, 427
    math anxiety, 427–428
    mathematics learning disabilities and, 423–426
    at secondary level, 429
    spatial relationships and, 425
    with time and direction, 426
    visual-motor abilities and, 425–426
    visual perception and, 425–426

problem solving
  in formal operations stage, 133
  in math instruction, 433–435
  reading as, 355
  in RTI, 42–43
procedural safeguards, 48
  special education laws, 294
processing functions, 142
processing speed, 83
processing speed tests, 67
professional licensing, 276–277
progress monitoring, 40, 43–44,
    54–55, 439
Project READ, 375, 376
pronunciation, 413
proprioceptive system, 231
psychological processing
    disorders, 141
psychostimulant medications
  neurochemistry of, 207–208
  for treating ADHD, 206–207
Punished by Rewards: The Trouble
    With Gold Stars, Incentive
    Plans, A's, Praise, and Other
    Bribes (Kohn), 137
puzzle cards of combinations, 450

Q

questioning strategies, for
    reading, 356

R

rapid automatized naming (RAN),
    319–320, 335
rapport, building, 87–88
rating scales, for ADHD, 200–202
READ, 375, 376
read-along method, 353
readiness, 84, 135, 136
reading, 341–381
  adult literacy organizations, 279
  assessment, 363–364
  comprehension and, 368–377
  computer technology and, 379
  connection with writing, 359–360
  elements of, 347–359
  English-language learners and, 362
  enjoyment and appreciation of,
      377–378
  fluency and, 351–353
  formal tests of, 364–365
  games, 366
  importance of, 377–378
  informal measures, 363–364
  intensive instruction in, 264
  phonics and word-recognition
      skills, 347–348
  phonological awareness and, 347
  portfolio assessment of, 363–364
  "Themes Instruction Program"
      for, 357

vocabulary and, 353–354
  vs. listening, 327–328
reading aloud to other audiences, 353
Reading Blaster, 379
reading comprehension, 354–359
  active interaction in, 356
  basal reading series and, 368–369
  before, during, and after reading,
      357–358
  for informational materials,
      358–359
  for narrative materials, 358
  reader's experience and, 355
  strategies for improving, 356–357
  teaching strategies for, 364–365
  as thinking process, 355
  views of, 355
  See also reading strategies
reading fluency, 351–353
  automaticity and, 352
  English-language learners and, 362
  repeated readings and, 353
  sight vocabulary and, 351–352
  strategies for improving, 353
  syllable recognition and, 352–353
  teaching strategies for, 364–365
reading problems
  consequences of, 342–344
  content-area, 359
  cultural and linguistic diversity
      and, 343
  dyslexia, 345–346
  impact of math skills, 424
reading strategies
  basal reading series and, 368
  building meaning with vocabulary
      and concepts, 370–374
  building phoneme awareness, 365
  cloze procedure, 373–374
  cognitive learning strategies for, 375
  computer technology for, 379
  directed reading-thinking
      activity, 355
  Dynamic Indicators of Basic Early
      Literacy Skills and, 366
  for English-language learners, 362
  expanding vocabulary, 371–373
  Fernald Method, 376
  for general education classroom,
      344–346
  general education instruction
      strategies and, 344–346
  to improve fluency, 367–368
  to improve reading
      comprehension, 368–377
  K-W-L technique, 369–370
  language experience method, 369
  literature-based reading
      instruction, 361
  multisensory methods, 375–377
  neurological impress method,
      367–368

Orton-Gillingham Method, 376
phonics methods, 366
predictable books, 367
read-along method, 353, 368
reading vocabulary, 354
reading-writing connections
    in, 374
repeated readings, 353
response-to-intervention (RTI)
    and, 344–345
whole-language reading
    instruction, 361
Wilson Reading System, 376
for word recognition, 347–348
Read Naturally, 367
Read Please, 379
Read Please Plus, 379
reasonable accommodations,
    91, 275
  See also accommodations
rebound effect, 207
recall, 414
receptive language disorders, 321
receptive language modes, 310
Recipe for Reading (Traub &
    Bloom), 376
reciprocal questioning, 337
reciprocal teaching, as interactive
    dialogue, 152
recorded textbooks, 379–380
Recording for the Blind and Dyslexic
    (RFBD), 379
rectangular array approach, to
    multiplication, 448
referral, in IEP, 38, 49–50
rehearsal, for improving
    memory, 145
reinforcement, 183–184
  for behavioral challenges, 183–184
  finding effective reinforcers, 184
  impact of negative, 390
  in language acquisition, 313
  theory, 183
related services, 286
repeated readings, 353, 367
representational level, in math
    instruction, 432–433
residential facilities, 110, 114–115
resiliency, lack of, 163–164
"resolution session," in IEP
    process, 48
resource rooms, 110, 113–114
response cards, 178
response-to-intervention (RTI)
  approach, 30–31, 39–40
  benefits of, 41–42
  concerns about, 42
  definition of, 39
  IDEA-2004, 295
  as IEP prereferral process, 49
  problem-solving approach to,
      42–43

Tests of Cognitive Ability of the Woodcock-Johnson III, 67
"test-study-test" method, 414
  vs. "study- test" method, 414
test-taking strategies, 262
  in general classroom, 69
textbooks, recorded, 379–380
texting, 33
text readers, 33
text-to-speech programs, 33, 379
Thalamus, 20
Themes Instruction Program, 357
theories of learning, 129–153
  behavioral psychology, 136–140
  cognitive learning theories, 147–150
  cognitive psychology, 140–147
  developmental psychology, 131–136
  learning strategies instruction, 151–153
  role of theory, 130–131
thinking process, 355
Three Billy Goats Gruff, The, 367
Threshold Program, 277
throwing activities, 241
time concepts, 452
time for thinking, problem solving, 451
time management
  accommodations for, 93–94
  in specialized instruction, 85
  strategies for improving, 210
time-out, 181–182
toddlers. *See* infants and toddlers; preschool children; young children
topic sentences, 409
TouchWindow, 239
tracing, for handwriting, 416
transition plans, 260–264
  content of, 261–262
  developing, 263–264
transitions, 287
  IDEA-2004, 295
  for secondary students, 260–264
traumatic brain injury, 9, 10
traveling assignments, 178
troll talk, 328
troublesome words, 335
tutorial instruction, 265
tutoring, 115–116
  classwide peer, 95
  cross-age peer, 94
  peer, 94–95
  same age peer, 94
  tutorial programs, 265–266
twin studies, 27
2-weeks facts, 450
two- and three-word sentences, 333
Type to Learn, 407
typing skills, 407–408

U

Universal Design for Learning (UDL), 34
University of Kansas Center for Research on Learning, 151, 273
U.S. Supreme Court, 300–304
  key cases in education decided by, 301–302

V

VAKT (visual, auditory, kinesthetic, tactile), 376
Venn diagrams, 148, 393
verbal comprehension tests, 67
verbal cues, in handwriting, 417
verbal/linguistic intelligence, 81
vestibular system, 230–231
Vineland Adaptive Behavior Scales, 58
visual cues, 328–329
visual memory, 265
visual-motor abilities, 425–426
visual perception
  activities for, 234–235
  definition of, 234
  as developmental indicator, 226
  difficulties with, 141, 231
  mathematics and, 425–426
  reversals and, 234–235
  spelling and, 413
visual processing, 83
visual reinforcements, 451
visual/spatial intelligence, 81
vocabulary
  building listening, 330
  building meaning with, 370–374
  building sight, 351
  building speaking, 334–335, 337
  direct instruction and, 354
  expanding with classification, 371–372
  exploring sources of, 372
  indirect instruction and, 354
  mathematics, 444
  multiple word meanings, 371, 372
  National Reading Panel on, 354
  oral *vs.* reading, 354
  providing concrete examples for, 372
  as semantics, 316
  stages of word learning, 354
  teaching strategies for, 354, 357
  word webs for, 373
voice recognition systems, 33, 395–396
volunteers, 117
Vyvanse, 206

W

wait-and-fail method, 343
walking activities, 241
Web pages, 397
Wechsler Intelligence Scale for Children, 4th edition (WISC- IV), 66, 67
Wernicke's area, 27
whole-language reading instruction, 361
Wikispaces, 397
Wilson Reading System, 376
Wind in the Willows, The (Grahame), 378
Woodcock-Johnson III Tests of Achievement, 68
Woodcock-Johnson Psychoeducational Battery III, 67
Woodcock Reading Mastery Tests, 68
word analyzer region, of brain, 27, 28
word combinations, 335
word finding, 319
Word Finding Intervention Program, 320
word-finding problems, 320
word-frequency approach to spelling, 402
word-pattern approach to spelling, 402
word-prediction programs, 395
word problems, 451–452
word processing, 33
  advantages of, 394–395
  electronic keyboards, 394
  keyboarding, 395
  presentation software, 396–397
  programs, 396
  software, 396, 397
  strategies for using, 412–413
  for students with learning disabilities, 33
  voice-recognition systems, 395, 396
  Web pages, 397
word-recognition skills, 347–348
  combining, 351
  context clues, 351
  phonics and, 347–351
  sight words, 349–350
  strategies for improving, 365–366
  structural analysis, 351
  task analysis, 99
  teaching strategies for, 364–365
word-recognition tests, 61
words
  in language development, 384
  lexical, 373
  multiple meanings of, 371
  multisyllabic, 398–399
  as primary means of communication, 385